Acclaim for Charlotte Gray's

CANADA

A PORTRAIT

IN LETTERS

1800-2000

A BEST BOOK OF 2003, *The Globe and Mail*
A BEST BOOK OF 2003, *The Vancouver Sun*

In *Canada: A Portrait in Letters 1800–2000*, Ottawa historian Charlotte Gray achieves the near-impossible, creating an enthralling, thought-provoking and frequently moving volume from more than 200 letters and 200 years. Gray [is] one of Canada's most significant popular historians . . . [and] *Canada: A Portrait in Letters* should find a permanent home in most Canadian home libraries. . . . It is a treasure trove not of history but of *our* history . . . a celebration of the written word, of the now almost forgotten joy of correspondence, the frisson of letter in a voice long unheard."

—*Ottawa Citizen*

"A new book from Charlotte Gray is always worth celebrating. She not only loves history, but she's a superb writer. . . . Gray takes joy in delving into the everyday details of life in the past, and she transmits her joy to the reader. [She] does a fine job of mixing the major players with the minor in her latest effort. . . . This book is a gem. Encore, Charlotte!" —*Calgary Herald*

"Each letter is a revealing window into our collective memory. To have them collected in a single volume is a gift." —*The Vancouver Sun*

"Charlotte Gray has a knack of making Canadian history come alive. . . . With correspondents both famous and previously unknown, it's uncanny how Gray always provides a clear social context for each letter writer."

—*Toronto Star*

CHARLOTTE GRAY

CANADA

A PORTRAIT

IN LETTERS

1800–2000

ANCHOR CANADA

COPYRIGHT © CHARLOTTE GRAY 2003
Anchor Canada edition 2004

LIBRARY AND ARCHIVES CANADA CATALOGUING IN PUBLICATION

Gray, Charlotte, 1948–
    Canada, a portrait in letters, 1800—2000 / Charlotte Gray.—Anchor Canada ed.

Includes index.
ISBN 0-385-65875-3

    1. Canada—History—Sources. 2. Canadians—Correspondence.
3. Canadian letters. I. Title.

FC89.G72 2004   971   C2004-904107-X

COVER IMAGES: (woman) Bettman/CORBIS/MAGMA, (stamp) Canada Post Corporation,
    National Archives of Canada POS-002250, (W.L. Mackenzie King) National
            Archives of Canada C-003176
COVER COLLAGE: based on an original work by Kara Kosaka
COVER AND BOOK DESIGN: CS Richardson
MAP DESIGN: CS Richardson

Printed and bound in Canada

Published in Canada by Anchor Canada,
a division of Random House of Canada Limited

Visit Random House of Canada Limited's website: www.randomhouse.ca

FRI   10   9   8   7   6   5   4   3   2   1

For Alexander, Nicholas, and Oliver

Contents

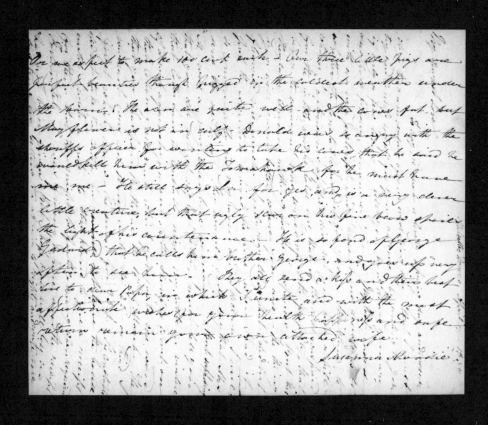

Susanna Moodie crammed all her news for English relatives onto one sheet of paper, to save money.

INTRODUCTION

LETTERS HAVE A MAGIC ALL THEIR OWN. WHEN MY MAIL ARRIVES EACH morning, the mere sight of a particular envelope addressed to me can induce a rush of expectation or foreboding. When I am sifting through someone else's correspondence in an archive, I am mesmerized. Hours vanish as I dive into the unrequited passions, servant problems, sibling rivalries, or political ambitions of another life. I never know what angels or demons will be released as I open each envelope, but as I unfold its contents I know the plot will move on. Like locks of hair, letters encapsulate some essential element of the personality of whoever holds the pen. I can almost hear the writer speak to me, across time and distance. I am drawn into a conversation with an unseen and often unknown protagonist.

The physical heft of a personal signature or a handwritten page has a potency that no phone call or e-mail can match. One of the most unforgettable instances of this I know is the letter that arrived for the Mohawk poet Pauline Johnson (Tekahionwake) in March 1898. In February, Pauline had attended her mother's funeral in Brantford, Ontario. Now, two weeks later, she was startled to recognize her mother's handwriting on the envelope. As she felt death approach, the elderly Emily Johnson had roused herself to write and mail a letter to her beloved daughter. When the fateful letter arrived, Pauline could only finger the envelope nervously. Months went by, and still she did not open it. Years passed, and it remained sealed. When Pauline died fifteen years after her mother, the letter was found, unread, tucked among Pauline's brooches in her jewellery case. It signified Emily's enduring presence in her daughter's life—part of a conversation that Pauline did not want to end.

Over the past months, as I selected the letters to include in this collection, I felt as though I was eavesdropping on history. It is not the conventional history of Canada, filled with nation-building heroes and great events. It is a history that goes in fits and starts, that speeds up in times of prosperity and slows down during periods of anguish. People write letters when they are separated from loved ones by emigration or wars, or when they are desperate for help in poverty and famine. They write letters when they are lonely, or in love. And for the most part, they write about the texture of their daily lives, rather than the achievements of politicians or leaders. I found no mention of Confederation in the private correspondence I discovered from 1867, but the arrival of the telegraph or the railway in a small community was always cause for comment. "History may intend to provide us with grand patterns and overall schemes," Margaret Atwood once commented, "but without brick-by-brick, life-by-life, day-by-day foundations, it would collapse." The letters in this volume capture that life-by-life, day-by-day reality.

But letters are more than a record of the past. A letter is rarely written with a view to posterity: instead, it captures the unique moment at which it is composed. The actual writing happens over a greater period of time than a conversation, allowing the writer to explore her thoughts or reflect on his circumstances. In September 1846, for instance, William Hutton, a successful farmer and schoolteacher near Belleville, Ontario, sat down to write to the mother he had left behind in Ireland years earlier. He mused about the dilemma common to immigrants: which is my country? "Dear Mother, A blessed day of rest amongst its many gratifications gives me that of writing *home*, a phrase, I suppose, we shall not forget till grandchildren scattered around shall cause us and our children to regard our own cottage as that sacred place."

This is history as it is being made, spontaneous and unselfconscious. Listen to Lucy Maud Montgomery, telling a friend about her first major literary breakthrough in 1907: "Well, I must simply tell you my *great news* right off! To pretend indifference and try to answer your letter first would be an affectation of which I shall not be guilty . . . Last fall and winter I went to work and wrote a book. I didn't squeak a word to anyone about it because I feared desperately I wouldn't find a publisher for it. When I got it finished and typewritten I sent it to the L. C. Page Co. of Boston and a fortnight ago, after two months of suspense, I got a letter from them accepting my book and offering to publish it on the 10-per cent royalty basis!" We know about the significance of this moment, and the enormous success of *Anne of Green Gables*. But Maud's letter allows us to travel back in time and hear her as she stood on the brink of a brilliant career.

The mere act of putting pen to paper may be cathartic for a correspondent. In the first half of the nineteenth century, the mail service was so unreliable that early settlers had little confidence that their letters would reach their destinations. Yet they wrote letters in quantity: the volume of immigrant letters from this period is wonderful. It is as though a one-sided conversation with family back home eased the isolation of life in the backwoods. "My dear brother," signed off John Capling in 1832, in a tragic letter to his brother in England in which he described the death from cholera of his wife and four of their eleven children soon after their arrival in Upper Canada. "Remember me to all relations, and all enquiring friends. I hope, by the blessing of God, you are all well, as I thank God it leaves me, and the remainder of my family, at present. I hope you will write to me, as soon as you can." The intensity of John's loneliness is overwhelming.

Writing a letter appears to offer a particular kind of personal therapy for those caught up in the uncontrollable circumstances of war. In 1916, young George Haddow unburdened himself to his family in Canada about the brutal fatigue of life in a military camp in England. He concluded his diatribe: "I feel like tearing this letter up now I have it finished, but I did that once before and it takes too much time to write them. When you can't unload yourself of what occupies your mind about eighteen hours a day, you have to shoot off a little hot air somewhere."

Similarly, in 1992, a Canadian peacekeeper in Sarajevo wrote to a correspondent in Nova Scotia: "I am really sorry as this is not a letter for anyone to read, but it helps to get it off my chest, as we don't talk about it among the soldiers. I wouldn't dare say this to my wife, so you are helping out a lot by reading this whether you realize it or not." He desperately needed to record on paper the horrors of the Serbo-Croat conflict, as one way of working through his own confused emotions. Other, more literary types might have used a personal diary for these experiences, but this pragmatic young soldier required a friendly "ear."

Not every letter is intended solely for personal consumption. I have included several letters to newspapers and a handful of official letters. These are public statements, geared to attracting general interest or provoking debate. Often the letter I have selected catches a stage of our history. In 1899, the Toronto *Globe* published an inquiry from a reader who recalled the clouds of passenger pigeons he saw during his boyhood in Ontario: "They would flock together by the thousands and after the young were able to fly they would return south until next spring; but where they are gone I would like to know." Other times, a letter to the editor is a chance for an expert to correct a widely held false assumption. In 1987, Canada's uncrowned master of the letter to the editor, the indefatigable Eugene Forsey, waded into the constitutional negotiations then under way: "The proposal for a 'triple-E' Senate (equal, elected, effective) includes provision for six senators from every province. That alone is enough to prove that it is just flailing the air, whistling in the wind, blowing soap bubbles."

Any anthology is a jigsaw. I was pleased to discover that a coherent, if untidy, picture surfaced on my jigsaw. The picture was of the emergence of a nation. I chose as my starting date the year 1800, just after the arrival of Loyalists fleeing the American Revolution, and before the flood of immigrants from Europe to British North America. Correspondents in a handful of wealthy eastern cities and a scattered collection of squalid settlements wrote the early letters. Most were insecure and hard up, with little notion of their colonial neighbours, let alone events in Europe or elsewhere. By 2000, my closing date, I was reading about the concerns of a settled and prosperous people who took for granted the idea that their sovereign nation had a role to play in global security.

At the same time, themes within this larger picture surprised me. I knew I would read about the back-breaking work of settlers in western Canada in the late nineteenth century, but I had not expected such aching loneliness. The desperate shortage of women out west led many a young immigrant to implore his family to find him a wife and ship her out. (The shortage of women affected our predecessors in different ways. Impecunious writers yearned for wives. Wealthier correspondents expressed a need for servants.) In the letters from the post–First World War period, I anticipated a growing sense of nationalism among Canadians. But I did not realize that there was an explosion of anti-British sentiment. In 1924, Norman Robertson, who would go on to become one of Canada's most distinguished diplomats, was exasperated by the snobbery of his fellow students at Balliol College, Oxford. "When people take it for granted," he wrote to his mother in Vancouver, "that an Oxford first class [degree] is somehow on quite a different plane from a U.B.C. first [class degree] they are, to put it mildly, talking through their hats."

A particularly dark strand that threads through this collection is the development of racism. At first, for example, relations between First Nations and non-natives were wary but respectful. Some settlers, such as Frances Stewart (see Letter 20), enjoyed meeting their Indian neighbours.

Dog trains provided the earliest winter mail service to missionaries and traders north of Lake Huron.

All too soon, however, contempt seeped into the prose of non-natives. By 1856, James Ross, son of a Hudson Bay Company factor who had been a leader in the Red River Colony, was imploring his sisters not to absorb the growing prejudice against mixed marriages: "What if Mama is an Indian! Does that detract from her rights and claims as a mother?" By the early twentieth century, it was not only First Nations who suffered discrimination. Immigrants from countries other than England, Scotland, and Wales were also feeling the brunt of prejudice. Racism began to retreat after the Second World War, but as Irshad Manji wrote in 1990, the children of new Canadians still find themselves stranded uncomfortably between two worlds.

How did I find the letters to include in *Canada: A Portrait in Letters?* First, my wonderful researcher, Deborah Van Seters, combed the catalogues of the Robarts Library at the University of Toronto and of several other institutions to locate volumes of published correspondence. Deborah passed on to me more than 2,500 letters that she selected from her wide-ranging search. Next, I wrote to every Canadian historian who I thought might know of unpublished treasures from their own research that they would be prepared to share with me. I was overwhelmed by the enthusiasm with which many academics responded to my request: this book is much strengthened by their support. Lastly, I described my project in articles in the *Globe and Mail* and the *Ottawa Citizen* and invited readers to send contributions. Some of the most touching letters came from this source, including the 1916 letter from a young Canadian soldier in England who hated military life, and the 1984 letter from an Ontario couple to the birth mother of the child they had just adopted.

I read close to 3,000 letters from these sources. There were so many intriguing glimpses of our past that this collection could have been three or four times longer than it is. I set myself particular criteria for selection. I looked for letters that captured a moving private moment, such as Willie Wallace's fears that he had lost his feet to frostbite in Manitoba in 1881, or a telling public event, such as the election of Pierre Trudeau in 1968. Letters that described familiar events seen from an unexpected angle had great appeal, whether it was the 1837 uprising in Upper Canada described by the governess to Sir Francis Bond Head's children or the murder in 1970 of Pierre Laporte in Montreal mentioned by a Quebecker who was also preoccupied with learning to knit. And intimate moments of famous Canadians—such as Isabel King's horrified letter in 1898 to her son Mackenzie King, when she learned he was engaged—were irresistible.

The Three-Penny Beaver stamp, showing the valuable fur-bearing mammal on a field of trilliums, remained in use from 1851 to the late 1860s.

I tried to find letters from every region, ethnic group, and level of society. I was thrilled when the diction of the writer was audible, as it was in an 1857 letter by George Cann, sent to me by George's great-granddaughter, Lois Daly of Calgary. George was the lighthouse keeper on Flint Island, off the Cape Breton coast, and his wife, Ann, had travelled to North Sydney to stay with relatives while she had a baby. George wrote: "I think I com and see you wen the roads gits good I feel quite lonsom when it is stormy I was glad to hear that you ware well caul the baby ann mary."

Yet I know significant voices and events from our history are missing from this collection. I don't have enough letters from First Nations or from immigrants from non-European countries. There are many letters from and about writers and artists, but few written by scientists or athletes. Milestone events such as Newfoundland joining Confederation in 1948 are missing. I never found letters that reflected the arrival of gramophones (let alone sound systems) or computers in our homes. As I approached the present day, my sources dried up: fewer people write letters, we all move house more often and discard papers more ruthlessly, important personal collections have yet to be lodged in archives or made available to the public. There may be letters that fit these gaps, or there may not. As every historian, amateur or professional, knows, finding the raw material of history is a hit-and-miss affair.

Most of the letters appear here unedited. But I had to trim some letters in order to avoid testing a reader's patience and to shoehorn everything I wanted into a manageable length. I hope I have done so, in each case, without sacrificing the writer's meaning or unique voice. Another, unexpected problem was grammar. Many of the earlier letter writers had little knowledge of "standard" English: punctuation and grammar were not part of their education. I did not want to distort the voice by "cleaning up" the style, but I didn't want the letters to be unintelligible either. In the end, I did the minimum to make each letter comprehensible to a modern reader. Not every change to punctuation or spelling is signalled by square brackets.

I have identified each letter by its place of origin as well as its date, author, and recipient. Identifying its origin for a modern reader often proved a slippery business. Place names shifted as governmental structures changed and settlers pushed westward. In 1800, Nova Scotia and Cape Breton were separate provinces: they were united only in 1820. Quebec was known as New France until 1791, Lower Canada until 1841, and then Canada East until Confederation in 1867. Confederation was the date when Ontario came into being too: it had been known as Upper Canada until 1841 and then as Canada West from 1841 to 1867. For much of the nineteenth century, most of the huge territories to the west of present-day Ontario (and including most of western and northern Ontario) were owned by the Hudson's Bay Company and known variously as Rupert's Land or the North-Western Territory. Portions of this vast land were carved off to create the provinces of Manitoba (1870, enlarged in 1880 and 1912) and Saskatchewan and Alberta (1905), and the Yukon Territory (1898). The existing provinces of Ontario and Quebec also swallowed up more land. Meanwhile, Vancouver Island was a separate colony from 1849 to 1866, when it joined the mainland colony of British Columbia, which had been created in 1858. Over the past months, as I assembled this anthology, I repeatedly resorted to the *Concise Historical Atlas of Canada* (University of Toronto Press) as I struggled to keep tabs on shifting boundaries and changing labels. Correspondents themselves often called the settlements in which they lived by outdated or mistaken names, so I have done my best with the kaleidoscope of possibilities.

If letters provide an idiosyncratic account of the past, some of the idiosyncrasy reflects communication technology itself. When Peter Russell, author of the first letter in this collection, wrote to Serjeant Shepherd in 1800 from the little military outpost of York, in Upper Canada, he used a quill pen on homemade paper. The sooty ink soaked into the soft rag paper, and Russell frequently had to scratch out untidy blots with a sharp blade. Since this was January, Russell took care that the ink didn't freeze in the inkwell. As an official communication, the letter was eligible for the government mail service to England. However, even as Russell trimmed his nib and chose his words, he knew that the missive would not reach Shepherd, in England, for months. Mail service was dependent on the seasons. The letter would have to wait until April, probably at either Quebec City or Kingston, until the heavy ice along the St. Lawrence opened up and navigation could recommence. The voyage by sail across the Atlantic would take at least five weeks, and if the boat foundered in a storm, Russell's letter would not arrive at all.

Many of the residents of British North America in the early nineteenth century had little use for letter writing. Living on the margins of the literate world, the majority had an insecure grasp of written language, poor handwriting, and the dimmest acquaintance with punctuation. The minority of settlers who wrote to distant friends and relatives rarely used the expensive government mail service. Even the more affluent ones preferred to rely on a more informal service: the goodwill of travellers who happened to be going in the right direction by steamer, boat, wagon, or sleigh. Most travellers were prepared to tuck a few letters into their packs as they journeyed up or down the St. Lawrence or across the Atlantic. But this "by favour" mail system was even less reliable than the official system. As Jane E. Harrison points out in *Until Next Year: Letter Writing and the Mails in the Canadas 1640–1830* (Hull, Que.: Canadian Museum of Civilization, 1997), if sickness, thieves, or any other misadventures waylaid the traveller, the letters in his pack might disappear. If his pack was soaked during a storm or shipwreck, the rag paper was reduced to illegible mulch. Delays were staggering: a letter written in Quebec City in July 1829 did not reach its destination in the Red River Colony until April 1830.

Yet these hazards could not quench the urge to communicate. From the moment that the sisters Susanna Moodie and Catharine Parr Traill, those two inveterate letter writers, set foot on Canadian soil in 1832, they felt compelled to record their experiences for friends and relatives in England. "I fear my long letters will sometimes weary even your patience," Catharine confided to her brother-in-law Canon Richard Gwillym in Lancashire. Since the official mail service based its charges on the number of sheets of paper used, Susanna would cram all her news onto a single sheet, turning the paper and overwriting earlier paragraphs, to save money. (Once I got used to this "cross-writing," I found it surprisingly easy to decipher.) Since prepared, gummed envelopes had not yet been invented, Catharine would carefully fold her closely written sheet, with a small square left blank on the outside for the address, then seal it with wax.

As postal services improved, Canadians began to send elaborate Valentine cards to their sweethearts.

During the 1914–1918 war, Canadian soldiers sent home cryptic postcards that revealed their state of health but not their whereabouts.

As the population of British North America swelled, mail services within the continent and across the Atlantic improved. In 1840, the British Post Office contracted Cunard Steamship Lines to provide a regular mail service between Halifax and Liverpool. In 1844, envelopes were introduced, and letters began to be rated on weight rather than number of sheets. And in 1851 a twenty-three-year-old Scots immigrant, Sandford Fleming, designed British North America's first postage stamp: the Three-Penny Beaver, the first stamp in the world to portray something other than a monarch.

New technologies shrank the delivery times for mail. In 1853, the railway mail service was introduced. The letter that once took over a week to travel from Montreal to Toronto by stagecoach would now arrive within thirty-six hours. In 1867, the new Dominion of Canada could boast a network of 2,333 post offices. In 1886, a daily trans-Canada railway mail service was introduced from Halifax, Nova Scotia, to Port Moody, British Columbia. As

volume increased, costs fell. By 1899, Canadians had to pay only 2 cents to mail a letter anywhere within the British Empire.

This was the heyday of the mail service. There were deliveries two or three times a day within major cities, and the service was as swift and reliable as a courier service today. In 1900, Mackenzie King, an ambitious young civil servant who would soon enter politics, could drop a line to a colleague inviting him to dinner at the Rideau Club, receive his colleague's written acceptance, and have the dinner all within twenty-four hours. However, outside of cities and the central corridor of railway mail service, it remained a challenge to ensure that letters reached the post office. "[The hired man] is going to Priddis tomorrow and will mail this and bring back any mail there is for us," wrote Monica Hopkins, a British-born farmwife living in the Rocky Mountain foothills in 1910. "I'm always afraid when he goes off with my precious letters that he will either dump them in the creek or lose them somewhere on the trail. I always tie up the mailbag myself and hang it carefully over the horn of the saddle; even then, I'm sure something will happen to it. The mail is such an important part of my existence that the very thought of losing part of it is most upsetting."

In the early twentieth century, the telephone arrived and dramatically changed the nature of letter writing. The metal contraptions in wooden boxes, screwed to front hall walls in middle-class residences, supplanted many of the notes, billets-doux, chatty letters, and terse written instructions that litter nineteenth-century collections of correspondence. Subscribers could now book appointments with chimney sweeps, discuss dinner arrangements, or spread the news of a new grandchild, without lifting a pen. Yet the telephone could not extinguish the urge to communicate by hand and to share feelings expressed more easily on paper than orally. And the mail service was still the only link between Canada and Europe.

When I published an appeal for family letters that I might include in this anthology, I was almost overwhelmed by the wealth of material from the 1914–1918 war. I could fill a whole volume with missives covering those years. Choosing the ones to include here was the most difficult task I faced. So many young men (and quite a few women) wrote home about the brutality and horror of the European trenches. Communication technology allowed those letters to reach their recipients: in 1911, the Militia Department had organized a military mail service to keep the boys in touch with home. But it was the slaughter of so many Canadian soldiers that ensured the survival of their correspondence. Those poignant bundles of letters from the front, neatly tied with ribbon or binder twine, were all their grief-stricken families had with which to remember the sons and brothers who had marched away so proudly. Only now are the grandchildren or great-grandchildren of those young soldiers discovering these packages, in trunks and attics. Did it take two generations for Canadians to come to terms with the carnage of that war? Perhaps. By comparison, few of the letters written during the 1939–1945 war resonated with the same raw fear as those from the earlier conflict.

Canadian letters continued to ebb and flow across continents and oceans throughout the twentieth century. Airmail service (costing 5 cents a letter) was established between Montreal and Toronto in 1928, and across the Atlantic in 1939. More mail meant that services had to be "streamlined." Soon same-day delivery was a thing of the past, and in 1951, letter carrier deliveries in cities dropped from twice to once a day. By the 1960s, a favourite Canadian pastime was complaining about the post. Eugene Forsey recorded in 1967 that a letter to him from the minister of justice had taken nine days to travel three blocks. Sixteen years later, a personal letter from the chief justice of Canada took eight days to reach him. With gleeful sarcasm, Forsey observed in a letter to the *Globe and Mail*, "Seven blocks in eight days is certainly a notable improvement over three blocks in nine days." The Canadian postal service gradually slithered into its current "snail mail" status.

When I arrived in Canada in 1978, I followed the example of so many earlier immigrants. I started describing my impressions of the New World in a weekly letter to my family back in England. The letters (stuffed into cardboard folders by my mother) are a record of what I thought might interest the recipients. I know from personal experience what a distorted picture letters present: my own letters linger on anecdotes of children and cottages but skate over disappointments and setbacks.

My letters have grown less frequent over the years, as I switched first to transatlantic telephone calls and then to electronic mail. Like the telephone before it, e-mail has had a dramatic impact on letter writing. Gone is the magic of handwriting, or the revealing personal signature. The crackle of creamy vellum paper or the lingering scent of lavender water as a nineteenth-century love letter unfolds belongs to another era. Yet the ease of hitting the Reply button, without the fuss of stamps and envelopes, allows a faster, freer, and more frequent style of communication. We're writing more than ever before, and each e-mail user is likely to have a wider circle of correspondents.

The last letter in this anthology is actually an e-mail between two sisters, tapped out on a keyboard in Italy and arriving within moments on a screen in Saskatoon. Eda Bannister's message to her sister Marie is as chatty and intimate as any conventional letter. But as Eda herself recognizes, a blinking screen does not give the same thrill as a handwritten envelope, waiting to be opened. An e-mail rarely offers the careful exploration of feelings or description of events that letters have always offered. Those of us who love letters applaud her for signing off, "Anyways, I will write, a real letter, soon."

Unscrupulous land speculators promised guileless emigrants an easy life in British North America, according to this cartoon, published in London around 1820.

PART 1: A SURGE OF SETTLERS
1800–1850

WHEN I TRY TO PICTURE BRITISH NORTH AMERICA AT THE DAWN OF the nineteenth century, I am reminded of my first flight across northern Ontario in 1981. I looked down onto a landscape of trees, lakes, and rocks— without a human habitation in sight. "Where are all the people?" I asked.

There were people here in 1800. Thousands of Indians and Innu roamed over the wilderness that stretched, unmapped, to the north and west. Some of these peoples cultivated crops; others were nomadic, following herds of caribou and buffalo. First Nations outnumbered the approximately 350,000 people of European origin who clung to the shores of the Atlantic and the banks of the St. Lawrence River. Yet contact between the different peoples was minimal, and the Europeans had as yet made little impact on the vast landscape. Once new arrivals had left the shoreline behind them, they often asked, "Where are all the people?"

Nevertheless, an administrative grid had already been superimposed on the landscape by busy imperial administrators. Twenty-four years earlier, the thirteen prosperous and well-settled British colonies to the south had gained their autonomy as the new United States. Now the remaining British colonies faced the challenge of building their own societies, and resisting pressure from the south to split with the mother country. There were seven outposts of Britain: Upper and Lower Canada, New Brunswick, Prince Edward Island, Newfoundland, Nova Scotia, and Cape Breton (which became part of Nova Scotia in 1820). Nova Scotia boasted the largest military presence, the closest ties to Britain, and a fine colonial capital in Halifax. Lower Canada, with its predominantly French-speaking population, tumultuous history, and well-heeled seigneurs, claimed the greatest wealth and almost two-thirds of the total population of the British colonies. Its walled capital was already two hundred years old and by far the largest of the colonial cities. Below Quebec City's ramparts, noted Thomas Ridout in 1811, the masts of two hundred ships at anchor in the St. Lawrence formed "a forest of three or four deep for six miles." But most of the other towns and villages perched on the shoreline were muddy settlements dominated by churches, gristmills, and breweries. French-speaking Canadians, most of whom had been in North America for generations, remained loyal to their church and their seigneurial system, while the link between English-speaking communities and Britain was an economic and a psychological lifeline for their residents.

British North Americans scrabbled to make a living from the fisheries, the woods, and the land. Communications were poor, and the wilderness threatening. Social, political, and economic activities were regulated by the seasons: during the bitter winters, life slowed to a glacial pulse. Drinking and praying (the immigrants were steeped in Christianity) were the only year-round activities. Even the relentlessly cheerful settler Catharine Parr Traill advised friends in Suffolk, "The badness of roads in this country, the slowness of conveyance, want of proper artificers etc. etc. are seldom taken into consideration by writers who write only to sell a book." Her sister Susanna Moodie wrote more despairingly of the isolation:

> Oh! Land of waters, how my spirit tires,
> In the dark prison of thy boundless woods . . .

Hundreds of kilometres to the north and west, in Rupert's Land (an area covering present-day northern Quebec, northern Ontario, all of Manitoba, most of Saskatchewan, southern Alberta, and much of the Northwest Territories), lay the fur traders' realm. Tales of those grizzled and taciturn traders were the staples of early Canadian history. Their network of trading posts included the sturdy stone buildings of Fort Albany and Rupert House on James Bay, and Fort York and Severn Fort on Hudson Bay, as well as the inland posts of Cumberland House on the Saskatchewan River and Fort Chipewyan on the Mackenzie River. It was a bleak existence in the distant north: as James Gunn, a mason at York Factory, wrote dolefully, "This country is very bad and always getting worse every way." Company employees had little to do with the colonists further south who were seeding a new nation on the northern half of the continent. The fur trade was dominated by the Hudson's Bay Company, with its headquarters in London. HBC (nicknamed "Here Before Christ") ships entered Hudson Bay from the north. Only the HBC's rivals, such as the Montreal-based North West

Company, brought their furs down the Ottawa River to Lower Canada's bustling ports, where they could carouse in taverns and brothels. Fur and fish remained the major exports of Britain's North American possessions.

Thanks to the British naval captains James Cook and George Vancouver, the broad outline of the continent's northwest coast was known. But Spanish, American, and British authorities were still squabbling about its ownership, and it remained *terra incognita* to British colonists in the east.

In the next half century, however, much changed. Lumber replaced furs as the colonies' major export. The land slowly filled up, as ships that had transported squared timber from the noisy wharves of Montreal, Quebec City, Halifax, and Saint John to Britain returned, after 1820, loaded with immigrants from the British Isles. Most of the newcomers were fleeing poverty—unemployment and social dislocation triggered by the Industrial Revolution in England and Scotland, and by the potato blight and starvation in Ireland. By 1850, the combined populations of Canada West and Canada East (now almost equal in size) constituted 2 million of the 2.5 million British North Americans. There were demands from both the new settlers in Canada West and the old-stock French of Canada East for a greater degree of political control over their own affairs. In 1837, uprisings in both Upper and Lower Canada had challenged the power of British governors and the colonial cliques that supported them. The uprisings persuaded London to send out John Lambton, Earl of Durham, to sort out the problems.

Lord Durham is one of the more colourful and canny personalities in our past, and I was happy to find a revealing letter from his wife, written in Quebec City in 1838. The Durhams toured the Canadas in considerable state, and Lord Durham's famous report led to a forced union of Upper and Lower Canada in 1841. And by 1848, the residents of "the United Province of Canada" were granted "responsible government," which ceded to them control of domestic affairs and election of their own rulers. Thanks to the efforts of Robert Baldwin and Louis LaFontaine, the forced union allowed French- and English-speaking Canadians to meet on equal terms: the French did not have to surrender their legal system or language. As the far-sighted statesman Baldwin wrote to his Quebec counterpart LaFontaine, "There is, and must be, no question of races. It were madness on one side, and guilt, deep guilt on both to make such a question." The smaller Atlantic colonies, however, had to wait several more years for ties with Britain to be loosened.

During these fifty years, British fears of the Yankees to the south gradually subsided. But north-south relations were seldom tranquil: there was a war in 1812 and a lingering sense that Yankee political principles, accents, and manners were antithetical to those of the British Empire. The motto that Ontario asserts even today—"Loyal she began, loyal she remains"—captures the guiding sentiment of those early settlers. Working-class immigrants revelled in their new-found freedom: "In Glasgow, I had to labour sixteen or eighteen hours a day," remarked a Scotsman who had taken up land in Lanark County, Upper Canada, "and could only earn about six or seven shillings a week—here, I can, by labouring about half that time, earn more than I need: there, I was confined to a damp shop—but here, I enjoy fresh air." Nevertheless, English-speaking Canadians continued to find the tie to the mother country both lucrative and reassuring. In bustling market towns north of the American border, employers preferred to hire newly arrived British immigrants, who would doff their caps, rather than American labourers who harped on the idea that all men were equal.

In the first half of the nineteenth century, letters were the only way of transmitting information over long distances. Family letters were stuffed with information: the price of wheat, the cost of land, births and deaths, styles of house decoration (the editor and future premier Joseph Howe was amused to discover copies of his newspaper the *Novascotian* used as wallpaper in a house near Sherbrooke, Nova Scotia). The political debates of the years 1800 to 1850 rarely crop up in the correspondence of this period. For most colonists, survival was the most pressing concern. There were so many daily dangers and pressures. Diseases like smallpox and cholera might wipe out whole families in days. A farming family that had spent long years clearing the bush might see its hopes destroyed by a forest fire or a run of failed harvests. Conflicts with the United States spawned fears that foreign soldiers might ransack property. An armed uprising offered an unsuccessful farmer like John Moodie the chance to escape the bush and defend the rule of British law. For most people, the arrival of responsible government signified not so much a triumph of democracy as a crescendo of intercolonial tensions.

And the wilderness still threatened. There was so much more of British North America to explore and "tame." The north and west remained unmapped, despite efforts by Sir John Franklin and others to chart the interior and find the Northwest Passage linking the Atlantic and Pacific Oceans. The western border between British territory and the United

States was still in dispute—a dispute that would not be completely resolved until 1872.

Nevertheless, the inexorable flow of European immigrants moving westward had begun. As early as 1812, Scottish settlers had reached the rich farming area around the junction of the Red and Assiniboine Rivers. Each advance by the newcomers meant further erosion of the territories and livelihood of First Nations such as the Cree in Lower Canada, the Algonquins and Mississauga in Upper Canada, the Metis and Plains Indians in the centre of the continent. Newfoundland's Beothuk people— "these unfortunate Savages," in the words of the colonial official John Bland—were completely exterminated; other groups withdrew north, hoping that Queen Victoria, "the Great White Mother" in faraway London, would guard their interests. They hoped in vain. Decimated by alcohol and disease, they were already heavily outnumbered.

By mid-century, a transportation system of canals and roads had developed, moving people and freight between colonies. Steamboats had cut the average duration of the voyage from England to Halifax from forty to twelve days. The telegraph linked the Old World to the New (although it depended on American lines to bridge the distance between Halifax and Montreal). Railways had begun to conquer the deep silence of winter: British North America's first, flimsy railroad track was laid in 1836. Britain's transatlantic colonies, no longer so unsettled, poor or isolated from one another, were inching towards nationhood. If I had travelled up the St. Lawrence River in 1850, I would have found many a booming little town, teeming with people. Many, like the letter writers represented here, would have told me anecdotes about their survival against the odds. And underneath the friendly gossip, I would have been able to detect a growing sense that British North America was becoming more than just a collection of bleak and sparsely populated colonies. It was now "home" for a growing population. If the creation myth for the United States was, in the historian Niall Ferguson's words, "the struggle for liberty against an evil empire," the creation myth for Canada was the struggle for survival on a raw and windswept landscape. Thanks to their fortitude, those hard-working and law-abiding settlers would achieve nationhood by peaceful means. An admirable patriotism and sense of purpose had developed. And also, it must be admitted, a whiff of the self-righteousness that has also characterized Canadians' self-image. As Mrs. Beikie wrote in 1813, "God seems to be on our side."

I

1800: UPPER CANADA

PETER RUSSELL TO SERJEANT SHEPHERD IN LONDON, ENGLAND

As the nineteenth century dawned in the vast wooded wilderness of Upper Canada, a handful of small European settlements were strung along the northern banks of the St. Lawrence River and Lakes Ontario and Erie. The hamlet of York (which would be renamed Toronto in 1834) consisted of fewer than 300 people and a scattering of wooden and clapboard houses. Yonge Street was still an ox-cart track. But with its military garrison, new brick legislative buildings, and fierce attachment to British manners and customs, York strikes me as the perfect backdrop for a Jane Austen study of small town manners. Within the colony's gossipy elite, slights and grudges were taken as seriously as if they had occurred in Mayfair. So when a Mrs. Small cast a slur on the reputation of a Mrs. White at a social event, Mr. White retaliated in the manner of a gentleman. Peter Russell, the colony's first receiver general, undertook the doleful task of explaining the outcome to Mrs. White's brother, in England.

York 9th Janry. 1800

Sir,

I take up my pen under the deepest Affliction to inform you of the Death of your Brother in Law Mr. White, who was shot in a Duel with Mr. Small, Clerk of the Executive Council of this Province, in the Morning of 3rd. [January], and expired at my House in the Evening of the next day. Though under the most excruciating Torture, he retained his Senses & understanding in their fullest force to within an Hour of his Death, & wanted for Nothing which the tenderest Affection of my Sister & myself with the best medical Aid to be found here could possibly supply. But the Wound was mortal from the first, the Ball having entered on the right Side between the two lowest Short Ribs & striking the Spine probably partially dividing some of the Bundles of Nerves that pass from the Vertebrae caused an instant Palsy of the lower Extremities & the most painfull Spasms. Knowing his dissolution to be inevitable he submitted to his Fate with a most pious & Christian Resignation to the divine Will & forgiveness of all his Enemies.

The Circumstances which led to this unfortunate Event are briefly as follows:

Mrs. Small having at one of the Assemblies in the Course of last Winter publicly Slighted Mrs. White in a most pointed Manner (as that Lady can best inform you) Mr. White being exceedingly exasperated was unfortunately impelled by the Violence of his Resentment to Communicate to Mr. Smith the Acting Surveyor General, who is now in England, some Circumstances to the Prejudice of Mrs. Small's Reputation which that Gentleman very imprudently (though in some degree authorised by Mr. White to do so) related to Mrs. Elmsley and the Chief Justice. Insinuations arising out of this Story having lately reached Mrs. Small's Ears, She urged her Husband, it is presumed, to do her Justice—and having demanded from the Chief Justice the purport of Mr. Smith's communication he called upon Mr. White in the afternoon of the 2nd. [January] to avow or deny it immediately. Mr. White answered that it being very possible that Mr. Smith might have said more or less than he told him, he had better obtain from himself the exact Tale he had Communicated to the Chief Justice & he should then very candidly tell him what parts of the Relation were true or false. Mr. Small, not satisfied with this, insisted on Mr. White going out with him immediately, which our friend having unfortunately agreed to, they met the next Morning, Mr. Small accompanied by Mr. Sheriff McDonell & Mr. White by a German Officer of the Name of De Haen. The Event you know.

Mr. Small has surrendered to Justice & is in Custody. Warrants are out for the apprehension of the two Seconds, who I am told propose to surrender before the day of Trial. I shall keep [Mr. White's] Boys with me until Navigation opens when I shall forward them to Mr. Osgoode at Quebec, who I have no doubt will procure them a Commodious & safe passage to England, under the Care of some proper person who will deliver them into your Hands . . .

2

1800: NEW BRUNSWICK
DR. JOHN CALEFF TO MAJOR HAILES IN FREDERICTON

Smallpox was endemic in North America. The killer disease, with its trademark sup-purating sores, first arrived with European fur traders in the seventeenth century and ravaged the native population; it went on to pose a major public health challenge throughout the colonies. But in 1798, vaccination was introduced into the continent, and in 1800, when there was an outbreak of smallpox in New Brunswick, the military authorities quickly imposed a mass vaccination program. The local doctor in St. Andrews reported on its success.

Saint Andrews,
23rd June, 1800.

Sir,

I wish to mention to you for the information of General Carleton that there hath been upwards of Three Hundred persons inoculated with small-pox in this Town & neighborhood, within about five weeks past, and all doing very well, except a Miss of five years, so refractory as to refuse medicine and even drink, and deceased the 7th day of eruption.

Mr. Lindsay's and three other families have been shut up by reason of their spouses being in circumstances not proper to receive the small-pox, one of the familys was inoculated 3 days ago, and expect to inoculate the rest on the morrow.

The disorder among women, and babes at the Breast, hath been of the lymphatic kind, and of course very troublesome, the subjects had dieted for more than a month (which to me proves erroneous) and but few had any symptoms till the 13th day after inoculation, and as low a state as some persons had brought themselves I found it necessary to give more Physick than to those who had not dieted even a day.

The people of St. Stephens keep a constant guard against any persons going among them that may endanger their taking the Infection, they say it would ruin their sawing and fishery, but mean to take it by and by, where are about 300 persons not having had the disorder.

I pray you Sir to present my high respects to the General and hope to have the honor to do so personally ere His Excellency may leave the province, which Report says he certainly will do by and by.

I have the honor to be with the greatest esteem,
Sir, your most obedient & most humble serv't,
John Caleff

3
1800: UPPER CANADA
JOSEPH WILLCOCKS TO HIS BROTHER RICHARD WILLCOCKS IN DUBLIN

The New World offered a new life to immigrants prepared to make their own way. Irish-born Joseph Willcocks arrived in York with letters of introduction to a cousin who had emigrated some years earlier from Cork, and sent home glowing accounts of his success as a merchant. Joseph quickly perceived that his relative would be no help to him. But he equally quickly attached himself to a better patron, Receiver General Peter Russell, and soon prospered. He could not resist a braggadocio tone in a letter home to his brother Richard Willcocks. Joseph's tongue-in-cheek humour amuses me: he noted wrily that the only man hanged so far in the colony was Irish, and the only person prepared to hang him was a fellow Irishman.

Upper Cana York
3d. November 1800

Dear Brother,
There is no new occurrence here worth relating when there is you shall know it remember me to all my friends, let me know particularly about my dear Fathers health. I wish he knew how much I am respected here, in fact I feel as if I was regenerated. I am here among rational beings, Men though they are high in rank & fortune know themselves to be Men & will be friendly & kind to you, but at home a Puppy Ensign A Clerks Clerk or a Sneering Atty [busybody] . . . will because he has unjustly usurped the appearance Of Loyalty look down uppon the rest of mankind with contempt.

However I shall drop the Subject, tho' you know I have some reason to speak on it, and give you a sketch of my [cousin] Mr Willcocks's circumstances & character . . . From the Letter my Father received from him previous to my leaving Ireland we should have supposed that his Property and circumstances were very extensive, particularly his mentioning to be Mayor of Cork. Tis true he was Mayor but at the same time a Bankrupt, and I have been since led to understand that from the repeated habit of being so, he was well acquainted with all its concomitant circumstances and left Cork rather at the Debtor side of the Book. On his arrival in this Country he became a Merchant, as they are called, and one of the most respectable of that Tribe, but at Home we would call them little Country Dealers. However by this Species of Huxtry [self-promotion] he enroled his name on the real Merchants book for nearly 2000 pounds, and from which, his present circumstances would not enable him to expunge a single Guinea. Tis true he has large tracks of Land but they are heavily Leaden with this debt, so much so, that I fear they will all sink under the Burden . . . Think my Dear Richard, what my fate [would] have been if solely left to the Guardianship and Dependency of this Family. Their utter incapacity to promote my Interest would have, I am afraid, reduced me to commit some very desperate act, had not Providence . . . stept forward and raised a friend for me who has it both in his power and inclination to assist me. I mean Mr Russell.

There are several Irishmen here and to the Honor of our Country the first and only Man that has been hung here was an Irishman. It happened since I came here, it was for Forgery, there was no getting a Hangman until at length another dear Countryman who was in for Robbery, with the promise of a Pardon & twenty Guineas to carry him out of the Country filled the Office with the most unpardonable Ignorance. The Gentleman who was to die fell three times from the Gallows. It fulfilled the old adage: put an Irishman on the spit and you will get another to turn him. I have met a very great loss by the removal of Colonel Smith from York Garrison. He was uncommonly attentive to me. He had also a very pretty sister that I would have been uncommonly attentive to if she carried more metal; indeed she is a rarity for there are few Pretty Girls in the Country, but you know beauty will not make the Pot boil, which consideration alone prevented me from assuming an air of Seriousness. Love & runaway matches I never was an advocate for, such proceeding may fill the belly of Women but not of men . . .

Labourers Wages here are extravagantly high, never less than from 6 to 10 Irish Shillings a day, Carpenters & Masons from 9 to 14. These Wages are general through America, sometimes more but never less, so that no Man can make Money except those who have large families that can Labor. In this Province, Mutten is 6 1/2 d. and Beef 4d the pound. In Lower Canada Mutten 2 1/2 Beef 1 1/2 d a Boushell of Potatoes 2d. bread 1 d a lb but Groceries very high and Waring Apparel excessively high I paid 5s a yard for a piece of Irish Linen Yesterday, at home it would be three, Madaira 2s2d per quart & Cheaper, Claret is not drank here, Port good 1s.10d a quart.

The heat of Summer is insupportable & the Cold of Winter Intollerable, there are many instances of Persons being frozen to death and a Winter dose not pass by with out several noses, fingers, and feet being lost. For my part I dred the Winter altho I have one of the most Comfortable rooms in this Province. In fact Mr Russell thinks nothing to good for me. We have an elegant pair of Horses, and a Sled that will be fine Sport in Winter if not too Cold, but we have a great many very valuable Skins some of which are for the purpose of Sleding.

There was great depredations committed the night before last by a flock of Wolves that came into this Town, one man lost 17 Sheep, several others lost in proportion. The perpetrators escaped with impunity. We let lose a Pack of Hounds after them but from their Scattering after the different Scents we had no diversion. When the Snow comes we will have fine fun tracing them & the Deer of which there are great abundance. I assure you that as for the Wild Ducks and Pidgeons they surpass any mention I could make of them. Fish of all kinds are in this Lake We will get a Salmon of 20lb weight as good as ever was killed at Island Bridge for an Irish Shillg., frequently less, You may think this underrating the matter but I assure you it is a fact. The Indians spear them . . .

4

1801: UPPER CANADA
COLONEL THOMAS TALBOT TO THE DUKE OF CUMBERLAND,
BROTHER OF KING GEORGE III, IN LONDON, ENGLAND

Influential connections back in England were the key to success for many ambitious land speculators in Upper Canada. The Anglo-Irish eccentric Colonel Thomas Talbot was one of the most successful land developers in British North America. After military service on both sides of the Atlantic, he immigrated to Upper Canada and began to acquire land, and promote settlement on it, in the London district. By 1836 he had secured a large fortune and the settlement of twenty-nine townships over a huge area along the north shore of Lake Erie, and lived in his "castle" at Point Talbot. His prosperity was due to his own labour and to judicious manipulation of royal friendships back home.

Skitteewaabaa [Port Stanley], Upper Canada,
May 16th, 1801.

Sir,

Although I am separated from England by some thousands of miles Your Royal Highness will find that I am not beyond reach of proving trouble-some, to which intrusion I am led, by command of Your Royal Highness, when you condescended so far to interest yourself in my welfare, as to desire that in whatever manner I could find your influence necessary to solicit it. I am now to have the honour to acquaint Your Royal Highness of my safe arrival in my favourite Settlement after the most propitious passage and as I am persuaded that Your Royal Highness will be satisfied, I will add, I find my situation quite what I could have wished—but I have one request to make which, if Your Royal Highness will have the good-ness to exert yourself in carrying into effect, will complete my happiness in this world.

Owing to some neglect of General Simcoe's [lieutenant-governor of Upper Canada 1792–1796], I find that the necessary Warrants for my lands were not issued previous to his quitting the Government of this province. Since then there have been new regulations adopted which ren-ders the possession of lands more expensive and difficult of obtaining than when I left the Province in 1794, and as I flatter myself, that Your Royal Highness will admit that I am as loyal a Subject and equally enti-tled to the Degree of *Hidalgo* [landed gentry] as other *adventurers* in a new country, I throw myself on Your Royal Highness's power to have it con-firmed, and to prevent its producing discontent, I will beg leave to point out a mode for its execution.

There are parcels of land under the name of *Townships* granted in this country to Heads of Societies, which possibly may in time prove beneficial to the proprietor. Now what I have to petition to Your Royal Highness is that you will have the goodness (I may add *charity*) to ask of the King the grant of a Township in the Province of Upper Canada for yourself, exempted from the fees to Government and obligations of location—for instance, *The Township of Houghton in the County of Norfolk on Lake Erie, or any other adjacent one, which may not be already granted*. Which, when Your Royal Highness has procured His Majesty's Patent for, it must be transmitted through the Secretary of State for the Home Department to the Governor and Council of the Province of Upper Canada, in order that the necessary Provincial Deeds may be made out for possession.

Your Royal Highness can on receiving the Royal Patent, make a legal transfer of the Grant to me, and permit me to request that you will have the goodness to cause duplicates to be made of the transfer, as the conveyance of letters to this Country is irregular and uncertain. My Sister Barbara will take charge of them or any other Communication Your Royal Highness may honour me with, she having the directions how to forward them . . .

I promise myself the enjoyment of every comfort in this Country excepting that material one, of seeing those I most respect and love. A small income provides the necessary luxuries in this Province to a Settler as his own industry and labour procures him provisions. I am out every Morning at Sunrise in my smock frock felling and burning the Forest to form a farm. Could I but be seen by some of my St. James's friends when I come home to my frugal supper, as black as any chimney sweeper, They would exclaim, "What a damn'd blockhead you have been, Tom." But I say, no, as I actually eat my homely fare with more zest than I ever did the best dinner in London. It is time that I should beg a Thousand pardons for this intrusion, but I am satisfied of the goodness of Your Royal Highness's heart, and sincerely praying that you may experience every blessing of this life, I have the honour to be with the most unfeigned gratitude,

> Your Royal Highness's
> Most Dutiful and Faithful Servant,
> Thomas Talbot.

5

1802: NEW BRUNSWICK
EDWARD WINSLOW TO THE *ROYAL GAZETTE AND NEW BRUNSWICK ADVERTISER* IN FREDERICTON

I expect hearts sank in Fredericton public meetings when the bombastic landowner Edward Winslow stood up to voice his strong opinions. A lieutenant colonel in the British forces during the American Revolution, he was forced to flee his native Massachusetts in 1782 and move north. He played a crucial role in the establishment of the province of New Brunswick in 1784, as a haven for Loyalist troops: he determined it should be "one of the most Gentlemanlike [provinces] on earth." Winslow had nothing but contempt for faint-hearted comrades who deserted the shabby little town on the Saint John River. As far as he was concerned, they were beneath respect if they deserted Britain and returned to New England, and he had little good to say about those who moved to the lusher pastures of Upper Canada, even though they maintained allegiance to the British crown. Under the pseudonym "Tammany," he frequently fulminated in the pages of his local newspaper.

Fredericton

July, 1802

Dear Sir,

It is an observation made by a late traveller: "That the people of America have a strange propensity to change their situations." He says, "It is not an uncommon thing to see families, who have encountered and overcome all the obstacles which naturally arise in forming new settlements, and are just beginning to realize the comforts and enjoy the sweets of their own labour, consenting to abandon their possessions, and engaging anew in the same scenes of difficulty and distress." Had that judicious writer pawed through the Province of New Brunswick, he would have seen instances of this disposition which might have excited a greater degree of astonishment than any which he could possibly have met with in the back parts of the United States.

It is an established fact that the Province of New Brunswick has been principally settled by an order of men who call themselves Loyalists—men who fought in the service of the King during a long war, and who, at the unfortunate termination of it, made an election to plunge into a wilderness with their wives and children rather than submit to the humiliating and degrading necessity of soliciting mercy from those whom they were in the habit of considering rebels.

Actuated by the same laudable and manly spirit they persevered, and they combated difficulties, fatigues and toils which, in a bad cause, they would have sunk under. Here they soon obtained a constitution or government similar (so far as was practicable) to the British. Lands were assigned to them, and cherished by a temporary bounty from a benevolent Sovereign they went to work with a degree of alacrity which was never exceeded. Huts were erected which at first were hardly sufficient to shelter their families, and little holes were cut in the forest. A few potatoes and a scanty crop of rye were the only rewards for the immense labor of the first and second years. During the 3d, 4th, 5th and 6th, although the prospects brightened a little, the difficulties were great and many discouraging circumstances occurred; but under all this pressure of care and perplexity the voice of murmur could scarcely be heard among them.

At the expiration of fifteen or sixteen years the scenes are materially changed. Enter the habitations of the Farmers in almost every part of Province now and, with very few exceptions, you'll find them tight, warm and comfortable, you'll see the man and woman surrounded by a flock of children—robust, hearty and useful, clad in homespun, feeding upon their own mutton, with bread, butter and cheese in abundance. In instances you may discover not only the comforts of life, but luxuries procured by their over-plus produce, which never fails to find an easy sure market—or by their winter exertions in masting, getting timber, &c, for which they receive the most liberal wages. Their barns and out-houses contain a stock of cattle, horses, sheep, swine, &c, of more value than their ancestors in [New] Jersey or New England ever possessed for three generations before they were born. Enquire among 'em for a Grievance and they'll not be able to point out one:

> Are you oppressed with taxes ? No.
> Does anybody interrupt you in matters of conscience ? No.
> Do the laws afford you sufficient protection ? Why yes.

This is the unexaggerated state of the Province now, and this too at a time when one half the countries in the world have been ruined by a calamitous war.

Notwithstanding all which, among the very people I have described, a few giddy, eccentric, and discontented characters have appeared who, forgetting all the favors which they received from our government, have made a voluntary sacrifice of their former honorable principles and professions, have sold the lands that were granted them, and meanly skulked into the United States. There they have made their submission; there they have become literally "hewers of wood and drawers of water"; and as an act of grace are permitted to eat, drink and vegetate. But in place of being buoyed up under affliction by the reflection of having done their duty as honest men and faithful subjects, they are compelled to consider the most meritorious actions of their lives as the most atrocious offences which they ever committed.

These men and their leaders will furnish subject matter for a future essay. I shall therefore quit 'em for the present and pass on to another class, who are not quite so culpable, but who appear to be influenced by the same extraordinary caprice—I mean those who have lately removed with their families to other parts of the King's dominions, particularly Niagara.

In comparing the two countries I declare that I have no intention of casting a reflection upon the Province of Upper Canada. I have a high respect for the government there, a good opinion of country, and sincerely wish it prosperity. The final determination of a few changeable people with respect to the place of their residence is matter of no importance either to them or to us, and the remarks which I shall make will perhaps apply with equal force to those who would wantonly and inconsiderately leave that Province and come to this.

The principal object I have in view is to enquire whether there is any sufficient temptation offered to induce a Farmer, who has conquered the great difficulties of making an establishment here, to disturb the peace of his family and to undertake the arduous task of removing to a place so difficult to approach and so remote. It is obvious that there is no essential difference between the constitutions and the laws of the two Provinces. Allow that in Canada the climate is more mild, the winters not so long, the land if you please easier cleared, and the crops (particularly of wheat) more abundant. Possibly these considerations might have afforded good reasons for an original preference, but let us put against these advantages the acknowledged unhealthiness of the climate, the impossibility of selling that part of their produce which they cannot consume, the immense prices of many of the necessaries of life and the total want of winter employment. Would any man in his senses readily barter sound health for fevers, agues and debility? Would he relinquish a Farm, cleared with his own hands, which supplies him with everything he wants and something to spare, for a redundance of wheat, which he can't sell and a surplusage of Pork which he can't find salt, to save? . . .

I call upon speculative readers of all denominations, between the two great extremes of Philosophers and Fools, inclusive to account for that passion or propensity, or whatever else you may call it, which causes some of the children of men thus voluntarily to surrender the peace, comfort and happiness of themselves and their families.

Tammany

6

1807: UPPER CANADA
THOMAS RIDOUT TO HIS PARENTS,
THOMAS AND MARY RIDOUT, IN YORK

Fifteen-year-old Thomas Ridout had to study hard in the little boarding school in Cornwall run by Dr. John Strachan, the stern Scots teacher who would later become bishop of Toronto. Strachan's ambition was to make his pupils British patriots and Christian gentlemen. Perhaps the most important aspect of Strachan's school, however, was that it allowed Thomas, son of an important official in the colonial administration, to mix with the scions of York's other leading families—the group that controlled the political and economic interests of Upper Canada and would come to be known as the "Family Compact."

Cornwall,
10th January, 1807.

My Dear Parents,

I am afraid you may be angry with us for not writing for so long a time, but there have been no opportunities. I come on middling well, and am going into book-keeping on Monday. I got a quire of paper to-day from Mr. Strachan, to make my book. Mr. Strachan has not struck me yet, nor has he been angry. We have finished our grammar and are learning it by heart every morning. It is very cold weather here and excellent sleighing, and very fine skating for the boys who have skates. It is snowing very fast now. We had about a week's play at Christmas and now and then half-days, but very seldom. The boys say that Mr. Strachan is going down to Quebec to see the Bishop in June, and that the vacation will be then. The boys had a frolic upon the ice yesterday with three pecks of apples which Stanton bought, and after his apples were gone they were as bad as ever teasing him. We stay up every night till about twelve or one o'clock and we have got so used to it that we don't mind it. We repeat four problems a week, and I am two from head. The day after New Year's Judge Anderson invited sixteen of the boys down there, and George [his brother] and I were of them. He threw about a bushel of apples to scramble for now and then, and I got as many as I could carry, and half a bushel of hickory nuts; and they had a dance, and all the boys danced except Robert Anderson, his grandson, and I. George danced very well.

I am, my dear parents,

Your affectionate son,
Thomas G. Ridout.

7

1807: NEWFOUNDLAND
JOHN BLAND TO HIS EXCELLENCY JOHN HOLLOWAY,
GOVERNOR AND COMMANDER-IN-CHIEF OF THE ISLAND
OF NEWFOUNDLAND, IN ST. JOHN'S

In the British colony of Newfoundland, relations between fishing communities and the indigenous Beothuk people had deteriorated steadily since Europeans arrived to settle the island in the sixteenth century. Angry fishermen repeatedly took brutal action against any "Red Indians" (the Beothuk painted themselves with red ochre) caught stealing their fishing equipment or stores of dried cod. The story of the Beothuk is one of the saddest in Canadian history: devastated by European diseases and clashes with well-armed settlers, by 1800 their numbers had dwindled to about 300, from a high of around 2,000 a couple of centuries earlier. Colonial officials such as John Bland struggled to improve relations.

Bonavista,
22nd September, 1807

Sir,

Since my return hither I have learnt that an Indian Canoe had been taken on the North part of this Island and carried to St John's and that enquiries had been made respecting the manner by which our Fishermen had become possessed of this Boat. From all I can learn of this transaction, as the Fishermen concerned in it belong to Bonavista, no other mischief happened than that of depriving the poor Indians of their Canoe.

Government has frequently expressed a wish that some means could be suggested of effecting a friendly intercourse between our People and the

Native Indians of this Island, but nothing serious has hitherto been attempted towards so desirable an end.

Without reference to correspondence with former Governors on this subject I will take the liberty to propose to Your Excellency that a small and select military party be stationed in the Bay of Exploits with a guide during the winter season and should it afterwards be found necessary one of the King's schooners during the summer months when the Indians resort to the sea coast in order to provide food for the winter. It is during this period that they are often met by the Northern Fishermen and unhappily interrupted in their endeavours to make this provision. There can be little doubt under present management that one at least of the two modes proposed would be successful in securing some of these savages, and common sense would then suggest what was further necessary to conciliate their good will and improve the intercourse.

The good to result from a successful attempt at conciliation must be an end to a long course of hostilities between our Savages and the native Savages of this Island, in which many lives on both sides have been lost, and, I am sorry to add, there is too much reason to believe that the mischief with respect to the latter has been more extensive than is generally known.

That the condition of these unfortunate Savages would be considerably ameliorated by an intercourse with us can admit of no doubt, for they are an ingenious people, as all they do plainly evinces.

It would be useless, Sir, to enter upon long descriptions of this question. Your Excellency I am sure, independently of the pleasure of doing good, must discover the general advantage of effecting the measure proposed.

> I have the honour to be, with great respect, Sir,
> Your Excellency's most obedient, humble servant,
> John Bland

Bland's efforts were in vain. By 1829, the entire Beothuk people had been wiped out. The extermination of the Beothuk was both a Newfoundland tragedy and a dreadful foretaste of what lay ahead for aboriginal peoples in the rest of North America.

8

1808: UPPER CANADA
TIMOTHY NIGHTINGALE TO QUETTON DE ST. GEORGE IN YORK

Cash was scarce in Upper Canada; farmers along the shoreline of Lake Ontario were often forced to buy goods on credit from York merchants. If the harvest failed and the merchant in question was the hard-hearted Quetton de St. George, resident of the first brick mansion in York, a farmer like Nightingale faced the loss of his farm and a spell in debtor's prison.

Whitby
May 28 1808

Sir.

As Anderson has disapointed me about taking my farm I am like to disa-point you about the Money due you it is out of my power to pay you unless I sell my farm which if for Sale I have offerd to sell for three or four hun-dred Dollars less then the Value of it but if You know any body that will buy it plese to send them and I will take the same that Anderson was to give in order that you may get your pay or I will let you have half of it for twelve Shillings an Acre which is worth Double what I offer it to you for or I will deliver my farm to you and you may let it out till you get your pay I cant offer anything more if I cant sell and you wont Comply with these terms to gaol I must go . . .

From your Humble Servant
Timothy Nightingale.

NB You need not send no officer any more only send a line and I will come up immediately and go to gaol if you say so.

Whitby
July 22 1808

Mr Saint George Sir,

I have ben atrying to get the money for you to pay you which you know that twice I have ben disopinted I am agoing to make potash to see if I cant pay you that way if you will Let me alone till I can turn my self to make it part this fall and part in the Spring I shall do my best to pay you I will pay you

the Interest of the money from this date you draw no Interest after Judment
but if you will wate I am willing to pay you Interest if you put me to gail I
cant be in the way to pay you then but to spend what I have and then sarten
you wont get your pay from your humble sarvant,

Timothy Nightingale

9

1811: LOWER CANADA
THOMAS RIDOUT TO HIS BROTHER GEORGE RIDOUT IN YORK

*The largest and most impressive commercial and military centre in British North
America during these years was Quebec City. In his letter to his brother in York,
Thomas Ridout, en route to London to receive a commission in a British regiment,
marvelled at the city's defences and its wealth.*

Quebec,
5th July, 1811.

After a journey of nine days, I arrived at this place, which far surpassed my
opinion of it. There are near two hundred sail lying in the river, they form
a forest of three or four deep for six miles. I came from Montreal for nineteen shillings, including provisions which were nothing but a bit of ham
and a loaf of bread. We were shockingly crowded in the boat, there being
ten passengers with their baggage, the crew, and 12 barrels of potash. I only
delivered Mr. Stuart's and Macaulay's letters. I am to breakfast and dine
with Dr. Macaulay on Sunday. He inquired a great deal about you and his
friends at York. John [Macauley] is now a first lieutenant at Cadiz, and
expects after that to go to the East Indies. James [Macauley] is at
Annapolis, New Brunswick. George [Macauley] has been taking me round
part of the ramparts this afternoon. There are great works going on now,
round towers and half-moons are building in front of all the gates, and the
double wall is continued down through the Quebec suburbs. They are in
great expectation here of war with the Yankees, and the works are accordingly carried on with great industry. There are two or three additional reg-
iments expected from England.

Montreal is nothing to compare with Quebec in regard to bustle, business or anything else. Consider what the loading and unloading of two

hundred sail must make! In coming to anchor, we passed close under the stern of the *Everetta*. She is the prettiest vessel here. I saw Captain Patterson on the deck. The quays and lower streets are completely covered and crowded with bales and men. One half of the crews of the ships look to be made up of boys between nine and fourteen years old, nice, smart little fellows.

I was at the market this morning, it was well supplied with everything, particularly strawberries, of which I dare say there were ten or twelve bushels, nice fresh butter on leaves, gooseberries and cakes of all kinds. Better mutton and beef than at Montreal.

10

1811: UPPER CANADA
SHERIFF JOHN BEIKIE TO THE CHAIRMAN OF
THE QUARTER SESSIONS IN YORK

The bitter winter of 1811 began in early November and was hard on everybody in the rough-and-tumble settlements of Upper Canada. But the sufferings of those confined within York's squalid, unheated log-house prison, with its dirt floors, moved even the sheriff to compassion. He wrote to the judicial authorities to express his concern.

Sheriffs Office
York 4th December 1811

Sir

I beg leave to state to you that the prisoners in the Cells of the Gaol of the Home District suffer much from Cold and Damp, there being no method of communicating heat from the Chimnies, nor any Bedsteads to raise the Straw from the Floors which lie nearly if not altogether on the ground— therefore I have to request that you will represent these matters to Your Brother Magistrates, and suggest, that a small Stove in the Lobby of each range of Cells, a rough Bedstead for each Cell—together with some Rugs, or Blankets will add much to the Comfort of the unhappy Persons confined and it is to be hoped will remove the grievance complained of to, Sir,

Your most obedient Humble Servant
(Signed) John Beikie
Sheriff

Sheriff Beikie's appeal resulted in the acquisition of "two small mettle stoves" and a consignment of bedsteads, blankets, and rugs.

II

1813: UPPER CANADA
MRS. JOHN (PENELOPE) BEIKIE TO HER BROTHER
JOHN MACDONELL IN HAWKESBURY

Mrs. Beikie, like her husband the sheriff, was known to be brave and forthright. An occasion for plain talk arose after the United States declared war on Great Britain in June 1812 and attacked British settlements, troops, and ships along its northern border. After the tragic loss in October of Major General Sir Isaac Brock, then commander of the forces and administrator of Upper Canada, at the Battle of Queenston Heights, hostilities became sporadic and confused, with several failed American attempts at invasion. When the Yankees briefly occupied York, in 1813, the troops seemed more interested in plunder than power. Penelope Beikie, whose husband and son were both fighting for the British, soon saw the invaders off her property on Front Street. She must have been a formidable woman, as she stood at her door, armed with the certainty that "God seems to be on our side." The half-hearted war drew to a close the following year, with the Treaty of Ghent.

York, May 5, 1813

Brother:

I am told you are low spirited since you were surprised by the Yankees at St. Regis; but I think it was a providential surprise for you to save your life, for, had not that been the case, I am convinced you would not have suffered yourself to be taken alive. We all have reason to be thankful to Providence, for never did I pass so awful a day as the 27th of April, with my two poor fellows in the heat of the battle. I never prayed more fervently, or said that beautiful psalm ("He that dwells in the help of the Highest shall abide in the protection of the God of Heaven, etc.") more devoutly, since my father's death, than I did that day. It is a beautiful psalm, and He who strengthens the weak gave me more strength and fortitude than all the other females of York put together; for I kept my Castle, when all the rest fled; and it was well for us I did so, our little property was saved by that means. Every house they found deserted was completely sacked.

We have lost a few things, which were carried off before our faces; but, as we expected to lose all, we think ourselves well off. Will you believe it? I had the temerity to frighten, and even to threaten, some of the enemy, though they had the place and me in their power. Poor William Swan [a Yankee acquaintance of the Beikies] was one of their majors, and behaved by no means like an enemy; he came without leave, and staid a night with us. I believe that through him we were treated with civility by their officers. Should he fall into our hands, I hope it will not be forgotten of him. They so overloaded their vessels with the spirits of this place, that I am told they have thrown quantities of pork and flour into the lake.

I really attribute this visit to the vengeance of heaven on this place, for quantities of stores, farming utensils, etc., sent from England in the time of General Simeon [Simcoe], were allowed to remain in the Kings stores and nothing of them did they [the colonists] ever get. Now, our enemies have them, to do with them as they please. I think we deserve all we have got. Keep up, your spirits, my dear John, for God seems to be on our side.

12
1815: UPPER CANADA
JOHN BALDWIN TO QUETTON DE ST. GEORGE IN FRANCE

John Baldwin, younger brother of the lawyer and politician Dr. William Baldwin, was a former partner of the prosperous merchant Quetton de St. George. When the latter returned to France in 1815, Baldwin took over his York store. Baldwin gleefully antici-pated regular shipments of French goods, which would make his store one of the finest in York. Now that the Yankee war was over, the town was booming and demand for lux-ury goods growing. I can imagine his dismay when he opened the stock that his former partner sent from France . . .

York
Sept 4th. 1815

Dear Sir
Yours of the 17th Augt I received by Major Simons this morning, and feel so much vexed that I can Scarce feel disposed to write to see other people get-ting goods into this town & me nothing comparatively. The Invoice of the goods by the Traveler was something but unfortunately it consisted to much of things we did not want such as *coars trash of Cloth* Scarlet, ditto blankets, a Trunk of Slippers so small that no one will by them as they will not fit

anyone, Natty Blue & white Calico as coars as *Tow Cloth*, a Trunk of coars Hosiery so coarse that not a Lady will buy a pr., not a pr. Of fine muslin or fancy goods amongst them, a few pieces of cambrick & other articles, excepted a trunk nearly full of Suspenders which are so dear & common they will never sell, a parcel of Sarsanet which we had the house full of before, and many other things in same way & & &.

So that the *devil* take Depending on the goods from England I say we have not any sewing Silks, no white thread, not an oz of tea either hyson or green, no *Crockery* or Glassware, no white wine, no Shrub, chocolate, gingers and many other things, not a yard of Irish Linen in the Store these 5 months—no light pocket Handkerchiefs nor any in the english Invoices and not a yard of Superfine Cloth has been in the Store since I belonged to the concern. All this is too bad. Since the new goods has come to town I have don no business at all and owe Wilmot $3200. This is to bad entirely. Young gets all the custom that is going . . . I know of no Store in town we are like but our neighbour Mr. Wood . . .

> I am dear Sir, Yours Truly
> J S Baldwin

From what you write to my brother I find you are going to marry. I wish you joy with all my heart. We hope you and Mrs. St. George will pay us a visit.

13
1818: UPPER CANADA
A LANCASHIRE FARMER TO HIS MINISTER IN ENGLAND

With the end of the Napoleonic Wars in Europe in 1815, the flow of emigrants from Great Britain and Ireland became a flood. Land speculators and emigration agents ensured that letters home from successful settlers were given widespread circulation. The comments from this phlegmatic Lancashire farmer on the shortage of manufactured goods were undoubtedly accurate, but his claims for the abundance of grapes, cucumbers, and melons seem rather far-fetched. And he never actually mentions winter . . .

Charlotteville, Aug. 30, 1818

Dear Sir,

According to promise, I now with pleasure hand you a few particulars of my journey. From Quebec it was tedious, expensive and disagreeable, a great part of the way being up rapid streams, only navigable for small craft; over Lake Ontario we had a pleasant sail, and good accommodation on board a schooner also over Lake Erie in another. It is necessary to observe that from Quebec all the way up the country the land kept improving even to this place, which I believe to be the most fruitful and delightful country I ever beheld, and the friendship of some of the first-rate people is such, that you'll scarcely credit it. On our arrival here, we were taken into a gentleman's house, and for five weeks the whole of my family were entertained free of expense. We sat down daily to as well-furnished a table as any in Preston, with wine &tc &tc. And to the honour of Scotland, of which he is a native, and of great respectability in this province. We are seven miles from the Court House, where the Assizes are held, to which I have been invited.

I have given up all idea of the United States, and shall remain one of his Majesty's Loyal Subjects, for various reasons, some of which I shall enumerate. Government, for the encouragement of Settlers, give grants of land. Myself, my son Edward and the young man who accompanied us have each received a grant of 200 acres of fine land. At present I am on an old settled farm of 300 acres, belonging to the before-mentioned Scotch gentleman, Col. Nichols. The rent is paid in grain, say one third. I purchased the crop in the ground, which puts us in possession of all the necessaries; the buildings are bad, but it produces both summer and winter keep for any number of cattle, also corn for our own wants and fruit in the greatest abundance, of cherries, plumbs, pears, peaches and apples in such plenty, we shall make cider &tc. Grapes hang in clusters would astonish you, and that *Natural*, we can gather any quantity.

In short, the soil and climate is such that a great many of the flowers as well as the fruit which are cultivated in England grow here spontaneously, besides a vast quantity of both not common there and many unknown. We have had not less than a ton of cucumbers and melons of four or five sorts. To raise them, you have only to dibble the seeds, either in field or garden, with no other preparation but plough or spade, which produces in abundance.

On the other hand, we want manufacturers of every useful commodity; industry, whichever way applied, is sure to meet with more than ample reward. Wearing apparel of all kinds brought from England meets with a ready market . . . yet there is very little money in circulation: they generally pay in produce, as wheat, . . . rye, flour, cyder, ashes, whisky. Had I come here ten years ago, I should have been as independent a man as any on your side the Atlantic; I really wish all my friends on this side. On my departure from England, some of them were inclined to send such goods on a venture, as they dealt in, which I objected to, not knowing how they might succeed. For the most part, they would have proved successful. Please to inform Messrs. P. and B. that if they had fifty ton of iron here, it would make 3,000 pounds; also Mr. Jno. T. that his goods made up and in hide would produce the like. Women and Children's shoes; Men, for the most part, wear strong half boots, some shoes; hats will be equally successful. Barley and hops grow here in plenty, yet few know the use of them as regards brewing and malting, also shumacs and sassafras.

14
1819: RUPERT'S LAND
COLIN ROBERTSON TO GEORGE MOFFATT IN MONTREAL

Far to the north of the Canadian settlements strung along the American border, the Hudson's Bay Company held sway over the vast territories in which it had held trading rights since 1670. But from the 1750s, the HBC, based in London, England, was challenged by a rival in the fur trade, the Montreal-based North West Company. In 1819, Colin Robertson was put in charge of fur collecting expeditions out of Norway House, the HBC's administrative centre perched at the northern end of Lake Winnipeg. Robertson, a hard-nosed Scotsman, was determined to beat the NWC. When he arrived at Norway House, however, he was horrified by the dissolute behaviour of the HBC men at a time when the HBC directors were planning negotiations with its rivals. Robertson confided his frustrations to his old friend Moffatt, a Montreal merchant.

Norway House

Here I am so far on my way to the North, but in the centre of trouble and vexation. The men belonging to the Sascatchwine [region of the HBC organization] opened their kegs at this place and have almost traded every article of wearing apparel belonging to our Irroquois, and as these men are much in debt, a fresh outfit must be a loss to the company. I can get no satisfaction from the gentleman in charge, as his men possitively declare they are masters of their own property. But this is not the worst, not being able or willing to wreak their vengeance on the N.W. [Company] for past injuries, they rose up in a body on my poor Canadians [HBC employees from Lower Canada], and I have no hesitation in saying, that had I not been present some thing serious would have happened. Mr. Archbald McDonald who was very zealous in keeping order was threatened with a ducking in the lake. I had no idea the sascatchwine men were in such a state of insubordination. Their master too, got quite outrageous in consequence of some slip slop talk which my old friend Bird had stuffed into his head.

The gentlemen clerks, whom Governor Williams handed me over, have opened a communication with the rum bottle, and every other night a dreadful crash takes place among their crockery ware, and if the fate of the North West Co. depended on the number of broken cups, their existence would be of short duration. I am fond of conviviality myself, but this kind of horse play is a thing I have never been accustomed to.

But the most painful circumstance of all is the discovery I have made respecting Mr Archbald McDonald whom I thought the very essence of management, from the direction of our affairs at Fort Wedderburne, but according to Mr. Miles' account is a lump of indolence and inactivity. He was stretched on his bed all winter under a feigned sickness and it was Messrs. McVicar and Andrews who conducted the business of the Post. Mr. Miles would have made his communication at Rock, but had no opportunity, and it was only after he embarked in my canoe, that I became acquainted with the real state of affairs in Athabasca; however I am saddled with the gentleman now, and must do my best.

Clarke is in high spirits as to his new enterprise being determined to divide the trade with the N.W. [Company] this winter. Here you will no doubt exclaim, "This is rather too much, John, remember you have not an Indian to your name." I shall be off from this dissafected place tomorrow.

Within a couple of years, partly thanks to the efforts of Robertson and Moffatt, the coalition of the two companies was secured.

15

1821: UPPER CANADA
A. BOAG TO HIS SISTER IN GLASGOW

In June 1820, 200 families sailed from Greenock, near Glasgow, to Quebec City. From there they made their way, by water and rough track, to land that had been secured for them in the Upper Canadian counties of Lanark and Renfrew. The first winter was bleak for the new immigrants: they had arrived too late to plant any crops, many succumbed to malaria, and the nearest Presbyterian church was some miles away, in Perth. But Boag was happy because he was finally enjoying an independence he could never have won in the teeming slums of Glasgow. I suspect he wrote so positively to his sister about his new country because he and his father desperately needed a housekeeper.

Lanark, Upper Canada
24th August, 1821

My father and I are settled on the 11th lot of the 6th Concession of Lanark township; he is on the front and I am on the rear; it was a 200 acre lot. The land is pretty good; we have cleared together, and have seven to eight acres in crop: we will have between five to six hundred bushels of potatoes. I intend to clear on my lot this winter. I never was so happy in my life. We have no desire to return to Glasgow to stop there, for we would have to pay a heavy rent, and here we have none: in Glasgow, I had to labour sixteen or eighteen hours a day, and could only earn about six or seven shillings a week—here, I can, by labouring about half that time, earn more than I need: there, I was confined to a damp shop—but here, I enjoy fresh air: there, after I had toiled until I could toil no more, I would have the mortification of being a burden—but here, two or three years' labour will give me more than will keep me in sickness, as well as in health: there, it is all dependence—here, it is a fair prospect of independence. Now, dear sister, if I had to come here again, I would come readier than before.

16

1821: UPPER CANADA
ANNIE POWELL TO HER BROTHER,
GEORGE W. MURRAY ESQ., IN OGDENSBURG, NEW YORK

I love Mrs. William Dummer Powell. She was the wife of the Speaker of the Legislative Council and chief justice of Upper Canada, and the most waspish gossip within the Family Compact. Mrs. Powell might be living in a colonial backwater, but she never let standards slide. She attended every ceremonial occasion in the legislature, every assembly and ball held in York, which by 1821 boasted a population of 1,600. A duchess in a Restoration comedy could not have been haughtier than Mrs. Powell, as she dismissed the late Queen Charlotte with a snort and requested a new gown from her brother, George W. Murray, a merchant in northern New York State.

York, 1 December, 1821

My Dearest Brother,

Mr. Powell's labours commenced on the 21st when at an unusually early period the Legislature was called together, 2nd. Dec. . . . . In the midst of all these causes of anxiety I have been obliged to do what under other circumstances would have been a matter of choice and source of amusement, attend a Coronation Ball given at the Govt. House, as soon as the farcical mourning for our unlamented Queen expired. It was numerous and splendid: between 150 and 200 people present, a proof of the increase of Society here at present augmented by the members of the Legislature . . . Eliza says I must have a black satin or black figured silk gown. Neither can be got here. Mr. Robinson would take charge of so small a parcel for me.

Your affectionate sister and faithful friend.

17

1822: RUPERT'S LAND
JOHN FRANKLIN TO ADMIRAL JOHN BARROW
IN LONDON, ENGLAND

In 1819, Captain John Franklin arrived in North America to map the Arctic seaboard and explore the turbulent Coppermine River by canoe. It was a gruelling expedition,

VICTORIA ISLAND

Coppermine R.

Franklin's Route
1819-1822

Great Slave Lake

largely because Franklin underestimated the severity of Canadian winters and his Indian guides proved unreliable. The party was forced to eat lichen and, it is rumoured, even their own leather boots to survive. When Franklin finally reached Great Slave Lake, he had to explain to his boss in London, the redoubtable Sir John Barrow (second secretary of the British Admiralty and founder of the Royal Geographical Society), the grim events that had befallen the expedition.

Great Slave Lake
April 5 1822

Dear Sir,

It gives me the deepest concern to communicate to you the distressing tidings of the melancholy death of my Friend and Companion Mr. Hood. We continued on the sea Coast in the prosecution of the objects of the expedition until the 21st of August when we commenced a journey across the barren grounds, in which the party Suffered incredible hardships from famine & fatigue owing to the want of Indian Hunters and the premature appearance of Winter. The strongest of the party were reduced to extreme weakness by frequent long fastings and walking for upwards of a month together through deep snow in a country destitute of firewood. And Mr. Hood Suffered partly from his less robust frame of body and partly from a peculiarity of constitution which exposed him to severe bowel complaints whenever he attempted to eat any of the mosses or lichens upon which the rest of the party derived some Sustenance whenever they could be pro-cured. On the 7th of October after [two?] others had sunk from fatigue W Hood finding himself unable to proceed at the pace at which the others were obliged to walk to give them a chance of reaching Fort Enterprise while their strength remained proposed to stop behind, in expectation of relief being sent to him by the first party of Indians that might be met. Dr. Richardson and John Hepburn a seaman prompted by Friendship which their mutual distresses had cemented, agreed to remain with him. They were left in a Tent about 35 miles from the Fort, whilst I with the rest of the Men proceeded in hopes of being enabled speedily to send them assistance.

George Back, a naval officer and artist, accompanied John Franklin on several expeditions and caught the bleak landscape of the Far North in this 1825 winter view of Fort Franklin, northeast of Great Bear Lake.

The next day four of my party became so much exhausted that they were quite unequal to the fatigue of travelling forward even at a moderate pace, and at their request received permission to return and join the officers behind. The remaining few five persons reached Fort Enterprise on the 11th of October, but in a perfectly debilitated state. To our infinite disappointment we neither found provision nor trace of the Indians, nor could we learn where to search for these Men.

You will easily imagine the deep affliction the unexpected circumstances occasioned and the painful apprehensions for the safety of my Companions in the rear which instantly excited . . . my mind and we were totally unable to advance further in search of the Indians and had to remain in the most pitiable condition Subsisting only on Singed deers skin, the Soup of pounded bones gathered from the Ashes heap, and an occasional mixture of Tripe de Roche [lichen] until relief arrived from the Copper Indians on November 7th, Sent by Mr. Back who had been Sent forward from the Copper Mine River to search for them.

During the interval Dr. Richardson & John Hepburn arrived at the House and communicated to me the mournful intelligence that Mr. Hood had fallen by the murderous hand of Michel, the only man who had arrived at their Tent out of the four who had parted from me on October 8th. This man had become regardless of the authority of his Officers and refused to either assist in collecting wood for the fire or to go ahunting, an occupation which he alone of the party had strength to follow. [He had] been on several occasions properly checked & reprimanded by Mr. Hood for this conduct, in consequence of which he had expressed a hatred towards him, but which his other two companions never could have supposed he would have carried to the dreadful [length] he did. On that particular morning, Dr. Richardson & Hepburn had gone from the tent, the former to gather moss at some distance, the latter to eastward so near the Tent as to overhear Michel and Mr. Hood in high conversation apparently disputing. Both of them heard the report of the gun which they supposed to have been discharged by Michel for the purpose of trying it, having left him in the act of cleaning his Musquet and therefore they did not go immediately to the Fire. After a few minutes had elapsed Michel called to Hepburn and said Mr. Hood was dead. He went to the spot immediately, and on observing the fact called to Dr. Richardson. On examining the wound, the Doctor perceived the ball had entered in the back part of his head, and was Convinced that the fatal shot had been fired by a second person because the musquet was too long to have been placed in the proper Situation to inflict such a wound and discharged by the same person. Hepburn on first hearing the report had perceived Michel stoop down and pick up something close behind where Mr. Hood was left Sitting, but Mr. Hood was shaded from his sight by a thick cluster of willows. Though they discovered much Confusion in the Manner & countenance of Michel, at the time, they did not consider it would be prudent to let him perceive they had any Suspicion of his having Committed the dreadful deed.

After they had recovered from the shock this awful scene naturally occasioned they united in prayers to Almighty God and then prepared for their departure for Fort Enterprise on the following day, where Dr. Richardson & Hepburn arrived on October 29th. The Manner of Michel's death is [reported?] in my official dispatches.

In transmitting to you this Statement I have performed the parting request which my dear Friend made of me in the event of his death. He thought the mournful intelligence would give too serious a shock if communicated directly to his Father, and I must beg of you to impart the distressing information to his family in the manner you conceive best calculated to alleviate the deep affliction they must naturally feel at such an irreparable loss. The greatest Consolation his associates [derived] under their sorrow at his desolation emanated from the knowledge that he had been [living] in a state of daily preparation for his awful [end] and that at the moment when the fatal act was committed he was supposed to have been reading Bickersteth Christian Help, which had fallen to the ground and was found laying open by his Side. The many documents he has Contributed during the progress of the Expedition bear unequivocal Mark of his great talent, energy and zeal. I must add to them my grateful sense of the unremitting attention and the valuable assistance he rendered to me on every occasion and whilst I deplore his absence most sincerely on my own account I feel his loss no less strong with respect to the profession to which he belonged being Convinced that had his Life been spared by the blessing of God, he would have proved a distinguished ornament to it [on] any [branch] but especially to that towards which he had recently directed his attention.

As soon as the opening of the Navigation will permit, we shall proceed to York Factory in the expectation of getting a passage to England by the next annual [Company ship] where I hope we shall arrive by the last week in October. I shall then [do?] myself the pleasure of Calling upon you early as possible, and give [you] any other information which may be required respecting my lamented Friend's debility and death.

After reading about the grim Coppermine Expedition, I have never quite understood why Sir John was so eager to return to the north in 1845 on his ill-fated attempt to discover the Northwest Passage. Exploration gets into your bones, I suppose.

18

1822: UPPER CANADA
EDWARD BLEWETT TO THE REVEREND JOHN STRACHAN IN YORK

By the 1820s, York had become a magnet for immigrants from eastern Canada as well as the British Isles. Local magistrates struggled to impose justice and good order on the crowded streets of a town that was doubling its population every few years. For malefactors who regarded their sentences as unfair, there was always a last resort—an appeal to the Reverend John Strachan, now rector of York and one of the most important and influential members of the provincial government.

York

Apl. 21 1822

An intire releance on your well known Humanity to the unfortunate Prisoners give me more than common confidence that you will pitty the most unfortunate of man my name is Blewett. I was born in Noviscocia where my Parants now Live and are considered respectable but I have disgraced them it would break their hearts, did they now know that their child was doomed to an ignominious punishmt. of being Publickly whipped in the Public Market. I was found guilty at the last assises of Stealing four plains. I work for the Person I took them from. I confesd. to him what I had done thinking it would induce him to pay me for my work what he owed me. I had no friend to state my case to the Judges. a poor Stranger in York I pleaded guilty. I know not nor would not do otherwise. God knows my heart. I am not a hardened thief. If Revd. Sir your great Goodness will induce you to state my case to his Excellency to remit that part of my sentence of being Publickly whippd. while I have Breath. shall be insensently offered up for your Protection and happiness the time is left to the direction of the Sheriff and I am afraid it may be put in execution tomorrow.

Mr. Blewett's petition was granted, and the sentence of whipping was remitted.

19

1829: UPPER CANADA

MISSISSAUGA INDIANS OF RICE LAKE

TO SIR JOHN COLBORNE IN YORK

The Reverend John Strachan was not the only authority figure receiving petitions from those who felt that colonial justice was a little rough. As settlers swarmed across the landscape, looking for good farming land, indigenous peoples were increasingly under threat. Sir John Colborne, lieutenant-governor of the Province of Upper Canada (1828–1836), was responsible for ensuring the security of Canada's native peoples. Their obvious respect for Crown authority (which they shared with the immigrants who encroached on their lands) seems extraordinarily deferential to a modern sensibility.

To His Excellency Sir John Colborne K. C. B. Lieutenant Governor
of the Province of Upper Canada &c. &c. &c.

The Petition of the Messissaga Indians of the Rice Lake in the New
Castle District.

Humbly sheweth,

That we and our Fathers having been in a long sleep have lately been roused
up by the word of the Great Spirit, our eyes are now open and we see that there
is light and truth by Jesus Christ for Indians as well as for our white Brothers.

That our hearts are grieved for the abuses which are done us by some
white men. Our hearts are true and we will speak plainly, white men seize
on our furs, and take them from us by force, they abuse our women and vio-
lently beat our people.

That your Red Children look for protection, We pray that late abuses,
which we have suffered may be inquired into. Some white men tell us that
we have no right to complain of Roberies on our hunters, and violence on
our women, we believe you know, and if white men do not understand that
Red men are to be protected, you will please to say, to what priviledges in
law the Indians are entitled to.

That we are poor in lands and have few places for hunting, much of our
hunting grounds are covered by white Settlement, and the small remainder left to us are invaded by the hunters from Lower Canada, they come
upon our hunting grounds, and wantonly kill and destroy all the animals
old and young, that come in their way. We have told them of their injustice
and urged them to depart; but our words are feeble and they will not listen. None but our Great Father can make them hear, when he speaks they
must obey.

And your Petitioners further pray, that in case the existing Laws do not
afford to the Indians a mutual and just protection, that Your Excellency may
be pleased to recommend a Legislative Enactment whereby Offenders may
be brought to Justice, in a Sumary manner.

York Jany. 27th. 1829.

Signed	their marks
George Pautash	

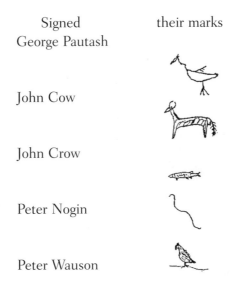

John Cow

John Crow

Peter Nogin

Peter Wauson

20

1831: UPPER CANADA
FRANCES STEWART TO HER COUSIN LOUISA BEAUFORT IN IRELAND

Relations between North American natives and newcomers were not always hostile. Many settlers were disposed to be friendly, recognizing how much they could learn from the continent's original residents. Frances Stewart and her husband, Thomas, arrived in Upper Canada from Ireland in 1822 and built a large log home on the Otonabee River, close to present-day Peterborough. The Stewarts had Chippewa neighbours. Frances, mother of eleven children and a cousin of the Irish novelist Maria Edgeworth, sent long reports about her new life to her Irish relatives.

Dec. 20th

There is an Indian encampment about a mile from us in the woods near Mr. Reid's, we are beginning to get acquainted with the poor people who are terribly shy, so much afraid of our dogs and the turkey cock that we seldom get them to come near. They go frequently to Mr. Reid's and are much delighted looking at prints or maps. Every Sunday seven or eight Indians and their wives sit round the table looking at them. I went to the wigwam one day where the Indian families live. It is seven or eight feet wide, of an oval shape, made with poles covered with birch bark and branches of evergreens, spruce and pine;

*I have only to look at Frances
Stewart's cheerful face to know that
she would rise to the challenges of
life in the bush in Douro
Township, near Peterborough.*

the floor covered with branches of hemlock strewed over the ground, then skins and blankets spread over that, and on this they sit through the day and sleep at night; a fire in the middle of the rude building, a pole across on which they hang bits of venison to dry and smoke. One squaw whose baby was a few weeks old was making a little frock of cotton for it quite neatly, putting green braid on the band and around the top; another was preparing a deerskin for making moccasins: another making a pair of the same; and still another making a basket. An old Indian whose name is "Squire Martin" was making a pair of snowshoes, his son a boy [of] eighteen was helping him. The boy, whose name was Jim Bigman, was our interpreter, he spoke English well. Four squaws and a boy came to me today with baskets, they sat a long time by the kitchen fire. I showed them some beads I had in ancient days on a gown, the squaws laughed, being much pleased and promised to bring me some more baskets for them. I want to tempt them to come here. I am in better health than I have been for two years. Mr. Stewart has gone for the first time to take his seat in the Legislative Council at York.

21

1832: UPPER CANADA
MARY RYERSON TO HER BROTHER JAMES LEWIS IN GRIMSBY

Mary Ryerson, wife of a Methodist minister and prominent Loyalist, John Ryerson, followed political events in Upper Canada with keen interest. She watched from the safety of her house in York the street demonstrations during an 1832 by-election, in which the fiery reformer William Lyon Mackenzie challenged the power of John

Strachan and his fellow members of the Family Compact. The red-haired Scot's attacks on the local oligarchy in his newspaper, the Colonial Advocate, *were so venomous that his Tory opponents had already expelled him from the provincial legislature for libelling its character. Mary was eager to describe events to her brother, a farmer in Grimsby, in the Niagara Peninsula. I enjoy these accounts from someone who had a ringside seat and stayed aloof from the political battle until she saw how events unfolded.*

My Dear Brother & Sister:

Being entirely alone this evening except my little children who are both asleep, I thought it good opportunity of dropping a few lines to you. We are all well at present for which we have great cause to be thankful to our Gracious Redeemer for his long continued goodness & mercy to us. I hope these few lines may find you & your family enjoying the same blessing. I am told it is very sickly in town—four or five funerals in a day.

Mr. Mackenzie had his election yesterday. I thought that there never were so many people in the town of York before. The procession came down Yonge street upwards of 50 sleighs & took Mackenzie about a mile up, agoing strait where the election was held. After he was elected the procession proceded back to town & [it] was thought there were more than a hundred sleighs, with many cheers by the way. His constituents presented [him] with a gold medal which cost a hundred and fifty pounds. They went to the Governor's & gave him a salute and then went to the parliament house. When the members heard them acoming, they adjourned & every one took his hat and ran. I have not heard since noon from the house. They had kept closed doors the first part of the day and would not so much as let the reporters in. I have not heard since. Mackenzie's expulsion from the house & the

Fiery William Lyon Mackenzie led the opposition to Upper Canada's lace-cuffed autocrats.

Governor's reply to the petition presented to him by our Conference has caused a very great excitement and it is hard to know how it will terminate.

We have had good sleighing ever since we were over & cannot see why Levi does not come over [unless] he is waiting for the snow to go away. I thought certainly he would have come over last Saturday. I hope that him & Hannah will come next Saturday without fail. If all is well I wish very much that you & Betsy would come over & mother. If you have apples to sell I think you would sell them very soon for half a dollar a bushel, or a dollar and half a barrel; that is the price for apples here. I hope Levi will fech us some lard & a few cabbages. They are dear here.

Please remember me to all enquiring friends. Tell mother I think she might come over if she wanted to. I wish to be remembered affectionately to her.

No more at present but remain
>   your affectionate Sister,
>   Mary Ryerson

P.S. McKenzie has got his [seat] today about noon. I wish you would write soon.

22

1832: UPPER CANADA
JOHN CAPLING TO HIS BROTHER IN SUSSEX, ENGLAND

In the 1830s, as unemployment soared in the British countryside, the number of families emigrating to colonies overseas swelled dramatically. Many emigrant letters contain searing accounts of hardships, but this is one of the most heartbreaking. John Capling (who also spelled his name Caplin or Capelain) was a labourer in the south of England when he heard about a scheme to finance the emigration of deserving families to British North America. In November 1830, he was given one pound ten shillings by his parish: the following year, he sailed to Canada along with his wife, Jane, and their eleven children, and several other families from his village in Sussex. Conditions on the emigrant ships were so bad that they were often called "death ships": cholera and typhoid were rampant in the overcrowded holds.

Huron Tract, Upper Canada,
August 28, 1832

My Dear Brother

I take the opportunity of writing these few lines to you, to inform you of our distress and trouble. After a very rough passage of twelve weeks, by the help of the Almighty God, we arrived safe to land, except the loss of two babes, Ned Luff's youngest and Wm. Tickner's youngest child. But we then thought ourselves safe, but the Almighty was pleasd to send a very great affliction upon us. In a few days after we arrived at our intended place of settlement I lost my poor little Mary for the first, then my poor dearest wife, then my two youngest, and little Edmund, all in the space of eight days. And what was more hard for me I was obliged to wrap them up in the rinds of trees and dig holes and put them in myself.

But, dear brother, I am not the only one the Almighty was pleased to send the affliction upon. Poor Joseph Kinshott was the first; and his sister, Nathan Morley's wife, were next; and, I am very sorry to inform my poor brother in law, poor Bob is gone: likewise the two young Landers. There was 32 of us that came up into the woods together, and there is twelve of the 32 dead. The complaint was the cholera morbus; they all died in the space of a fortnight. There [was] none laid ill but a few days. Dear brother, I should like to know what my brother in law should like to be done with poor Bob's things: he had no money. I think his things to [be] worth 6 pounds; [it] is now in [the] possession of Nathan Morley.

My dear brother, I am very sorry to send you this unpleasant account, but it is all owing to the affliction the Almighty was pleased to send upon us: for I can see [a] good prospect for a good living to be got. Flour is 7 dollars a barrel, which is 3 ½ bushels. That is the highest price; after another harvest, it will be lower, no doubt, as we shall all grow our own, and now it is brought a long way up the country. Mutton I kill, and sell out. I can afford to sell it 3 d. per lb., beef 2 ½ d., butter about 9 ½d: but I shall keep a cow and make my own next summer. I have nothing, no keep for a cow, this winter. Dear brother, if my brother William could take the heart to come, there shall be a home for him, as soon as he comes; for I have got a comfortable house up, and 100 acres of land, full of timber, and he shall have part of it. But I will not persuade any one to come, tho' I can see much better prospects here than in England. If he should, let him bring what ready money he can and not provide a parcel of things, as I did. For things is as cheap here as in England and tools cheaper. Let him bring a few one-sided oats, a little barley, gooseberry and currant cuttings.

My dear brother, remember me to all relations, and all enquiring friends. I hope, by the blessing of God, you are all well, as I thank God it leaves me, and the remainder of my family, at present. I hope you will write to me, as soon as you can. I remain your affectionate brother,

John Capelain.

But John Capling was stoic. Left with seven surviving children, ages six to twenty, he settled on 100 acres and prospered. In 1832, Lower Canada authorities tried to contain the spread of cholera and typhus by establishing Grosse-Île, just off Quebec City, as an inspection and quarantine station at which every immigrant ship sailing up the St. Lawrence had to stop.

23
1832: RUPERT'S LAND
THOMAS SIMPSON TO JAMES HARGRAVE, YORK FACTORY

James Hargrave was the administrator of York Factory, the Hudson's Bay Company entrepôt on the shores of Hudson Bay, and nerve centre of the HBC's vast trading empire. He coped with the heaps of trade goods to be sorted for the various districts, the mountains of pelts collected throughout the north and shipped back to London each summer, and the piles of invoices and accounts. He also enjoyed hearing about life in HBC outposts, and Thomas Simpson, an HBC trader in New Fort Garry (present-day Winnipeg) several hundred kilometres southwest of him, was happy to supply details to his boss.

Private

New Fort Garry
19 Dec. 1832.

My Dear Sir

I received your several favors by the Boats and feel much obliged for your kind attention to our business matters. I fear you will be grumbling at the requisition I now send, it is so dissimilar to that I gave in two years ago, but I told you so at the time. It has been calculated with great care, and there are many articles of which I would have asked for a still larger supply had I

York Factory, established on the permafrost in 1684, was the Hudson's Bay Company's most important trading post.

not been *ashamed*, such as Tools of all descriptions, white enamel Beads, green & 2 ¹/₂ pt [point] striped Blankets, crockery, and window glass—in which we are always deficient, but I shall take care that will not be the case in making out the Indent for Outfit 1835. The few things I have ordered on my own account I would be much obliged by your getting put apart for me. This is all I have to say on business, and now for a word or two of news.

In the month of October we had a terrific fire which threatened the safety of the whole settlement part of which had a very narrow escape especially McDermot's house, Mr. McMillan's, and Joseph Spence's; the fire went completely round the latter while the old man was asleep without touching the Wheat or haystacks, but it consumed hundreds of the latter out in the plains. The [Experimental] Farm had a very close shave, and Mr. McMillan had a general turn out of his people to plough in the middle of the night tearing up the ground round the Stackyard. At the Forks the fire came close to the outer fences when it was arrested by a large potatoe field which covers the rear of the Establishment.

On the 2nd [of October] at day break a most extraordinary meteor was seen by the Bishop, Mr. Jones and other credible witnesses in various parts of the Settlement, passing up from Lake Winipeg. Its body appeared about

the size of a nine Gall. Keg, but differently shaped, its section being ellipti-
cal, with a long bushy tail emitting fiery sparks. Its course was steady and
regular travelling very slightly elevated above the earth at the rate of a horse
at gallop. In passing Mr. Sutherland's, it descended so low as to brush the
tops of the willows, and desperately frightened a woman, who was standing
at the wood pile at the time, and threw herself on her face expecting that
the whole would be in a conflagration about her. Near the Forks it was
observed to shape its course up the Assiniboine, and was subsequently seen
at Manitobah. It has given rise among the "knowing ones" to divers fearful
prognostics of Cholera and other terrible calamities. Speaking of Cholera
we have alarming but apparently exaggerated accounts of its ravages in
Canada and the States from Michilimacinac through David Aikin (the Am.
Fur Co.'s Clerk at Pembina) who was here on a visit six weeks ago. One of
the victims he mentioned is Henry McKenzie of Montreal. I do not think
there is a shadow of danger here, but the Indians have heard the story, and
not a man will venture near the American Post at Pembina for fear of catching infection from their goods. This is a "ruse de guerre" of Nolins (who is
trading there) and a most successful one.

We are exceedingly well housed here in the new buildings; but I have
been so desperately busy for weeks back and have kept such late hours that
I scarcely know at this moment what I am writing.

Mr. Burns has been slaughtering all the pheasants in the neighbourhood;
I hope you are more successful than the two last winters in your partridge
hunt, and that I shall soon have a long "yarn" from you narrating your adventures since we parted; meantime with every kind wish

Believe me
My Dear Sir
Most sincerely yours
Thomas Simpson

24
1833: NOVA SCOTIA
JOSEPH HOWE TO SUSAN HOWE IN HALIFAX

Joseph Howe, future premier and lieutenant-governor of Nova Scotia, first made his
name as owner and editor of the newspaper Novascotian, *which under his leadership*
became a source of lively criticism of the government. He frequently travelled around

the province, selling subscriptions to his newspaper, gathering local news, and writing home to his wife in Halifax. It was a good thing that this cheerful, well-educated man had a sense of adventure: country roads were poor and lodgings unreliable.

Antigonish, Tuesday Morning
[September 24, 1833]

My dear Susy

I wrote you a terribly long letter on Sunday night—intending to defer my next till after I had received your letters in Pictou—but the fates have decreed that I am to be a prisoner for the day and I may as well devote a portion of it to your service. I finished all I could do here yesterday (I am sorry to say it was not much—for money is as scarce in the country as in town) and should have been on my way to the Gulf Shore before this—but it is pouring rain with a cold north easterly wind, and I have ordered a fire and must trust to my book and pen for entertainment.

I may as well begin where my last left off and give an account of myself since I left you for I have little else to write about. The worst of my perils were passed after I emerged from the forest upon the West Branch of the St. Mary's River. Nearly all our Rivers, towards their head are divided into several branches, which go off in different and often in entirely opposite directions receiving the tributary streams from the numerous hills among which they wind, and finally pouring their waters into some common channel, which bears them onwards to the ocean. The east branch of the St. Mary's goes off past the lower end of the Lochaber lake till it penetrates to the district of Pictou, the West Branch down which I had to travel trends away in an opposite direction towards Musquodoboit. The ride downwards for 15 miles to the Forks (which is so named because here both branches blend their common currents) was pleasant enough—tolerable farms are scattered along with spaces of woodland between, and are either on the one side or the other of the River as its windings leave the intervale to the left or right. I got to Archibald's at the Forks, which is a plain but comfortable place—half farmhouse and half inn—in time for tea, and amused myself during the evening with an old volume of sacred dramas.

Thursday morning it rained, and as Sherbrooke was ten miles off and destitute of any house where one could be moderately comfortable, if storm stayed, I determined to stay where I was and passed the forenoon fishing in the river—but with no great success, as the season did not answer well for trout. As it cleared up about dinner time I rode down to

Sherbrooke—stayed a couple of hours and got back to the Forks by bed time. The next morning it rained a little, and as I had 30 miles before me to Antigonish with no Inn on the road, I determined to wait for settled weather. To beguile the time I got a gun, and went into the woods for an hour, during which time I shot six partridges—knocking down three at one shot. I wish I had been near enough, or had any conveyance by which they could have been sent to you.

As the day brightened up I left them and took horse. But when about half way, it came on to pour, and as there were none but highland cottages on the road, I left my horse at one of these, and paddled myself over the Lochaber Lake to the house of a subscriber named Brown—a Glasgow man, who had just commenced a new clearing when I was here before, but had in the two years made a snug little farm. Here I should have been comfortable enough, but as every room in the house smoked my eyes suffered severely. The people were very kind and did all they could to make me welcome. As they had seen better days there were some remnants of decent furniture and some excellent books, which I should have enjoyed more but for the smoke.

You would be astounded to see how the poor settlers in the country live, and how many shifts they make to supply their wants, and do without that great indispensable Agent of the towns—Money. Many families do not see a pound in the twelve months—although perhaps they may owe some money on their farms and some more to the Merchant; and although they will often pay 20, 30 and some of them 50 pounds of debt in a year. Butter, Grain, Cattle, potatoes, and, where they live near brooks and rivers, logs are their common mediums. These latter they cut and prepare in the winter and raft down to the nearest saw mill in the spring. Archibald at the Forks told me he paid 400 pounds for his farm in this way, and during a good part of the time was obliged to pay 10 per cent on the money he was from time to time obliged to borrow. You may depend I borrow some [fair?] lessons of content from these people—some inducements to perseverence and activity in a walk of life more laborious to the mind perhaps (although that I doubt) but certainly not so severely harrowing to the body.

But to return to the Browns—the man was a weaver, and subsequently a grocer in Glasgow, and is an uncle to the Stayley Brown from Yarmouth who spent the evening with us last winter—a very well read and agreeable person . . . Brown came out to Yarmouth, at the request of his Brother—but finding the land bad and the prospect not promising he subsequently moved to Sherbrooke, but lost nearly all he had before he could get into any profitable way of business. He finally determined to settle on a piece of wilderness land which he had taken for a bad debt—and with his wife, a son and five daughters removed to the Lochaber, where they cut down a few acres of trees and raised a little log house, which still forms half of their present dwelling.

In this hovel, said the old woman, "I married three of the girls within a month after we came here—two of them in one day—and one on another—two of them hae goun to Merrigomish with their lauds, and one o'them lives a bit up the glen. Before we left Sherbrooke the girls were aye sayin' to their Father, 'Oh! dinna gae to the woods'—but every thing was going out there and nothing coming in—and I and the old man thought that if we did not get settled somewhere they would be marrying and leaving us [alone] at last. So up we came—and sure after, as I tell ye, two were married in the smoke of this little cabin. After the third one was gone, the Auld Man began to lose heart, and although we did all we could to cheer him—the stumps and the stakes—and the poor living and the loss of the children would some times come over him—but Agnes, the youngest, promised him that she would stay with him three years, ask her who would—and though it is more than that she has kept her word, and she might, I dare say, if she'd like, been married long since."

You may remember that I was in love with the sylvan appearance of the Lochaber or College Lake when in this country last. Then the ancient woods were scarcely broken upon on either margin, and the whole scene was as beautifully wild as it had been a thousand years before. Now every lot has been taken up—clearings are making and log houses are building in every direction—and in a few years more there will scarcely be a tree to be seen. When I left Brown's in the morning—the good humored girls filled one pocket full of cakes and the other of maple sugar—that I might not be hungry on the way. There was one method that they had adopted of perpetuating and extending my words—the walls were plaistered with *Novascotians*, and furnish an inexhaustible fund of amusement to all visitors who are able to read.

I got to Antigonish on the afternoon of Saturday—too late to do much. Sunday I went to the Chapel and heard the Bishop preach—partly in English and partly in Gaelic—he is no great orator in the former—but seemed to berate his flock pretty roundly . . . Yesterday I spent the day collecting, and rode down the harbour where some subscribers lived about ten miles—there was much cleared land and pleasant scenery which I had never seen. I dined with McDougal, who has a fine little girl, and spent the evening at Mrs. Manor's, who seems to have sacrificed her happiness for the sake of a husband. She has got a half stupid sot—and I believe but little property after all. Good bye for the present.

Yours
Jos Howe

25

1834: UPPER CANADA
CATHARINE PARR TRAILL TO
JAMES AND EMMA BIRD IN ENGLAND

Catharine Parr Traill arrived in the Peterborough area of Upper Canada from Suffolk with her husband, Thomas, and James Bird, son of close Suffolk friends, ten years after her friend Frances Stewart (see Letter 20). When the Traills moved into their new log home, Catharine was eager to describe to James Bird's parents how they were all doing. If I had been a pioneer, I would have liked Catharine as my neighbour. A perennial optimist who faced the trials of pioneer life with equanimity, Catharine wrote hundreds of letters to friends and relatives in England over the next sixty-seven years.

Westove, Douro
7 January 1834

My Dear Friends,
Having an opportunity of sending a packet free to England I gladly avail myself of it to assure you of my unaltered regard to tell you that I am well and happy and unite with my dear Partner in every wish that kind feelings and friendly hearts can offer for the continued prosperity of you and yours. As there can be no theme as interesting to you as what relates to your poor absentee I shall speak of James [Bird], before I dwell on more selfish matters and indeed it is with pleasure I assure you that he is well in health and appears to be steady and attentive in his conduct, improving I think in every respect since last I wrote to you. James has his youthful faults and who has or had them not at his age, but on the whole he is a good boy and I hope will prove himself worthy of parents of whom he is justly proud. He has his ups and downs in this country, all classes have their trials and hardship, they may

be called with truth, and James's situation does not exempt him from his share. They will I trust fit him the better for a settler's life when he becomes his own master, a period as yet distant. At present he is become intimately acquainted with the customary work of a Canadian farm. I could edify his Suffolk friends by telling them of chopping, underbrushing logging making brush heaps and log heaps, burning and branding a fallow, sowing and harrowing in wheat and rye, planting corn ie. Indian corn, for we do not here mean all sorts of grain by the term corn as at home, setting pumpkinseed and turnips, raising potato-hills etc. He could talk very learnedly of Raising-Bees, Logging Bees, Carpentering Bees and Husking Bees. Discuss the merits of Buck & Bright, the orthodox names for Canadian oxen, go through the logging exercise with

The perfect pioneer wife: Catharine Parr Traill, author of the best-sellers The Backwoods of Canada *and* The Female Emigrant's Guide.

stentorian lungs till the silent echoes of Cockfield Park or the Grove rang with—Hor Bright! Buck and hor round wo gee! Buck and many other unintelligible expletives that would wholly stam [confuse] a Suffolk horse-driver of untravelled wit. How the quiet little anglers of the ponds and tiny streams about his native village would stare to hear fishing by torch light on big lakes in a canoe made of the bark of birch trees and instead of a little hook a trident or a hook big enough to haul forth a whale or Leviathan himself. In short, my friend, your boy could set the whole village of Yoxford gaping with his feats of skill and knowledge. I do not know but he could even discourse in the Indian tongue, at all events he could give fine accounts of the Squaws and their swarthy spouses and their "Pappouses", ie. babes.

We are now comfortably settled in our new house. We moved into it on the 8th of Dec., late enough in the season, but many untoward and unavoidable delays happened to retard our getting the house sooner habitable.

When writers in this country speak of the rapid manner in which houses are put up upon one day or two they mean the icy walls merely. If you do not mean to live in a habitation divested of all comfort, much longer time is required. The difficulty of measuring sawn board is inconceivable especially if it so happens you are distant from a sawmill or a town. The badness of roads in this country, the slowness of conveyance, want of proper artificers etc. etc. are seldom taken into consideration by writers who write only to sell a book. When they talk of the advantages and comforts of a settlers life they pass over the intervening and necessary hardships and privations and talk of the future as if the present—but I was telling you of our new home.

Its situation fronting the Katchawanook Lake, I think I have described to you in a former letter. The inside of the building gives us a nice parlour with glass door opening towards the Lake (which by-the-by is now a sheet of ice on which I took a long walk a week or two back) a window looking towards the South and commanding a view of the Little Lake and its pretty wooded islets with a portion of my brother's clearing. We have a small but pleasant bedroom opening from the parlour and a kitchen, pantry and store closet. A cellar below the kitchen and an upper floor which can be divided into three bed rooms.

In the parlour we are kept warm and cheered by a Franklin stove a very handsome adornment to our room. The floor is covered with an Indian mat plaited by my friends the squaws from the inner bark of the [cedar]. We have a handsome sofa with brass railing which also [serves] as a bed for one or even two persons. I have made blinds for [the] windows of green cambric with white muslin draperies which have a light and pretty effect. These with the white painted chairs, a stained table, book case and some large maps and prints of General LaFayette, Kosciusco, Fox, and Brougham form the *tout ensemble* of our log sitting room. I hope you will say we keep good company for Backwoods men, though it be somewhat radical of its kind.

Now to my fond eyes the greatest adornment of our log house is my precious darling a most energetic and lively creature the joy of my heart and delight of my eyes. He is sitting at this minute on his doting nurse Isabella Gordon's knee with half closed sleepy blue eyes "devouring wittles" according to the phrase of a Suffolk settler of small degree and great appetite in our vicinity. In good truth my little James grows bravely and governs the house, the same way that Theseus son governed the world. He can say mamma quite plainly begins to creep and step with help though only 7 months today. I should think him the eighth wonder of the world only you my good friends have the tenth and eleventh . . .

My dear husband begs to be remembered to you both. He is the kindest most affectionate of partners.

What a pity I chose a short sheet of paper. I find I could have scribbled over a long one if only in discoursing on my boy, but must have done for it is bed time and sleeping awaits. With deep affection and sincere friendship believe me now as ever my kind friends your attached,

Cath: Parr Traill

26

1836: UPPER CANADA
WILLIAM ROBINSON TO THE REVEREND T. SOCKETT,
CHAIRMAN OF THE PETWORTH PROJECT, IN SUSSEX, ENGLAND

There was much land in Upper Canada, but there were few labourers for hire. Most immigrants, escaping from oppressive landlords and employers in the Old World, were determined to be their own masters in the New World. But landowners already established in British North America needed hired hands. One such landowner, William Robinson, hoped to persuade a few new arrivals to come and work for him rather than plunge straight into the bush to carve out farms. In particular, Robinson was looking for employees who would display British deference rather than Yankee insubordination.

Ekfrid Park, near Delaware,
London District, Upper Canada,
14th October, 1836.

The Rev. T. Sockett,
Chairman, Emigration Society, Petworth, Sussex.

Sir,
Understanding that you preside as the chairman of the Petworth Emigration Committee, I take the liberty of addressing you, presuming that the same good, which has hitherto been experienced by the many individuals which you have been the means of placing in a comfortable situation in this country, will be followed up during the ensuing spring, by your society sending

Field of stumps: after settlers had built themselves a cabin in the backwoods, they faced the back-breaking labour of clearing and fencing their land.

out more settlers; and being myself in want of labourers on my farm, I beg leave to make the following proposals to those families who may feel inclined to embrace the offer.

First, I will give employment to two men who have wives and children, who are of good reputation for sobriety, honesty, and diligence. The wages that I offer to these men are 30 pounds per annum, with a house rent-free, as much fuel as they wish and the keep of a cow winter and summer, together with as much land for a garden, or other purposes, as their families may require.

Secondly, I can offer a place to a young woman of steady age and disposition, who has been in service, and can produce testimonials for activity, industry, and capability, as a house servant of all work. And should the families not have a boy of 12 or 15 years of age who has been brought up to farm work, I will also give employment to a youth of the above description, with his board and lodging, and washing; his wages commencing with fifteen shillings per month, and yearly a proportionate increase, with his capability and worth.

My object is, to have people about me whose services I can rely on, at all seasons; and I am persuaded, that the only means of obtaining that end, is to get out families direct from England, who, by being kept together, are less liable to contract wandering habits; and when comfortably housed round their domestic fire-side, with every comfort that reason can dictate, will be more induced to conform to stationary habits, than embrace the roving propensities that too many of the emigrants in this country are addicted to. I have also other reasons for offering employment to families previous to embarkation, and who, on their arrival here, have employment, and a home, ready to their hand; for the more intercourse they have with the older inhabitants, the sooner they lose their native character, imbibe loose habits, become Yankeefied (if I may be allowed the expression), insolent, and independent; for which reason, I would avoid giving employment to any person who came to this country by way of the United States. I am, myself, an Englishman, and although not long a settler, have been in the country some years, in the service of the British Government; but as yet have not lost sight of the good old English manners and habits; and those about me, acting with and for me, I wish to observe the same . . .

Emigrants on their arrival here have much misery to contend with, and for a length of time after, that is, when establishing themselves on wild lands; and happy are those who have the good fortune to meet with an employer, who is disposed to place them in a comfortable situation, and aid them in procuring of those comforts without which, life is only a misery; and when they find those blessings bestowed on them, the only means they have of shewing their gratitude is, by faithful servitude. The District of Country from which I now write, is much wanting of able labourers, and particularly mechanics, such as carpenters, a blacksmith, a wheelwright, and in fact, almost any tradesman would find employment, as public works are now commencing, which will for years afford constant work. Having a tolerable large tract of land here, by way of encouraging mechanics, I would engage to settle them, by giving each, at a nominal rent for 3 or 5 years, village lots of about 5 acres, upon which to erect a house, and to cultivate, at periods when their mechanical exertions were not required. By this means, they would at once find a home and employment; during which term they might, if industrious, amass a sufficiency whereby to better their condition, if possible, or to remain with their families, friends, or connections, forming a social society amongst themselves. An able tradesman will earn his dollar per day, besides his board . . .

I shall be happy to hear from you on this subject, and if your Committee think proper to entertain a favorable opinion of my proposition, I will thank you for timely notice, so that I may make suitable arrangements previous to their arrival. In conclusion, I beg to say, that I consider this portion of the London District worthy of the attention of your Committee, as a part of Upper Canada well calculated to the settlement of the majority of the Emigrants, that you may think proper to send out next year; and I shall feel pleasure in assisting Mr. Brydone, or any other person you may select as superintendent, if such services are deemed of any utility, and this part of the Province eligible. It is healthy, well watered, and excellent soil.

> I remain,
> Sir,
> With much respect,
> Your very humble Servant,
> W. Robinson.

27

1837: UPPER CANADA

FANNY BRIDGMAN TO FANNY WEST IN ENGLAND

Tension simmered during the 1830s between the colonial officials in Toronto (formerly called York), who ran Upper Canada, and those excluded from power. The reformers included merchants, artisans, and the settlers scattered throughout the backwoods. Their most colourful (if not most effective) leader was the rabble-rousing journalist and former mayor of Toronto William Lyon Mackenzie. The tension finally erupted in 1837. That year, twenty-nine-year-old Fanny Bridgman, from Kent, was governess to Julia Bond Head, daughter of the lieutenant-governor of Upper Canada, Sir Francis Bond Head. Sir Francis was a high-handed and rather stupid man who loftily dismissed Mackenzie as "a madman." Sir Francis badly underestimated the reformers' demand for more voice in who might buy land, where roads should be built, and how their taxes should be spent. Until the last minute, he was also blithely oblivious to the fact that similar demands were also being made by the discontented "Patriotes" of Lower Canada, where Louis-Joseph Papineau led an uprising in late 1837. However, to Fanny, the lieutenant-governor was a hero, as she described in a letter to her childhood friend Fanny West.

Government House,
Dec. 15th 1837.

My dearest Fanny

I have no doubt you will be astonished to hear that our peaceful Province has been threatened with civil war, and that an insurrection has actually broken out and been crushed it is hoped for ever, or at least for a very long time. I will endeavour as well as I can to give you a faithful account of what has occurred . . . There were various rumours that the radicals were assembling at Newmarket, a place at a considerable distance up Yonge Street (all our roads are called Streets). On Saturday the 2nd [December] there was also a report that they intended to attack Toronto, in consequence of which, although no one thought they would really come, 50 special constables were sworn in, there were patrols in all the streets, and on Monday Sir Francis issued a Proclamation calling on the Militia to hold themselves in readiness. Things were in this state till Monday night, the 4th, when about 12 o'clock a Mr. Powell came breathless to Government House and told Sir Francis that the rebels were in great force within 3 miles of Toronto, and intended to attack us that night. He had a very narrow escape and had he not acted with great courage and determination we should not have been aware of their approach and had they got possession of the town our situation would have been dreadful as it was their intention to burn it to the ground. It appears he was riding up Yonge Street with a friend and that near the turnpike they were met by McKenzie, one of the leaders, a notorious radical, and some others, who endeavoured to make them prisoners. McKenzie presented his pistol close to Mr. Powell's face, it snapped [misfired]. Mr. Powell then fired at him, but his pistol also snapped, he then aimed at the other man who immediately fell from his horse, as Mr. Powell thought shot dead; it was however ascertained afterwards that he broke his neck when he fell. Mr. Powell then jumped from his horse, ran into the bush and made his way to Toronto with all speed.

We were very much frightened, I had been in bed some time; we all got up directly and dressed ourselves. Sir Francis with a guard of 12 armed men took Lady Head and all the females of the family to the Solicitor-General's house, as being a place of greater safety than Gt. House, as that was the first place the rebels intended to attack. Mrs. Draper received us with great kindness, and there we passed a miserable night, as you may imagine, apprehending all sorts of horrors. On leaving us, Sir Francis went down to the Town Hall, where he was joined by all the principal people, and there made every arrangement to receive the rebels—they however did not come that night. It seems that under Providence the death of Anderson, who was the most determined and blood-thirsty of their leaders, was the cause of their stopping. McKenzie wanted them to proceed, but they were divided and afraid we should be too well prepared for them. We remained at Mrs. Draper's until Tuesday evening, when the Archdeacon came to Lady Head from Sir Francis to say it was his wish that we should go on board the "Transit" steam boat, as he no longer considered Mrs. Draper's house safe.

We heard then that the rebels were at the top of the College Avenue, which is close to the town. We saw also the smoke from Dr. Horn's house which they had set on fire. You can have no idea of the state of excitement and terror in which we were. The scene on board the vessel was most distressing. There were several families on board beside Lady Head's and they were all in the greatest distress and fear for their husbands, brothers, and sons who were exposed to danger, as every one had taken arms. Although I was very much frightened and felt very deeply for them all, I was rejoiced and comforted to know that all who were dear to me were far away and in safety. During the night we were moored out in the lake, and in the morning we came back to the wharf, so that we could see and hear all that was passing in the Town. On this day, Wednesday, volunteers were coming in from all parts, it was a joyous sight to see them arrive and did one's heart good to hear the cheers of those who came down to receive them . . .

On Thursday Sir Francis, at the head of 2500 men, went up Yonge Street to attack the rebels; they were soon put to flight after a very slight resistance, and Montgomery's tavern, their place of rendezvous, burnt to the ground as likewise the house of Gibson, one of their leaders. The name of the place they fixed upon as their station was most appropriate, namely Gallows Hill. Only 3 of our men were wounded. McKenzie made his escape and has not yet been taken. 1000 pounds are offered for him. You may suppose that the party on board the steamer were most anxious all this time—I never passed so long a day in my life. At length the Mayor came to us and brought the rebel's flag, which he presented to Lady Head. He told us that the victory was complete, that the rebels were flying in all directions, and that Sir Francis had pardoned many who were brought up prisoners.

This act of mercy must I am sure have gained him the hearts of these poor deluded creatures, many of whom were so affected, that they burst into tears. He is indeed a noble character, uniting great firmness and decision with so much humanity and goodness. He is as kind and amiable in

private life as he is just and honorable in his public character. He sent the
carriage down to the wharf for us on his return, and on Thursday evening
we had the happiness of being once more in safety under the same roof we
had left in such alarm and which none of us expected to see again.
Everything is now going on well. Government House is a scene of great bustle and business—full of gentlemen from morning till night. Volunteers
continue to come in every day—on Saturday 500 came from Yonge Street
and on Sunday 1100 more; there is now however, thank God, no occasion
for their services, the business is done. Sir Francis has issued a
Proclamation to say that there is no further occasion for the resort of Militia
to Toronto. We are to have a body of 1000 men, who are to be stationed at
the Garrison for the protection of Toronto and the neighbourhood. There is
a guard round Gt. House night and day. It is really delightful to see so many
brave men ready to defend us to the utmost.

The town that was so peaceful and quiet is now like a garrison. Every one
is armed, horsemen are galloping in all directions and bodies of armed men
are to be seen marching about. There has been only one person killed on our
side, his death is very melancholy and has cast a gloom on our otherwise
bloodless victory—Coll. Moody, a gallant, courageous man, who lived about
15 miles up Yonge Street, had on Monday received certain intelligence of the
intentions of the rebels. He wrote a despatch to his Excellency informing
him of this and sent it by a servant; fearing however that he might be
stopped, which was the case, he determined to go to Toronto himself and set
out for that place accompanied by 4 other gentlemen. They soon came up
with a party of the enemy, through whom Col. Moody and another pushed
their way. But meeting another party, amongst whom was McKenzie, they
were again stopped. Coll. Moody fired his pistol; he was immediately pulled
off his horse and it is said that while on the ground one of the wretches shot
him through the body. He was taken to Montgomery's Tavern where he died
after lingering 3 hours. The number of the rebels was, I believe 700 although
it was said there were 3000. The inscription on the flag in Lady Head's possession is "Bidwell and the glorious <u>manority</u>, 1837 and a good beginning" on
one side, and on the other "Victoria 1st and Reform."

Bidwell was the radical speaker of the House of Assembly. Sir Francis has
allowed him to expatriate himself; he has left Canada for ever. McKenzie the
radical printer and editor of the paper called the Constitution is wandering
about the country. He is the most daring and cruel of them, the prime agita-
tor of all radical meetings and of the conspiracy . . . It was McKenzie's plan

to come to Gt. House., and he was heard to say nothing would satisfy him but Sir Francis's head. It is very well known now that it was their intention had they been victorious to hang the Governor and his principal officers, to burn the town and put everyone to death.

We have heard of one escape Sir Francis had—on Thursday when in pursuit of the rebels one of our party saw a man take a deliberate aim at him from a tree, the ball passed close between him and his servant who was close behind him. The man who saw this went under the tree and shot the villain dead on the spot. The rebels have lost a great many men, but the number is not known. There are 200 prisoners, among whom is Montgomery.

Decr. 29th. I add a few lines dearest Fanny to tell you that although the rebellion is put down here that we are still in a very critical state in consequence of McKenzie making his escape to Buffalo, where he has induced a great number of Americans to join him, about 800, to attack our Frontier. He has taken possession of Navy Island which is about 3 miles above the [Niagara] falls. There he collects his men, arms, cannons &a and threatens us with an invasion. It is supposed by those who know best that the American Government will prevent their people from joining these rebels and cut off all communication between Navy Island and the United States, and most earnestly is it to be hoped that this will be the case . . . as our situation would be most dangerous were they to assist our enemy.

Our frontier is however strongly defended by no less than 1300 horse and men. From the situation of Navy Is. it is almost impossible to attack it, certainly not without great loss of life, as on account of its proximity to the falls the rapids would carry the boats over the falls. There was a rumour that they intended to attack us to-day; we have not however received any intelligence to confirm this. You cannot imagine dear Fanny how anxious and I must add how frightened I am. There is something so dreadful in war and so unnatural in civil war that I quite shudder when I think what may be the result of all this. It is however a great blessing and comfort to know that we are under the protection of Him who never fails those who trust in him. I pray that I may have faith sufficient always to feel this. I was very happy to hear you had been so gay and happy—it always gives me pleasure to know of your happiness. I am sorry to hear your dear Mamma still continues weak and ill. I hope to hear a better account next time—pray remember me most kindly to her. Tell her I very very often think of her kindness to me. I trust I shall yet have the pleasure of seeing her once more.

God bless you dearest Fanny. I know you will excuse my entering on the subject of dress &tc. just now. Should these unhappy disturbances end favourably and I feel again at liberty to think of those subjects you shall have my full opinion. Once more God bless and preserve you. Believe me ever yours most affectionately

F. L. Bridgman

Give my best love to your sister & remembrances to all . . .

28
**1837: UPPER CANADA
CHIEFS JOSHUA WAWANOSH, EDWARD OGEEBEGUN,
AND GORDON MEGEZEEZ TO CHIEFS KANOODUNG,
MAUSHKENOOZHA, WANNEDEGOOSH,
AND JOHN KIYA RYLEY, NEAR LAKE ST. CLAIR**

While the settlers of Upper and Lower Canada decided whether they were for or against the reform movements, led by William Lyon Mackenzie in Upper Canada and Louis-Joseph Papineau in Lower Canada, the native peoples realized that their interests would be best served by staying on the sidelines.

St. Clair mission
14 December 1837

Dear Brothers,
we last evening received a letter bringing us bad new respecting the troubles which exist in our country, of which we were sorry to hear.

You enquire whether we think it best to take any part in these affairs. we can inform you that we consider it best to spread our matts to sit down & smoke our pipes and to let the people who like powder & ball fight their own battles.

We have some time ago counselled with the Indians around us & we are all agreed to remain quiet and we hope that all the Indians will do so, as we can gain nothing by fighting, but may lose every thing.

We should be glad to see you but cannot come at present, we send this by one of our Chiefs who will have a talk with you on the subject.

We have no fear that you who are wise will go astray, but we fear that some of those who are in the west on Lake Huron may be misled by designing white men & should such as are yet foolish be induced to commence war on the whites of any party, we should all be more hated by the whites than we are now.

We would just observe that we cannot be compelled to go & fight for any party, we mention this fact in order that should you be called on you may know that you are free men & under the controul of no one who has authority to make you take up arms.

29
1838: LOWER CANADA
LADY DURHAM TO HER MOTHER, LADY MARY GREY, IN ENGLAND

Louisa Lambton arrived in Canada in May 1838 along with her daughter Mary and her husband, Lord Durham, who had been asked by Prime Minister Lord Melbourne to prepare a report on the Rebellions of 1837. The British government was anxious to find a way to secure harmony in Britain's North American colonies without incurring any costs. During their brief stay in the colony, the Durhams made every effort to entertain the leading figures in Quebec society, but Louisa did not find everything to her taste. I suspect that some of the ladies she met in Quebec City might have found her "grande dame" manner a bit much.

Quebec City
Monday June 14

My dearest Mary,

I do not know when the *Hastings* will sail as the Admiral arrived last night & she will now await his orders, so that I send my letter to morrow by New York.

Lambton has been very much in want of the Admiral who has been long expected, & though I trust He has had the means of doing all that was necessary, I am very glad he has come to assist him. Every one tells me that all things go on in the Province as one could wish but the Pirates and the Frontiers are a plague, & the turmoil in which we have hitherto lived I think very tiresome. In short, I give many a sigh to home on many accounts . . .

The Drawing Room took place last night, & I am happy it is over though it was much more easily got through than I expected. There were about 200 ladies, every one that ought to come, & a much larger number of gentlemen but they went by so very quickly that it looked a very short time, & I was neither hotter or more tired at the end than I was before it began. The ladies had all done their best in dressing, & were smarter than I expected, but seemed in a great fright. That they are also when they come to dinner, particularly with Lambton, though he does all he can to put them at their ease. I cannot help telling you that the one he took out to dinner the other day, who had been given to him as the highest person present, ate jelly with her knife!

This is a beautiful place to see for a day, & we shall be glad to have been to Niagara, but it does give me a pang when I hear of other girls in England, to think that my dear [daughter] Mary is passing her time in society like this. If it ends with this year well & good, but I dislike the thought of remaining so much on every account, that I shall not be able to trust to our going so soon till I see the preparations actually begun. George [her hus-band] has not been quite well this day or two, the sudden change & heat of the weather have I think affected him, but I trust that he will soon be right again. He was not the better for another expedition we had with the *Hastings* people the day before yesterday, to the Chaudiere falls, which I think are much prettier than Montmorenci, but after landing from the Steamer we had to go 2 or 3 miles in the carioles of the country, & we were caught in a heavy rain & had to [come] back in a hurry, we were nearly jolted to pieces. Lambton had been kept at home by business, & as it turned out I was very glad. The heat has been very overpowering for the last few days. I don't know that I should have found it so if I had been able to sit still in a cool room till evening, but this I could not do & I have besides, been tormented by [bed]bugs at night, so that I have scarcely had a good sleep since I came to this house. In general, I am not a victim to those creatures, tho I am dreadfully disturbed by the notion of them, but this time they have attacked me more than the children. Every bit of furniture we have is new, but they crawl out of the floors, & it seems one cannot get into a house any where out of England without having some nuisance of this kind to encounter. However I trust we shall soon overcome these difficulties. The kitchen & eating at the Chateau is still a plague—worse for the servants than for us—but we are making our rooms very comfortable.

Pray give my best love to Papa & all. Excepting George's little indisposi-tion we are all quite well, Good bye my dearest Mary.

Yr. most affect.
Louisa

30

1838: NORTH OF LAKE SUPERIOR
THE REVEREND JAMES EVANS TO MRS. EVANS IN COBOURG,
UPPER CANADA

James Evans was a cheerful young Methodist missionary who was commissioned by his church to spend a year among the Indians on the north shore of Lake Superior, near present-day Nipigon. He had already acquired a good knowledge of Algonquian languages during a sojourn at the St. Clair Mission (present-day Sarnia). He left his wife and daughter at Cobourg and wrote home frequently, although he had to depend on infrequent Hudson's Bay Company expeditions to take his letters south. The nonchalance with which he describes sailing in a small canoe across Lake Superior in a November hurricane is staggering.

Mishebegwadoong
2nd October 1838.

My Dear Wife and Daughter

. . . Our prospects on Lake Superior are not by any means discouraging, but many things conspire to make our mission tedious, first we started too late by three months, as we should have left St. Clair in April at the latest instead of in July and we are now consequently winter-bound at this place instead of being three or four hundred miles further on . . . Brother Hurlbert has not yet left for Fort William, we expect the vessel hourly, we are keeping batchelors hall, and as we are so admirably qualified to cook for ourselves we have proclaimed "independence" and take our turns in doing the housework. Could you have seen the dumplings which we had yesterday, so nicely rolled up as if full of preserves while they contained but a few dry morcels of dried apples, dried I suppose sometime during the present century, and then boiled dry in our kettle, we had indeed a dry dinner, but ills seldom come single, we had so much, not having yet measured ourselves with apple dumplings, that we fried it for supper, eat it cold to breakfast, and put the remainder into our soup for dinner and then threw it away. So I leave you to guess the quality of apple dumpling thus thrown from pillar to post and at last given to the dogs. I suppose they ate it when hungry.

But upon the whole we live very comfortably. We have a great abundance. We have set our gill nets a few times and we have now packed for winter consumption four barrels of trout and whitefish superior to anything ever seen in your country. I went one day last week and set eleven snares a little way from the house and yesterday I brought home three fine large rabbits. These make fine broth and pot pie on which we have just dined. These animals are very numerous; some of the women here catch more than a thousand each during the winter. They are very fine eating.

Sunday 7. Last week a family arrived from the interior and came to see us about religion almost first thing; there has not been an evening during last week but we have had all the Indians present when we had family prayers. Yesterday the head chief of the tribe, a fine looking fellow, arrived and we were highly gratified in seeing him leading all his people to our wiggewaum in the evening in order to hear of the "good way", in fact no missionary can seek these people more faithfully than they seek him and I am anxiously looking for their return in the spring as the Chief informs us that his people will desire to be instructed and that they will do anything which God's servants direct them to do. I hope on snow shoes to see some of them in their hunting grounds during the winter. I must do something if it be only to kill time. I can't spend the long winter of seven months without some active employment. We have had some snow, about a fortnight ago it snowed nearly all day; however, it is all gone except on the mountains where we can see their snowclad summits giving us notice of the winter's approach . . . We had more than forty in our congregation today both forenoon and evening . . .

Saturday 13th. Today we have had a fall of snow but the weather is moderate. This is a vast extent of country here. The H. B. Co. have Posts from this to the Hudson Bay and from Labrador to the Pacific Ocean, and in all this region of thousands of square miles but two missionaries are to be found—church ministers—and one or two R. Cath. Priests . . . We had in our congregation last Sunday an Indian cannibal. It is well known that he and an old woman (a witch looking character) killed and eat two Frenchmen about two years ago, he is a sour savage looking fellow and looks as though he could eat anything. He however declared his intention to strive to serve the Great Spirit and acknowledged that he has been a very wicked man.

Saturday 20th October. Today the long looked for vessel arrived from the Sault Ste. Marie and brought letters and papers. Br. Hurlbert had two letters from his wife and I had one letter from Br. Stinson and the *Guardians*.

October 25th. Br. Hurlbert left here last Tuesday for Fort William so that I am now all alone . . . I expect God willing to start as soon as the ice clears in the spring and purpose visiting the Peak, Lake Nippegon in the interior, Lake St. Joseph, Lake Sal, Lake Winnebeg, Lake of the Woods, Rainy Lake and return by Fort William down Lake Superiour. You will of course discover that I shall scarcely reach home in time for [the Methodist] Conference, as I cannot leave this on my proposed route before the fifteenth or twentieth of May.

November 1st. Here I am never long in one place. I now write in my cloth tent on a small island about half way between where I commenced this letter and the Sault De Ste. Marie. I have thought it necessary for the prosperity of our mission to go to the Sault this fall and am now on my way with a small canoe and two Indian boys. I received a letter by the vessel from Br. Stinson and he appears to be particularly anxious that we should if possible locate a mission at or near that place. I am now going thither to see whether the chief Shingwaug has received a missionary from the Church of England and if not, should he wish it, to promise him one as early as possible from our Society.

We left Mishebegwadoong on Monday about noon, we have got along very well but the weather is very cold, the rocky shores are covered with ice as were our oars and paddles and canoe all the way. Yesterday we were met by a heavy gale from the Southwest. Several times we attempted in vain to land, as the surf beat on the shore with too much violence, and we were compelled to keep the lake, with a tremendous swell increasing every moment. The wind fell an hour before sunset and we got within three miles of our landing place [before dark] when the wind arose again with redoubled fury and we were tossing about three hours in the dark while the white foam of the majestic waves of Lake Sup. often threatened and sometimes even ventured into our little bark, but the blessed Lord saved us, we are now under the lee of a small island safe from harm. I shall rejoice to get your letters at the Sault. The weather today is more mild than for two weeks past and I hope it will continue so until I return.

I cannot deny myself the pleasure while scribbling altho my fingers are cold to give you a little description of my present establishment. Well, I have overhead a good cloth tent, not quite air proof to be sure, on one side in front lays our little canoe and on the other side heaps of pine tops extending some distance in front as wind breakers, between these is our camp fire before which my moccasin soles are cooking while my back chills. My present stock of provisions consists of about two pounds of rusty pork, half a pound of worse butter than you ever found at St. Clair and half a small loaf of good bread with fourteen potatoes and a little bit of tea and sugar. It still blows a hurricane and looks likely to blow on.

Nov. 6. 1 have this moment rec'd your kind letter and all its accompanying tokens of friendship and Christian sympathy. I have only room to say I thank Br. Mulkins for his politicks, Sister Rogers for her literature and Sister Boulton for her apologies. And may perhaps as soon as possible trouble the firm of Mulkins Rogers and Boulton with a letter. I am much obliged to my academic correspondents for their kind epistles which accomplished all they anticipated in giving me pleasure. I shall if all be well embrace an opportunity when matter accumulates sufficiently, to return the compliment. But as to politicks, there is here no Government and consequently no politicks, and being savages we have no literature, and among such uncultivated characters you would scarcely look for apologies. May God bless you in your various spheres of labour, Amen.

And now I had nearly forgotten to tell you who sent this mammoth sheet and mammoth letter, and lest you should be lost in conjecturing, I just beg to subscribe myself,

> Your loving husband and father
> James Evans.

31
1838: LOWER CANADA
EUGENIE SAINT-GERMAIN TO LADY COLBORNE IN QUEBEC CITY

Joseph-Narcisse Cardinal was a notary public and elected member of the Legislative Assembly of Lower Canada who had made his Patriote sympathies clear during the second uprising in Lower Canada, in November 1838. Sir John Colborne, commander-in-chief of British forces in Canada, suppressed the Patriotes with great severity; Cardinal was sentenced to execution. Cardinal's wife, Eugenie Saint-Germain, mother of five small children, sent a passionate appeal to stay the order of execution to Lady Colborne.

Chateauguay, Lower Canada 1838

To Lady Colborne,

My Lady,
You are a wife and you are a mother! A wife, a mother, under the stress of hopelessness, forgetting the rules of etiquette which separate her from you,

falls at your feet, trembling with fear and a broken heart, to ask You for the life of her beloved husband and the father of her five children! The death sentence is already signed! The fatal hour approaches!

Tomorrow, alas! Tomorrow!!! God! O God! I have no strength left to face such a horrid end. I would be stronger if another life did not depend on mine. But my miserable child will never see daylight! He will die with his mother under the gallows where his father, who deserves a better destiny, will have perished. O God! Is it in this way that you punish? No, No forgive me that blasphemy. Only men have recourse to such vengences. Only men kill the innocent with the guilty . . . guilty . . . What am I saying? And my husband, of what was he pronounced guilty? The most that one could say is that a bit of excitement, a weakness perhaps, led to his ruin . . . By character very timid, mixing little in society, not enjoying life except amidst his family who adore him, he took no part in the trouble which preceeded the final scenes of disaster. It was in his house that he was surprised by a sudden and unexpected movement. He did not make victims; on the contrary, he himself is a victim. That is his only crime, and for that crime, (if it is one), hasn't he already atoned? Hasn't he already suffered too much? And during the time of his imprisonment in his solitary prison, neglected by all, we, your humble petitioner and her children, haven't we suffered sufficiently for him? Formerly, happy with him, although in a humble condition, were we not banished from our home by the torch and brutality of an incendiary? Were we not stripped of everything, even our clothes? Weren't we obliged to live on bread provided by the goodness of God, and given to us by charitable persons, who for the love of God, take pleasure to distribute it to those who are in need?

And you, My lady, what heavenly treasure has not been placed in your hands? Have you not been given an immense influence over the heart and the spirit which today governs our destiny? Act like those charitable individuals of whom I have spoken, use this treasure for your eternal advantage, for that of the husband who you cherish and for your children who are your glory and happiness. Oh! humanity is certainly not banished from this land by vengence, humanity must have taken refuge in the hearts of women, without a doubt, in the hearts of mothers, such as yours. Humanity will speak from your lips—it will be persuasive, eloquent, irresistible. It will stop the sword of death, ready to slay all the victims. It will bring joy to the hearts of all the wretched who dread tomorrow's dawn. It will be heard even in heaven and will be written to your credit in the book of life.

I have the honour to be
My lady
Your, very humble and afflicted servant
Eugenie Saint-Germain, wife of Joseph-Narcisse Cardinal

Eugenie Saint-Germain's petition had no effect. The following day, she became a widow when her husband was executed for high treason in Montreal.

32
1839: NEW BRUNSWICK
JAMES ROBB TO HIS SISTER JANE ROBB IN SCOTLAND

Fredericton, the capital of New Brunswick, was always intended by its founders to be a "haven for the King's friends." In 1838, twenty-four-year-old James Robb, a graduate in medicine of the University of Edinburgh and the Sorbonne, arrived there to teach at the newly founded King's College, which was intended to produce an educated elite to govern the province. Robb found himself in the midst of a lively community that valued intellectual discussions and scientific pursuits. Robb added to the city's lustre: his collection of botanical, geological, and mineralogical specimens would become the nucleus of the scientific collection of the University of New Brunswick. But ferns and rocks were not enough to fill the vacuum in this young man's life. Fredericton was a small town on the fringes of the civilized world, and his nostalgia for family and friends in Stirling is heartbreaking.

King's College, Fredericton,
26 February 1839.

My dear lassie,
Will has forgotten me, and Mama has forgotten me and everybody else, so I will just forget them for a time and have a tête à tête with you. You are a good, kind, well behaved attentive little creature and I thank you for your long letter full of news. If you love me, however, you must repeat the dose. I get nothing here but business, business, business and it is quite a relief to get an easy good natured lassie like you to wreak my quizzicality upon. Now, Miss Robb, remember that I am one and that you are many, remember that I am alone and that you are altogether, that I am oppressed and overburdened with work and that you are comparatively idle, remember that you have all the distractions of a city about you and that I have only a village and some snow. Remember all that I say and try to persuade yourself and any

good natured people in your neighborhood to write me a little oftener . . .

I am working away again at the old work, lecturing, examining, scolding, fuming and fretting like fun. I have three lectures a week and two examinations and every thing must be prepared the same week: now in all conscience that is enough and if you just had one lecture to deliver in a week I think you would look rather out of humor. I guess as how you would.

I'll begin popular lecturing again and am always obliged to give up gaieties and amusements altogether: in fact if I had not constant work to do I would rage at you all from "dear Sir" to "yours truly". The popular course is geology and I flatter myself it is popular too but I can't gain by it, in fact I will lose. I had to send tickets to Government House and the Legislative Council and the House of Representatives and a dozen or two of my private friends. Do you know, lassie, that it is one of the oddest things in this world to look grave and lecture to people whose wine you were drinking the night before or to demonstrate the interesting peculiarities of a Megalosaurus and a Megatherium to the young lady with whom you danced or trifled the night before. But so it is, and I try to look as sagacious as possible. I never did imagine that I had much of the look of a pedagogue, and hardly can flatter myself that I have yet attained it. In fact I am often tempted to think that I am too much of a Gentleman ever to be a superlatively excellent teacher. If it was only lecturing as in our Scotch colleges or as at Popular Lectures it would suit me to a hairsbreadth and I might ever hope for all the renown which a lecturer is entitled to from the world; but here there is much more to be done. All the gaieties and absurdities of a miniature capital come in to lead off the minds of the young men . . . The House of Assembly fights for a week every year about the College charter and well they may. King's College has cost New Brunswick about 37,000 pounds already and it has only been in action about 8 years. There are we eating up their money and sending out but few students. Why should they not grumble? In fact to tell you the truth, if there be not some speedy improvement you will soon hear me begin to grumble and growl at matters as well as the worst radical among them. This is but a poor province on the whole, and things are miserably dear in it. I can't conceive how the people here keep their daughters in such good dresses.

My money does not go a great way. Everybody here, almost, is in debt. Some have great homes and little substance. A Fredericton party would however astonish you, because official people, be their office ever so small, always make a great show. Many of them give only one party a year and that one is a good one. Others give them once a fortnight and they are meagre enough. I go everywhere and anywhere when I am at leisure, or rather I go to all the people *of the set*. There are two sets in Fredericton. 1st, the Government officers, Clergy, and professional men—that is my set. 2d, shop and store keepers; and businessmen. There I am found by exception only and on rare intervals. It is death without benefit of clergy if you are caught out of your set. The Scotch are rather in the background here, and my friends are either bluenoses (natives) or English: Peters, the attorney general, Street the solicitor general, Shore of the Executive Council and Coster the Archdeacon give very pleasant parties.

Do you know that we are going to have war [with the Americans] here? . . . The disputed territory is a tract of about 10,000 sq. miles at the head of the St. John River. When the U.S. rebelled, the boundary between the British Colonies and the U.S, was left unsettled or rather it was settled on paper. But when the commissioners went to fit it in nature they could not agree upon what was meant by the terms of the Treaty, so they disagreed. After much palaver it was referred to an Umpire but the U.S. would not accept his decision. Now the General Government of the U.S. always recognized the right of Britain to the jurisdiction of the land in dispute. But the particular states (Maine and Massachusetts) to which the land adjoined conceiving that the warden appointed by Great Britain to prevent the timber from being felled on the disputed territory did not do his duty said, "We'll stop the depredations ourselves," and accordingly they send a sherrif and land agent and 150 armed men to drive off lumberers But the lumberers get ahead of the Yankies and surprised the lawyers and land agents while they are asleep, pop them on to a sledge and drive down to Woodstock 41 miles above Fredericton where they get a warrant made out for the men they had seized and gallop them down to Fredericton.

They go to Government House: "Major General Sir John Harvey Lieutenant Governor of the province of New Brunswick etc. May it please your excellency we have brought 3 prisoners." "My dear fellows," says Sir John, "I am much obliged to you: take them to the Attorney General or the Constable." So they drove them through all the town followed by all the dirty boys hooting and squealing. Then the Attorney General was at Council, so they drove again followed by same crowd to the Province Building and there all the House of Assembly and lawyers' clerks came running out with their hats off to look at them and they were galloped off in custody of the sherrif to a Hotel still attended by log hopping friends—the lumbermen with blanket, great coats and fixed bayonets. Then everybody was in excitement and alarm. "Oh the horrid men, the horrid men," said Mrs. Peters, the Attorney General's wife, whom I had met that evening. "What fierce brigands!" said another girl, whose ideas of ferocity must have differed very much from mine. For when I attended at their examination next day I found 3 quiet well shaved Americans looking quite as like green-grocers as fierce brigands at bay. At last they sent them off on parole. In the meantime our Land Agent (a British Crown officer) is seized by way of reprisal and walked to the States where he now lies. (His son Win. McLauchlan is my student). The Governor of Maine makes a blustery speech, talks of foreign dungeons and eternal disgrace to his citizens, gets 500 men sent to take possession of the territory and talks of drafting 10,000 more, orders 800,000 dollars to begin the war with, etc. etc.

Meanwhile, all the troops in New Brunswick go up to oppose them. The militia and volunteers are ordered into Barracks. There was a ballot for men on Saturday, but I escaped—chances one to 7. Another ballot soon chances 1–3 so that if I don't look sharp I will have to shoulder a musket yet. Right Face, march, present, fire, etc. How delightful, not to say interesting . . . But certainly matters are come to a pretty crisis when the defence of a country is trusted to me and such as me . . . But there is no danger. If the worst comes to the worst I will try to get appointed surgeon to a provincial regiment. Two or three of our students are obliged to go.

I wish I could see you among my lady auditors next Saturday. I would astonish your weak nerves. Oh how nice lectures! Oh how lovely lectures! Oh what delightful lectures! Oh my! Did you ever—no never—are as common as peas. By such expressions is my merit signified. By such emphatic phrases is their satisfaction shewn. But I have competent judges besides the ladies and *their* opinion is of more value. Excuse me, but you know I am not very partial to the sex.

I gave a horrid lot of commissions to Will in my last letter and I hope he will fullfill them. Positively you must get me a lot of letters next time and collect all the news. Tell me the works you read and the works you do, tell me your companions and your joys and your sorrows . . . I am often dull and low spirited for want of congenial society. It is really a horrid bore to be obliged to live forever with boys.

I sincerely hope that my health and strength will last till the end of this winter. But I have hard work and rarely get more than 6 or 7 hours sleep. I think I ought to be getting a parcel of books, etc. soon. May God bless you my dearest Sister and may you be an honor and comfort to us all and to my dear Mother in particular. May we all live to meet again, if not on earth, at least in Heaven.

33

1839: UPPER CANADA
SUSANNA MOODIE TO JOHN DUNBAR MOODIE IN BELLEVILLE

Susanna Moodie, sister of Catharine Parr Traill (see Letter 25), also arrived in Canada in 1832, and with her husband, John, attempted to establish a farm out of the wilderness near Peterborough. Unlike her sister, Susanna did not minimize her difficulties. The Moodie farm never prospered and there were always creditors knocking at the door. So in 1838, John Moodie took a job as paymaster to the British forces in Belleville, in order to earn some badly needed cash. Susanna and her four children (who were frequently sick) were left in the bush, with only neighbours like Agnes Caddy to help her. Susanna was a more than competent housewife, but she was also a passionate woman who found separation from her beloved John almost unbearable.

Melsetter
March 20, 1839

My Dearest Husband,
Banish all your gloomy forbodings, our dear children are quite out of danger, though a cough hangs on both of them, especially my lovely Johnnie [age five months], but I do not feel uneasy about it; as the spring advances I hope they will lose it entirely. I cannot keep Donald [three years] indoors, and the poor moccasins that I can manufacture out of old cloth, keep his feet constantly wet, which is one cause of the obstinacy of his cough. Dunbar [five years], who is no better off, is quite stout and well, and grows a very noble looking boy. His love for Agnes Caddy, is almost a passion, and he is always there. You would laugh to hear the little creature talking to her, just like a man desperately in love. He always sleeps with her, and says that he can't sleep if his head is not on his dear Addy's bosom. "Oh my dear little Addy; I love you better than any sing in the world." Addy is very kind to her wee pet, and makes him so docile and obedient, that he is quite a pattern to all the rest.

Your kind letter was a great comfort to me. To know that you love us, and think of us in all our sickness and privations atones for them all. How precious that love and sympathy is to your poor Susy no written language can

For Susanna Moodie, author of
Roughing It in the Bush, *it
never rained but it poured in
the backwoods.*

tell. In it, is concentrated every better thought and feeling of heart and mind. Oh, that I were indeed deserving of the love and esteem I so much covet. But, then, I should be too happy, and perfect happiness is no denizen of earth. I rejoice, in your having paid that miserable M'Donald dun [bill], and so much off the bank debt, you are an excellent Johnnie. I shall send Jenny [her servant] down to Crawfords with the 5 dollars and a note, some day this week. The other 5 dollars I must give to Jurys as I promised and I am glad to have something to stop their clamours, for they grow very impatient, and pay me a visit about once a month. An annoyance which I am forced to bear patiently, and treat the inflicters with civility. I must thank you very much for the shawl, which will be doubly prized, as a present from the beloved. I long to be with you—to see, to speak to you, to hold you to my heart once more. Three of the long months are passed. They have been months of sickness, anxiety and sorrow, and worse than all, of absence from you. There are times when I almost wish I could love you less. This weary longing after you makes my life pass away like a dream. My whole mind is so occupied with thinking about you that I forget every thing else . . .

The dear Traills are gone—I am doubly lonely now. Many tears have I shed for their removal, we have been on such happy terms all winter. They have been so kind to me especially poor [Thomas] Traill. One knows not the value of a friend till one is left alone in this weary world. The poor children quite fret after their good Aunt [Susanna's sister Catharine]. On Monday, Donald and Katie [seven years] went up to Stricklands in the ox Sleigh with George Godard to return the wheat we borrowed off [her brother] Sam in the fall. They did not come home untill three o clock in the afternoon. Old

Jenny asked Donald if he had had his dinner. "Oh no Jenny," said the poor innocent. "Dear Auntie Traill gone so we got no bread." "Yes Mamma," said Katey, "Aunt Strickland never gave us a bit of bread, but we went to see dear Aunt Traill's desolate house to console us, but it was cold and empty. Every thing was gone but the clock, and that was striking hours for nobody to listen to, and when I thought of dear Aunt I could not help crying to think she was gone."

It was strange, Katey noticing the striking of the clock in the empty house. It was a feeling connected with the highest range of poetry. Yet she has not the least idea of rhymes, and seldom remembers them in her little hymns correctly.

Poor Traill, with many tears begged me to remember them most affectionately to you. He left me his stove for the parlor, which has made the house warmer and more comfortable, and has given me a small pit of potatoes. Jenny has picked the whole cellar over, an awful job. There were about sixty bushels of rotting frosty potatoes to remove. I doubt whether we shall have enough good for seed. Well, I trust it will be the last year we shall have to stow them in that cellar. I begin to get tired of the woods, and now the dear Traills and Mrs [Shairp] are gone, I care not how soon we follow . . .

The Wolsleys have not as yet taken possession of Traill's house, and I shall not be able to call upon them till I get a pair of shoes. By the by, dearest when you are in funds, if you could buy me a pair of Indian Rubbers it would save shoe leather in the bad roads, and they would last for some time. Mr. Crawford tells me, that he fears you will not be able from the nature of your situation to come and see me. I have a strange longing to come and see you. But perhaps you would not think it prudent. Mrs Caddy would take Katey and Dunnie during my absence. Aggy remains with the dear Hagues, and Mrs Traill would take Donald and I should bring my wee darling Johnnie to put into his dear father's arms. Ah, this is one of my day dreams. But it amuses my loneliness. The coach hire would be the sole expence as I have friends at Peterboro and Cobourg who would give me house room.

My health is better than could have been expected, having had to sit up so many nights, with anxiety and want of rest. Do not therefore make yourself unhappy my dearest love. Had the poor little dears died, I should not have told you. It would have done no good only made you suffer. Thank God, I can speak of their danger with calmness now. Do dearest write me soon and believe you live ever in the prayers and affectionate thoughts of your faithfully attached and grateful Susanna. All the little dears unite in kindest love to dear Papa. Poor old Jenny is behaving better. We have had no run of sap, worth gathering yet.

March 25

Dearest Moodie

The Sheriffs Officer is here and has seized our cattle for the sum of 23 pounds on the account which you have just paid—viz—Macdonalds or Askews. It seems the writ was issued before you made payment. Why did not Bethune inform you of this? They will give you a fortnight or so to settle it up before the creatures are taken away. This, alas, has doubled the original debt, but it cannot be helped. I feel so agitated I can scarely hold my pen. The officer will be the bearer of this. Adieu, God bless thee ever.

S.M.

Do not buy anything for us till these horrid debts are paid. You can pay Askew himself he lives at Kingston . . .

34
1840: NOVA SCOTIA
JOSEPH HOWE TO
JOHN MORRIS IN HALIFAX

Joseph Howe, the newspaper editor, had now emerged as a no-nonsense reformer. He had little time for corrupt officials or British pretensions and was frequently challenged to duels by high Tories who disliked his politics. In general, he thought anybody who "engages in [duelling] lightly must be a fool—he who is fond of it must be a villain." When Howe received a challenge from John Spry Morris, second for Provincial Secretary Sir Rupert George, he made it clear that he thought a resort to firearms a poor substitute for political debate.

The great Nova Scotia patriot Joseph Howe, who would be the provincial premier (1860–1863), had little time for government bureaucrats or Confederation.

April 24, 1840

Sir,

Your note of this day's date, covering one from Sir Rupert George, has just reached me, and in reply to both, I have to state that I see no occasion for consulting any friend upon the subject of them—but, at once, and without hesitation decline the hostile meeting to which they point.

Having never had any personal quarrel with Sir Rupert George, I should certainly not fire at him if I went out, and I have no great fancy for being shot at whenever public officers, whose abilities I may happen to contrast with their emoluments, think fit to consider political arguments and general illustrations insolent and offensive.

> I am Sir,
> Your obedient humble servant
> Joseph Howe

35
1840: RUPERT'S LAND/HUDSON BAY
LETITIA HARGRAVE TO HER SISTER
FLORENCE MACTAVISH IN SCOTLAND

Letitia MacTavish married James Hargrave, chief officer of the Hudson's Bay Company main supply depot at York Factory (on Hudson Bay), in Edinburgh in 1840. Almost immediately, James Hargrave took his twenty-seven-year-old bride back with him to the bleak settlement on the edge of the Arctic, where Letitia's first reaction was "to turn my back to the company & cry myself sick." However, with Scottish fortitude, she made the best of her bleak new life. Because she was one of the few non-native women living in the HBC territories, her letters to her Scottish family give us a unique picture of life in the fur trade. An early letter describes her first journey across Hudson Bay. Her transcriptions of Inuit words were accurate.

York Factory 1st. Sept 1840

My dear Flora

I began and continued a sort of diary but in the hubbub of leaving the ship and my being so unwell I could do nothing. Mr Hargrave & Margaret lost the sheet containing our adventures in Hudson Straits so that I must remember what I can. On first entering, we were becalmed among the ice

& lay 2 days off Savage islands. For 24 hours night & day we were beset with Huskies [Inuit]. They were heard shouting for at least 2 hours & a half before they reached us which they did in light canoes with a hole in the middle. Each holds one man & a few tusks of ivory (walrus teeth) which they brought to traffic. There were 34 canoes. We moved so slowly that they kept up with us all the time: 3 hours after their arrival the luggage boats came up manned by women & laden with children, husky dogs, images or dolls in imitation of themselves. There were several large boats holding the various families of the gents in the light ones. Almost every woman had a huge fat child in her hood & when they saw anything in the sailors hands that they wanted they seized the babies, pulled off their one article of dress, shrieking *pilly tay* (give me), threw the weans who squalled like any white back into the hood. If they did not get quiet, they put their breasts some how over their shoulders & continued their *pilly tay*. When a saw was shown them, the whole fleet got into commotion & screamed *cutty swaback*. A gimblet was *billy linga*. They would give any thing for them but poor wretches except a few seal skins & the walrus teeth they had nothing worth trading. When they got any thing a broken pair of rusty scissors or horrid old iron off a barrel (the hoop) they rubbed their tongue over it. They use their boots as you used to do your wide sleeves—that is, put every thing into them, pot lids & darning needles.

I gave one some needles. He tried to stick them into his trowsers but always pricked his fingers, so after licking both finger & needles, he said *coonah* looking very knowing, & handed them over the ship's side to his *coonah* (wife). They were evidently quite ignorant of the use of water & nothing more horrible than the old black dirt of the ladies can be imagined. They rub themselves all over with grease & from the hood being always dragged down by the child's weight, their necks & shoulders are blackened by wind & weather. I got a [carved] doll & will see if it can get a place among the [smoked buffalo] tongues [which will be sent back to Scotland]. The hood is on the head & the tail behind is too short, but the carriage & shoulders are the very thing & the shape of the face. They keep bawling *Chimoo Chimoo*, signifying good & *aha* when pleased which indeed they always seemed. The men looked well, each in his beautiful canoe, but the women gathered together in the luggage canoes were hideous.

While the canoes were round us, a shouting & yelling arose & off they all paddled towards a berg, where on looking through a glass an unfortunate seal was discovered. Their clamor stupefied the animal & he stood quietly till they harpooned him on which he fell head over feet off the ice into the water. Any thing like the rapidity of their progress I never saw. All the men's canoes were there. They cut the seal up, ate what they wanted (they don't cook) & then divided the remains faithfully among them. When they returned to the ship each man had a lump of red seal behind him. Every moment they would put a hand back rub it over the store & lick the fat & blood off the paw with great satisfaction. We had great difficulty in getting rid of them, they followed & made such a noise & the smell they left was insufferable all about for days. Although only one man had been allowed to come on board, yet he managed to drag his wife up by a leg & arm. Hargrave & I were standing on a pigs' house when she came up & before I could escape she had her arms about my waist dancing & singing till I thought we should have either got over board or down among the pigs.

They plait their hair in tails both before & behind & are certainly well sized & not the wretched looking objects they are often represented. They are a little fat I confess, but had they been clean they would many of them have looked well, particularly the men who seem very strong. They wear often a queer sort of spectacle to save their eyes, wich are probably affected before they put them on by the snow both on land & water . . . They all appeared very happy & good natured to each other.

This early watercolour of an Inuit man fishing from an inflated walrus hide confirms Letitia Hargrave's description of the Inuit's skill with harpoons.

The day we got out of the Straits was very rough & we were all in bed sick. It was by far the worst day I had for constant sickness. We were 6 days crossing the bay & during that time, the fog was so dense that we got no observation so that it was an agreeable surprize when on Sunday 9th the sun appeared & at noon we found ourselves 20 miles north of York & the beacon in sight. We arrived at the bar about 6.P.M. that evening but on crossing the tide had turned & there we were ashore. It was alarming as she lay much on one side but providentially the night was calm. Next morning, however, she did not get off & we left her in the yawl at 4 o'clock & after partly sailing, partly rowing, we reached [York Factory] about half past 7.

I forgot to say that on Friday we got into some very thick ice & feared that we might have been kept. The bells were kept ringing for a while by the thumps but by dint of management we escaped. A large white bear came out on the ice. We had seen one in the straits & by my running on deck I got a few days threatening of an attack of earache but it was very slight. Mrs. Finlayson's hands & my feet suffered dreadfully from chilblains. They broke & swelled so that I had to wear mocassins & she could not put on her gloves. This was in the straits. I had to wear my fur tippet in the cabin & every thing else I could get. The others sported blanket shawls, Mrs. F. having been deluded into paying 13 pounds for a cloth cloke grudged to wear it & in fact it was such a weight that she could not go up the steps with it. I now . . . wear my black shawl when I go out & the thin cotton drawers & mousseline gowns which have struck astonishment into every one by their showiness.

We were only once damaged by the ice. I was in bed & the shrouds & scuppers at my side were torn away. Nothing could be more wearing out than the never ending bump bump bumping & then rumbling under or past us. Sleep was impossible. It was like the loudest thunder & the ship quivering & flying right back which is always a good thing as she is less liable to injury. The water was beautifully smooth, not a ripple upon it & the shape of the different pieces of ice large & small very diverting to those who could sit & look on deck. Mrs. Finlayson had a horror at being blown up & as there was gun powder under our cabin would not listen to the proposal of a fire. I was sure I would die of cold, the Doctor insisted on my having one, and from the first made a hubbub about my sitting & sleeping in the state of health I was in, in a room which was washed twice a week & never dry, as there was no window but the sky light. One day I got faint at dinner & had to scud into my berth so the Doctor fought & had a fire &

I got thawed & never suffered from extreme cold for the few days we were longer on board . . .

I have written on scroll paper in consideration of postage. Give my love to Hector & Alexander. I often wish very sorely that I could see Alex & many a good volley Willie gives me for saying it. I know I will like York as well as any other place if I ever get over the constant wish to hear from you. Hargrave I think will go back to Scotland at last if we live but at the very soonest that will not be for ten years. Of course I mean to remain. I fear you will hardly read this.

With kindest love from Hargrave & myself believe me ever
My dear Flora

Your most affectionate sister
Letitia Hargrave

36

1840: RUPERT'S LAND/HUDSON BAY
JAMES GUNN TO HIS FATHER, GEORGE GUNN,
IN THE ORKNEYS, SCOTLAND

James Gunn was an Orkneyman who entered the Hudson's Bay Company and crossed to North America in 1836. He worked as a mason at York Factory. In 1840, when the HBC ships were making their annual voyage carrying furs and men back to England, he wrote to his father, a farmer back in Naversdale on the island of Orphir in the Orkneys.

October 24
York Factory

Dear Father
I embrace the uppertunity of writting you this fue lines to let you know that I am in good helth at present thank god for his merciful kindness towards us. I received your letter the tenth Agust which was Considered very erly. The ship came from Orkeny in 7 Weeks to York and I was in the second boat at the ship. I received the Bundle which you sent me Safe and was very glead to receive it. I sold some of it T[w]o pair of Trousers one pair of shoes I sold. I am to Send A Bill of four pound sterling, Two pound to my brother Adam and two for A fue things from my brother John. I want one pair of Best White Molskin Trowerses, one worsted frock, one pair of shoes, two pair of stockings.

But the money it run short. Mind let my brother John pay himself for making out of the first end. And for the Fraight and if it cant run to the things that I mention never mind pay yourself in the first place and you will send it out as usually. When you writt me the next year let me know how times is rowling at home. I hope you will writt me same as usual.

If God spairs me I think <u>I shall be home the next year a look if I should go off again, it will not be to this place that I will goe to again</u>. Dear Parents Try to scool Morison my brother well and put him to a good Trade, a ships Carpinter is the best trade I know now. Without a trade a man is nothing. <u>This country is very bad and always getting worse every way</u>. You will Give my compliments to all my Cosens in Tankerness, in Nearhouse, and likwise the people of Coat and my friends in Orpher. I add no more at present,

> Your Effectonate Son till Death,
> James Gunn

Not surprisingly, given his discontent, James Gunn left the Hudson's Bay Company service in 1841. His letter to his father was never delivered, and for 160 years was stored unopened in the "Lost Letters" collection in the Hudson's Bay Company Archives. James was not the first member of his family to join the HBC. In 1806, his aunt, Isabella Gunn, arrived in Canada disguised as a man and calling herself John Fubbister. She worked alongside the other Orkneymen until she gave birth to a boy, James, at Pembina in December 1807. Once her gender was known, she was not considered capable of a man's job and was relegated to the laundry tubs at Albany. She returned to Orkney and ended her days in the poorhouse in Stromness. Audrey Thomas's novel Isobel Gunn *presents a fictionalized version of Isabella Gunn's story.*

37

1840: UPPER CANADA
ROBERT BALDWIN TO LOUIS-HIPPOLYTE LAFONTAINE
IN MONTREAL

Out of the discontent and uprisings in Upper and Lower Canada during the late 1830s emerged two politicians who shared a new vision for their country's future, in which French and English had equal rights. Between them, Robert Baldwin and Louis-Hippolyte LaFontaine developed the intellectual framework for a self-governing Canada. LaFontaine, a Montreal lawyer and reform member of the Assembly of Lower Canada, had travelled to London in 1837 to plead with the Westminster government for constitutional reform. The following year, Baldwin, a Toronto lawyer and Reform member of the executive council of Upper Canada, met Lord Durham when the latter was in Canada and urged him to recommend a more democratic form of government for the colonies. This letter, the first in a lengthy correspondence, marks the start of a long, respectful, and important friendship.

Robert Baldwin, a Toronto lawyer, worked closely with a Montreal politician, Louis-Hippolyte LaFontaine, to ensure equal treatment for Upper and Lower Canada.

Toronto 26 Nov, 1840

My dear Sir,

My professional engagements during the last Term prevented me till now from acknowledging your politeness in sending me the pamphlets connected with the subject of your seminary, which I shall not fail to read with that attention which the consideration of everything so important as I understand this to be to our Lower Canadian fellow subjects demands from us.

I had been informed of the paragraph [criticizing LaFontaine] in the *Herald*, though I had not seen it. I have however been so often the subject of misrepresentations myself, that I am always slow of belief in matters of this nature, particularly when the information comes from such a source as the *Herald*.

I sincerely regret the [adversarial] position of parties . . . in Lower Canada, and am therefore more anxious for the proclamation of the union, as the first step towards changing it, and mitigating the evils which appear to me to have grown up under it. There is, and <u>must be no question of races</u>. It were madness on one side, and guilt, deep guilt on both to make such a question. But, my dear Sir, while the Reformers of Upper Canada are ready to make every allowance for the unfortunate state of things and are resolved, as I believe them to be, to unite with their Lower Canadian Brethren cordially as friends, and to afford them every assistance in obtaining justice, upon precisely the same footing in every particular as ourselves, it is, be assured, not to the adoption of a course of proceeding leading necessarily to collision, and tending to stop unavoidably the whole machinery of the constitution, that they look for the accomplishment of this just and necessary object; but on the contrary, to the harmonious working of the constitution itself, by means of the new principle which . . . no one can now doubt is to be applied to its practical administration, coupled with that forbearance, moderation, and firmness on the part of the people, which so long as it compromises no great principle, affords the best assurance of the possession of fitness for the exercise of political power.

Believing these to be your sentiments, and those of a large majority of your friends, I am I confess becoming impatient of the present unnatural state of things, though I take it for granted that there must be some necessity for its continuance, which my not being sufficiently acquainted with the state of Lower Canada prevents me from properly appreciating.

My father and brother request me to present to you their best respects,

> And believe me, my dear Sir, to remain
> Yours truly, Robt Baldwin

From 1840, the two men forged an alliance to promote equal treatment of Upper and Lower Canada: in 1842–1843 and again in 1848–1851, they were joint premiers of the united Province of Canada.

38
1842: CANADA WEST
GEORGE CHILD TO HIS MOTHER,
LYDIA CHILD, IN CANADA EAST

When George Child was fourteen years old, he accompanied his father, Marcus, from their home in the Eastern Townships of Canada East to Kingston, Canada West, where the parliamentary session of the united Province of Canada was temporarily convened. Marcus Child was a merchant and potash manufacturer who had recently been elected to represent Stanstead in the Legislative Assembly. According to George's sister, George was sulky and obstreperous at home, but once in Kingston, the youngster was homesick. When he tried to go home on his own, however, he hit a major snag. The colony's banking and commerce were still largely unregulated, and every little (and insecure)

local bank issued its own paper currency. If the bank failed, the paper (including a
$2 bill given to George by his father) was worthless.

Kingston 28th 1842

My Dear Mother

I am under the necessity of writing you a letter as I think it is my duty to do
so. I will tell about Kingston it is very dirty every thing is thrown into the
streets you can think of it is very limy the water is bad but I think it was
intended for a very large nice town but it is altogether different from that.
The most splendid thing that I have seen yet is the soldiers . . . band they
play most beautifully they march to church on every Sunday. Their are very
fine buildings of lime stone. But I forgot to tell you that I have been to two
soldiers funerals march slowly the music very solemn the drums were covered with black & when we got up there the soldiers that had guns stood
each side of the grave & loaded and fired. The musick beggan on a very high
tone and died away slowly the drums beating the same time. I started for
home on Tuesday the 20th and went to Ogdensburg in the *Gildersleeve*. She
is a very nice clean boat. I pass the thousands islands which was a grand
sight & on my way I saw Major Richardson house. He is in Kingston now.
I arrived in Ogdensburg in the afternoon and found every thing wright as a
book. But when we were going to Kingston, father bought a couple pair of
braces at Ogdensburg and pa handed the man a five dollars bill. He gave
back in change a two dollar bill from the Agricultural Bank in Toronto
[which] has been down this five years. Father handed me the bill and said
that I might have it if I could get it changed in Ogdensburg. I went to get it
changed the man said he never gave pa such a bill and I could not get it
changed. I went back to the hotel where the mare was and paid my bill and
started for home again when I got out of Ogdensburg, the roads were so bad
that it took from four o'clock until eleven in going 13 miles. I got to a tavern
there stopped over night. In the morning I started on again. They told [me]
that the roads were good but I found them so bad that I turned around and
went back. When I got back to Kingston fathere said that we would go
home in ten or fifteen days. I shall wait until he goes home. You write to me
in your letter how is Gerzy my horse . . . I am your son ma

G.M. Child

39
1843: CANADA WEST
MARCUS CHILD TO LYDIA CHILD IN CANADA EAST

Marcus Child liked Kingston little more than his son did, but he enjoyed the cama-
raderie among legislators and his jovial humour would probably go down as well in
today's House of Commons as it did in the 1843 assembly. He lobbied doggedly for his
constituents and pressed for better local roads and protection for spawning fish in the
local rivers. However, he was anxious that the Legislative Assembly should find its per-
manent home in his own province in Montreal, where the residents were more wel-
coming and the water quality better than in Kingston.

Legislative Assembly
28th Oct. 1843

My Dear Wife
Today one month of our Session has passed, and for the time, more business has been done (and we may hope well done, too) than was ever before
done, in the same time by a colonial Legislature. Nothing new, however,
since yesterday. I write to you every day—immediately after Breakfast I go
to the House and it generally happens that the clerks are not ready to serve
the committees till 11 or 12 o'clock consequently I read what I can find in
the Newspapers that is worth reading (which is little) and then I look out
for a pen & some quiet place (scarcely ever to be found) and fill a sheet to
my dear Lydia. This is a most beautiful morning—the Lake is calm, sky
clear & air warm, so that it is comfortable; without an over coat, the snow
treads down, but is not yet wet, but as the sun gets up, it will rapidly melt.
    Saturday is with our House, a holiday. Nevertheless, members are from
one accord so desirous to finish the public business, so as to go home to
their wives and children, that they work as much as on any other day; and
perhaps more so. Kingston is no place for pleasurable relaxation. Last
Saturday, the Governor General and the Hon. Speaker of the Assembly
entertained large and joyous parties at dinner. I send you a bill of fare with
which the Speaker treated his guests. Capt. Moore, who sat a little to my
left and proved a great wag, as well as one of the first of song singers,
Anglefied some of the dishes: "Le Quartier de Chevreuil Roti"—a quarter
of a roasted horse, and "Les Charlottes Russe Glacées"—Charlot's glasses,
which when understood round the table made a good deal of fun. We had
English, Irish, Scotch, Canadian, & voyageur songs, in the chorus of which

most of the company joined, and a more joyful set of folks is scarcely to be found in Canada than the Hon. Speakers guests were. They were mostly Lower Canadians. And a little circumstance which occurred on my walk to the Pavilion in company with Mr. Turgeon, a French member [from] below Quebec (who by the way gave us one of the best french songs during the evening . . .), when he found, from the little conversation we had, that I was a Lower Canada Member, he put his arms round me and gave me a fraternal hug, with the expression "bon ami du Bas Canada". And it is a fact that Lower Canadians are really attached to each other and the more so in an unsocial place like this. In our House there are men belonging to the medical profession and civil rank from the Lower province, and although Kingston has such, no notice has ever been shown by the latter to the former. And it is generally known among our members that the Kingstonians resolved in public meeting before the Opening of the present Parliament in 1841 that in consequence of the expense it would endure, they would give to the members of neither House or of the government no dinner, or other parties. The consequence is they have no communication whatever; and was I to give my opinion, I should assign this as one of the strongest grounds of dislike which the Lower Canadians entertain against this place and will go very far in carrying it to Montreal. Next week the matter, I hope, will be forever set at rest at any rate there will be a larger majority for Montreal than I expected two weeks ago. Now we are sure of nearly 30 majority.

Save the bill of fare as a curiosity! As soon as Elizabeth comes home I shall write to her. In the meantime I shall keep up my letters to you as often as I can and hope you will do the same. You should have some paper brought in and then you will perhaps write oftener . . . Nothing is new in the Cabinet. Sir Allen N McNab [Allan Napier MacNab, a prominent Tory from Hamilton] is up in the Gore District agitating against the removal of the Seat of Government to Montreal. These upper Canadians are as fickle and boisterous as the surface of their Lakes. I have little sympathy with them or for them any way. Love to all

M Child

Marcus's hopes were realized: Montreal, the pre-eminent city of British North America with a population of 40,000, became the permanent capital of the Province of Canada.

40

1843: CANADA WEST
SOPHIA EASTWOOD TO HER PARENTS,
THE STANDENS, IN SUSSEX, ENGLAND

Sophia Eastwood arrived in Canada with her husband, Alfred, and seven of their
nine children in 1843. Two children, Thomas and Laura, were left with grandpar-
ents. The Eastwoods were ideal immigrants: they had the skills and stamina required
for life in the bush because they had farmed back home in Sussex, England. But
their early months were hard, as they tried to find land they could afford, first in
Canada East (Quebec) and then in Canada West (Ontario), and watched their
scanty savings dwindle.

Bloomfield
July 6, 1843

Dear Father and Mother,

We hope these few lines will find you and our dear children in good health
as thank God it leaves us out here at present. When we wrote to you last
we had just arrived at Quebec. Alfred and I went ashore there on the
Sunday. We went to see the Plains of Abraham where the battle was fought,
and we saw the Monument that was erected on the spot where General
Wolfe was shot. It was a great sight to see the batteries and wagon loads of
cannon balls that lay around them.

The steam vessel came and took us on the Monday afternoon at five
o'clock and we arrived safe at Montreal on Tuesday about twelve o'clock.
There we hired a room for which we gave one shilling and threepence a day.
The children and I stopped there and Alfred went down [on foot] to Brome.
He found Brooker and Stevens that went from Frant [a Sussex village close
to their own] but not doing so well as he expected and he did not like that
part of the country. It was very cold and stoney and could not grow any
wheat. It was a hundred miles there and he was gone nearly a week. When
he came back, we thought we would go further up the country so we took
shipping for Kingston which cost us four pounds ten shillings. We were
three days and three nights going.

Thomas, your father says I am to tell you that we saw more islands than
ever you read of. We went through ninety locks, through little narrow places
where there was just room for the vessel to go through between rocks and
woods and then out into the wide lakes again. We saw trees tacked together
and a fire on them, and a tent that men lived in made of the bark. They

floated on the water and they went up and down the river lumbering in the woods in them. We went to Bytown [renamed Ottawa in 1855] and we saw the house Colonel By lived in when he was Governor out there.

When we got to Kingston we met an English gentleman who was very kind to us and took us into a storeroom of his. We stopped with them for a week and he advised Alfred to go to a place called Picton about seventy miles from there. Edgar and his father went, and the children and I stopped at Kingston. There another gentleman offered them a house rent-free until Alfred could suit himself to something. So he came back and fetched us all up there to a place called Bloomfield about five miles from Picton. It is fine open country, where we are and there are large cultivated farms. The farmers are almost all Quakers.

It seems here that every man must have land before he can do anything for himself. None here will employ a man steadily, only for a few months in the summer and there is no such thing as to get money of them. They will let you have anything they have got except that.

The gentleman whose house we live in has taken Sarah to live with them.

As Sophia Eastwood's letter describes, and Frances Anne Hopkins's water-colour The Lumber Raft *illustrates, loggers' rafts were large enough to carry tents, campfires, and dozens of men.*

She has been there a fortnight and likes it very well. She is to have two dollars a month. Edgar went to a situation yesterday for three months. He is to have seven dollars a month.

Dear Mother, if you were here and had got a farm you might ride in your four wheel carriage, for here they all have a pair of horses, and the wagons and gigs keep continually running all the day long. I will just tell you what they say about here, that tis a heaven for women but a bad place for men and horses.

We hope you will write us a long letter when you receive this and send us word how you are getting on and how your crops are. Please tell us how your hops look and how you get on with your dairy. We cannot get any cheese here. The farmers make it and sell it in the fall. Butter is one shilling and sevenpence a pound; meat is very cheap, but clothing is very dear where we are and earthenware is a most extravagant price. We are troubled to get anything to use. We ought to have brought that with us of all things.

We are just as well off as I thought we should be. We have not got a chair or a table or a bedstead belonging to us. Our being obliged to travel so far and getting no employment it has taken all our capital nearly.

Tell dear Laura to send word how many chickens she has got, and accept our kindest love from

Your affectionate son and daughter

Sophia's stalwart confidence paid off: the Eastwoods finally acquired property in the backwoods north of Belleville, close to present-day Rawdon. Sophia lived on the farm for the rest of her life, dying in her ninety-fourth year in 1893.

41
1846: CANADA WEST
WILLIAM HUTTON TO HIS MOTHER IN IRELAND

The dispute between Britain and the United States over the exact location of the boundary west of the Rockies threatened to spill over into armed hostilities in 1846, and William Hutton, an Irish-born schoolteacher and farmer in Belleville, was infuriated by what he perceived as a Yankee land grab. Hutton was a hard-working, community-minded citizen, who took intense pride in the growing prosperity of his family and his country. Unlike the Moodies (see Letter 33), he had the advantages of owning fertile land near to markets, so his success is not surprising. I find that his pride verges on smugness, but I am prepared to allow him a sense of relief that he had escaped Ireland before the dreadful potato blight and ensuing famine. His mother, back in Summer Hill, near Dublin, must have thought that Canada was the New Jerusalem after receiving this letter.

Sidney, nr. Belleville
Jan. 18th, 1846

Dear Mother,

How shall I begin the long chat I love to have with you this blessed evening of a peaceful Sabbath, when family prayers are over and our dear ones talking of going to their rest, except Joseph, who can now only chat to us on paper, having returned to College last week. His journey thither was not a very pleasant one, having been overturned; but fortunately into a snowbank and without receiving any injury. Our winter has been a most delightful one; our natural railroads uninterruptedly fine and our weather overhead splendid; a bitterly cold day not yet having assailed us. This, united to the more comfortable state of our house and our being better defended from the cold, has made us all enjoy this winter beyond all others. These are not the only mercies either, for prosperity of every kind attends us—excellent crops, excellent prices, excellent times, excellent children, and not less important, excellent health.

All we have to fear at present is the approach of war. Our unprincipled [American] neighbours (politically speaking) seem to have the hump of acquisitiveness much too large and require a very tight rein to be held upon them to prevent them from coveting too practically our beauteous colony. We sincerely hope that our dear old Mother Country will continue to cherish her children, though remote, and will, in proper time, take the most Christian means to teach our grasping neighbour that the rights of her children must be respected. I cannot contemplate the idea that odious, detestable and Unchristian War must be had recourse to in these enlightened times, when there may be found so many other ways of deciding a dispute about [the Oregon] territory. Their braggadocio style of speaking and writing (denying that any European power has a right to hold lands on this Continent) is extremely galling to the subjects of dear old England, and some means must be taken to silence them, and that effectually and promptly. War is hateful and would be extremely injurious to us, as we have such an extensive and undefended frontier. It would be the means of preventing Capitalists from investing their money in our Colony and would indeed retard our progress exceedingly, if not put us back half a score years. The very necessity of having war would show that one nation or another was retrograding instead of advancing in civilization. But the British inhabitants here will not give up a kind and indulgent and dear old parent for a younger one without a desperate struggle. She would only be a Mother in Law; we could not love her with filial love. If they would only let us alone, we would do very well, "with plenty of bread and butter".

No such year for the prosperity of every class has been known in Canada. Our produce *all* sells high for cash . . . We never spent so cheerful and happy a Christmas since we were married. On our wedding day, the 30th of December, we had a party of 57 from town and country. We had an excellent spiced round of our own good beef and two fine turkeys and ham and fowls in abundance and custards and apples, etc., etc., in every shape; the produce of our own dairy and barnyard and orchard; and a most delightful evening we had, dancing till about 3 the next morning. All appeared to enjoy themselves much. The fiddler played in the hall between the parlor and drawing room, and both rooms were full; one 15 by 21, the other 16 by 18. They were the cream of the country, being the best educated amongst us: lawyers, doctors, and clergymen, their families and a few merchants . . . We had only three farmers; but there is a very apparent desire on the part of many of them to educate the rising generation, and such times as these are, by giving them the means, will foster the inclination. If there be no better motive to excite them, *ambition* will do much in a few years.

Our party cost us very little, as we paid for our wine and spices in wood; made our jelly (most beautiful) out of our pigs' feet; made also apple jelly, excellent; and blancmange unsurpassed, and trifle most charming. We had to borrow chairs, dishes, glasses, etc., etc., pretty largely but had not one broken. The party is universally spoken of as the Party of Parties and was the first we ever gave in Canada. We danced the quadrilles altogether, not caring much about the polka, and country dances appear to be out of the question. Mary dances very prettily and Sarah and Lizzy are about to learn. Anna does not enjoy dancing much. Our whole family had not been together before for 3 years. We hired no one extra to assist. The girls did almost everything and are, from long experience, complete adepts . . .

21st. I have just had the threshing machine threshing out our wheat and eleven men to attend it. In a day and a quarter we had about 215 bushels which will make 44 barrels of flour and 2200 lbs. of bran, which will feed

Mama's cows all Spring and give us plenty of milk and butter and some money for our hay season and harvest. We hope flour will be at least 30 shillings per barrel of 196 lbs., but all depends upon the state of your markets at home. I do not wish poor people with you to starve, but I may rejoice that, under the circumstances of such high prices at home, we have plenty to dispose of and at a fair remuneration.

As to poverty here, it is out of the question. The higher agricultural produce is, the better for all classes, as we are a colony of farmers. At the same time we are all poor, but want is an entire stranger in our country. This is perhaps the greatest recommendation to Canada, and to a merciful man a blessing not to be recompensed by a more enlightened state of society such as you enjoy; because along with the enlightenment you have to witness the miseries of the human race. If we were only sure of peace and a continuance of British rule. I would not change countries with you for a consideration. Very many speak of my fortunate location in this most beautiful and thriving district.

The children brought in fresh eggs yesterday, so mild has been our winter, at least 3 weeks earlier than last year. We wish we were near enough to send you some of them, so beautiful are they. We begin to count now for our year's supply. Last year we had 200 dozen or 2400 and sold 100 dozen. This year we have twice the number of hens but I do not think they will be so profitable as the fewer numbers. Fanny was able to oblige her friends all winter with packed ones and gave a great many away. Her cows too will soon be calving, so that her spring work is at hand and her spring means will be very early available this season. The girls will have plenty of spinning to do as soon as the weather gets warm. Nothing pays so well as our wool when manufactured at home. In the meantime, Anna is keeping a regular school every morning till dinner time and the girls are coming on pretty well. Lizzy makes an excellent attempt at speaking French words; she seems to have an ear for it. I expect to be about a fortnight absent from home at this time [inspecting schools]. With very dear love to my Father, Mary, Mira and all dear friends . . .

> Your ever loving son,
> William

42

1846: CANADA WEST
HENRY CHANTLER TO HIS BROTHER JOSEPH CHANTLER IN NEW YORK STATE

The Chantlers were a close-knit Quaker family of weavers who arrived in the New World from Surrey in 1832 and settled in the prosperous farming area fifty kilometres north of Toronto. The unmarried men in the family quickly discovered that, in pioneer Canada, men heavily outnumbered women. When Henry Chantler heard from his brother Joseph that the latter had found a wife in Ogdensburg, New York, his envy was almost palpable. If I was his new sister-in-law, I would have some reservations about meeting a man with such repressed passion—although I would have been gratified by his poem.

Newmarket Whitechurch

Nov. 12th 1846

Dear Brother,

I wish you with your better half much joy in your Hymenial change. I was not a little surprised when I found in your letter of the 28th Sept that you had united in the bands of Matrimony and have transformed yourself into a Married Man. I am happy to hear also that you are united to one who is kind, affectionate, tenderhearted, and of a respectable family. I still remain unmarried and the day seems far hence when I shall be able to pronounce the assertion "I am a married Man." Though at times I feel wrought up to a sense of my own oneness and when I serve up my soul with the thoughts of being comforted with one of those creatures you talk of, my heart throbs with the greatest emotion sometimes starts off on the trot rears, pitches, bounds, and leaps to the canter rendering it difficult by times to keep from being overthrown. But when I reverse the train of thinking it settles down into a perfect calm and seems ameliorated by being unattached.

But no more of this, let me give you a detail of things less grave than that of Marriage Courting or Love, for certainly they are these things clothed with solemnity though often contemplated with mere bubbles of thought.

I have my health as usual it being by times scarcely probable but I still continue teaching school in the same place and expect to remain through the winter. My school at present numbers 45, and I have prospects of having a very large school in the winter season. Alfred [his brother] still remains at his trade as firm and as staple as the Alpine hills and as steady as a town clock. Nath [another brother], I am sorry to say is not doing much for himself he has been sick all summer or nearly so and is now without a place. Esther is well and Brooks the same, both and in fact all of us are anxious to see you; we are particularly so now when we anticipate the pleasure of seeing the person you must assuredly bring with you. We would all be glad to hear how you are situated what wages you get &tc. the next time you write.

Esther with all your connexions here send their best and most precious Love to you & M[ary] A[nn Millard], hoping that you enjoy true happiness in every sense of the word, highly recommending too the peace you talk of, which as you say is the principal thing. Though earth with all her Laurels, crowns, thrones, Sceptres, pomp, pride and gaiety be collected in one wreathe it is not to be placed on a paralel, with that peace of mind—the soul and life of man. Receive this as flowing from the heart of your affectionate brother.

H. Chantler

TO M[ary] A[nn Millard]

Dear Sister in Law
Though I have never had the privilege of beholding your face yet I form your appearance in my imagination. You will pardon my presumption in taking this liberty of addressing you. As it comes through the medium of your connexion with me influenced by the warmest affection towards you perhaps this will merit your excuse.

> Remember me who'll think of you
> And often long to see
> Though billows roll between the homes
> That nurture you and me
> Wilt thou permit a wandering thought
> To cast its flight on me
> Whose heart is filled with deep desire
> And friendly love to thee
> Remember too a married life

Is always filled with care,
But at the theme of Love have vent
And give to J— his share.
If through the day thy anger rise
Or something go Amiss
Be reconciled before you sleep
An seal it with a Kiss.

Your H. Chantler

43
1847: CANADA EAST
ELIZA STACEY TO HER FATHER-IN-LAW,
EDWARD STACEY, IN ENGLAND

Pretty, loyal Eliza Stacey knew all too well the dark side of her marriage vow: "For bet-ter, for worse . . ." Her charming husband, George, was a reckless and improvident man, who was saved from London's debtors' prison only by his father's influence. The practice of sending family "black sheep" off to the colonies was already well established among the English middle and upper classes, and the elder Mr. Stacey was adamant: George and his long-suffering wife must leave England. The Staceys were exiled to Sherbrooke, Canada East, where George started farming and made friends with other English immigrants. But he was soon fighting off creditors, and Eliza found herself liv-ing hand to mouth and forced to appeal once again to her father-in-law.

March 1847

My dear Father-in-law,
I have noticed through life that my spirits have never been duly elated, or my hopes of worldly advantage apparently about to be increased, but the hopes are frustrated and more than equally depressed by disappointment. Certainly such is the fallacy of relying upon worldly expectations.

Some time ago George was sued by a man of the name of Crosby for a debt of 12 pounds which he had been owing a long time, and as he had not liquidated it they sent a bailiff to put an execution on the house and seized what comforts we were blessed with. George advised his lawyer on this debt, and was led to believe that things were going on favourably.

We had not felt guilty of this debt, for the whole affair is due to an unscrupulous rogue, and the lawyer had agreed. The fellow hired our horse about four years ago, on which he rode to Montreal so hard, and in such terrible weather, that he killed him. We never heard from him, nor were we paid one farthing for the hire of the horse nor its loss. We had given the matter up as a bad debt, and thought that the 12 pounds George owed him would serve to settle the hire and loss of our horse. But not so.

Last Wednesday after supper the bailiff arrived in a sleigh, arrested George and took him to Sherbrooke gaol. You can imagine my distress and tears, and poor George was distraught at leaving me suddenly with everything to do, and my baby due in about two weeks' time. No entreaty served to bring mercy, and George was driven away in the bitter cold to the prison he had been condemned to once before.

After all this time we had put George's debt out of our minds and considered we had been generous to the rogue Crosby, and now we are told that our debt, with the interest and legal expenses, might come to near 100 pounds.

George has been taken at the worst time of the year, for he and Fred [their son] were busy logging, and he has a hired man in the house to assist. The ground is hard and at its best for dragging the timber. I am afraid to dismiss the hired man, for how can I manage? I expect to be confined in two weeks' time, and Fred cannot carry the whole farm upon his young shoulders, and if we cannot get the timber out we shall fall into terrible trouble at sawing time.

I have worked very hard all the time of my pregnancy. I now never lay my weary body full of pain on my bed but I think that before morning those pains may change to those of travail, and assisted only by my children, and the labouring man in the house, how can I survive? To be without the comfort of my husband's consolation at such a time is indeed hard to bear.

During the winter we have brought our bed into the kitchen, the cold being so intense that our bedroom was icy. We made the bedroom into a convenient lumber room. George and I fixed next week to put it again in order for my use during my approaching sickness. How can I now do it?

How long George will be held in prison I do not know, but at least they are not seizing everything we have, so perhaps it is the lesser of two evils.

Fred visited him the day after he was taken, and he is going tomorrow with Alfred [another son]. George wished me to send little Eugene to be his companion. He has always appeared to be fondest of him than of any of our babes. He is a great talker and very original, but I have not allowed him to go.

George knows I am writing to you. I have always received so much kindness from you, it relieves my over-burdened mind to pour out my troubles to you. I cannot do so to Papa, particularly in his present weak state. I am glad Dr Atkinson was able to help his gout, and the high manner in which you speak of him and my dear sister is very gratifying. Sarah-Ellen has always been the most dutiful of daughters. She would not think of coming out to Canada some years ago because she was certain her place was with her parents.

I feel most particularly your goodness in consulting the doctor about George's leg, and sending a prescription for him. I do so hope it will benefit my dear husband.

Adieu, my dear Father. I dare not dwell longer on our serious situation for fear of distressing you too much, and causing myself an upset just at this time when I can least sustain it. I must keep calm for the babe's sake.

We do not feel responsible for this debt, as the weight of it is on Mr. Crosby's side, not on ours, and we have been generous towards the rogue. It has not brought us any reward.

> I remain, your deeply afflicted daughter,
> Eliza Stacey

Edward Stacey bailed his son out on this occasion, but poor Eliza continued to lurch from crisis to crisis with her improvident husband. See Letter 56.

44
1847: CANADA WEST
JAMES THOMSON TO HIS FATHER,
ALEXANDER THOMSON, IN SCOTLAND

As the century progressed, the flood of inventions that characterized the Industrial Revolution began to reach the margins of the British Empire. The telegraph revolutionized communications across the vast Canadian land mass. News that once took more than a week to travel from Montreal to Toronto now flashed from one city to the next. The description of the arrival of the telegraph in the little St. Lawrence River community of Edwardsburgh (present-day Cardinal), sent by James Thomson, a baker, to his father, makes this one of my favourite letters. He also mentioned his community's generosity towards the Irish and Scots in the old country, who were fighting the potato blight, eviction, and dreadful poverty.

Edwardsburgh C[anada] W[est].
March 24th 1847

Dear Father

The sleighing has been beautiful all winter and still continues good. I had twenty miles of a sleigh ride yesterday evening. We had one cold day in February. I dont know how far the thermometer was below the freezing point but I thought my nose and ears was not far above it when going to breakfast.

We are to have a telegraph along this road to connect Montreal and Toronto with Buffalo and the principal towns in the US. The wire is to be supported on posts 20 feet high 30 to a mile. One of the poles is close by our door. The people here, the great majority of whom read but little and consequently are not over stocked with scientific knowledge, have curious ideas of the telegraph. It would make any one smile to hear two or three of them discussing the matter among themselves. Some think that a letter will be put in the wire & pulled along with a string, Others think that the invention consists in applying some unknown power to the letter which makes it go without a string. Others who object to this theory will ask them how it will get past the top of the poles without being torn and how will it do in a heavy shower. Although they can thus silence others, they allow that they themselves know no more about it than a cow does about fiddling. One old woman, a neighbour of ours who has seen over fourscore winters, believes that railways, steamboats and telegraphs are the invention of the emissaries of his Satanic Majesty and are the means [of] bringing down famine on her native land. If they set up a pole at her door she is determined to set fire to it.

We are at present doing something for the relief of the distressed Irish & Scotch. A meeting of this Township was held at Spencerville a few days ago when a commitee was appointed to receive contributions in Money or grain the whole to be converted into Flour or Meal and sent home. Mr. McPherson is a member of commitee for the neighbourhood and Mr. Elliot below. We opened our list at noon yesterday and before night we had about 10 pounds from twenty subscribers which from a small neighborhood and comparitively poor people is very liberal. McPherson headed the list with 1 pound 10s. The writer of this followed with 1 pound 5s. Most of the others gave from 1 pound to 5 s. I think by the end of the week we will have about 20 pounds including grain. Mr Elliot was boasting that he would beat us. We shall be glad if he does. He is to give five pounds himself. In our list we opened two columns, one for the Irish and one for the Scotch, so that contributors could give to either or to each nation as they pleased. I see the majority have given a half to each. Only two or three that were called on refused to give something. It certainly is the duty of everyone to do all in their power in such a case. Our fields are extensive and have hitherto been fertile but we know not how soon the labour of the husbandman may fail and the fields give no meat.

James Thomson

45
1848: CANADA EAST
LORD ELGIN TO EARL GREY IN LONDON, ENGLAND

Throughout the 1840s, political dissatisfaction simmered in the united Province of Canada, as the British government resisted Canadian demands for responsible government. But the tide began to turn in 1847, with the appointment of the judicious and progressive Lord Elgin as governor general of Canada. He accepted the arguments of LaFontaine and Baldwin that equal treatment of French- and English-speaking Canadians would help bring harmony. And as he confided in his letter to Earl Grey, the new colonial secretary in London, he hoped it might also prevent an unholy alliance between French-speaking Lower Canadians and Irish Catholics on both sides of the border who were virulently anti-British.

Private

Montreal. May 4, 1848

My Dear Grey,

I mentioned in my last that some anxiety was felt here in reference to a projected political demonstration. M. Papineau and his satellites were, it was understood, laboring to bring the Irish and French together to listen to inflammatory harangues on the exciting subject of Ireland. It was supposed that when the Irish blood was up, they might be induced to commit some act of aggression, as, for example, to attack the Government House or military stores, and that the collision ensuing thereupon might furnish a pretext for interference on the part of American sympathisers. The chief apprehensions prevailed among the military authorities. I enclose the copy of a note written to Sir Benjamin D'Urban by Colonel Holloway,

Commanding Officer of Engineers and placed in my hands by the former which will enlighten you as to the nature and grounds of these apprehensions. I kept myself in full and frank communication with my Council, who did not share these alarms, but acted nevertheless with good sense and propriety. I need not give you details, but the upshot of all was this: that although no steps were ostensibly taken by the authorities to prevent a meeting, M. Papineau found to his disgust, when the appointed day arrived, that if he attended it, he would be unsupported by any French Canadian or Irishman of influence. He thought it therefore adviseable to decline to be present. The meeting was put off to a later day, but that day too has passed tranquilly as the first.

These are, I think, facts of some importance. Bear in mind that one half of our population is of French origin, and deeply imbued with French sympathies, that a considerable proportion of the remainder consists of Irish Catholics, that a large Irish contingent on the other side of the border (fanatics on behalf of republicanism and repeal) are egging on their compatriots here to rebellion, that all have been wrought upon until they believe that the conduct of England to Ireland is only to be paralleled by that of Russia to Poland, that on this exciting topic therefore something of a holy indignation mixes itself with more questionable impulses, that Guy Fawkes Papineau—actuated by the most malignant passions, irritated vanity, disappointed ambition, and national hatred which unmerited favor has only served to exasperate—is waving a lighted torch among these combustibles; you will, I think, admit, that if we pass through this crisis without explosions, it will be a gratifying circumstance, and an encouragement to persevere in a liberal and straightforward application of Constitutional Principles to Government.

I shall not hazard a conjecture as to what might have taken place ere this, had my late Council been still in office; but I may mention that one of their number, an honest and worthy man, has congratulated me more than once on the seasonable change of administration.

I have peculiar satisfaction, therefore, under all these circumstances, in calling your attention to the presentment of the Grand Jury of Montreal which I have sent you officially, in which that body adverts to the singularly tranquil and contented condition of the Province.

I am very anxious to hear that you have taken steps for the repeal of so much of the Act of Union as imposes restrictions on the use of the French language. The delay which has taken place in giving effect to the promise made, I think by Gladstone, on this subject, is one of the points of which M. Papineau is availing himself for purposes of agitation. I must moreover confess that I for one am deeply convinced of the impolicy of all such attempts to denationalize the French. Generally speaking they produce the opposite effect from that intended, causing the flame of national prejudice and animosity to burn more fiercely. But suppose them to be successful, what would be the result? You may perhaps *americanise*, but, depend upon it, by methods of this description, you will never *anglicise* the French inhabitants of the Province. Let them feel on the other hand that their religion, their habits, their prepossessions, their prejudices if you will, are more considered and respected here than in other portions of this vast continent which is being overrun by the most reckless, self sufficient and dictatorial section of the Anglo Saxon race, and who will venture to say that the last hand which waves the British flag on American ground may not be that of a French Canadian?

Another subject on which I am very solicitous is the free admission of Canadian products into the States. At present the Canadian farmer gets less for his wheat than his neighbour over the lines. This is an unfortunate state of things. I had a long conversation with Mr. Baldwin about it lately, and he strongly supports the proposition which I ventured to submit for your consideration about a year ago—*viz*, that a special treaty should be entered into with the States, giving them the navigation of the St. Lawrence jointly with ourselves on condition that they admit Canadian produce duty free. An arrangement of this description affecting internal Waters only, might I apprehend be made (as in the case of the Columbia in the Oregon Treaty) independently of the adjustment of questions touching the navigation laws generally. I confess that I dread the effect of the continuance of the present state of things on the loyalty of our farmers. Surely the admission of the Yankees into the St. Lawrence would be a great boon to them and we ought to exact a "quid pro quo".

I enclose half a newspaper containing a translation of an article in the *Avenir*, Papineau's paper, with his declaration of war, [and] a reply in the *Revue Canadienne*, La Fontaine's organ, and a commentary from the Conservative *Herald*. It will give you an idea of our politics in this quarter.

> Yrs very sincerely
> Elgin & Kincardine

P.S. It is the Irish not the French from whom we have most to dread at present.

Earl Grey considered Lord Elgin's letter so important that he passed it on to Queen Victoria.

46
1849: CANADA EAST
THE REVEREND WILLIAM RUFUS SEAVER TO MEHITABLE HOMER SEAVER IN MASSACHUSETTS

This is the kind of eyewitness account of a major event that brings history alive for me. The subject is the furor caused by the Rebellion Losses Bill—a furor signalling that the transition to responsible government would not be easy. This bill, modelled on successful legislation in Canada West, was introduced to compensate people in Canada East ("les Canadiens") whose property had been damaged in the Rebellions of 1837 and 1838. Premier LaFontaine, determined to heal the wounds left by the Patriotes, introduced the Rebellion Losses Bill into the united Province of Canada legislative assembly in Montreal. But since the bill would offer compensation to some rebels as well as those who had remained loyal to British authorities, his English-speaking Tory opponents saw it as a sign of French domination and their own loss of power to "les Canadiens." When the bill was passed, and the governor general agreed to sign it on April 25, riots broke out. Lord Elgin found himself being defended by French Canadians from the wrath of those who, in other circumstances, were his natural allies: Tory Upper Canadians.

On that day William Seaver, who supplemented his income as a Congregational minister by keeping a shop in the city, was preparing to move house. Hearing the commotion, he rushed into the street. For the next few days he divided his time between witnessing events and recording them for his wife, who had gone to visit her parents in Massachusetts.

Montreal April 25th 1849

My dear Wife,

I'll attempt to give you an account of what I am doing and what other people are doing for great things have been talked of to day. I begin by saying that I am glad you and the children are not here, for we are on the Eve of another rebellion, not however a *French Canadian* Revolt but a Rebellion of quite another stamp, and I have no doubt but that ere I close this I shall have to tell you of *martial law, and fires and blood and murder*—Today the Governor came to town on horseback attended as usual by an aid and his Groom, went home about 3 o'clock and every one supposed the business of the day concluded and his excellency had gone to dinner. But in about an hour more he came again to town *in state* attended by his officers and a Guard more than usually numerous. What is all this about? was at once the enquiry. It was not supposed that it could be to give the Royal Sanction to any bill, for before such a sanction is given it is customary to give public notice to that effect and call out the soldiers in front of Parliament house and fire a salute with much more parade etc. but on this occasion there was no notice given and no display nor anything to indicate that the Royal Sanction was to be given to any measure, but it was rumored that the Bill for indemnifying the Rebellion losses was now to be sanctioned . . . On the report spreading through town (which it did like wildfire) an immense mob assembled and surrounded the Parliament house to see what his Excellency intended to do—and when it was finally announced that he had really given the Royal Sanction to the Bill, then there was trouble. As his Excellency left the House for his carriage at the door he was assailed with stones, clubs & rotten & good eggs by thousands, and he was struck in the face with an egg, his carriage windows broken etc. but by the speed of his horses, he was enabled to escape with no injury except to his carriage and his equipage.

I stop here for the cry is raised that the *Parliament House* is on fire. "Fire, fire" is the cry, and from my shop door I see the red flames light up the heavens . . . I go—more after I see what the row is about.

April 26th. Tis too true. Last night about 8 o'clock while Parliament was still sitting a mob (it can be called nothing else though composed of some of our most worthy citizens) assembled around the House, and commenced the destruction of the building, by breaking windows etc. Soon the doors were broken open and a stout fellow sprang into the speakers chair with the exclamation, *"I dissolve Parliament."* This was the Signal— and immediately in the face of the members, and an immense multitude of spectators the Gas Pipes were fired in a dozen places, and the building wraped in flames. The "Golden Mace," sacred emblem of Royalty, was seized by the infuriated mob and borne into the street amid shouts of derision & scorn. The Members barely escaped with their lives, and that splendid Building with its rare paintings, all the records of the Provinces from the first settlement, all the acts of Parliament, that Library, worth alone, 100,000 pounds, all, all, are distroyed. That splendid portrait of the Queen, which you may remember, was droped into the street, and torn into a thousand pieces. All was lost, nothing saved, and the structure now is but a heap of smoking ruins. The loss to the city cannot, be less than 300,000 pounds. The fire Engines were not allowed to play upon the fire at all, and it was only on the arrival of General Gore with a body of soldiers that the engines were allowed to approach for the protection of other property. To day there is a terrible excitement in Town no business doing at all. The Guards at Monklands are all doubled, also the Guard at the jail. To day about 20 of our citizens are arrested on the charge of arson & sedition and Committed for trial, *without examination*. Tis said the jail is to be attacked and these men rescued tonight, and no doubt there will be some trouble. I'll try and finish tomorrow—

Apr 27th. Dear wife, Truly we are in a great crowd, *Some fun* & some *not so funny*. All was excitement yesterday, and about 8 ½ o'clock last night a friend came into the store and says, "Seaver, you better shut shop the mob are coming." I went to the door and one would have thought all hell was loose. St. Antoine Street was full of men armed with sticks etc. Fortunately for me they stoped at Mrs. Smith's Boarding House, where several of the members of Parliament board, (opposite Gravel's the Carriage Maker) which gave me time to shut the store before the mob reached my place. Mrs. Smith's House was attacked by the excited people and all the windows broken and furniture destroyed. Previously to this the mob had destroyed the Houses of the Honerables Mr. Hinks and Holmes and gutted them of the furniture etc also attacked the *Pilot* office (the Government Paper) and broken the windows there. From Mrs. Smith's Boarding House they passed my store, and then the cry was "To Lafontains, to Lafontains"—Mr. Lafontain you will remember is the *prime minister*. I went with the crowd of course, on reaching the house (which by the way is the Splendid Cut Stone House built by Bourris the Brewer, who failed last spring and whose property was sold at the Bankrupt Court this past winter, and was purchased by the Hon. Mr. Lafontain, and is just newly and splendidly furnished for the 1st of May, but not yet occupied, situated back of Place St Antoine and in front of Bellevue Terrace) it was surrounded by an immense assembly who very cooly and deliberately set fire to the out Buildings in 3 or 4 places, broke the windows of the House, forced open the doors, and commenced the work of destruction, breaking crockery, china, mirrors, opened the Wine vaults, threw mahogany chairs Tables, bedsteads etc of the most costly and splendid discription out of the window, ripped open the feather beds and mattrasses, and scattered the contents in the yard. By much labour and perserverance of Mr Phillips' and some private gentlemen the House was not burned though fired in many places, but the out buildings were all burnt. Such a work of destruction you can scarce conceive of, 'tis horrible. The Soldiers will scarce do duty for the anger is all directed against the Governor and a Canadian Ministry, and the rioters are all mostly those men who are truly loyal, and who in '37 fought *against the very men* whom the *Canadian Ministry* now proposes to indemnify out of the pockets of British subjects . . . The soldiers and officers all rather sympathize with the rioters and as yet no attempt has been made by the Military to suppress the disturbance except to make room for the fire engines to save adjoining property. The engines were not allowed to approach Mr. Lafontain's House till the soldiers came and formed a guard around the house. At Two o'clock this afternoon there was an asemblage of some Thousands on the "Champs de Mars" which in no way cooled off the excitement, tho, I am not able to say what was done except that resolutions condemnatory of Lord Elgin's conduct were unanimously passed . . .

28th. I went out last evening Friday—'Twas our church prayer meeting. After we had assembled Mr. Hayne said there was too much disturbance in the street in front that the meeting had better be closed and people retire to their homes. Much was done, on going into the street (Great St. James) I found 300 or 400 men assembled, of two opposite parties: Viz, the [French] Canadians vs the English speaking portion of the community. They proceeded through Gt. St. James, Notre Dame & Craig streets into the Quebec suburbs thence to the Government House which was guarded by 300 *Canadian* militia (The Governor daren't trust *British* Soldiers) with Colonel Laclie also a *French Canadian*, at their head to defend the house and quell disturbance. These 300 militia were armed at government expence with Muskets and cutlasses. The English body, unarmed except with clubs and sticks, on perceiving the preparations made by the Canadian Government to receive them, they all retired and only a few shots were fired, which wounded two or three men, though I believe not seriously. Both parties will meet again tonight fully armed and there will be bloody work in the streets without doubt . . . Col. Gugy is a leader of the mob (English) and after an adress which he made on the "Champ de Mars," he was taken on the shoulders of four stout fellows and bourn in triumph through the streets.

Much more of disturbance I might write you but it is time to close. The quarrel is a war *of Races—English-speaking people* will not be ruled by a [French] *Canadian* Government, and none can see what the end of these things will yet be. Shall it be the extermination of the Canadian Race? God only knows. But we are in trouble enough now, and blood will be shed worse yet than in the Rebellion of '37. The papers I send you with this will give you some more particulars. Have no fear for me, I am only a looker on, and shall take care to keep out of harms way . . . I send you $5, and will continue to remit to you as I can spare it, use all the money you need, enjoy your visit, Write me often, Send me papers. Don't waste so much paper when you write, but fill up your sheets. You've got *brains* enough only *stir* them up. Be active, both in thought and Action . . . Kiss the children. Their pictures and yours are comforts for me, and they don't make a noise. I've not half done, but must close. More when you write me—I can't read this over for corrections so excuse

Your affectionat husban
W R Seaver

The riots lasted two days and involved thousands of people. Four weeks later, the government decided that the legislature should be moved from Montreal, which was considered too susceptible to ethnic tensions. It took some years for the British government to decide where a new capital should be located, and more years to build appropriately monumental buildings in the little lumber town of Ottawa, balanced on the border between Canada West and Canada East. Yet despite William Seaver's fears, Canada would not see such violence again for decades. Thanks to the efforts of intellectuals like Louis-Hippolyte LaFontaine, politicians like Lord Durham, populists like William Lyon Mackenzie, and settlers like the Traills, Eastwoods, and Moodies, the country was achieving a shape and a political stability that had seemed unthinkable a bare fifty years earlier.

A *new nation needed a new legislative building. The original
Parliament Buildings, a masterpiece of Gothic revival architecture,
took six years to build (1859–1865) but were destroyed by fire in 1916.*

PART 2: A NATION TAKES SHAPE

1850–1900

AROUND 1850, BRITISH NORTH AMERICA WAS COMING INTO FOCUS AS the Canada we know today.

On historical maps for the mid-nineteenth century, the country still looks weirdly untidy and tipped heavily towards the Atlantic. In 1850, there were six British colonies in North America: the united Province of Canada (comprising the former Upper and Lower Canada), New Brunswick, Prince Edward Island, Nova Scotia, Newfoundland, and the newly created Crown Colony of Vancouver Island. Considered as a whole, British North America remained fragmented and incoherent, with unsettled boundaries and immense territories that were still unexplored. Settlers continued to face all the hardships of pioneer life: the weary toil of clearing the land; the fear of fire, harvest failures, and disease. And the weather! The topic of Canada's dire climate threads its way through so many letters! As the weary, frostbitten pioneer Willie Wallace noted in 1881: "I have concluded that the climate of Manitoba, so far as its settled character is concerned, is a perfect fraud."

In the next half century, the face of Canada would be transformed. From a disparate collection of colonies with primitive economies, Canada would emerge as a united nation ready to supply the world with its wheat and mineral wealth. Its heartland would become an industrial powerhouse, linked by a mighty railway to outlying regions. And letters from these years speak more directly to a modern reader. I can imagine George Brown, the constitutional reformer from Upper Canada, enjoying the yellow sands and gently lapping waves of Prince Edward Island while attending the 1864 Charlottetown Conference, and writing wistfully to his beloved wife, "After all, Anne, there is something in the sea." I can almost hear Captain Samuel Anderson, of the Royal Engineers, chortling at the poor health of the Americans he met at a Manitoba dance in 1874: "[It] is not to be wondered at when you consider that they live in heated houses, on a diet of pickles and candies, and gobble their food at such a rate that it has been calculated that the average time an American takes for his dinner is 6 ½ minutes."

In letters written during the second half of the nineteenth century, I found a new note: a distinct culture had begun to emerge, along with an appreciation for a flatter social structure. The colonists were less radical than their Yankee neighbours, yet less conservative than their relatives in the mother country. Countless immigrant letters reflect the hard-earned satisfaction of ordinary men and women (including runaway slaves from the southern States) who had achieved an independence and comfort out of the reach of those they had left behind. Nathaniel Carrothers, an Ulsterman who flourished in southern Ontario, wrote to his brother in Northern Ireland, "The farmers [here] will make well this year as [they] have not to hand their hard ernings to the Landlord as with youes." There was little respect for the social pretensions that some immigrants tried to import from Britain. Describing an Alberta neighbour who, like him, had arrived from England, a hard-working rancher named Claude Gardiner wrote with disdain in 1895: "He is one of the usual English sort who does nothing but play polo and drinks and plays the fool generally."

What triggered the transformation of Canada during this period? The momentum towards a union of the provinces was well under way in central Canada by the late 1850s. The Province of Canada had achieved a measure of self-government and was developing a taste for more power and a place in the world distinct from Britain's. However, French-English tensions meant that the "united" Province of Canada was anything but united.

The four Maritime provinces were another matter: they enjoyed local autonomy and were content to rely on their resources of "wood, wind and water." But the outbreak of the American Civil War in 1861 left all the British colonies feeling vulnerable to American aggression. Then there were the cross-border raids by the Fenians, a ramshackle bunch of Irish-American nationalists intent on banishing the British presence from North America. At first the Fenians had a comic opera touch to them, until the popular Ottawa politician D'Arcy McGee was shot in 1866 by, it was alleged, a Fenian assassin. With almost indecent haste (and dyspepsia-inducing festivities), a modest 1864 conference on Maritime union in Charlottetown, Prince Edward Island, became the first step in a process that would lead to a confederation of British North America.

Within three years, and despite the misgivings of many participants, the Province of Canada (now split into Quebec and Ontario), Nova Scotia, and

New Brunswick became the Dominion of Canada. Sir John A. Macdonald was its first prime minister, and its capital (to nobody's satisfaction) was the shabby lumber town of Ottawa. Two years later, the Dominion completed the biggest real estate deal in British North American history. It paid the Hudson's Bay Company $1.5 million—a huge sum by the standards of the day—for the whole of the vast territory of Rupert's Land, covering present-day northern Quebec and Ontario, all of Manitoba, and most of Saskatchewan, Alberta, and the Northwest Territories. All this territory was then renamed the North-West Territories. Canada was taking shape.

Confederation established the legal and political structure of the new nation, but it needed technology—plus rich dollops of political largesse—to pull it together. The technology was the railway. The promise of a transcontinental railway brought British Columbia (formed in 1866 when the two separate colonies of Vancouver Island and British Columbia, a colony since 1858, merged) into Confederation in 1871. "Go where it will," wrote Alexander Robb from Nicola Lake, British Columbia, in 1871, "it will be of immense benefit to everyone." Ottawa's pledge to Prince Edward Island to pay its railroad debts enticed the smallest colony into the union in 1873. By 1885, a railway system that stretched 8,000 kilometres from Halifax to Vancouver—*a mare usque ad mare*—sewed together a nation vast in territory but still, at 4.3 million, tiny in population. Only Newfoundland, of Britain's nineteenth-century North American colonies, remained outside Confederation.

The railway system nearly bankrupted the country: railway scandals dogged Sir John A. Macdonald's governments and led to electoral defeat in 1873. But the Canadian Pacific Railway reinforced Ottawa's authority. This was never more evident than in 1885, during the Northwest Rebellion. The charismatic French-speaking Metis leader Louis Riel had already led a successful uprising in the Red River area in 1870. Now he attempted to defend the territorial interests of the Metis and some Indian peoples in Saskatchewan. His efforts were doomed, thanks to the CPR. Dominion troops arrived by train in the west within eleven days of the first shot being fired. In November 1885, Riel (alongside eight Indian chiefs) was hanged, despite his questionable mental stability and in the face of outrage in Quebec. Prime Minister Macdonald had demonstrated the power of Ottawa and the danger of inciting Indians to sedition. But Riel's execution left a legacy of racial animosity within the Canadian federation that is still with us.

The transcontinental railway had a further nation-building impact: it made western Canada accessible to Europeans who felt restless or oppressed in their homelands. The bulge in the mailbag from western Canada in this period reflects the rise in the number of officials and ranchers there. To a modern reader, the most disturbing aspect of many of these letters is the hostility and contempt some writers display towards native peoples. Decimated by unfamiliar diseases such as chicken pox and tuberculosis, and starving because European hunters had wiped out the buffalo on which they had depended, First Nations were in an unhappy state. But the newcomers were content to lay the blame for their predicament on the prairie peoples themselves. "On arriving we heard that the Blackfeet at this place were starving & a few dying every day, & the most alarming rumours were in circulation that they were killing cattle wholesale," Elliot Galt wrote in 1879. "Fortunately the truth was grossly exaggerated . . . they are a miserable lot & won't do anything for themselves."

At first, western cities were slow to develop. Lovisa McDougall, whose husband opened a grocery store in Edmonton, noted in 1879, "Their are lots of people comming and going all the time. Their are only 4 white wemon here besides myself." A global economic recession stalled development through the 1870s and 1880s, but the brakes came off in the final decade of the century. By the end of the century, Edmonton's population had topped 10,000. People surged west, lured by the promise of free land. Immigrants from Germany, Scandinavia, the Balkans, the Ukraine, Russia, and the United States crammed into CPR immigrant cars, gazing out of the windows at the miles of empty prairie on which they would homestead. With CPR rail cars ready to take their wheat to market, most prospered. A landscape once dominated by bison and Indian bands would soon be the breadbasket of the British Empire. The most popular image of Canada for decades to come was of acres of golden wheat waving in the prairie breeze as far as the eye could see. Which of us cannot summon up a mental picture of those golden acres, imprinted on our memories by years of Canadian calendar art?

Agriculture was not the only activity to thrive. Sir John A. Macdonald (who returned to power in 1878) had introduced a system of tariff protection for Canada's fledgling industries: steep import duties were imposed on goods that Canadian factories could manufacture, such as nails, screws, blankets, and threshers. Canadian industry took off and the economy boomed. Cities like Montreal, Toronto, Hamilton, and London grew exponentially. The population of Montreal, still the largest city in the Dominion, doubled between 1871 and 1891; Toronto's tripled; Winnipeg's rose from 240 residents to 25,000. Merchant princes and banking magnates built magnificent homes which boasted all the new inventions of the era: gaslights, running water, telephones, and, from the mid-1890s, electricity.

Those of us who like to imagine ourselves in previous lives are always tempted to place ourselves within these plutocratic ranks. For the majority of Canadians a century ago, however, life was grim. Wages were low, hours long, and there were no pensions, health care insurance, or paid holidays. In Nova Scotia, boys as young as ten years of age could be sent down the mines, and after their twelfth birthdays they could work up to sixty hours a week. Henry Swift, general manager of the Springhill mine in Nova Scotia, struggled to keep the mine open despite sagging pit props and underground floods: "My mind is at all times fully occupied with thoughts to make the work a success, enough of worry to Kill a man." Only a day after he wrote those words, the mine killed him. It was only a matter of time before the appalling conditions in urban factories, remote mines, and the railyards of Winnipeg would persuade the workers to organize themselves into unions, and to demand improvements.

As these letters attest, however, as the end of the century approached, a mood of optimism prevailed. Despite the inequities, everybody's standard of living was slowly rising. The gold rush miners who toiled over the Chilkoot Pass in 1898 symbolized the fervent belief in Canada's untapped mineral resources. The North-West Mounted Police who controlled entry to the Yukon from the summit of the passes embodied the national faith in "peace, order, and good government." And in Ottawa, the dapper and debonair Liberal prime minister, Sir Wilfrid Laurier, moving easily between the two different worlds of French and English Canada, healed the wounds of the 1880s. He was the perfect symbol for the new nation of Canada, its 5.3 million citizens ready to embark with unprecedented confidence on a new century. Canada, in Laurier's felicitous phrase, had found "the sunny way."

47
1851: NEW BRUNSWICK
THOMAS H. JONES TO DANIEL FOSTER IN MASSACHUSETTS

Thomas Jones, who was born to slaves in North Carolina, had had four different own-ers before his thirtieth birthday. In 1849, he and his family escaped to New York City, where Thomas became a well-known anti-slavery speaker. But in May 1851, a friend warned him that slave catchers were after him, and Thomas fled to the Maritimes via the Underground Railroad, an informal network of safe houses and people who helped fugitive slaves. As he wrote in this letter to a minister with the Massachusetts Anti-Slavery Society, arrival on Canadian soil had a powerful impact on a man who had hitherto never felt truly free. Thomas was one of around 30,000 escaped slaves who found their way to Canada before the American Civil War.

St. John, N[ew] B[runswick]
May 5, 1851

Dear Brother:

From my knowledge of your generous nature and kind Christian hospitality, I know it will be a source of pleasure to you to be informed of my safe arrival here on British ground. Quite free from terror, I now feel that my bones are a property bequeathed to me for my own use, and not for the servitude or gratification of the white man, in that gloomy and sultry region, where the hue of the skin has left my race in thraldom and misery for ages.

O, my dear friend! how good it is to live on the poorest fare, where the mind may apply its immortal powers to the contemplation of heaven and heavenly things, unawed by the monsters who would tie us to a tree and scourge us in our nakedness for attempting to worship the Creator in spirit and in truth!

The atrocity of the hideous system under which I groaned for more than forty years was never so strikingly demonstrated to my mind as it has been by breathing under the auspices and protection of a Government that allows all its children to go abroad in the true liberty of nature, every person free to frequent the altar or the sanctuary to which Conscience would lead him; no cause for degradation but vice, and no lever of promotion but virtue and intelligence.

I begin to see clearly, and to hope with reason, that the Refugee Law [which allowed slave owners to pursue fugitive slaves in "free" states] has or will awaken the world to a sense of our deep wrongs; and I feel warranted in saying, that the nations of the earth will soon give an expression of opinion upon our cause which will shame the Southern white man out of his cruelty, and cause him to unchain his sable victims. The Ethiopian will ere long be redeemed from his bondage, for Jehovah will be his Emancipator, as he is his King, Creator and judge.

As to this Province, I have found a home of refuge, full of true, warm, generous Christians, whose hearts, abounding with the love of God, are full of sympathy for the slave, whom they will help to free in due time, as far as human means can extend. The citizens of St. John have received me in the spirit of brotherhood, and only that my mission calls me beyond the seas, I might remain here, and be an instrument of good for many years to come.

In a few days, I proceed to Halifax, and thence to England, as soon as circumstances will permit. Hoping that you will remember me to every kind friend taking an interest in my destinies, I am, Your brother in Christ,

Thomas H. Jones

P.S. Wherever I preach or lecture, I am followed by enthusiastic houses.
      T.H.J.

Thomas never went to England, but he travelled throughout the Maritimes giving anti-slavery lectures before returning to the United States in 1853 and writing a memoir.

48

1852: CANADA WEST

TUNIS SNOOK TO HIS FATHER

Among the perennial features of family life are those carefully argued letters to parents from students who cannot quite make ends meet. A young man with the intriguing name of Tunis Snook was one such petitioner. The need for lawyers in Toronto, chief city of Canada West, grew in step with its swelling population and commercial development. Tunis was eager to answer that need: he was studying for the degree of bachelor of civil law at Trinity College while articling with the well-known legalist John Hillyard Cameron and preparing for his Law Society exams. Tunis's ambitions were admirable, but his expenses were heavy.

Toronto,
March 4th, 1852

Dear Father,

I am much pleased in being able to verily say that I derive much benefit from Trinity College law lectures. There are upward of thirty in the law class, part of whom are barristers and attornies.

I am happy to say also that the Osgoode Hall debating club yields much advantages to all its members who take the proper interest in the society. I believe I stand as high in the society as any other member although several attornies and barristers of some years practicing belong.

I am very much engaged in study at present and would be much better engaged had I more law books of my own to read during the night time.

You no doubt might think it very singular that I complain of not having law books, as a student is generally supplied by the office. But the fact is Mr. Cameron does not keep his books at the office, nor does he lend them. Although there are nine students in the office I very seldom see a book in the office except those belonging to myself or some of the other students. It is very difficult to read up the lectures without books to study at night. I mean to say I can study at Osgoode Hall in the day time between the hours of ten and five, excepting office hours, but during the evenings and mornings I have only my own law books to which I can resort.

I have purchased the following books during the last two months, namely Burton on Real Property, Cameron's Rules, Angel on Limitation, Angel on Intercourses, Rules of Court, Smith on Contracts, Books for noting 2,

Roseve on Evidence. The above books have cost me considerable, but I could not do well without them.

I will now give you a further statement as to my expenditure since I left home:

	Pounds, shillings, pence
Travelling expenses to Toronto	1.1.3
board at 16/3 a week	13.0.0
washing 6/3 per month	1.5
1 overcoat (lion skin)	2.5
1 pair boots	0.17.6
4 pair socks	0.6.6
1 pair gloves	0.3.9
1 handkerchief	0.3.9
1 gold ring at half price	0.10.0
1 new cup	0.11.3
1 new hat got yesterday	0.18.9
postage	0.7.6
pens paper ink etc.	0.3.9
2 pencils one lost	0.3.1
2 pocket knife one lost	0.2.6
1 bb vest	0.15.0
pair suspenders	0.2.6
cab fare for 3 times changing boarding house	0.3.9
pd fee to join Osgoode Club	0.5.0
paid dues to classical club	0.10.0
hair oils, hair dressing	0.7.6
hair brush	0.3.9
2 bottles sarsaparilla	0.7.6
I will then add the cost of the books	
before mentioned	5.0.0
	29.12.7
Tuition at Trinity College	1.5.0
	30.17.7

There are various items that I have not mentioned but I only gave you this statement to show you the costs of necessities which necessaries if you question my word, I can produce to your satisfaction when I return home. I wish you to keep all my letters so that when I move home I can show you all I say I have purchased. I need say but little more as you will take from this letter that I will want money before long.

You will oblige me much indeed if you will assist me on or about the first of next month.

We have about a foot of snow here and the weather is very cold. I long to get back to sweet home.

> Which I remain,
> Tunis L. Snook.

49
1853: CANADA WEST
MARY BIBB TO HORACE MANN IN NEW YORK CITY

Schoolteachers throughout rural Canada in the nineteenth century were overworked and underpaid. Their pupils' parents were usually too poor to pay fees and regularly kept the children away from school to help with farm chores. Mary Bibb, who worked in the Sandwich area of Essex County, faced an additional problem: she and her students were all newly arrived blacks who had fled from American slavery. Blacks were allowed to settle in Canada, but black children in the Sandwich area could not attend white schools, and the provincial government would not support the only school that was open to them. Mrs. Bibb explained her predicament—and her solution—to Horace Mann, an American educator.

Windsor, Canada West,
January 20th 1853

Sir—The interest you have always manifested in the elevation of the colored people, has encouraged me to acquaint you with my humble effort to establish a school in Sandwich irrespective of color.

We moved to Canada about three years ago, at which time I opened a school (there being none except the French and English Catholic) for the benefit of those who had recently arrived in the province from Republican oppression. Being desirous of doing that which would result in the greater good to this people, I charged each person enjoying its benefits 6 cents per week, thinking there could be none found too poor to pay so small a sum. Experience soon proved that very few of those attending the school did pay.

We then took measures to secure the Government annuity, which amounted to $16.60 for my labor of one year and six weeks. [When that ran out within two months] I then felt that duty compeled me to abandon the school for it required too great a sacrifice of my domestic duties to continue without compensation. My successor was Mr. Jackson, who kept the school six weeks. It was reopened by Mr. Russell who did not collect enough from the people to sustain him although his board and rent was given.

You will perceive that in all, the school was continued near four months during the whole year and that too with two teachers. It was then I resolved on the experiment of starting an Independent School that should be free to all irrespective of color at least.

The result has more than met my most sanguine hopes; having increased from five on the 13th of Sept. 1852 to fifty-two in January 1853, being just four months. Should you feel like doing something to promote so humble an effort, please consult:

Rev. Samuel J. May, Syracuse, N.Y.
Mr. Mumford, Detroit, Mich.
Judge Woodbridge, Sandwich, C. West.

Yours in haste
Mary E. Bibb

50
1853: BRITISH COLUMBIA
HENRY TUZO TO HIS SISTER ANNA MARIA TUZO IN MONTREAL

The size of British North America was beyond the comprehension of most of its resi-
dents: few ventured more than eighty kilometres from their homes. But in 1853, an
intrepid twenty-one-year-old medical graduate joined a Hudson's Bay Company expedi-
tion for a transcontinental journey that was as challenging as a voyage to the moon is
today. In letters to his family in Montreal, Henry Atkinson Tuzo described sights that few
of his contemporaries had seen or would ever see. His destination was Fort Vancouver,
where he would be a company physician. During its seven months of travel, the expe-
dition was frequently guided and fed by members of the First Nations whose territory it
crossed, but Henry reflected all the prejudices of the day as he wrote of "hostile bands"
and "roving tribes with which these plains are infested."

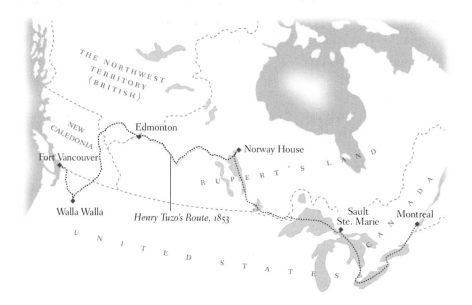

Henry Tuzo's Route, 1853

Fort Vancouver
Decr. 10th, 1853

My dearest Sister,
It affords me the most sincere pleasure once more to sit and write home
again, and most heartily thank that kind & watchful Providence which has
(although far far away from you and home) brought me once more within

the bounds of Civilisation. I have safely arrived at my destination and by Gods Mercy have escaped all the perils of my dangerous voyage. I have safely passed through the territories of hostile indians and leaped the furious Dâlles [falls] of the dreaded Columbia . . .

You have asked me to give you account of my trip . . . Having started from [Montreal] on the Railway at Lachine I took my passage on board the steamer from Carillon and here I overtook the Express Canoes on their way to the Interior. These I assumed charge of and proceeded as far as Sault Ste. Marie with them . . . At Sault Ste. Marie, Sir George Simpson [governor of the HBC] joined the canoes, and from this date 23rd May we pressed on across Lake Superior and up the River Kaministiquia traversing Sturgeon Lake, Lake of the Woods and many others to the Winnipeg River descending which we arrived on Lake Winnipeg, and after a prosperous trip across it of three days, we got safely in to Norway House on the 17th of June.

On this part of the route the Establishments (or forts as they are called) of the Company are small but numerous. They are Two Mountains, Coulonge, Lac des Allumettes, Mattawa, Nipissingue, Lacloche, Sault Ste. Marie, Paque, Michipicoton, Ft. William, Rat Portage, Forts Frances, Alexander and Berens River—as well as many others. The greater number of these are merely a Collection of Log Huts with a few goods for Indian trade &tc. The route of travel is decidedly bad and difficult as you may imagine when I tell you there are upwards of Seventy Portages between Montreal and Norway Ho. There are also many bad Rapids & Falls particularly on the Winnipeg River . . .

The weather on this part of my journey was fair for the season of the year and although at times cold and uncomfortable, yet upon the whole the trip was far from being unpleasant. Sir Geo. Simpson came to Norway Ho. for the purposes of attending what is called the Northern Council which is a meeting of Fur Traders convened from all parts of the Country for the purposes of consulting one another about matters connected with their business. When this is over they proceed to York Factory on Hudson Bay to obtain a supply of goods for trading, which they take with them to the interior. This occupies about six weeks and instead of going with them I stayed at Norway Ho. to rest myself agreably here in shooting, sailing and reading besides enjoying a considerable amount of professional occupation.

On the 30th of July the Brigade of Boats bound for the Saskachewan River arrived and in one of these I embarked with three other Clerks who were to be my travelling Companions to Fort Vancouver. After a tedious passage of over six weeks we arrived at Edmonton on the head waters of the Saskatchewan.

During the early part of the voyage the weather was not very fine, but as soon as we arrived on the plains or prairie country the occasional rain suddenly cleared and continuous fine and sunny days prevailed. On these Plains we were obliged to Camp together at night, with loaded arms and trusty watch-men in case of an attack from Indians but by the Mercy of Divine Providence we were not disturbed by any hostile band. As a precautionary measure we were also in the habit of putting out our Camp fires at night so as not to attract the attention of the roving tribes with which these plains are infested.

The Saskatchewan is a swift and muddy river with only two portages on it and runs from the Rocky Mountains into Lake Winnipeg. On it we passed Cumberland House, Forts Nipawin, Carlton, Pitt and Edmonton, all these are stockaded and defended by Bastions bristling with cannons. I must not omit to mention an incident which occurred while I was at Carlton. It became nec-essary to obtain meat for the Brigade, all the Pemmican being exhausted. In order to accomplish this the Buffalo had to be hunted and all the passengers myself included accompanied the Hunters. We left the Fort with about 50 Horses and 18 mounted men besides 12 Carts. After travelling for two days in search of animals we at last spied them; the whole plain as far as the eye could reach was black with Buffalo. The whole cavalcade approached as near as was prudent without disturbing them. The carts halted and we started in full pur-suit on horses trained for the purpose & exceedingly fleet. When the animals took alarm the roaring and dust were tremendous but onward we went. The hunters killed Eleven—and the carts came along and cut them up to take away. The next day 9 more were shot and I was the only passenger who suc-ceeded in securing one as a trophy. I cut out his tongue and cooked it for sup-per. I will remember even at this moment the terrific fury which was pictured in his face and how he toss up the turf with his paw when he received a shot from my rifle immediately seconded by another. It was a thrilling scene to wit-ness the death struggles of such a monster.

Fort Edmonton, which may be called the Capital of the Prairie Country, consists of a few buildings surrounded by stockades with a population of about 70 men and their families . . . There are several hundred horses belonging to this establishment—besides a garden and some cattle. There is also a windmill here but no wheat in cultivation to grind in it. It is at this post that the Blackfoot, Blood and other tribes of ferocious Indians princi-pally trade their furs &tc.

From thence, after having stayed several days, the whole Columbia Party started with horses and proceeded in a northerly direction as far as Ft. Assinaboine on the Athabasca River. This occupied eight days. The weather was warm and I enjoyed myself remarkably well.

After a short stay at this place we embarked in Boats to proceed to the head waters of the river in the Rocky mountains. This was accomplished in Twenty Days, and I assure you I was not a little pleased when Jasper's House appeared to my delighted vision. Every where surrounded by tall Ridges of the Rockey Mountains —and as far as the eyes could reach there was nothing presented to them but perpetually snow-clad peaks and shining glaciers the result of a sum-

Henry Tuzo travelled across the continent at a time when the prairies were still "black with buffalo."

mer sun. The magnificence [of the scenery] baffles all description. We are here already within three ridges of the Back-Bone of North America and nothing is to be seen around but Snow, Rocks and the clear blue sky—with occasional stunted vegetation. The place abounds with game. Beautiful White Fish are here in abundance besides Moose, wild sheep and Goats and many other fur-producing animals. At this romantic place we remained three days and then took our departure, after having mounted ourselves and tied luggage on the backs of horses. These horses are beautiful creatures. They are born and die perfectly wild in the mountain recesses. They live out all winter and roam in large bands in search of food. When wanted for use some are caught and broken in as riding and pack animals.

With these creatures we travelled for 8 days up hill & down dale perpetually surrounded by snowy mountains whose peaks are almost continually obscured from view by passing clouds. But onwards we went now meandering along the Valley of the Athabasca and again climbing some adjacent hill until we arrived at the height of land in the pass between Mt Hooker & Mt Browne which is about 6400 ft above the level of the sea. Here I saw what is called the Committee's Punch Bowl, a small Lake, from one side of which runs the Athabasca into the Arctic Ocean and from the other the Noble Columbia into the Pacific. Although there was no snow at the foot of the mountains, yet here it was 3 ft deep and as cold as I ever felt it in Canada—besides being quite barren and very bleak.

To arrive at this point we ascended for 6 days and now we came down in half a day as many hours what had taken us so long to get up. You can imagine how steep and long this hill must have been! It was like coming from the Clouds down to the Earth, from perpetual snow to a mild and genial Ocean, from trees of two feet in heighth to those of enormous dimensions. All this change is very remarkable and strikes the observer forcibly. This hill is called the Grand Côte. We slept a night at its foot and the following day after a gallop of 36 miles down the banks of the Columbia arrived at the Boat Encampment, the highest navigable point on the river, and here we met the Boat wh. was to Convey us down Stream—to our destination.

The weather on the mountain was fine but we had one snow storm, and it frose very hard at all times So that we were uncomfortable after getting our legs wet in the fords on the Athabasca and Columbia River, which we were under the necessity of crossing upwards of 80 times on the road. The Boats on this river are built after the model of Canoes and managed by paddles in the hands of Expert Iroquois from Canada.

We embarked in one of these and you may imagine how swift the mountain torrent of this stream is when I tell you that we descended upwards of a hundred miles a day in some places. The rapids are almost innumerable and most terrific . . . The Shores of some of them are Covered with graves of the victims of their raging waters and knowing this fact it is not without peculiar sensations that a stranger for the first time approaches the summit of a dangerous leap above a rapid or the vortex of an irresistable whirlpool below. Not the least unpleasant part of this mode of travelling is the thorough ducking that one gets in passing through the tremendous waves at the foot of a heavy rapid through which the tiny boat is hurled along at a lightning speed. The lives of all the passengers depend on the skill of the Guides at these perilous moments and they deserve praise for their courage.

After descending in this manner for five days we [arrived in] Coville in the State Territory . . . On the 6th November we left this place and again travelled down stream to Walla Walla. The weather was cold and wet, as the rainy season had commenced—and I felt it more as there was a scarcity of wood. I can compare this section of the Country to nothing more apt than what I have read of the deserts of Arabia in fact it is nothing more than a sandy plain without water or any other vegetation than wormwood and sage with a few <u>Cacti</u> here and there. Fort Walla Walla is built of mud and an ugly place it is but there are plenty of beautiful horses. One of the chiefs here owns some 5 or 6000 besides an enormous number of wild Cattle. The principal food used by the Indians is Horse Flesh and I assure you it is not unpalatable. I was obliged to eat some as there was no other meat at the Fort.

Finally on the 17th Novr I arrived at my destination. It would take a good deal to induce me again to traverse the same route. But on the whole my trip has not been without its pleasures although mixed up with a good many hardships. It had novelty . . . if nothing else to recommend it. I have seen many tribes of Indians, their manners and Customs besides travelling a route which is seldom or never gone over by any but those belonging to the Company. I think I have written a long enough letter this time as you have asked me. I have already read those letters from you and mamma the latest one Oct 10th and have written one dated on my birthday. Send me some long letters and often and I will do the same. Believe me to remain

Your affecte Brother
Henry Tuzo

Henry Atkinson Tuzo later became manager of the Bank of British North America in New York and died in England in 1890. His grandson, John Tuzo Wilson, was an internationally renowned geophysicist who developed tectonic plate theory.

51
1855: CANADA WEST
WILLIAM DAVIES TO HIS BROTHER JAMES DAVIES IN ENGLAND

The growing prosperity of Britain's North American colonies attracted immigrants eager to start businesses as well as own land. In 1854, a twenty-three-year-old entrepreneur named William Davies arrived in Toronto with his wife, Emma, and their infant daughter, and immediately bought a pig, slaughtered it, and started making sausages. He soon had a stall in St. Lawrence Market, had expanded into other pork products, and, as he was eager to tell his brother in Berkshire, was doing well. The "Lady in the Sleigh" who made a special journey to buy his sausages must have been one of Toronto's first epicures.

Corner of Agnes & Sayer Sts
Toronto.
January 28th 1855

My Very Dear Brother,

I was very pleased to receive 2 letters from you & one from Mother dated 14th & 21st on the 16th January, the fruits you see of going via Halifax. I recd. the Paper about a[n] Election the 23rd July & the one of the 11th November on the 26th January. I have had no others, I should like to get the one continuing [Charles] Dicken's Lecture at Reading. I was very pleased to hear you were all well & I am thankful to say we are except Emma . . . I don't know if I told you she had engaged a Nurse, one who attended a fellow passenger & is there still. By the bye this man who came with us got a berth as Bookkeeper & Cashier as soon as he got here at 150 pounds & he is going to England 1st class by the next Collins Steamer from N.Y. for the firm. He was very fortunate. He expects to be partner soon but he has no more money than I have so he may be wrong. He was a Schoolmaster.

Trade is rather better than when I last wrote. If I could take 20 pounds per week it would do for we get Good Profits. The Pork costs 3 1/4. I sell the Lard 7 1/2, Prime Pork 5d, some parts 4 1/2. Heads & Feet I boil with the rind & bones & sell it when put in Basins at 4d which pays Cent per Cent. We call it Head Cheese. You would be amused sometimes to see me cleaning 10 or 20 sets of guts. It is a cold job I assure you for it is done in cold water. I use 10 or 12 sets per week for sausages. My trade you see is no sinecure. I have an idea of making a Good Thing of the Sausage & Pork business if I live till another winter & get to handle 200 pounds which I hope to do. I have good reason to believe I could sell 300 lbs per day of Sausages. If I made Hog Puddings I could sell a great many but I have not time, or convenience for it. I would rather have a good Grocery Trade but unquestionably the former pays best. My Lard, Sausages &c begin to be esteemed already. A Lady in a Sleigh came for some yesterday, so do others from the other end of the city. Farrow has paid me 5 pounds & we have bought a Bed & got about 6 pounds 10 now & a Stock of Meat, so I may riggle along even now, but it will be close work when Doctor, Nurse &c come to draw. The Weather is very cold & we have a foot or so of snow, but instead of making a "dark picter," as old Tommy Hilliard said, it is a very light one for it is a busy time in Toronto when there is good sleighing. You have to watch it as you walk down St for there is no sound but the Bells. It is very pleasant riding. I have ridden home from the market with them when I have bought things. It is very easy for the Horses when it is good sleighing. Some of them are very smart & drawn by good horses richly caparisoned with Plated Bells on Red Morocco & the Sleighs lin'd with Buffalos & Choice Furs.

. . . I did not observe anything particular in the keeping of Xmas day here more than in England . . . We had a Goose & had Farrows to dinner & Tea . . .

If you were here you would not think the Free Niggers were confined to Lower Canada, for we have a matter of 8 next door & we meet them at every step. A Slaveholder tried to catch one & take [him] back last Summer, & the free Niggers caught him & took him into the Bush tied him to a Tree & horse whipp'd him. The Constable of Maryland wrote to Chf Police Montreal asking him, to go halves in the rewards & take them to the Frontier & the said Constable would be there to receive them off him. Of course the Montreal man did not.

This is a terrible place for Fires. About a month ago a Cabinet Factory [the Jacques and Hays furniture factory] employing 250 was burnt down & 30 or 40,000 pounds of Lumber mostly Walnut burnt, I saw it, it broke out just as we were in bed. It was an awfully grand sight. Had the wind not been favourable (it was very high) it would have burnt down a Brewery & a large Vessell on the Stocks nearly ready to Launch. Last week the Queen City Steamer was burnt to the water. She plied between Toronto & Hamilton. She had not been in long. Had not the Bay been frozen she would have been at the Wharf on which I was but she was at Queen's Wharf at the opening of the Bay . . .

Within a few years, William Davies was making a very "Good Thing of the Sausage & Pork business," and had laid the foundations of the large export meat-packing and pro- vision business which long bore his name. When he died in 1921, at age ninety, it was part of Canada Packers Ltd.

52
1855: NEW BRUNSWICK
FREDERICK ROBB TO HIS GRANDMOTHER
ELIZABETH ROBB IN STIRLING, SCOTLAND

Freddy Robb, age nine, was a boisterous little boy whose father, James, taught sci- ence at King's College in Fredericton (see Letter 32). Freddy's grandmother in

Stirling, Scotland, never met her grandson, but she kept in close touch with her Canadian descendants and often sent unusual gifts to Freddy and his four siblings. In 1855, two years after London's Great Exhibition, she sent him a model of the Crystal Palace in which it had been held. How many children today write such beautiful thank-you letters?

Fredericton,
26 December 1855

My dear Grandmama,

The holidays are come now, and I have time to write you a letter. We went to church on Christmas day, and went to the Chief Justice's to the Christmas tree in the evening, and got such lovely things. I got two nice knives, and a pair of skates, and a lot of other things, and the others got very nice things too. I hope you are quite well, we are quite well now. Those were such lovely things you sent us, those two books were so nice, and the chrystal Palace. I thank [cousin] Alfred for the nice boxes of sugar plums that he gave me, and I hope he is quite well. I do wish he was out here that I might play with him. Mama says she has been wanting a letter from you for she has not had one for a long time. Our little sister Harriet Amy is a dear little thing—she is very fat and merry, we all like her.

Papa and Mama and all of us send their love to you, and our cousins.

Seven months later, heartbroken James wrote to his mother: "My poor boy Freddy—the eldest and best of the five spared to me . . . went to bathe in the river for the second time only on Friday last and somehow unaccountably fell and was drowned dead . . . Oh God! How mysterious are thy ways."

53
1856: CANADA WEST
ROBERT JONES TO WILLIAM STILL IN PENNSYLVANIA

One of the most literate and ambitious former slaves to come to Canada via the Underground Railroad was Robert Jones, who left Virginia and settled in Hamilton with his wife, Eliza. William Still, chairman of the Pennsylvania Abolition Society, noted approvingly that Robert had a "decidedly clear idea that coloured men [should] prove themselves qualified to rise equally with other branches of the human family." The notion of racial equality was foreign to most British-born Canadians, and there

were no land grants and little sympathy or education for fugitive blacks. But Robert
reported his own success, in the face of prejudice.

> Hamilton, C. W.,
> August 9th, 1856.

Dear Friend,

I take this opportunity of writing you these few lines to inform you of my health, which is good at present, &c.

I was talking to you about going to Liberia, when I saw you last, and did intend to start this fall, but I since looked at the condition of the colored people in Canada. I thought I would try to do something for their elevation as a nation, to place them in the proper position to stand where they ought to stand. In order to do this, I have undertaken to get up a military company amongst them.

They laughed at me to undertake such a thing; but I did not relax my energies. I went and had an interview with Major J. T. Gilepon, told him what my object was, he encouraged me to go on, saying that he would do all he could for the accomplishment of my object. He referred [me] to Sir Allan [MacNab] . . . I took with me Mr. J. H. Hill to see him. He told me that it should be done, and required us to write a petition to the Governor General, which has been done . . . The company is already organized. Mr. Howard was elected Captain; J. H. Hill, 1st Lieutenant; Hezekiah Hill, Ensign; Robert Jones, 1st Sergeant. The company's name is "Queen Victoria's Rifle Guards."

You may, by this, see what I have been doing since I have been in Canada. When we receive our appointments by the Government. I will send by express, my daguerreotype in uniform.

> My respects, &tc. &tc.
> Robert Jones.

54
1856: CANADA WEST
JAMES ROSS TO HIS SISTERS IN THE RED RIVER COLONY

Alexander Ross was a larger-than-life character in the Red River Colony (in present-day Manitoba), and when he died in 1856, aged seventy-three, his widow and children

*were devastated. A former HBC factor, the ebullient and benevolent Ross had been
sheriff of Assiniboia, commander of the volunteer corps, police chief, magistrate, commissioner, and court examiner. He also wrote several fur trade classics, building on
both his own experience and the tales he heard from his wife, an Okanagan Indian. By
the mid-1850s, however, racial prejudice was building in the colony: as more white
women arrived, so did the British belief in "pure blood lines" and rejection of the many
Indian and Metis (mixed blood) people in the community. James Ross, at school in
Toronto, wrote home to console his sisters in their bereavement, and to remind them
that their mother deserved the greatest respect.*

Knox's College, Toronto
Christmas Eve 1856

To my beloved sisters
Isabelle, Mary, Sally, Henriette,
& Jemima, and brother Sandy,

I think it is my duty to write you all at this time, seeing that we have been
deprived of our dear dear Papa. He is at last taken from us! And we are left
almost like a flock without a shepherd. I am sure the house at Colony
Gardens must be a lonely place now. How different from former years! That
place was all life—people visiting—friends coming and greeting each other
joyfully. All without was stirring, all within, joy and gladness. Mama would
look out for her children to meet there on Saturday evening. William &
Jemima would be down—Geordy & Mary—James & Sally—Papa & Mama
and all the rest. Oh! How happy—talking about everything. But now, now—
how is it now! Ah, how different! Only 6 short months ago, a dear brother
was taken from us—the oldest brother in the family—one who was so kind,
so gentle, so affectionate to us all—and one to whom we all, I am sure,
looked as our main hope when papa should die and one too who was
esteemed by all who knew him. But <u>he is gone never to return</u>. We may
think of him with love and regret—with pleasure and even with pride—but
he is gone. Who would have thought it? Only 31 years old, and just when he
was beginning to be so useful. Well, our next only hope is our revered papa.
We thought the loss a great one when William was removed—and so it was.

We however looked to Papa. The 6 months are over and Papa is cut down
too! Can anything be more pitiful than our condition? Just think—an aged
mother and one daughter left to occupy the big house. On her right hand,
one daughter (a widow) and four children—on her left, a daughter-in-law

(also a widow) with five children. Is it not enough to make one weep! That once strong family is reduced to helplessness. But, my dear sisters, hard as is our lot, we must not be discouraged. I have given you the dark side of the picture—there is another side to look at, tho' perhaps we can hardly call it a <u>bright side</u>. There are many things that should comfort us. In the first place, we have reason to believe that Papa has gone to heaven. Is this not one great comfort? Consider what would have been your thoughts if it was believed Papa died and only passed off in order to suffer. Oh! We could not bear the thought. And then, consider he was a very old man. We could not expect him to live much longer. He was not killed—he was not cut down without a moment's warning—he did not suffer very much or very long—he did not leave a bad name behind him. All these things should comfort us somewhat. In fact his death took place in as favourable circumstances as possible. There is nothing to grieve us but just that he is taken away. All people die—so must he. Consider again, he did not leave Mama in poverty. If he did, matters would surely be far worse than they are. Mr. Black has given me some account of Papa's will, and I am delighted to find that our dear Mama has been well looked to. It would have been sad indeed if she and Jemima & Sandy had nothing. Yes, and I would add Isabel. But you have all had portions. Let us be thankful for this. Of course, those who are married could always get along.

Now, I appeal to you sisters especially (as Sandy is so young yet) to mind how you conduct yourselves. Pardon me if I <u>seem</u> to speak with too much authority or presumption. I can assure you it is only <u>apparent</u> not <u>real</u> presumption. I do not wish to dictate to any of you, but allow me to speak to you in affection, though with firmness and strong feeling. I must tell you to beware how you conduct yourselves. Be on your guard. Remember, dear sisters, that we at present occupy a certain standing in the community. Owing to Papa and William—and to our connection with your worthy minister Mr. Black—I say, owing to these things, we have a certain standing and respectability, and we must keep it. Don't think that because Papa is taken from us, nobody will mind us—nothing of the kind. We will be held in esteem for Papa's sake—and we must show ourselves worthy of that esteem by our own doings. It seems generally the case that halfbreed families dwindle into insignificance as soon as they lose their head. But why should it be so? The families themselves are to blame. Never do anything mean. Never say anything mean or unbecoming—anything of which you would be ashamed. Whether with the higher or the lower classes always act and speak respectfully—even in trivial matters. Observe, I don't mean you to be stiff and proud—nothing could be more distant from my mind. You should be humble-minded, gentle & kind—yet there is a <u>kind of pride</u> which you should have that is <u>self respect</u>. Papa has left property and money, but he has left a name too and the name of Mr. Ross will for many a day to come be mentioned with profound respect. The Scotch people will for generations to come revere the name of him who did so much for them. And who besides Papa was so much esteemed by the whole settlement? This being the case, would it not be too bad if we acted unworthily of him? . . .

One thing more that I must press on your attention is <u>Economy</u>. My dear sisters, let me urge you <u>to be economical</u>. Do not be oversparing—supply yourselves with all acquisitions. Do not be too scanty. Be well furnished, but guard against extravagance. You have now money to yourselves, but mind it is your all. If that is spent you have no other place to look to. In saying this, I refer particularly to you Jemima. It was very different before, for no matter how you spent, you always had a sort of feeling that there was an unfailing source somewhere, and that there was no fear. But you are it all now. What if any one of you be reduced to nought. Oh! Let me never hear of this. It would grieve me, grieve me, grieve me to hear that any one of you was brought to want! You need not be, if you manage rightly. You have 5 or 600 pounds each.

. . . A third point I must mention is: <u>Kindness to one another and to Mama</u>. I am sure I need hardly hint this, for you will all feel the necessity of it at once. Be kind to each other. Let there be no coldness—no petty jealousies (I cannot imagine there can be any) no casting off of each other. Feel that you are dependent on one another. How much happier you can make yourselves by so doing! And especially be tender and affectionate to Mama— our Mama—our dear mother—our only remaining parent. Who would be so hard-hearted as not to love their mama. Cheer her up, show her all respect. Perhaps halfbreed children are not respectful enough towards their Indian mothers. Let us be however. What if Mama is an Indian! Does that detract from her rights and claims as a mother? Does that free us from the duty of loving, obeying and respecting her? Nothing of the kind. We are bound by every consideration—by natural duty and scriptural injunctions—by everything sacred and dear—by all our finer feelings—we are bound, I say, to revere and love and cherish our aged Mama. Yes, and remember the personal qualities that ought to endear Mama to us. Who more tender-hearted? Who more attached to her children and more desirous of their happiness? Who more attentive to their wants—anxious about their welfare? <u>None</u>. She has all these qualities in a wonderful degree and these are the endearing qualities of a mother. These are the essential qualities of any good mother. What avail those accomplishments in etiquette and fussy nonsense of which she happens to be destitute? Do they constitute the mother? Does a certain amount of reading and writing—skill in saying "Good morning" and "Please take a seat?"—some knowledge of dressing and promenading—some glib of the tongue—Do these make the mother all that she aught to be? I ask again: "What avail they" when not accompanied by a warm motherly heart? Better far give me my Mama with her Christian meekness—her kind affection, her motherly heart—than the cold-hearted so-called <u>lady</u>—who prides herself, it may be, in her fine shape—her clever but foolish joking—her superficials and secondaries of writing and hairbrushing and gait and posture! Yes, I would have no difficulty in chosing. I admire education and accomplishments—none could more—but these are not in my estimation the <u>first</u> requisites of a good mother.

Last year, when I was in R. River, I observed on one Sabbath morning just as we were starting for church, that Jemima (excuse me, dear Jem, for mentioning this) seemed unwilling to go into the cart and ride down <u>with mama</u>. I could not say whether it was because she disliked the cart or why; but I felt grieved at it <u>because I thought it was a slight on mama</u>. I felt this so keenly that, although my horse was saddled and I was about to jump on, I told Baptishe to unsaddle him—that I wanted to ride with mama, and so I did. I jumped into the cart, drove mama down, spoke to her cheerfully the whole way down and walked into church holding her hand, opened [the] seat for her and saw her comfortably seated. Now, I do not think I ever told Jem. The reason why I did not accompany her on horseback, but that was the reason. I trust that act will show you my feelings in regard to mama, and that you will do the same, as occasions offer.

My dear sisters, I have only to say in conclusion, let us be much in prayer. Let us wrestle with our heavenly Father for grace and consolation and guidance. Let us often come to a throne of grace. Let us remember each other before Him. Oh! Is it not a blessed thing that we have a kind, sympathising High Priest on high! We have reason to be thankful even for our present condition. Some one once said: "We have to thank God for every hour that we are not in hell!" How true! Before parting with you I must recommend to your kind attention <u>our little brother Sandy</u> "the child of their old age"—the Benjamin of our number. Be kind to the <u>laddie</u>. Train him up in the way in which he should go.

Farewell! Farewell!! The Lord guide and conduct you all. The Lord comfort and encourage you. The Lord bless you now and for ever. And the Lord bring us at last to that happy happy land, where death-divided friends shall meet to part no more. Amen.

In sadness, but in warmest brotherly affection, I wish you a "happy New Year." And believe me, my beloved sisters & brother,

> To be, even until death,
> Your affect. Brother James Ross

55
1857: NOVA SCOTIA
GEORGE CANN TO ANN CANN IN NORTH SYDNEY

George Cann was appointed keeper of the newly built lighthouse on Flint Island, off the coast of Cape Breton, in 1856. In December that year, his wife took a boat to North Sydney to stay with relatives while she had a baby. Ann Cann left her son John (age ten) and daughters Sarah (six) and Mary (five) with her husband in the lighthouse, which was perched sixty-five feet above the Atlantic Ocean. I imagine they all got, in George's words, "quite lonsom" as they listened to huge rollers crashing onto the treacherous rocks below them.

Flint Island Janury 1857

Dear wife to let you know that I am well it afords me much pleasure and I hope you are injoying the same blesing I received your leter on the tenth of Janury John is well he has lernt fore verses in the testment to day he says he like to se Will tell the children I will bring them Carys chickens [stormy petrels] wen the ise gits strong I think I com and see you wen the roads gits good I feel quite lonsom when it is stormy I was glad to hear that you ware well caul the baby ann mary and Peter is well mary seldom lafs the weather rather Cald weare in want of nothing at present John says to tell his Gfather he like to see him and so should I and you and mother tow Rite and tell us all the noose mind how you spell this

> your affetnate husband
> G Cann

George and Ann had ten children before George died in 1869, aged forty-six. He was lighthouse keeper until his death, and his son John succeeded him as keeper of the Flint Island lighthouse.

56
1858: CANADA EAST
LOUISA STACEY TO HER GRANDFATHER EDWARD STACEY
IN LONDON, ENGLAND

Louisa Stacey, eldest daughter of George and Eliza Stacey (see Letter 43), was only four when her debt-ridden parents were packed off to Canada in 1836 by George's irate father. Louisa remained in England and was raised by relatives in Derby. She finally joined her parents in the Eastern Townships when she was a teenager and their circumstances had improved, but remained in close touch with her beloved grandfather in London. She followed British imperial exploits with interest and often confided to him her nostalgia for the intellectual pursuits she had enjoyed in England.

Sherbrooke
January 1858

My dear Grandpapa,

We have had five very interesting and amusing lectures in the new school house this week on *phrenology*. We subscribed in the settlement and raised 10 dollars for the series. The lecturer, Mr Nicholls, is an American and if he had had a superior education he would have made a splendid lecturer. As it is, he is sometimes at a loss for words, and occasionally a grammatical error is observable.

He dined with us yesterday (now we are better off we can sometimes entertain), and afterwards he felt our *bumps*. He said in placing his hand on the top of my head that there was too much heat there and asked me if my head did not very often ache, owing to my having too much to use the organ of firmness, very much as mistress, and having the care of the young ones. He advised me to keep my head wet with cold water. He did not feel Papa's head (indeed I doubt if he would have been allowed to), but from the look he said he had an even temperament, and that there was no one like him around here, and none in whose presence he took more pleasure.

But perhaps you are not a believer in phrenology? I always was, and feel the shape of the head must tell much of the person's character and capabilities.

I wish there could be a lecturer like him every week, for it raises the minds of all, and made me realize how much I miss the intellectual converse of Miss Oliver at Derby. The children were deeply interested, and he read their characters well.

I must tell you of one very pretty thing he said when I had been playing on the piano. He said that "Music, poetry and devotion were the flowers in the garden of nature"!

Having no church here is sad indeed and a great drawback. Sherbrooke is the nearest and there is nothing elevating for young or old.

What a sad pity it is that Sir Henry Havelock is dead in this terrible Indian Mutiny. We were much shocked when we heard the sad news, even before we knew how much his country appreciated his gallant conduct and his heroic relief of Lucknow. We also grieved to hear of the death of Sir Henry Lawrence, that great Christian, and the brave holder of Lucknow. May that gallant siege soon be lifted and its survivors, women, children and men, brought into safety after all these months of peril and near starvation.

We are having a strangely mild winter, and I saw in the paper yesterday that a fine pansy had been picked in a Toronto garden last week, a thing never known before!

I hope my young cousins enjoyed the Christmas Revel at the Crystal Palace, and the beautiful dissolving views at the Polytechnic. We should love to hear more of their doings.

Believe me, dear Grandpapa, to remain your affectionate Granddaughter,

Louisa

57

1858: PRINCE EDWARD ISLAND
CRITCHLOW HARRIS TO HIS MOTHER,
MARTHA CRITCHLOW HARRIS, IN ENGLAND

Immigrants did not always believe they had made better lives for themselves in the New World. Critchlow Harris, forty-three, a sometime gentleman farmer, was a chronic depressive who found Prince Edward Island as unsatisfactory as his former existence near Liverpool, England. His mother, Martha Critchlow, still in England, tried to help him financially, while his long-suffering wife, Sarah, spent much of her time encouraging him to look on the bright side of life. After two years on the island, the Harrises were still unsettled, having failed to buy an attractive farm at Long Creek, near Summerside.

Charlottetown
September 20, 1858

Dear Mother,

. . . You say in your letter, "I cannot help feeling your gloomy forebodings have urged you to make precipitate changes which you must now feel were unwise." If you mean by thinking that I have acted unwisely in coming to this Island you are right; but if you think I have done so by not going to Long Creek, you are wrong, for I am truly thankful that circumstances prevented my going there. As far as this place is concerned I do not think I could do any better elsewhere than where I am, although I am convinced that I cannot make the two ends meet by farming. No one can, except those that have labour within themselves. We have too many people already in this Island— they are leaving it in numbers. In fact, there is nothing for them to do in it. Everyone seems to be head over heels in debt.

Two vessels are to sail to New Zealand between this and the first of November next, and two more are to sail next spring. There are a much greater number of Persons wanting to go there than can get Passages in these vessels. In fact, the well-conducted part of the Inhabitants are endeavouring to get away, but the great difficulty with them is to get rid of their property. There are neither purchasers for the land, nor money to pay for it. In this place money is very scarce, little or no specie in the Island, and few Island or Treasury notes. The latter are at a discount of ten per cent. I only wish I could get out of the miserable place. If I can only get this winter over, I will endeavour to get away next spring. I only wish I could get a situation, for I have not strength to work upon a farm. I am greatly troubled with heartburn and head ache. In fact, I am too tired to eat my meals. I am quite done up at the end of each week, and on Sunday I am fit for nothing. No one is more willing to work, but I cannot stand it. When you see Miss Grace Rice, tell her that I do not think everyone can do well by farming in this country: there is scarcely a farmer in this Island who is out of debt. A person can do better by farming at home, although he has more Rent and Taxes to pay than in this country. It is deplorable to see the state of things in this Island . . . Oh, that I could once get back to Old England, and obtain some small situation!

I do not know what we should have done but for Mr. Thomas Stretch.

He has been very good to us. The fact is, I could not have been able to get food for my family but for his assistance. I am endeavouring to sell some of my furniture. In fact, I dread the winter. I have had nothing but a Horse and Cow until within the last week. I have been compelled to borrow a cart and plough from my neighbour, Mr. Haszard; but I saw he was getting tired of it, and there was a sale last week in the neighbourhood, so I purchased some things very cheap (a list of which I enclose). I have to pay for them on the 16th of next November, but I do not know how I shall manage it . . .

Sarah appended a note: "How thankful I should be if Critchlow would take your valuable advice and not give way to despondency." Despite the slow start, the Harris family flourished on P.E.I. One son, Robert, became a prominent painter and another, William, the best-known architect in Atlantic Canada.

58
1859: VANCOUVER ISLAND
SIR JAMES DOUGLAS, GOVERNOR OF BRITISH COLUMBIA,
TO SISTER SUPERIOR IN VICTORIA

Although British prejudice against mixed marriages and "half-breeds," already rampant in eastern Canada, was spreading westward, society remained open in the rough-and-tumble atmosphere of Pacific seaports. In Victoria, capital of the Crown Colony of Vancouver Island, Sir James Douglas and his Metis wife, Amelia, wanted a good education for their two daughters, whose mixed heritage was no bar to acceptance at the fashionable convent school run by the Sisters of Saint Ann. But convent rules forbade pupils to go dancing, and when Sir James's daughters attended an official ball, they were threatened with expulsion.

To the Reverend Mother Superior,
Saint Ann's Convent,
Victoria, British Columbia

His Excellency, the Governor, presents his respects to the very Reverend Mother Superior of Saint Ann's Convent, and acknowledges the receipts of her esteemed letter, dated the 15th of this month.

His Excellency learns with admiration the principles of rule which the Reverend Mother Superior proposes to maintain in regard to dances.

His Excellency desires to inform the Reverend Superior, that in general, he does not permit his dear daughters to frequent dances, but some occasions occur, as for example, the assembly of last Tuesday, when his position and public duty require his presence. Such occasions do not occur frequently, but if the Reverend Superior looks upon them as infractions of the convent regulations, His Excellency will be reduced of necessity, though with regret, to withdraw his daughters from the school.

Finally, His Excellency begs the Reverend Superior to accept his expression of very high esteem.

Government House
March 17, 1859

Sir James's protests were useless. His daughters and eleven other daughters of Victoria's governmental elite were asked to leave the convent.

59

1859: VANCOUVER ISLAND

FIELDING SMITHEA TO AMOR DE COSMOS,

EDITOR OF THE *BRITISH COLONIST*, IN VICTORIA

Canada's west coast has always been a magnet for outspoken eccentrics, charismatic leaders, and mavericks. One of the most interesting was a man called Fielding Smithea, an articulate and passionate advocate of black civil rights on the west coast of North America. Disturbed by racial tension in California, he joined a group of blacks who moved to the bustling port of Victoria in the late 1850s. There he worked as a messenger in government offices and frequently lectured and wrote to the local paper, the British Colonist, *on the evils of racism. Slavery had never flourished in Canada, because it was unsuited to agriculture and commerce here, and it had been abolished within the British Empire in 1834. Nevertheless, Fielding found plenty of ammunition for his polemics about the insidious discrimination he found in the British colony.*

Victoria, V[ancouver] I[sland]

June 10th, 1859

Mr. Editor:

Have the colored people realized their fond anticipations in coming to Vancouver's Island? I answer *no*. And if not, what is the position they occupy in this colony? I answer decidedly a degrading one, and certainly one not to be borne by men of spirit.

It is a fact generally known that in the United States of America, the colored people labor and live under many disadvantages, the result of prejudice. Yet while this is a truth, there are many States in which colored men vote and enjoy all the rights of citizens. Hence we have in many of the northern States colored men practicing the law, medicine, and many other professions. We enter their colleges, and graduate in common with white students. In many of these colleges they have colored gentlemen professors and teachers . . .

We went to California in common with others, to make money [in the gold rush], and very many were successful. In the early history of California, the very worst men, shoulder-striking, devil-daring fellows, fought their way into office, and when in, they tried to pass a law prohibiting any more colored persons and Chinamen from emigrating thither, and those already there must register their names in a Recorder's office, and though they did not accomplish their diabolical purpose, yet we took the will for the deed and considered ourselves, not only outraged, but more degraded than ever. Hence we held mass meetings, and discussed the question of where we should go. Some said to Sonora in Lower California, others into Central America; but just at that time there was some talk about Vancouver's Island, where the majority concluded to go. A Roman general said "Veni, Vidi, Vici," and I can say, we came, we saw, and even conquered difficulties, but we have not conquered that mildew-like feeling that lurks in the hearts of our enemies, i.e., prejudice.

Having from early boyhood cherished a friendly feeling for the British Government, which was the result of her liberal policy towards the colored people generally, we had hoped on coming here to occupy this virgin soil; that we would enjoy all the rights and privileges enjoyed by others, but how sadly have many of us been disappointed. All the hotels, inns, and whiskey shops, are closed against us, and a colored gentleman was ordered out of the cabin of the steamer *Gov. Douglas* the other day. He had a cabin ticket. They shut us out from their concerts, and a member of the church says give him $500 and he will build a gallery in the English Church, in which to huddle us together. I know nothing of English law, yet I believe the course these men pursue is contrary to all law, human or Divine . . . I am informed that there is in town a secret association of wicked white men, whose ostensible purpose is to keep colored men out of the jury box, and from serving on the Grand Jury. Now for myself, I care not if I never fill any office here, but in the language of one, "Fiat justitia, ruat coelum." . . . Some of our people whose susceptibilities are not so keen upon the subject of human rights, say having the law in our favor we ask no more. It is well said, "if ignorance is bliss." But when I consider how many ways there are to evade the law, I subscribe to no such doctrine, for there is a power behind the throne stronger than the throne itself, and that power is public opinion. Were it not so, men would have no regard for human society.

In view of these facts, I contend that the position we hold in this colony, is not only humiliating in the extreme, but degrading to us as a class. I will not now stop to enquire why it is that we are thus treated, hated and despised. Enough to know that it is so. I know some among us are inclined to whitewash these matters over, saying there will be a better state of things hereafter. But the obnoxious seeds of prejudice are so deeply rooted in the white man's heart, which he directs against us with such burning force, biting like an adder and stinging like an asp, that we naturally suffer from its deadly effects.

It is said that in war colored men make good and brave soldiers, but I think in the common walks of life they are viewed through different glasses. I believe it utterly impossible for the African and the Anglo-Saxon races ever to live together on terms of equality. *I am as firmly fixed in this opinion as I am that some day I shall go to judgement.* I am not alone in this feeling, for I reflect the views of very many of our people, even in Victoria, unless they say one thing and mean another.

When I contemplate the vast multitude of colored people scattered throughout the United States of America, the Canadas, and the West Indies, my heart yearns for the day when God, in his providence will gather us together in some favored country, where we cannot only be men, without any restraint, but grow and become a great nation like others; this inward desire does not only predominate over all others, but it does in very deed *consume me gradually away.* Yet *homo sum, atque nihil humani me alienum puto.* [I am human, so any human interest is my concern.]

F. S.

Smithea returned to San Francisco in 1869 and was a delegate to the 1873 Black National Convention. The same year, Amor de Cosmos, another unconventional character, who had changed his name from William Alexander Smith, was briefly premier of British Columbia.

60

1860: CANADA WEST
W.R. BARTLETT TO JAMES BEGAHMIGABOW,
ACTING CHIEF OF MUSKOKA, IN PENETANGUISHENE

This letter, with its horribly finger-wagging tone, indicates the depressing deterioration in the position of Canada's native peoples. In 1857, the legislature of the Province of Canada passed the Gradual Civilization Act, with the object of absorbing native peoples into European settler society and culture. Three years later, the British government in Westminster transferred responsibility for Indian matters to the Province of Canada. Mr. Bartlett, a senior provincial official, made it clear to the Algonquin bands that native leaders had better learn English if they hoped to be taken seriously.

Indian Office, Toronto
October 10, 1860

With reference to the document handed me last spring at Penetanguishene signed by Chief William Yellowhead of Rama in which it is stated that you are the present chief of Muskoko, I have the honor to inform you that your appointment has met with the approval of the Superintendent General of Indian Affairs, and I am to instruct you to continue to act as chief during the minority of the late Chief Megis's eldest son who, when he is old enough to perform the duties of that office, will fill the place of his late father.

In conveying to you the Superintendent General's decision, I would beg leave to add that, as it is desirable that every Indian chief should be able to read and write, young Megis will be expected to avail himself of every means that may be afforded him to acquire the elementary parts of a common English education in order that he may qualify himself in some measure for the office he is to fill. He should be also made aware that the Department will not appoint any Indian of intemperate and dishonest habits to the office of Chief.

61

1863: VANCOUVER ISLAND
LIEUTENANT EDMUND VERNEY TO HIS FATHER,
SIR HARRY VERNEY, MP, IN LONDON, ENGLAND

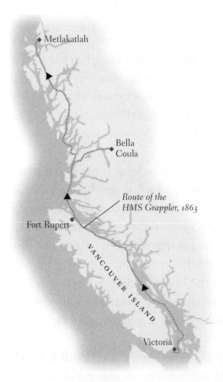

Metlakatlah

Bella
Coula

Route of the
HMS Grappler, 1863

Fort Rupert

VANCOUVER ISLAND

Victoria

Edmund Hope Verney was only twelve when he joined the Royal Navy in 1851. By the time he arrived on Vancouver Island in 1862 to command the gunship Grappler, *he had distinguished himself in the Crimean War and in India. Pious and rather stuffy, Edmund did not enjoy the louche society of colonial Victoria. However, on long and dangerous cruises among the uncharted inlets and islands of the Pacific Coast, he was deeply impressed by both the scenery and the work of Anglican missionaries, as he explained to his father, a well-known Liberal MP in London.*

H.M.S. Grappler, Nanaimo, V.I.
October 1, 1863.
My dear Father,
On the twenty-seventh ult. we left Victoria on our northern cruize . . . It is pleasure indeed to have [Parson] Dundas with me, not only because I shall enjoy his society and have a companion, but also because my own men, and those settlers whom we shall visit will have the benefit of his ministry.

October 5. We reached Fort Rupert last night, and this morning started across to the mainland to seek for the *Beaver* [a Hudson's Bay Company survey ship], to communicate with her and obtain any information we can about the coast; we have not yet succeeded in finding her, and are anchored tonight at the head of the first reach of "Well's pass" which you may see marked in the chart: tomorrow I intend to go round Broughton Is. and out by Fife Sound, when I shall probably pick up the *Beaver* somewhere. The weather has been fine, the sea like glass, and the scenery of surpassing beauty: what is marked in the chart as Broughton Island, is really a group of islands of every size, and covered with trees: in the absence of correct charts the navigation requires considerable care.

October 10: On the sixth we fell in with the *Beaver*, and proceeded on to Shuchartie Bay, to the north of Fort Rupert, where we fell in with the *Carolena*, Mr. Duncan's schooner from Metlakatlah. His assistant, Mr. Cunningham, was on board, and he came to us with several of his Christian Indians. They came down into my cabin and were interested in looking at all one's little &cs: afterwards they sang some hymns to us very nicely together. They were a very attractive set of fellows, and when they sang their expression of earnest solemn piety was very touching. They were all very cleanly dressed, and polite in their manners: one was almost absurd in his extreme politeness: and all spoke a few words of English, such as "thank-you, Sir", "good-night" &c. One of them, Robert Hewson, goes with us as pilot and Interpreter . . .

October 15, 1863. This morning we left Bella Coula, and hope to anchor tonight in Restoration Bay. Yesterday morning, I pulled up the river to the Indian village, in my gig, and having assembled the chiefs, made to them a short oration through the medium of an interpreter: they had stolen a shovel and an axe from one of the settlers, which I required them to give up; this they did, as they were much frightened at the appearance of the gunboat, and the articles were humbly brought to the *Grappler* in the afternoon. No punishment was inflicted on the thief, as there had been a regular row, in which some Indian heads had been broken, and the natives had got considerably the worst of it.

The Bella Coula Indians are a very degraded set, they speak a harsh dialect most grating to the ear. We saw them herding together like animals, some quite destitute of clothing.

October 18. After leaving Restoration Bay, the chart was found to be so totally incorrect as to be of little or no use, and on the night of the sixteenth we anchored in a narrow channel from which there was no second outlet. Yesterday we had to retrace our steps, and, after going much out of our way, found ourselves in Milbank Sound in the afternoon. A canoe came alongside, and an Indian pointed out to us an anchorage: we steamed up to it, and found it to be a very small bay, but affording good shelter from the S.E. wind then blowing, and indeed it became so thick with rain and fog, that I hardly thought it prudent to go out again to look for a better anchorage. The bay was open to the N.W. and at midnight the wind sprang up suddenly, and it blew very hard from West, and W.N.W. for a couple of hours: we dragged our anchor, and drifted alongside the rocks, where we lay till the weather moderated a little, with five fathoms of water on the off side. The corner point of the bay sheltered us just enough to keep the water tolerably smooth. At about three, we hove in our cable, and steamed out in the dark, to my intense relief. We had nearly reached the middle of the East end of the Sound, when we passed a solitary rock to windward: from the darkness of the night, and the plainess with which we could see the white foam breaking over and around the black rock, it must have been less than a ship's length from us. After a night of the greatest anxiety, we anchored this morning at daylight in another bay, three or four miles from the first. I trust I may never spend such a night again . . . Verily the navigation of these unsurveyed waters calls for the utmost caution and circumspection.

October 22. Yesterday morning we left Milbank Sound, and anchored in Carter's Bay, on Saturday we hope to arrive at Metlakatlah [close to Prince Rupert]. Our course continues to lie through the most beautiful inland navigation, presenting fresh points of beauty every hour. Now it is some grand and lofty snow capped mountain, then some bold cliffs and precipices, then perhaps a sweet little valley, with a torrent rushing down and emptying itself in one broad foaming sheet into the water, or down the steep bare face of the rock comes a slender waterfall, streaming down over the smooth water-worn surface, with many a sheer descent, or slightly glancing off from crag to crag.

And all this is the view from one's own windows, as I may call it, unaccompanied by all the vexations of travelling, bad servants, bad food &c: and it is additionally delightful because I have a charming companion in Parson Dundas.

Some Indians came alongside this morning in a canoe, from whom we bought some beaver, and mountain sheep: I have already eaten beaver, but do not like it much. It is said that the mountain sheep is particularly good.

October 24, 1863. Yesterday morning we arrived at Metlakatlah, and in the afternoon, Dundas and I walked over the village, and heard the children read and sing. Fancy fifty Indian children singing "see our oars with feathered spray", and well known catches, pronouncing the words quite as well as English children would, and singing quite as correctly. Mr. Duncan has done nothing incredible at Metlakatlah, as some of his admirers would fain have you believe: he has not converted whole tribes, and miraculously imbued them with a love of eau-de-cologne and kid gloves. But he *has* brought some hundreds of the natives from a state of the most degraded barbarism and the blackest heathendom to a state of civilization and outward christianity which may be quite placed on a par with that of an ordinary English village. The conditions under which a man may become a resident at Metlakatlah are that he must give up all heathen practises, he must obey Mr. Duncan, and he must become a hearer of the Word.

So now there are those people living decently: feeding on nearly the same food as before, with perhaps a few more vegetables; their houses clean, their persons decently clothed, their children educated: superstition banished; the old heathen distrustful scowl vanished, and in its stead a manly open expression of countenance: willing to labour and earn money, and then to spend it wisely: paying taxes, making roads and gardens, building good houses, and forming little trading societies: tea-totallers, when they can get tea, strict observers of the sabbath, living in very general harmony . . .

October 26. The moment the bells ring for church, every one issues from his house, and they walk up to church in two long lines: there is no waiting for a second bell; none of the thousand and one excuses which we find for staying away from church in England; no one prefers cooking his sunday dinner to going to God's House, no one remains at home because he has no clothes good enough to go to church in; none are too young or too old; all come forth, dressed at least neatly and cleanly, and in two long ranks, march reverently up to the Mission House: it is indeed a very striking sight.

All the houses are, of course, built of logs, which make them warm and comfortable: in the centre of each is some earth and gravel on which are placed the blazing logs, while the smoke ascends through a hole in the roof. Some of the houses have regular chimneys, while others have stoves, and some Indians have gardens round their houses: in process of time, every Indian will have a stove in his house, and a bit of garden in front of it, besides a potato-patch elsewhere.

The soil is remarkably good, and the culture of potatoes very remunerative: Mr. Duncan has a schooner flying between Metlakatlah and Victoria, to help the Indian trade. When one sees what Mr. Duncan has succeeded, by God's blessing, in bringing these Indians to, one is filled with indignation at the conduct of the Hudson's Bay Company, who by example and precept have thrust the poor degraded creatures into still lower depths of vice. I ought rather to say the servants of the company, for I know that they have rules about performing Divine Service every sunday, and establishing schools for the Indians which look fair enough on paper. But I know that even now, it is customary for their steamer, the *Labouchere*, to trade on

Sunday, and neither in fort nor steamer is Divine Service ever performed. I now close this letter: it is going by canoe to Fort Simpson, to go down to be mailed at Victoria by the steamer *Labouchere*.

Believe me, your affectionate Son,
Edmund Hope Verney.

Verney's Pacific voyage is commemorated in many of the place names that appear on the nautical charts of the Wells Passage area. Claydon Bay, Hammersley Island, Fremantle Point, and Hope Point all bear names associated with the Verney family.

62

1864: BRITISH COLUMBIA
ARTHUR BIRCH TO HIS BROTHER JOHN BIRCH
IN LONDON, ENGLAND

No sooner is a government centre established than the bureaucrats start complaining about their workload. Arthur Birch, a twenty-seven-year-old clerk in Whitehall's Colonial Office, arrived from England to be colonial secretary in New Westminster, which had become the capital of British Columbia (a province separate from the Crown Colony of Vancouver Island) in 1859. His main job, as the number two official in the young and scarcely populated province, seems to have been signing documents. Arthur's descriptions of the social mix in the settlement would have shocked the recipient of this letter, his brother John, a banker in the City of London, but John's mouth must have watered as he read about the Fraser River teeming with sturgeon.

New Westminster
7 May 1864

My dear John

I do believe that I shall be able to write you a long letter if I begin at once as the steamer has just arrived by which we find that we have missed the Mail from Vancouver to Frisco & there will be no other for 8 days.

I am really very hard worked & see no end at present to arrears. I have a very good set of Clerks in my office, all gentlemen & willing to work. I muster six, that is, 4 as Colonial Secretary, & 2 as Auditor, which latter I had no idea I was in for; and we now have a Revenue of 130,000 pounds & spend a good deal more, and so not a penny can be spent until I have signed & approved the Requisition. My signature alone takes up ½ the morning. At present I begin work at ½ past 7 a.m. with the Governor in his study—breakfast at ½ past 9—at my own office at ¼ past 10 where I now remain till 5 p.m.; but up to 2 days ago I had to be in Chair at Legislative Council Chamber by 2 o'clock & kept there without moving until 7 p.m. I own to having funked this very much at first but I am very satisfied with the way I got through and I was not shy of calling Hon Members to "Order" and giving several very unpopular casting votes, but I always made a short Speech explaining my reason for so doing which I fancy was generally well taken. I found I was expected to give a Whitebait dinner at the close of the Session but I kept silent wishing to keep such popular entertainments [until] I want popularity.

I have got a very nice little Wooden Office & my room is charming now though I fear very cold in Winter. It is close onto the Fraser [River] & the balcony & the verandah overhang the water. All the Indians are down now fishing and it is great fun to watch them spearing Sturgeon which here run to the enormous size of 500 & 600 lbs. The Indians drift down with the stream perhaps 30 canoes abreast with their long poles with spear attached kept within about a foot of the bottom of the River. When they feel a fish lying they raise the spear and thrust it at the fish seldom missing. The barb of the spear immediately disconnects from the pole but remains attached to a rope & you see sometimes 2 or 3 canoes being carried off at the same time down river at any pace by these huge fish.

My own sport has been at present very limited having only been out 2 evenings. Last night at 5 I went down to a small stream close by with my fly rod & by ½ past 6 had caught 5 Trout of 3 lbs & 2 2lbs. On the other occasion I took a canoe from below my window & paddling with a rake had in about an hour over 600 Smelts in the bottom of the canoe. The rake is so about 8 ft. long. You sit right forward and use the Rake as a paddle bringing it behind you into the boat. Each stroke sometimes I would bring up 9 or 10 at a stroke— very large Smelts & delicious eating. It is great fun & I want to be at it again.

I fancy the shooting here is a myth but I have had no time to judge . . .

We had a Ball in our town on Thursday last—there was not a single unmarried Lady present so I am in no danger here at any rate. All the Ladies are in an interesting condition with the exception of the Lady Mayoress who is a Grandmother but is Mad upon Waltzing & so are all the rest of the Ladies and it is not otherwise than dangerous or to say the least of it painful work.

We are over run with Mosquitoes & fleas; The weather is very bright and warm with sharp frosts at night, which keep back the garden. We can get no gardener so we have established a system of rivalry between the four, each having his row of beet, carrots, onions, lettuce &c &c, and as we have no rake or hoe we find the weeds very troublesome . . .

Don't advise anyone to come out here on speculation as we are over run with decayed gentlemen—the boots [handyman] at the Hotel is the son of a Dr. in Harley Street and has met me in "Society". Clifford, the son of a Clergyman in Somersetshire, is chopping wood for the Public Offices, half the stokers on the River Steamers are decayed Gentlemen & the numerous lawyers about the place are all Captains or Majors. And on the other hand we have a Tailor from Montreal & a Lumberman from up country our richest Members of Council.

We are very religious in our regulations having passed a Law for white ties every day at dinner, Holmes appearing in Uniform. This is one of the only ways of keeping up civilization in a place like this. Have you any money to spare if so send me some. I can allow you 10 p.c. & first rate security . . . Give my best love to all & Julia.

Ever Yours
A.N.B.

New Westminster lost its capital status in 1867, when Victoria was made the permanent capital of the newly united colonies of Vancouver Island and British Columbia. Arthur had returned to Whitehall the previous year; he went on to serve in Ceylon and Malaya.

63
1864: NOVA SCOTIA
GEORGE BROWN TO ANNE BROWN IN ENGLAND

George Brown, founder of the Toronto Globe *and Upper Canadian reform leader, was a major player in shaping Canadian history. As a senior member of the Province of Canada delegation, he attended the Charlottetown Conference in September 1864, along with legislators from the three Maritime provinces. The participants laid the foundations of Confederation and, according to Brown's letter to his wife, also had fun—unthinkable for a constitutional conference today! Champagne flowed and a mood of gaiety prevailed as the "Fathers" approved the "banns of matrimony between all the Provinces." The festivities were enough to bring on a bilious attack.*

Halifax
September 13, 1864

My Dearest Anne,

I wrote you a hurried note last evening just before dressing for a public dinner given to the delegates by the Government of Nova Scotia, and fully expected to have been by this time well on in our voyage to Shediac. But we were not able to leave as we expected. A storm came on about the time I closed my letter, and it gradually increased until the hour our party broke up, when it blew a regular gale. The steamer was in consequence storm-stayed and is so still, and our route will now be changed. We remain here today and start by land tomorrow morning for Windsor, where we take the steamer for St. John, New Brunswick. From St. John we will either take the steamer to Portland and return to Quebec by the Grand Trunk R.R.; or take rail from St. John to Shediac and go thence by our own steamer up the St. Lawrence. If you look at one of "Nelson's Maps" you will see exactly where we are and where we are going.

But whichever route we take, it is greatly to be feared that our arrival at Quebec will be delayed until the 19th or 20th, and as I have much public and private business to transact before sailing for England, it is too evident, I am very sorry to say, that our meeting . . . will have to be postponed a week or two later than we calculated upon. It is very provoking, my own dear Anne, that we should be so long separated—but there is no help for it under the circumstances of the case.

Our party from Quebec consisted of [George-Étienne] Cartier, John A. [Macdonald], [Alexander] Galt, [William] McDougall, [Alexander] Campbell, [Hector-Louis] Langevin, [D'Arcy] McGee and myself—beside the clerk of the Executive Council Mr. Lee, the clerk of the Attorney-General, Mr. Bernard, and a shorthand writer. We had great fun coming down the St. Lawrence—having fine weather, a broad awning to recline under, excellent stores of all kinds and unexceptionable cook, lots of books, chessboards, backgammon and so forth. Our first stopping place was at Gaspé, a pretty little fishing town in Canada, where the population turned out *en masse* to receive us, amid firing of guns and other rejoicings. Mr. LeBoudillier, M.P.P., gave us a most hospitable reception at his mansion and conducted us over the great fishing establishments of the place. In the afternoon we sailed out of the beautiful little harbour in the same distinguished manner of our entry!

From Gaspé our course was direct to Charlottetown, the little capital of little Prince Edward Island. I was up at four in the morning!—Thursday morning—to see the sun rise and have a salt water bath. We had just reached the westerly point of Prince Edward and were running along the coast of as pretty a country as you ever put your eye upon. The land all along the shore rises gradually up from the sea for a space of two or three miles, and this slope all round the island is well cultivated and when we passed was clothed in bright green verdure.

About noon we came to an inlet which we entered, and running up for some miles what appeared to be a river but was in fact but an inlet of the sea, amid most beautiful scenery, we came suddenly on the Capital City of the Island. Our steamer dropped anchor magnificently in the stream and its man-of-war cut evidently inspired the natives with huge respect for their big brothers from Canada. I flatter myself we did that well. Having dressed ourselves in correct style, our two boats were lowered man-of-war fashion and being each duly manned with four oarsmen and a boatswain, dressed in blue uniform, hats, belts, etc., in regular style, we pulled away for shore and landed like Mr. Christopher Columbus who had the precedence of us in taking possession of portions of the American continent.

Our brother delegates were there before us. Five from Nova Scotia, five from New Brunswick and five from Prince Edward. Newfoundland goes heartily with the movement, but was not notified in time to take part in the proceedings. At two o'clock the Conference was organized by the appointment of Col. Gray, Prime Minister of Prince Edward, as President of the Convention.

The urbane George Brown, founder of the Toronto Globe, *relished the balls, badinage, and backroom deals of the 1864 Charlottetown Conference.*

You are aware that the Conference was originally summoned merely to consider the question of a union of the Maritime Provinces and that Canada was no party to that arrangement and had no interest in it. We came then, not as recognized members of the Conference, but unofficially to discuss with them the propriety of extending their scheme and seeing whether the whole of British America could not be included in one Government. The Conference was accordingly organized without us, but that being done we were formally invited to be present and were presented in great style to the Conference. Having gone through the shake elbows and the "How d'ye do" and the fine weather—the Conference adjourned to the next morning at 10, then to meet for the serious despatch of business.

In the evening the [Lieutenant] Governor, Mr. Dundas, gave a large dinner party to as many of the Party as he could conveniently receive—I being one. He is a very nice fellow, son of Dundas of Dundas in the neighbourhood of Edinburgh. His wife is English, of the name of Atkinson—a very agreeable person. During our stay they were very kind to us. The Government House is very pretty—handsome grounds around it and the sea washing up gently to the very door. After all, Anne, there is something in the sea. I was the guest of Mr. Pope, the Provincial Secretary, during my stay on the island and was very glad to get to bed that first night.

On Friday, we met in Conference and Canada opened her batteries, John A. and Cartier exposing the general arguments in favour of confederation— and this occupied the time until the hour of adjournment at three. At four o'clock, Mr. Pope gave us a grand *Déjeuner à la fourchette*—oysters, lobsters and champagne and other island luxuries. This killed the day and we spent the beautiful moonlight evening in walking, driving or boating, as the mood was on us. I sat on Mr. Pope's balcony looking out on the sea in all its glory.

On Saturday the Conference resumed its deliberations, and Mr. Galt occupied the sitting in opening up the financial aspects of the Federation and the manner in which the financial disparities and requirements of the several Provinces might be arranged.

When the Conference adjourned, we all proceeded on board our steamer and the members were entertained at luncheon in princely style. Cartier and I made eloquent speeches, of course, and whether as the result of our eloquence or of the goodness of our champagne, the ice became completely broken, the tongues of the delegates wagged merrily, and the banns of matrimony between all the Provinces of B.N.A. having been formally proclaimed and all manner of persons duly warned there and then to speak or forever after to hold their tongues. No man appeared to forbid the banns and the union was thereupon formally completed and proclaimed!

In the evening, Col. Gray gave a grand dinner party at his beautiful mansion. His wife is daughter of Sir John Pennefather, Commander of the Forces at Aldershot [England]. She seems a most excellent person. She has three daughters—one here and two at Aldershot on a visit to their grandmamma. You will like her very much when you see her. I half promised to make a run down to Aldershot and see her daughters, while in London.

On Sunday I attended the Free Church and heard a very grand discourse from a licentiate whose face was familiar to me but whose name I did not learn. The afternoon and evening we spent quietly at home. Mrs. Pope is a very plain person with a large family of strong, vigorous, intelligent, and good-looking children—eight of them all steps and stairs kicking up a precious row occasionally. Her grandfather was Governor of the Island and she is related to all the old families upon it. She was born on the island and was never out of it in her life! Many of the people here are in the same position and are not withstanding amazingly civilized. Mrs. Pope has a governess for her children, beautiful grounds for their recreation, and a capital library.

On Monday the Conference resumed its sittings, when I addressed the members on the Constitutional aspects of the question, the manner in which the several Governments general and local should be constructed, and the Judiciary should be constituted, what duties should be ascribed to the general and local legislatures respectively and so forth. My speech occupied the whole sitting. At four, we lunched at the residence of Mr. Coles, leader of the Parliamentary Opposition. He is a brewer, farmer and distiller —and gave us a handsome set out. He has a number of handsome daughters, well educated, well informed and as sharp as needles. The evening I passed on board the steamer, playing chess and catching lobsters over the side of the steamer. On Tuesday the Conference resumed its deliberations, earnestly discussing the several details of the scheme. The Canadians this day closed their case, and left the Conference to decide what course it would take on their propositions. At four o'clock Mr. Palmer, Attorney-General, gave the delegates a grand luncheon at his residence. He is a very agreeable, amicable man—a person of good sense and ability who has seen much of the world. His family are in mourning, so that we did not see the ladies. In the evening Mrs. Dundas gave us a grand ball at Government House—a very nice affair, but a great bore for old fellows like me. I stayed half an hour or an hour and then bolted off quietly.

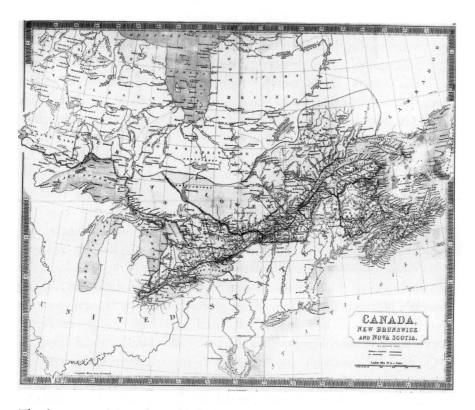

*The first map of Canada, published in Confederation Year, 1867, included
only the Atlantic seaboard and the Great Lakes basin.*

On Wednesday, the Conference gave the Canadian Delegates their
answer—that they were unanimous in regarding Federation of all the
Provinces to be highly desirable, *if the terms of union could be made satisfactory*—and that they were Prepared to waive their own limited questions
until the details of our scheme could be more fully considered and matured.
It was agreed that the Conference should stand adjourned until Monday
the 12th Sept., then to meet at Halifax. That afternoon, the Canadian delegates received on board our steamer the Governor and Mrs. Dundas and a
number of ladies, and entertained them in grand style. I was not present,
having been laid up at home with a bilious attack, the natural result of such
a round of dissipations.

On Thursday, we made our parting visits, rode into the country and
amused ourselves generally. In the evening, we were entertained at a

grand ball by the inhabitants of the island in the Parliament Buildings. It was a very grand affair—two bands of music, fine supper, and so forth. I went for an hour, but escaped about 12 as the supper was approaching . . . From the ball, all came on board the steamer and we fired up Steam and sailed for Pictou.

Midnight: This is all I can get through, have been kept up to the ears all day. We start at six this morning and I have yet to correct the Reporter's notes of my speech. So goodby my own Anne. Love to the little Darling.

> Your own loving
> George

64
1865: CANADA WEST
ANN SLATTERY TO HER SISTER IN IRELAND

The governors of municipal workhouses in Britain and Ireland often shipped groups of women across the Atlantic to become servants in British North American households (and get them off their rolls). Twenty-three-year-old Ann Slattery left her infant daughter, Jenny, with her sister in the Limerick Union workhouse when she and sixty-nine other Irish girls were sent to Canada West. She found a position as a maid of all work with a Kingston family but, as she told her sister, ached for her family.

> Kingston, Canada West,
> 1865

. . . A Stranger has a great deal of trouble to meet with before they are settled; my dear Sister I would have sent for Jenny before now but I am not intended to stop in Canada. I will go to the . . . States. It is much better place for a servant but my dear Sister please god if I am spared health, I will have her and early in spring I am doing very well at present I am living with a gentleman's family the name of Corbett they are a very good family. I have four dollars a month but still I am not inclined to stop in Canada; my dear Sister it is very lonesome to be here alone You will meet many strange faces before you will a friends but we must persevere.

Oh how happy I would be if I had a relation to spend my leisure hours with; I think I should be happy once more, but my dear Sister I am happy so long as God spares me healthy, but when my work is done I sit down and thinks of the pleasant home and loving faces I used to gaze on and tell my troubles to, but please God I will soon have some of my dear Cousins out to talk to, and then I shall be happy my dear Sister I send my love to all your family and kiss them for me, let me know how all the neighbours is; and give them my respects and that I am doing well and hopes before long to see them . . .

65
1865: CANADA WEST
EGERTON RYERSON TO HIS DAUGHTER
SOPHIA HARRIS IN LONDON

Pretty daughters can wind their fathers round their little fingers. This was certainly true of Sophia Harris, daughter of Egerton Ryerson, the Methodist minister who had become Canada West's superintendent of education in 1844. They corresponded frequently after she married the lawyer Edward Harris in 1860 and moved from Toronto to the Harris family home, Eldon House in London, Canada West. Well-educated and independent-minded, Sophia found life in Eldon House, with an autocratic mother-in-law, boring and restrictive. Egerton was in a dilemma: he knew the Harris marriage was rocky and he wanted to make his daughter happy. But he also had doubts about her priorities . . .

Toronto,
Sept. 5, 1865

My dearest Sophie,
I confess I read your letter of yesterday with some surprise. Not knowing that it contained anything *peculiar*, I was going to put [it] in my pocket & read it in my study after prayers; [but] your Mamma wished me to open & read it before prayers; so I read it out. To my surprise, your Mamma wishes me to comply with your request & send you the money—though she does not approve of the proposed expenditure. I must say I regret it myself. A passion for jewelry should rather be resisted than cherished, as it gains strength by indulgence, & is sometimes attended with very painful consequences, especially when one is not rich.

You have done well, & made your way hitherto, without so costly an ornament. Col. Lowry & the officers of the 16th [Regiment] invited Ella last week to a "garden" party in the old Govt. grounds; and one of the officers referring to you, said you were the most charming woman he had met, & spoke in a manner to indicate that this was the opinion of all. I was gratified to hear this, & could not but think how superior are the diamonds of the mind & heart—a cultivated & refined mind, pure, generous & cheerful feelings & affections—to the diamonds of the hand. *I* think you are more charming in simplicity, than in the most splendid ornaments.

As Edward has so kindly furnished you with pin money, I think you ought not to make such a purchase without his knowledge & approval. Perhaps this suggestion is superfluous, but I have thought I would make it. I have no doubt he would value the ornament more highly if his knowledge & consent were united to your wish in the purchase of it. A diamond is always worth something, but seldom brings what one gives for it.

Having thus said all that is in my heart on the subject, I herewith enclose you a *cheque* for $30, as I have no money from the Bank; & I hope you will be guided aright in your decision.

I have given Mr. Lunn of Montreal, a letter of introduction to you. He will probably call upon you sometime Friday.

I beg you will regard the cheque as a free gift, not as a loan.

Your ever affectionate Father

66

1866: CANADA WEST
NATHANIEL CARROTHERS TO HIS BROTHER
WILLIAM CARROTHERS IN IRELAND

This letter from a successful immigrant captures not only his solid farming competence but also his unmistakable Ulster accent. Nathaniel Carrothers was a no-nonsense carpenter who worked on construction projects in London as well as acquiring several hundred acres of prime agricultural land. He was one of seventeen members of the Carrothers family who had emigrated from County Fermanagh in Ireland to Upper Canada between 1835 and 1847, and settled in and around London. As Nathaniel had earlier written home, the Carrotherses had "bettered their condishion by coming to America far beyont what it was possible for them to have done had the stopped in Ireland." Nathaniel's staunch Protestant Conservatism infused his contempt for the Fenians, the Catholic Irish Americans intent on invading Canada in the 1860s.

Westminster [Township]
January the 29th 1866

Dear brother

I once again take up my pen to write to you hoping that these few lines may find you and famely in good health as the lave me and famely at present thank god for all his goodnes; with the ecception of my second son Joseph who has been in a state of bad health for two years and dont seem to get beter it is a liver and stomack complaint that eals him, he has tried three docters and none of them seem to do him any good. Last spring we got every thing ready to send him to Ireland for two or three months in the summer, and when we told the doctor who is a Scochman he would not hear of it; he said the climate in Ireland was to cold and damp for his complaint and that it was sure to make him worse but he advised us to send him north on our freshwater lakes avoiage; so we sent him; he was a way two months and felt better when a way but since he has come home I see no improvement in him.

I see by your letter to Joseph that times is better with youes, and that youes are all hard at work to make money for your land lords; this is all write so long as your famely stick to gether and is content. This has been a very dry summer hear and the winter so far very mild; we have had hardly any snow yet; the prices for every thing has been unusly dear, the farmers will make well this year as the have not to hand their hard ernings to the Landlord as with youes.

I have sent youes som newes papers so that you might have some Idea of the kind of aniables that we raise; such as was shown at our Chrismas market. The provendisial fair was held in London this year and was a large one it lasted five dayes; and as many as forty thousand visited the grounds some dayes.

James Stewart and two of Edwards boyes came down to the fair and made us a visit. We had a young man a Mr. Armstrong son to Willey of the woods who came to see this country make us a visit last winter, he stopt a week with me, he coud tel me a good dale about my old friends and acquaintance a bought Greenhil, and he liked this country so well that the whole famely has come out this harvest, they have bought a farm of two hundred acres with a good breck house and other suitible buildings on it for seven thousant Dollars. I went to see them after the came the distance of 16 miels and we had jouvel time of it. The were stoping at the house of my old friend and acquaintence Mr James Armstrong of Latin, the are all delighted with this country. I have bought since I last wroute to you two hundred more acres of land for John and Joseph my two eldest sones, there is one of them 75 acres cleared and on the other 50 acres. John is maried and is living on his, the other I have rented to a man at 100 Dolars a year. The cost four thousand dolars which is semething more than eight hundred of your pounds; so I have got 100 acres for each of my sones so that may liv comfertible with out toiling all their dayes to make the rent. I have been talking to a good many that lives on rented farms hear and the say that the woud rather live on one in this country than there. Ther is a scoch man living on a rented farm near me and he has saved as much money as has bought him self a farm last year.

I have been thinking had you come to this country when you were thinking of it with such a famely of sons how wel of you woud have been and how well it woud have been for them besides toiling all their dayes in Ireland. If you would send one of the boyes out to this country to see their friends and the country how the woud like it before the go renting a farm there and be not likin to live here and wishing to return, I will pay his passage home a gain and I am shure he wil be much the wiser after it; I have had strong nosions of going back to see the old country and you in times that are past, but I suppose that I never shal now.

There has been deaths and mariges among the friends hear since I wrout last. Brother Thomas has beried his wife and is maried a gain to a scoch woman, but I supose Brother Joseph has sent you al perticulars; we had a visit from Polwel gaham he was going from the easteren part of this provence to the westren to see his brother. You mentioned nothing about the fenians in Ireland in your letter to brother J but I see by the news-papers that you have trouble some times of it. The have large meetings in the states and make boistring speeches how the will invade Ireland and free it from british rule and make it a republick of their owen, the allso talk about taking Canada. There has been some feer that the woud cros the lines this winter and rob and plunder and carry what the coud a way with them, but I think the poor devils is putting their time and money to a bad use as the never will be able to do either.

The thing that is causing the greates excitement in this part of the country is the discovery of oil which is under the earth in large quantiteys in this part of Canada which is going to become a sourse of welth as great as the gold miens of Californa or Austrila; there has been hundreds who has made a fortune of it the last year. This oil is caled rock oil and is got by boring a hole into the earth [until they] come to the rock which is from 40 to 50 feet and into the rock three or four hundred feet [until they] come to the oil and when the strike a good vain the oil will rise to the surface and flow over and run away; there is hundreds of such wells and hundreds of them sinking this winter some of them yeilding 300 barrels a day it is worth 10 dolars a barrel there is severel wels sinking in and neare Londond. Write me a letter as soon as you get this and let me know all you can about my old friends and neibours and rememer me to all enquiring friends and neibours; and wife and all the children and I remain

Nathaniel Carrothers

67

1868: RUPERT'S LAND (PRESENT-DAY MANITOBA)
CHARLES MAIR TO HIS BROTHER HOLMES MAIR
IN PERTH, ONTARIO

With each successive year, the growing demand for good agricultural land exacerbated competition between different ethnic groups. Charles Mair, an Ontario poet, was the kind of self-confident blusterer who made everything worse by trampling over local sensitivities. In 1868, in the wake of Confederation, Mair went to the troubled Red River Colony, near present-day Winnipeg, as paymaster to a road-building party. When he arrived, the Red River colonists (most of whom were Metis) were vehemently resisting a takeover by Canada. However, they were in a vulnerable position: after a grasshopper plague ruined harvests and the Hudson's Bay Company removed its support, the colony's economy was failing. Mair became an instant expert on the shortcomings of the whole community (few of whom he had actually met) for the benefit of his brother in Perth, Ontario.

Head-Quarters, Mistamiskano,
November 19th, 1868

Dear Brother,

I received your long and welcome letter yesterday, and also the papers, but not yet the [weeklies] you mention, and which I miss very much. They will yet come along, I have no doubt, but tardily; as the irregularity of the mails to Fort Garry is simply a matter of course. I wrote to you from Fort Garry, and Dr. Schultz [local leader of a noisy pro-Canada party] has instructed the editor of the *Nor' Wester* to send on the paper to you and James [their brother] regularly. Our trip over the prairies was a stupendous novelty to me. You can imagine nothing like it; but I shall not dwell upon it here . . .

After putting up at the Dutchman's hotel there, I went over and stayed at Dr. Schultz's, after a few days. The change was comfortable, I assure you, from the racket of a motley crowd of half-breeds, playing billiards and drinking, to the quiet and solid comfort of a home . . . Altogether, I received hospitalities to my heart's content, and I left the place thoroughly pleased with most that I had met. There are jealousies and heart-burnings, however. Many wealthy people are married to half-breed women, who, having no coat of arms but a "totem" to look back to, make up for the deficiency by biting at the backs of their "white" sisters. The white sisters fall back upon their whiteness, whilst the husbands meet each other with desperate courtesies and hospitalities, with a view to filthy lucre in the background.

We crossed the Red River to St. Boniface, opposite to Fort Garry, the Doctor driving me out in his gig, and drove over the virgin prairie for thirty miles due east, to Oak Point, which we have dubbed Mistamiskano, and where we have established our head-quarters. The country traversed is a beautiful one, covered with a tall, luxuriant hay which springs from a loamy surface in many places four feet deep, resting upon clay of any depth. Inconceivably rich, indeed, is all this country; boundless and rich beyond all description or comparison. At Oak Point, we rented a house from a half-breed . . . Here also begin the woods which stretch clear through to the Lake of the Woods. This wood consists mainly of small poplar, a sort of bastard red pine, a few cedars, and vast quantities of red willows, or quawpe-mug as the Crees call them. It in no respect resembles a Canadian forest, but rather the growth which springs up in place of a pinery when a fire has swept it away, with this singular difference, however, that it rests upon a perfectly level country almost, and is nourished by rich loams, instead of rock and sand. The poplar is the firewood chiefly used here, and is burnt when dry. Few of them are over six inches in diameter, but they burn briskly and give much heat. About ten miles from here, a shanty has been built, and twenty men are now at work upon the road. Of course, through such a country as I have described, there is little difficulty in the work of destruction. The timber is small, the country is level and free from stones (except boulder), and there is an easy drainage into the numerous rivers (creeks we would call them in Canada) which invariably cut their way for twenty feet or more beneath the surface. I was out at the works today, and the cleared portion of the track looks very fine and straight. Certainly, when all is grubbed out and graded, it will be a magnificent road.

There are not many Indians in this neighbourhood at present, most of them being away in pursuit of peltries. The word "wigwam" is never heard here. In speaking of an Indian's home it is called a "lodge". The "lodge in some vast wilderness" that Cowper sighed for, can be had cheap here—dirt cheap. It is composed of skins stretched over some eight or nine poles standing on end on the ground, and converging to a common centre near the top. The smoke from the fire, which is built in the centre of the lodge, issues out of the top, and, though very comfortable with its buffalo robes and skins of all kinds, it has a very rakish and *Ojibway-ish* look. I never look at one without fancying to myself that it is full of wolves inside. This is the Nor'West Indian's house, and they are to be met with everywhere from Rainy Lake to the Mackenzie River. It looks odd, however, to see them scattered about the village of Winnipeg, where the "poor Indian" comes to barter and drink fire-water.

Next spring, I shall have an opportunity of smoking the calumet [peace pipe] with the fierce Plain Crees and the Blackfeet, who come down on horse-back annually to have a "talk" and smoke the pipe of peace with their "Father" at the stone Fort. These are the real Indians, wild and eloquent; and the Doctor tells me it is a strange sight to see them at their dances and medicine mysteries, circumscribing that little speck of civilization—the future city of Winnipeg. Many of the Sioux, who committed the horrible outrages in Minnesota [the massacres of 1862], are now about Lake Manitobah, and the Doctor is coming out next week to take me back to the village for a trip up the Assinniboine some seventy-five miles, to Portage la Prairie and Lake Manitobah. At Portage la Prairie will be the most flourishing city in this great West, for many reasons, which I will defer giving until I have been there.

So far as I have yet seen, the country is *great*—inexhaustible, inconceivably rich. Farming here is a pleasure—there is no toil in it, and all who do farm are comfortable, and some wealthy. What do you think of a farmer within a bowshot of here, being worth seven or eight thousand pounds sterling, and selling to the Hudson's Bay Company last week 5,000 pounds worth of cattle: a man who came from Lower Canada nineteen years ago, not worth sixpence.

The half-breeds are the only people here who are starving. Five thousand of them have to be fed this winter, and it is their own fault, they won't farm.

They will hunt buffaloes, drive ox-carts 500 miles up and 500 miles back to St. Cloud, at the rate of twenty miles a day: do anything but farm. Hitherto, it was so easy to live here that it didn't matter whether they farmed or not; but the grasshopper put a stop to that last summer, and now they are on their beam-ends. As for the farmers: Scotch, English and French, not one of them requires relief, other than seed wheat, which they are quite able to pay for. This is the true state of the case here, but it does not lessen the claims upon humanity. It will take 40,000 pounds to feed the people through to next fall; but the 40,000 pounds will be forthcoming.

As for the future of this country, it is as inevitable as to-morrow's sunrise. The climate is delightful. The weather just now, and there is no appearance of a change, is clear, cloudless, bland and inspiriting; and the thermometer has not sunk below 30 degrees for a week. In deep winter, there are short spells of severe weather, but they are short; so they all tell me, and certainly my experience so far justifies the assertion. I never felt such fine weather in November in Canada as we have here just now: and there is an exhilaration in it quite new to me. But enough for the present . . .

I enclose you a feather of the prairie-chicken; also an oak leaf picked up "in the Land of the Dacotah," 150 miles south of this. The hay enclosed is the celebrated prairie "wire-grass;" the other article is a strip of wild sage which grows extensively on the prairies. The finest hops I ever saw were growing wild at Eagle River, Dacotah Territory.

Charles Mair's letter was published in both the Toronto Globe *and the Montreal* Gazette. *On the strength of it, Mair was appointed special correspondent to the* Globe.

68

1869: RUPERT'S LAND (PRESENT-DAY MANITOBA)
LOUIS RIEL TO THE EDITOR OF *LE NOUVEAU MONDE*
IN MONTREAL

Copies of Charles Mair's letter, with its offensive comments on Metis and Indians, quickly found their way back to the Red River Colony. The Metis leader Louis Riel despatched a stinging reply to Le Nouveau Monde, *a Catholic newspaper published in Montreal that upheld the rights of the Metis settlement. Riel, one-eighth Indian and seven-eighths French Canadian, was a clever, ambitious, poetic dreamer, who resented the way that English Canadians consistently underestimated and dismissed the Metis people. The following year, Riel would lead a successful rebellion against Dominion authorities and secure separate provincial status for the Red River Colony.*

Red River,
February 1, 1869

Mr. Editor:

Please be so good as to give me a little space in the columns of your journal, in order that I too may write of Red River.

I cannot resist that desire since I have read the enormities which a journal of Upper Canada, the *Globe*, has just uttered, in publishing a letter of a certain Mr. Mair, who arrived in Red River last fall. This gentleman, an English Canadian, is, it is said, gifted in making verses; if such is the fact I should advise him strongly to cultivate his talent, for in that way his writings would make up in rhyme for what they lack in reason. Scarcely a month after his arrival in this country, Mr. Mair desired to describe it and its inhabitants. He succeeded rather like the navigator who, passing by a league from the coast, wrote in his log: *"The people of this country seemed to us to be well disposed."*

"The climate of Red River," says Mr. Mair, in his letter, "is most agreeable." On the 19th of November there were not three degrees of frost. I had heard it said, of course, but I know it by experience now.

Well now! If he had arrived here in the night, and had been able to write down his impressions at once, he would have said in the same way: *"Here the sun never rises; the densest darkness constantly blankets these vast territories."*

That is rather like what he has done in speaking of the climate after two weeks' trial. He does not know that very often the ice sets by All Souls' Day; that we have snow storms, even in the middle of October; that last year, during the month of January, the thermometer stood continually at from -25 to -30 degrees centigrade and that very often we have it as cold as -40 degrees. This year Providence, which had already well tested us, has wished to spare us cold weather, but because of that it is not necessary to say that we live under the torrid zone.

The country, he adds, is of an inconceivable richness: those who wish to farm are all rich; only the half-breeds are in distress.

Well, I am a half-breed myself and I say that there is nothing falser than those words. I know almost all the names of those who received help this winter, and I can assure you that they were of all colours. There are some half-breeds who do not ask for charity, as there are some English, some Germans and some Scots, who receive it every week.

It was not, of course, enough for these gentlemen to come to mock the distress of our country by making unfortunate people driven by hunger, work dirt cheap. They had also to spread falsehoods among the outside world, to lead people to believe that the relief sent to Red River was not needed.

Happily there was other more trustworthy testimony published in the newspapers to contradict such tainted reports.

"One can", says he again, "judge of the richness of certain individuals by a sale of cattle to the Company, by a single settler. He sold 5000 pounds worth of stock." Indeed! Do you know that in estimating them at ten pounds a head, he would have to have had five hundred, to reach such a sum? Let us take a step further, for no one in R.R. ever had five hundred animals to sell, nor even a hundred.

He adds: "The future of the country is as inevitable as to-morrow's sunrise." That is what is known as casting a horoscope. And who indeed up to today has ever doubted the future of this country? Yes, unless indeed God causes an earthquake in this small part of the globe, this country like all others, will have some kind of future, but not that which Mr. Mair predicts for it.

I know some men who have more than two weeks' experience and who say the opposite to this gentleman. He says finally: *"The city of Portage la Prairie is destined to become one of the most important in the country: however, I shall not speak to you of it until I have seen it."* And why not? You speak of a great many other things that you have not had time to see or know; that would be worth as much as the remainder of your letter; as much as the scarcely courteous terms, I will even say barely civilized, which you use in speaking of the ladies of the country, who certainly by all reports are quite equal to the ladies of your country.

Be it said in passing, Mr. Mair, if we had only you as specimen of civilized men, we should not have a very high idea of them. If I wished to amuse myself by wielding the pen as you do for the sole pleasure of uttering follies to the world, I should have some amusing things to say on your account . . .

In other circumstances than those in which we are, I should not have taken note of the falsehoods of this letter. We are accustomed to see strangers arrive every year who come to look us up and down, and who then print in the newspapers or in big books their reflections more or less queer on us and our country. But after the bad times which have befallen on us, driven as we are to have recourse to public charity, I have thought that it was my duty to protest against falsehoods which could give the impression elsewhere that there was no need of relief in Red River.

L. R.

69
1869: ONTARIO
SIR JOHN A. MACDONALD TO JAMES O'REILLY IN OTTAWA

There is no doubt that, for all his failings, Sir John A. Macdonald, the first prime minister of the Dominion of Canada, was a tough-minded, sure-footed leader. When the garrulous little Irish tailor Patrick James Whelan was accused of the murder of Thomas D'Arcy McGee, an Irish-born father of Confederation, many Canadians believed that a Fenian conspiracy was involved. The trial was pure melodrama (Lady Macdonald, the prime minister's wife, attended court every day) and the verdict was a foregone conclusion. But others expressed doubts that there was enough evidence to hang Whelan. Macdonald had no time for such doubts, as he made clear to Crown Prosecutor James O'Reilly.

Ottawa, 12th February, 1869.
Private

My Dear O'Reilly,
You will see by the papers that Whelan said nothing on the scaffold. He left a short paper stating that neither Doyle nor Buckley participated in the murder, which he signed before O'Gara and Lees. In conversation with them he freely admitted his presence at the murder, [as] he did to Goodwin, and on several occasions to the Sheriff and Governor of the gaol, but he always denied that he fired the shot. I am satisfied that he did fire the shot, and that that fact is the reason that he did not offer to turn Queen's evidence. I attach no importance to the written statement. It has evidently been dictated by some superstitious feeling that as he had taken away one life, he would make amends by endeavouring to save two. The body was to have been given up to Mrs. Whelan, but information having arrived that there was going to be a great Fenian demonstration over the corpse at Montreal on its arrival, which would inevitably lead to bloodshed, it has, I

believe, been buried within the precincts of the prison, the ground being blessed and Christian funeral given, attended by the clergyman who was with him at the last. This was the arrangement last night when I went to bed, and I presume it was carried out this morning.

Thanks for your congratulations.

Yours faithfully,
John A. Macdonald.

P. S. to the effect that priest having declined to attend, body was buried without rites of Church.

70
1869: RUPERT'S LAND (PRESENT-DAY MANITOBA)
WILLIAM MCDOUGALL TO PRIME MINISTER
SIR JOHN A. MACDONALD IN ONTARIO

In 1869, the Toronto lawyer and MP William McDougall returned from London, England, very pleased with himself: on behalf of the new Dominion of Canada he had helped negotiate the biggest real estate deal in Canadian history—the purchase of all the Hudson's Bay Company territory for $1.5 million. He was immediately appointed first lieutenant-governor of the North-West Territories by Sir John A. Macdonald, and joyfully set out from Ottawa to assume his important new office. But his high-handed disregard for Metis land rights alienated the colonists, led by Louis Riel. McDougall was prevented from entering the Red River Colony.

Pembina,
31st October, 1869.

Private.

My Dear Sir John,

By this mail I send my first report from the North West Territories. I am sorry that it announces insurrection and possible bloodshed. The papers which accompany my report give you all the particulars that have reached me, except the rumours of this neighbourhood. These do not amount to much, and are not worth repeating, but one fact is significant, viz: that the half-breed settlers hereabouts, perhaps a dozen families, have been holding secret meetings at the instigation of emissaries from Fort Garry. I believe they have come to nothing as yet. Two of the most influential of these settlers called upon me today. The spokesman, one Marceau, of French Canadian origin, assured me that he had no sympathy with the movement, and refused to attend meetings. He said the half-breeds were ignorant, and that parties behind were pushing them on; that they had read, in the papers that "all the *law* was to come from Canada," and that "no one in Red River would be in the law" (meaning the Council): that the half-breeds would be all driven back from the river, and their lands given to others, etc. I assured him that there was no truth in any of these stories, and that his countrymen must not believe the statements read to them from Canadian newspapers, especially the *Globe*, as to the intentions of the Canadian Government.

He is to see me tomorrow and offers to go down to the barricade, and persuade his countrymen to go home. I mention this case to show how the injudicious remarks and statements of Canadian newspapers are made the occasion of outbreak and outrage in this distant region.

The worst feature in the case is the apparent complicity of the priests. It appears certain that at least one of them has openly preached sedition to his flock, and has furnished aid and comfort to the parties in arms. I regret to hear that all the priests in this country, with one or two exceptions, are from France, and have no sympathy with Canada or Canadians. There is probably some exaggeration in the papers accompanying my report, as the statements come through Protestant channels, but I have heard enough from other sources to satisfy me that the R.C. priesthood here cannot be relied upon to support the authority of the new Government. You must expect a call for volunteers from Canada to settle the country, with a good rifle among the implements of husbandry in each case.

I closed an agreement for the construction of a line of telegraph from Breckenridge to Fort Garry, of the terms of which you will all approve, do not doubt. If I find time I will send a copy of the agreement for your confirmation by this mail.

I saw all the principal railway people at Chicago and St. Paul, and learned their plans. There is no doubt that railway connection with Red River will be established next summer, and the only thing required to continue it to this point is a good charter in proper hands with a reasonable grant in land and money—$5,000 per mile of a bonus would be sufficient to build the line to Winnipeg, with a land grant equal to those of the Western States. But we must not allow this line, which is indispensable to the settlement of this part of the country, to retard our efforts to open our own Lake Superior water line. It will not do, I am convinced, to be at the mercy of the American lines. My own experience has satisfied me on that point. Both means of communication are necessary to the speedy settlement of the country, and will repay the cost in a few years.

We have had delightful Indian summer weather for the last three or four days, after the snowstorm . . . and the natives say it will last two or three weeks. All that this country, for hundreds of miles in every direction from this point, as I learn from hunters and settlers, needs to make it the northern farmer's paradise, is railway communication. Timber for fuel and fencing is scarce, but the railway and the steamboat will supply that as soon as the demand is urgent. So far, I am charmed with the prospect which everywhere opens to the eye of the tiller of the soil. Let us have law and order and public improvements, even on a moderate scale, and we will make this country the home of happy and prosperous millions in the lifetime of some of us who now have its destiny in our hands.

I will write you as soon as I reach Fort Garry, if ever I do, on the railway question as promised, as I have something important to suggest. I will only add I am not frightened and don't believe the insurrection will last a week.

> Yours most faithfully,
> W. McDougall

By the end of 1869, the Metis people had seized Fort Garry, Riel had become head of a provisional government for the colony, and McDougall had ignominiously retreated to Ottawa. The new province, named Manitoba, was a tiny rectangle of land (known as "the postage stamp province"); Manitoba did not acquire its current boundaries until 1912. However, McDougall had been half right in his analysis of the situation. When the Canadian Pacific Railway decided to route the railway through Winnipeg, the city's population exploded from 5,000 to 35,000. Settlers poured into the surrounding region, rapidly outnumbering the Metis.

71
1871: MANITOBA
SARA RIEL TO HER BROTHER LOUIS RIEL

There were ten other surviving children besides Louis in the Riel family, who shared their grandfather's Cree blood and their mother's French-Canadian Catholicism. Sara Riel, whose love for her brother Louis was as fanatical as her religious faith, was a Grey Nun missionary. In many loving letters to her brother, she expressed her belief that they both had a divine destiny.

St. Boniface General Hospital,
January 29, 1871

My dear Louis,

On Monday the 26th I received your affectionate and nice letter of the 6th. Thank you, my dear Louis, for the pleasure you have given to me. To talk with you, to read letters from you is something that alleviates the suffering Our Heavenly Father has imposed upon us. Thank you again and please, grant me this solace from time to time. I was glad to hear that you were better, and hope that our feeble prayers may at last be heard and that the Good Lord will reward you with good health. Health gives charm to this life . . . a favour for which we rarely offer to God our tribute of gratitude. I heard someone make that remark a few days ago, and realized how true it was in my own case. It occurred to me not too long ago, that I ought to thank the Good Lord for the blessing of good health.

I hope this letter finds you in as good health as it leaves me. Thank Heaven for this. I have been so well for the last month that I began to believe I shall yet become an old bone! One thing I did not like too much last year was that I seemed to have a desire to die. I gradually realized that my feelings have changed. If it is the will of God I would like to live many more years to serve Him and make up for lost time in doing so. It is our misfortune that while we are on earth, we can only deplore that we are not here long enough to become worthy of the rewards of eternal life. What a mission to be a Sister of Charity! Every day I appreciate more and more the role God has given me; to look after, to visit, to comfort, to give strength to the sick, to pray with them; to speak of God to them makes me feel good inside, as does the task of caring for children, teaching them and helping them get to know and love God. More and more do I love the bonds that chain me to Him. There is a wish in my heart which naturally would be yours too, if you were in my place, which catches me unawares a thousand times—to ask God for something which I leave you to guess . . . Time will tell whether my most intimate prayer for the past eight years shall at last be answered . . .

But where am I? This was not the point I intended to make, when I began. The lips run over when the heart is full and you will not blame me, will you? This reminds me of a thought I had the other night in the chapel, leaning against the altar rail. I go there often, to receive the Bread of Life that makes us strong . . . I was praying with all my heart for you, my beloved brother, I felt the pain of your suffering, I wept, bringing to the Sacred Heart of Jesus, my fears, my worries, and my pleas . . . Suddenly I thought of the many who cry, sigh and bemoan the strayings and indifferences of their brothers. Ah, my dear Louis, what a consolation! What happiness to know that my brother is how the good Lord wanted him to be; faithful to his religion, fulfilling his duties. Ah, my dear Louis, keep on doing that! Remain everywhere and always our Eldest! And I hope that along the same road, through the grace of God, beside you shall walk your sister who loves you and who commends herself to your prayers, and to those of our dear Marie.

I saw Mamma on Thursday, she was very well: knowing that you will come soon, gives her heart, as she says. Joseph and Alexandre are well and going to school. Dear little Alex studies like a man. He is not as shy and timid as he used to be. He walks with his head high and answers questions without embarrassment. Mr. Thibeault and Mr. Dugas have gone to St. Vital. These reverend gentlemen asked him why he goes to the chapel every night, "I come to pray for little Louis," he said. Octavie, Eulalie and Henriette have been at school since the 21st, last Saturday. They are well and not bored; they study and do their best. Sister Marie-Xavier is very satisfied with them. They told me they wanted to make up for lost time. The other day, Henriette decided that she was not able to learn English grammar. She went to Sister Marie-Xavier and told her so. Sister answered: "What, Henriette, you're joking, my girl! You, the most talented in the whole class, cannot learn grammar? I cannot believe that!" A few hours later Henriette handed in her grammar, her geography and Holy History.

I am proud and happy to be able to tell you about them. Write to encourage them. I was astonished to see them with their clothes as fresh and as clean as they were last fall . . . That time of freedom gave them the experience and made them better in every respect. They took Communion the next day to receive the Benediction of Heaven for their studies, and above all for our dear Papa who they miss so much.

Find consolation, strength and courage in the Sorrowful Heart of Jesus. So long, be happy, and remain healthy, that is what I wish for you. Believe in the sincere affection of your sister who embraces you.

S. Riel

By the time Louis Riel received this letter, the new province of Manitoba had been absorbed into Confederation and he was being vilified in Ontario for his role in the 1869–1870 Red River Rebellion.

72
1871: BRITISH COLUMBIA
ALEXANDER ROBB TO HIS SISTER SUSANNA ROBB IN IRELAND

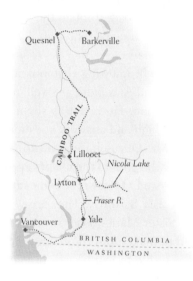

The Cariboo gold rush was just beginning in 1862 when Alexander Robb, twenty-three, left the family farm in Ireland to prospect for gold in British Columbia. The province was then one of the most isolated parts of the British Empire, and Alexander had to hike five hundred kilometres along a steep, rough trail, through unsurveyed territory, to reach the gold fields. Over the next few years he tried gold mining, labouring, and cattle ranching but never thrived. He did not enjoy the rough, all-male society of the frontier: "There is not within some thousands of miles of where I sit tonight one solitary individual who would care two straws if I were dead and buried tomorrow," he wrote his sister Eleanor, whom he had begged to send him a wife. Despite a succession of defeats, he struggled to remain optimistic about the future of the province.

23 May 1871,
Nicola Lake, BC.

My dear sister,
Your very welcome letter came to hand about three weeks ago and as I am going to start for Lytton (our Post Office) today I will take the opportunity

of answering it. Just fancy, it will take me 3 days to go down and as many more to come back and yet this is the only way unless by a chance that we have of communicating with the outside world. We did expect to have a direct mail of our own before this time and the legislative assembly actually granted us funds for carrying mail, but it appears that the governor vetoed the vote as he had no money to spare for that purpose.

You may have possibly heard that by a vote of the parliaments of Canada and this country we now belong to the Dominion of Canada or will be as soon as the home government gives its assent to the bill which we expect will be about the month of June or July. Great benefits are expected by some people from the change, and although I am not so sanguine as some are, still I have no manner of doubt but that it will do some good. Among other benefits we expect to derive from the confederation is that of having the full management of our own local affairs, of which we are in a great measure deprived under the present form of government. You see that our present assembly or parliament is composed of only one third of what we call popular members—that is, those who are appointed by the people, while the remaining two thirds are what is called official members and are appointed by the governor and are totally irresponsible to the people at large. It is very easy to see to what abuses such a system is likely to give rise. Of course where people have the voting of their own salaries, it is only likely that they will have good ones and the officials certainly do rate their services at a very high figure considering what they have to do while it is scarcely possible for any measure, however necessary it may be for the good of the country, to pass through the assembly if it interferes in any way with the interests of these gentlemen. Under confederation we expect these abuses will be done away with. All the members of the legislature will be elected by the people and it will be our own faults if we do not get laws to suit ourselves.

Another benefit which we are to derive from joining ourselves to Canada is that in the terms of confederation the government of Canada binds itself to commence a railroad from Canada to the Pacific Coast within two years and finish it inside of ten. Most people think that the road will be completed in a little over half that time and I understand that a party of surveyors have arrived already from Canada to look out for the best route for the proposed line. It is just possible that they may bring the road through this valley and at any rate it cannot miss us by more than fifty miles and we think nothing of that distance in this country. Go where it will, it will be of immense benefit to everyone as the very money which will be spent in its construction will be a big item among such a small population as this colony has got while the stimulus it will give to industry of all kinds will be of incalculable value to us.

I am very sensible, my dear sister, that this must appear to be a very strange kind of letter to write to you but I really have not got anything to say that I think would interest you. I am and have been in good health and with ordinary good luck I think that in two or three years more I will be not indeed rich or anything like it but at least out of debt and independent and you may be sure that the first use I will make of the first money I can get a hold of will be to take me where I can eat my Christmas dinner with you . . .

My object in going to Lytton now is to take down some butter and get things from the store. It is a very unpleasant trip at this season, as the snow is melting on the mountains and the creeks and rivers are very high. Fortunately there is now a bridge across the worst and largest river. Last year I had to ride my horse and make him swim across it and I do not care about taking such risks oftener than is necessary as it is both a wide and rapid river larger, I should think, than the Shannon (that is, at this season; at other times it is quite easy to cross almost anywhere). Give my love to father and all at home also to all my friends and believe me my dear sister your loving brother

Alexander Robb.

In 1874, Robb returned to Ireland, where he married, had seven children, and prospered. The railroad arrived in British Columbia ten years after he left; it passed through Lytton but went nowhere near Nicola Lake.

73
1872: ONTARIO
THE MARQUESS OF DUFFERIN, GOVERNOR GENERAL OF CANADA, TO SIR JOHN A. MACDONALD IN OTTAWA

How grand should Canada's head of state be? When Frederick Temple Blackwood, 1st Marquess of Dufferin and Ava, was appointed governor general of Canada in 1872, Ottawa was still little more than a lumber town. Its impressive new Parliament Buildings were surrounded by a squalid sea of shacks. But Dufferin, an Anglo-Irish aristocrat, was determined to infuse Rideau Hall with glamour and power. He believed that the great Dominion of the north should have a vice-regal presence as impressive as the American presidency. But as he pointed out to the prime minister, there was a small matter of cost . . .

Ottawa,

December 1872

Private and Confidential

My Dear Sir John,

I return you the volumes containing the debates on the Governor's salary which you were kind enough to send me, and which are sufficiently explicit. On the other hand, I feel that it will be necessary for me at once to face the question of my future expenditure. Since arriving in Canada, I have spent over 11,000 pounds, in other words 5,000 pounds more than my official salary. It is true that this includes several very heavy and exceptional items such as freight, purchase of horses, transport of carriages and servants from England, which would not recur in the current expenses of future years. But now that we are settled down at Ottawa, I have been able to ascertain pretty accurately what my regular outgoings are likely to amount to, and the estimate proves very far from satisfactory, as you will see by the table:

Per Month		
Ordinary household expenses	200 pounds	
Wages and livery	130	
Stables	60	
Firing and light	130	
Wine	10	
Washing	30	
Private Secretary	30	
Sundry	10	
	600	7,200 p. a.
Charities and subscriptions	1,000	
Travelling	1,000	
Sinking fund to recoup a portion of the excess of expenditure which has already taken place	800	

| Balls, parties, state dinners and occasional entertainments | 3,000 |
| Personal expenses | 0,000 |

It is to be observed the foregoing calculation is, in respect of what in England would be considered a modest establishment for a peer or ordinary country gentleman, and that neither in the number of my servants, nor in my kitchen, am I at all extravagantly provided. In the *household expenses* there are not included any entertainments beyond the ordinary dinners at which I have had the pleasure of receiving my Ottawa friends. To these, of course, there must be added a certain number of balls, parties, and other occasional hospitalities, which I should both desire and be expected to dispense. I find that the expense of a ball, including wine, can scarcely be kept under a pound a head. At Toronto our ball cost only 500 pounds, but on that occasion the Provincial Government contributed both the decorations and the lighting, so that only three balls a year would require the best part of 2,000 pounds.

The item for travelling expenses is calculated on the exact average to which they have come during the last five months, and if I am to visit New Brunswick and Nova Scotia next year, I can hardly expect it to be less, unless our steamer may make a difference. I hardly know as yet what my charities and subscriptions will amount to, but Lord Lisgar expended 1,000 pounds per annum under that head, and mine would probably not be less.

On comparing these estimates with my official salary, there results a discrepancy of a very startling and disagreeable character; indeed, it is only too plain that if I am to keep out of gaol, I must at once change my programme and make my role as

Rideau Hall was built in 1838 by Thomas MacKay, a contractor on the Rideau Canal. The conservatory (right) was added after the government purchased the house in 1868 for the governor general.

Governor General very different from what I had desired and intended it should have been, assimilating it more closely to the economical and sedentary tenor of existence adopted by my predecessors. This will be very distasteful to me, and quite contrary to my convictions as to the procedure which it is desirable the Governor General should adopt, but unless your ingenuity can discover a remedy, I do not see what else can be done. I am quite certain that the estimate I have drawn up is an economical one. At first, my secretary being in England, and we ourselves being new to the country, and too busy and hurried in our movements to attend to our weekly bills, a good deal of cheating and overcharging may have taken place, but since Mr. Pattisson's return, there has been applied to my domestic concerns the same care and vigilance which I have been accustomed to use at home, and what we have done lately could not have been done cheaper.

I had been told that everything was much less dear in Canada, but this is certainly not the case, or at all events the enhanced price of some things more than counterbalances the cheapness of others. Be that as it may, I do not think that I can manage to get on, according to my present way of life, under 13,000 pounds. If the excess of my expenditure over my official income was merely a matter of 500 pounds or 1,000 pounds, I should not regard it, or trouble you with my difficulties, but the prospective deficit is too serious to overlook. If I could throw upon the government the expenses of lighting and heating my official residences, and so much of my travelling expenses as were incurred in my official visits to the distant Provinces, the relief would be very sensible; but Parliament, if we are to judge from the debates you have referred to, may not smile on such contingent disbursements. On the other hand, as the Dominion Government acquires the consciousness of its growing dignity and importance, public opinion may develop a greater liberality of sentiment in all these matters.

I see the United States are about to increase the income and appointments of their President, and the shrieks of our own Civil Service are calling attention to the rapid rise in prices. All this may perhaps help, but at all events, I have thought it better to acquaint you with the present state of the case in order that on an early occasion we may take counsel together and determine on what footing it will be best to put my establishment in future.

> Believe me, My dear Sir John,
> Yours sincerely,
> Dufferin.

Dufferin succeeded in his ambition: he secured a larger budget and by the time he left Ottawa, in 1878, he had established a vice-regal style of pomp and ceremony that lasted for generations. He went on to serve as British ambassador in Russia, Turkey, Italy, and France.

74
1874: MANITOBA
SAMUEL ANDERSON TO HIS SISTER JANET ANDERSON IN SCOTLAND

The enthusiasm of participants at this slap-up military dance on the Manitoba-Dakota border in the depths of a prairie winter delights me. Captain Samuel Anderson, Royal Engineers, was a member of the survey party that set the boundary between the United States and the new Dominion of Canada. Working in temperatures as low as –34 degrees Celsius, the party struggled with both difficult terrain and discrepancies between American and Canadian calculations. However, the Canadian and American survey parties developed remarkable collegiality, as Sam described to his sister in Scotland.

West Lynne. Manitoba.
Dom. of Canada.
28 Feb. 1874

My dearest Janet,

We are just recovering from the effects of a dance we gave last night to our American neighbours which went off splendidly. Our men had a party two days before and had sent for 12 bandsmen from the regiment at Fort Garry, so we took advantage of these musicians being here to invite all the Americans over, and they all came, eight ladies and eight gentlemen. We asked them for eight o'clock but they were so eager that they arrived at ¼ to 8, and it was lucky I had got ready in time, for my room was used as the ladies' boudoir and I had to make everything as tidy as possible for the occasion.

One of the ladies had to bring her little baby and nurse (the child was about 10 months old) and the little one was as good as gold, slept in my bed a good part of the evening, and when he was awake, the nurse brought him into the room where dancing was going on and sat there for an hour at a time. When you consider that these good people had all driven 6 miles in sleds roughly covered overhead with canvass, it was a great undertaking to bring the little one too, in such cold nights as we have here. I was quite delighted to see the baby as the Mamma would not come without it, and it gave us no trouble whatever.

We had to cover the bare walls of the quarters with flags and various devices made up of swords and steel ramrods and pistols, and the men painted several devices for their own party, which came in most opportunely for ours. The two ladies belonging to our little community did all the soups and jellies, ices, &c. with their own hands and gave us a first rate supper. They lent us all their silver and crockery, and there was such a spread that it astonished ourselves just as much as our American guests. The dancing went on splendidly, ten couples to every set of quadrilles and lancers, & the set of lancers with ten couples requires people to have their wits about them to prevent its degenerating into a scramble. This was cleverly prevented by one of the American officers, as is the custom in their country, calling out the figures, so that after the first trial the drill was very creditable.

We had to scrub the floor, then dry it with pans of hot ashes put about in different parts of the room, then planed the floor & bees-waxed it. We did not begin to prepare until after breakfast yesterday morning, but there [were] many eager hands as willing as they were skilful, who helped to get the place ready. We had no carpets for the sitting rooms and staircase, so we had to nail down for the occasion blankets of many colours, and these made the place look very snug.

I was quite tired out by 2 a.m. but fortunately we were three gentlemen more than ladies, so that one was able to rest occasionally, but the ladies, never. They danced with great resolution and unimpaired vigour till 3.30 and then they began to dress for their journey. When I tell you that the operation of taking off their things took 3/4 of an hour, when they were eager to be quick and begin to dance, you may imagine the time it took to sort all the variety of mufflers, overshoes, cloaks and other paraphernalia and finally to get them all put on, and properly adjusted for the homeward journey. It was long after 4 when we saw them all packed snugly in the hay of 3 large waggons (mounted upon runners) then covered up with buffalo robes and wrappers and saw them off.

They all enjoyed themselves immensely and said they never danced to such delightful music, tho' it got very screechy towards the end, being nothing but brass instruments. One of the American officers said late in the evening in the fulness of his heart, "You Britishers know how to do the thing in proper style." It was quite marvellous—every one had contrived to produce a pair of white kid gloves for the party. The only thing that we could not get for the American ladies was sugar plums (or candies as they call them) and I am afraid they consider this as a grave omission, for I hear that some of the bachelors at the American Fort are going to give a party but they have to wait till the Candies, they have sent for, arrive from New York.

The lady who brought the baby was immensely delighted with my album, and she said there was [a] picture of a Miss Anderson in it that was lovely . . . Americans really appreciate the freshness and robustness of an English face, seeing that these qualities are so notably deficient even among their own beauties. This state of things among Americans is not to be wondered at when you consider that they live in heated houses, on a diet of pickles and candies, and gobble their food at such a rate that it has been calculated that the average time an American takes for his dinner is 6 ½ minutes. About the only things the ladies ate heartily at supper last night were first course, Crosse & Blackwells pickles, 2nd course ice creams. It was with fear and trembling that I pictured to myself the appalling results that might be reasonably expected from such a meal as this, followed by violent exercise . . . I am quite certain that if our lady guests have not a pain in their heads this morning, as some of us have, they must have pains somewhere else, after such a supper . . .

I had some measurements taken yesterday of the extent of this winter's frost and we find that the ice on the river (where there is a good current too) is 3 ft. 7 inches thick, and the ground is frozen to a depth of 5 ft. 9 inches. Last year at the same date the frost had penetrated to a depth of 6 ft. 4 inches, and the ice was 3 ft. 4 inches thick. This difference shows that the early fall of snow this year has kept the ground somewhat warmer!

The soil is wonderfully rich here, as the settlers raise wheat off the same plot of ground every year, & they never manure the soil or let it lie fallow. Our immediate neighbour, a half caste, has raised wheat from a little plot of ground, near his house sufficient for his family for a year, and has been going on this way for 22 years. Sometimes however the locusts come and eat it all up. This happened two years running just before we came here. They reap 80 to 90 days after sowing, & then hibernate for 6 months. This manner of life may suit bears, but is not attractive to English people.

75

1875: ONTARIO

ANNIE DAVY TO ADAMS DAVY IN PRINCE ARTHUR'S LANDING

When Annie Davy was expecting her third child, she and her husband, Adams, an engineer, decided she could not stay in the Lake Superior bush town of Prince Arthur's Landing (present-day Thunder Bay) while her husband worked on the Fort Francis Locks. Both the local doctors were drunks. Annie travelled to Toronto with her two little girls, Daisy and Dolly, rented a house, asked her mother to come from England to help at the birth, and prepared for the arrival of the baby she called "Betsey." But she knew it would be a long winter without her husband.

8 Little Jarvis Street,
Sunday Afternoon,
October 10, 1875.

My Darling Adams,

I was both surprised and pleased to find from your last letter which I received on Friday that you were at the Landing. It seems so much nearer home though you are still a long way off. I am longing to get your next letter for I hope to know then whether you are coming or not. I have been thinking so much about you today, dearie. I feel so miserable to think you are sick and I can't do anything for you. I do hope you are better. You can't think how I long to see you dearie. I want to know if you can come down for a little while (that is if you are not coming back this winter) if only for a week. I want to see you so much, dearie, and the change would do us both good. If I had the money I believe I would go up myself and see you. Perhaps they will let you have a holiday as you are not well and have worked so hard all summer. Do you think you can manage it? You do not say where you are staying but I suppose it is at The Queen's [hotel] . . . I suppose The Landing has improved, even since you were there in May. I am glad you think there is a chance of getting something from McAree [his employer], if ever so little, it will be better than nothing. You had better take what he offers, don't you think, or he won't give you a cent. Do they intend staying up all winter?

The enclosed letter came last mail so I suppose mother really intends coming this time. I wish you could come home before they arrive. I should like a little time to ourselves. For some things I am sorry they are coming and for others I am glad. It will certainly be a great help to us in the pecuniary sense and if ma will be agreeable and not grumble (the same as I did, dearie) I daresay we shall get on.

I am very busy preparing everything. We have got the sitting room finished with the exception of the stove. It looks so cozy and nice. I think you will like the carpet. I helped Minnie [a servant] put it nearly all down. Just as we were finishing it, Mrs. Moore came over and took my place. I was very glad for I had been down the city in the morning and did a good bit of walking which made me feel very tired. Friday evening Mr. Moore [a neighbour] came over and put down the oilcloth in the hall. He has cut it beautifully. Minnie has made the bedroom carpet but I am not going to put it down until my room upstairs is ready. Minnie is going to whitewash and paper it this week. I don't care if it is not very nicely done so long as it is clean, it will save expense. After my room is done I am going to get mother's ready (the one downstairs that I use) and then whitewash and paper Fred's room, then try to patch up this kitchen which must be used as a dining room and get the pantry whitewashed and make a bedroom of it for Minnie . . .

With regard to the stove, it will require, as you say, a great deal of attention and Mrs. Freeman says if I have <u>a coal stove</u> in the sitting room the heat from the pipe going up into my room will be sufficient. Mrs. Adams has another stove (a coal stove) a self-feeder that they do not want. I can have it for $12 (they paid $16 for it). If you like I will return the wood one and by paying $8 get the other one. Tell me in your <u>next</u> what I am to do. Everyone is taking in their coal. It is $7 a ton now and will be dearer in a week or so. This coal and wood business is a regular nuisance.

Last week I made some apple jam . . . it is so nice. I peeled and cored all the apples myself (16) pounds, also pickled some apples and made crab-apple jam. This week I hope to make grape jelly and I ought to do some peaches and pears. You see I have my hands full. I have got all "Betsey's" things ready which is one trouble off my mind. I am so thankful I am able to work as I do though sometimes I am obliged to give up. I don't think it will be long now and I shall be very glad when it is all over. Doctor never comes over . . .

Daisy and Dolly have been over to Mrs. Moore's for a short time. Daisy goes over alone and knocks at the door. She is a funny child. The other morning when I was dressing she was sitting in bed looking at me. At last she says, "Oh Mamma, what a big tummy you got. Get a big tummy like that again and you must go to bed." You can imagine how I laughed. She is now sitting at the table with a few bits of paper, the knob of a door and a pencil. She folds every piece of paper, then gives a knock and says she is just reading her letters.

Miss Dolly I have just brought in from the garden, where she was busy picking grapes. She has 3 more teeth nearly through. I am glad to say she has been very well lately.

Monday morning. Dearest Adams I am going to be as busy as a bee today but I am going to finish this first. I went down on Thursday to ask the man who I got the sofa etc from if he would let me have some furniture on credit until Christmas. He said he could not as he was selling off and wanted to leave Toronto at once if he could. Stewart, the man I got the other things from, would not give me credit either so my last resource was to go to Graham's up here. He was quite willing to oblige us provided you would send him your note for 3 months. He wanted to send the furniture on Saturday but I told him I would write and ask you first. It is certainly the best thing that can be done. Some of his things are more expensive than those in the city but it is a great advantage in having credit and the principle things will be for Ma and Fred and of course she will pay us again. It is not likely she will bring her furniture and if she did it would not do to wait until they arrive. He made out a rough list of what I should want. I will enclose my list which makes it a little less. The extra mattress which I have marked will be for Fred's bed . . . the one I got the other day. The servant will only have a straw one and don't you think I'd better get a double instead of a single for her? It will be more useful and there is only 40 cents extra on the bed and 25 cents on the straw bed . . .

Mrs. Freeman wanted a little money so I gave her $4 towards the last things we got. I thought he would be able to wait but he has been hard up. I have just one dollar left from your last $53. The man brought his bill for the last wood and I got $3. He wants the money this week. Can you spare four or five dollars, dearie?

I will enclose a list of how I have spent the money. And now dearie, I will say goodbye for a few days. Hoping to hear from you soon. With very best love and lots of kisses from us all,

> I remain, darling, your ever loving wife,
> Annie Davy

PS Write by return post if you can.

Betsey was born safely, although neither Adams nor Annie's mother arrived until several weeks later.

76
1871: QUEBEC
LOUIS-A. DESSAULES TO A FRIEND OF LOUIS-JOSEPH PAPINEAU

Nineteenth-century Quebec was deeply religious. But when Louis-Joseph Papineau, leader of the 1837–1838 uprisings in Lower Canada, was dying in 1871, he refused the last rites. As he had challenged the political status quo during his lifetime, so at his death he challenged the rigid Catholicism of the society that produced him. He relied on the bishop's respect for his family to allow him to be buried in the family vault at Montebello, the seigneurial manor house on the Ottawa River in which his family had lived for generations. His nephew described the final hours of one of Quebec's greatest heroes to a family friend.

14 September 1871

My dear sir,
I arrived last night from Montebello to find your kind letter of the sixth. You show an instinctive understanding of the recognition that this great personality deserves from the public. Never did he show the shadow of an idea inspired by interest, and devotion to duty was his only motivation throughout his life. Never was patriotism purer than in his case or more detached from any egotism or personal ambition. Never did he speak a word that did not come from his heart. He had a horror of anything which was not frank and sincere. This explains why, in dying, he did not want to make any declarations of faith in which he did not believe.

The local curé behaved as a worthy priest and a sensible man. He went with an offer of his services to which my uncle replied that he was always glad to see him as a member of the family, a friend of the family and as a personal friend, but, he could not lie to God and men and receive him as priest, that he did not believe in the revelation and that after fifty years of study and serious reflection on these questions he had reached the view that all religions have a quantity of good and of very beautiful things alongside a quantity of falsity and superstition, that all religions claim exclusive truth and none possess it more than the others, thus while believing as unshakably as anyone in the existence of God and in the moral duties of man, he could not accept religious cults which men had laden with so many superstitions, that his conscience forced him to renounce; that he saw the coming of his death with a complete calm, persuaded that God would not punish him for not having believed in dogmas that in his soul and his conscience he believed harmful to goodness and justice.

The curé noted in a friendly way that his example could have very sorry consequences in the country and that a word from him, even if not an explicit profession of faith, could do a lot of good.

"Would you, my dear curé, then have me arrive before God with a lie on my lips and as a hypocrite before men? Would you have me, in dying, lose my own self-esteem in professing beliefs that I don't have in my heart? Never during my life have I hidden my thoughts and would you have me do so just as I appear before God? It is then, more than ever, my dear curé, that I should be incapable of lying to God and to men, and if I am wrong it should be in good faith and with my trust in the mercy of my creator."

The curé noted that this conviction could perhaps give rise to problems around his internment in the mortuary chapel next to his late parents, and that he, as curé, would

Louis-Joseph Papineau, leader of the Patriotes in 1837, was a Quebec nationalist, an economic conservative, and a harsh critic of the Catholic church.

have to refer the matter to the Bishop in Ottawa. My uncle said he could not imagine any difficulties about his being buried in a chapel which was his own property, even though one could always upset his descendants by refusing them religious ceremonies in a space which was said to be desecrated.

"But," he added, "I cannot believe that, when I have always respected the wishes of my family and have always made every effort to ensure they got the religious ceremonies and comforts they wished; when I have always contributed to the cost of the church, including contributions to building new churches and convents which I know you so zealously wished, I cannot believe that one would even imagine excluding me from the last resting place which I have prepared for myself and my family. I want to lie in peace in the company of those who have been dear to me and if there could be any objection to such a legitimate wish, I would have to do what was required to see that my rights were respected. But I do not imagine that one could show such an extreme lack of charity toward me and I cannot think that the Bishop, who has always shown me great consideration and respect, would do so—not like that old fanatical bishop in Montreal—and he would never dream of excluding me from my own estate."

The curé then went to Ottawa and received instruction from the Bishop to do nothing which could give rise to unpleasant discussions. He came back happy to preside over the funeral wearing only his cassock and to deliver in the chapel the funeral service which had been signed by the relatives and friends, and all was well. Amédée Papineau wrote him a thank you.

I give you all these details so that you will have a precise understanding of what happened, because, naturally, it will be reported in many different ways and the smallest error in the story quickly gives rise to myriad absurd embellishments.

> Please believe me, very sincerely,
> Your friend,
> Louis-A. DesSaules

77
1879: NORTH-WEST TERRITORIES (PRESENT-DAY ALBERTA)
LOVISA MCDOUGALL TO HER MOTHER IN ONTARIO

Fort Edmonton changed little in the quarter century following Henry Tuzo's visit in 1853 (see Letter 50). When Lovisa McDougall and her husband, John, unpacked their bags there in August 1879, twenty-six years later, it still consisted of a Hudson's Bay Company post, a cluster of wooden buildings, and a population of 153 non-native adults. John opened up the Buffalo Store, a general store that catered to the local farmers and ranchers, while his young bride settled down to housekeeping. She was one of only five white women in the community, and two of them, as she wrote to her mother in Ontario, would not speak to her.

Fort Edmonton
August 28, 1879

My Own dear Mother
Since the last time I wrote you we have got comfortable settled. We rented a nice large house untill our own is finished. They are buisy building it but I

hardly think it will be done before spring. The house we have rented is very nice. The stoar is up stairs and we live down. I have 4 large rooms, sitting room, bedroom, kitchen and a large hall. It is not plastered, but finished of very nice. It is all wood work. I had to scour it all. My carpet just fits my sitting room. I have lace and blue damask curtains to the windows, some nice pictures, and the organ table for my books, and one we eat on. We have not many chairs, but 2 good ones, and I covered a little box with damask. So my room looks splendid. Johnnie is going to make a lounge this week. In my kitchen I have shelves for my dishes and we use the organ box for a table.

Henry [the hired man] eats in the kitchen. I have no cooking stove yet so I have a great times cooking by the fire place. I find it so unhandy, but Johnnie is getting 2 stoves from Winnipeg this fall. I bake in the frying pan and I am baking all the time, but Mrs. Coleman, one of the white wemon here, is going to set a batch of bread for me tonight and I will bake it in her stove. She lives not far from us. The fireplace is plesant in the evening, it is always coole here in the evening. My bedroom is of the kitchen, it is nice and large. I have it fixed very nice. I only wish you could come and see me now, it would be so nice. Johnnie says he wishes you could. Do try & come next summer. The boats carry passengers now from Winnipeg up here. Mrs. Walton gave me her houseplants before she left. The geranium is all in blossom, I have Migonette and balsams besides. I send you a little nosegay. We have a nice little cow we bought from Mr. Walton but I have not made any butter yet as I had no place to keep the milk so we gave it to the calf . . .

This week I had a halfbreed woman washing my bed clothes. They are all dry now and put away. I changed the feathers into the new bed tick this week to. All the things I brought from home are as good as ever. I did not use them before. Today

Lovisa McDougall found cooking and baking over an open fire "so unhandy."

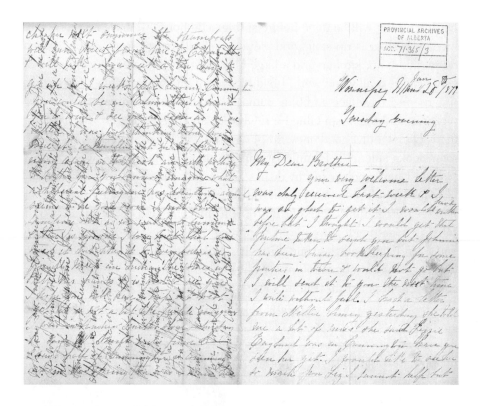

Lovisa's letters, recording her early struggles with housekeeping, took weeks to reach her family in Ontario.

Johnnie bought 2 pails of huckleberries. I intend to preserve some and use the rest for pies. I bake pies in a bake kettle and they are splendid. We expect to get 2 bushels of cranberries from Victoria and that will be all the fruit I will have for winter. I often wish I had some plums or cherries or something like that. I had a taste of plum preserves in Winnipeg but they were sent from Ontario. I get along splendid house keeping. I like it, and I do not find it a bit dull up here. Their are lots of people comming and going all the time. Their are only 4 white wemon here besides myself. 2 of them called on me but the other 2 are Hudson Bay officers wives, and the Hudson Bay Company is vexed at Johnnie for selling cheaper than they do, so I dont expect the wives will call on me. When the new Minister comes I expect to have a nice friend in his wife. Last week Johnnie took me out to Big Lake, the Catholic Mission. We had dinner with the Nuns, they were very nice. They have a beautiful flower garden, they gave me a nice boquet. I was asking them about making butter. They make splendid butter, I bought some from them. They told me to wash it in cold water after I took it out of the churn untill all the milk was out. Is that the way you do it? I wish you would tell me all you can about it please.

I must close now as it is late. Good by from Your Loving Daughter Lovisa

78

1879: NORTH-WEST TERRITORIES (PRESENT-DAY ALBERTA)
ELLIOT GALT TO HIS FATHER, ALEXANDER GALT, IN MONTREAL

Elliot Galt was a well-educated, athletic twenty-nine-year-old when his father wangled an appointment for him as secretary to Edgar Dewdney, Indian commissioner of the North-West Territories. Dewdney and Galt immediately travelled west and criss-crossed the prairies, where they enjoyed hunting wildlife. They apparently made no connection between the non-native appetite for hunting as a sport and the widespread starvation among Blackfoot Indians who depended on declining stocks of buffalo for food. Galt was more interested in western business opportunities than native culture—but so was his authoritarian father, who had served as the Dominion's first finance minister in 1867.

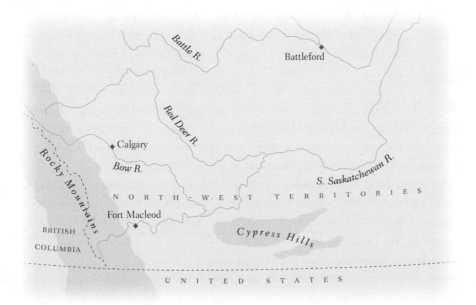

Blackfoot Crossing
Oct. 12th, 1879

My dear Papa,

I have just got through a long pow-wow with the Blackfeet Indians, & as I shall probably not be disturbed for an hour or two I shall give you an account of my doings for the last six weeks.

I was at Battleford for 3 weeks but neither saw nor did very much as the Indians had all gone South after the Buffalo. Gov. Laird was very kind & we struck up quite a friendship. Our journey from there to Cypress took 8 days & was uneventful save that Mr. Dewdney killed a Buffalo. I had no chance to get one, but no doubt shall capture one before long as I have seen a good many on the plains. We skinned the animal & took his hide which measured 9 feet. He really looked massive while lying on his side. Antelope are very numerous all over the country. You have to approach them very carefully as they are very shy, & travelling with a lot of dogs as we do, it is impossible to get nearer than 5 or 600 yards. Ducks are very numerous everywhere, & in the evening when near water there are thousands of them in the air. Geese too are very plentiful.

We only stayed a day at Cypress & borrowed a team from the Police to bring us on to Fort Macleod, our horses being pretty well played out having been on the go since the end of July. We travel with our four horse heavy team for our baggage, & a light covered wagon drawn also by four horses for ourselves. A cook & coachman complete our outfit. We are comfortable enough on the plains, sleeping in a large bell Tent, & altho' we have sometimes to use canned goods we are scarcely ever reduced to nothing but dry bread & bacon. The horses suffer a great deal while travelling at this season of the year, the prairies being burnt up & scarcely any feed left for them. We could not get along at all if we did not carry oats which weigh a great deal, & take up much room. Water too is very scarce & sometimes we have to go 40 or 50 miles without a drop. It is 170 miles to Macleod & took us 4 1/2 day of steady travelling, the road being none of the best.

Mr. Dewdney had previously engaged a house for me there, thinking I could not catch him, so we took up our quarters in it & Col. and Mrs. Macleod were kind enough to feed us at their house. I should not care to live in the house as it seems to be infested by skunks & the smell at night is intolerable. The Town as it is called is not very extensive, a couple of stores, a barber's shop, & the Fort besides a few private houses comprise everything.

On arriving we heard that the Blackfeet at this place were starving & a few dying every day, & the most alarming rumours were in circulation that they were killing cattle wholesale, & threatening the whites with extermination. Fortunately the truth was grossly exaggerated, & although they are in a pitiful state of want & destitution I scarcely think they will give us much trouble beyond the expense of funding them; they are a miserable lot & won't do anything for themselves. I am afraid that the Farmers who are coming up to instruct them will have to do nothing but feed them. There are 1200 of them altogether here & we brought with us 22 head of cattle & 125 Bags Flour & Sugar & Tea, so they will be in clover for a few days, but they will have to be provided for during the Winter some way or other.

Before coming out here I visited the Government Farm near Calgary, & nearly lost my life on the trip. I had a smaller tent to myself, & about 5

The Dominion government farms on Indian reserves were rarely successful, since Ottawa rarely supplied adequate seed or implements.

o'clock one morning I woke up with my Tent, bedding & everything else on fire & outside, the whole prairie was in flames. I had my feet slightly burnt, & my hair & beard were singed, but lost everything & had to go into Calgary without a hat or coat. My nightcap was burnt off my head. The men were sleeping in the wagon about 75 yards off & did not wake up until I shouted to them from the midst of the flames. They could not have put out the fire of the night before properly, as a strong wind sprang up during the night & must have blown some of the embers into the dry grass a few feet distant. It took us a couple of hours to put out the fire & I assure you I was quite played out when we had got it under.

I only spent a day at Calgary & found it a very pleasant place. I think I prefer it to any place I have seen yet in the North-West. The Bow River running close to the Fort is full of Trout but as I lost my rod by the fire I did not get any fishing. It is about the size of the Magog & this same style of River, being very rapid. The Bow River country is not what it has been cracked up to be. Its valley is very fertile but limited in extent. The fact is that this part of the country is only good for cattle grazing. There are frosts nearly every month in the year which play the mischief with crops.

The Govt has started a Farm 9 miles from Calgary on the Bow River, which is prettily situated, the intention is to grow as much grain as possible to be ready for a grist mill to be set up next year. Flour is very expensive just now. We paid today $10 a bag for a large quantity.

The scenery between Macleod & Calgary is very fine. The road skirts the Rocky Mountains almost all the way. They are all covered with snow & look very imposing after seeing nothing but prairie for some time. Quite a lot of snow fell last night & the ground has been quite white all day. They generally have one or two snow storms in October, followed by an Indian Summer. It is very pleasant travelling now, there are of course no flies. The nights are cold & it has been precious cold getting up early in the morning, but now we have a small stove which warms up the Tent very nicely.

This [Blackfoot Crossing] has always been a great place for Indians, & a most unattractive place it is; the Bow River is quite large here, it is fordable this year, but as a rule it is not.

The Blackfeet are not nearly so civilized as the Crees, & it is only a few years since it was unsafe for a white man to go into their country. While you find no end of half-breeds among the Crees, I believe there are not more than half a dozen Blackfeet half-breeds in the country. In the event of trouble with the Indians I believe the half-breeds would throw in their lot with them. I don't anticipate a row as the Indians are very poorly armed & are perfectly aware that if left to themselves must starve. Mr. Dewdney's management is I think very judicious, although the cost is going to be awful, as the Indians have to be fed, & the expense of bringing in provisions is very heavy. He is very patient with them & takes pains to have them understand clearly the present state of affairs, & tells them that if they want to be fed they must work. The trouble at present is that there is nothing to put them at, but in the spring the Farms will be in full swing, & it remains to be seen how they will do manual work.

The people about Macleod who have cattle accuse the Indians of killing a great many, but it is almost impossible to catch them in the act. Near Calgary where there are some 2000 Head only 12 are missing since the spring.

I expect we shall reach Cypress about the 25th inst. where Father Martin, a delegate of the American Govt. is waiting to accompany us on an important visit to Sitting Bull, who is at present camped near Wood Mountain. I am looking forward to this Trip with much interest as I am told the Sioux are very well armed, & I am convinced that we have more to fear from them than our own Indians. Afterwards we shall return to Cypress for a few days & then go on to Fort Benton, & homewards by Helena, & Ogden, so I am in hopes of seeing you early in December . . .

Oct. 19th. I have got back to Fort Macleod & am off to Walsh tomorrow. I see by the papers that you are going to England for good, but hope that I shall see you before you start. I shall be down about the end of Nov.

> Love to all at home.
> Yr. aff. son
> E. T. Galt

In 1880, Alexander Galt was appointed the first high commissioner of Canada in London. Elliot alerted him to valuable coal deposits in southern Alberta. Alexander incorporated the North Western Coal and Navigation Co., of which Elliot became general manager.

79

1880: ONTARIO

TED FFOLKES TO HIS MOTHER, MRS. HENRY FFOLKES, IN NORFOLK, ENGLAND

One group of immigrants determined to homestead or ranch in western Canada con-sisted of educated, middle-class young Englishmen whose prospects in Britain were dim. Lacking farm experience, many enrolled in a three-year course at the Ontario Agricultural College, founded in Guelph in 1874. Ted ffolkes, the amiable second son of a Norfolk rector, found the college routine a cross between Haileybury College, his private school in England, and the life of an underpaid farmhand. I'm not sure that his textbook Stonehenge and the Horse *would have been much help on the Canadian prairies.*

Ontario Agricultural College,
December 8, 1880

Dear Mother,

I wish you all a very merry Christmas. It is not of course the first time I have been away at Christmas, only I feel more entirely separated than before. I shall think of you all on Christmas eve. I dine with such a dear kind old lady, she always sends kind messages to me through [her son, a fellow-student] Frank's letters, asking after my family, etc. I am cramming now for Christmas examinations. I was so pleased to get all your letters. I got the cheque, and had to pay a great deal out, on farming-books, etc., such as "Youatt on Sheep," "On Cattle," "The Model Grazier," "Stonehenge and the Horse." We must have them for the lectures. Last Sunday there was a tremendous thaw, everything melted, and it was quite hot. I went to church in the evening; and it was horribly wet and sloppy. When I came out every-thing was frozen solid.

I wish I had got that pea-jacket Harold advised at Silver's. I have got no coat to work in, as of course my Norfolk jacket is too good—I mean that old home-spun; but it is cool work. My whole outfit was a mistake; as regards material, too good. Two good suits, and two really strong suits of rough tweed, are what a man wants, for a two years' equipment in this country. That knitted waistcoat of Aunt Fanny's was a godsend, but of course only to be used on swagger occasions! The most useful thing in my outfit was that woollen waistcoat with sleeves. I wear very little clothing in the house, so as to feel the difference when I go out. My costume indoors is: breeches, gaiters, slippers, flannel shirt, home-spun coat. Waistcoat, tie, and collar are quite unnecessary, not to say unheard of articles, as of course we have not time to change after work.

I forgot to tell you we have a literary society here. I had to debate the Friday before last on "Resolved that ambition is a virtue." I was on the negative side and lost it. Last Friday I proposed the following debate: "Resolved that Vanity is conducive to the happiness of man." The positives got the debate. Next Friday the debate is, "Chewing is injurious to the health." The fellows chew here to the most disgraceful extent, they make the walls and floors simply "hoggish." Besides the debates, poetry and prose are read. We have a president, vice-president, secretary, critic, a committee of five. Every member pays twenty-five cents, and is bound to perform once in every term. Last Friday, one of the old country fellows was censured and expelled from the meeting, for repeated disorderly conduct; he came in again, and in the end had to be carried out.

> Love to all,
> From your very affectionate son.

Ted ffolkes farmed in Manitoba and British Columbia, but returned east in 1895 and settled in Toronto with his wife, Agnes Strachan.

80

1881: MANITOBA
WILLIE WALLACE TO HIS SISTER, MAGGIE WALLACE, IN GLASGOW

The promise of a transcontinental railway triggered a land boom on the prairies. English-speaking Protestants from Ontario, the Maritimes, and the British Isles flooded into the new province of Manitoba, which had joined Confederation in 1871; in the next decade, its population rose from 12,000 to 66,000. In 1881, three Scotsmen took up land in Elton, near Brandon. Peter Wallace, age fifty-nine, and his two sons, William, twenty-two, and Andrew, fifteen, faced every pioneer trial with stoic good humour, as William recorded in monthly letters to his sister Maggie, who had remained in Glasgow to train as a teacher.

Elton, Man.
16 November 1881

My Dear Maggie,

We only received from your quarter a paper last mail—knowing well that your time would be more than fully occupied with your school duties we pardoned you, and more than that generously determined to forgive such conduct until next year. But after that we expect to be exceedingly jealous of our privileges, so you had better not fall into bad habits during this indulgence period.

Our neighbours on the southern half of the township are quickly taking advantage of their newly acquired Manitoba rights. They have appointed a committee and forwarded a petition to the Government for a grant to enable them to build a school and secure a teacher. The school is very much wanted, as there are a great number of children. When at Winnipeg I got acquainted with a young man who had a school appointment at Gladstone, about 18 miles west of Portage la Prairie. He had been there about two years. He was only getting $250 yearly and was, owing to this small salary, about to resign. He intended going to the Qu'Appelle to begin stock raising. You will understand from this instance that teaching is not here a very remunerative occupation. The teaching fraternity down in the lower Provinces are evidently as much in want of elbow room as their brethren in the old country. Before your certificate can be of service here you must have it attested by a J.P. or a clergyman and at Winnipeg undergo an examination that takes place only once a year, in August.

Since I wrote my last letter we have not been doing very much, although somehow always busy. The weather has been very severe and stormy. In fact I have concluded that the climate of Manitoba, so far as its settled character is concerned, is a perfect fraud. Undoubtedly during the summer time we had a long spell of delightful sunny weather but this was no advantage, as it made the ground very dry and unploughable. Later on we had a good many opportune showers, but they were real busters—short storms or tornados. Their severity far exceeded anything I could imagine. However, these and their effects became things of the past, and knowing people characterize the season as a "windy" one.

I had great hopes that the fall would realize the descriptions heard, and our haystacks were put up to resist wind but not rain. But alas, about harvest times, on came the rains quietly and steadily. At one time it lasted three days. It did our hay no little harm, but our neighbours who were harvesting suffered most. Some had only their crops cut and lying unbound, others had them in stocks very badly set up. No matter, all was soaked. Some of our oats were bound up soaking wet. A spill of dry weather, however, dried them thoroughly, and raised our dampened hopes, not to exalted pitch fortunately. We took the precaution of stacking them with straw and water tight. Many of our neighbours could not, and did not, do that. On came the rain again and consequently a great deal of wet grain has been thrashed. Knowing ones again styled the harvest a most extraordinary wet one.

Now I was disposed to overlook and forgive all this, as another year would most likely enable us to get better accommodation and give us more time to secure things properly—and the rain helped the ploughing very much. Time went on. "Now you will experience real Indian summer, no doubt about that, snow never falls here until the end of December," was what everyone said and I previously understood. Imagine our surprise then at a heavy fall of snow, falling shortly before I left for Winnipeg, and occasional falls during the journey, with the thermometer at zero. "Oh, this is only squaw winter. It will go away in a day or two and then you'll have Indian summer."

Papa and Andrew started out on the faith of this story when the weather appeared to take up, and fortunately they had the summer all the time. But this was a very so-so blessing. With the exception of two days, about noon the thermometer got above freezing point. and the Weather was not unlike Scotch March weather. So you may guess our Indian summer was no great treat. The comparatively mild weather hardly lasted a week: since then we have twice had snow falls and succeeding thaws.

One Sabbath however, early in the morning, it began in earnest to blow and snow. We were thoroughly storm-stayed. The heavy drift rendered travelling any distance, however short, dangerous, and it was awful cold. On Monday it cleared up, but hard frost. We started for the bush early in the morning. The thermometer registered 5 degrees below zero—a slight wind blowing made it bitter cold [for] walking nine miles.

I always take the future into consideration, and determined to reserve my moccasins for 60 degrees below zero or thereabouts, I had on only my top boots and one pair of socks. During the short time I was standing fixing up my load I felt my feet cold, and then almost immediately had no feeling in the greater part of them. I feared the worst and started home, not feeling very comfortable over the probable result. About sundown the wind began to rise and the cold increased thereby. I actually thought my legs sometimes were frozen completely, I could hardly walk. I seemed to have no feeling in them. The oxen, I thought, would never hurry up sufficiently. As it was, we got home about an hour after dark. Quickly I got off my top boots—the socks went along with them quite white with frost. Andrew got a basin of snow, and into it I put my feet, and with his assistance rubbed the frozen parts for a good long time. I am sure I had my feet on the snow for half an hour. The parts that were not frozen suffered dreadfully from the cold, but when I had the frost all taken out I thought little of this. My left heel was the most seriously affected. I have not yet any feeling in it, and expect the skin will come off. The big toe on my right foot has also been badly nipped, and the nail will come off of it. It is exceedingly painful—for three days I have been a prisoner in the house. I have now learnt the true value of moccasins and will act up to my knowledge hereafter. They are loose and soft—inside them you can put any number of socks, Now after this long freezing story see that you do not accuse me of letting you see the best side of everything.

When we got home we found the thermometer 10 degrees below zero. On Monday night it again became stormy and continued so until Wednesday evening. The wind was all the time exceedingly high, and the snow and drift blinding. Today it has cleared up and the sun is shining brightly. At noon we still had 23 degrees of frost, therefore it is not likely the snow will thaw until next spring. All around there are great deep wreaths: this will cause travelling to be very unpleasant until the surface gets hardened. Now do you not think after all this that I have just cause of complaint against the climate we have adopted? But I suppose that you will conclude that frozen feet have made me lose my temper on the subject . . . I discover I have gone beyond the limits of an ordinary letter. I expect my toes will be better next time I write, and I will be in a more amicable mood. Meantime I send herewith a newspaper to take away all bad impressions. We all keep well and unite in sending kindest regards to cousins and yourself.

> Your most affectionate brother
> Willie

Maggie eventually joined her family in Manitoba. The shortage of women on the prairies meant that Peter Wallace's sons ended their days, like thousands of other pioneers, as old bachelors living with their widowed sister in a family homestead established more than half a century earlier.

81

1882: NOVA SCOTIA
ANNIE AFFLECK THOMPSON TO JOHN THOMPSON

There is nothing more dispiriting than an election campaign that seems doomed to defeat. This was the kind of provincial campaign that the Tory lawyer John Thompson, who had briefly served as premier of Nova Scotia, was fighting in 1882. As usual he turned to his wife, the strong-minded and warm-hearted Annie, for comfort; as usual, Annie raised her husband's spirits with her love and encouragement. The Thompson marriage was a model political marriage, in my view.

Halifax,
Wednesday June 14th, 1882

My poor old tired Tory

I cannot tell you how glad I was to get your letter this afternoon. I know that you are feeling badly but surely child you cannot be sick that you are so dull, as you tell me. I wish that I could be with you for one or two minutes to talk square to you. You want to know how I'll feel if you are beaten, well child except for your being disappointed and bored to death, not one row of pins. You know I never thought it worth the journey down that all the honour to be had out of it was yours already and except that we never gave up a fight yet I wouldn't mind if you put on your hat and left them tomorrow. It is better to fight as long as you are started and be beaten than not to fight at all. So keep up your courage and I'll go part of the way to meet you coming home win or lose that can't keep you from me much longer. John is very much exercised to know why they should want another man instead of pa and that if you should not get in if you would only be a lawyer and if the other man would be Attorney General and if you would go to town every day. I am trying to get Mr. Frankie's short clothes ready for him. Yesterday I made him a new hood and he looks just as cute as can be in it.

Things are getting pretty hot here. I think they looked forward to you not being opposed and that you would be up on the wings of love to help them . . . The carpenter's bill was $46.90 and I gave him $20 telling him that he could have the balance on the twenty second $2 a day and the price of materials is the way he ordered his a/c. I think you will be pleased as all the leaks appear to be stopped.

So now my old baby you must not be such an awful baby until you get home again and then I'll see how far you can be indulged. I am going to North Street to post this so good night and lots of kisses

Annie

Thompson's government was defeated, as predicted, but within three years he was a member of Sir John A. Macdonald's cabinet in Ottawa. He served as prime minister of Canada from 1892 to 1894 and was knighted before his untimely death at age fifty.

82

1884: NORTH-WEST TERRITORIES (PRESENT-DAY SASKATCHEWAN)
JESSIE MCLEAN TO HER FRIEND LILIAN SHARPE IN ENGLAND

Western Canada was still the Wild West, as Jessie McLean, age twenty-two, enjoyed telling an English friend. Jessie lived in Prince Albert, a muddy, jerry-built settlement that straggled for five miles along the North Saskatchewan River. Her father, the Right Reverend John McLean, was Anglican bishop of the Saskatchewan Diocese, and Jessie, the eldest of eight children, was painfully aware of the limitations of pioneer life. Her father, seeking to raise her spirits, took her with him to England in 1883, and Jessie established a close friendship with Lilian Sharpe, a young woman her own age. Jessie obviously took pleasure in confirming her genteel English friend's stereotypes.

Prince Albert
29 September 1884

My dear dear Lilian,

I expect you will be thinking that after all my promises to the contrary, I have forgotten about writing. But such is not the case, dear Lilian, for if I could have written to you as often as I should have liked to, I fear you would have been decidedly bored with the number of my epistles.

And now first and foremost you must hear how very welcome your letter was to me. Just fancy, Lilian, it arrived here the day before we did, & Winnie put it away so carefully that she forgot all about giving it to me, until two weeks after our arrival. One evening my heart felt very "solemn" with some of those worries & troubles I used to tell you of, & I was longing for England again, when Maude handed me this letter, saying that Winnie had forgotten it, in all the excitement of our arrival. I opened it without even looking at the envelope, never dreaming of the treat in store for me, I turned to the signature & when I beheld the magic name of "Lilian" all my apathy vanished, & after devouring the contents thereof I was no longer "solemn hearted". So after all, Lilian, I forgave them for deferring my pleasure for a time.

And now for news of our trip. I sent you a paper from Winnipeg to let you know that so far we had arrived in safety. We were ten days there—just time enough to become rested for our prairie journey, & Papa telegraphed to my eldest brother to arrange with someone to meet us at Qu'Appelle i.e. the farthest point we can travel by rail. Bertie did not reach Qu'Appelle as early as we expected & we were compelled to wait there for four days. That was the most trying part of the journey. The best hotel where we remained gave anything but the best accommodation. The rooms were more like wooden boxes than anything else & you could not do much more than step into bed from the door.

We met Bishop Anson [of the new Diocese of Assiniboia-Qu'Appelle]. He was consecrated shortly before we left England, & and it seemed so nice to see him again.

Mamma & I used to go for long walks to pass away the time. I will never forget our first encounter with a snake. We were having a stroll one very warm day, when I happened to cast my eyes down & see a large snake just gliding under Mamma's feet. I said very quietly "there is a snake", & you should have been there to have heard the shriek with which my information was greeted. After Mamma had recovered her first alarm she started after the reptile with her umbrella in the most vicious way, & did not cease her exertions until it was left a corpse.

I can just imagine, Lilian, you drawing your skirts about you & saying in the most pleading tone, "Oh Jessie, please stop". By this time I am quite hardened to seeing the reptiles, but in this case, "distance (& the greater the better) lends enchantment to the view". Often in the tent after we had retired to rest, Mamma would say in sepulchral tones, "Jessie, do you feel the bed moving?" & I would be forced to reply that I was conscious of a gliding motion underneath. However we never had the courage to investigate whether our couch was really a bed of snakes.

We had several amusing adventures on the way, one of which I must tell you. One night after we had been in Camp some time, & it was quite dark, Mamma & I went off for a stroll in the direction of some bushes near. We were busy talking & laughing, until Mamma suddenly laid a trembling hand on my arm, with the question, "What's that?" in an alarmed whisper. I gazed before me into the darkness & saw with a fainting heart what looked to me like a black bear with a white nose. Imagine our horror, which increased more & more as the bushes commenced to crackle as if the adversary meant to show fight. We brave creatures were not going to be undone, and after a consultation carried on in loud tones, decided to pelt the animal with the largest stones we could find. We however looked in vain for any missile wherewith to attack the enemy, & at a louder crackling of the bushes, our courage all oozed out & we shrieked for Bertie [her brother].

Bertie immediately rushed to our aid & all we could say was "a bear! a bear!" He looked rather amused after he investigated the matter & we laughed steadily for about an hour, when he came & said, "it is only Papa". His white collar was our bear's nose. I really thought Mamma would injure herself laughing & after we had retired we could hear Papa chuckling away to himself. When we started off, we thought he, with the man & Bertie, had retired into their tent. You can imagine how hard it was to get away unobserved sometimes. The night we camped on the Salt Plain, which is 40 miles across, we had to walk about five miles to get out of sight.

We presented quite a formidable appearance travelling along. First, there came two large wagons containing our luggage, provisions, tents, cooking utensils etc. The man drove one & Bertie the other and we brought up the rear in our own carriage & horses which Papa drove.

We were only home three weeks when Papa, Mamma, & Winnie [her sister] this time, started off for Winnipeg again. Winnie will go on to London Ont., for the winter, but I expect Papa & Mamma back by the end of October. I have therefore been very, very busy with household duties & teaching Maude [a younger sister]. Fannie [a married sister] had a little son two days after they left & I have been over with her a great deal lately. I have a niece and nephew now. I dread to think of Winter without Winnie but she was so pulled down when we returned that she had to be taken away.

I have the banner you gave me on a bracket beside my bed & *Under the Surface* opposite on my bookshelf. Your painting also decorates my wall & I only want your photo to make my room complete. You see, I have told everyone so much about you that there have been several requests to see your photo & I have to reply that "I have not got one", but I hope it will not be for long.

How I should like a nice long chat with you tonight, Lilian. Do you remember the night we talked till four o'clock & I shocked you with some of my sayings? How little I dreamed then that there would be a reality some day in two or three things I said in jest then. But I must not become "solemn hearted" now & treat you to a dish of worry. They have opened a Sunday School down in the town as it was so far for some of the children to come, so the S.S. here is not nearly so large as formerly. However we have the children who live near. I have taught them Mr. Graham's hymn, and they were so delighted with it & can sing it quite nicely. They enjoyed so much hearing about St. Paul's Sunday School & were especially amazed at the number of children there. I am regarded as quite a curiosity among them since my visit to England . . . When Mamma returns I will have much more time for writing & I will then be able to tell you many things want of time has compelled me to omit. Have you laughed much lately? I have not had a good laugh for ever so long. My face has grown quite stiff and solemn looking.

Good bye, dearest Lilian. Much love to your Aunts and your sweet little self.

> Lovingly,
> Jessie.

P.S. If you want to cheer my "solemn heart", please write another letter like your last one very soon. Ever lovingly, Jessie

83
1885: QUEBEC
LOTTIE DALKIN AND LEILA GEGGIE TO ADOLPHE CARON, MINISTER OF MILITIA, IN OTTAWA

Discontent among Metis, Indians, and white settlers did not abate after the 1869–1870 Red River Rebellion. By the early 1880s, the buffalo had been virtually exterminated by white hunters; settlers continued to encroach on traditional Indian and Metis land, and aboriginal peoples were starving. The Metis asked Louis Riel, in exile in Montana, to return and help them: Riel, now convinced that he had a divine mission to establish a Roman Catholic state in the Canadian west, answered their call. A clash between mounted police and Metis at the tiny Saskatchewan settlement of Duck Lake on March 26, 1885, ignited the Northwest Rebellion. The young minister of militia in Ottawa, Adolphe Caron, immediately sent a militia force west to put down the insurrection. Within eight days, it had arrived in Winnipeg via the new CPR line. But Caron rapidly found his desk piled high with demands, advice, and suggestions from extraneous sources.

Quebec 13th April 1885.

Sir:

We, the Women's Christian Temperance Union of Quebec City, beg you to use your influence to prevent troops going to the North West from taking alcoholic liquors in the Stores, except in such small quantity as may be required for medicinal purposes. Lord Wolseley has proved in 1871 that even in that climate alcohol is unnecessary and we are specially anxious lest youths going to their country's defence should contract habits of intemperance which might in the future tend to their own [undoing] and that of the country they are now fighting for.

Trusting to receive a favorable reply
We are
Sir
Yours &c &c &c
(Signed) Lottie H. Dalkin, President
Leila Geggie, Secretary

84

1885: DISTRICT OF ALBERTA
JOHN MCDOUGALL TO HIS BROTHER-IN-LAW,
CHARLES AMEY, IN ONTARIO

I'm always intrigued by letters that show the writer struggling with the rights and wrongs of official policies. One such writer is the Fort Edmonton storekeeper John McDougall, whose young wife, Lovisa, wrote Letter 77. As the Northwest Rebellion spread, the McDougalls were horrified by the rumours (most false) of Indian atrocities and relieved to hear that troops were coming to protect them. But John also recognized that Indian grievances were legitimate.

Edmonton,
April 29th 1885

Dear Charlie

I expect you will all be very anxious on our account since this Rebellion has broken out in the Saskatchewan Country. It has turned out a much more serious affair than anyone here ever expected, and the worst feature of the whole concern is that of the Indians having joined in. They have been comitting some terrible crimes murdering and plundering saturating the dead bodies with Coal Oil and piling a lot of wood around them then setting all on fire, and dancing round and round. We hear some fearful yarns of how they have been carrying on. One young man that I was acquainted with and who had just been married to a young Ontario girl about three months ago was shot down by his wife's side and she was taken by the Indians and outraged by over a dozen of them, and traded from one to the other every day until she was about dead when they put an end to her misery by cutting her open. They have still got one white woman among them. So far, both Riel and the other Indians have met with so much success and have now had their own way for over a month that it has encouraged them a lot and they now think that they can carry everything before them and I believe it will take all summer to quell the trouble and can only be done after suffering the loss of many a brave young fellow's life.

I believe that Riel and the Half Bs can be put down easier and quicker than the Indians, but they both have a great advantage over the troops on account of them all having Horses and knowing every inch of the Country. They can do a lot of mischief and harm without as great a risk as the Soldiers who are nearly all on foot. The Rebels know also that their will be no mercy shown them if taken alive and so they will fight hard and they are encouraged by reports stating that there is a large number of feenians across the line ready and willing to assist them at any time if they require assistance. We were pretty badly alarmed here as we had every reason to be and we would most certainly have been in the same bad fix as the Fort Pitt and Battleford people if we had not sent for assistance in time and it did not start a day too soon as the Indians all around us were plundering and killing cattle, destroying everything they could not carry away. People had to run for their lifes, having their cattle shut up in the stables, the pigs in the pens, the doors of their stores unlocked, everything left behind, no time to think of anything, we were besiged on all sides. The mails could not come or go, no one dare travel far from home, and the worst of it was the settlers were all very poorly supplied with arms and ammunition and could make but a very poor fight if necessary. Guards and scouts were kept out all the time and scarsely a day passed but what we would hear reports, and every report worse than the last, and all turned out to be true, and the whole place town and country was completely paraylaised. Their was a mass meeting called and we decided to send for outside assistance and a young fellow offered to carry the dispatches to Calgary our nearest Telegraph Office 200 miles distant and through 4 or 5 Indian Reserves. He was supplied with authority to take horses wherever he found them, he started one night at 12 o'clock and rode that distance in 36 hours without any rest. That was a pretty good ride.

After he left we were kept in great suspense for 10 or 12 days until he got back again, bringing the welcome news of the troops coming which had a wonderful affect on the Indians. Those that had not done anything very serious returned to their work and the most of them started down to join Big Bear's Band. And as I said before they have gone too far and done too much to back out so they will do a lot more harm before they are subdued. I think though our danger here is about past unless Big Bear should be driven back this way and he might induce a lot more Indians to assist him in cleaning out the white people.

As they say, the H.B. Coy. had no right to sell this country for it belonged to the Indians and The Govt., since getting the country they claim, has not treated them right or as they agreed to do. There is general dissatisfaction among all classes of people in this country against the Govt. and for many good reasons. And I believe that this will be the means of having everything made right. I have a lot of other letters to right . . . have sent you some Bulletins giving further particulars.

John A. McDougall

85

1885: DISTRICT OF ALBERTA

CAPTAIN J. DROLET TO HIS FATHER IN QUEBEC CITY

Almost 3,000 troops were transported west in April 1885 to put down the rebellion. Most were from Ontario, but there were also two Quebec battalions and one from Nova Scotia. The campaign was an adventure for young men who had never before left home. Captain Drolet of the 9th Quebec Rifles was eager to make proper identifications of birds and wildlife before he returned to Quebec City in July. (The animal he could not identify was probably the American badger, Taxidea taxus.*) His address to his father is so formal that he evidently came from a very proper background.*

10 June 1885

My dear Governor,

I received this week your letters of the 13th, and 30th May last; they were left at Crowfoot or at some other place I suppose.

I am now in a pretty good room and I am very well, compared with the others. The Colonel sends me papers and as I have a couple of books and tobacco, I manage to get along pretty well.

I am gathering relics of the expedition. I have two Blackfeet knives and sheaths, a whip, some paint bags, a bullet pouch, moccasins, a pair of polished buffalo horns, a squaw's belt and some ornaments, so you see that along with my photographs and what I will get more, I will be able to fix up my room. The Indians pass here now and then so I am able to procure those things at reasonable prices.

We are enjoying beautiful weather and the prairie is covered with flowers of every description. We are in what is called a rolling prairie; it looks like the sea; sometimes you find yourself in a hollow and in front of you is a kind of wave.

The buffalo holes and small lakes are numerous, and are covered with ducks, plover, snipe, etc. Now and then you may see antelopes, but they are getting exceedingly rare, and, like the buffalo, will soon be a thing of the past. Skulls and ribs of buffalo are scattered all over the prairie and one may imagine how numerous they must have been before the building of the Canadian Pacific Railway; they are not to be seen except in the foothills of the Rockies and only in small herds.

The most curious animal here is the gophers. It is a kind of ground rat very much like our squirrel; they dig holes and live in groups of four or five. They are not afraid of us at all and are easily caught. Along with the gopher is a larger animal which is called badger by the people here. I do not believe it is the common badger, for it is not at all like the prairie badger described by Humboldt. If you could send me some of Audubon's, Humboldt's or Cuvier's books, I would be very much obliged to you, as I could see for myself if their descriptions of the prairie animals are accurate.

June 11, 1885. I had to leave my letter unfinished yesterday, so I will continue now; you see that I am as bad as yourself. I had to stop short yesterday to play the Judge; you may imagine the fine figure I did cut. Two Indians came to me to decide who was the owner of a lariat. They kept talking to me for about an hour, and as I understood their language as much as Hebrew, I did not know the deuce was the matter until a half-breed came and explained me the meaning of their gibberish. After he had explained everything, I did not know who the owner was more than before. So I just took a quarter out of my pocket and tossed head for one and tail for the other; tail turned up and I adjudged the lariat. This judgement is as good as Solomon's or anybody else's, the Recorder of the City of Quebec included. The next time Indians come to me to act as a Judge, I will ask a fee for my trouble.

Indians are numerous here today. They come by gangs of three or four with their squaws, papooses (children), ponies and dogs. Each gang has about three or four ponies and twice as many dogs. The squaws pitch the camps, raise the tepees (tents), light the fires and do all the heavy work while their lords and masters sit down and quietly enjoy a good pipe. It is one of the queerest sights to see these Indians, wrapped up in blankets of every colour, travelling in the prairie with their little ponies and dogs. The buck comes first riding on the finest pony of the lot, with nothing else but his rifle slung across the pommel of his saddle; then come the squaws leading their ponies by the bridle with their papooses on their back, and last but not least, the dogs.

The Indian dogs are never to be forgotten; some of them look like coyotes (prairie wolves); others resemble foxes, &c. They are as wicked as blazes, and I would pity the Quebec policeman trying to catch one of them to see if he had a medal.

We have a few white visitors occasionally, and it is always a pleasure to see somebody. This week I had the pleasure to meet Father Doucet, O.M.I. He remained some time in camp and I had quite a long chat with him. He acknowledged to me that it was perfectly useless to try to convert adults. The only thing they can do is to take children and instruct them. Some of them turn out good, but the great part forget everything as soon as they are out of school and, as a Church of England clergyman told me the same thing about his flock, I can say that the poor missionaries are not much repaid for their trouble.

Another visitor here is Mr. Goldfinch, a ranchman near Langdon. He is an ex-lieutenant of a Highland regiment, and as he is a perfect gentleman a visit from him is always a great treat. Col. Evanturel passed here today on his way to Calgary and will go back to Gleichen in a couple of days.

We are greatly troubled with mosquitoes. They come in crowds at night, and they are the cause that I say my prayers backwards more than once. We are literally eaten up by them, and the boys say the sweet souvenir of the

North-West mosquitoes will stay with them as long as they live. The train is in sight and I must cease wasting paper.

> My best love to all,
> Yours affectionate son.
> J. Drolet

86

1885: DISTRICT OF ASSINIBOIA (PRESENT-DAY SASKATCHEWAN) LOUIS RIEL TO JAMES WICKES TAYLOR, U.S. CONSUL IN REGINA

The Northwest Rebellion collapsed within weeks; Louis Riel surrendered to imperial authorities and was jailed in Regina. On July 6, a formal charge of treason was laid against him and on July 20 his trial began. Given Riel's religious passion, his lawyer proposed to defend him on grounds of insanity. But Riel refused that defence and, concerned that the Dominion government would let local justice take its course, appealed for help to the local American consul.

> Common jail at Regina
> 21 July 1885

Honorable J.W. Taylor
U.S. Consul

Sir

I am in the painful condition of being brought before the court at Regina, under charge of High treason.

I have the honor to let you know to inform you that I am not guilty.

I have the highest respect for the stipendiary magistrates before whom I have to answer. But their court is not the one to try my case; as that case had its origin long before the stipendiary court of Regina existed.

As American citizen I humbly appeal to the government of my adopted land for help through you. I assure you, my request is not inspired by any of those feelings which might have a tendency to create difficulty between the United States and England.

I am small and my humble condition prevents me from being heard by the British dignitaries of the Dominion. I am confident that if you would deign [to] write to the American government on my behalf, they would not refuse to say a good word in my favor: that good word would secure me a fair trial: and a fair trial would save me.

While in Montana I have exerted myself to be a good citizen, and I have worked in harmony with the U.S. authorities in the Territory. I have even had the honor to be appointed several times U.S. special deputy marshal. If I mistake not, there are in the Department of Justice at Washington documents which speak favorably of me.

In God I trust that a friendly word to the British Minister would go far to protect me from *inattention*.

Also, I have no means to defray the expenses of a trial such as the one I have to stand. I beg the American government to help me, that way, too. Please transmit my humble petition, if it is not altogether out of place.

Thanking you for all the favors that you have done me, in the past, and praying that you may be fully rewarded, I hope the Providence of God will spare me, through as generous a Consul as you and through as good a Government as that of the States.

> I have the honor to be very respectfully,
> Your h[umble] s[ervant]
> Louis Riel

No help was forthcoming from Taylor, and on September 18, Riel was sentenced to be hanged. The execution of Louis Riel had a lasting impact on Canadian history and exacerbated tensions between English and French Canadians.

87
1888: BRITISH COLUMBIA
ANNIE LEAKE TO SARAH GIBBS GOODERHAM AND ELIZABETH SUTHERLAND STRACHAN IN TORONTO

In 1887, Annie Leake, a forty-eight-year-old schoolteacher from Nova Scotia, was appointed matron of a rescue home for young Chinese prostitutes in Victoria, British Columbia. Vancouver and Victoria had had bustling Chinatowns with their own brothels and bars ever since 1881, when the CPR started bringing Chinese men to British Columbia to help build the railway. A trickle of wives and concubines followed the men, but many ended up on the streets. Annie's institution was financed by the Methodist Women's Missionary Society, a Toronto-based organization run by two formidable Toronto grandes dames, Elizabeth Sutherland Strachan and Sarah Gibbs Gooderham, to whom Annie sent regular reports.

Victoria B.C.
Jan. 23rd, 1888

Dear Mesdames Gooderham and Strachan,

I have thought that I would begin to note incidents as they occur, and thus make a letter more correct and interesting, than if written in a hurry, as I think my last one was. Mr. Gardner has rescued one girl since I came. He brought her in at mid-day. A fine-looking young woman, dark, but regular and pleasing features; good-natured and intelligent I think. She came in the whitest of cotton hose, and Chinese slippers, wooden soles, of course. Her person and clothing perfectly clean and of good material. But she brought nothing but what she had on. She has asked me for a clothes brush, as her clothes are getting dusty. She must borrow comb, towel, and some clothing, as I have given her nothing yet.

Mr. Gardner expects to come every Sabbath afternoon to give religious instruction in their own language. He did not come yesterday so I had to amuse the girls as best I could. I gave them a lesson in reading and writing, although our school work is not really commenced, as I am waiting for blackboard and slates promised. Then they had been interested in a group of my brothers that I have, so I got my albums and we looked at the pictures. They understand remarkably well, and give me Chinese words for many things—father, mother, sister, brother, etc. Some of the faces were of those who were in the Better Land. When I would tell them such a one had gone to live with Jesus, and of the beautiful home on high, they seemed interested. Of course Mr. Gardner has told them the "Old, old story of Jesus and His love" often. My father was among the dead, and a sweet-faced child of a friend—"So sorry," they say, and gave as much sympathy in the expression as if they were really Christians.

Feb. 2nd. We had a pleasing incident yesterday. A converted Chinese lad from Westminster was in town and called to see "The Home." It did me good to hear him talk. His English is very good, for it led me to see what my girls may become by the grace of God. This lad says that Mrs. Cunningham, of Westminster, was the first to talk to him of Jesus. Rev. Mr. Watson, now of Toronto, baptized him, I think. He intends going to Toronto in the summer, he says. He talked to the girls of the better way of living, or the difference between a Christian and heathen life. I think it did my girls good, as they have been real good and obedient today.

On Saturday last I had a letter from Miss Chown, Kingston, enclosing P.O. order for $10.00, which we spent for boots, and added a little for stockings. They have small, neat feet, and look very well in nice boots. Today we had an invitation to Mr. Gardner's, and the girls really looked nice in their best Chinese clothing and new boots—all but the *cue* and immense *ear rings*. But best of all, they really behaved like ladies on the street and at table. They know how to be real good, but are not always disposed. We all ate together, and they handled the knives and forks well, considering that at home they yet use the chop-stick, because we have nothing else. I have got them all started at knitting a pair of stockings for themselves. None knit well, to some it is quite new, but all will learn. We have also got started at school work. Blackboard was given, or lent; books, slates, etc., I had to buy, after waiting some time. It cannot be called a Model School yet, but sometimes I have real pleasure in teaching, at others they are full of whims; but I have seen just such children before in my life. It takes little to please—20 cents worth of clams will make them good-natured for a day—then it takes just as little to displease. And really I have only had them five weeks, but it seems a much longer time. They are bright and apt enough. One of the brightest left for China this week; she was also the most troublesome, but I was sorry for her to go so soon, as she seemed interested in learning to read and write. We are in hopes that she will go to some missionary when she reaches Canton, and continue her search after knowledge.

They are learning to be able to teach Chinese women. This is Mr. Gardner's hope, and no doubt the correct one—after they have been educated and converted, to send them home as Bible women [teachers] under the care of some missionary already in China. God is able to do this for us if we but have faith, and some of the girls, I am sure, are quite capable of being thus trained. Ah Yuk, the one who left, had her passage paid by a Chinaman who helped in her rescue and wished her returned to her parents.

March 3rd. I find that I have spent $40 for food for the girls during two months, which gives an average of about $2.50 for each girl per month. As I have said before, I have not yet spent much for clothing. The girls are working quite diligently at their first pair of stockings, when those are finished I will set them to work on pillow slips, sheets, and underclothing for themselves. I have not got the cotton yet. Shall put off until ready to make. A piece of good white cotton would be acceptable from any quarter, but if none comes in I must buy I suppose, even if I over-run in my bills before the year ends. You kindly ask if you can do anything for me. I would like some cards containing the Lord's Prayer. They are learning to read it from the blackboard, and I should like them to have it in print. Also some texts of scripture on cards, as large print as possible. I might find some such here, but I get out so little, and would have to pay high for them. We shall want copy-books and pens soon, and every little thing counts up, as you know.

I have nothing special to report just now. We are eight in family, all well, comfortable and happy, learning a little every day. I had a lady from Winnipeg, with two from the city, in yesterday. It is thought that the "Home" will grow in the favor of the friends of Victoria, as the girls learn to be industrious and obedient. I have some really fine girls, and can but hope and pray that the Lord Jesus will soon incline their hearts to love and seek to please Him. They often ask, "if Jesus no like." The last such question was "Jesus no like smoke?" One of their former habits was smoking, and they have continued it until all their material is used up. When I would smell the smoke, I would say, "Mamma no like." They know Jesus does not like stealing and lying, and yet they practise both when it suits them.

I shall make up the first quarter's report at the end of March.

> I remain, very sincerely yours,
> Annie Leake

88

1888: NORTH-WEST TERRITORIES
I.A. YEREX TO HIS PARENTS

Today it is hard to believe that there was once an extraordinary network of paddle steamer routes criss-crossing the north, before branch railway lines snaked up to isolated communities. The steamers' shallow draft ensured that they could stay afloat on mighty rivers that often shrank to trickles in hot summers. Intrepid travellers particularly enjoyed the trip across Lake Winnipeg in a lake boat, to connect to a riverboat that voyaged up the Saskatchewan River, calling in at Hudson's Bay Company posts and native villages. Mr. Yerex, an American tourist, appreciated the stateroom comfort and fine dining on the steamer Northwest, *but also discovered some drawbacks to steamer travel.*

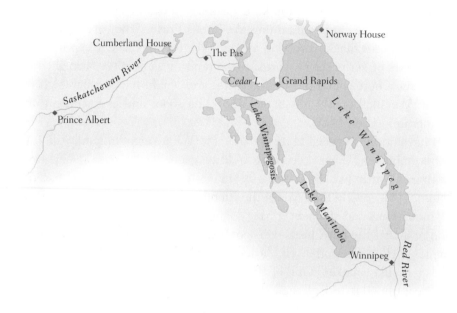

"Northwest"
July 22nd, 1888
28 mailed

Dear Father and Mother,

After a very pleasant voyage of three days on Lake Winnipeg I arrived in Grand Rapids on the 20th Inst. Grand Rapids is beautifully situated on a beautiful bay at the mouth of the Saskatchewan. About six white people live there, the balance of the population being composed of Half Breeds and Indians. The only means of existence are fur trading, fishing and trans-shipping from Lake boats to River boats and visa-versa. There is quite a large fishery and a fine Hudson Bay Post located there. A Rail Road and Telephone 3 ½ miles long connect the Lake and River boats as navigation is impossible for that distance over the Rapids.

We left Grand Rapids on the evening of the 20th and have since been winding very slowly up the great Saskatchewan. Navigation is very danger-ous on this end of the River, as Rapids are numerous, swift, and rocky and we have a number of lakes to cross. The "Northwest" is 200 feet long and carries four hundred tons. She runs swift on smooth water but a high wind on the lake will smash her to atoms. As I write we are lying in the lee of an Island waiting to cross Cedar Lake which is forty five miles long.

The cabin passengers are composed of some people from the Old Country and one Lady from Ont. bound for Prince Albert, some fur dealers and Hudson's Bay Co. men, the Dr. and myself—all very fine people (Myself included of course). It is very interesting as long as the boat is running as the diversity of the scenery affords us ample company in leisure moments, but when the boat ceases to move and we have a little run on shore to eat berries and be eaten by mosquitos, the scenery becomes monotonous and we hail with delight the signal for proceeding to a fresh scene. If you have not seen one of those large river boats running up rapids I am sure it would interest you. About a dozen Indians are harnessed in straps attached to a large York boat filled with rope about 6 inches in diameter. The Indians walk along the bank pulling the York boat about ¼ of a mile up the rapids. The large rope is then fastened to a tree or pier up stream and on the other end to a spool on the Steamer which is wound

Luxurious paddle steamers plied the extensive network of shallow lakes and rivers in the Canadian north in the late nineteenth century.

upstream by steam. This is repeated until we are out of the Rapids. In about 6 days more we expect to be near the scene of the [1885] Rebellion. We are having delightful weather. Millions of fish of all kinds and wild game in every direction. Good day—will see you again in a few days.

Monday 23rd July

We have not moved an inch since I wrote above. A gale blowing from the west. Cannot say when we will get out of this. My expenses are $3.00 per day, which accounts for my anxiety to proceed. We expect to reach Prince Albert in about a week when nearly half our voyage on this boat will have been completed. Twelve hundred miles on one boat—imagine—and on one river after three hundred and fifty miles on one lake and one boat. However, the accommodation is good, perhaps better than you could get on any boat on Lake Ontario. There are state-rooms for 80 cabin passengers and altogether over 1000 people could be accommodated on this boat. You will perhaps be surprised as I was to hear of such Enterprise away up here in the far north, but what is still more difficult to comprehend is this fact. Two days drive from Edmonton north connects us with boats as large as this which run nearly 3000 miles north or within sixty miles of the Arctic Ocean. The people of Manitoba know less of this northwest Country than the people of Ontario do of Manitoba or Montana. A lady correspondent of a Boston paper is on board with us and adds considerably to the enjoyment of all on board. I will endeavor to procure a copy of the paper containing her no doubt flowery description of this vast wilderness, and forward to you which of course will be months yet.

Thursday July 26th

On Tuesday we stopped 2 hours at one of the old Hudson Bay posts called The Pas—beautifully situated on the first raise of ground since we left Grand Rapids 140 miles. Up to this time we have not seen enough dry land to pitch a tent on. And here at "The Pas" there cannot be over 50 or 100 acres of ground. However, what there is, is good and presents a very imposing appearance after 3 days of muskeg. Two Hudson's Bay Coy. men, one Free Trader and a few hundred Indians comprise the population. Oh! I might add—a school teacher and a Church of England Clergyman . . . About 70 miles of very winding river with marsh on either side brought us on Wednesday morning to Cumberland House the chief Hudson Bay post for a district 1700 miles long. The chief Factor for the district (Mr. Belanger), who has been on the boat with us from Grand Rapids, will get off at this point, and we will miss him *very much*. He has been the life of the boat. A very fine jovial fellow with a heart that compares with his size (315 lbs). He invited The Dr. and myself to dinner. We accepted the invitation, & I assure you we enjoyed the moose steak and the nose which is considered one of the greatest delicacies in this part of the country. Cumberland House [is] beautifully situated on a gravelly point on Lake Cumberland on an Island with an evergreen background. An abundance of vegetation. We left Cumberland yesterday afternoon and do not stop for two days, unless stuck on a sand-bar which is quite a usual thing in this part of the river. The banks of the river have been gradually rising since we left Cumberland and have now reached about 5 feet and [are] rapidly increasing in height.

Saturday 28th July
For two days after leaving Cumberland we did not see a house and as yet have only seen 4 or 5. The banks of the river are now about 100 feet high with beautiful evergreen banks on either side. We have been making extra good time the last two days and consequently expect to reach Prince Albert some time to-night. The country on either side is high, sandy loam and partially covered with wood which is gradually growing less. The river is very wide and full of rapids. Two Mounted Policemen boarded our boat last night from Prince Albert to see if there was any whiskey on board. . . . We are within 17 miles of Prince Albert. Mostly prairie clay-loam. Dry land fine country. I will probably be here for a week. I will write you again after leaving P.A. and give you a description of the town & etc.

    With Love to all I will close abruptly as I have some business to attend to.

                    Yours aff'ly,
                    I. A. Yerex

Cannot write good as boat is always heaving. I.A.Y.

89
1889: ONTARIO
PAULINE JOHNSON TO ARCHIBALD KAINS IN NEW YORK CITY

Literary courtships have their own particular charm. Here is the rising young Brantford poet Pauline Johnson, with her unusual half-English, half-Mohawk background, flirting outrageously with one of her many male admirers. Archibald Kains, a rather conventional banker, was dazzled by Pauline's looks, paddling skills, and wit. She sent him an embroidered tobacco pouch; he replied with a photo of himself and a request to continue the correspondence. But in the end, I think, he found her a little rich for his blood.

Brantford, Sept 25th 89

My dear Mr. Kains

Your letter found me off in the country for a few idle days and some fresh air before the season closes and if there is one thing that could have, and did, enhance my holiday it was to know that my little gift pleased you and that my letter was not altogether unwelcome. If indeed more of its kind will ever give you any pleasure they will be heartily and readily sent you.

I do not know when anything has gratified me so much as your desire for my friendship. You tell me simply that you want it, but that means a great deal to one who honours and cherishes friends as I do, and though I gladly tell you now that you shall have all the friendship from my hands and all the faith from my heart that constitutes the chief elements of friendship that you wish, still I am not ready to admit that this is a new standing for us both to take. Please don't tell me Mr. Kains that it has not existed before, that we have hitherto been but rather well-meaning acquaintances, had I not regarded you as a friend—stranger though you may be. I would never have sent you any of my needlework nor would your photo be just where it is, on my writing desk with one or two whom I have known for years. And so if by writing to you I manifest what has all along existed, you shall have the letters. You will find me a moody fitful correspondent I fear, and you must take me just as I feel, without restraint or disguise. I never dissemble with those I write to, and you will have to put up with an expression of my ideas more than a list of town items—with my impressions of thought, observation and feeling more than bits of social news. Either you must let me sing to you when I am successful, complain when I am discouraged, write gloomily when I feel gloomy—or you must not hear from me at all. Will you choose?

It was my good intention to sit for some photographs this week but at the [Canoe] Regatta last Saturday I contracted a miserable cold in the weak side of my face and as my eyes are affected by it I am not beautiful to behold. But if you have any faith left in me I will ask you to believe me in the future, and probably next month my face will be looking in upon yours. The Regatta was the sporting event of the season here and of course

I was in my element although not yet permitted to paddle in the races. I had much fun following the course up, and my favourites all won. I was so sorry the Earl and Jiggs were not here. They would have enjoyed it and as I taught them to paddle I feel a little proud of my pupils.

I miss the Earl very much, for although latterly he has been [her sister] Eva's "chum" and I have stood on the second step of the stairs in his good fellowship, still one cannot be first always and I am very used to being second. I don't feel it now the way I did when I was a girl. I have my literary work and chum with my muse more than with any fellow being. Somehow I think I might well afford to be content with a second place as regards people and all persons. For have I not had the bestowal of a greater gift upon me than that which the whole world

Pauline Johnson was still living in Brantford, dreaming of a career as "the Mohawk poetess," when she penned lively letters to Archie Kains.

could offer? Here I am at the outset inflicting you with a harangue . . . I would have been terrified to write that to a woman. She would have thought I was in love . . . I wonder why women think that because you are fond of a person you must necessarily be in love with them, it is horrible. Bless me, if I were in love with Laddie and Puss and Jiggs and all the boys I am fond of I would never have any appetite left for breakfast, and I am painfully healthy.

Don't you think I had better stop writing or I will be reading you sermons and essays next. So as I leave you this peerlessly bright afternoon I go down to the boathouse and take out my canoe which takes the place with me of a cigar to a man. Evidently I am bordering on the "glooms"—I wish you were here, I would run you down the rapids today, and we would put up a sail in the quiet water beyond, it would be perfect and I would enjoy it even more than you would, for I love an appreciative comrade in a canoe and you would surely be that.

My mother wishes me to remember her most kindly to you. Eva is out of town or she would send a message also. And again, let me tell you how glad I am that I may be

> Your friend,
> E. Pauline Johnson.

Six weeks later, Pauline sent Archie Kains a photograph: "What do you think of me in my flannel canoeing shirt and tam? When you want to see me just me with that odd wild streak of gypsy life that is so strong in my nature—look at the enclosed." In the next five years, Pauline became one of Canada's best-known poets and performers, while Archie rose steadily in the ranks of the Canadian Bank of Commerce in the United States. They continued to write to each other until 1893.

90
1890: NOVA SCOTIA
HENRY SWIFT TO R. COWANS IN HALIFAX

In central and eastern Canada, industrial production was growing and exports of Canada's mineral wealth booming. But there was little concern for the safety and welfare of factory workers and miners. Nova Scotia's Springhill Mine, like the many coal mines scattered through Nova Scotia, was a particularly tough place to work in the 1880s. Each night, Henry Swift, general manager of the mine, catalogued the problems to his boss: injured pit boys and ponies, dangerous water levels, pockets of poisonous gas, decaying pit props.

> Springhill Mines,
> Nov. 11th 1890

Dear Sir,
I beg to hand in report of day's work.

Examined report in morning, found all favourable in general.

Went down the West Slope by traveling way which is being thoroughly overhauled and repaired. Should stand a few years when finished this time. Will take untill Christmas to complete.

It is all most discouraging repairing and renewing old work which should have been done years ago . . .

The steam have been coming through in the traveling way, rotting the timber and causing the roof to give way. Went in Stoney Level in Main Seam to the working face, found all looking well here. Balance will soon be ready to break off to go through to the 800ft. level . . .

Went up to the East Side of tunnel to Carmichael and Co. Chute. Found gas, nothing serious. Also D. Dawson & Co. Balance in East Slope stripping top coal down and breaking of the Bords will be a month before they will be clear of the Balance . . . Regarding the abuse of horses at North Slope. I am entirely ignorant of any horses being abused just having been somewhat overworked. Whoever is the informant I think his duty should have been to tell either Mr. Simpson, Mr McInnis or Myself. The stableman comes this evening to Mr. McInnis 5 pm to tell him almost in identical words as stated in the note. If he knew such was the case he should have informed Me. I have met him several mornings when going out always ask him how the horses were. His general reply was allright . . .

It has just come to light how the last horse got jammed in the North Slope. The Stableman had the horses out watering him in the dark. The driver came on him unawares before he could stop the rake jammed the horses. The Stableman never reported that matter to Mr. Simpson either.

It is rather hard lines to be taken to task for negligence in matters which a person are ignorant of and no information on them untill a note from you. I am very anxious that everything should go right and willing at any time to sacrifice my own personal interests to promote the Company's.

My mind is at all times fully occupied with thoughts to make the work a success, enough of worry to Kill a man. If my services are not satisfactory I wish to know it as early as possible as I am doing all I can to keep things straight and can do no more . . . As underground is much different than the surface a driver might abuse a horse without any one knowing.

Whenever any matters are reported to me I always investigate to the fullest extent and shield no one who I find in blame. And whoever is the informant, had he reported to me I should certainly have looked into the matter and brought it to your notice.

I am Your Obedient Servant
Henry Swift.

The next day, a powerful explosion in a mine shaft killed Swift, along with 124 others, in the worst mining disaster Canada had ever known.

91

1890: NOVA SCOTIA
ALEXANDER LYLE TO LEVI THOMAS IN MAINE

Testosterone pulses through this letter! Alexander Lyle was a fisherman renowned for his sense of humour and his partiality to what were known locally as "frisky girls." He and Levi Thomas grew up together in the tiny fishing village of Blanche at the southwestern tip of Nova Scotia, and when Levi moved to Maine to live with his sister, twenty-four-year-old Alexander frequently dropped him a note.

Blanch
Nov 23 1890

Dear frind i seved your letter some tim ago and was glad to hear from you and glad to hear that you was smart [well]. I am smart at prasant and hop that those few lines will find you the sam and i hop that you ar a making lots of muny so i can get som from you for times is very hard on Blanch now. We have not got any Markel [mackerel] yet and i dont expect we will get any of them this fall for it is a getting to let for them now and i am a goining to take up my nets next week. Well levi news is very scarce around hear now and I dont no what to right. You Must tell [your cousin] Sam that i sind my love to him and tell him that i should like to be there to kick his ass and tell him the first girl that he sees he must fuck for me for i have not got it this summer. Well levi girls is very scarce a round hear. I have not bee down to sandy Point only once sance you have been gon but i am a goining down soon. Lizzie goodick is married. Well I dont no as I have any more to right this tim. You must com hom soon as you can. so i will Close my letter by bidding you good after noon.

from you frind
Alexander S Lyle
to levi thomas

92

1891: MANITOBA
DAISY MACDONALD TO HER GRANDFATHER
SIR JOHN A. MACDONALD IN OTTAWA

Sir John A. Macdonald had already been prime minister of Canada for nineteen years when he ran once again in the 1891 election. His teenage granddaughter Daisy and her stepmother, Gertrude (known as Gay, and wife of Hugh John Macdonald, a Manitoba MP), both wrote to congratulate him: Gay asserted that the Conservative triumph meant that "the country is saved." But Daisy's note reflects family concerns about the old man's health.

Sault au Recollet
March 8, 1891.

My dear Grandpapa,

I am writing this to congratulate you upon the result of the Elections. I am so very glad you got in. You could not tell how hard your little puss prayed for you in my thoughts all the time. I hope you will be able to take some rest after these busy anxious days for I am afraid you will be ill. All the girls were so excited as they had some one of their relations interested in the result but we are nearly all conservatives.

> With love & kisses to all I remain,
> your loving child
> Daisy.

Daisy's concerns were justified. Within three months, the first prime minister of Canada was dead of heart failure at age seventy-six, and the Conservative Party began a long decline.

93
1892: QUEBEC
WILFRID LAURIER TO ÉMILIE LAVERGNE IN ARTHABASCA

Wilfrid Laurier was one of the most charismatic leaders in Canadian history, and he was well aware of his charms. But in 1892, the leader of the federal Liberal Party was in the political wilderness: despite his efforts to make his party a truly national institution, the Conservatives continued to dominate the young nation. Laurier, a married man of fifty-one, had an outlet for his anguish: his correspondence with Émilie Lavergne, the charming wife of Joseph Lavergne, his law partner in Arthabasca, Quebec. In his angular scrawl, Laurier poured out to Émilie not only his deep affection but also his political worries. Maybe it was a love affair; it was certainly a partnership of intellectual equals.

Montreal,
21 February [1892]

This has been a week of increasing fatigue, my dear friend, and I am . . . rather stiff in all the limbs today; that is the only complaint, but this is a day of rest [Sunday] & I will not go out of my room. I will thus, I hope, be again fresh for my labors tomorrow. Perhaps you are aware that I have been, for the whole week, constantly on the wing like a bird. One thought annoys me; it is that I did not fulfill my promise of sending you newspapers. I did not forget it, I can assure you my dear friend, but though scarcely credible, I never had one single moment alone to myself, which I could have given to the sweet task. I did not forget my promise, though it remained unfulfilled; but you my dear friend, did you as much as I remember it, surrounded as you are by scores of friends?

When this letter reaches you, you will have learned by the newspapers, that my efforts have been perfectly useless. My friends [running in two by-elections] are mowed down & buried under tremendous majorities, there is manifestly a revulsion of feeling in the West. What are the causes? . . . I have yet nothing positive but I am more and more of the opinion that the real cause is a revival of the old hostility between English and French. My friends are most loyal to me. I had many evidences of their personal devotion, but there exists in the great mass of the people of Ontario a conviction sprung from late events & carefully nursed by the enemy that Frenchmen are boodlers [corrupt], & that I am not in consequence to be trusted. I am given the full credit of not being a boodler, but that I would be unable to stem the current of boodlism. My opponents yell themselves hoarse, shouting and repeating that statement. They are not above boodling themselves today. I have reason to believe that they are strong at it even now, but the idea that Frenchmen might do the same, is a consideration which makes them wild.

I leave on Tuesday for Ottawa. If I were in such pecuniary circumstances that I could afford it, I would feel inclined to make a strong, even bitter fight, but I am not in such circumstances & I must listen not to the voice of resentment but to the voice of reason.

Will you be able to send me a word. You know how it will make me happy; no I am sure you do not. Remember their old friend, to your little ones.

Again and ever of all your friends, the truest.

W.L.

Four years later, the Liberals won the federal election, and Wilfrid Laurier served as Canada's first French-speaking prime minister for the next fifteen years. He broke off the relationship with Émilie around 1900.

94
1895: NORTH-WEST TERRITORIES
CLAUDE GARDINER TO HIS MOTHER,
MRS. EDWARD JAMES GARDINER, IN ENGLAND

By the 1890s, the foothills of the future province of Alberta were flooded with settlers, many of them ne'er-do-well Englishmen, banished from Britain by their exasperated families, who supported them with remittances. These "remittance men" were more interested in cards than cattle and posed an embarrassment to fellow-countrymen who genuinely wanted to make a new life in the last best west. In 1894, a horse-loving city lad called Claude Gardiner, twenty-five, left his family in London, England, to take a "situation on a ranch." For several months he worked for a former North-West Mounted Police sergeant called Bell, who expected him to spend twelve hours a day in the saddle and live on a diet of bacon and beans. Bell then tried to persuade him to buy the ranch. Claude reported to his mother the course of negotiations.

Macleod,
June 6, 1895

My dear Mother,

The business with Bell is all off. I heard from Winnipeg and they confirmed Mr. Gigot's advice which was not to go in unless Bell agreed to have a count on the cattle and this he would not do. Bell says it knocks the cattle about to brand them over again. You have to do this when you count them or you cannot tell afterwards what cattle have been counted as you do not always get everyone the first time of rounding them up. I think Bell was afraid he had not got the number of cattle he claims or he would not have objected to have a count on them. I wish Mr. Gigot had given me his opinion sooner in the deal so I should not have wasted so much time.

I left Bell yesterday and have taken a room in town while looking about. I can live very cheaply in town in a nice clean place, a Temperance Hotel they call it. You bet I slept last night. I have not slept in such a bed for a long time. I was glad to leave Bell's house in town; it is small and full of children and I had to sleep on the kitchen floor.

I have been to look at a ranch in the Porcupine Hills that is for sale. The H.B. Co. have a mortgage on it and they are going to sell it. They have the deeds of the place so that one cannot be turned off it by anyone. It is very good land and grows a good crop so that one has something to help besides the cattle. Of course, I could homestead next to it and so get a good sized ranch. The place as it stands now is 160 acres or a $1/4$ section. There is a house of several rooms, stables, corrals, etc. There is also a good spring which runs winter and summer and does not freeze up. I shall not decide about this place for a week or two so as to see if anything else turns up that is any good.

Tell Father that the boots he wrote about would not be any good to me. I always wear high riding boots with high cowboy heels on them like a lady's shoe; they are very comfortable and the heels prevent one's foot from slipping through the stirrup. With regard to six shooter, a Colt's Frontier to take an American .44 cartridge is the best thing; I can get cartridges for either .44 or .45 American. I don't know which is the best size, some use one and some the other. Plated is better than blue as it does not rust so easily.

I have heard talk about Canon Hollard's son being out here. He is close to this place but the account one hears of him here is very different to what you hear of him. He is one of the usual English sort who does nothing but play polo and drinks and plays the fool generally. His horse ranch is a myth. I believe he has some polo ponies and that is about all. The old canon came out here to pay his debts and his son fed him about as roughly as he could, so the old man did not stop long. I think young Hollard is going back to England soon.

Nearly all the Englishmen out here go on in the same way, pony racing, etc., and are the laughing stock of all the Americans. The article in Longmans on why the Englishman is a failure is quite true. The man knows what he is writing about but most of it applies more to the States and farming than it does to the cattle business. There is a lot of dancing here. They have a dance every week, also there is tennis playing, etc., but an Englishman that goes in for that sort of thing is considered no good. I must finish this letter I am writing it in the office at the Hudson's Bay. Hope Grandpa is better now.

Claude

The roundup is on now and it is raining like anything today. I am glad I am not out.

95

1898: ONTARIO

ISABEL MACKENZIE KING TO HER SON
WILLIAM LYON MACKENZIE KING IN MASSACHUSETTS

This letter is one of the most blatant exercises in maternal manipulation I have ever come across. Isabel King adored her twenty-four-year-old son, William Lyon Mackenzie King. A brainy, ambitious Harvard graduate, Billy had all the qualities that Isabel's father, the Little Rebel of 1837, and her husband, the unsuccessful lawyer John King, lacked. Isabel relied on Billy for emotional and financial support. She expected him to pay off his father's debts, help with his brother's education costs, and find suitors for his two sisters. So when Billy told his parents that he had proposed to a German woman several years older than himself, Isabel was horrified. A fiancée represented a threat to the whole family's future.

Toronto
Wednesday 6 a.m. [April 6, 1898]

My dear Billy,

For hours I have been lying awake thinking of you. I have never crossed you in your life and I do not intend to do so now but I think there are many things to think about before you take this step. The struggles have been long and hard at home and I hope you will not think me selfish when I say I had counted on you to help to lift the cloud. Things are looking brighter than they were but no matter which way we turn it must take time to lift the burden off our shoulders.

The girls are not growing younger and the advantages you have had they in a great way have been deprived of and your father and myself desire to give Max a chance for a university training as well as yourself. This last year he has not spared himself and I am most anxious to encourage him. You are but a boy yet and the whole world is before you with prospects such as we never could have looked to at your age and even if you engaged yourself to a girl you could not marry for some time and experience tells one [that] long engagements are not fair to a girl or even to yourself. In your loneliness I sympathize but who has not told me again and again that in books we can find everything? Perhaps you have changed your mind and find so much learning is a weariness of the flesh.

No Billy, there is lots of <u>easy flesh</u> and though I would be the last one to tell you to live the lonely life of an old bachelor I would tell you to

Isabel Mackenzie King never let her son Billy forget his family responsibilities; without him, she believed, the family would starve.

consider before you step into matrimony. Come home and let us talk it all over dear boy and feel that wiser old heads than your own may teach you what in the future you will thank them for. I have had lots of dreams of sitting besides you at Cambridge and having you talk as you used to do . . . I have built castles without number for you. Are all these dreams but to end in dreams? I am getting old now Willie and disappointment wearies and the heart grows sick. Sometimes when I hear you talk so much what you would do for those that suffer I think charity begins at home and as you do so shall it be done unto you. I am not grasping for myself but I do feel for your sisters and I know you who have such a big heart will not forsake me. I am afraid these Harvard young men have contaminated you but, when you come to your sense, you will look at all "things" in the light we do.

I have waited till the dawn would break to write to you and I trust an answer will come that will relieve my mind. I am very wearied. But that is nothing new for Mother, it is only one more lesson not to put your trust in anything under the sun.

Goodbye: may every blessing attend you is the loving wish of your Mother

Write by return of mail.

Mackenzie King's engagement soon crumbled, and he never married. Instead, his relationship with his mother became increasingly intense.

96

1899: MANITOBA
ALMON JAMES COTTON TO W.F. MCCREARY, COMMISSIONER
OF IMMIGRATION, IN WINNIPEG

A.J. Cotton became known as Manitoba's "Wheat King" after he filled twenty-eight railway cars with the record harvest of number one hard Manitoba wheat grown on the farm he rented in southern Manitoba. As the century drew to a close, the energetic and enterprising Cotton decided to buy his own property in the Swan River Valley, 525 kilo-metres northwest of Winnipeg. He was outraged when he discovered that large sections of adjacent land had been granted to the Doukhobors. Thanks to the patronage of Count Leo Tolstoy, 7,400 of these Russian pacifists had escaped persecution in their homeland and headed for the Canadian prairies. Cotton made his feelings clear in a letter to the Winnipeg-based federal commissioner of immigration.

Treherne
January 30, 1899

Dear Sir,

My attention has been called to a very serious matter dealing with the government in regard to settlers in the Swan River Valley on Range 29 with especial reference to township 35 in that range. In this township there are 35 homesteads taken up by Canadians and a number of those are from Treherne who homesteaded in that township and all have been notified by the Department of Interior that they can get out and take up homesteads [in] some other part as this range is reserved for the Doukhobors. Now I claim this is an Injustice to those homesteaders. They all wish to remain there as they are satisfied and have gone to a great expense to get there and settled. They are going to stoutly rebel against the government if they allow the Doukhobors to settle among them. I say it is a shame on any government to act in this manner.

My brother-in-law W. I. Ford took up land there for himself and his father, and last summer drove from here to Thunder Hill and underwent difficulties and hardships to locate there, and then drove back again last fall and just before Xmas loaded a car here of effects and implements and took [them] out to Thunder Hill and drew this 55 miles and put up his buildings and just came here on the 27th on his way to Ontario to bring up his father and mother and another load of effects for their homesteads. He told me they were just served with notices about the 23rd to vacate the homesteads unless they wished to have those Doukhobors for neighbors. Now this is interfering with their private rights. They are British subjects and should be treated as such. If the government wishes any moving to be done let the Doukhobors do it. There is plenty of land west of this range that is vacant for all of them and such being the case, why interfere with the Canadian settlers who had no assistance? I am a Grit to the back bone but such treatment of our own Canadians (and a number of them have served their three years in the Volunteers) is a disgrace to any government. Mr. Ford told me last night that in the Swan Valley a petition will be presented to the government signed by those settlers that they wish to have British rights and do not intend to move out, hoping the government will not settle any Doukhobors in Range 29 in the Valley. And if this is not done there is not a Grit in Treherne but will turn their backs on the government. One Tory here has been served with a notice of the above and has sent it down to Hugh John [Macdonald?] for him to look over and have his opinion. Now, Mr. McCreary, by all means advise the government to be cautious in dealing with those Canadian settlers and meet their wishes, as one of them are worth 25 Doukhobors to this country. And whatever the government does let it satisfy the settler and encourage him. Don't tramp on him and turn him out for a Doukhobor. There is land enough here for all. And if there is an advantage to give let the British subject come first.

This is of Importance to me also as I applied for two sections of land there and intend going there to farm on a large scale, but my land is in Range 28. I have been the means of bringing a large number of settlers to this country from Ontario and all are doing well and I have spoken up for this country wherever I went and wrote about it in the press and always spoke up for the Grit government and intend to do so as long as they protect the settler. Hoping to hear from you in this case.

I remain Yours Truly,
A. J. Cotton

97

1899: ONTARIO

D.C. BLACK TO THE EDITOR OF THE *GLOBE* IN TORONTO

Over the course of the nineteenth century, the population of the northern half of North America had risen from less than half a million to over 7 million. The buffalo was not the only endangered species: the influx of immigrants had a disastrous impact on much of the indigenous fauna and flora. John James Audubon once reported flocks of passenger pigeons—or wild pigeons—numbering between 1 and 2 billion, and one flock in Michigan covered forty-five kilometres in length by five or six kilometres in breadth. By the end of the nineteenth century, however, hunters and hungry farmers had taken their toll.

Appin, Ontario
February 4, 1899

Dear Sir,

I noticed a short item in yesterday's *Globe* by G. C. T. Ward saying it would be a matter of much interest to many if, through the *Globe*, anyone who has seen wild pigeons in recent years would make it known. Well, Mr. Editor, I had the pleasure of seeing nine of them in a wheat field near the village of Glencoe last fall, and they are the first I have seen in 25 years. They did put me in mind of the olden times. When I was a boy I used to spend a great deal of my time trying to strike them with sticks. They have often taken over half a day crossing over our farm, flying very low, as they seemed to be very tired. They would make for the townships of Stephen and Hay on Lake Huron shore, among the hemlock and pine trees until the hatching season would be over. They could be plainly heard cooing three miles away. They would flock together by the thousands and after the young were able to fly they would return south until next spring; but where they are gone I would like to know. To see a few of them is to me as seeing a dear old friend.

D.C. Black

The last known passenger pigeon died in the Cincinnati Zoological Garden in 1914.

In the early twentieth century, immigrants poured into "the last best west," lured by Canadian government campaigns in Britain and elsewhere.

PART 3: A HALF CENTURY OF BATTLES
1900–1950

THERE IS AN ARTLESS CONFIDENCE IN THE LETTERS I FOUND FROM Canadians at the dawn of the twentieth century. Whether it is the excitement of Lucy Maud Montgomery of Prince Edward Island, when a publisher accepted her manuscript in 1907, or the exuberance of Monica Hopkins of Alberta in 1910, as she cantered over the prairies in her nightdress, the emotion almost leaps off the page. Visitors could not miss it. A twenty-seven-year-old British politician visited Winnipeg in 1901 and was bowled over. "Fancy 20 years ago there were only a few mud huts—tents," Winston Churchill wrote to his mother. "And last night a magnificent audience of men in evening dress & ladies half out of it, filled a fine opera house."

The nation was growing by leaps and bounds—immigrants poured into the west and two new provinces, Saskatchewan and Alberta, joined Confederation in 1905. The economy boomed, thanks to new mining technology, a rapidly expanding web of railways, better agricultural machinery, and the development of hardy, high-yield grains like Red Fife wheat.

But there is also a terrible poignancy to these youthful high spirits. Ghastly ordeals lay ahead. Even as the optimism brings a smile to my face, I know it will be shattered in the next fifty years by bloodshed, hardship, and racial and regional animosities. This section of *Canada: A Portrait in Letters* is far longer than the others because the events of these years meant that loved ones were frequently separated and wrote to one another more often. The sheer volume of correspondence I found was far greater than for other periods, as families struggled to maintain ties and morale. The content of many of those letters was more painful and intense than the cheerful exchanges of information of other times.

As the century began, however, Canadians regarded the most pressing threat to be the imminent death of the only sovereign most of them had ever known: Queen Victoria. Canada was proud to be one of the largest patches of imperial pink on a globe girdled by British power. When conflict erupted in 1899 in South Africa between British colonists and Boer farmers, 7,000 English-Canadian men volunteered to fight under the British flag in the first major Canadian military expedition overseas.

The Boer War brought into focus two tensions within Confederation that would undermine future governments. The first was conflict between Quebec and the rest of Canada: the zeal of English-Canadian volunteers was not matched in French Canada, where the war was dismissed as an imperialist adventure that Canada should ignore. The second tension focused on Canada's place within the British Empire, and particularly its role in imperial defence. Should Canada have its own navy, and would a Canadian navy automatically join in all Britain's adventures abroad?

I have always found silver-haired, silver-tongued Prime Minister Sir Wilfrid Laurier one of the most captivating leaders that Canada produced. But he tried to dodge these issues. His stumbles earned him the nickname "Waffley Wilfy" and, combined with his government's proposed free trade deal with the United States, led to his defeat at the polls in 1911. He was replaced by the Conservative leader, Robert Borden, a much more plodding fellow, a Nova Scotia lawyer who wanted business to boom and Canada to do its duty on the world stage.

The tensions were temporarily submerged in 1914, when German aggression in Europe erupted into war. With full public support, Prime Minister Borden assured Britain that Canada was "ready, aye, ready." By February 1915, the 1st Canadian Division was in French trenches.

But euphoric patriotism soon gave way to grim shock as the lists of dead and wounded lengthened. The cost of the war both in human lives (Canada's casualty rate was particularly high) and in financial terms was immense. Hardly a family was untouched by grief or by the haunting fear of loss. Letters written from First World War trenches still have the power to make the reader gasp, or cry. I am deeply moved by Alwyn Bramley-Moore's insistence, in letters to his children in Alberta, that *not* all Germans are cruel, whatever wartime propaganda suggested. I am nauseated by the idea of rats' whiskers tickling my ear as I sleep, as described by Mayo Lind of Newfoundland. I grieve that these two talented writers, along with so many other brave young men, never came home. They remain buried on the battlegrounds of France.

"The Great War" (as it was once known) shook up many of the old assumptions. The great cliché about this period is that it allowed Canada to "come of age as a nation." There is some truth in that, although I'm always suspicious of stirring generalizations that meant nothing to those on the ground. And if it was a kind of rite of passage, it was a particularly merciless one. As the war dragged on, it reignited the old tensions. Public opinion in Quebec was outraged when a shortage of volunteer recruits for the Canadian Corps obliged Borden to introduce conscription. The province remained predominantly agrarian, and French-Canadian farmers, who had little interest in Canada's commitment to its European allies, were horrified at the idea that they and their sons should leave their fields at harvest time. Westerners and working-class Canadians were equally incensed by Ottawa's high-handed wartime policies. At the same time, Borden himself wondered whether British generals were carelessly using colonials as cannon fodder. He turned out to be far more than a plodder. His rage at the way Canadians were treated is almost incandescent in a letter he sent to England in 1916: "Procrastination, indecision, inertia, doubt, hesitation and many other undesirable qualities have made themselves entirely too conspicuous in this War."

But back in Canada, dissatisfaction simmered within just about every Canadian group and region by war's end, in 1918. During the war, thousands of women had taken jobs in offices, in munitions factories, and as drivers, and had tasted financial and social independence. Now they refused to fade quietly back into the kitchen. Instead, they challenged the assumptions that had governed their mothers' lives. "There seems to be something terribly wrong on the prairie," one hard-working and bitter farmwife wrote to the local paper in 1918. "A woman gives up her life for her child and it is all right, but if a man's best mare is sick, how quick he can get a veterinary in."

When the soldiers returned to a Canada of rising unemployment and poor working conditions, their discontent contributed to widespread social unrest. The idealism of war—"making the world safe for democracy"—was snuffed out in the summer of 1919, when 30,000 workers in Winnipeg went on strike for six torrid weeks. They failed, however, to secure higher wages or shorter hours. The following year, the farmers of Ontario and the west united to form their own political party, the National Progressive Party, to counteract what they regarded as the bully influence of eastern big business. They campaigned for lower tariff and rail rates, more aid to farmers, public ownership of utilities, and a more open democracy. Meanwhile, the Maritimes suffered both declining demand for coal and iron (which led to ugly strikes in Cape Breton) and the loss of railway facilities.

Canada seemed to be splitting along its seams. Could anyone sew the nation back into one whole cloth?

William Lyon Mackenzie King, Liberal prime minister from 1921 and an expert in compromise, struggled to keep all these competing interests in balance through the 1920s. Always more concerned with domestic harmony than with imperial unity, King quietly asserted Canadian control over its internal and foreign policies. The "Roaring Twenties" arrived in Canada largely thanks to a return to King's canny protectionist policies: wheat sales soared, the railways returned to profit, Ontario industry hummed. Good economic times were mirrored in another development during these years—an explosion of Canadian culture. Artists like Lawren Harris and his fellow members of the Group of Seven and poets, writers, and critics including Hugh MacLennan and B.K. Sandwell strove to reflect a North American landscape and society in their work, rather than traditions inherited from European forebears. By 1930, a publicly owned national radio network was already under discussion.

Few, if any, Canadians realized how shaky were the foundations of the post-war prosperity of the late 1920s. The economy rested on a mere handful of industries: pulp, paper, wheat, minerals. When the New York stock market collapsed in 1929, the country was plunged into a depression, made far worse by brutal droughts on the prairies. It was a calamity. The yield per acre in southern Manitoba fell from twenty-seven bushels of wheat to three bushels. Farming families starved. Thousands of city dwellers were thrown out of work. Children were forced to leave school in the struggle to make ends meet.

Politicians and charities were inundated with desperate pleas for help that are as searing today as they were at the time. Who can read this appeal to the Alberta Division of the Canadian Red Cross without wincing? "The family consists of three boys, 10, 7 and 4 years with the mother very sick on roughly constructed bed with two baby boys (twins) three days old. The one room farm house, roughly constructed of logs, draughty floors, keeps the children shivering, and very sick mother on bed with no bedding of any kind nor clothes, no shoes or caps nor stockings. The children's clothes made of old sacks and patched finally played out and no clothes of any kind for baby boy twins. The father of these children can not get work of any kind." In Newfoundland (still a self-governing dominion) the Depression's impact was so harsh that the island was forced to surrender to government by London-appointed commissioners in 1934 in order to get help from Britain.

The Depression dragged on year after year. At this stage in our history, few people expected the federal government to step in and help; Ottawa's role was to cut costs and erect tariff barriers to foreigners. Yet hunger gnawed. And there was a sense that the country owed something to those who, only a few years earlier, had risked their lives for Canada: "It certainly doesn't make me feel very nice to think I helped to defend a country that will not help me in times when I and my family need it badly," a father of five small, starving children wrote to the Ontario premier in 1934. It was only towards the end of the decade that a handful of intrepid academics and politicians raised the notion that perhaps the state had some responsibility for the social and economic well-being of its citizens. Meanwhile, most Canadians were too preoccupied with their own problems to notice what was happening elsewhere. They preferred to avert their eyes from disturbing events in Europe; appeasement was cheaper and less controversial than arming for a conflict that would surely divide the nation.

Escape from the Depression years came at a cost: the outbreak of another world war. The country's major industries finally got rolling because in 1939 Canada once again told Britain, "Ready, aye, ready." By 1941, more than 250,000 men and 2,000 women were in uniform. Over a million Canadians (out of a population of 12.5 million) had seen service in the armed forces by 1945. Over 42,000 (two-thirds the toll of the First World War) died.

Prime Minister Mackenzie King may not have had Wilfrid Laurier's charm, but he had far more cunning. He knew that, for the third time in this half century, the major challenge would be to maintain national unity. Once again, English Canada was gung-ho to fight while Quebec was as resistant to conscription as it had been in 1916. King managed to finesse the conscription issue by evasion ("Not necessarily conscription, but conscription if necessary"), but there was a dark racial underside to the federal government's determination not to rock the boat. When Jewish Canadians begged Ottawa to admit Jewish refugees from Nazi policies, almost all received an unequivocal no. When Japan joined the war in 1941, the Canadian government clamped down on the Japanese-Canadian community in British Columbia: families were split up or relocated elsewhere, and their property was confiscated. At the time, in an atmosphere of fear and suspicion, many Canadians trusted that their government was making the right decisions. In retrospect, Canadians can only be appalled. I still get chills down my spine as I read the 1942 letter from Muriel Kitagawa, as she packs up four small children for the trip to a Japanese internment camp: "We are Israelites on the move. The public is getting bloodthirsty and will have our blood Nazi-fashion . . . My nights are filled with exodus nightmares."

Hitler's war ended in May 1945. But canny Mr. King had already taken steps to avoid the discontent that erupted at the end of the previous war and a renewal of the Depression. Even before the soldiers returned, Canada was given its first unemployment scheme. There were family allowance cheques for mothers and pensions for the elderly; low-cost mortgages were available to those with enough wartime savings for a down payment; veterans were eligible for low-cost mortgages and education and training opportunities. Thanks to Imperial Oil's discovery of a gusher in Alberta in 1947 and increased trade with the United States, a post-war economic boom began to develop.

In 1948, William Lyon Mackenzie King, the nation's longest-serving prime minister, finally retired. He had moulded Canada into the social democracy we recognize today. The following year, Joey Smallwood brought Newfoundland into Confederation as Canada's tenth province. By 1950, the words "Dominion" and "British" (long a source of irritation to French Canadians) had been dropped from Commonwealth terminology and, in the patrician Vincent Massey, Canada had its first Canadian-born governor general.

By mid-century, Canada had emerged as a nation with its own culture and character. In the previous fifty years, the population had doubled to over 14 million (largely because of natural increase rather than immigration), and most young Canadians now had little sense of loyalty to a distant "home country." First Nations continued to live on the neglected margins of society, but groups such as the Ukrainians and the Greeks, who had immigrated before the Second World War, had been absorbed into the mainstream. There was a new pride in nationality which emerges in many of the letters from Canadians abroad. Young Arthur Wilkinson, writing proudly to his mother in Ottawa after Canadians had played a pivotal role in the disastrous 1942 Dieppe raid, noted how "the Limey's attitude towards the Canucks seems to have changed considerably. They were tops in the raid and did their job well."

The sweet innocence of 1900 had evaporated by the time Canadians heard that an atomic bomb had been dropped on Hiroshima in 1945. "From false fears good Lord deliver us," wrote a shaken Canadian diplomat, Escott Reid. Yet a bracing self-confidence was visible in the arts, in sport, and in attitudes to the rest of the world. Canada enjoyed economic and industrial momentum and was now ready to flex international muscle. A generation of diplomats, seasoned by war experiences, were eager for the country to participate in multilateral initiatives and institutions. They were prepared, in Escott Reid's words, to write "notes on the pages of history."

The country emerged strengthened from the shadows of a British Empire now in rapid decline. The 1945 federal election revealed that an increasingly urban populace had embraced a new, less naive confidence—a belief that government would look after its citizens. And as the shadow of war receded, the characteristic Canadian delight in the ridiculous re-emerged. Who can resist the picture of the nun flying down a hill on skis, as described by Nathalie in a letter written in 1949 in Quebec: "When she was coming down, the wind filled out her cloak and she looked like the superman we saw the other day at the movies"! The incongruous clash of nineteenth- and twentieth-century images in this description captures both the past and the future of a mature nation prepared for a post-war world.

98
1900: BRITISH COLUMBIA
MALI TO THE MAGAZINE *ALL HALLOWS IN THE WEST* IN YALE

All Hallows School, founded in Yale, British Columbia, in 1888 by Anglican nuns, was an unusual institution: alongside its white students were thirty-five Indian girls, sent (in the words of one of these girls) "to learn white people's ways." A young woman called Mali, who attended the school from 1885 to 1897, recorded her own difficulty in reconciling the two cultures in a letter published in the school magazine. The federal government had banned the elaborate Northwest Coast Indian feasts known as potlatches, which involved days of feasting, dancing, and gift-giving, in 1884, as part of a deliberate campaign to suppress aboriginal culture. Mali, who respected both Christian and traditional beliefs, challenged the government's policy.

1900

Dear Sisters,

After an absence of many years, I went back to live among my people for a few months, and I saw again some of their customs which must appear to white people as very strange, and sometimes very wrong—but I think it is because they do not understand.

The Potlatch is always one of our chief affairs. It is our way of paying for the burial of our dead. The Indians would not think it honouring the dead, just to pay in money the people who help to bury their dead, just the same as they pay the people who build their house. That is a common way, but to pay for a funeral they have to save for years, and the workers are willing to wait for *long* time, years and years, to be paid in what we think the right way. I think you would call it etiquette, and the Indians are very particular about it.

The Potlatch and the Indian dance always go together, and they are always held about the fall of year . . . I will try and tell you in a few words about the Indian dance. It is not full like the white peoples' dance, it is always rather mournful and makes you feel inclined to cry. The dance I went to this Fall was given by Chief Sam. It was a big affair, but he had his son Peter and his daughter Mary to help him. He had a large number of friends from North Bend, and Spuzzum, and all the Yale people, and some from the Lower Fraser too.

The guests were all comfortably settled in old Tom's big house. Poor Tom can no longer see, but it is astonishing how he went about talking to his dear "tillicums," and knowing almost everyone around him. So Tom entertained them until supper time. Chief Sam would often come in and tell his guests, in a long speech, how glad he was to see them, and thank them for coming, because he knew they had come a long way from their homes to comfort him. You see it was something like a funeral feast, although Chief Sam's wife died nearly nine years ago. The funny part was that Sam could only talk in Yale Indian, and a great many of his friends were Thompson and they could not understand, but they knew he meant something kind.

When supper was over the dance began, first some planks were put round the room in front of the people who were sitting on the ground, and then small sticks were given to them. There was no kind of music but every one just beat time, who knew how, to the dance and every one who could sing the dancer's song joined in it, but if any one made a mistake in beating time, that offended the dancers. The first one who danced at this party was an old woman, and she began moving slowly, waving her arms about to the time of the beating sticks, and the singing and all was so mournful. Then it got a little louder and faster, and then louder and faster still, but altogether in time, singing, beating and dancing. When the old woman got tired, someone else began, and so on till all had their turn. I do not mean everyone danced, only those who knew how, and they were mostly the very old people. Old Tom, blind as he is, danced as good as ever, better even than the others. One man danced too much, he danced until he could not stand, he was like a naughty child wanting sweets and not knowing when he had had enough, but no one else did that I am glad to say. It was very late when everyone went to sleep. The next day there was nothing done, but dancing and singing and beating time began in the evening.

And it was that second evening, Chief Sam and his sons piled blankets and Indian-made blankets in a heap in the middle of the room, and the real business of the potlatch began. All those who had helped to bury Sam's wife, and his brother's wife and child had to receive first. Tom made a speech explaining everything, then one by one each blanket was lifted up and given to the person it was intended for. After Sam's *debt* was paid, what was left was given away to other people. Sam's potlatch was not a very grand one, because he is an old man and poor, but everyone got something, either in money or strips of Indian-made blanket, no guest went away empty-handed and he was glad, he said, that nothing went wrong, no gambling or drinking until they fell ill.

Though the dancing and the song is so sad it always makes the people cry, and sometimes become hysterical. It is not that the dance is wrong, but the people have to learn self-control.

Formerly the Indians used to go and dig up their dead and wrap them round in new blankets to keep them warm. But now the Government does not let them do like that, and being Christians they begin to understand slowly that they must leave their dead undisturbed, and in God's care until the Resurrection Day.

Potlatch is an old custom, and I do not think the Indians will ever give it up. But it is changing in some ways, and people are not so extravagant as they used to be in giving them. It is a very solemn kind of meeting of the living, in memory of the dead.

There is someone at home who is thinking of having a small potlatch for his little son, who died a long time ago. I think if some of our friends, I mean our *real* white friends like the Sisters, and Miss Moody would come, they would see for themselves: you cannot understand unless you see, and the Indians would be so glad, and there would be a chance to teach them more to be good Indians and Christians too, and not what they often feel, that to be Christians they must leave off being Indians and try to be like white people, giving up even what is harmless in their old customs.

Mali

All Hallows School, with its rare effort to educate natives and non-natives under one roof, was closed in 1920. The ban on potlatches remained in place until 1951.

99

1900: YUKON

WILLIAM OGILVIE, COMMISSIONER OF YUKON TERRITORY, TO CLIFFORD SIFTON, MINISTER OF THE INTERIOR, IN OTTAWA

When is an "evil" a "necessary evil"? In 1896, the discovery of gold in Bonanza Creek, a tributary of the Klondike River, jump-started the Klondike gold rush and gave birth to the city of Dawson. By 1900, Dawson was the largest city west of Winnipeg, with a population of more than 40,000, and a reputation for "yellow liquor, green cloth and women in red." A flood of complaints about Dawson's dance halls and gambling houses reached Clifford Sifton, Ottawa's minister of the interior. Sifton promptly instructed the Yukon's governing council to shut down these dens of iniquity. I particularly enjoy the way that Commissioner William Ogilvie, a consummate bureaucrat, imparts some surreptitious education about the realities of Yukon life to his minister in Ottawa.

The officers and men in the Yukon division of the North-West Mounted Police had their hands full imposing law and order in the Klondike.

Sept. 12th, 1900.

Sir,

I beg to acknowledge the receipt of your letter of the 14th of August informing me that you had decided to suppress gambling and dance halls in
Dawson. Major Wood informed me that he had received a letter from you
on that matter, and he and I will hold a formal discussion on the question
as soon as possible and decide what steps we will take.

I desire to point out to you that this question has been seriously thought
over by the members of the Council individually and collectively in
Council. At first each one of us thought, and, I may say, were strongly of the
opinion that these vices should be stamped out; but after a sojourn in the
country, and after devoting much attention and consideration to it, it was
deemed best to allow it to go on as it was; and I may say that the members
of Council are still of that opinion.

Today, it may be said, that all the gambling in Dawson is done in the gambling halls, openly and subject to the observation of anyone and everyone:
consequently what the miners call a square game is generally played. It was
felt to be absolutely certain that if open gambling was suppressed, the gam-
blers would resort to secret methods, and the result would be much worse
than the present system.

It may be accepted as an axiom that a great many men in mining camps,
as well as elsewhere, will gamble. Now, very often, they resort to the gambling table in an intoxicated condition, and it is self apparent that men in
that condition stand a much better shew for fair play, than they would have
in a secret den. It is held as something beyond doubt in the minds of all
the members of the Council, and the public generally here (that is, the
practical public who are unprejudiced in any way in discussing such questions) that the vice would be very much worse practised secretly, and
would be a great deal more trouble to the authorities and involve much
more loss to the public, than openly. For this reason, it was not stopped.

Again, with reference to the dance halls and dance hall girls: dance halls
are an evil, which no-one attempts to gainsay; but at the same time they are
like many other evils, considered absolutely necessary under certain conditions. To abolish them would be to throw a lot of women into a more vicious
life, as many of these women would not resort to ordinary prostitution but
would be leeches on the general mining public.

Box rustling, as it is called here, that is dance hall girls and theatre girls
selling liquor in the boxes, has often been discussed, with a view to its

suppression, but no decisive step was taken, as it could not be very well seen what could be done to suppress it entirely. As long as human nature is what it is, this evil will exist in some form or another, and no legislation can be enacted which will abolish it. I say this with regret, as, personally, I would like to be able to say that no such vices existed in the Yukon Territory. I believe that I am voicing the views and sentiments of the majority of people—that is, practical people—both in the Council and generally, in making these remarks.

As gambling has been permitted in the past and considerable expenditure has been gone to in connection with it, it would be unfair to suppress it immediately; consequently the matter will be well ventilated, and the public generally will understand that its existence is limited, so that those who have invested capital in it will be in a position to withdraw without serious loss. I think this attitude is only fair and just.

"The Belgian Queen" was one of the gold miners' favourite dance hall girls.

> Your obedient servant,
> William Ogilvie
> Commissioner.

Within a couple of years, most of the dance halls and gambling dens had closed without any action from Ogilvie. Prospectors had moved on to the newly discovered gold deposits in Alaska.

100

1901: MANITOBA
WINSTON CHURCHILL TO HIS MOTHER,
LADY RANDOLPH CHURCHILL, IN ENGLAND

Canadians had rarely seen or heard a more dashing and captivating speaker than twenty-seven-year-old Winston Churchill. The British MP for the Lancashire riding of Oldham had caused a sensation in South Africa by his derring-do as both a reporter and a serving officer. He then crossed the Atlantic to cash in on his celebrity status with a North American lecture tour on the Boer War. The tour netted him £1,600— the equivalent today of about $200,000. By far the warmest reception he received came in Winnipeg.

22 January 1901,
Winnipeg

My dearest Mamma,

Your letter and some rubbish in the American newspapers alarmed me a good deal with the prospect of another general election and another battle at Oldham which I really do not think I should . . . have had the strength to fight. Your cable and one at the same time from Captain Middleton reassured me that there would not necessarily be a Dissolution.

So the Queen is dead. The news reached us at Winnipeg and this city far away among the snows, fourteen hundred miles from any British town of importance began to hang its head and hoist half-masted flags. A great and solemn event: but I am curious to know about the King. Will it entirely revolutionise his way of life? Will he sell his horses and scatter his Jews or will Reuben Sassoon be enshrined among the crown jewels and other regalia? Will he become desperately serious? Will he continue to be friendly to you? Will the Keppel [Alice Keppel, the new king's mistress] be appointed 1st Lady of the Bedchamber? Write to tell me all about this to Queenstown. (SS *Etruria* leaving New York on the 2nd prox.)

I contemplated sending a letter of condolence and congratulations mixed, but I am uncertain how to address it and also whether such procedure would be etiquette. You must tell me. I am most interested and feel rather vulgar about the matter. I should like to know an Emperor and a King. Edward the VIIth—gadzooks what a long way that seems to take one back! I am glad he has got his innings at last, and am most interested to watch how he plays it.

I have had a most successful meeting at Winnipeg. Fancy 20 years ago there were only a few mud huts—tents: and last night a magnificent audience of men in evening dress & ladies half out of it, filled a fine opera house and we took $ 1,150 at the doors. 1,230 [people]: more that is to say than in cities like Newcastle. Winnipeg has a wonderful future before it. At the back of the town there is a large wheat field 980 miles long & 230 broad—not all culti-vated yet, but which will some [sic] feed the whole of the British Isles. I called the town "Great Britain's Breadspot", at which they purred. They are furiously British and a visit to them is most exhilarating. But of course you must have passed through on your last journey round the world . . .

> Always your loving son
> Winston

PS. I have been reading "An English Woman's Love Letters". Are all Mothers the same?

Please send letters and complete files of papers—*Times, Spectator, Saturday Speaker, Punch* etc to Queenstown to meet me.

Most Canadians were shaken by the death of the only monarch they had ever known. In Toronto, there was such a stampede into fashionable mourning that Eaton's ran out of ladies' black gloves. The future British prime minister visited Canada frequently. In 1929, he wrote to his wife, Clementine: "Never in my whole life have I been welcomed with so much genuine interest & admiration as throughout this vast country."

101
1902: SOUTH AFRICA
BERTIE LECKIE TO HIS SISTER ALICE LECKIE IN ENGLAND

English Canadians had never felt closer to the "old country" than when Britain declared war on the Afrikaners in South Africa in 1899, and they were given the chance to rally to the imperial cause. This was Canada's first major overseas adventure, but the boys sailed off under the Union Jack. Among the 8,000 volunteers who went to fight the Boers were the two Leckie brothers, Jack and Bertie, born in Nova Scotia, who spent a year with Lord Strathcona's Horse. After a brief respite in Canada, they returned enthusiastically to South Africa with the 2nd Canadian Mounted Rifles. Both had been struggling to survive as prospectors in British Columbia and found life in uniform a welcome change.

Western Squadron, 2nd CMR
Newcastle, S. Africa,
March 2

My dear Alice

Here we are at the front with the rest of the regiment which had gone ahead of our squadron. As I told you we did not land at Capetown, but sailed the same day for Durban, arriving there the evening of the 25th. We lay at anchor off the port that night and went into the harbour the next morning, and immediately commenced entraining the horses and troops for Newcastle. We left in four trains of which Jack had charge of one and I of another.

It was awfully slow travelling as they side-tracked us for any other kind of train. We saw nothing of Durban scarcely, as we had to work hard until the troops were aboard the train. It was a fearfully hot day. The night on the train however was cool. My train left at about seven p.m. and we break-fasted at Pietermaritzburg about 5 a.m. next morning. We caught up with the trains ahead of us at Mooi River and spent some hours there taking the horses out and feeding and watering them. It was interesting there as it was

Bert Leckie enjoyed life on the dusty veld, since the camps were well organized and the "grub . . . A-1."

the furthest south the Boers ever got in Natal. At Estcourt we crossed a trainload of Boer prisoners (369 I think) recently captured in the Free State. They were mostly an ugly lot. I had quite a chat with some of them. One was the Adjutant of General Viljoen [who had recently been captured] and he was anxious to know where the General had been sent. He seemed a nice young chap. I gave him cigarettes and cigars to some of the others. They were travelling in open trucks but were well fed and well looked after. Our train was drawn up alongside of theirs and it was strange to see the Canadians handing them their rations from the car windows, and shaking hands when they said good-bye as the train moved out.

The men all sleep with rifles beside them, and bandoliers at the heads so as to rush out in case of night attack . . . Yesterday the [Eastern Squadron of the 2nd Canadian Mounted Rifles was] driving about 400 Boers right in our direction and [was] going to call us out; but a regiment was sent out from town to intercept them, and the Boers all surrendered. It was a good haul and it was hard luck we were not in it considering it was so close. Botha with 1400 men is supposed to be across the hills to the East from us, and these were on their way to join him. It was stated last night that seven hussars were killed very near to us who were out exercising their horses without being armed. We do not stir from camp without arms. Things are in pretty good shape however just now, and the blockhouse [concentration camp] system is working to perfection. Old Timers think fighting will be over in a few months.

We and our horses will probably remain here in camp before going on a trek for a week, and then we will probably join some column. This is a very healthy place and Jack and I are feeling very fit at present. Although we have rain occasionally the weather has been very fine. Natal all through is the finest country I have ever seen as far as appearances go . . .

Jack and I are both in splendid health. This country and life appears to agree with us both. I am heavier now than I ever was. Our grub for men and officers is A-1. Mail goes out today so no more at present.

> Your loving brother
> Bertie

The Canadian troops distinguished themselves in hostilities: their tenacity and stamina proved a match for the Afrikaners' unorthodox guerrilla tactics. But the final few months of the war were a dismal grind, and both Leckies contracted enteric fever. They were relieved to return to Canada, and their mining ambitions, by the end of the year.

102

1904: NOVA SCOTIA
ANNIE BURBIDGE TO ELLA LATHROP

In the early twentieth century, marriage was not simply a stage in a young woman's life: it was the most desirable state and her whole future. When twenty-year-old Annie Burbidge became engaged to Jack D. Clark, she abandoned her teaching career and devoted herself to acquiring a trousseau and preparing for a partnership in which Jack (who had already rented a large, furnished home without consulting her) would make all the decisions.

Morris St. School
Halifax, N.S.
Jan. 25th 04

Dear Ella,

I know you are waiting to hear all about my preparations for the eleventh. I do wish you could be here for it, only two weeks and a few days more—I have to teach until the Friday before. Isn't that cruel?

Where shall I begin? With my "trousseau" I suppose. I haven't very much but [what] I have I think is pretty good.

Mother made all my underwear and I wouldn't exchange them for the best ready-made. There is a lot of work in everything and the material is all of best. Am I boasting? I don't mean to, I want you to have as correct an idea of everything as possible.

I will send you a sample of everything I have, in the dress line, except my tailor-made suit. I was not fortunate enough to be able to get any from the tailor . . . My wedding dress is not finished; it is white silk with chiffon yoke and under sleeves. I have a pretty green dress, trimmed with reside silk yolk covered with lace; a broad silk girdle and long cuffs of silk and lace . . . With this dress I have a grey hat, trimmed with silk the same shade and a egret (Is that correct?) My every day suit is blue (Norfolk style) and I have a dark grey hat trimmed with red velvet.

I wonder if you would care about seeing the plan, as Jack sent it, of our house. I will copy it exactly as he gave it to me. You knew that he had rented a house furnished.

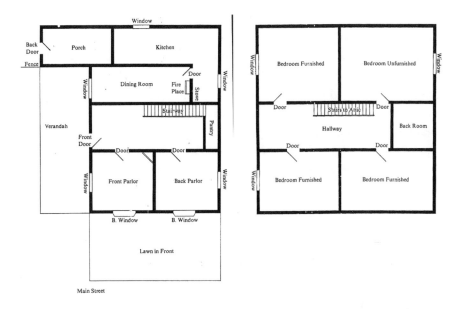

This is as Jack sent me. I expect this corner room has a window in it; but when you come to Kentville you can see for yourself. Of course I have no idea of the proportions.

Are you not tired of hearing all about wedding? My next letter will probably be written under different circumstances. I cannot realize it yet; it seems as if the preparations were all for somebody else.

Sincerely yours,
A. Winnifred Burbidge

103
1906: WESTERN CANADA
"BIG MIKE" TO *WESTERN HOME MONTHLY* IN WINNIPEG

A continuing concern in the west was the shortage of potential wives; according to a 1910 government pamphlet, "there are three male immigrant arrivals to every female arrival." Big Mike decided to take his problem to the correspondence column of the Winnipeg Western Home Monthly, *where rural women recorded their own isolation and lack of traditional support and family networks.*

August 1906

Editor:

I would like to correspond with some of the fair writers in the *Western Home Monthly*. I am young, temperate, a member of Christ's church, have a half section of land, good horses and cattle. I would like to have a good strong woman for wife who would milk cows and feed calves, and raise plenty of fowl and keep a good garden.

Big Mike

104
1907: MANITOBA
JACOB PENNER TO HIS FAMILY IN RUSSIA

"Stalwart peasants in sheepskin coats" flooded into western Canada from eastern and central Europe, in response to the vigorous promotion of immigration by Clifford Sifton, interior minister in Wilfrid Laurier's government. Among those arriving from Russia in 1905 was Jacob Penner, a Mennonite teacher who had been involved with the Russian Social Democratic Party, along with his parents and family. In his early years in the west, Penner used "America" and "Canada" interchangeably and was ambivalent about the New World's charms.

702 Sherbrooke Str.,
Winnipeg, Canada,
23 February 1907

Dear N. N.

In our first winter here I wrote you a letter, but as you know, it was lost. That I haven't written until now is due to the fact that from the beginning I was not well here, and people in such a frame of mind don't communicate easily. I became ill very soon in America. This cancelled all of my plans, since I did not intend to stay in America. Even now I would not hesitate for a moment and return if I were well.

But I do not want to say that America has made only a bad impression on me. On the contrary, we have experienced during our time here that America has many good sides, but we have a hard time adjusting to the new circumstances, customs and views—indeed, to Americanism. This is not a simple matter, as one might think, and we see it in the immigrants who arrive here as adults and for the rest of their lives feel strange here. It would be the same for Americans in Europe. I believe that one does not value one's fatherland until one is in a strange land, and that is our situation now. We often long for our homeland, and yet our parents and siblings are happy that we are here. In material terms it is better for us here, compared with the last ten years in Russia.

We all have positions now and are earning well. In the last while I too have felt better, now that I have employment again. I am working in an office belonging to two doctors; I keep the books and correspondence and answer the telephone. It seems as though the telephone will do away with the writing of letters, like the telegraph. Almost everything is now done by these means. Long-distance has been perfected here to the point that one can be understood to a distance of 1000 miles, and Winnipeg is now connected with all important centres within 1000 miles by telephone.

We are now in the deepest winter here . . . We are still having a difficult time adjusting to the climate here in Canada. It is said of Canada that there are 13 months of winter in a year. In any case, the farmers can only begin seeding after May 1, and are busy with this into June. The winter weather is very steady; when the cold weather arrives it remains cold until spring. A midwinter thaw never occurs here, so one can never use a wagon in winter. There is a thick snow covering 4 feet at present. But what makes the cold bearable is the dryness of the winter. There is mostly bright sunshine and for this reason the cold is not as noticeable as in regions where the winter is humid.

The summer too does not have much pleasantness. Either it is uncomfortably cool or so terribly hot that we from Russia are not used to it. And then the mosquitoes! It is hard to describe what a pestilence they are. Doors and windows must all be covered with screening in the summer, otherwise one cannot survive. To take a walk in the woods during the mosquito season means to return with thickly swollen hands and face.

Fruit trees do not flourish in the Province of Manitoba, but on the coasts there are very good gardens. Because one cannot plant gardens here the life of a farmer is not attractive to us Russlanders. In addition there is the loneliness of farm life here; since there are no villages, every farmer lives on his farm and since the farms are at least a half-mile apart, but often 2 to 3 miles, there is no sociability. All this together makes for the fact that we are not interested in moving out of the city, although land may be had for the asking.

As far as the growing of grain is concerned, it is hard to imagine a better place for it than Canada. Here the best wheat in America is grown, and in addition, there are no crop failures here. If grain had better prices the farmers would become very rich, but the price is always very low.

Taken all in all, the life of a German farmer in Russia is immeasurably better than that of the American farmer. The latter would never admit this, but it is true. First of all, there is the village life, compared with the loneliness of the farm, and secondly the beautiful gardens which one can have in South Russia. Here people on the land can only plant forest trees and wild cherry bushes. It is said that in America all the work is done by machines. This is true in part, but not for the farmer. His machines and tools may be more advanced than those in Russia, but he still must work like an ox all his life. Not every farmer can afford hired help; it is too costly and too hard to find. Even well-to-do farmers only take on help for a few months during harvest, and then they have to pay 2 to 3 dollars a day in wages. It is also necessary to be very quick with this work since the summer is very short . . .

For the workers [in cities], conditions are significantly better than in Europe. No one need be unemployed here and work is well paid. The average daily wage is two dollars for general work. Tradesmen do especially well here. The proverb: "the trades have a golden floor" is true here in the fullest sense. Tradesmen work nine hours a day and earn the following: carpenters 3.5 to 4 dollars, painters and decorators 4 to 4.5 dollars, blacksmiths and locksmiths 5 dollars and bricklayers 5 to 7.5 dollars.

Commerce and industry are also doing very well here. The American is a very clever businessman and very energetic. Even the Jews are behind the spiffy Yankees in business matters and it seems as though they will not do well in America. This [flourishing] situation is due to the general prosperity of the people. Doubtless, the industry and commerce in Russia would do well also if the 80 or 90 million peasants were as well off as the average American.

Our city of Winnipeg is rising with American speed. Ten years ago Winnipeg had 30,000 residents and now there are 120,000. Every year buildings worth more than twelve million dollars are built here, and the city administration spends huge amounts every year for improvements and beautification of the city. So now most of its streets are paved with asphalt. A number of gigantic American firms have been established [such as the huge Eaton's store] . . . I scarcely believe that Moscow or Petersburg has anything like that. In this store, 1200 persons are employed. Of these 700

are salespersons, 150 are office personnel, cashiers, etc., 100 who unpack
and pack the goods and 80 who deliver them. Goods that are bought here
are delivered to one's home; one needn't take anything along, even if it is
small. Apart from these employees another hundred or more look after various other tasks. The whole business is run with gigantic machines, powerful enough to run a large factory. They power the various installations in the
store, like the elevators, which lift the customers from one floor to the next.
No one walks up the stairs anymore. These machines also generate the
electricity to light and heat the building, as well as the compressed air
which moves the money to the cash registers. Every salesperson has a pipe
nearby which leads to the cash registers. The money is put into a box by the
customer and pushed into the tube, upon which the compressed air, which
is constantly in the pipes, quickly moves the box to the cashier, whereupon
a receipt is rapidly sent back by another pipe. Such a business could not
possibly exist in a large city in Russia, but here it does very well. The number of customers is also very great. From morning till evening all six floors
are full, so that one can sometimes hardly make one's way through them
and it becomes a little unpleasant.

A superficial observer will at first be of the opinion that America is a
very happy land, but when one becomes familiar with the circumstances
and looks more closely, it is apparent that there are still many negative
aspects. First of all, life here is very expensive; food and clothing are two
and three times as much as in Russia . . . Especially unpleasant in this land
are the impossibly high railroad ticket prices. For example, the [journey]
from Ekaterinoslav to Petersburg cost only 12 rubles. Here the same distance costs 65 rubles. On the positive side, the coaches are not divided into
classes here. There is only one coach type and the worker is as comfortable as the capitalist. This comfort is limited to the railroad coach though,
because in the circumstances of ordinary life the capitalist is as privileged
by fate as elsewhere in the world. Or perhaps even more, since when one
speaks of the darker aspects of American life then the first thing to mention is the incredible power of the organisations of the capitalists, the so-
called trusts. These trusts are truly the despots and tyrants of America, and
one can scarcely imagine the harmful effect that they have on the whole
of life. Here money has the greatest power, and since the trusts have most
of the money, they can do as they please—and their pleasure is selfish . . .
At first I was very surprised that the American people would stand for that,
but when one gets to know the Yankee soul a little better, then one realizes

that every American has the quiet hope of one day becoming a member of a trust.

The American has another characteristic expressed in the saying: Help yourself. Everyone who cannot help himself cannot survive. It is because of this that there is so much blameless unhappiness in this country. The battle for one's existence is carried out with incredible intensity, or, as I would call it, with a bestial ruthlessness. He who is clever and less choosy in his methods in achieving his goals will usually have great success, and the weaker one succumbs or collapses completely. But this is the case elsewhere as well, and if one considers the relationship of people to each other, one finds that they are like a chaotic virgin forest, where the mighty giant trees stretching to great heights, take all the room and sunshine for themselves, while beneath them innumerable small trees and bushes carry on a bare existence. But if our institutions were built on rational foundations our life would be like a garden in which every tree would have equal space and sunshine.

Jacob Penner.

Jacob Penner was active in the Winnipeg General Strike of 1919, and in 1921 he became a founding member of the Communist Party of Canada. From 1934 until 1961, he served almost continually as alderman for the North End on Winnipeg City Council.

105
1907: PRINCE EDWARD ISLAND
LUCY MAUD MONTGOMERY TO EPHRAIM WEBER IN ALBERTA

We all know that Lucy Maud Montgomery was a gifted fiction writer, but I find her letters even more enthralling than the Green Gables books. In rural Prince Edward Island, the thirty-two-year-old's career as an author had not yet begun, but she was polishing her skills in correspondence. One of her correspondents, whom she had met through a mutual friend in 1902, was Ephraim Weber, a homesteader in Alberta. Her letters to Ephraim were an important creative outlet for Maud, who had reluctantly abandoned her ambitions to be a teacher in order to care for an elderly grandmother in the family home in Cavendish. In 1907, she could not wait to share some important news . . .

Cavendish, P.E.I.,
Thursday,
May 2, 1907.

My dear Mr. W.,

We are just in the middle of housecleaning! I fear that statement will be more or less wasted on a mere *man*. If it were made to a woman she would appreciate the compliment of my sitting down to write her after a day of it. For the past four days I've been scrubbing and whitewashing and digging out old corners and I feel as if all the dust I've stirred up and swept out and washed off has got into my soul and settled there and will remain there forever, making it hopelessly black and grimy and unwholesome. Of course I *know* it won't but knowing is such a different thing from *believing*.

Well, I must simply tell you my *great news* right off! To pretend indifference and try to answer your letter first would be an affectation of which I shall not be guilty. I am blatantly pleased and proud and happy and I shan't make any pretence of not being so.

Well, last fall and winter I went to work and wrote a book. I didn't squeak a word to anyone about it because I feared desperately I wouldn't find a publisher for it. When I got it finished and typewritten I sent it to the L. C. Page Co. of Boston and a fortnight ago, after two months of suspense, I got a letter from them accepting my book and offering to publish it on the 10-per cent royalty basis!

Don't stick up your ears now, imagining that the great Canadian novel has been written at last. Nothing of the sort. It is merely a juvenilish story, ostensibly for girls; [but] as I found the MS. rather interesting while reading it over lately I am not without hope that grown-ups may like it a little. Its title is *Anne of Green Gables* and the publishers seem to think it will succeed as they want me to go right to work on a sequel to it. I don't know whether I can do that and make it worth while however.

The Page Co. is a good company. Not one of the topnotchers, of course, such as Harpers or Macmillans: but it has published several successful books by well-known authors, including Charles G. D. Roberts and Bliss Carman.

I signed the contract today; it is a fearsomely legal looking document all red seals and "saids" and "whereases." There is only one clause in it I don't altogether like. I have to bind myself to give them the refusal of all the books I may write for the next five years. The insertion of such a clause is rather complimentary, I suppose, but I'd rather not have to agree to it. However, I've done so and the rest is on the knees of the gods. I don't suppose the book will be out before the fall.

While I'm on the "trade" subject I might as well finish with it. I've had several successes lately; formerly I would have been delighted over them but now they are quite cast in the shade by my big fish.

The *Housekeeper*, Minneapolis, have accepted [a] 20,000 word serial. I am to be paid the tenth of May. Don't know what I will get but they pay well for short stories. I want you to see this story but it won't be out till next year and they want my photo to publish in their prospectus! Ha-hum!

The *Home Magazine*, Indianapolis, published by the Reader Co., recently accepted a short story to be paid for on publication. This is a new place for me.

The *Blue Book*, Chicago, paid $20 for a short story. The editor also asked me to write a 12,000 word serial of mystery and adventure but I told him I couldn't. I haven't the knack of such stories so it's no use my wasting time over them.

I got my check—for $35—from *Gunters* at last. They have another of my stories in their April number and I presume I shall have a hard time to get my cash also. I don't intend to send them any more.

There, that's enough about *me* and *my doings*. Now for your letter . . .

You ask if I am ever troubled with friends I like not liking each other. Yes and yes and *yes*! I should think I know all about it. It is terrible, isn't it? Sometimes my spirit fairly cringes within me at the horror of it. I have two friends in especial whom I love and who hate each other and we are all three constantly being thrown together and my friendship with each is more or less spoiled and embittered by their antagonism . . .

I congratulate you on discovering the—Bible! I did it a year ago, though and have been reading it—really, *reading* it—ever since; but as my rate of progression is slower than yours you will soon outstrip me. I can't get over much more than seven chapters a Sunday—I'm just beginning the Psalms now. It *is* a wonderful book—the crystallized wisdom and philosophy and experience of the most deeply religious people whoever existed. Could anything be more vital and truer to our own experience than this: "Hope deferred maketh the heart sick"? . . . When I was a child a school teacher gave me a whipping because I used the expression "by the skin of my teeth." He said it was slang. If I had but known then what I know now!! It is in *Job*—those very words. *Ruth* is a delightful thing: "Where thou goest I will go: thy people shall be my people and thy God my God: the Lord judge between us if aught but death part thee and me." Was ever the loving self-sacrifice and self-effacement of womanhood better or more exquisitely expressed? . . .

Fourteen pages isn't bad for a girl who has been housecleaning all day! I wonder if it's absolutely necessary to houseclean? I wonder if nine-tenths of the things we think so necessary really are so! But I shall go on house-cleaning and wondering! I may have given up belief in fore-ordination and election and the Virgin Birth; but I have not and never shall be guilty of the heresy of asserting that it is not vital to existence that the house should be torn up once a year and scrubbed! Perish the thought.

> Yours sincerely,
> L. M. Montgomery

106

1907: ONTARIO
JOHN DAVIS TO MAGGIE NICKLE DAVIS IN SMITHVILLE

In 1907, John Davis and his partner, George Mitchell, opened a law practice in a tent on the remote and muddy main street of Latchford, north of North Bay. Latchford was enjoying a boom thanks to the discovery of huge quantities of silver ore nearby. There were rich pickings for land speculators, but as John told his wife, it was far too rough a town for her and their four children (Helen, John, Maggie May, and Dewitt). Instead, Maggie remained in the family farm in Smithville, on the Niagara Peninsula, and once a month John travelled the 650 kilometres south to visit.

Davis & Mitchell
Barristers, Solicitors, Notaries etc.
Offices: Latchford, Cobalt and Haileybury
Latchford

May 5, 1907

My Dear Wife,

This is Sunday afternoon and I am going down to North Bay on the 8.15 train tonight so as to be ready for work tomorrow morning in North Bay. We get to the Bay at about 11 o'clock to night. I expect to stop at the Queen's Hotel while I am there. I expect to be engaged nearly all day at the Registry Office. Then I have to leave there at about 5 o'clock Tuesday morning so as to be at Haileybury to defend a man at 10 o'clock a.m. I will not stop off at Latchford on my way up from the Bay.

I have done considerable work this week but there has not been much cash in it. I have a stenographer now and pay her $5.00 per week. She will look after the office while I am away. I have written Mr. Adams to know when he will be ready to do the work [on the Smithville house in which Maggie was living] but have not received any word from him as yet. I intend to write to Mr. Joseph Martin for the address of another mason so that I can go on with the work should Mr. Adams not be able to do the work when we are ready for him. A poor fellow just came up from Bobcaygeon the other day and cut his foot the day after his arrival. He started for home on the next train accompanied by a doctor. Tonight another unfortunate goes down to Toronto for an operation for appendicitis should he last that long. Everybody has their own troubles and we should be thankful that ours are no greater than they are. Sometimes I get tired of being up here.

If we had our home paid for in the completed condition in which we hope to have it soon and had $1000 in cash besides, I think I would be in a condition to go to Welland for business with a branch office in Smithville. Things seem to be shaping that way at present. But you know we often are disappointed in our expectations. However we have very [little] reason to complain as we have accomplished very much of what we planned. I purchased a lot here for $200 from the Trustees of the Presbyterian church but I have not paid any money yet. I hope to collect sufficient funds from here for that purpose. The lot is number 226 of the townsite of Latchford. I own lot 123 of the Latchford townsite and will have the transfer in my own name after May 15. You may remember that I told you that I bought lots 123 & 141 for $200 and got $20 commission and sold lot 141 for $175. Of this amount $125 has been paid by Geo. Roberts. He is to pay the balance of $50 on the 15th of May. Then I will send away the $175 to D. E. Johnson, Ottawa. I hope to make a few more turns like that as they pay better than practicing law. I presume you have got the cheque for $18 in my other letter.

Well Maggie I was at church today but did not get much inspiration from the sermon. I can get a great deal more from the Bible itself. I hope the Smithville congregation get a good live preacher with a wife interested in all good work. I am still working on the text "He that will do His will shall know of the doctrine whether it be of God". I am surprised at the drinking, gambling and swearing there is among young men here. I should be very very sorry indeed to think that either John or Dewitt would ever do any of those things. I realize more than ever how important it is for a boy to go to Sunday school and learn to love and fear the God who made him. The psalmist says "The fear of the Lord is the beginning of wisdom." Out here I see men with their faces cut and bruised and bleeding staggering about the street slobbering, vomiting, cursing, and falling in the dirt and filth of other men and without any money to buy a meal all because they have spent it for drink.

They have so abused their minds that they cannot say no and have so abused their bodies that they are unfit for work.

A man or a woman or a boy or a girl is like a tree. Each year they grow into the physical and mental shape they are going to be—straight or crooked as the case may be. I hope John and Helen are doing their level best to pass their examinations and to grow strong in the right so that when they are grown they may be a power for good and able to say NO.

I trust this will find you all well and send kisses to you all.

Your affectionate husband,
J. S. Davis

107

1908: NOVA SCOTIA
WANDA WYATT TO HER FATHER, JAMES (NED) WYATT,
IN SUMMERSIDE, PRINCE EDWARD ISLAND

Wanda Wyatt was thirteen and her sister Dorothy fifteen when they were sent from their home in Summerside, Prince Edward Island, to the Edgehill School for Girls in Nova Scotia. Ned Wyatt and his wife, Cecelia Lefurgey, were determined their daughters should be well educated; since Ned was an MPP and travelled a great deal, it was also convenient for the girls to be at a boarding school. The family exchanged letters almost daily.

Edgehill, Windsor, N.S.
Sept. 13th 1908

Dear Papa

We received your welcome letter, *welcome indeed*, last night.

I am writing under a disadvantage being in a room with a lot of other girls who are certainly making a lot of noise.

We are getting acquainted with two or three girls. It is pretty lonesome but I guess we will be all right in a few weeks time.

There was one little girl we thought had run away last night at supper time on account of being lonesome and there was excitement for the time being but after a search she was said to have been found at the Station with another girl, so the story runs.

We had a nice bath last night and bathe our chests in the morning.

We had our clothes checked the night you left but have not as yet put our winter things back in trunk. The teacher who checked our clothes said she thought it would be more convenient for me to have another laundry bag, but I think that if we don't get our laundry bag back in time we might put our clothes in the one bag. Just as mother thinks though.

We took our entrance exam yesterday it was certainly easy all except the history which was just about right. The grammar was to give definition of a noun, adj., trans. verb, etc. Analyze "My little sister has large feet", & give the plural of man, tooth & knife. Arithmetic was L.C.M., multiplying sum, finding area of a floor, write in words _____, in figures _____. History, give some account of Jacques Cartier (Frenchman) or, William the Conqueror, or Elizabeth, or any English King.

We were put into form 3.C. We start Latin all over again in a different method & french we have to learn in a room behind. I think. I'm not sure. If we have to do the work a room ahead or the same room as our exam we certainly will be pretty far back. The French takes us back I guess . . .

Hard to know what the bells all mean but do what the other girls do, or ask some one.

We are both lonesome only wish you & mother were here but keep us well posted be sure.

Good Bye your loving daughter Wanda

108

1909: QUEBEC
LOIS SYBIL HARRINGTON TO EDWARD WINSLOW-SPRAGGE

One of the winter highlights of early twentieth-century Montreal was the elaborate castle constructed each year out of blocks of ice at Fletcher's Field, at the base of Mount Royal. Lois Harrington, granddaughter of McGill University's first principal, Sir William Dawson, was among the thousands who enjoyed the carnival atmosphere. A few days later, on her twentieth birthday, she described the outing to her fiancé, Edward Winslow-Spragge, a travelling salesman in western Canada.

Montreal
February 15, 1909

Dear Edward,

I'm feeling old enough to be your grandmother today—"old age creeps on apace"—I can scarcely imagine that my teens are gone forever and that now I am just twenty, not even sweet twenty or blushing twenty, merely plain twenty.

Thursday we went to see the storming of the ice palace, it was just great, you could see all the torch light procession winding in and out through the trees on the mountain before they got down to the palace. They have some wonderful effects with coloured lights—at one time they made the whole palace look like a stone castle and then they sent up fireworks with deep blue stars. You cannot imagine how pretty it looked. I never got into such a crowd in my life. The whole of Fletcher's Field was a seething mass; we were in the middle of it and simply could not move.

One little boy tried to shove his way right through Mother. She got mad and gave him a jab, and the kid yelled out at the top of his lungs. "Gee! That big fat lady gave me a poke in the ribs." Of course, everybody roared with laughter. The crowd certainly was fascinating. There were darkies, Chinamen, villains, McGill students, squeaking infants and respectable citizens (comme moi!).

Well, bon soir,
from Lois

109
1910: MANITOBA
WILLEM DE GELDER TO HIS FAMILY IN HOLLAND

This letter gives a rare insight into the life of an immigrant hired hand, who probably didn't speak the same language as his employer. Willem de Gelder, a young Dutchman, went to work for a prairie farmer named Burrill in Elgin, Manitoba, and found he had signed on for backbreaking work, uncertain wages, and winter unemployment. After several weeks on the farm, he described his loneliness and low morale to his family, back in the Netherlands.

Elgin,
28 August 1910

It's strange, but if the truth be told, I don't know the [Burrill family] a hair better than when I first came here. For that matter there's no time to make closer friendships or have a pleasant chat. The boss isn't as friendly as he formerly was. The whole family is oppressed by the bad harvest and the boss is often out of humour and dissatisfied. The bad harvest also has an effect on my pocketbook, the boss told me he couldn't give me more than $10 per month and couldn't keep me this winter. That was quite a disappointment for me because I had figured on $15. But maybe it isn't that bad if I can't stay here this winter, because if I stayed I couldn't earn much, perhaps not a cent. But if I work in a factory I will be able to earn the whole winter through.

The boss is dumb and he will stay that way; every day I see that he is dumber than I thought the day before. He lives in his own little world and knows nothing about what goes on outside it. The children don't go to school, as it is the custom in this neighbourhood not to send the children to school until they are 10 or 12 years old. They then stay in town the whole week and come home on Saturday and Sunday, and naturally they don't get any instruction now from pa or ma; "No Sir, too busy."

Elgin is a small town with 500 inhabitants, about as big as Linschoten, and it has *five* churches, an Anglican church, one Mennonite church, and three others. All have ministers with good incomes of a $1,000 or more dollars, the highest is probably $1,500 or $2,000. I don't know if the people go to church very often, but the boss went once when a new preacher came, mostly out of curiosity I think. When he came home he said he was a nice fellow and that he would probably get a good salary. Before meals the boss pinches his eyes shut and mumbles a short and unintelligible grace. The children cover their mouths with their hands, and after the grace, shout triumphantly that they have listened.

There's a hotel with a bar and supposedly quite a bit of drinking is done, mostly whiskey but also beer and "Holland Gin." In the winter, when there is nothing to do on the farm, the farmers and cowboys are in town all day long, and a lot of drinking is supposed to go on. The five preachers are busy trying to turn Elgin into a dry town, but it doesn't particularly meet with the approval of the citizenry, and for rather strange reasons. They are not opposed to it because it would curtail their drinking, but because the hotel-keeper would lose his livelihood. They can't understand why the preachers are so hostile to him when he is so "awfully good" to them. Every year he gives them each $50 in the collection plate. He also pays good wages to his help, the two bartenders each get $30 a month, and the two girls each get $20. Real American! The barkeeper makes tremendous money, and he is quite open and above board, and says that he made so much on such and such a day. For example, they had a plowing match in Elgin one day and he took in $1,500 over the bar.

They still haven't got a domestic help on the farm, they have been trying to get one, but there are none to be had even for $15 per month; it's enough to make a Dutch domestic's mouth water. The girls prefer the towns and cities where they can also earn good money.

Dinner is composed of a slice of pork sometimes boiled and sometimes fried, and some potatoes (boiled or fried), and bread and butter. Dessert is a dish of compote, mostly prunes, 3 to 7 in number, and everything is topped off with a cup of tea. Sometimes there are vegetables, but it's a real occasion if there are carrots or wax beans, they simply don't care for them. But even a dinner like that tastes marvelous when you've worked hard and only had a frugal breakfast in the morning. The potatoes which they grow here are generally much larger than in Holland, a potato as big as your fist is no curiosity. Disease is uncommon here because the ground is too dry, but potato bugs (a sort of caterpillar) are a scourge. If you don't watch out, they will eat all the leaves off the plant before you know it.

We've been very busy this week and the boss has been going at full speed. The work kept us occupied all last week and the first half of this one. The first couple of days the work really bothered me because the sharp wheat cut my hands and wrists and made small wounds. This was extremely painful, especially in the evenings after work, when the horses were rubbed down and the salty dust irritated my wounds. So I used my imagination; when I went to the field I put on a coat and gloves. That worked fine, however in two days I had mittens, because the fingers were totally worn off, but my fingers had slowly got used to the work anyway. You can see that you can get accustomed to anything.

Stooking the sheaves is pretty hard work, that is it gets heavy when you have to do it the whole day long, in a bare field under a blazing sun. When the grain is ripe you naturally have to cut it as quickly as possible, and every day saved means more bushels for harvesting. And because the boss doesn't want to increase the days it takes to harvest, he increases the length of the day; we begin an hour or an hour and a half earlier and finish two hours later. Just imagine it, up before dawn and finished after sunset. You have to make sure that the stooks are stacked firmly and can withstand a push, in this case a wind, because it can really blow here. Especially on warm days you get a calm, and then a cyclone comes along and upsets everything if it is not set firmly on its feet. Wednesday, this work was finished and we began bringing the sheaves in. The boss and I get the sheaves with a big wagon, and bring them to the yard, where we make big stacks. It's not easy to handle the sheaves with a fork, and lay them just so on the wagon, so that the kernels are towards the inside. This work will probably take two weeks, then a couple of days of threshing and my work will be done here.

The threshing is done mechanically. The boss doesn't own a thresher (one costs $3,000). Someone in Elgin has one, and he comes to the farms and threshes for so much a bushel, depending on how easy the grain is to thresh. A machine like that can thresh about 500 to 2,500 bushels per day. You begin threshing in the morning at 4:00 o'clock and finish about nine in the evening. All the ordinary chores of the morning have to be done before four, such as currying the horses, feeding, watering, and breakfast for ourselves. Those promise to be hard days, but never mind, they are only a few of these and after the threshing I will get a few days rest. I wrote a letter to the Salvation Army, asking them if they would write me and let me know if they had work for me here or there at about mid-September. I still haven't received an answer. Some days we skip dinner and only have breakfast and supper.

Will

The following year, de Gelder filed for his own homestead in Log Valley, thirty-two kilometres north of Morse, Saskatchewan. He farmed there until 1923, when he abruptly sold his property and disappeared.

110
1910: ALBERTA
MONICA HOPKINS TO HER FRIEND GILL IN AUSTRALIA

Monica Hopkins was the impetuous daughter of a Methodist minister in England. She surprised her parents and herself when she became betrothed to Billie, a young Irishman who eight years earlier had built a log cabin in the Alberta foothills. In preparation for married life in the Canadian west, Monica attended a domestic science college in Leeds, England, to learn how to launder, gloss, and iron her husband's dress shirt fronts and collars. Then her parents waved her goodbye as she and her new husband sailed away. The cheerful young housewife soon found that ironing was perhaps her least useful skill, as she and her Australian friend Helene learned the hard truths of ranching.

Enmore,
Priddis,
September 1910

Dearest Gill,

Have you ever ridden a workhorse with harness on instead of a saddle for
four miles over open range clad only in your nightdress, a dressing gown,
and a pair of sand shoes? It sounds like one of those nightmares where you
are being presented to Royalty dressed only in a vest! But I have done it and
only yesterday. You will be wondering what led up to this rather unusual riding costume so I had better start and tell you all about it . . .

Yesterday Joe [the hired man] went haying with Billie in the morning and
then went looking for some horses in the afternoon. About two hours after
they left Helene came rushing in to tell me that the stallion was hung up in
the barbed wire fence quite near the west gate. She had been down to the
mine but there was no one there. I [was sick in bed but] got into my dressing gown and some canvas shoes and we started off armed with an axe and
a pair of wire cutters. Heaven knows what we intended to do with them but
we couldn't get near the horse. He was simply crazed with fear and tore
himself worse than ever when we went near him. We didn't know what to
do but we realised he would bleed to death if we didn't get some one here,
so Helene said she would try and get the saddle horses in and in the meantime I would start off on foot to get the men. If Helene got the horses she
would catch me up and I could return to bed.

As we were right at the west gate a quarter of a mile on my way, I said I'd
go on and not return to the house for more clothes and started off as I was.
I was pretty wobbly at first, partly from weakness and partly from worrying
over the horse, but soon I got over my shakiness and was able to walk and
run in spurts. I kept looking back hoping to see Helene but there was no sign
of her. I crossed the creek by jumping from rock to rock and didn't get very
wet and at last reached the hillside where I expected to find them, only to
discover that they had finished there and moved on up the creek another
mile. I was getting pretty desperate and started to call the boys' names at the
top of my voice—"Billie-e-e-e", "Joe", "ah dam the country", "Billie-e-e-e"
went wailing up the valley.

I was told afterwards that Joe said to Billie that he thought he heard
someone calling. Billie replied that he heard a coyote howling somewhere
(the brute!). Another despairing yell of "Joe" and Joe said he would take his
horse and see if there was anyone calling. In the meantime I was so tired

that I just sat and wept and Joe nearly rode over me as he came galloping along. I told him what had happened and he raced back to tell Billie and then tore past me on his way home just shouting to me that Billie would be along with the team right away. I crawled under a bush to wait and must have slept for a moment for as I opened my eyes at the jingling of harness I saw Billie shoot past me on one of the team and leading the other, and disappear round a poplar bluff. I got up and started off again, only for home this time, and was wearily plodding along when I saw Billie coming back, wild eyed with the old team puffing and blowing. He had realized that he must have passed me somewhere. I took care that he didn't miss me this time!

He hoisted me up on Hetty's back and she seemed a mile wide. I tried sitting sideways on at first but slid off almost at once so we decided that astride was the only thing. Billie had to split my nighty up the side and with the dressing gown flapping and my pigtails waving in the breeze we started for home. In the meantime Joe had met Helene at the gate. She had had an awful time getting the horses and had at last corralled an Indian cayuse we have; she had saddled her up and was loping along when Joe arrived. When Helene had heard that Billie was bringing me back she returned with Joe to give what help she could.

When we reached home they had the stallion in the stable but he was still bleeding badly. He had cut the fetlocks right through to the bone. They made me go back to bed though I didn't want to and insisted on getting up for supper. I ate an enormous meal, the first for several days. That ride back must have joggled the chill out of me for today I'm feeling very fit, and the stud too is better. Billie thinks he may live now but his foot will always be crippled and unsound and of course his value has depreciated very much . . .

Tomorrow we have two boxes each of peaches and plums to preserve. I have never done anything of this sort before and I approach the experiment with alarm. I can't forget that I have been used to paying three pence for a single peach and I haven't yet got used to having them by the dozens and eating them as if they are as common as cherries at home. I have still much to learn but I can't help feeling a little proud of myself that I have come through the first year of my life here without making any very big mistakes, or making Billie ashamed of me.

It is amazing to think that I have actually been here a year. The months have simply scampered past. Sometimes I feel that I am just holidaying here and it won't be long before I am back in England again. Other times I feel as though I have been here all my life and the past [is] just a dream. I can't help smiling when I look back and think how absolutely "green" I was. The new life that I had taken on so cheerfully was so entirely different from anything I had ever experienced before. As you know I had lived the normal life of a minister's daughter, not by any means a model minister's daughter I regret to say. I had lived in several of the largest English cities and had often stayed in the country with friends who had farms, but nothing had prepared me for the difference in every way that I am finding out here . . .

I have loved every minute of it. So many interesting things have happened. I have met some very nice people, all sorts and conditions, and found them all very kind and often very helpful in advising a rather bewildered English woman in the ways of her adopted country. By now I realise that this is essentially a man's country and that a woman has to practically sink her own identity and take on her husband's interests. For a woman to come out here and by "here" I mean isolated places such as this and not like country life would be fatal. It would be impossible for any woman to fill up her days doing housework, for in 99 percent of the houses here the necessary work can be done in a few hours daily. In many it can be done in much less than that, so that she would have many hours on her hands that she would find hard to fill. Books and sewing help out but more than that is needed and you can't be out riding and visiting every day so that interest in her husband's pursuits is absolutely necessary. Another thing I have found out is that it is useless grousing over the inevitable. So many unexpected things turn up you might as well meet them with a smile. It makes life so much more pleasant all around. If you treat life as a joke and not take it too seriously then you'll be happy here. If you don't, then Heaven help you, for no one else can.

I think the thing that I found most trying was the unexpected visitor. It nearly always happened on the days that we had got down to the far end of the joint and were making do with odds and ends. Usually when we were finishing the little we had, the dogs would start barking and some one would announce that a rider, or riders, were coming. Billie would go to the door and shout "Put your horses in the stable and come and have a meal." I would scuttle around and feel fearfully ashamed if I couldn't put up a good meal on the best china and silver, but now I'm hardened and just add an extra cup and saucer and plate and let the visitors take "pot luck" along with us. If there is nothing else they get bread and cheese and the familiar four pound tin of jam put before them.

I entertained a French count two weeks after I arrived here and all we had was six eggs, the heel of a loaf of bread, and some rock buns. There was nothing else in the house . . . When Billie came and told me of our visitor and when I heard whom it was I felt dreadful. However the count was very charming. He told me, "In France I am a count, but in Canada I'm no account!" He ate the scrambled eggs and complimented me on my rock buns!

Well! That's enough about me. You will be able to glean from it that the year has been a happy one. Please God the future ones will be the same.

. . . Last week was the Priddis Fair and we went down for it. It's quite a social event so we dressed in our best "bib and tucker." . . . We had been invited to stay to supper with Mr. and Mrs. Dennis and go over to the hall afterwards where there was to be a dance. I can't say that Billie was very enthusiastic, but Helene and I were very anxious to go and of course he gave in. It was the first dance we had been to in this country and we were longing to see what it would be like. It was really good fun but of course quite different from any we had been to before . . . The orchestra was comprised of a piano and two violins and was quite good. We did not know many people there: we found out afterwards that the elite do not attend the dances and they expressed surprise at our being there.

They can stay away if they want to but they miss a great deal of fun by doing so; anyway, I always did prefer the "hoi poloi"! Helene and I were very amused at the mode of introductions. Streams of young men were dragged up by a perspiring M.C., "Mrs. Hopkins meet Mr. Jones; Miss Cunningham, meet Mr. Jones," and we would smile sweetly and the young man would bob his head and another take his place. At first they all seemed too shy to ask us to dance but eventually Helene was flying around the room, simply dazed at the rapidity of her partner. I followed soon after, more sedately as becomes a matron! The quadrilles were what we loved to watch: a "caller-off" directs the dancers and each figure has a different set of rhymes. Towards the end of the dance the tempo gets more rapid and the ladies are simply lifted off their feet and hurled around and around. I still laugh, as I think of the expression on Helene's face as she found herself flying around, her feet off the ground, as two youths whipped her and another girl around as fast as they possibly could. It's simply impossible to be dignified. You just hang on to your partner's neck and pray Heaven he won't let go of you. After our decorous Lancers these dances were simply marvellous and jolly good fun too. I asked to join in but evidently being married and

English it was supposed I wouldn't care for it. Helene being an Australian was not supposed to be so superior.

Between the dances all the females sat on one side of the hall on the narrowest forms I've ever sat on. On the opposite side of the hall the men gathered; when the music started up for the next dance the males dashed across the floor to their favourite partners and the most popular ones had several suitors claiming her for the dance.

The supper was served to us in the hall. We all sat in the same way, sheep on one side and goats on the other. The cups were brought around in a washtub and we all took one. No saucers were provided but the refreshments were ample and delicious: sandwiches and cakes in profusion were passed around. I found myself copying my neighbour and placed an open handkerchief on my lap and simply took a piece of everything. About 2.30 Billie came and asked in a very martyred tone as to when we proposed to go home. We weren't a bit tired but we still had a long drive ahead so we said we were ready to go any time. Billie hurriedly departed to hitch up the team before we would change our minds; as it was, we almost had to drag Helene from the arms of her partner so loath was he to let her go. It was nearly four o'clock before we tumbled into bed after having spent a really delightful time full of interest and fun . . .

Jenks is going to Priddis tomorrow and will mail this and bring back any mail there is for us. I'm always afraid when he goes off with my precious letters that he will either dump them in the creek or lose them somewhere on the trail. I always tie up the mail bag myself and hang it carefully over the horn of the saddle; even then, I'm sure something will happen to it. The mail is such an important part of my existence that the very thought of losing part of it is most upsetting.

Our love to you both,
Monica

Billie and Monica Hopkins had no children but continued on their ranch (named Enmore after a ship captained by Billie's father) until 1918, when they relocated closer to Priddis and went into the sheep business. Monica's fellow citizens loved her cheerful personality and get-on-with-it approach to life; before her death in 1974, she was a leading member of the local church's Women's Auxiliary, the Priddis Red Cross, and the Priddis-Westoe Women's Institute.

III

1910: WESTERN CANADA
"IN-THE-DEPTHS" TO THE *FARMER'S ADVOCATE* IN WINNIPEG

"Dame Durden" was the pen name of the advice columnist for the Farmer's Advocate, *and each month lonely prairie wives poured their hearts out to her. A frequent theme was the prejudice against non-British: "I have a nice friend among the English here," wrote one Scandinavian newcomer to Manitoba, "but for the most part they would as soon dream of associating with the animals as with us." Another letter writer who identified herself as "In-the-Depths" from "Western Canada" described the subtle snobbery within homesteader society.*

October 12, 1910

Dear Dame Durden:

We have taken The Advocate about a year and I don't think I ever read a better paper. As I was standing in my kitchen all alone washing, just now, my heart was made to ache. I saw two women pass, about a quarter of a mile from our house, going towards town, which is ten miles from here. I suppose they were women that live within two or three miles of us, though I couldn't just recognize them from here. One was in a democrat [carriage] by herself; the other in a buggy, also by herself. How I would liked to have gone with them for a ride! But they didn't even look towards the house, just kept laying the whip to the horses, as if they couldn't go fast enough. I never get to go off the place scarcely, just stay home and attend to the stock, while my husband goes with the thresher and other places to make money. We came here about a year and a half ago from one of the middle states, where we were born and raised. We bought a half of a quarter section of land without seeing it; paid too much for it, and paid cash. We laid out about fifteen hundred for stock and farming implements. We have a good two storey house, but haven't fixed it up on the inside much yet, as we are very dissatisfied and might leave any time. It seems to me people regard us as very poor people. The most of them came once. I had met some of them at one of the neighbor's houses and noticed they played cards most of the time, I told them I didn't know how to play, and I didn't think I would like the game anyway. So I didn't have any cards for them when they called on me. I entertained the best I could under the circumstances, but it seemed the day was very dull for them. I was used to music and singing and talking where I came from. I sold my organ and all my nice furniture back East, and you may be sure I miss it all. But I had my big oak heater shipped here and bought a new cooking stove, iron bedstead, one rocker and some other things, and keep my naked floors scrubbed white and am considered a good cook, So I don't understand why we are slighted even if we don't ride in a rubber-tired buggy or automobile . . . It is true we have two good neighbors, but they have several little children and can't come often. Is it possible some people can't be interested only with cards? I thought at first with all the hard work, and loneliness, I would surely die or go insane, and I believe I would only for the Bible and your paper.

In-the-Depths

"You poor, dear, lonesome soul. I ached for you when reading your letter," replied Dame Durden, who advised her correspondent to learn a few card games because her neighbours were "thoughtless, that's all."

112

1910: ALBERTA

THE REVEREND MARTIN WEBBER HOLDOM TO HIS STEPMOTHER, GRACE HOLDOM, IN ENGLAND

The young Anglican priest Martin Webber embraced life in the newly founded Alberta township of Castor, east of Red Deer. Recruited by Bishop Pinkham of Calgary to serve the surging prairie population (Alberta's population grew from 73,000 to almost 500,000 between 1901 and 1916), Martin developed a genuine love for the prairies and for the hard-working settlers to whom he ministered. His parish covered 1,600 square miles, but he met his outlying preaching obligations regardless of weather or distance. And he threw himself into the local recreations . . .

December 19, 1910

Dear Mater,

Tuesday, December 13: Had to go down to play a curling match in the evening. Curling is a great winter sport and I enjoy it thoroughly. The staves are very heavy, about 50 pounds apiece. A great deal depends on the knack of throwing them. We played in a covered rink about 25 yards long. There is a waiting room heated with gallery for spectators. The old curlers wear Scotch bonnets and jerseys. When they get excited, they often play all night. The club has about 60 members and we are affiliated to the Royal Caledonian Club. I have been elected chaplain. Certainly, it is great fun. Tom Finlayson is a great hand at it; business and everything has to go if he is down to curl. It is a game with tremendous possibilities and requires a lot of skill. Sweeping the ice is a great feature. I swept until my arms ached. With practice, I think I shall make a pretty good curler.

Wednesday, December 14: I was happening to look out of my window at about 10:00 P.M. when a great light blazed up in the east. There was no doubt something was on fire. Rushing on our clothes, Field and I were soon running towards the blaze. In a minute or two the fire bell was clanging, and we could see dark figures hurrying from all directions. We could not make out what it was at first, until someone said it was the curling rink, and sad to say, so it was. It was in full blaze when we got there. Nothing could be done; we just stood round and watched it burn. Most of the curlers had managed to save their beloved staves.

The bank manager, who was there at the outbreak, told me how it happened. The janitor of the rink was drunk. He poured a little gasoline on the stove to make it burn up, spilt a little on the floor, which caught fire, and then being frightened, overturned the can. All that the players could do was to get outside; $1,000 worth of lumber gone in a few minutes. In about a quarter of an hour the chemical fire engine turned up, but as the team of broncos refused to come within a quarter of a mile of the blaze, it was not much good, and they had to take it home again amid the cheers of the onlookers. You can understand how thankful we were that the building was outside the town limits. It gave us a very good example of the havoc a fire would make in the town . . .

> Your very affec. Son,
> Martin W. Holdom

113
1914: ONTARIO
CLARE LOUISE CAMPBELL TO HER FRIEND
DINAH MEREDITH IN ENGLAND

In August 1914, the British Empire declared war against the German and Austro-Hungarian Empires. Toronto was abuzz with war fever and rumours of German spy activities. The streets were filled with crowds cheering columns of young soldiers off to train at Valcartier, Quebec. Victory, it was believed, was only a few months away, and no youth wanted to miss the fun. A debutante named Clare Campbell wondered which swains would be left in the city.

509 Huron St.
Sept. 1st [1914]

Dearest Dinah

I was wakened up this morning at 8.15 by our clever little hound jumping on my bed with your letter in his mouth. He is the smartest thing—does most of our shopping for us now!

If you haven't had the most exciting time! Didn't you go through Paris at all, on your dash for life through France? It really is a crime your trip ended so terribly.

I don't expect we really feel the war as much as you do in England—but it is bad enough here—it is the most desolate town you ever got into!

You said you hoped no one we knew has gone to the front! I can't think of more than five or six of our friends who haven't gone! Last Saturday was the saddest day I ever spent. Gay and I went to see the 48th off. Their route to the station was jammed with crowds of people, yelling, cheering & crying! And of course a beastly mob got right in front of us blocking the view successfully with umbrellas & we couldn't see a soul. This was near the Armouries, and they were going to the little C.N.R. Station near the Evangelia Settlement to get the train. So we flew down to King, got on a car & got out to the Don Bridge ahead of them, where there was another huge crowd. However by the help of our winning manners and a strong good-natured onlooker we forced our way to the front of the line—had a beautiful situation—I shook hands with almost everyone we knew! Never Again!—tried to be bright & cheery with a lump in my throat like a pumpkin! I think they are too wonderful for words.

I pinned my hopes firmly on a few who would be left. But last night Ned

Martin came up to see me, he was one of the few, and announced that he was busy qualifying for the Q.O.R. [Queen's Own Regiment] having only got back from his holidays. Also that Felix, Jack Harmon, Reg. Geary, Sydney Burnham & Ted Doheny were in his company. Must tell you something funny that happened while Ned was here. The doorbell rang at about ten o'clock, and as we were expecting no one & I heard two men's voices talking on the porch, said I in jest, "Ned, stick close behind me while I open the door, possibly they are German spies."

I opened the door & two large sized tough individuals demanded to see Dad at once. Dad hadn't been very well & was in bed, so I asked if I could take the message & one said, "Yes! You could—we're from the police station . . . and we want that wireless machine taken out immediately!"

Well! If you could have known my terror for a minute & the relief that followed, because all amateur machines were ordered to be taken out at the beginning of the war, but as Gordon has sold his set last winter (it was useless) he [never] thought to take down the arial off the roof. The men had seen this & suspected messages were being sent out secretly, to the Kaiser probably! I told them the set was not in commission, but they said, arial must come down at once. So Gord dashed home from work today & pulled it down with fury! Think though, if you had come home to find the Campbell family had been shot for spies, on account of the German name too!

Have you heard that Clifford & Phyllis are *married*? They dashed in one afternoon when he could get in from the camp at Long Branch & did it, with only the immediate family there. Poor Phyllis is nearly crazy, as he has gone with the 48th. Another hurried wedding of last week was that of Chuck & Helen, & for practically the same reason: they wanted it before Trumbull went off.

Oh! this is going to be a jolly winter allright!

Just can't wait to see you two once more—hustle up & come home—I am trusting to luck that you'll get this before you sail.

> With loads of love
> Clare Louise

114

1915: ALBERTA

LEA PANQUIN TO THE *FAMILY HERALD AND WEEKLY STAR*'S MAPLE LEAF CLUB IN CALGARY

Thousands of children in rural Canada contributed letters to the children's pages of their local newspapers. In return, they received membership pins and a sense of fellowship with other young people. The Maple Leaf Club was particularly popular among immigrant families in the west.

April 14, 1915
Coleman, Alta.

Dear Maple Leaves:

I am writing you a few lines to let you know if I am a german or a english or a french or a belgian. I am a belgian, and now it is war I cannot go back to my country. But when it is going to be finish I think my parents will go back, and I too. I like very much coleman now it is cold. I go to school everyday. I do the work with my mother. I know some little girls who are in the Maple Leaf Club. I like the teacher who teaches me at school, she is very kind to the children. My brother go to school too, he is in the same room as I am. My little sister is only two years old, so she is not going to school.

Lea Panquin

"I am glad this little Belgian is safe on our old Tree," the children's page editor wrote, "but hope that before long she may with safety return to her own country."

115

1915: HALIFAX

PERCY WINTHROP MCCLARE TO HIS MOTHER, GERTRUDE WINTHROP, IN MOUNT UNIACKE, NOVA SCOTIA

"Winnie" McClare was only sixteen when war broke out, and the minimum age for recruits was eighteen. But the eldest of eight children, who worked on his father's Nova Scotia farm, was swept up in war fever. Soon after his seventeenth birthday, Winnie could resist the call to arms no longer. But he needed his mother's assurance that she would not notify officials of his true age.

MacNabs Is,
Halifax
22 July 1915

Dear Mamma,

Just a line to let you know I am well and there is [an] urgent call out for more men, men, men, and my name is going in for the 40th Regt. Percy F. [Freeman, a cousin] and he [*sic*] is trying hard to get in the 40th Regt.

Last Friday there was a Capt. (I forget his name) from the front here and he said that the men at the [front] are happy as can be. He made a long speech, told us how they live and everything about them. Said they had a jolly time. All I need is you concent.

I asked Percy F. about the month's furlough and [he] said it was for Regts going across soon. He said he didn't think I could get it.

> Your loveing Son,
> Winnie

Winnie travelled to England on the Empress of Britain *in 1916 and entered the trenches for the first time on April 8, 1917. The nineteen-year-old was killed in action one month later.*

116

1915: ENGLAND
ALWYN BRAMLEY-MOORE TO HIS DAUGHTER
DOROTHY BRAMLEY-MOORE IN EDMONTON

Sometimes the clear-headed integrity of a long-dead writer seems to illuminate the untidy scrawl on a creased page. Alwyn Bramley-Moore was a middle-aged Alberta MPP and author of Canada and Her Colonies, or Home Rule for Alberta. *When war was declared, he felt he owed it to England, the country of his birth, to enlist. (More than half the members of the Canadian Expeditionary Force were British-born.) In regular letters to his wife and five children in Edmonton, he sent shrapnel souvenirs and encouragement in their studies. He also urged his children to think for themselves, and not to believe all the propaganda about German atrocities. The Bramley-Moore family had met German immigrants in Canada, and Alwyn guessed that enemy soldiers might be as inexperienced and apprehensive as his young Canadian colleagues.*

Alwyn Bramley-Moore wrote loving letters from the front to the five children he would never see grow up.

July 25th / 15
Hut 24, 23rd R.F.
Gidea Park, Essex

Dear Dorothy:

I am glad you have all done so well at your exams and I hope you will have a good rest and go for a change somewhere. You mustn't despise the country as you can get lots of fun on a farm.

That story about Major Anderson's legs being cut off is a lie from what I hear. Nobody here knows anything about it. And prisoners are not allowed to put any stamps on their letters, so he couldn't have written underneath one. You mustn't believe all the wicked stories you hear. Germans and Austrians are just the same as we are, some kind, some cruel, none of the Germans you knew were cruel. And of the two boys George and Billy who worked on our farm; George was an Austrian and he was a nice boy. Billy was almost as much Russian as Austrian, and though sulky perhaps, he was nice enough . . .

I have a wretched time now and hope soon for a change. They seem to treat us more as criminals [than] as volunteers; they bother you about such stupid things.

I hope you will play plenty of indoor games together when winter comes; there are enough of you to make things very pleasant if you all try to be cheerful to one another. We must learn to make ourselves happy. No more news just now so—

    With lots of love to all
    from your affectionate Father

Lance Corporal Bramley-Moore of the Princess Patricia's Canadian Light Infantry was shot and killed by a German sniper in March 1916, after six months in the trenches.

117
1916: ONTARIO
PRIME MINISTER SIR ROBERT BORDEN TO SIR GEORGE PERLEY, CANADIAN HIGH COMMISSIONER IN LONDON, ENGLAND

As Canadian casualties in Europe mounted, Conservative prime minister Robert L. Borden became exasperated by the Dominions' lack of input into British military strategy. His fury increased after a visit to London in 1915, where he was almost ignored and saw the lack of coordination among departments. Were colonials regarded simply as cannon fodder in the desolate, muddy landscapes of northern France? The prime minister sent an angry note to his representative in London, for transmission to Colonial Secretary Andrew Bonar Law.

Ottawa

January 4, 1916

My dear Sir George Perley,

I beg to acknowledge your letter of the 15th November enclosing copy of correspondence with the Right Hon. the Secretary of State for the Colonies touching my message as to information and consultation during the War.

Mr. Bonar Law's letter is not especially illuminating and leaves the matter precisely where it was before my letter was sent.

During the past four months since my return from Great Britain, the Canadian Government (except for an occasional telegram from you or Sir Max Aitken) have had just what information could be gleaned from the daily Press and no more. As to consultation, plans of campaign have been made and unmade, measures adopted and apparently abandoned and generally speaking steps of the most important and even vital character have been taken, postponed or rejected without the slightest consultation with the authorities of this Dominion.

It can hardly be expected that we shall put 400,000 or 500,000 men in the field and willingly accept the position of having no more voice and receiving no more consideration than if we were toy automata. Any person cherishing such an expectation harbours an unfortunate and even dangerous delusion. Is this war being waged by the United Kingdom alone, or is it a war waged by the whole Empire? If I am correct in supposing that the second hypothesis must be accepted then why do the statesmen of the British Isles arrogate to themselves solely the methods by which it shall be carried on in the various spheres of warlike activity and the steps which shall be taken to assure victory and a lasting peace?

It is for them to suggest the method and not for us. If there is no available method and if we are expected to continue in the role of automata the whole situation must be reconsidered.

Procrastination, indecision, inertia, doubt, hesitation and many other undesirable qualities have made themselves entirely too conspicuous in this War. During my recent visit to England a very prominent Cabinet Minister in speaking of the officers of another department said that he did not call them traitors but he asserted that they could not have acted differently if they had been traitors. They are still doing duty and five months have elapsed. Another very able Cabinet Minister spoke of the shortage of guns, rifles, munitions, etc., but declared that the chief shortage was of brains.

> Believe me,
> Yours faithfully,
> R. L. Borden.

In June 1918, Prime Minister Borden had the opportunity to make his views known directly to the British prime minister, David Lloyd George, at a meeting in London of the imperial war cabinet. After a furious description of the ineptitude of British generals, the usually mild-mannered Borden strode across the room, seized Lloyd George by the lapels of his frock coat, and announced that no more Canadian soldiers would cross the Atlantic if such incompetence continued.

118
1916: A CPR TROOP TRAIN
STUART TOMPKINS TO EDNA CHRISTIE TOMPKINS IN EDMONTON

As the German army advanced west, Prime Minister Borden used his 1916 New Year's message to pledge 500,000 soldiers from a total population of barely 8 million to the imperial war effort. Stuart Tompkins, an Alberta school inspector, received a commission in the 89th Alberta Overseas Battalion. He described to his wife how the soldiers acquired a mascot and were feted en route across Canada.

Sturgeon Falls,
Ontario
May 28, 1916

Dearest:

What a hot almost oppressive day it has been. We have been seeing sights since morning. At 12 o'clock we stopped at Cartier and had a walk down the track and back. It was not enjoyable in the dust and heat. We were at Sudbury an hour and a half ago. It has become a real smart progressive looking place and even the ladies were out to see us. It was quite interesting. One demure maiden went the length of the train and shook hands with the 484 [men] on board. She didn't seem enthusiastic, doing it apparently as a matter of duty. How like Old Ontario. She came up to a group of us officers and for the life of me I could not think of anything to say to cover our embarrassment. But she didn't worry. She hoped us shyly a safe return and left it at that.

By the way I must tell you of our bear—which was taken on the strength of the regiment at Jackfish. I don't know its length over all or its weight but it is about the size of a pup. He has been appointed provisional regimental mascot, and will still have to qualify before the imperial authorities. His appearance is always hailed with shrieks of delight but everyone clears passage when he lunges with his tiny paws . . .

Well honey we are back to the land of the elm and maple. As I look out I can count an odd dozen, and the whole country side is the most luscious green and cows and chickens and barns everywhere.

I bought an extra supply of stamps at the last station so look out for letters . . . I know they are illegible and not worth while but maybe you will find a few grains of wheat in the chaff. Captain Muncaster and I have been discussing *wives* this afternoon.

Stuart

Stuart Tompkins relieved the tedium of night watches in the trenches by studying Russian, and after the war he became one of North America's first experts in Russian history. The bear cub, named "Winnie" after Winnipeg, where it was taken on board, was placed in London Zoo once it arrived in England. There it became a favourite of A.A. Milne's son Christopher Robin and went on to become the model for Winnie the Pooh.

119

1916: SUSSEX, ENGLAND
GEORGE HADDOW TO HIS FATHER,
THE REVEREND ROBERT HADDOW, IN MILTON, ONTARIO

Some Canadians found war a disillusioning experience before they had even reached the front. The boredom of training camps in Britain and culture clashes with the English eroded their enthusiasm. George Haddow, a Presbyterian minister's son from Milton, Ontario, was a twenty-two-year-old graduate of the University of Toronto when he enlisted in the 4th Cyclists Corps of the 74th Infantry Battalion, Canadian Expeditionary Force, in 1916. He found army life, and military triumphalism, almost unbearable.

14 June 1916,
Shoreham Camp,
Sussex

Dear Father,

I have been very much worried since coming back from London because the 4th Div. Cyclists have been shoved bodily, without any chance to transfer, into the 74th battalion infantry, and there is a strong rumour going around, even the officers credit it, that we are going to be put into the infantry too. Most of the 74th have gone to France, but our fellows are in the base battalion at Bramshott in a platoon with chinamen and all kinds of nice company. They were given absolutely no choice and men who were expecting commissions and had all kinds of money to back them had no more chance to escape than anybody else.

This life is hopeless. The Cap., who was a very decent fellow, got drunk one night about a week ago and while riding his motor cycle ran into another cyclist and both got smashed up pretty badly. Ever since we have been under the 2nd in command who is cordially hated by everybody. He insists on treating everybody like a dog and in trying to make you feel as though you were an inferior order of being. The whole idea of the army seems to be to try and suppress individuality totally and the life is not a fine, healthy, free life as some people seem to think but the filthiest, unhealthiest, most crushing, exhausting and hateful anyone could imagine. It is nothing more or less than slavery. You do exactly what your superiors tell you and if you disobey or are unable to do it you are put in jail or made to break stones or something like that.

When Earl, Scott and I met in London we all agreed that we felt as though we didn't give a rip who won the war or what came out of it if it would only stop right away. I haven't been feeling well lately and too tired and listless to do anything but lie on my bunk between parades—and when you're feeling tired and have no place to lie down but on a few boards in a dirty bunk house you feel pretty homesick. There seems to be such an impassable barrier between the army and getting back to a decent life. Under ordinary circumstances it's nothing to be so far from home and everybody you love. If it comes to the worst you can get home in a couple of weeks or less. But here you are bound to a slavery from which there is no escape. And how can anyone take an interest in his life when his work is to learn to kill men? If you aren't doing that, it is either monotonous drill or else a route march that exhausts you or, worst of all, the most menial kinds of dirty work.

We got back from London shortly after eight Monday morning—I am continuing this Friday evening. Sunday night I only got three hours sleep as I had to get up at four o'clock. As soon as we got back to camp we had a nine mile route march on an empty stomach. We had an easy afternoon—only signally, but I felt too tired to write that evening. Tuesday morning as I was not feeling very well, I paraded sick—principally so I could get the morning off to get rested up. The doctor gave me a few pills but they weren't much good and I had to drill a little while after the afternoon parade to make up for the time lost in the morning. But there is no use trying to take preventive measures. Nobody will believe that there is anything the matter with you until you're so sick that you have to go to the hospital. If I'm not feeling better in a few days I think I'll see a doctor in Swindon. Wednesday morning I was put on officers' mess. Washing dishes, scraping pans etc. with the officers' cook and the batmen. One thing I got three decent meals. I was on from 7.30 am till 9.00 in the evening with only half an hour's intermission in the afternoon to parade for my pay . . .

I had a very pleasant visit to Oxford two weeks ago. The first day I was disappointed with the city but the second day, Sunday, I began to get the charm of it and left with the greatest reluctance. I've lost my desire to finish my education there though. The old world may be very interesting to visit but Canada's the only country to live in. There are too many people over here and the average Englishman hasn't the same spirit of personal independence that the Canadian has. The English serjeants are regular bullies. The way they treat the men when drilling them is a positive shame. A Canadian would never stand for it. The arrogant way in which some Englishmen look at the other people of the world and especially the way in which they speak of Americans is enough to make one's blood boil. There is no doubt that Canadians and Americans are far more alike than Canadians and Englishmen. I have lost every spark of Imperialism I ever had, and if I ever get back to Canada no more mixing in European quarrels for me.

Of course I have been exaggerating as usual. If I got the chance, I should come to Oxford, but I really think it is better for one who is going to spend his life in Canada to get most of his education in America, and then to visit European universities in the vacation or in off years. And of course in our world today, you can't separate the Old World from the New. They are so intimately connected in every way. I am not sorry that I enlisted but I wish I had considered a little more before jumping right into it. Sometimes I think I must have been crazy to reject Austin Campbell's offer of a clerical serjeantry. The work of the cyclist corps seemed about as good as anything to me at the time, but I haven't had anything but fatigues, a little platoon drill and a few route marches since coming over. Some of the fellows have had bombing and bayonetry and most of the N.C.O.s are now taking a musketry course; but there doesn't seem to be any possibility of getting wheels—we shan't need them if we are transferred to the infantry . . .

I shall have to stop now as it is a quarter after ten and we have general fatigues tomorrow morning. I feel like tearing this letter up now I have it finished, but I did that once before and it takes too much time to write them. When you can't unload yourself of what occupies your mind about eighteen hours a day, you have to shoot off a little hot air somewhere. Of course you know my tendency towards hyperbole. It really isn't so bad. We have a very comfortable camp here and are having a cinch of a time compared with what some poor fellows are having. Bill and I correspond pretty regularly and it is apparently much stiffer at Thorncliffe [training camp] than here. He hasn't had his six days yet, can't get weekends and has a hard time to get a midnight pass.

Much love to you and Marion and everybody at Bonnie Brae [the family home in Weston, outside Toronto]. I have some Pear's soap and the smell of it reminds me of the times we used to come home from [the] Eel river tired but satisfied . . . Your letters and those of all my dear friends are a great comfort and help. I have had a regular deluge lately and have an enormous pile to answer.

George

Despite his reservations, George Haddow studied at Oxford University after the war and subsequently became a professor of English literature at McMaster University in Hamilton, Ontario.

120

1916: FRANCE

MAYO LIND TO THE *DAILY NEWS* IN ST. JOHN'S

Newfoundland, an independent dominion in 1914, enthusiastically supported the imperial war effort. The Newfoundland Regiment served both in the Gallipoli campaign and in the trenches of France. Its exploits and its esprit de corps were recorded for the St. John's Daily News *by Frank Lind of Bett's Cove, who acquired the nickname "Mayo" thanks to his taste for "Mayo Tobacco," produced by Imperial Tobacco of St. John's.*

France,
June 29th, 1916.

We are out to billets again for a short rest, returning to trenches tomorrow, and then . . .—but never mind that now.

Again our boys have brought honour to themselves and Newfoundland, but I have no doubt Newfoundland is ringing from one end to the other with news of the great success of our raiding party, which under Captain Bert Buder, Lieut. C. Strong, and Lieut. Greene, D.C.M., played havoc with the Huns. About fifty of our men made an attack on the Germans, and although we have to regret the loss of several of our brave fellows killed and missing, also several wounded, yet the casualties on the enemy's side amounted to about 400—score another for Newfoundlanders. Our chaps are the talk of the whole line; every man held his life in his hands, and none knew if they would ever return alive; all heroes as brave as any that ever went over the parapet. You ought to have heard the praise given them by the Colonel, also by General Cayley.

. . . No doubt you have the official list of wounded and killed, so I had better not comment on it now. Some are missing, we hope they may turn up O.K. Some of them did not turn up until twenty-four hours after the raid. George Phillips of A Company got back next day, "tattered and torn," but what a hero, for George slept in a German dug-out the night before, (cool!), and as far as we can learn the Germans are wondering yet what struck them. Our fellows charged right into their trenches carrying all before them and in a word played "hide and seek" with the Huns, chasing them in and out through the traverses, and dropping bombs on them everywhere. Fully 400 Germans were knocked out by fifty brave fellows. The Germans never want to have another visit from the "White Indians," as they call us; for one day they put up a notice in their trenches, "When are the White Indians from Newfoundland coming over." They know now that some of them have been over, and likely will know more later.

These Germans have a great fancy for putting up messages over their trenches for us to read. One day they put up, "We sympathize with you in the loss of Kitchener." We did not know what it meant until that evening the news came to us that Lord Kitchener and Staff were drowned. How strange that the Germans should know about it before we did; but they seem to know everything. No doubt, the sinking of H.M.S. *Hampshire* was planned before she left England.

The other day somebody saw a German digging and fired a shot at him; down drops Mr. Sausage, and held up his shovel signalling the result of the shot, and up he got to dig again, but he didn't signal the next shot—don't ask why!

Our bombers have done great work and are ready to do even more when the time comes. Lance-Corporal Arch Gillam is in charge of 8 Platoon Bombers, and he has a good team with him: J. Pennell, F. Freake, T. Seymour, G. Abbott, N. Dean, G. Madore, and last, but not least, the unconquerable Joe Andrews. Joe came out to the Peninsula, and not getting enough of it there, he determined to do away with some Germans before seeing Newfoundland again, and here we find Joe Andrews going about like an armoured cruiser ready for action, and goodness help Germany when he gets going. He is a very accurate shot with bombs and rifle. Joe is also a good singer, and helps to pass many a weary hour when out for a rest.

Did I tell you about the mud here yet? Well, just a word, it is mud and slush from head to toe. We are quite used to it now, and would you believe it, we enjoy it. Yes, it is great fun, for believe me, a man can get used to anything, and when this bunch gets back they will be the hardiest lot of men in the world. Here we face danger, awful danger, every hour, looking over the parapet sometimes during a beautiful clear sky, gazing across "No Man's Land" to the enemy's lines, perhaps at just before dawn. It is wonderful how our boys have hardened to this life—shot and shells—and some shells you bet—flying all around them, yet not a flinch. Ah, I wish I could just, in imagination, take you into the trenches. I wish I could illustrate to you just what it is like, but I cannot. No pen could describe what it is like, how calmly one stands and faces death, jokes and laughs; everything is just an every day occurrence. You are mud covered, dry and caked, perhaps, but you look at the chap next you and laugh at the state he is in; then you look down at your own clothes and then the other fellow laughs. Then a whizz bang comes across and misses both of you, and both laugh together.

Now, just for a minute come into our dug-outs . . . in the trenches. So in we go; I only want to tell you about the rats; they are in swarms, and big monsters. I never thought rats could grow so big, and there we find them roaming about the dug-outs, looking for our rations. They chew our clothes, our equipment, everything they destroy, and roam around the dug-out so cool, many of them bigger than any cat I ever saw, and as we enter they just look around as much as to say: "Oh, so you're back again," and then they go digging in to our iron rations. We chase them away; they go just a little way and stop again, and if you go up and kick them, why they only turn and snap at your boot. They consider themselves part of the establishment, and have come to stay, and when we lie down for a rest we can feel them walking over us in swarms. The only thing is to lie stiff and let them have their fling, but it nearly drives a man's patience out of him sometimes when he feels a rat's whiskers tickling his ear. They just stroll about on us and calmly look at our shoulder badges to see what regiment we belong. The weather is rather cold at nights, but the beautiful summer will soon begin here.

The other day some of us visited Gus Manning's grave. I am sure his friends will be glad to know that he is not forgotten by his comrades. I think his grave is by far the best amongst that lot of heroes who have died for King and Country. Officers and men from all parts of the great British Empire lie there. I wish I had been able to take a photo to send you, but alas! cameras are not allowed here. At the head of Sergt. Manning's grave is a beautiful cross, standing above all the others, and at first appearance it seems like marble, the work is done so nicely, and is a credit to Gus Lilly and Lew Stone who made the cross and did the painting, with inscription, and on the grave are many flowers, showing the esteem in which Gus Manning is held by his comrades.

Our cooks are still busy on the job cooking under fire, but B Company, at any rate, are always assured of regular meals, while the redoubtable Hebe Wheeler is in charge; for Hebe only laughs at shells; he must bear a charmed life, for he has had many narrow escapes. Only two days ago when they were moving the Field Kitchen across a dangerous place, a shell knocked the cover of one of the boilers off, and at the same time sent Jack Thompson's helmet spinning into the soup; but who minds that, "steel soup" is a change anyhow. Just after that their horse was killed, but nothing daunted, Hebe Wheeler, Reg. Masters and J. O'Driscoll fastened themselves into the shafts and brought the kitchen to safety. These are only some of the many incidents that occur every day. Sometime when we return we shall be able to tell you lots and lots of things that time and circumstances will not allow now.

Now, don't think that although we are here in the midst of the greatest war ever known that we don't enjoy ourselves when we get a chance, for a football match is going on at present just outside our shell-torn billet. We have many pleasant hours by holding impromptu concerts, and some of our chaps are great comedians. Then talking about humour: we will never forget "Bush" Callahan when he came across a German dug-out filled with Germans. "Rod" knows a few German words, and he sang out, "how many men in this dug-out?" The Germans, thinking, no doubt, it was one of their officers, replied: "Eleven." "Then," said "Bush," as he threw in two bombs, (time fuse five seconds), "share these amongst you." Oh, if you could have heard the roar of those bombs in that confined space, the screams of the "baby killers," and the patter of Callahan's feet as he beat a hasty retreat. It was a grand stunt, but "Bush" Callahan thinks that nothing. "Not a bad haul," he said, "eleven at one go." . . .

I will ring off for this time but will write again shortly, when I hope to send you a very interesting letter. Tell everybody that they may feel proud of the Newfoundland Regiment, for we get nothing but praise from the Divisional General down.

> With kind regards,
> Frank

Two days after Frank wrote this letter, the Newfoundland Regiment stormed Beaumont Hamel in the opening day of the Battle of the Somme. Of the regiment's 790 members, 710 were killed, wounded, or missing. No unit among the Allies suffered more heavily. Frank Lind was among the 272 men who were killed that day.

121
1916: FRANCE
FRANÇOIS-XAVIER MAHEUX TO ANGÉLIQUE MAHEUX
IN BASKATONG BRIDGE, QUEBEC

Letters from army privates, who bore the brunt of trench savagery, are rare. I find this letter particularly touching because the writer acknowledges how he himself lost control in battle. Frank Maheux was a thirty-four-year-old Quebec logger who had crossed the Ottawa River in November 1914 to enlist with the 21st Battalion, commanded by Colonel Sam Hughes. Frank's motives had little to do with patriotism and everything, as he told his adored wife, Angélique, to do with escape from the lumber camp and the promise of regular wages and meals. Once he arrived in France, his initial bravado wore thin, especially after he watched many of his comrades die in the bloody carnage of the Battle of the Somme. Frank wrote in English, the way he spoke.

François-Xavier Maheux confided to his wife some of the blind brutality of war.

Sept 20th, 1916
In France

Dear wife and children,

Rec'd your letter glad to see that you are well, hoping my letter will find you the same well dear wife I am very well I past the worse fighting here since the war started, we took all kinds of prisoners but God we lost heavy, all my camarades killed or wounded, we are only a few left but all the same we gain what we were after, we are in rest, dear wife it is worse than hell, the ground is covered for miles with dead corpses all over and your Frank past all true that without a scratch, pray for me dear wife, I need it very bad, I went true all the fights the same as if I was making logs, I baynetted some killed others. I was caught in one place with a chum of mine he was killed beside me when I saw he was killed I saw red we were the same like in a butchery, the Germans when they saw they were beaten they put up their hands up but dear wife it was to late, as long as I leave, I'll remember it. They attacked us one morning some poor man came running to me no rifle, no bombs and the Germans all around us I gave order to the poor boys to jump on the parapet so they all jumped on the parapet we had a better chance but we lost our trenches for a few moments but dear all our men were killed or wounded, another regiment came up to help, it took us a few minutes to clear them we were just finishing when we got orders to charge the Germans we went lines after lines, our mens dropping all over, we advanced over 2 miles it was great to see the poor boys from Canada going ahead, but it cost us heavy price. I don't know where the boys [are], they are not here . . . I won the stripps of sergeants . . .

The average survival for front-line infantry in France was a year. Frank was one of the rare soldiers who lived through the Battles of the Somme, Passchendaele, and Vimy Ridge. After treatment for gonorrhea and a foot injury, he returned to Canada, Angélique, and his three children in 1918.

122
1917: FRANCE
PRIVATE DONALD ROSS TO HIS MOTHER,
MABLE ROSS, IN ONTARIO

Donald Ross was only seventeen when he enlisted in the Canadian infantry. Suffused with patriotism, he was determined to do his duty, but from the start, he was lonely and frightened.

Somewhere in France;
1 January 1917

Dear Mother,
My cold has left me quite deaf. This morning a couple of shells landed within 10 yards of me but I did not heed them. But the dead certainly make me creepy. I never was quite so bad. The mud is terrible, over your boots, everywhere. You would not know me now if you saw me. I am covered head to foot and cannot get it off me . . . Katie [his sister] said in her letter that

they are going to send me a parcel. Would it be too much trouble to ask you to send one every week?

> I am your loving lonely son
> Pte. Donald Ross.

Dear Mother,

I wrote you a few lines this morning but I still have the letter in my pocket as I did not get a chance to hand it in I will write off a few more.

First I want to thank you for the parcels I received the second one today at noon. The old chum [tobacco] just came in the nick of time and everybody is admiring the pipe but think it is a little out of place in here. A big rat just ran out doors from under my feet the place is alive with them but they do not bother us at all as they get plenty to eat from the dumps. I want you to thank Janie MacDonald Aunt Allie and Uncle Andrew and Mrs Phillips for me. I will write to them the first chance I get but I don't get much chance here. I won't have a chance to make any Oxo here but as soon as I get the chance I am going to try it. Never be worried when you do not hear from me at times for there are times when I cannot get even time to sleep. And if anything was to happen you would be notified at once you see I always carry my paybook and your address and fathers were both put in by the paymaster.

However you know that I will write you a few lines every opportunity I get. Well the photo is far better than I expected. I still have your picture. I carry it in the bible over my heart. The bible that Mr Underwood was so kind to send me. Well I wrote you Xmas but maybe my letter will not sound very good. I will acknowledge that I was pretty sick Xmas with a cold but am feeling much better now. There is a fellow in this battalion from Ottawa only sometimes his mother sends him a parcel every two weeks and he gets them quite regular. I still have a parcel coming from Auntie one from Pearl and one from Bee. I have not heard from Abby. I also have one coming from the young ladies patriotic Assn in Colborne.

Will close now but love to one and all

> Your loving son
> Donald Ross

In September 1918, Donald Ross became lost behind enemy lines, stumbled into a German-held trench, and was shot. During his two years in the army he had written 275 letters home.

123
1917: FRANCE
AGAR ADAMSON TO MABEL ADAMSON IN ENGLAND

The Battle of Vimy Ridge on Easter weekend, 1917, was a defining moment in the Canadian war effort. Thanks to careful preparation, the battle-hardened Canadian Corps managed to capture the seemingly impregnable landmark. Agar Adamson, a bon vivant and acerbic observer, had joined the Princess Patricia's Canadian Light Infantry as soon as it was formed in 1914, although he was forty-eight years old and blind in one eye. By 1917, he was the Princess Pats' lieutenant colonel, and he led the regiment into battle. He also recorded the action in daily letters to his wife, evading the censor by giving the casualty count in code.

Top of Vimy Ridge,
April 10th, 1917.

My dear Mabel,

We took all our objectives yesterday pushing off at 5:30 A.M. in a rainstorm. The 4th Division on our left, not yet in line with us, having failed in two attempts to gain their objective. We have our flank in the air and are suffering from enfilade fire in newly dug trenches.

A snow storm in progress. Sladen killed. 10 officer casualties, including 3 killed, Pearson shot through lung and spine. Have had him taken out. Other casualties so far equal double Beverley Street number [Mabel Adamson grew up at 152 Beverley Street, Toronto]. I think we can hang on. Our Brigade did splendidly. Pipes played this Battn. over [the top] and are doing great work carrying stretchers, I hope I may get this out by one of them.

Ever Thine,
Agar.

P.S. Our observation over Vimy ridge is magnificent and if we can hold them till the Artillery push up, we have a commanding position. This Battn. took 400 prisoners, Agar.

In the battle of Vimy Ridge, Canadian troops gained more ground, guns, and prisoners than any previous British offensive had done. But there were 10,602 casualties, including 3,598 men killed.

Top of Vimy Ridge,
12th April 1917.

Still hanging on wonderfully, well dug in. 4th Division now up in line with us. Their losses heavy. We are suffering a lot from machine gun fire and snipers well hidden and difficult to spot. Also artillery fire, though very general and not concentrated on any one spot.

Estimate of our losses impossible to collect accurate returns. Should not be more than Beverley St. by 3 less 50.

No determined German counter-attack yet launched though R.F.C. [Royal Flying Corps?] report enemy massing in great numbers in front of us. I feel we can stop them in my particular front if their Artillery does not find us too continually.

Agar.

> Vimy Ridge,
> April 1917.

We have done very well, though suffered a lot. The town named after the Ridge will be well in our rear. So far, the fighting has been of an open character. The Germans falling back, fighting hard rearguard action; every place is mined and the whole country, including dugouts and cellars, a mass of booby traps . . . All the wells are poisoned. Every prisoner had a photo of one or more most repulsive naked women. One of our Divinity student sergeants made an officer eat three most filthy postcards. A German Major refused to be sent with prisoners to the rear, except in charge of a Major. He will trouble us no more. Our roads in the new area are very bad, having been smashed by our shell fire. We are having great difficulty in getting guns, etc., up.

Agar

> Vimy Ridge,
> 12th April 1917.

My dear Mabel,
We have pushed them back and are on the outskirts of the town named the same as the Ridge. Awful weather. Men absolutely done, awaiting news of a relief which must come. Things have gone splendidly and men awfully cheered. In consequence, if we only had summer instead of winter weather, we could endure more.

Thine. Agar.
P.S. Eaton of Ottawa killed.

Of the twenty-nine officers who went to France with the Princess Pats, more than half were killed. Agar survived, but by 1918 he was exhausted physically and emotionally.

124
1917: ONTARIO
TOM THOMSON TO HIS FATHER, JOHN THOMSON, IN LEITH

Back home, ordinary life went on peacefully for those who, like the painter Tom Thomson, were not involved in the war. Since 1912, Thomson (who was rejected for the military on medical grounds) had made regular trips from his home in Toronto to Algonquin Park to sketch: in the summer of 1916 he worked as a park fire ranger. Although his large oil paintings were already fetching high prices, Thomson still struggled to support himself. In April 1917, he returned to the park, bought a guide's licence, and set out to record the daily unfolding of spring.

6 April 1917,
Mowat P.O.
Algonquin Park

Dear Father: I have been up here for two weeks making sketches. Had intended going up home for a day or two before coming here but wanted to be here before the snow was gone so could not spare the hour. The lakes are still frozen over and will be for two or three weeks yet and there is still about two to three feet of snow in the bush so I expect to get a lot more winter sketches before the snow and ice are all gone. Tom Harkness and Walter Davidson were in to see me the day before I came here also Mrs. Andrews and Low Julian (I don't know if the last name is spelled properly or not) but I don't think they enjoyed the show a great deal as they are taking lessons from Manley [probably Charles Manly, who taught at the Ontario College of Art] the worst painter in Canada.

Am stopping at the Post Office here until the ice goes out when I will start to camp again. have tried fishing thro the ice two or three times but have had no success yet have caught some "ling" which is a cross between an eel and a fish but they don't use them up here.

I did not send any paintings to the O.S.A. Exhibition this year and have not sold very many sketches but think I can manage to get along for another year at least I will stick to painting as long as I can.

I got quite a lot done last winter and so far have got some pretty good stuff, since I came here and expected to do a great deal between now and June.

Have not decided if I will stay here the whole summer or not. Hoping you are all well. I remain your loving son.

Tom Thomson

In the next three months the thirty-nine-year-old painter completed sixty-two sketches. On July 8, he disappeared; his body was recovered from Canoe Lake eight days later.

125

1917: ONTARIO

EVELYN KELLY ALBRIGHT TO FRED ALBRIGHT IN FRANCE

The war brought English-speaking Canadians together and gave them a sense of inde-
pendent nationhood. Celebrations for the fiftieth anniversary of Confederation illus-
trated the growing patriotism, as Evelyn Albright described in a letter to her husband,
Fred, who was serving in France. The Albrights lived in Calgary, where Fred had a law
practice, but Evelyn was enjoying a two-month break with her sisters in Ontario and
looking forward to her husband's return.

1 July 1917,
Toronto

Darling One:

We have had the most wonderful day. Yesterday it rained so that today there
was no dust. The sun shone all day, but there was a lovely breeze, so that
the day was neither too hot nor too cold. I washed my hair this morning,
and Ora and I cut out a dress for me. Here we go out for our meals in the
middle of the day, so to-day Ora and Elleda and I took Mr. & Mrs.
Dickenson to the Wentworth Arms for dinner. Afterwards we drove to the
Beach and along the new highway as far as Oakville. The road is paved (pardon the blot, but my pen wasn't working right & I shook it) and there are
charming homes along it. Really, England hasn't much more beauty than
this country around here, except maybe for the flowers and the hedges.
Coming back we stopped at Mr. W. D. Flatt's at a garden party for the Red
Cross. Their grounds are in the lake shore, and have most beautiful trees.
We went out by the shore—the bank is high there, and sat under two huge
chestnut trees, for about an hour and a half, just talking, or not, and watching the water and the ships. I said tonight to Ora, "If only the boys could
have had to-day, in the midst of their present life." We came home through
crowds and crowds. Everybody was out with the whole family it seemed. It
did seem as if the world and his family was having a well earned holiday.

We came home for supper, and then went to a patriotic fête in the cricket
grounds. There was a big choir, which sang "Oh Canada" & the Hallelujah
Chorus and led all of us in the singing of the songs on the enclosed card,
Bruce Carey was leading, and really, it was the most enjoyable thing. Before
us lay the green, green grounds, then as a background rose the tree covered
side of the mountain. About a hundred little white clad kiddies danced and

played on the green grass, before and after they did their "stunt," which was a Maypole dance most beautifully done. There were two bands which played. Once they played "Pack up your trouble in your own kit bag, and smile, smile, smile," and everyone was asked to sing. A man sang "Rule Britannia" and all were asked to join in the chorus. Adam Brown, aged 90, made a speech. He had been present at the first Confederation exercises, 50 years ago. A man who also had been present then, opened by leading in the "Lord's Prayer" which everyone was supposed to repeat. The End was a tableau "Confederation." First a woman in bridal robes with 2 children came in and took a seat on a throne covered with a Union Jack. Then the first four provinces, each bearing the coat-of-arms of that province, came in turn and as each came an appropriate air was played by the band. B.C. was preceded by an Indian youngster who went back & beckoned her in, when she was welcomed by all, as were all the late comers. Before Manitoba came a little Indian child, who also went and beckoned her in. She was a young girl. Before Sask. & Alberta came in, two young cow-boys, with big rakes came in from either side and bumped into each other, then each went and called its respective province. Then the lady in white got off her throne and "Canada" I guess it was, came in and got on the throne & the lady in white did homage and then disappeared. Whereupon the band struck up "The Land of the Maple" and then "God Save the King." It was such a charmingly simple celebration we were all delighted. One coloured balloon was sent up, and we saw a few rockets. I never heard a fire cracker all day. Are we learning some sense?

It was a year ago, wasn't it, that you first went out to camp, and it rained and oh, you came home. How glad I was that night. May it be an augury of your soon homecoming to your loving wife.

Fred never came home: he was killed in his first engagement, the Battle of Passchendaele, on October 26, 1917. Evelyn Albright became an associate professor of English at the University of Western Ontario and died in 1979.

126

1917: FRANCE

MARY DOHERTY TO HER AUNT MRS. H.A. DOHERTY

IN NEW BRUNSWICK

Twenty-five-year-old Mary Doherty was one of 2,504 Canadian nurses who served in military hospitals overseas. From a field hospital in France, Mary wrote to relatives in the Maritimes about her encounters with boys she had known growing up who had been wounded in the fighting. She also passed on a piece of poetry by a medical officer.

No 3 Can. Gen. Hosp.

B.E.F. France

11–8-17

My Dear Aunt H:

Have intended writing you for a long long time but over here the days just seem to go and I accomplish so little I am almost ashamed.

I am on night duty once again. Tonight most of the patients seem to be sleeping fairly well so I hope to get several letters written. The wind is rather light and there is no convoy reported so far. I have an awfully good orderly on with me. We have three wards one hundred beds in all. The weather has been simply terrible. We had 21 days of nothing but rain and wind. You can't imagine it. Well what do you think of me—a real aunt no less. I can't imagine Florrie [her sister] with a baby. Can you? I always think of dear Grandma and her story "Nancy of Nancy" . . . Florrie says mother is delighted and that she has never seen her so happy before. Would love to be home but will just have to wait. I had a letter from Jim McSweeney a short time ago but it was written from Sussex so there was little Rexton news in it. I have not heard from Harry for some time. I have written him twice. How is Hugh—poor boy—I hope heaps better.

I am including a bit of poetry by Col. McRae. He is in charge of medicine here. He has written several very good things. How is Miss H. and is she still with you. I wrote to Aunt W. some time ago but the naughty thing I have not had a line from her. Must say good night. Heaps of love, M.

In Flanders' Fields

In Flanders fields the poppies blow

Between the crosses, row on row,

That mark our place. And in the sky

The larks, still bravely singing fly;
Scarce heard amid the guns below.

We are the dead; short days ago
We lived, felt dawn, saw sunsets glow,
Loved and were loved, and now we lie
In Flanders' Fields.

Take up our quarrel with the foe!
To you from failing hands we throw
The torch; be yours to hold it high!
If ye break faith with us who die
We shall not sleep, though poppies grow
In Flanders' fields.

One of the sisters—a Miss Glass, a very well educated girl, a graduate of the Royal Victoria College (McGill)—thinks the fourth word of the third verse should be struggle instead of quarrel. What do you think?

Do write <u>real soon</u>
Love, M.

127
1917: NOVA SCOTIA
BERTHA BOND TO SANDY WOURNELL IN FRANCE

At 8:45 A.M. on December 6, 1917, a Belgian vessel collided with a French munitions carrier in Halifax Harbour: nineteen minutes later, the munitions ship exploded in a giant blast that rocked the city. Sixteen hundred buildings were levelled, including Kaye Street Methodist Church. In the manse, the Reverend William Swetnam, his wife, Lizzie, his daughter, Dorothy, and his son, Carman, were gathered. Lizzie and Carman were killed instantly; Dorothy was trapped under heavy ceiling beams; the house was on fire. Next door, the Swetnams' neighbours, Ethel and Bertha Bond, emerged from the dust to find their own father dead. In a letter to her fiancé, Bertha described the panic.

December 10, 1917
Kaye Street,
Halifax

It may be beyond my power of thought to collect enough to put on paper but I want you to see my hand writing first because that may convince you that I am all right. Both Ethel and I had a most miraculous escape and for that we are so thankful, but Sandy when we got out of the house and found our dear dad, it made us, well, I can't describe the sensation I had. He had just gone to the mill to get some sugar which was in a barrel inside the door and there we found his body. Our greatest comfort is that his death was instant and that he was ready to go. You know, Sandy, that neither Ethel nor I are of a collapsing nature, so, as hard as it was, we had to cover the body and leave it.

I wasn't half dressed. We had been up late the night before, so that morning Ethel said for me to take another nap and she would get the breakfast so I didn't wake up till about nine o'clock. Then I hurried into my underclothes and corsets, stockings and an old pair of boots which I didn't button. Then I put on a heavy bath robe and went into the bath room and I was there when the explosion occurred. The first shock didn't stun me but the [Kaye Street Methodist] church fell and I saw it go. Maybe a shell struck it or maybe it was simply the concussion: then in another instant I was knocked into the hall, face down and walls and I don't know what all began to tumble in and I felt the stuff piling up on my back. I was sure that was the end of me and all I was thinking of was you. I remember saying, or rather thinking, your name over and over but when I hit the floor first and for a few seconds I was stunned and if I had never lived I'd never have known what happened to me or felt any pain, but as it was I began to move and wiggle out from under the stuff.

My face and head was bleeding considerably—I could tell by the look of the floor and also by the way the blood was dripping off my chin but for all that my knees didn't shake a particle. I called Ethel and at the same time she called me and she came scrabbling up what was left of the stairs and met me at the top, She says she never expected to see my face whole again by the look of it then and I felt sure too that it would have to be patched up but I might as well tell you now that I don't expect to have a scar—only two new upper front teeth to replace the ones that were broken off.

The robe I had on went I don't know where—I didn't see it so I picked up a flannel dress and put it over my head as I followed Ethel to go outside . . . [We] finally landed at the parsonage.

I didn't expect to find a soul there, but I did. Little Dorothy was unhurt, but so completely hemmed in that her father was doing his best to saw her out. The other two were gone . . . By now the fires were blazing in pretty good shape . . . I'll never forget Mr Swetnam's look when he saw us and if we hadn't gone she'd never in this world have been saved. Then it was time to run so we ran to our place and grabbed what clothes we could. We got upstairs and I thought of my [engagement] ring. It had been in my jewel box on the bureau. I found it among the plaster but the tray had gone. In a minute I located it, but no ring. I just had to get it, and I did, also my watch which was in the mess. We had no time to hunt for anything more or any way of gathering or carrying it so as we went we picked up a few clothes, I picked up enough odd pieces to finish dressing later and all the old coats in the coat room we took.

We rigged out the two Swetnams and were ready to leave when I dropped my load and went to see if the safe was anywhere. It flashed through my mind that if it had been a shell from sea another might come and so I opened it up first try—ripped open a couple of little cushions and dumped everything in the safe into these rude bags—shut the door and when we got out Ethel didn't know what I had done. It was a dreadful hustle.

Out of a population of 50,000, over 1,600 people died and 9,000 were injured, including 200 by flying glass. The Halifax Explosion was the largest man-made explosion before Hiroshima.

128
1917: ONTARIO
JANIE SMYTHE TO FLORA DENISON IN TORONTO

As the men disappeared to Europe, women took their jobs in factories and on farms. Their strengthened role in the national economy added force to the "Votes for Women" campaign, spearheaded since 1906 by the Toronto journalist Flora Denison. The federal election of December 17, 1917, was the first in which women were allowed to vote. But only certain women—those in the armed forces and the wives, mothers, or siblings of those serving. One of Denison's correspondents found some irony in this restriction.

22 Glengrove Ave. W.
Toronto Dec. 18, 1917

My Dear Mrs Denison.

It is befitting that you should be the first one I should write to since I recorded my *first* vote. It was a proud day yesterday for me and an hour which you and others have by unceasing devotion to the cause, made possible. I may now be recognized by humanity at large, as having a complete number of organs and faculties with more or less average mental ability to use them! In a word, am equal of my husband, at least technically speaking. I have my vote owing to my sister nursing soldiers. Stepmothers are not fully qualified for such a high honour as voting. I trust that when next we shall meet that I shall bear myself with true and becoming dignity in my new state of equality . . .

Janie Smythe

The following year, the right to vote in federal elections was extended to all women.

129

1918: WESTERN CANADA
"DISCOURAGED WOMAN" TO THE *FREE PRESS PRAIRIE FARMER*
IN WINNIPEG

It is fascinating to track the growing political consciousness of women through the correspondence columns of newspapers. "Women's pages" were one outlet for demands for more attention to their legal, property, and health needs, in both the private and public spheres. Too often, as this prairie farmer's wife explained to her fellow readers, women seemed to get less respect than livestock.

January 2, 1918

Dear Editor,

In reply to the letter signed "One of Us," I would like to say a few words. I do certainly feel grateful for the kind letters that I have received in answer to my letter in your paper, "A Discouraged Woman." Maybe I am a little selfish and inclined to dwell too much on my own trouble and sickness, but God knows I wrote with the full intention of helping some other woman to stop before she gets in such bad shape as I am in.

Since writing the last letter the kind neighbor I spoke of is dead. She has four little children, and was always so strong and well I can't realize she is dead, and her three days' old baby as well. They [were] getting on fine as far as money goes. Her husband put up a beautiful new barn this fall. It did not matter that his family still lived in the two-roomed log shack he built when they homesteaded here. As long as his horses and cattle are warm and dry what matter, if the log shack was cold and damp. He will build a house after a while. Now the poor woman is in her grave he won't need to.

There seems to be something terribly wrong on the prairie. A woman gives up her life for her child and it is all right, but if a man's best mare is sick, how quick he can get a veterinary in. How terrible to lose a mare worth 250 dollars! But there are lots of women now. As one man said to my husband the day of the funeral: "Do men ever stop to realize what it means for a woman to bear his children, give the best years of her life for him and them, and then be glad to die?" I think a man should be compelled to build a decent house and have a well near the house before he can take a wife on the farm. Also, he should be compelled to have a doctor in times of confinement and not depend upon a neighbor at such a time. My trouble all comes from that cause, too little care and getting about too soon.

Well, dear Editor, this is a long letter, but will you kindly print it. If it only helps one woman I shall be satisfied. Again, thank the other members for their kindness and sympathy.

Discouraged Woman

130
1918: FRANCE
ALEXANDER GORDON TYRRELL TO HIS MOTHER,
JESSIE ROBERTSON TYRRELL, IN TORONTO

More than 20,000 Canadians served in the war with the British air services as pilots, observers, and ground support. One of the young fighter pilots who saw service in France in a Sopwith Camel was Gordon Tyrrell, from Toronto, who joined the Royal Flying Corps in 1917, when he was twenty. Like Billy Bishop, Gordon relished dogfights at dawn, as he described to his mother.

73 Squadron,
R.A.F. B.E.F.
France, Oct 10/18

My Dear Mother,

I'm afraid my letters are getting a bit behind but I know you wont mind when I tell you just how busy I've been and how much moving about we are doing. This is the time of our big push and daily the roar of the guns grows fainter and our balloon line is pushed farther and farther east. May it so continue . . .

In a big push our first show usually comes off at dawn. The three flights each spend between an hour and an hour and a half over the lines and often that is the completion of a day's work. Of course we cannot leave camp and are constantly "standing by". This gets very tiresome and often a little snooze or a scrounge fills in an afternoon. When the weather is "dud" it is very miserable as we really have no place to go except our tents. The mud is terrible and our clothes, bedding and all get very damp and disagreeable. It is really wonderful but nobody ever, or very rarely, seems to get sick . . . I have had a couple of warm baths in the past month and am just the "same sweet son" that I used to be. These consisted of two, two gallon petrol tins, of hot water and one of cold in a canvas bath about a yard square and a half or foot high. And, oh yes, I did wash my head in the last one, and then got one of the motorcycle mechanics, who used to be a barber to cut my hair. So I am fixed up there, for awhile anyway . . .

Gee it is hard getting up for a dawn show nowadays. And last Saturday we had our first touch of frost. But it is the most satisfactory time of the day as there are no huns astir to bother us and we can so pay full attention to the ground. The tanks had gone thru the wire and our infantry were advancing towards a small wood when suddenly from the corner of said wood I saw the flashes of a machine gun. I dived and sent a good long burst towards those flashes. Turning quickly I was regaining my height when I noticed a red light come from the wood. This must have been a signal to "Archie" [the flyers' term for anti-aircraft fire], for shortly after, as I was preparing for another dive, he started to send "them" up in earnest. I had a hot time for a couple of minutes. Twice again I dived watching closely but observed no more firing from the woods. Each time I had a warm reception but got away OK with a few holes in my wings . . .

The next day it was very "dud" so a bunch of the fellows got a tender and went up to the line around Gorry, where there had recently been some very terrific fighting. But I stayed and had a fine little fire going in our tent and wrote a letter to Berta and to Isabela. The fellows returned late in the afternoon tired, cold and hungry. They had seen some awful sights and I'll bet not many of them will want to go again. One thing in particular was a hun "Glycerine Pot" where human bodies had been used for its manufacture. The Australians had it all roped in and were charging 50 centimes admission. Isn't that a terrible burial for their "heroic dead"?

Monday I received your letter with the clipping about Len [a close schoolfriend who had been killed]. It is actually the first semi-official word that I'd had and you may imagine what a terrible shock it was to me. I can't even yet realize the truth that the best pal I ever had has gone out into the Golden West. A feeling of bitter hatred and of revenge fills me whenever I think of it, and yet again the helplessness and hopelessness of war makes me pray to God that such a thing had never been. And above it all, I am more firmly decided to see this thing through. Whatever the costs, and I know my brave family will "back me up" too.

Tuesday on the early show I had my first real fight with a Fokker. While engaged in straffing, I had thoughtlessly wandered some considerable distance over the enemy lines, and had also been separated from the remainder of our flight. At about 2000 feet I had just turned west when I noticed three of the enemy suddenly emerge from a cloud about a thousand feet above and in front of me. Let me here explain that this particular type of enemy machine is very fast, having great powers of diving and climbing speed. Their tactics are a swift dive, a burst of shots, and then a tremendous zoom up to safety again. It is almost fatal for them to come to close grips, as our smaller machines can actually turn twice to their once. Considering the odds against me I shoved my nose down for home. Instantly one of them dropped towards me, but as I stalled up under him "seeking a bead", he turned quickly aside. This gave me a chance to again drop my nose and beat it. In the instant he had stall-turned onto my tail and as I glanced back I saw him rapidly gaining to within firing distance. But I also noticed that the other two huns were not joining in the fight and so decided to turn on him. I side-slipped steeply to the right and just as I heard "pop! pop! pop!" pulled the old bus [plane] up and around to the left as I have never done before. Gee! I must have gone around fast. The blood rose to my head and I made one complete circuit and was again going west before I knew where I was. The hun evidently thought I was some stunt merchant for the next I saw of him he was climbing east as fast as he could towards the clouds. And do you know what flashed thru my mind at that time? "Two minds with but a single thought." But that is not all. Oh no! The best is yet to come for as I watched him a formation of eight of our scouts appeared thru the clouds and found themselves right on his tail. Yes only one thing could happen and believe me it did happen too. I saw him go down in flames.

That afternoon we flew to our "new" aerodrome which is only a short distance away. It consisted of a field full of shell-holes built on top of a hill. And, wonder of wonders, everybody landed OK. There were a lot of Yanks on rest in a ruined village nearby. They sure are a great bunch, full of "pep" and enthusiasm. Of course the war is new to them yet.

Our kits didn't arrive till late that night and we all had to work hard to get a bed. The cook and staff got drunk and so we had to fix up some bully-beef, bread, jam and tea for our supper. I never tasted anything so good for a long long time . . .

I have had very few letters and no parcels for a long, long time, but am waiting patiently. Everybody out here is very cheerful that the war will soon be over, so here's hoping. Give my love to our dear family and friends and keep lots for your dear self.

> Ever your loving son,
> Gordon.

Gordon returned to Toronto in 1919 and lived there until his death in 1981 at the age of eighty-four. In 1924, the Royal Canadian Air Force came into existence, but it lost its separate identity with the unification of the Canadian Armed Forces in 1968.

131

1919: SASKATCHEWAN
KENNETH LYON TO THE *FREE PRESS PRAIRIE FARMER* IN WINNIPEG

Those families that had not lost a son in the war often suffered the loss of a loved one in the Spanish flu epidemic of 1918–1919, in which about 50,000 Canadians died. Yet daily life on prairie farms carried on, as eleven-year-old Kenneth Lyon described in a letter to the Free Press Prairie Farmer's *Pathfinders Club for boys.*

Box 146, Admiral, Sask.
February 12, 1919

Dear Pathfinders:

I have been reading your letters ever since we took the paper. And I want to become a member, too. I will be 12 years old on the 7th of March. I have 3 ½ miles to go to school. The name of my school is the Clifford school. Our school was closed in October on account of the flu. I am in the fifth grade. My teacher drove her car and I rode with her. I cranked it for her. Sometimes when it was cold we boys had to push it down the hill to get it started. We have a car. It is a Ford. I like to run a car. I have shot 12 jack rabbits and an owl this winter with a shotgun. We live nine miles from town. My papa let me have a piece of ground this year and I got 12 bushels of wheat from it. I was in the Boys' and Girls' Pig contest this summer and I got 7th prize. The prize was $4. I brought a $50 Victory Bond with my money. I have a brother that enlisted in 1916. He was killed in action on Oct. 30. He was 25 years old.

Kenneth Lyon

132

1919: ENGLAND

GEORGES VANIER TO HIS FATHER, PHILIAS VANIER, IN MONTREAL

Georges Vanier, a twenty-six-year-old lawyer in Montreal, was one of the first to sign up for the 22nd (French-Canadian) Battalion when it was formed in 1914. Vanier spent four years in Europe with the "Van Doos," as the regiment was soon known. Three months before the November 1918 armistice, he was wounded in battle and his right leg was amputated. While recuperating in a London hospital, he reflected on the death of the French-Canadian hero Sir Wilfrid Laurier and a world shattered by "the Great War."

Canadian Red Cross Hospital à Londres,
24 avril 1919

Mon bien cher papa,

Your letter of 8 April, which I received this morning, gave me much pleasure. Thank you for your kind thoughts and your good wishes on my birthday.

I share completely your pessimistic views regarding Europe and even the whole world. Wars are not over: they are only beginning. I do not foresee another war like the one we have just lived through but I do predict several social and revolutionary wars. There is no doubt that England right now is going through a domestic crisis which will have serious consequences.

I do not defend Russian Bolshevism—far from it. However I do realize it is the sort of violent reaction that inevitably follows an autocratic regime when the people are oppressed and <u>kept</u> in ignorance of their rights and responsibilities. The situation in Russia before the revolution was dreadful. The aristocracy gradually became more and more decadent. You only have to read *The Last of the Romanoffs* by Charles Rivet to appreciate the desperate situation of the Tzarist regime. Reading this historic book written by *The Times* correspondent in Petrograd instills in you such a strong repulsion that you remain deeply marked by it.

The Times this morning speaks of a "manifesto" from the French socialist group. The constitution and the laws of France could suffer considerable modifications. Even Canada will have its own internal crises—I already see elements of separatism between west and east. The next election will be a contest between those who support and those who oppose the tariff . . .

I was deeply touched by your transcription of a passage from the newspaper containing the ideas of Sir Wilfrid [Laurier] on death and life after death . . .

> Very devotedly your son,
> Georges

Georges Vanier's concerns about social unrest in Canada seemed justified when the Winnipeg General Strike broke out a week after he wrote this letter. Vanier himself went on to become a distinguished Canadian diplomat, and to serve as governor general of Canada from 1959 to 1967.

133
1919: SASKATCHEWAN
SARAH RAMSLAND TO HER PARENTS IN MINNESOTA

Step by step, women inched their way into public office. When Sarah Ramsland was a thirty-seven-year-old teacher and mother of three children, her husband, Max (who was the Liberal MLA for Pelly riding), died. Although there had never been a woman legislator in Saskatchewan, she ran and won in the Pelly by-election. As the province's only woman MLA, she was isolated in the House. But she won the admiration of colleagues and voters by her determination to improve rural education and to make divorce laws fairer to women.

Regina, Saskatchewan
November 29, 1919

Dear Mother and Father:

Well the ordeal of taking my seat in Parliament is all over, and my name goes down in Saskatchewan history. I was given a very warm welcome, and as one man said to me today I had attained an honor no other lady in Sask. could attain in being the first lady member: I have received many compliments and congratulations, but you can rest assured that it has not affected my head in the least and I only wish I was more worthy of the many nice things said about me. Everyone tells me I was so very calm and undisturbed as I went through the introduction, but if I looked that part I was not feeling that way.

After I took my seat as a real member there was great applause and when the House adjourned I was surrounded by crowds of people waiting to meet me. A number of women's organizations was there from the city to extend a hearty welcome also Govt. members and private members. One woman's organization here in the city invited me as Guest of Honor at a luncheon in one of the best hotels in the city next Thursday.

I was out at the Buildings this morning and to my great surprise here I was escorted to a special room with a card on the door, "Lady Members Room." That is something no other private member has. One Govt. official said to me it was all ready for me except the rocking chair and that was coming. This room of mine has a nice table, large mirror, telephone, writing paper, easy chairs and I certainly appreciate very much the courtesy I am receiving. Max had many friends here in Regina, and among the members of the Govt. and that is one reason for them being so kind to me, and although my position takes me among men and has since I began my campaign and entered into politics, but I was told by a man in Kamsack who opposed me and admitted he did that he heard it on every hand that although going into politics [and] going through a hard campaign I had been a perfect lady in every way and I held the respect of everyone by the lady-like way I concluded myself. I told him if for one moment I thought I could not be the same lady I had always tried to be I would never have entered politics. And I am sure my own good judgment will be used in every instance and my vote during my political [career] can <u>never be bought</u>.

I miss the children but I know they are getting the best of care . . . I must close . . .

> Lovingly,
> Sod

134
1920: ALBERTA
KOST KLYM TO HIS UNCLE IN UKRAINE

Between 1891 and 1914, 170,000 Ukrainian peasants arrived in Canada. Among them was Kost Klym, a giant of a man who spent most of his working life as a coal miner and who, alongside many of his fellow-countrymen, was interned as an "enemy alien" in 1914.

> P.O. Box 332 Canmore, Alta.
> 02 July 1920

Dear Uncle:

I was very delighted with the letter you wrote to me and I thank you sincerely for it and the fact that you do not ignore me. I know that you consider yourself in the same category as the average laborer. I feel well and wish you good health and all your family.

I am getting along not too badly, generally like an average coal digger. I work every day now and earn $6.00 for an 8-hour shift. I work on the day shift. In 1918 I worked on a contract and earned $10.00 a day, but left that job in the spring, for I did not want to work that hard; and since I worked a long time in water, I damaged my feet to a certain degree. I could work out in the open, but something always pulls me into the mines, but it is hard to last long on mine work. When one works out in the open, the pay is so low that one can't exist on it. In these mountains everything is very expensive. Besides I'm tired of moving from place to place. Had I not considered to travel to the Old Country, I would have been in Manitoba long ago.

I have saved close to $800, since I have been released from internment, that is, since April 22 [1916]. I was interned for two years. Now I seldom receive letters from the [old] country, although I write home fairly often.

From autumn until mid-February, I wrote three and three letters in March and April and received not one reply.

However, during these last two months, I received two. They always write that there is "beeda", hard times, and want me to return home. But there is no peace there, so why go? If there were peace, I would go.

Best wishes to your whole family, until we meet again.

Yours, Kost Klym

Kost Klym never returned to Ukraine.

135

1922: ONTARIO

DR. J.B. COLLIP TO DR. H.M. TORY IN ALBERTA

Bert Collip, a biochemist from the University of Alberta, was working in Toronto with the illustrious physiologist Professor J.J.R. MacLeod in the fall of 1921 when he was invited by Dr. Frederick Banting to join the team investigating the internal secretions of the pancreas. Banting already knew that the key to the treatment of diabetes lay in these secretions; the challenge was to isolate and extract the secretion in a form that was pure enough for use in humans.

182 Soudan Ave
Toronto
Jan 25/22

Dear Doctor Tory

I have received your letter of January 18th. In reply I will be pleased to accept your offer of the Chair of Biochemistry in the University of Alberta according to the terms outlined by you in your previous letter to me . . .

Since last writing you I have had such a phenomenal break in my research that I must tell you some particulars. Last Thursday Jan. 19th I finally unearthed a method of isolating the internal secretion of the pancreas in a fairly pure and seemingly stable form suitable for human administration. It was tried out in one case in the clinic with such encouraging results that today $5000 has been placed at our disposal to secure apparatus, four assistants etc. to rush the work for the next four months in the hope that we may establish a block of clinical evidence which will prove either the value or the worthlessness of this substance in treating diabetes in the human. There are three of us associated with Prof. Macleod in the work. Dr. Banting a surgeon and Mr. Best a recent graduate first demonstrated the feasability of use of pancreatic extracts. I was invited to share in the future developments and definitely took over the chemical side as well as a part of the physiological side of the problem. We some time ago succeeded in producing a potent extract which produced marvellous effects on dogs but which if injected into humans produced abscesses. While we were confident that we had established the potency of pancreatic extracts prepared in a definite manner, an apparently insurmountable barrier lay before us. It was useless for human administration.

The problem seemed almost hopeless so you can imagine my delight when about midnight one day last week I discovered a way to get the active principle free from all the "muck" with which it appeared to be inseparably bound. On the advice of Prof. Macleod and others I am keeping the process an absolute secret.

We have decided not to patent it but to offer it to the University. The response was as I have indicated. I am to go ahead and prepare the material which is to be given a thorough tryout. If it is pronounced satisfactory I will direct the establishment of a manufacturing plant in connection with the Connaught Labs. If it should be pronounced unsatisfactory no harm has been done. When it has been proven, if proven it is, the method will be published in fullest detail for the world at large.

As it appears now we will have seven papers on the subject. In three of these I will be senior and associated in two others.

I have told you these facts because I am sure you will be interested but also in order that you will be able properly to interpret any wild newspaper talk which you may chance to see.

I would prefer that no publicity be given our present actions until we are finally able to report success or failure in the human.

Yours sincerely
J. B. Collip

Although Collip had played a crucial role in the discovery of insulin, quarrels with Banting persuaded him to return to Alberta. He would become a world-famous pioneer in endocrinology and serve as dean of medicine at the University of Western Ontario from 1947 to 1961.

136

1922: ALBERTA
GERTRUDE CHASE TO HER MOTHER IN WASHINGTON STATE

Who today can imagine dressing their daughters in clothes made of flour sacks, dyed pink, or surviving a winter on moose stews? But that was how Gertrude Chase, an American who homesteaded in northern Alberta with her husband, Webster, lived. I think Webster was handier with a rifle (and perhaps the whisky bottle) than a spade, so the family subsisted on Gertie's vegetable patch, chickens, and cow.

Feb. 11, 1922
Halcourt, Alta.
Canada

Dear Mother,

We received your letter of Jan. 1 a short time ago. Have been in very good health so far this winter. Am sorry to hear that you have been sick. How are you now? Have you gotten entirely over it?

We have had very little snow here this winter till just this month. Did not have enough for sleighing. Have plenty now. Have had some very cold weather this week. 30 below zero over night. The same tonight.

It has been very dull here all winter no work any where hardly for the men. A lot of them around here have gone up into the woods to trap for something to do to make a little money. But they dont seem to get much fur. Some dont get any. They dont know how I guess. We got a little money through threshing and that keeps us in flour etc. this winter along with what potatoes and garden stuff we raised and some moose meat. The moose are large animals you know. We take some carrots and onions and potatoes and rice and a moose bone and make a mulligan quite often. I dont know what I would do if I was to get a new dress. I havent had a good one for so long. Things have been so high here ever since we have been here. They are coming down a little now but they dont get much for their grain now. We can raise fine potatoes on this place. They are nice and mealy. Our place is a flat along the river of sandy loam, just right for potatoes. I would like to try some strawberries here of the ever bearing kind, I think we could make a fair living off the place with things like that . . .

I think its the best life there is myself, if we just had some neighbours, but we are three miles I think from the nearest. I have seen no women since fall. There have been lots of men at our place to go moose hunting all winter but

I havent been away from home myself since threshing stopped in October. Before that I stayed here all winter and summer without going away at all. So I dont know just what to think about it. I cant say I like to live that way. There is no school near and Alice is nine and should go to school. So we will either have to move out soon or send her somewhere to go to school. It is hard to keep the children's clothes in condition and get ready to go anywhere with so many of them and then so far to go anywhere. We cant go to an entertainment at Halcourt as it is ten miles or so from here. Well as I have my health I guess I shouldnt complain perhaps. I am sending the picture you were asking for. I wish I had a good picture of the children I could send you. You ought to see the baby. She has brown eyes and her hair curls. Cant you have your picture taken in town and send us a good one sometime?

Tell Pete to write. I'll try and answer. Alice would like to write to you. She can write good but doesnt know how to read or spell much yet. Is good at figures. Cora went to school 1 month last fall while Webster was threshing at Halcourt. She learns good. Florence is a big stout girl same as ever and full of mischief, will be 5 in March. Ruth is quiet and more like Cora. Well the house is getting cold, I have to stop and go to bed, it is getting quite late. Write soon.

From Gertie

P.S. If you should happen to have any old clothes you could send don't send anything unless it is worthwhile. That is unless it is fair condition. Not to many holes and thin spots you know.

137

1923: SASKATCHEWAN

A YOUNG MOTHER TO MARGARET SANGER, EDITOR OF
THE BIRTH CONTROL REVIEW IN NEW YORK CITY

No information about contraception was publicly available in Canada until 1969, and most physicians refused to tell their patients how to limit their families. Many women turned to an American source: The Birth Control Review, *published in New York by Margaret Sanger. The review's letters page reveals the desperation of many Canadian mothers. I wish I knew the end of the story for this woman.*

August 1923
Saskatchewan

Dear Mrs. Sanger,

I sincerely trust you will pardon me for writing you this letter, but I have just finished reading your book, *Woman and the New Race*, and I could not help but feel that you were a true friend to women, and some way I felt that you might be able to help me.

I am a young married woman nineteen years old and I have a dear little baby boy five and a half months old, and I am expecting another baby in four months. Now, we are not in a position to support more than two children as my husband and I both work hard for a living. I love my baby and I want to give him a fair chance in life. I have a good husband and he don't want to see a big family in want any more than I do. I have good health at present, but oh! Mrs. Sanger, how long would it be good if babies came to me that fast, and once health and happiness are gone, what is the use of asking help then? Now is the time, and if you could only tell me how to prevent conception you would make me the happiest woman in Canada. Oh! I would be so thankful. If it is impossible for you to do this, is there any way I could find out, or must I go on and lose all that is sweet in life and bring into the world a big family which I could not take the proper care of? Where I might raise two as they should be, and we would all be happy. As you perhaps know, Birth Control has not advanced very far in Canada as yet and I am afraid you are my only hope. Oh! Mrs. Sanger, if you only would help me, I would never forget your kindness, you who are trying so hard to lead us to freedom. May God bless you and your good work.

138

1924: ENGLAND
NORMAN ROBERTSON TO HIS MOTHER,
FLORA ROBERTSON, IN VANCOUVER

There's an unfamiliar note in this letter: a Canadian impatience with British pretensions. When a clever and self-assured young graduate of the University of British Columbia arrived at Oxford University on a Rhodes Scholarship, he entered into activities at Balliol College with a mixture of enthusiasm and skepticism. Norman Robertson was not afraid to challenge long-held assumptions of British superiority.

Oxford,
February 25, 1924

Dear Mother,

Haven't heard from home for quite a while but assume that your letters are somewhere in the thousands of mail bags held up at Plymouth. No one has had any Canadian mail this week so we will place the blame on the dock strike. The new departure in stationery and letterhead does not signify anything except that I have another half hour to put in before I can leave an extremely dull and unintelligible lecture. The general subject of the course is Modern Realism but for ten days now the lecturer has never been within striking distance of his subject. Just now the old sophist is holding forth on the frailties of symbolic logic about which I share the turkey's amiable sentiments and do not care a single damn. However I'm stuck here till one so shall thus improve the shining hour.

I have really no news at all. Last Sunday I had tea with Les MacLennan at Mrs. Gerrans. You will notice how scrupulously careful I am to keep on the right side of people who write home to Vancouver. Tomorrow night I will probably go to the [Oxford] Union of which I am at long last a member. Friday night [Bertrand] Russell speaks at the Labor Club and on Saturday I am going to see *She Stoops to Conquer* at the Playhouse. Tomorrow Toggers [Torpids, an intercollegiate rowing competition] start. They are rowed on the next six days. It is an ordeal that I'm not looking forward to. My last day on the river will be a week tomorrow. I certainly hope I can stick to this resolution . . .

Well at last the mail has come. Four letters from home this morning. For over a fortnight the dock strike has held up the American mail but although the men are not yet back to work, it is not likely that mails at least will be tied up any longer. All the letters in a bunch leave one quite breathless and I don't know where or how to begin to answer them. So I'm tacking this letter onto the tail of a scrawl I started almost a week ago. It is my first experiment with a quill pen—written during a very dull lecture. Well what do I know. Nothing that seems worth writing about. Things never happen in Oxford. There is no such thing as news. We just go on as we have gone on for nearly two terms now. One's nights and days are all controlled by the [rowing] coach, when you get up & when you go to bed. What you eat at every meal & tea etc. When flu was raging they actually gave us quinine pills as a preventative. At least the pills were more palatable than the ammoniated variety. But it did seem foolish and trivial. Last Friday I entertained at breakfast in my rooms. Really a sumptuous repast. Ten people sat down to a five course breakfast culminating in poached eggs on beef-steak. I have not yet rec'd the . . . account but it was a good breakfast anyway and I pretty well owed it. Torpids are half over. This afternoon will be our fourth race since Thursday. Rowing is [a] very unpleasant way of spending a fine afternoon. Always leaves me positively ill at the finish. However as a crew we have done quite decently. It is hard to explain about . . . bumping races [which] are most complicated affairs. However on Saturday we cadged our share of immortality by doing something which had never been done before. Oxford epitomizes that Toryism which believes that nothing should ever be done for the first time. When Balliol II bumped Balliol I the consternation in official circles was immense. There was no precedent for a second boat bumping the first boat of the same college. I don't know what will be the final decision. Meanwhile *Times* and *Morning Post* are speculating on possible outcome. Three more days and then I blossom out as an aesthete . . .

Have not done any work so far this term. This despite two essays a week. I've two tutors, one in economic history, one in ethics. They are both young and presumably have taken good degrees. The economics man is a stickler for efficiency and neatness. Keeps most relevant information in an easily accessible filing cabinet and can repeat most textbooks from memory. And that is absolutely all that can be said for him . . . The man in Ethics is infinitely worse. He is a Greats [classics] tutor and supposedly a first class man. He is both ignorant and quarrelsome. I'm not in a huff over anything special. That is just my serious opinion of him that most people share. He rather fancies himself as an exponent of the Socratic method of eliciting truth by question and answers. After I have read an essay for him, he sits in thoughtful silence for some minutes trying to remember what the essay was about. When this attempt fails he asks me for a digest of the paper in words of one syllable . . . All he wanted was a lodgment for his quibbling . . .

Oxford is a beautiful city to live and loaf in. Balliol I like and would unwillingly be elsewhere. Englishmen I find very agreeable and "affable". I've made many friends and have never time on my hands. All these sides of the Rhodes I do enjoy. There are many things over here that we will, in the nature of things, never have in Canada and U.S.A.

But there is just one item in the 100% Oxonian's credo that I will challenge whenever and wherever I can. And this is the confident assumption that the lesser breeds without the law who've never been to Oxford or

Cambridge lack the intellectual acuteness & distinction that is supposed to inhere in Oxford gentlemen.

When people take it for granted that an Oxford first class is somehow on quite a different plane from a U.B.C. first they are, to put it mildly, talking through their hats. The average in Balliol is of course higher than the average at home. But after all, that average at Balliol is supposed to be higher than in other colleges. More people over here are comparatively well read than at home. But after all, why shouldn't they be? Most of them are wealthy, all come from comfortable middle-class homes, as many people in U.B.C. do not. But except for the cult of aesthetes from whom, thank God we are free in U.B.C. there is nothing that really matters over here that can't be matched in Canada. This is rank heresy, but like most heresies it has the truth within it . . .

Be very careful of yourself and go easily for a while yet. I am keeping very fit and it is up to you to follow suit. Love to all.

Norman A. Robertson

Norman Robertson returned to Canada and in 1929 joined Ottawa's Department of External Affairs. He became one of the most important diplomats of his generation and served as high commissioner in London, ambassador in Washington, and under-secretary of state for external affairs.

139
1924: EDMONTON
EMILY MURPHY TO WILLIAM DEACON IN TORONTO

Emily Murphy (1868–1933), who wrote under the name "Janey Canuck," was a leading activist for women's rights. "The world loves a peaceful man," she said, "but gives way to a strenuous kicker." In 1916, when she was appointed to the bench in Edmonton, she became the first woman judge in the British Empire. She had a deep compassion for the plight of the poor and desperate, of whom there were many in Alberta as crops began to fail. She was particularly appalled by capital punishment (which remained on the statute books in Canada until 1976), as she told her friend the Toronto critic William Deacon.

The Police Court
Edmonton
August 14, 1924

My dear William,

. . . I was down at the Provincial jail to-day and the Superintendent Blythe
and the Deputy Minister of Public Works were with me. I was making a
report on conditions at the jail for the Social Service Council of Canada.

In the death cell, old Picarello [convicted of a brutal murder] had drawn
a picture of the hangman on the wall—"a downcast hangman who had no
job," he said—but the hangman got the job alright. It must have been a grim
satisfaction to that official as he bound "Pic" and bound him up to know
that he had "Finis" up his sleeve . . . When the Warden entered his cell,
[Picarello] fainted . . .

The Warden tells me that the death watch is changed every four hours
because this official must never take his eyes off the condemned man. If
left longer the watchman's eyes get heavy and he falls asleep. Don't you
think this is almost as bad as execution—to be observed for every instant?
This alone, might drive a man to murder . . .

Superintendent Wm. Blythe was born on the jail farm over 50 years ago
when it was the headquarters of the Mounted Police. He was a bugler in
their band, as a boy, and lately was appointed the Superintendent . . . He
is a lusty, likeable fellow and has a wife who makes a wonderful dinner.
Our waiter who came and stood at the dining room door with a [tray]
upon which Madam laid the dishes from the table, was a gentleman
convicted for a breach of the new liquor act in Alberta, but I pretended I
didn't see.

In one of the cells I talked with a man who is to die on August 30th for
killing his child in a fit of rage. He wasn't a murderer to me. I have written
the Minister of Justice [Ernest Lapointe] (but no one knows not even the
prisoner) saying this should be culpable homicide under 261 of the Code,
and that the sentence should be commuted to life imprisonment. He and
his wife were lovers as boy and girl and lived on adjoining farms in the
States. He came here 11 years ago, and went to an arid district. In all that
time, he never had a crop and I think his nerves broke under the strain, and
so he destroyed what he had been trying to protect. It must be so for he is
loved by his relatives, and even by his neighbours.

I didn't cry—only the men with me [did]. It would be foolish to bid him
be strong and then be weak myself. And I told him too, about all the strong

young men alive to-day who would die before him, in the next 6 weeks, and of what Sir Walter Scott said,

> "Come he slow, or come he fast,
> It is but death that comes at last."

He is quite a fine looking man but his hair has turned white this last month or so, and his hands were clammy as I held them in mine . . .

There are two women in the Fort awaiting trial for murder, but I could not stand anymore. One is watched all the time by the girl convicts, because she has attempted suicide by hanging on two occasions, and nearly succeeded.

Don't show this to Sarah, it would sadden her. I don't know why God lets me look into hearts like these. Maybe, He knows I need it to keep my balance true. I often feel it would, otherwise, be quite easy to fly without even a propeller. It must be the altitude here that causes this.

> Always affectionately,
> Janey Canuck

Emily Murphy was one of the six women who challenged the exclusion of women from the definition of "persons" in the British North America Act. They appealed the Persons Case all the way to the Privy Council in England, which agreed, in a landmark 1929 ruling, that women were in fact persons.

140

1925: OTTAWA

PRIME MINISTER W.L. MACKENZIE KING TO ELIZABETH CLOUGH IN SOUTH AFRICA

In 1925, the Liberal leader William Lyon Mackenzie King had been prime minister for three and a half years; only the support of the new farmers' party, the Progressives, guaranteed his precarious hold on power. King's public image was of a sober and rather colourless leader, but a more whimsical side appeared in his private correspondence. When a letter addressed to "Dear Government" arrived from a little girl in South Africa who was worried about "red-skins" being locked up on reserves and not being allowed to shoot "Grizzily Bears," King sent a personal reply.

Ottawa,
March 28th, 1925.

Dear Elizabeth,

I cannot begin to tell you how very pleased the members of the Government of Canada were when they received your letter.

Some of the letters they receive are so very hard to read—not beautifully written as yours was—and sometimes people ask for the most extraordinary things! You would hardly believe me, I am sure, were I to tell you all the things the people in Canada ask for!

The only difficulty about your letter was that each Minister thought *he* should answer it. However, I was very firm and told them I was the one to do it.

I then spoke, at once, to the Minister of the Interior, who looks after Indians, and he tells me, Elizabeth, that there is nothing you need worry about. It's like this. Supposing the Indians had all gone a-hunting, some one might come and settle on their lands or steal their tents—all kinds of

Prime Minister Mackenzie King's public face was dour and serious, but he showed a surprising streak of whimsy when dealing with a little South African girl.

dreadful things—while they were away. So the Government just puts up big signs "This land is reserved for our Indians,"—and no one dares to touch anything. But the Indians are never shut up, Elizabeth, and if any Grizzly Bears come, they can always shoot them if they feel like doing so. You say you are coming to Canada when you are fifteen. That is splendid. The Minister of the Interior says that if he is still Minister of the Interior (you never can be quite sure), he will see that we have a good supply of Indians on hand.

The Minister of Defence says that if he is still Minister of Defence, he will give them plenty of ammunition with which to shoot the bears. And I feel sure that some one else—probably the Minister of Agriculture—will arrange for the grizzly bears—so that's all right, Elizabeth.

But there is something I want you to tell me—about South Africa. This Government has never been there but perhaps some day they might feel like going. Now is it true, Elizabeth, that when you have your tea in the garden, lions sometimes come and sit down beside you?

And when you go for a walk, do you have to be *very* careful, for fear a rhinoceros or a hippopotamus might want to walk with you?

It would be apt to make the Government *very nervous*. There is so much you must tell me when you come. Of course, I know you always ride on elephants.

But I shall have to say good-bye now. It was very nice of you to write (we all thought the letter paper beautiful!) Will you let me thank you again for the Government and with all good wishes, say at present Good-bye Elizabeth.

Yours sincerely
W. L. Mackenzie King

141

1925: BRITISH COLUMBIA
DUTCH EMIGRANTS TO THE EDITOR OF
DE NIEUWE TILBURGSCHE COURANT **IN HOLLAND**

In 1925, as part of its campaign to entice immigrants with appropriate skills to particular regions and industries, the Canadian government lured Dutch agricultural workers to marshy areas on the west coast. A Mrs. Rutten, in the north of British Columbia, sent exaggerated and misleading propaganda back to her hometown of Tilburg, in Holland, and probably got paid a per capita sum for each Tilburger she attracted. One

group of her recruits, however, wrote home to the local newspaper, warning readers that
Mrs. Rutten was a hard-hearted liar.

British Columbia

1925

Dear Editor:

In April of this year we emigrated to Graham Island in Canada due to the insistence of Mr. and Mrs. Rutten, both Tilburgers. The above-mentioned had distributed a circular in which the primary contents came down to the following:

1)   The government has contracted the construction of roads here which provides regular work at $3.75 a day.

2)   You can catch fish here and sell them to a cannery in Tow Hill.

3)   The government grants free land which when developed can be sold for $25 an acre.

4)   In order to get here everyone must have 426 Guilders passage money and at least $25 (62.5 guilders) landing money.

Thus far their circular. Now the truth.

The fellows (nearly all Tilburgers) came here about the middle of May after a long trip which had taken almost four weeks. First to Massett from where they were sent to Tow Hill supposedly to dig clams. It was said that you could earn $7 to $8 a day at it. They moved on about 30 km. further and lived there on the beach in a very big house in which there was nothing. The fellows, for the first time, suffered hunger there. Lacking a pot or pan, they ate raw potatoes. They even ate an eagle, a black crow and a sea gull (this only serves to prove that they were truly hungry). How were the earnings? The first days they weren't able to do better than 50 cents a day, that's all together, 7 people. But of course this was a period of training, even though when they knew how to do it, and there are truly good diggers among them, they were never able to earn more than $1 or $1.50 a day per person. So that was the first lie.

Mrs. Rutten told us then that it would get better and that everything was fine, as a result the fellows regularly wrote good letters home.

Finally, after three months, we began on the much-promised road work. We moved again, about 16 km further on and worked there not quite

2 months when the work was stopped because, according to the engineer, the road was useless because no people lived there. Most of the fellows, before they began work on the road, had contracted some debts because they could not earn a living.

Just as the work stopped, three new boys arrived, misled by the Ruttens' alluring circular and reassured (so the fellows later found out) by the fine letters which they had written home at the urging of Mrs. Rutten. After being bored in Tow Hill for 14 days and making only debts, because there are no people and no work, we began other road work, however this was 100 km further on. The road to the place, which had to be traveled primarily on foot, was for us a true "via dolorosa." We each carried about 60 pounds of freight on our backs and traveled on an almost impassable road. As a result we arrived at our destination more dead than alive and were allowed to rest on plank beds. We were there for three weeks, then the boss stopped the work because he saw that it just wouldn't work any longer. For that matter, 3 of the boys had already become sick because of the sleeping accommodations. Our beds regularly got soaking wet from the damp that came out of the ground.

Then back to Massett; but during the three weeks, the road that we needed to go back on had flooded and so we crossed a lake on a raft of tree trunks. It still surprises me that nobody drowned because it was an extremely dangerous trip, even though it ended well. Then we had to walk a distance of 12 km and following that we were taken to Massett in a boat. When we arrived there it was 8 o'clock in the evening and we had left home at 7:30 a.m., so we had been underway for about 12 hours. We arrived in Massett dead tired and hungry and passed the night, without food and bed, in a house about 20 steps from that of Mrs. Rutten. When we told Mrs. Rutten where we were and asked her for a lamp, because it was dark, her husband replied that he wasn't going to pay any attention to us.

Now the fellows had had enough and they decided to leave the island. As three of them didn't have a cent, one of the boys asked the aforementioned lady if she would lend them some money against security, but she refused. When she heard that all the fellows were prepared to help the three empty handed ones, she loaned us enough money to get to the next place but at security of three times the value.

We are now off the island and we recommend that anyone who wants to emigrate to Graham Island on the importuning of Mrs. Rutten first seeks some good information about the place.

Now something about the place:

Every fellow got 160 acres of land in his name. We went to see it once, but two of the boys almost drowned in it. It's completely under water and we heard from everyone here that the land is completely worthless. We also have a real farmer with us and he says the same thing. For that matter if the soil was good and you could grow enough on it, then you still couldn't sell the produce because there aren't any people here to buy it. At Tow Hill, which is 20 km from the land, there are 40 people in the summer (mostly Indians) and not one in the winter. In Massett, that's another 30 km further on, there are perhaps 40 whites and 400 Indians, although the latter buy little or nothing, so that you can freely say that there are no people in those places.

In closing, Mrs. Rutten says that she earned her money (and she has a lot) on the island. This is absolutely untrue as she earned all her money in Prince Rupert, thus not on the island . . .

But let everyone be warned by this letter. There's nothing there now and it will never become anything. The connections are nothing either; there's not one good road, there are no people and the land is good for nothing.

We thank you dear editor for the space and we remain with the highest regards,

> A. Smulders, B. Laurijssen, J. Bisschop, H. Kemps,
> J. Couwenberg, A. Kemps.
> Old Colonists of the Golden Gate

142

1927: BRITISH COLUMBIA
AMELIA CARVER TO THE EDITOR OF *SCHOOL DAYS*
IN VANCOUVER

The era of uppity girls was about to dawn, and red-haired Amelia seems to have been in the vanguard. She knew that her strong sense of self and habit of questioning conventional wisdom would get her into trouble at junior high school, but, judging from her letter, her sense of humour might allow her to escape.

British Columbia,

1927

tor:

__d hair and a bad temper and I am going to Junior High School when it opens in September. I am signing my real name, but I am never called by it. My parents must be dead because I lived in the Orfunidge until I was nine years old, when a kind man and his wife adopted me, so now I have their name. I am real dumb at school being a farely good speller but a poor writer and fractions and decimals drive me crazy. Do you think I could grow up and be a nurse without knowing decimals and fractions? I think I could put two-thirds of a spoonful of medicine in three-quarters of a glass of water and I know I could make the patient drink it by holding her nose, but I never could divide seven-eighths of a bottle of castor oil by five-thirds of a tablespoonful and reduce it to its lowest terms.

I have selected my first patient as the girl who stood behind me when I went to see the Prince come in on August 18th. I pushed a policeman aside and stood in the front row with my hat off. My hair is so bright it could not help but catch the Prince's eye, so he smiled at me. Then, would you believe it, this tall bleached blonde behind me proclaimed to all around that the Prince smiled at her and began powdering her nose. If I had her for a patient I would first wash her face and scour it with a brick to get down to the natural skin and then I would give her a dose of bitters that would not be measured out in fractions. If this is published I will write a letter each month telling how I get on at Junior High School. Even when I have done my best I know there will be trouble.

Yours truly,
Amelia Carver.

¹43
1927: NORTHWEST TERRITORIES
EDGAR CHRISTIAN TO HIS PARENTS IN WALES

When eighteen-year-old Edgar Christian heard his Uncle Jack's invitation, he was suf-
fused with excitement: this would be the adventure of a lifetime. Jack Hornby's name
was already a legend in the Canadian Arctic: an eccentric loner, he had twenty years'
experience living and travelling in the Far North. He asked his young English relative
to join him and another Englishman, Harold Allard, for a winter on the Thelon River
in "the Barren Ground," 600 kilometres from any non-native settlement. In May 1926,
the threesome set off from Edmonton in high spirits, but during the brutal winter that
followed, disaster struck. The caribou, on which Hornby depended for survival, never
came. First Hornby, then Allard, succumbed to death. Edgar Christian was left alone in
a log cabin that was pitifully exposed and inaccessible. As he felt his own death
approach, five days away from his nineteenth birthday, he scribbled two last notes.

May 1927
The Windsor
on Dominion Square
Montreal

Dear Father
My Address is not the above but I hope this finds you one day.

  Jack Hornby always wished to see the Country sometime before he gave
up the Life in Arctic Regions & wanted someone with him & I was the one

this time. I realize why he wanted a boy of my age with him & I realize why one other should come in order to make sure I got out safe, but alas the Thelon is not what it is Cracked up to be I dont think. I have now been trying to Struggle by myself for over a month & help my other poor pal but Spring is Late here & I cannot get fresh meat although have always had food to eat at times some jolly good meals only a few days ago which did not put me in condition to hunt fresh food but the weather blew cold & to day June 1st has seen me with fine weather food but not fresh & unable to get fresh being too weak & played out.

Adamson Corona Hotel Edmonton finds 2 trunks of mine & In on[e] that Bible & Prayer Book which Jack refused to let me bring do not be annoyed but I know why now & Jack alone was one man in this world who can let a young boy know what this world & the next are.

I Loved him he Loved me. Very seld[om] is there true Love between 2 men!

Bye Bye Now Love
& Thanks for all
you have Ever done for
me Edgar.

Dear Mother
feeling weak now can only write Little. Sorry Left it so Late but alas I have Struggled hard.

Please dont Blame Dear Jack He Loves you & me only In this world & tell no one else this but keep it & believe.

Ever loving & thankful to
You for all a Dear Mother
is to a Boy & has been to me
Bye Bye Love to all
& Dulc Rits Fred Charls
& Gwen
Edgar

In August 1928, the RCMP detachment in Chesterfield Inlet telegraphed to Ottawa that the "bodies of Hornby party of three men" had been discovered in a cabin on the north bank of the Thelon River. "Death apparently due to starvation."

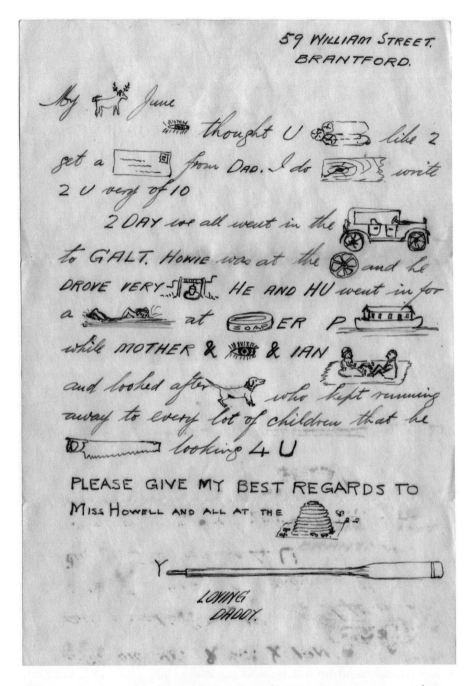

June Copeland, a seven-year-old from Grimsby, Ontario, was nervous when she went to camp, but her father wrote reassuring picture letters to her.

144
1927: ONTARIO
WILLIAM DEACON TO B.K. SANDWELL IN TORONTO

Wilson MacDonald (1880–1967), in the words of one biographer, was "a barn-storming versifier with unbending faith in his own greatness." This popular poet, who was a great hit as a public performer, was also cantankerous, opinionated, and, as the critic Bill Deacon warned the writer Bernard Sandwell, a difficult house guest.

November 14, 1927

Dear Sandwell,

Wilson MacDonald, whom Merrill Denison has aptly named the world's most imperfect guest, will be with you on Thursday; and it may be as well to forewarn you. In a sense you will be held responsible for his atrocities, and you will naturally hold me responsible for not telling you so here goes.

He is an anti-prohibition fanatic. He likes a good drink of strong liquor, but he only takes one on an occasion, one per diem.

Though himself approaching 50 years of age, he objects to associating with older people—particularly women. He does not like to associate with married people, particularly married women. That is why he hasn't been at my house in years. He desires to be perpetually surrounded by virgins from 16 to 21 years of age, and they must be pretty. He can relish a dozen to twenty of these at a time. Fear not. He will not copulate with them, but simply likes to play around with pretty girls—very much his inferiors in age and brains. The ideal entertainment is a dance at which only the undeflowered are present, and he is the only male.

He is a strict vegetarian.

He objects to everything that is set before him in the way of food—particularly dainties, and tells you how bad they are for you to eat, and what a healthful diet consists of and how well he can cook. (He does, in fact, everything well—he is the best tennis-player, skier, skater, poet, dramatist, piano player, watch-repairer etc., ad infin.)

His pet antipathy just now is Robertson of the Wpg. *Free Press* who knocked his book (I admit the article was spiteful and unfair) but still if you don't want a tirade of 3 hours keep off critics and reviewers.

Underneath it all he is a most sweet and lovable chap; only until one knows all his prejudices getting on with him for even a few hours is an almost unbearable strain. I speak as his best friend. I curse him out every six months or so and vow never to speak to him again, but I always do. He's a dear soul, who has lived too much to himself, that's all. I don't say it is up to you to provide either the one drink or the 20 virgins, but guessed you might be preparing some little treat, and it would be as well not to have it consist in a platter of roast pork with a 250 pound matron to talk to him while he eats.

Treat him as you like. I have just warned you. Step easy, and don't contradict him, even when he insists the moon is made of green cheese—

There is no record of how the visit went.

145
1929: ALBERTA
DR. MARY PERCY TO HER PARENTS IN ENGLAND

Twenty-five-year-old Dr. Mary Percy chose to leave a comfortable Birmingham home in 1929 to take up a medical posting in Alberta's Peace River area, 600 kilometres northwest of Edmonton. Percy lived in a three-room shack with only her dog, Brutus, for company, and served as doctor, dentist, public health officer, and coroner for a district that covered 900 square kilometres of wooded boggy land. There were no roads, and the nearest medical aid was in the town of Peace River, 120 kilometres to the south. Her exuberant letters home capture both her sense of adventure and contemporary English attitudes to the scattered population of Metis, native peoples, and Eastern European immigrants of the region.

Northern Alberta
11 November 1929

Your letters of October 13th and 21st arrived last Friday. Dudley seems to be a very good place for mailing letters, better than anywhere except Manchester and London. The letter from Weston should have arrived a week before but didn't. I'm always awfully glad to get your letters and know you are so well.

I'm just waiting for the kettle to boil, so that I can wash up my supper things and get to bed. (It's 9:30 p.m.) It's getting cold again tonight and there's a gale coming up from the west. We've had another week of perfect weather, cold at night (down to 10 or 15) but sunny and warm in the day.

You can't think how weird it feels at night, living all by myself in this little house. I've got the whole valley to myself. There's not a light to be seen.

All around are old burnt-off tree trunks, very white in the moonlight, and the Spruce trees are intensely black against the sky and make a noise like the sea in this wind. The sound of the river has almost gone, now it's freezing over. It feels as though Brutus and I are utterly isolated in the middle of this immense country.

There's something overpowering about the size of Canada. I get the sensation sometimes that these people are tiny beings struggling with their backs to the wall against something enormous that is bound to beat them. And when I see acres of land cleared and broken I feel a queer sort of triumph and then, seeing the country from one of the surrounding hills, I realise what a little scratch on the surface it is. All round, shutting it in on every side, is bush and forest and muskeg, unmapped and untouched.

That's something queer about Canada. I keep noticing it—not only that it is big but that you can't help feeling all the time how big it is. Even though you can't see more than a mile or so around, you still feel that it goes on for thousands of miles. I can't make out the cause of it. It seems to be something apart altogether from one's knowledge of geography. Do you get what I'm driving at or does it sound merely mad?

Kettle's boiling. I'd better wash up.

Tuesday Nov. 12th
This is a funny beginning to a letter. But I was in a funny mood last night, the effect perhaps of reading *Wuthering Heights*.

What a very long time my letter of Sept. 19th took to arrive. Did you notice by any chance what day it was posted? A half-breed took it out for me. The roads were practically impassable after the rain. I don't know how many days it would take.

Thursday Nov. 14th
I don't seem to be getting on very fast with this letter. I keep getting interruptions.

Yesterday I took advantage of a very warm fine day to wash the three pairs of curtains in this room. (Why, oh why, did I choose biscuit colour?) Between carrying in the wood and the water, doing the washing, carrying in more wood to heat the irons, ironing curtains and sewing on their 42 rings and putting them up, they took half the day.

Oh, you pampered beings who get hot water by turning the tap, you

should just try this life! Getting water from a half frozen river is really exciting. You see, the ice gets thinner and thinner as you get nearer the water.
It's hopeless unless there's a handy rock. Well, there are lots of rocks, as
you'll see from the photos I sent you, but they're awfully awkwardly
arranged! Also, standing on a very rounded rock covered with a thin layer of
ice while you reach over to get a bucketful of water is no mean balancing
feat, I assure you. Even when you've got your water, turning round on afore-
said slippery rock and then stepping from one slippery rock to another to get
to the bank has its excitements. I went through yesterday, I mean one foot
only, but goodness, it was cold.

Bother! Have just missed a truck that might have taken this letter out if
only I'd finished it sooner.

The mail is in tonight or tomorrow. I don't know whether I shall go over
tonight to see. It's been snowing all afternoon. They're going to move the
Post Office 4 miles north to Rousseau's in a week or so, now the Post Office
6 miles south (North Star) has been opened. It's obviously unfair to have
two offices 6 miles apart and there's nothing for the next 18 miles. Think of
doing 36 miles in mid-winter just to see if there are any letters for you! Of
course I shall have to do 8 miles but then I'm reasonably certain of having
some letters when I get there.

It started snowing very heavily this afternoon. I thought we were in for
3 or 4 feet of snow but it stopped again. When I went down to feed Dan the
river was half frozen and the ice snow-covered. The water was a sort of blue
black colour and it was snowing hard. It looked just like one of these
American films. It only required a woman staggering through the snow
clutching a baby!

These half-breeds are funny. Last week one of them called me out late at
night to see a baby who was teething. (I didn't go. I've met the lady and the
baby before. She thinks that as she doesn't intend to pay anything she may
just as well call me out as come down to see me.) Today, a half breed
brought a boy of 6 with *pneumonia* 12 miles in an open Ford car in a blinding snowstorm to see me! I suppose he didn't know it was pneumonia, but
with a feverish child, getting pain in his chest on breathing, and with a res-
piration rate of 50 to the minute, you'd have thought he'd have suspected it,
wouldn't you? He told me that the Kiddie's breathing began to get faster at
dawn this morning. As a matter of fact, the kid's jolly bad. He was an elegant pale blue when I saw him. I don't like his chances; I'm glad the snow
has stopped. I'll be able to get a lift in a car tomorrow. I promised I'd get out

on horseback (it's only 6 miles away) if the snow was too deep to get a car through . . .

I do meet some priceless people on this job, visitors as well as patients, and now I've got yet another class of visitors—men enquiring how to get to various places. This is the penalty for having a pretty good all-round knowledge of the district and a home-made map, compiled very laboriously from land office lists with the names of the majority of the people on it. So newcomers, generally unable to speak English, go to Bissette for direction and Bissette saves himself much time and trouble by assuring them that I have the only map in existence and sending them over to me! You see me dragged from my bed in the early hours of the morning (i.e. at 8 a.m.), expecting nothing less than a broken neck, greeted on the doorstep by a Ukrainian who enquires if I am the doctor—in other words says, "Meeses Doktor?" and when I say I am, bursts into Ukrainian. I assure him in my best Ukrainian that I don't understand and get another burst of Ukrainian. (All this on the doorstep at temperature of 10 degrees Fahrenheit, me in my dressing gown.)

Eventually, he either gives me a bit of paper with his section number on it or makes me understand the name of the man he wants. Then I get out my map and, having found the place, tell him how to get there. It's often 10 minutes work to explain, pointing in the different directions and showing him how many miles on my fingers! It's difficult to be sure they understand because they all say "yes, yes, yes." It's often the only English word they know! I know a few words of Russian, Hungarian, Polish, Ukrainian and Cree but I get them mixed! But all the Eastern Europeans call me Mrs. Doctor. I don't know why. Still, this game of directing people is all very well. Three times in one week have I been fetched out of bed. Oh goodness! I do laugh when I remember how I used to pine for fresh air and exercise this time last year.

This is just the life for me, you know. I haven't been quite so busy lately and so Dan has been very frisky. He tried to run away with me last week!! (I was riding without a bridle or bit. Somebody borrowed mine for a couple of days.) I may say I let him run and, when he showed signs of slowing down, I kicked him on again. I did the 10 miles to Second Battle River in 20 minutes less than usual! He won't try that game again in a hurry. But it's a great sensation galloping across open prairie. And now the pup can keep up. We have some great times.

Saturday Nov. 16th

Well, I have had a day of it! Started with two patients before breakfast and have been at it ever since. Set a fractured femur for an Alsatian puppy this morning!

The little boy with pneumonia is doing awfully well. I went out to see him this afternoon and had a glorious ride. It was a perfectly lovely day.

I hope to get this down to town tomorrow.

Mary Percy continued to work as a physician in the Peace River region for over forty-five years, treating five generations of patients. In 1931 she married a rancher and fur trader, Frank Jackson, a widower with three children; she and Frank had two children.

146
1930: BRITISH COLUMBIA
EMILY CARR TO NAN CHENEY IN OTTAWA

The artist Emily Carr (1871–1945) was determined to record the vanishing villages and totem poles of West Coast native peoples, despite lack of support from the staid Victoria society in which she had been raised. One of her few confidantes was the Ottawa artist Nan Cheney, whom she met in the summer of 1930 when Nan visited British Columbia during some marital problems. By now Carr's work was receiving long over-due recognition, but her sense of neglect and isolation remained undiminished.

646 Simcoe Street
[Victoria]
Nov. 11 [1930]

My Dear Nan Cheeney [*sic*]

I was tickled to bits to get your letter and to think of you in your own home again with your own man. I . . . found my eyes leaking. Well I'm out and out *glad* & may you both have a long and happy life ahead. Probably you just had to go through that time to clear things up.

I am so glad your show was successful & hope the Can. Geographic take the set. [*Canadian Geographic Journal* bought two paintings that Cheney completed during her trip.] You did get some good work in while out West & I'm shure the old beloved West helped you. Gee! how I love this West of ours, in spite of the terrible Tabby Cats who spit venom. The Arts & Crafts Ex[hibition] has been on. It was just *aweful*, made one *sick*. I was for not sending in but one of the old Tabs. persuaded me & Miss [Edythe] Hembroff would not send unless I did. So I swung in 6 of course they loathed them. 2 oils & 4 water colors. Instead of Yowling about them they tried just ignoring them & me . . . they just did not [exist] nobody made one remark or one mention of them. (The oils were two of my largest) & they were filthily sarcastic the one day I went, saying, "Oh how gracious of you to deign to come to the show" etc. They made me feel just sore & whipped really. I don't think I'll send again. What's the use? Somehow I feel they just degrade Art make it mean & little, & I feel it hurts one's work & outlook. It would be best to stay apart. One hates their ideals bemuddied. and really Victoria's idea of Art is degrading. Miss Hembroff (you remember she was at my party) she's been studying in Paris. She sent in a pencil sketch of a nude. One of the filthy old men said the most revolting things to her face about it, talking of it in the lowest terms of "nakedness." They refused to hang it.

I went over to Seattle 10 days ago & saw the North West Show, it was quite interesting. I had a lovely visit all were so good to me. I've been working like a nigger repainting 4 canvases. I took them as far as I knew two years agoe but I felt I wanted to carry them further now. I am to have a show in Seattle, 32 canvases (by invitation) probably going to other Western Cities as well so I wanted it to be as presentable as possible. have several new canvases as well. I have to get the things off by the 16 of the month so am some busy. [Carr's solo exhibition at the Seattle Art Institute was held from November 25, 1930, to January 4, 1931.]

 . . . Thank you for your invitation I'd shure love to stay with you but I doubt if I shall get over again for many a Moon. Next year I'll have to stay put last year I was so movable & it costs too much to do it always. lots of love & good luck to your work & your life.

from yours,
M. Emily Carr.

147

1931: QUEBEC
"A DISHEARTENED MAN" TO PRIME MINISTER
R.B. BENNETT IN OTTAWA

The collapse of the New York stock market in October 1929 marked the end of the fragile prosperity of the 1920s. The Great Depression of the 1930s affected Canada more severely than any other country. Between 1928 and 1933, annual per capita income in Canada fell by 48 percent, from $471 to $247, and one in five Canadians became dependent on the government for survival. P.W.L. Norton was one of the many Depression victims who laboriously explained to the millionaire prime minister in Ottawa the crushing circumstances that faced him and his family.

Sherbrooke
Pro. Que
Canada
Jan. 5th. 1931

Rt. Hon. R.B. Bennett,
Prime Minister of Canada

Dear Sir:

Always beining Conservetive and hearing you speak in the 54th Armory Belveredere St. Sharbrooke when you were here; I am taking this time to write you: I am a painter and paper hanger and Decorator by trade: I havent done any work since June 28th 1930; I have a Wife and three girls ages 13 yrs 11 yrs and 9 yrs. My Wifes family in Lincolnshire England have been helping us out; Ive been going and regoing to the City to get work: all I get is We will see what can be done: Our rent is back from Nov. Dec. 1930 and this month God only knows where we are going to get it from: I have asked & asked the City to help, and they say its been turned down for some reason the reason they wont tell: Today I whent to get 3$ to keep us for a week and Mr Valcourt of the City Office said I couldn't get it because someone said we had a radio: We have never had a radio: He sent Mr. Lesseau from the City Office to search our home from top to bottom bedrooms and bathroom under and over: Then he says he don't have to give us help if he dont want to: I ask you Sir "who was this money given to and what for?" is it for a man to crawl on his hands and knees to get a loaf for his family:? I ask you Sir how do you think we live on $3 a week and can't get that because some people make up a lie: What sort of a country have we: I dont want help: I want work I'll do anything to keep my family. A few lines from you would be a good help Thanking you for your time

I beg
To Remain
A disheartened Man
P.W.L. Norton

148
1931: ONTARIO
VERA ERNST TO HER PARENTS

One of the few professions open to women in Canada in these years was nursing. Vera Ernst, the teenage daughter of an Ontario farmer, was thrilled to be accepted as a trainee at Listowel Memorial Hospital and to don its full-skirted blue uniform, starched white cuffs, and snowy apron. Nurses in training provided cheap labour for understaffed hospitals, but nothing could dampen Vera's enthusiasm.

Memorial Hospital
Listowel, Ontario
January 7th, 1931

Dear Mother, Dad, Audrey and Grandma.

Since coming here I have many things to tell you. I took the stage from the station to the hospital and sent my trunk by an express sleigh to the nurses' residence which is three blocks east of the hospital. On arriving I was met by the superintendent, Miss Alice M. Woodard, a tall elderly lady with greyish black curly hair. I liked her as soon as I met her, but more so do I like Miss Sadie Brown, her assistant. The latter gives the instructions and accompanied me on my first visit to the wards.

I had to wait in the front office until the bell sounded two strokes to summon the nurses to the dining-hall.

Miss Woodard came from her imposing desk and I rose from the chair I had been sitting on to await her bidding. She beckoned me to follow her down the hall to the swinging door of the dining-room, to which many of the nurses had already assembled. The moment Miss Woodard entered there was a rustle of starched uniforms, as the nurses quickly rose to their feet to show respect to the superintendent. They looked askantly at me, as if to pity me. I was introduced to all the nurses, and after I was assigned the chair next to the head of the table. Miss Woodard took the lead in sitting down and the nurses followed automatically. She spread a large white linen serviette over her lap, and rang a little hand bell for the food to be brought. Naturally she was served first, and one by one those on her left received her plate of steaming food until it finally came my turn. The plates were white with a dark blue band around the rim and the food was the same for all at the table.

Directly after dinner I was taken to the Nurses' Home, a large red brick building, the door of which is always locked.

My room is beautiful, nicely papered and having pictures hanging about. The floor is covered with shiny linoleum with a hooked mat in front of each white cot. There are two dressers and two wooden chairs, one beside each bed. The bed linen consists of two white sheets, pillow cases, a white blanket and white crinkley cotton spread. At the foot of the cot is folded a red woollen blanket in case extra warmth is needed. Miss Minnie Richards is my room-mate. Since she works at night, I have the room to myself. The window faces Penelope Street.

The telephone at the Residence rings in the morning at a quarter to six to summon us to the hospital by six thirty, at which time we are to be at the breakfast table. Breakfast consists of half an orange or half a grape-fruit, toast, cereal, either hot or cold, as we choose, eggs or bacon. After breakfast the nurses-in-training must assemble in the office to answer roll-call and repeat in unison the Florence Nightingale Pledge before going on duty at 7 a.m. We have to back out of the office as we dare not turn our backs on the superintendent.

My first duty is to dust and clean the office, empty the waste paper basket, and fill the ink-well. Then I have to clean second floor bathroom, mop second floor hall and bring up morning nourishments to patients, help those unable to feed themselves. After the food is eaten I have to gather up the patients' trays and take them to the kitchen, where the dirty dishes are piled to be washed. This is done by the cook, but I put the dishes away afterwards. At ten o'clock I get my lesson from Miss Woodard for one hour, then help get the trays ready for dinner. After I have my own dinner, I gather up the trays from the bedsides of patients. At one o'clock I go off duty until three p.m. and can hardly wait to get outside the hospital to read my mail, which is left at the dinner table, but dare not be opened until the nurses go off duty. Today I received a letter from Rev. Harvey Hallman, who promises to call on me when he comes to the City Mission to preach.

After three o'clock I help the nurses with whatever they want me to do. At five p.m. we have supper. I help with the trays again and at six p.m. I go to the three bathrooms, on first, second and third floors to see that all is tidy.

DON'TS I have to obey:
1. Never speak to a senior nurse unless about a patient.
2. Do not go down the street with uniform on. Uniforms are referred to as war outfits.
3. Never answer personal questions asked by patients, nor speak to the help in the kitchen.

DO—
1. On entering a ward always knock and say, "Good-morning" or whatever time of day it is.
2. Ask a patient how he or she slept.
3. Do work quickly and quietly.
4. If a doctor speaks, stand still.
5. When a graduate nurse comes into the room, rise and stand still as long as she is standing.
6. When a senior nurse asks you to do something say, "Yes, Miss".
7. We have to make our own beds.
8. Lights in our bedrooms have to be out by ten o'clock.

Our Residence is called the Orphans' Home. Miss Woodard has special rooms we dare not enter. She reminds me of Mrs. W. D. Gray at Gotham corner, tall and so prim.

I saw a little girl taken to the operating room yesterday afternoon, Dr. Andrew Gordon Shiell performed the operation. He is a tall, dark-haired fellow with a quick step and an abrupt manner, but I like him.

There are a great many things to do in helping the nurses, but I enjoy it so far. I'll write you before long again, so do not worry about me.

Your loving daughter,
Vera.

149

1933: ONTARIO
BERTRAM BROOKER TO HIS FRIEND
LEMOINE FITZGERALD IN WINNIPEG

Bertram Brooker, British-born, was eager to encourage Canadian artists to be more open to international influences and not limit themselves to traditional techniques and landscape as subject matter. He regularly reviewed contemporary art and became the first Canadian painter to exhibit abstracts in 1927. Brooker was a key founder of the Canadian Group of Painters (1933–1945), which was an outgrowth of the Group of Seven but had a membership drawn from all of Canada. He corresponded frequently with his fellow artist Lionel Lemoine FitzGerald, principal of the Winnipeg School of Art.

Bertram R. Brooker, *Writer*
107 Glenview Avenue,
Toronto, Canada
March 20th, 1933

Dear LeMoine,

Since the first of the year I have been unusually taken up with business, pleasure, painting (very little), writing, travelling, and God knows what. When I look at the date of January 12th on your letter I feel very guilty, but I have been hoping for a spell when I could really tell you something. Unfortunately, now that I have the time there doesn't seem to be such a great deal to tell.

You know all about the new Group, of course. We had a very nice evening at Lawren [Harris]'s house to get the thing started, and I have really not seen any of them, except [Arthur] Lismer and [Charles] Comfort since that evening, and neither of us have discussed the thing very much. Between ourselves, however, I am a little afraid that a strong nationalistic bias, which always gets into the utterances of the old Group, either public or private, is going to continue very strongly in the new Group. Comfort and I were the only ones at the meeting who raised our voices in protest against this rather insular attitude. We both felt, for example, that the very name of the new Group—Canadian Group of Painters—puts undue emphasis on the word "Canadian." However, we did not press the point, but we did stress the feeling we both have, that paintings, even by Canadians in Canada, need not necessarily be confined to any sort of nationalistic tradition. The question is one of such subtlety that it's not much use trying to talk about it in a letter.

While in New York a week or two ago, I saw a show of International art from twenty countries. The Canadian exhibit consisted of a Harris, Jackson, MacDonald, Lismer and a Casson, and when I came into the room where they were, I felt that all, with the exception of the Jackson, felt curiously out of place in the exhibition. They seemed to lack the quality which is difficult to explain, but which I can only call "painting." Alex [A. Y Jackson] is a painter. The others seem to go off either in a decorative, or romantic, or philosophical direction. You will perhaps be amused at hearing me talk in this kind of strain, in view of the kind of thing I do myself, but I don't pretend to be a "painter" in the strict sense in which I am using it here.

I am afraid this will sound very puzzling to you, and perhaps I had better leave it and talk to you about it this summer, because I fully hope to be up with some of the family, at least, and look forward to seeing as much of you as your time and mine will permit.

The only painting I have done this winter is as follows: two rather interesting still life sketches of fruit in a new sort of way for me. An outdoor snow sketch of a barnyard that came off rather well with an interesting sort of zigzag pattern, from foreground to horizon, running through it. I have done a few other sketches both indoors and out, but they didn't amount to anything. Then I worked for some time on a life size sitting nude with an interesting drape of a sort of monks cloth. The figure and this bit of drape are perhaps the best painting I have done so far, but the head is no good at all, and the whole thing has a sort of still life quality about it. I doubt whether I shall try to go on with it.

I have nearly completed a 24 x 30 [inch] of some trees sketched this summer at Newcastle, and treated in somewhat the same way as the two fruit pieces that I spoke of above. I have made it a snow piece instead of a summer scene, and although rather eccentric, it is perhaps a little bit interesting. I have just finished a 24 x 30 which is a very abstract still life, the main objects being spheres. The thing really is an experiment in texture, and is perhaps only interesting on that account. Last of all, I have done a landscape about 30 x 40 of Glen Major, a very hilly spot about 30 miles north of here. Comfort and Ogilvie and I chased up there one Saturday afternoon a couple of years ago, and I had often thought of painting up the sketch. I have done so now in a semi-abstract fashion, with a very unified colour scheme, and most of the people, who so far have seen it, seem to think it comes off very well.

I am sure you will appreciate that any adjectives used in describing these things are all very relative, by which I mean that I am simply comparing these things with previous work. I didn't send anything this year to the O.S.A. [Ontario Society of Artists annual show] for the first time since I started painting, partly because I hadn't anything really suitable, and partly because the hanging committee was of a calibre deserving of being ignored . . .

With best regards to all the Fitzgeralds, I am,

> Very cordially,
> Bert

Brooker published the first Yearbook of the Arts in Canada, *dated 1928–1929, and went on to win a Governor General's Award for Fiction in 1936.*

150

1933: SASKATCHEWAN

MRS. THOMAS PERKINS TO PRIME MINISTER

R.B. BENNETT IN OTTAWA

By 1933, bread was only a nickel a loaf and a good dress shirt cost $1. But this was far beyond the means of most prairie farmers, who were struggling to keep body and soul, and their marriages, intact. Annual incomes in Saskatchewan had fallen by 72 percent since 1929 and the entire province was heading towards bankruptcy. One elderly farmer's wife wrote to the prime minister in despair.

> Kingdom, Sask.
> Sept 28 1933

Dear Sir it is with a very humble heart I take the opportunity of writing this letter to you to ask you if you will please send for the underware in the Eaton order made out and enclosed in this letter. My husband will be 64 in Dec. and his nuritis very bad at times in his arms and shoulde have had very little crop for the last three years: not enough at all to p live and this year crops around here (West of Saskatoon) are a cc ure. My husband is drawing wood on the waggon for 34 miles.

The cruel combination of drought and depression drove many families to leave Saskatchewan in the 1930s, hoping to find work elsewhere.

draw hay too, for feed for horses this winter. He has to take two days for a trip, and sleep out under the waggon some times. He is away for wood today and it is cold and windy. So I am writing this in the hope that you will send for this underware, as we really have not the money ourselves. I have patched & darned his old underware for the last two years, but they are completely done now, if you cant do this, I really dont know what to do. We have never asked for anything of anybody before, We seem to be shut out from the world altogether we have no telephone Radio or newspaper. For this last couple of years we have felt we could not afford to have them. We used to enjoy your speeches on the Radio also the Sunday Church Services, as we cant get out very much in winter. If I can only get this underware for my husband I can manage for myself in some way. He has to be out in the cold, where I can stay in the house, for the truth of this letter I refer you to Rev. J.B. Jackson, Paster. United Church. Kingdom or Dr. A.J. Portens M.D. Saskatoon Sask.

Thanking you in advance I remain yours truly
Mrs Thomas Perkins

Mrs. Perkins's appeal was heard. Two weeks later, she had a letter from the prime minister's secretary. "While you can realize Mr. Bennett has been inundated with similar requests," he wrote, "nevertheless in view of the health of your husband I have forwarded to the T. Eaton Co. Limited, order for high grade, heavyweight Wolsey underwear, which I trust you will receive in due course."

151
1934: NEWFOUNDLAND
LADY HOPE SIMPSON TO HER DAUGHTER BETTY IN ENGLAND

In February 1934, the Great Depression brought Newfoundland to its knees: the self-governing British colony was declared bankrupt and a commission of government was appointed by London. Among the first commission members to arrive in St. John's was Sir John Hope Simpson, who took charge of Newfoundland's fishing, forestry, mining, and agriculture. Meanwhile, his wife, Lady Hope Simpson, recorded in letters to her children her own dismay at the colony's poverty.

Newfoundland Hotel,
26 February 1934

Darling! it is so lovely today. The children are sliding & tobogganing about & shouting & skating along the streets & the sledge bells ring so merrily, and there is fresh-fallen snow over everything & the sun shining on all.

But it is terrible to know of the awful poverty behind this joyous scene. It is unbelievable. The dole is so small that it is only just sufficient to keep life; it is given in kind (food) once a month; & of course a hungry family finishes its ration long before the end of the month. And it does not allow for clothes or rent or anything else. There are poor creatures living in the town in shacks without doors & without any heating in this bitter cold. That is why Lady Anderson [wife of the governor] & other people are at work & working their fingers to the bone. And it is not just here. All over the island, the poor people are in desperate case. Women stay in bed till 1 o'c. because there is nothing to get up for. In other places, the people never go to bed because they have no blankets, so stay huddled together round whatever fire they have. One trouble here is that there are so many tiny communities scattered along the coast—fisher folk whose ancestors settled just here or there because there was enough fishing for perhaps one or two families. And many of the villages, & towns even, are so inaccessible in the winter—

they can only be reached by sea & in the winter it is almost impossible to get to them. There has been terrible misgovernment—worse, terrible immorality in the government. The people have been exploited—the natural resources have been wasted & gambled away. Wealthy men hold huge tracts of land—hundreds of thousands of square miles & pay 2 [shillings] an acre & do nothing to develop it—just hold it in the hope that sometime it will be wanted & they can demand huge prices for it.

The politicians have demoralized the people. They say, "Appoint me & I'll give you this & that." So that the people have grown accustomed to having everything done for them.

The stories we hear!

And yet—they are a fine people really, & if they get a decent government and a chance to recover, they will do well.

Lunch-time, & Daddy will be in directly.

152
1934: ONTARIO
WILLIAM KINGSMAN TO MITCHELL HEPBURN, PREMIER OF ONTARIO, IN TORONTO

The Depression continued to bite even deeper. Politicians' offices were flooded with pleas from desperate citizens. In wealthy Ontario, where the farm machinery manufacturers, automobile industry, and steel producers all laid off workers, annual incomes had fallen by 44 percent since the 1929 crash. Conservative premier Mitchell Hepburn faced the dismay of voters who felt abandoned by the country for which they had fought in the Great War of 1914–1918.

December 17, 1934

To Mr. M. Hepburn

Dear Sir,

I am very sorry to have to trouble you in this way but I am sure you will understand and help me if possible.

I live in the township of Elfrid in the county of Middlesex, I am a married man with five small children. I have been working cutting brush on the roads and being paid by the council. I have only had about 18 days work in the past year and now they say they will not give me any more work because they say I do not deserve it, and I want to know why.

My wife is to have another child in March and they even say she has no right to be that way when we are so hard up. I wonder what Canada would do for soldiers in case of war if my father and others had said that. I myself am a returned man with four years of service for my country. It certainly doesn't make me feel very nice to think I helped to defend a country that will not help me in times when I and my family need it badly.

This county have also employed on the roads young single men and sons of farmers who are quite well off. Now I ask you is that even fair to the other farmers, a few of the farmers have been very good to me and I don't like to see them imposed on either. I would certainly appreci-

Frequent marches by the unemployed during the 1930s did not persuade governments to provide more relief.

ate it if you could have a man investigate this matter and I will answer all questions truthfully.

I was on relief last winter and the winter before and had to take so many insults and slams about it that I don't feel like asking again, in fact I have been given to understand I would be refused.

My little children are going to school right now with no underwear on and when the real cold weather comes I shall have to keep them at home.

It takes all the money I can make to pay my rent and buy groceries and even then I can't buy what groceries they should realy have. I do not ask them to keep me in luxury or even to keep me at all and I have never refused to work when they give it to me but now they say they won't do that.

I cannot understand why my little children are not as much entitled to a living as others are.

I have tried to get other work and there simply isn't any around here to get.

They told me that the money they were having the work done with was a special relief fund but if so why was it not kept for men who are or would be on relief otherwise.

Hoping you can have a man look into this matter as soon as possible and clear it up.

Thanking you very much, in advance.

> I remain
> Yours respectfully
> Wm. Kinsman

The standard reply sent out to such letters from the premier's office included the line, "I am sorry there is no way I could be of assistance to you at the present time . . . I can only trust that things will brighten."

153
1935: SASKATCHEWAN
GREY OWL TO WILLIAM DEACON IN TORONTO

The conservationist and writer Grey Owl was an international celebrity by the 1930s, who wrote and spoke about the need to respect native culture and the environment. He lived in Beaver National Park, where he ran the beaver conservation program. But in 1935, he received a letter from the Toronto critic Bill Deacon. "Met an acquaintance of yours, from the woods who says you are all Scotch without a drop of Indian blood in you; and suggests you assume the Red Brother for artistic effect," Deacon wrote. "Do you want to deny the charge? What proofs of origin have you?"

> Beaver Lodge
> Prince Albert National Park,
> Saskatchewan
> May 10, 1935

Dear Mr. Deacon:

Received your kind letter & the Australian review. Kind of reaching out, eh? Have just sent away the ms. of a book for children, 45,000 words, 18 sketches besides thumb-nail sketches for chapter headings. Lots of Wild Life; nearly every animal in the woods depicted. Believe my sketching technique is improving.

Now about my friend who suggests I have no Indian blood, but am all Scotch. Firstly, the only people who have known me real well since I came to Canada 30 years ago, are bush people & Indians of the type who do not go to Toronto, nor speak of "artistic effect." No one living in this country knows anything of my antecedents except what I have chosen to tell them.

If I have not analysed my blood-mixture quite as minutely as some would wish, let me say here & now that here are the component parts.

> Mother— $1/2$ Scotch (American)
> $1/2$ Indian
> Father—   Full White, American,
>   *reputed* Scotch descent.

Therefore I am a quarter Indian, a quarter Scotch & the rest reputed Scotch, tho unproven.

Now there it is. You may know that all persons of $1/2$ breed "nationality," also all persons having less divisions of Indian blood, are known as half-breeds. I never even stopped to figure the thing out. My friend whom you met, has only my word for it that I have a drop of Scotch blood. Some people, you must know, object to having a "native" accomplish anything. As my whole life-training, my mentality, methods, & whole attitude is undeniably Indian, I have given credit for anything I may have accomplished to the people whom I look on as my own. Unfortunately most men of my type, in whom the Indian, at first glance, is not so strikingly apparent, spend much time denying their Indian blood, & claiming to be French or smoked Irish or something. This I refuse to do. Give all credit for my small success to the white people, (no offence intended) & leave the Indians, who taught me what I know, holding the bag? No sir. it is the admixture of Indian blood that I carry, with some pride, that has enabled me to penetrate so deeply into the heart of Nature; yet undoubtedly the White part has enabled me to express it adequately.

There are thousands of mixed bloods like myself kicking around the North; some favour the Indian, some the white; those that favour the white deny their Indian blood which makes me mad as a wet hen. It is a strange anomaly that my wife who is nearly fullblood Indian, could not, when she married me, speak 10 words in any Indian language, even her own, & knew no more about bush life than a young miss from the sidewalk on Yonge

English-born Grey Owl's protestations that he was part Indian were so vehement that perhaps he convinced himself.

Street. I, who was 3 parts white, was the better Indian. Civilization plays strange tricks on us. Right now, so quickly she picked things up, Anahareo can shade many a practiced woodsman, both in skill & courage. This last attribute is her most outstanding characteristic.

When I first commenced to write a few articles, the Editor asked who & what I was & I said I was a bushwhacker, a man of Indian blood. What I meant was, I was tarred with the brush, & felt I was admitting something. I expected he would at once turn me down. This has happened, socially, before, & often since. The artistic effect I never even thought of. I figured I would write a few articles till I got enough money to move the beaver to Ontario, & then quit, & follow my natural way. That the writing business would assume the proportions it since has, never even occurred to me. When the Government took me up, they used the word Indian in describing me, as they said "breed" was derogatory, God knows why. I did not figure I should call myself a white man, because when it was found out, as it eventually might be, that I had Indian blood, down I go with a wollop. I feel as an Indian, think as an Indian, all my ways are Indian, my heart is Indian. They, more than the whites, are to me, my people.

So my good friend was astray even in his knowledge of my Scotch ancestry. I can only claim of a certainty ¼ Scotch. His evidence is unreliable.

I do not intend to deny the "charge" publicly. The Government is very strict on me avoiding any debate whatsoever. It is a queer paradoxical situation; the one thing that I was so particular to tell about, for fear it would be found out & so destroy me (apart from my sense of justice to these people), that same thing is now denied in the form of an accusation! . . . If I hadn't been part way successful, no one would care three hoots in hell what I was. Dogs will bark & snap at my heels, but I will, as you advised yourself, just keep on going, no matter who says what . . .

A man can call him [sic] a Chinaman so long as he keeps on buying the drinks, but let him try to step out of the rut & do something, & see all the hands reaching to pull him back again. It would take very little, just a touch or two of discord & I will fold up my foolish pieces of paper & my piles of crazy notes & notions, & go back into the obscurity to which I belong, where I can at least be happy. Somehow all this public stuff has me buffaloed. Perhaps a fellow will get used to it. But the temptation comes very strongly at times to drop everything & hit for the North, where I don't have to wonder if some Smart Alec hasn't twisted some of my statements to suit his fancy, & got me in wrong with somebody. It is only the beaver that hold me. I will be faithful to them, so long as either they or I shall live. My wife & daughter can follow me, but they cannot. And they are so utterly dependent on me for their safety. Always they know I am there; I am part of their lives. And they trust me. So I stick. Though I wouldn't give one acre of Northern Ontario for 5,000 square miles of this depressing Western Country. Homesickness has me down at times, & I sit for hours beside a fire, thinking of my few, but good friends at Bisco [Biscotasing, his previous home north of Sudbury, Ontario]; they seem to be so far away & unattainable. You have heard the wind singing in the pine trees perhaps? There is no tree in this country can reproduce that sound. And then I hear that some one of my old acquaintances is taking what he considers, poor fellow, to be a rap at me. I wish some of them knew how I feel about them, counting the days till I see them again.

Though nothing has been decided, there is talk of me touring Great

Britain on a lecture tour. If it materializes I intend to stop off in Toronto, & may call on you for a little advice.

Pardon this very long & very dull letter. Blame it on nostalgia; it is a hobby of mine. I suppose a man of any strength of character would push it out of his life, but I can't; too firmly rooted in the pine lands, & white water, & the smoky, balsam scented tents of the Ojibway Indians . . .

With best wishes I am,

> Yours sincerely,
> Grey Owl

After Grey Owl's death three years later, it was revealed that he was entirely English in origin and had come to Canada in 1905. His real name was Archibald Stansfield Belaney.

154
1936: QUEBEC
JEWISH IMMIGRANT AID SOCIETY OF CANADA TO
THOMAS A. CRERAR IN OTTAWA

As Europe drifted towards a second international conflict, Canada remained preoccupied with the domestic economy and resolutely neutralist. Prime Minister Mackenzie King believed that Hitler was "a simple German peasant." Jewish Canadians strove to bring the persecution of German Jews to the notice of the minister of immigration and colonization.

February 18th, 1936.

Dear Sir:

On January 20th, you were kind enough to receive a delegation representative of Canadian Jewry who placed before you the position of the Jews in Germany. In the period of three years since the advent to power of Chancellor Hitler's party, the Jewish population of Germany has been subjected to a most brutal and ruthless persecution. This persecution has been gradually and steadily intensified and has culminated in the far-reaching repressive legislation passed in the autumn of last year at Nuremburg.

The persecution of our people goes on relentlessly and it is becoming increasingly evident that official government policy aims not only at the pauperization of the nearly half million German Jews but their complete destruction. It has become almost impossible for Jews in Germany to sustain life and in the considered opinion of well-informed observers of the German scene the victims of this cruel and ghastly persecution can only escape oppression by fleeing the country. Tens of thousands of unfortunate people have already left Germany and have been absorbed by sympathetic countries in many parts of the world. France, Belgium, Holland, Denmark, Switzerland, Czechoslovakia and other European countries have accorded hospitality to a considerable number of refugees. Palestine has taken nearly 40,000, the United States about 10,000, the United Kingdom, South Africa and Australia a considerable number.

Even a casual reference to the authoritative and unbiased report that Commissioner James MacDonald made to the League of Nations, a copy of which report was left with you, will doubtless convince you that the unfortunate Jews left in Germany today merit some humane consideration.

Motivated by a natural desire to save at least some of these victims of racial and religious persecution, we respectfully request that a limited selected number be permitted to come to Canada. Before the world-wide depression extended to our Dominion, immigrants from Germany and other Northern European countries seeking admission to Canada were granted the same entry privileges and preferences as immigrants from Great Britain and the United States. It is on behalf of this type of immigrant that we pleaded with you when we interviewed you recently.

World conditions generally have improved and our own Canada has been making progress and is on the road to recovery and while we recognize that the time may not be yet altogether ripe for a broad immigration movement, we believe that a small number of specially and carefully selected men would not materially accentuate the present employment situation.

Under these circumstances, and having regard to the calamity which has befallen our German co-religionists whom neither sex nor age exempt from every type of persecution and humiliation, and having further regard to the limited number whom we are seeking to bring out, we hope that early action will be taken so that at least some suffering might be mitigated.

We undertake to distribute throughout the country those who may be brought over, to properly take care of them, and to prevent any of them from becoming a charge on the public. We have in the past kept faith with the authorities and have always honored our pledge to provide for immigrants who have been brought in under our auspices.

Knowing how generously Canada has responded to former appeals on behalf of victims of religious persecutions, we look to your favorable consideration of our request.

Yours truly,
JEWISH IMMIGRANT AID SOCIETY OF CANADA
Lyon Cohen
S. W. Jacobs
Samuel Bronfman
Samuel Factor
A. J. Freiman
A. A. Heaps,
Honorary Presidents
Benjamin Robinson,
President.

The request was turned down. No Jewish refugees were accepted into Canada until after the war.

155

1936: ONTARIO

C. GARDINER ESQ. TO MARY SUTHERLAND, MEMBER OF THE NATIONAL EMPLOYMENT COMMISSION, IN OTTAWA

Between 1930 and 1935, weekly wages across Canada fell by 30 to 50 percent. With one in three people out of work in the 1930s, there were frequent demands that men should be given preference for jobs and married women should be discharged. Such demands often landed on the desk of Mary Sutherland, an employment commissioner in Ottawa.

16 Todd Street
Galt,
Ontario.
November 19, 1936

Dear Madam,
I have read in the paper with a great deal of interest your speech on jobless women, and as you invite ideas, I will try in my humble way to supply mine. First I would have every married woman who applies for a job or is already

working fill out a card stating where her husband works and how much he earns, if he has steady work, and a living wage, said living wage to be set by Government, if husband has hospitals bills to pay or such like.

Well if husband earns a living wage the wife should be discharged to make way for the young single girls who also want to get married and raise a family, also those who have school and want to help keep their parents who are sometimes out of work in this way I am sure we could save a lot of families from been on relief, I venture to say that in Galt alone if all the married women were fired whose husbands have good jobs, we would not have a single unemployed person out of work, you don't have to take my word for it take a census of the married women working and find out for yourself.

Now it took a Hitler in Germany and also a Duce in Italy to put the married women out of industry and make way for the men and the young people who leave school, why not some one here in Canada who has courage enough to tackle this question, it does not need to work a hardship, if the woman's husband is sick all right let her work, if he can't find work let her work till he does, but make him look, if he does not earn a living wage find out why he don't, this is important, as some imployers say his wife work he makes enough, if the woman is a widow she would be classed as single, this would all be on a card she would have to fill out sent to all factories and office and stores. Now I can hear the cry always raised about womens rights, that fine they have a lot of rights in good times, when there is lots of employment, but what right have they who have husbands to provide good wages for them, to deprive the young workers male and female of the chance to advance, and also the young girls leaving school of the chance of going to work and helping their parents, in a local office a girl got married to a young man who has a real job in the city everyone thought she would quit her job several girls applied for job, but did she no, she did not but they did buy a new car a couple of months later, this only one of the many cases I could name for you . . .

I hope you will not resent my ideas. I have only said what my thoughts have been in my mind for a long while, I hope you may find this usefull in you work, I dont mind if you use my idea's if you feel they are worth while but I would request that you keep my name private, I would also like to hear from you personally on this subject for or against.

Yours
C. Gardiner Esq.

Mary Sutherland replied, "The practical difficulties in the way of taking employment from one group of persons and giving it to another group are so large that any benefits are lost sight of in the general dislocation."

156
1938: PARIS
FRANK PICKERSGILL TO HIS FRIEND HELEN MAGILL
IN WINNIPEG

I would love to have met Frank Pickersgill, an attractive and brave young man who filled his letters with careful observations, perceptive analyses, and extraordinary joie de vivre. The twenty-three-year-old Manitoban was typical of his generation. He had soaked up the disillusion with war expressed by writers like Ernest Hemingway, but was also eager to explore Europe for himself. As a post-graduate student in Paris, he immersed himself in current political developments and became fluent in French. He was in Germany when the Munich Agreement, which bought a temporary peace between Germany, France, and Britain at the cost of Czechoslovakian independence, was signed. As Frank told a girlfriend in London, he was revolted by both Britain's action and Adolf Hitler's rhetoric.

Maison Canadienne, Paris,
September 26/38

Dear Helen:

Today and tomorrow at any rate will decide whether it would be safe for you to come to France or not—I imagine though that if you were going to stay in Europe, France would be as safe as England—I don't know what the hell is going to happen. That bastard is going to make another of his inflammatory speeches tonight. Jack [Frank's brother, who worked in the Prime Minister's Office in Ottawa] cabled me to Germany telling me to visit Switzerland. I took it to mean get out of Germany. The consulate hinted broadly on Friday and I left Germany on Saturday.

My God—I don't think there'll be conscription in Canada this time, but Canada will probably be in there anyway. I've got to start working out my morals in the matter right away I guess. If I hadn't spent those three weeks in Germany I think I would C. O. the business as far as Canada was concerned. But having been there is the best anti-German war propaganda I've ever seen . . .

You have no idea how quickly public opinion can be changed in Germany.

Three weeks ago people snapped their fingers at the possibility of war. All this last week in Munich everyone had become convinced that a war with Czechoslovakia was inevitable. Simply, the dead weight of all the newspapers in Germany printing eight pages a day of atrocity stories, horror stories, etc.—at least one inflammatory speech by a big shot or sob-interview with Sudeten "refugees" over the radio every night—all the thing of course becoming more intense all the time. It is so painfully obvious that they want the control of Czechoslovakia that one would wonder how the common people can possibly be taken in by the crusade talk. Of course the present Godesberg plan gives the Germans all they want because it means in actual fact the control of Middle-Europe. So that if the Czechs give in now, the war, when it finally comes, will be so much worse than the one that might have to be fought now.

Even now I think the odds are against a war. The Germans are obviously scared to death at the prospect of a war with France and England—they're not gambling on winning a war against France and England but on scaring France and England out of the picture once again. I don't think even yet Hitler has gone so far with the Czech business not to back out if he has to and I think he will even now if France and England make it perfectly plain that it's going to involve fighting them too.

God what a country. It was an interesting three weeks but about as depressing as any I've ever spent. The thing is so much worse now than four years ago that the place isn't recognisable—I heard [Hitler's speech at Nuremberg] over the radio. I'm glad I didn't see it in the flesh—I think I wouldn't have remained sane. It was bad enough over the radio. That was National-Socialism *en fête*. If it had been merely barbaric it wouldn't have been so bad. Honestly that nation is, I think, possessed by the devil—I see now what Dostoyevsky meant in his novel. The inspiration behind their "culture" isn't merely subhuman or uncivilized. It's worse than that. In Munich I went to visit the exhibition of Nazi art at the New Museum of German Art—it is incredible the effect that stuff has on one. An absolutely unheard of unity of inspiration hangs over the place like a fog—and a sinister fog, because the pictures are really unpleasant. I felt an almost insane desire to grab an axe and go to work on the place. Of course the superficial objection to the exposition is that it reeks of sadism and homosexuality, but there's something lying behind that even which is much more sinister . . . And not only there. The thing hangs in the air of the country. Honest to God I feel superstitious. I imagine Italian Fascism must look like the incarnation of sunny health and sanity by comparison. When I saw the sloppy dirty cheery French customs officers at Kehl I could have hugged them. And then at Strasbourg the train filled up and I never would have dreamed that the crowded noisy disorder could be so glorious. I just sat in the corner of the carriage and grinned and giggled like a loony for about an hour. No wonder these people love their country.

The hateful thing about Germany is that in their off moments you like the people so much—that makes it all the worse when they get caught up in this grip of their religion. If they were always hateful or contemptible the country wouldn't be so depressing at all. It's not the people you are revolted at—but just this alien spiritual force which seems to have got hold of them. God this must sound like insane superstition. If my impressions were unique I would say I had projected my own feelings into the thing and had let my imagination run away with me—but they're by no means unique . . .

As you can see I've been turned into a first class subject for war propaganda. But I still think it would be suicidal for Canada to participate. And yet as I say that doesn't solve my own personal problem in the question—which would never have arisen, damn it all, if I hadn't gone and visited the bloody country . . .

Love,
Frank

157
1939: ROMANIA
FRANK PICKERSGILL TO HIS MOTHER, SARA PICKERSGILL, IN WINNIPEG

During the first ten months of the war, Frank stayed in Europe, writing articles for the Canadian press. During the summer of 1939, he spent several weeks in Poland. As a Canadian citizen, he travelled under British auspices and was in Bucharest when Germany, in defiance of British and French warnings, prepared to invade Poland. As one of his friends described Frank, he was "brawny, tough and huge, and in wonderful spirits."

British Consulate,
Bucarest,
Roumania,
August 28, 1939

Dear Mother:

I'm here in what for a while, at any rate, will be the safety zone . . . I doubt if this country will go to war (unless Hungary attacks them) until Poland looks done for. Then they'll probably be forced in. The atmosphere is very much that of a neutral onlooker—sympathetic, though, to France, England and Poland.

The last days in Poland were pretty harrowing: I came to have a much more sympathetic view of Poland before I left as a result of leaving the Klobskis and seeing the other people. I particularly liked Mr. Fulde. His estate, as I've told you, is only 25 miles from the German frontier and of course will be all smashed to hell in the first week. He has built it up and is very attached to it—the morning we all left, Thursday, he was mobilized into the civil government of Kalisz, and when he left he nearly broke down. Poor man. He's a quiet, very kind, peaceable sort of person—and you know what happens to civil governors of towns in occupied territory. He'll be shot as soon as the Germans go in. I wish from a personal point of view that this damned awful thing had started last September before I made a lot of personal friends all over Europe who are going to be shot to pieces . . .

I can't really believe yet that it's possible—it's sort of like trying to imagine yourself dead. Up until this minute I suppose I really thought of bombs, machine guns, etc., as properties of an opera or something and not really for serious use. We can even talk calmly about the bombing of Madrid, because we didn't know any of the people who were bombed. I imagine that's why I haven't yet been at all frightened: I couldn't really bring home to myself the reality of these things.

Those people were pretty wonderful really, the last hours before the household broke up: I think the Germans are going to have a hard time conquering that country. When all the men are killed the women will start in on the invaders with their bare teeth!

The point I think is the Poles know what they're fighting for, and most of the poor Germans don't really. They're just bewildered—and how long they'll go on blindly trusting the omniscience of the Führer once they start getting their heads blown off it's hard to say. Czechs and Austrians will almost certainly revolt in large numbers . . .

You should have seen the Jews in the Roumanian legation at Warsaw! They all had brand new Palestine passports and were getting transit visas through Roumania en route to Zion! This crisis has caused an amazing conversion of Polish Jews to Zionism. Polish anti-Semitism is fairly understandable. The Jews have been pretty well-treated and (especially in the face of Nazi invaders) you would expect a certain degree of loyalty. But not only are they clearing out of the country, dashing to and fro and doing their best by their panic to demoralize the country, but they have in their own little way done their best to create a crisis in the Polish monetary situation by hoarding coins because of their fear of the devaluation of paper money (bad economics incidentally which is curious in Jews). There is, of course, an incredible number of them in the country.

Well, Mother . . . there's not the slightest need to worry. I'm perfectly safe, and I have a mother, father, brother and sister in the British Government. This trip is almost turning me into an Imperialist! You can't imagine how nice they've been . . . I've already borrowed money from them and will continue to do so until I leave Roumania.

Remember that here I'm quite secure and don't worry.

Love,
Frank

Frank never returned to Canada. The Germans captured him in 1940 and interned him in occupied France. After a daring escape in 1942, he joined the Canadian forces in London and in June 1943 was parachuted into occupied Europe on an intelligence mission. He was quickly caught and imprisoned by the Gestapo. On September 12, 1944, Frank Pickersgill, age twenty-nine, was executed in the Buchenwald concentration camp.

158

1939: CHINA

**DR. NORMAN BETHUNE TO HIS FRIEND
JOHN BARNWELL IN CANADA**

Norman Bethune, a thoracic surgeon from Montreal, had joined the Communist Party and served in the Spanish Civil War, where in 1936 he organized a mobile blood transfusion service. In 1938, age forty-eight, he left Canada again, to join the Chinese

People's Army in its struggle against Japanese invaders. There he was a tireless and inventive surgeon and teacher, and a committed participant in the Communists' struggle. But as he admitted to a fellow Communist in Canada, he was often beset by loneliness.

On the border of north western Hopei,
China,
Chin-Ch'a-Chi Military District,
August 13/39

Dear Comrade,

It seems such a long time since we last met and so much must have happened to you. It has certainly happened to me. These last (nearly two years) now, have been very full, so full that I hardly know where to start to describe them to you. So this account will be a disconnected one at best. But I am anxious that you should receive one letter at least of those I have written you, for I have written before, but I am supposing that you never received them as I have had no reply. That is what I have come to accept, more or less resignedly, as part of this life. The mails are very irregular. It takes at least 5 months for any letters to reach me after they have arrived in China. I calculate that I get only 1 in 25. Books and periodicals are even worse. I have received none in one and a half years. My reading consists of years old San Francisco papers used as wrappers for sugar, tea and cakes by merchants. I am thoroughly conversant with the doings of the "smart set" and the vagaries of Hollywood, but of anything of importance, I know less than an Arctic explorer. He, at least, has a radio, I have none. It was three months before I knew that Madrid had fallen!

The work that I am trying to do is to take peasant boys and young workers and make doctors out of them. They can read and write and most have a knowledge of arithmetic. None of my doctors have ever been to college or university and none have ever been in a modern Hospital (most of them have never been in any hospital) much less a medical school. With this material, I must make doctors and nurses out of them, in 6 months for nurses and 1 year for doctors. We have 2,300 wounded in hospital all the time. These hospitals are merely the dirty one-story mud and stone houses of out-of-the-way villages set in deep valleys overhung by mountains, some of which are 10,000 feet high. We have over 20 of these hospitals in our region which stretches from Peiping in the north to Tientsin in the east, south to Shi Chia Chuang, west to Tai Yuan. We are the most active Partisan area in China and engaged in very severe guerrilla warfare all the time.

The Japanese claim they "control" this region. The claim is absurd. What they control are the large towns and cities of the region which is an entirely different thing. There are 22 cities. They hold these. There are 100 large towns. They hold 75. There are 20,000 villages. They hold none. "Holding" a city means something like "holding" a tiger. You feel rather proud of "controlling" such a big fine beast but rather afraid also of what he may do if you relax your vigilance.

The Puppet Governments set up by the Japs seem to work in a sort of fashion in the cities. In the countryside they are complete flops. Our own local governments are the only ones recognized by the people. To them they pay their taxes. Japanese taxes are pure and simple robbery and extortion, capricious, uncertain and based on the simple gunman principle—"How much have you got?" Our taxation is a fixed tax on the land such as the peasants are accustomed to paying for centuries. This year 1939, the taxes for 1940 have been paid as usual a year in advance. 90% of the customary amount ($1,200,000.00) has been already paid.

My own opinion is that the Japanese can never conquer China. I think it a physical impossibility. They haven't the troops to do it. The country is too big, the people too numerous, the feeling against the aggressor, among the masses too intense. Even at present, the Japanese army is nothing but a police force. They seem held up in their advance. And in the meantime, China is building an enormous army of 20,000,000 men. Next year this army will take the offensive.

The war will be a long one. We want it to be protracted. We are planning on a war lasting at least ten years.

The Anti-British sentiment in China is a purely Japanese manufactured article. The real Chinese feel very friendly to England and America.

We must help these splendid people more than we are doing. We must send them more money and men. Technicians of all kinds are badly needed, doctors, public health workers, engineers, mechanics—everybody that knows some technical specialty well. Last year I travelled 3165 miles, of which 400 miles were marched on foot across Shansi, Shensi and Hopei Provinces. 762 operations were performed and 1200 wounded examined. The Sanitary Service of the army was re-organized, 3 textbooks written and translated into Chinese, a Medical Training School established.

It's a fast life. I miss tremendously a comrade to whom I can talk: you know how fond I am of talking! I don't mind the conventional hardships—heat and bitter cold, dirt, lice, unvaried unfamiliar food, walking in the mountains, no stoves, beds or baths. I find I can get along and operate as well in a dirty Buddhist temple with a 20 foot high statue of the impassive-faced god staring over my shoulder, as in a modern operating room with running water, nice green glazed walls, electric lamps and a thousand other accessories. To dress the wounded we have to climb up on the mud ovens—the k'angs. They have no mattresses, no sheets. They lie in their old stained uniforms, with their knapsacks as pillows and one padded cotton blanket over them. They are grand. They certainly can take it.

We have had tremendous floods this summer. It's been hellish hot and muggy. Rain for 2 months coming down like a steady shower-bath turned on full . . .

I dream of coffee, of rare roast beef, of apple pie and ice cream. Mirages of heavenly food. Books—are books still being written? Is music still being played? Do you dance, drink beer, look at pictures? What do clean white sheets in a soft bed feel like? Do women still love to be loved?

Dr. Norman Bethune repeatedly risked his life for the causes in which he believed, finally dying of septicemia in northern China.

How sad that, even to me once more, all these things may become accepted easily without wonder and amazement at my good fortune.

Goodbye for the present, dear friend and comrade.

Beth

Bethune never tasted coffee or ice cream again. Three months after writing this letter, he contracted septicemia during a makeshift operation, and within days he was dead. He is a hero in the People's Republic of China, thanks to Mao Zedong's essay "In Memory of Norman Bethune."

159

1939: ONTARIO

DOROTHY MACKENZIE TO HER SISTER RUTH IN TORONTO

Against the background of global conflict, life in Canada went on with its own private tragedies. Tuberculosis continued to be a major health hazard, for which the only treatment was isolation, rest, and nutrition. Dot Mackenzie, the thirty-eight-year-old wife of the headmaster of Lakefield School, Ken Mackenzie, was among those afflicted, but she was optimistic she would recover.

Lakefield Preparatory School
"The Grove"
Lakefield, Ont.
October 25, 1939

Dear Ruth,

Good news! Good news! Today for the first time since a year ago June, I have been for a walk. I went around to my old garden (some ski slacks and a coat pulled over pyjamas—as I'm not allowed to dress yet). I hadn't seen the garden since June, and now there are only little autumn crocuses blooming—however, I've had lots of bouquets all summer from it.

I have been waiting to write letters until I had some definite news of myself. A week ago Tuesday I drove in for an X-ray, but it wasn't until a week later, yesterday, that Dr. Cameron came out and told me what changes in routine would be made as a result of finding wonderful improvement. I am to spend six hours outside reclining in the wheel chair every day (in bad weather, on the verandah bed). Always before, I only went out on sunny days, and of course I haven't been out at all this summer. A walk of 15 minutes a day to be increased 15 minutes a week so in a month I'll be walking an hour a day! Beside the walk and going out again I may have the evening meal at the table with the family. Not being allowed to dress has advantages for I must start gaining again, says Dr. Cameron. Clothes which I'd worn two winters ago and which I was thinking of wearing again, will be too small again. Milk and cream and porridge are on my diet sheet once more—and although it's a new one, the only other change is that I may have a little lettuce now.

It's rather cold for knitting outside—I'll spend from 10 to 4 out, so I won't get so many socks knitted for the Red Cross. I have made three pair so far. Everyone here is working most enthusiastically. Billy goes down to the village twice a week, dressed in spotless uniform to lecture on First Aid to a class of 25. Hubert Eisdell has just finished his second large knitted scarf for the Navy.

Tommy tells us Peaches [her niece] has been highly congratulated on a composition she has written at the Mothercraft Hospital. It is the best they have ever received there. The Duke [nickname of a family friend] returned to this country yesterday from England. He went over the week after war was declared, and it took three weeks on the way. He says it is practically impossible to join the British Army—he has tried half a dozen times without success. We have several Old Boys in the [Canadian] Army and Navy and nearly every day one writes to Ken for help to get in. This is certainly a queer war—terribly hard on sailors of all nationalities.

Everyone is well here. We are having lots of rugby games and cross country races these days. Tomorrow is our Cowley Race, a social event here. Friday is Ken's fortieth birthday. Hoping this finds you all well.

Lovingly yours,
Dot

Five months later, Dorothy Mackenzie died. Canadians had to wait until the 1950s for effective anti-tubercular drugs.

160
1940: ONTARIO
MARIE WILLIAMSON TO MARGARET TOUT SHARP
IN LANCASHIRE

Remember the photos of "evacuees"—lines of solemn English children, in belted woollen coats and carrying little leather suitcases, disembarking at Halifax Harbour? Bill, Christopher, and Tom Sharp, along with several hundred other British children, arrived in Canada in 1940 to stay with distant relatives and escape the German bombs. For the next five years, Marie Williamson wrote regular reports to their mother in Lancashire about the boys' progress in Canada, so that Margaret Sharp might feel she was with her children on a daily basis. Among the English boys' first unfamiliar experiences were mosquito bites, burning sunshine, and corn roasts.

> Paradise Lodge,
> Haliburton,
> Ont.
> 14 August 1940

Dear Margaret,

The boys have been with us ten days now and I should certainly have written you earlier. However I knew Theresa wrote you of their safe arrival and the boys have been writing since, and I thought I would have a second letter from you soon, as I did yesterday.

We were delighted that the boys were able to leave as soon as they did—so many seem to be held up indefinitely—and so glad to have them with us. As far as can be seen there has not been a sign of homesickness which is remarkable, and they are adapting themselves splendidly to what must be an entirely strange way of life. They are all three so different we can scarcely believe they're brothers! I don't think you did Bill justice in your letter, or perhaps you had no way of knowing how he would respond to responsibility. He is simply splendid, thoughtful and helpful and so good with Christopher and Tom and spends hours playing with Tom and entertaining him in a constructive way. He is so anxious to fit in to our household and to see that the others do. When I got your letter yesterday I spoke to him about going to Vivien Ratcliffe and he is quite agreeable, though he asked if he could see the boys often, which of course he can. I really think it will be a little fairer to Bill not to be with them, as while he is with them, he takes so much responsibility. The Ratcliffes have a boy of 15 and I will be glad to have Bill able to take advantage of all possible new experiences . . .

They have been introduced to life in the wilds of Canada with a vengeance. I had arranged for us to holiday here long before there was any thought of the boys coming and as all the little cottages are the same size there was no way of getting more accommodation so all of us had to fit in to what we had intended 4 to occupy. However since the weather has been nice (it was rather bad at the start) Bill and Peter have slept in the tent. C & Tom are very anxious to sleep in the tent but I wanted to make sure of dry warm weather for C. to be out and it does get damp at night. There are a lot of cottages built along the lake with a central Lodge which supplies ice, water, linen etc. and collects garbage and sells supplies. The cottages are equipped for housekeeping but any meals we want may be had very reasonably at the Lodge dining room. So we get dinner there and prepare our own breakfast and supper. It is a very safe place, not rocky, the ground sandy so rain soaks in immediately and fairly well wooded. The lake is not a particularly attractive one in this country of lakes, having a muddy bottom but there is a bathing place which the Lodge keeps raked so it is sandy and clean a good way out and the slope is very gradual . . . Today the boys are constructing an elaborate canal and water way system along the edge.

There are lots of expeditions they could go on if it were not for the mosquitoes—they are usually over by this time of year but we have had so much rain this year that they are very bad still in the wooded places or high grass. Bill and Tom got badly bitten when they first came but we got that cleared up and now with more precaution they are getting on all right.

We were so delighted when Tom caught his big fish—I have never seen anyone so pleased as he was—but so modest and he kept insisting that he had had help in pulling it in so it wasn't quite all his doing!

August 17

I am ashamed to have had this unfinished so long! There is so much I could say that I keep thinking I can't possibly finish it! . . . We get [the boys] to keep their shirts off a good deal of the time and they are all getting brown— each one turns a different shade, their complexions are so different. Tom's face is all golden pink like a peach. They are looking very well indeed and their appetites are splendid and a good example to my two . . .

The boys, that is Bill, Christopher, and Peter, went to a corn roast which the Lodge gave last night. I think they enjoyed it—it was the first time they

Summer cottages and mosquitoes were a whole new experience for the English evacuees staying with Marie Williamson in Toronto.

had had corn on the cob and while Bill said he quite liked it C. was rather noncommittal. John said the corn was not particularly good, it is too early in the season. Bill is very eager to learn everything new and compare things Canadian with things English. For a boy so young he is remarkably free from any prejudices of any kind and I have noticed in all his dealings with the others he has a highly developed sense of justice and fairness . . .

We have asked the boys to call us Uncle John and Aunt Marie—Cousin always seems an awkward title for a child and we want something more intimate than Mr. and Mrs.

It must have been dreadful for you to part with the boys, it is such a difficult decision to make. Please don't worry as to whether you did the right thing in sending them alone. I tried to [tell] you that we would be glad to have you if you came, but we are perfectly willing to assume the responsibility of them without you. After all, we can only give them the same care and thought we do our own, in fact we love them as though they were our own. Anyway, the regulation you speak of, which permits a mother to escort her children, applies I believe only in cases where a child or children are under 5 years. I do hope you are successful in getting the teaching position. I am sure you must feel anxious to have your days filled with the boys gone.

We are taking some pictures of the boys here and will send them when they are printed.

> Affectionately,
> Marie

161

1940: ENGLAND
LESTER (MIKE) PEARSON TO MARYON IN OTTAWA

As first secretary in the Canadian High Commission in London since 1935, the diplomat Mike Pearson had a front-row seat on Britain at war. His office in Canada House overlooked Trafalgar Square, which was only a couple of hours away from Luftwaffe bases in Germany. His wife, Maryon, and two children, Geoffrey and Patsy, spent most of the war years in Ottawa, so he wrote them regularly about London in the Blitz.

> Canada House
> London
> Oct. 1st, 1940

My Darling,

This has been a rich week for me—since last Wednesday I have had two letters from you, two from Patsy and two from Geoff. What care I of bombs or breadbaskets or flaming oil drums or anything else when I get so many and such cheery letters from you three. The airmail letter came in less than 5 days—less time than it often takes London letters to reach us now—in existing circumstances. It was wonderful that you were finding things satisfactory in Ottawa and that your friends were rallying around in such fine style. I'm sure you are going to have a happy winter there, and the children too. Patsy's note from Ottawa showed that she was right at home already. I am anxious now to hear how Geoffrey likes it. His two letters were from Toronto and Winnipeg. I was really very touched by the one from Toronto. I think I had better quote what he said (don't let him know this.) "Mummy and Granny think it is very silly of you not going to an air raid shelter as soon as you can. Work is important but I think your life is more important to us. Dear me, I seem to be giving you lectures, but anyway thats what Mummy and Granny said".

Very good advice too. But if we went to a shelter every time the sirens went these days, Hitler's raiders would win; that's what they want us to do, stop work and disorganize life. But we have a good compromise; as soon as the sirens go, we station a roof watcher with glasses and when he sees danger up above he presses the button which sends us below. I was on this duty last Friday and saw two formations flying over, but as they were south and going from east to west I kept my twitching fingers under control.

I'm getting lots of sleep at night—that's the main thing—now the most rackety barrage, like last night's, merely makes me turn over. You soon get used to the noise. I suppose soon we won't be able to sleep without it. Of course we are lucky—luckier than most—the people in town who are in upper floor apartments or the poor devils who have to spend the nights in tubes or surface shelters. What they will do when the bad weather starts, God knows. Though by then things may be pretty well organized—or even the Germans may have let up on London!

There is much less disorganization of transport than there was a few weeks ago. Trams and buses are running, even when the latter take strange courses, and the tubes too. Everybody gives lifts; lorries fill up with typists going home or dignified black-coated City men coming to work. People are getting quite chummy with strangers! Certainly Hitler and his gang are a very long way from demolishing or disrupting this city . . .

(There go the sirens—second this morning and it's not 10—but last night was the quietest for a month.)

Last Sunday afternoon we played some golf at Roehampton and we were amused to read the following notice in the club house: "Hazards the result of enemy action may be disregarded." By the way the convent next to us was partly burnt out the other night by an incendiary bomb. It needn't have been if someone had been on hand to deal with it. Those things are only dangerous when they are left alone.

This is a lovely Autumn morning—how wonderful it must be up the Gatineau [Hills, north of Ottawa] now—and how lonely I feel when I think how far away that is. There are times when even my cheery nature gets a wee bit down—but not often or for long. Two things always pull me up again—the thought of you and Geoff and Patsy safe and happy in Ottawa and not forgetting me, and the thought that, after all, I'm doing my job keeping things going here as smoothly as possible in spite of difficulties. The staff watch you pretty carefully these days—me more than the H.C. [High Commissioner Vincent Massey] because they see me more, and they take their cue from me more or less. Which sounds egotistic, but isn't meant to be so. If I get down early, they do; if I stay late, the others are more willing to. If I'm cheerful about everything it helps the others to keep so. I make it a point now of seeing a good deal of the employees during the day—dropping in to their offices. They are certainly a loyal crowd and the Canadian Govt. should be mighty proud they're here carrying on . . .

Mike

Mike Pearson left London in 1942 and in 1945 attended the founding conference of the United Nations at San Francisco. Three years later he left the civil service and entered politics: he served as Liberal prime minister from 1963 to 1968. He died in 1972 and was buried at Wakefield, Quebec, in his beloved Gatineau Hills.

162
1941: NOVA SCOTIA
MINNIE PAYZANT WARD TO MRS. STAN GILBERT
IN NEWMARKET, ONTARIO

Nova Scotians welcomed the men and women in uniform who congregated on the East Coast throughout the war. The Imperial Order Daughters of the Empire busied itself with rummage sales, recitals, bake sales, dances, and home visits. Minnie Payzant Ward, an elderly member of the Dartmouth chapter of the IODE, so enjoyed a week-end visit from Dr. Stan Gilbert, an army dentist stationed in Halifax, that she wrote an enthusiastic letter to his wife and two sons in Ontario.

Terrace Bank
287 Portland Street
Dartmouth,
Nova Scotia
Thursday, October 27, 1941

My Dear Mrs. Gilbert
Your very delightful letter came this morning and I can assure you that Stan was a grand person to have for a visitor, he just made the house very

much alive; you see I live alone except for my Maudie, she has been my house-keeper for over twenty-three years, she is a wonderful person for me to have, I just could not keep house without her, I always say that she is my boss! But it is hard to always keep a house homey when you live alone, so, knowing your husband, you can just understand how much brightness he brought along with him; I shall always be so glad to have him come at any time to spend a week-end, a welcome will always be waiting for him, I only wish you could come along also, if you should be down this way some time, remember our latch is always down and I would love to see you.

We have a busy life in these sea port towns, just as I wrote the last sentence the door bell rang, it was 10:30 p.m., Maud went, and three sailor lads came running in just for a few minutes, so we talked and had lots of fun, and then I left them and betook myself to the kitchen and fried them some bacon and eggs with lots of toast and tea, that is always their favorite supper, they all came out to the kitchen and had a feast; you just can't realize what a joy the sailors are, they are so wholesome, I may never see those boys again. Last week our H.M.S. Shannon Chapter, I.O.D.E., had a pantry sale, really I never saw things sell so quickly, you see our town is just crowded with brides of the different services, they haven't much more than one room to live in, so cannot do much cooking, they just love a pantry sale; then tomorrow evening we are sponsoring a recital by a colored girl, Portia White, she has a lovely negro voice, and is giving us the programme she intends to put on in Toronto in November, I do hope she does well, she is a daughter of a pastor of our colored church, the man who has trained her voice, feels she has great possibilities, he is taking her on a concert tour; on Saturday morning we are having a rummage sale, and next week a dance; between them all we hope to make between three and four hundred dollars, to keep our war work going, this all is only for one month; next month we must do more, so you see we have to be on the job all the time. I was so interested in all Stan told me of you, the boys and your home, I shall certainly come and see you all if I should be in Toronto. Goodnight, I must be off to bed. Remember me to the boys.

Very sincerely,
Minnie Payzant Ward

Portia White, often called "Canada's Marian Anderson," went on to achieve international fame as a classical concert singer in the 1940s and 1950s.

163

1942: BRITISH COLUMBIA
MURIEL KITAGAWA TO HER BROTHER
WES FUJIWARA IN TORONTO

For some Canadians, the outbreak of war triggered a terrifying outbreak of hostility towards them. After the Japanese attack on Pearl Harbor in December 1941, the Canadian government ordered the removal of all Japanese Canadians residing within 160 kilometres of the west coast. Muriel Kitagawa was the Vancouver-born mother of four, including newborn twins, and a writer with New Canadian, *a newspaper for Japanese Canadians edited by Tommy Shoyama. Her husband, Ed, had worked in a Canadian bank for twenty-two years. In letters to her brother Wes, a medical student in Toronto, Muriel described the chaos and paranoia within their community.*

Vancouver,
March 4, 1942.

Dear Wes:

Just got your air-mail letter. I'll try to tell you as much as I can get down on paper.

We are Israelites on the move. The public is getting bloodthirsty and will have our blood Nazi-fashion. Okay we move. But where? Signs up on all highways . . . JAPS KEEP OUT. Curfew. "My father is dying. May I have permission to go to his bedside?" "NO!" Like moles we burrow within after dark, and only dare to peek out of the window or else be thrown into the hoosegow with long term sentences and hard labour. Confiscation of radios, cameras, cars and trucks. Shutdown of all business. No one will buy. No agency yet set up to evaluate. When you get a notice to report to RCMP for orders to move, you report or be interned. "Who will guard my wife and daughters?" Strong arm reply. Lord, if this was Germany you can expect such things as the normal way, but this is Canada, a Democracy! And the Nisei [born in Canada of Japanese parents], repudiated by the only land they know, no redress anywhere. Sure we can move somewhere on our own, but a job? Who will feed the family? Will they hire a Jap? Where can we go that will allow us to come? The only place to go is the Camp the Government will provide when it gets around to it. Ah, but we are bewildered and bitter and uncertain.

As for Eddie and us, the Bank is worried about us. At any rate, there is so much business that he has to clear up for the removees that no hakujin [foreigner] can do, so though we don't know for certain, he may have to stay till the last. We may stay on with him or move first to wherever we have to go, either to Camp or to some other city where there is a Branch big enough to let Ed do routine work behind the counter, but never at the counter as he is doing now. Perhaps we can move together. I don't know. This uncertainty is more nerve-wracking than anything that can happen. I don't know whether to pack all my stuff or sell it. I can take only the irreplaceables. I hope that by the time we go the twins will be big enough to stand the trip in some discomfort. But again I don't know. I may have to cart 12 bottles and 6 dozen diapers. By myself or with Ed, I don't know. Much as I would hate to sell my books I may have to. My wedding presents, all those little things that are more valuable than furniture or $300 radios, what to do with them? If we go to Camp we shall need more blankets, warm clothes, which we haven't got at all . . . winter or summer I wear cotton dresses. In any case, wherever we go will be colder and hotter than Vancouver. We can't even get around to saying good-bye to friends. Our whole way of life is disrupted. My nights are filled with exodus nightmares.

The war triggered a terrifying wave of racism, in which Japanese Canadians were deported from the coast and lost homes, property, and liberty.

My friends are so sorry for me . . . now that I have four kids, twins at that . . . they daren't phone me for fear of hurting me. So I heard. They are so kind. They come and mind them when I want a bit of time for myself. They wash dishes for me too. But now it's every man for himself and devil take the hindmost. Just the same, I am worried about Eiko and Fumi and Uncle and Aunt Toyofuku, Nobi, and the rest of them. When shall we ever meet again if we scatter? *Don't you dare come here!!* I'll lose you for sure if you do, then where will we be? You sit tight and maybe if Ed isn't transferred, he may find a job where you are, even as a house-servant if he has to. At least we will be together. The Nisei would have been so proud to wear the King's uniform! Even die in it. But not as Helots, tied to the chariot wheels of Democracy. "Labour within or without Canada" . . . who knows but the "without" may be the hot sands of Libya, hauled there as front-line ditch-diggers. And you know that most of the people here call this a "damned shame," this treatment especially of the Canadian-born? It's just the few antis who have railroaded Ottawa into this unfairness. Talk about opportunists. Was there ever a better excuse for them to kick us out lock stock and barrel?

I'll try to salvage as many of your books as possible, but honest Wes, I can't promise. You see, we don't know what's going to happen next. Maybe we can move everything . . . maybe we can take nothing. Just depends on whether we go to Camp or to some other city.

So the saga of the Nisei begins. I, too, mean to survive this. This is the furnace where our worth will be tempered to white-hot resilience or not at all.

Pray for us all, you who are in "safe" areas. For me, whose faith these last few years is sorely tried and wearing thin. Gosh, your first year at school has been a hell of a time. Don't mind my cusswords . . . we're doing nothing but.

Tommy [Shoyama] has bedded down at the [*New Canadian*] office since the curfew tolled. We visit in the mornings, and do our housework at night. Every night, when Ed is late getting home and the minute hand gets nearer seven, I sweat blood, wondering whether he'll make it before he's nabbed. He's so busy at the office transferring accounts and helping the Japanese straighten out their affairs, that he stays till the last possible minute. I sweat and sit fuming and helpless. And he can't leave the house before eight either.

So there you have a blurred picture of what life is like here. I'll keep you posted.

Martial law on the coast in the States. 120,000 Japs on the move inland.

But there they don't have to join Gangs, or go to Camps . . . which may be better or worse I don't know. The watchword is "I don't know."

I'm glad you are in Toronto.

Love,
Mur.

In 1942, 20,881 Japanese Canadians, 75 percent of whom were Canadian nationals, were shipped to detention camps in British Columbia or to prairie farms. Lives were disrupted, an entire community destroyed, and property confiscated and sold off. Muriel and her family received special permits to join her brother in Toronto, where they remained after the war. Tommy Shoyama subsequently became the federal deputy minister of finance.

164

1942: ONTARIO
NORAH EGENER TO FRED EGENER IN EUROPE

More than a million men and women, one-tenth of Canada's population, served in the armed forces during the Second World War. For newlyweds such as Norah and Fred Egener, the war involved long separation. During their first seven years of marriage, they spent only two and a half years under the same roof. While Fred trained in England and saw action in Italy and Holland, Norah established a home for their two infants near Owen Sound, Ontario. But each ached with loneliness and longing for the other. They exchanged hundreds of intimate letters in which they confessed their depressions and tried to give each other courage and hope.

June 15

Fred dearest:

. . . I am now at the cottage . . . Mom and Dad were down yesterday and took Marg [her aunt] back up town for a week, so I am alone with the children [Waide and Cynthia] and the maid. It is the first time I have had them alone since Cynthia was born, and it is a real treat . . .

I am quite prepared to take that rolling pin to you dear if you ever go away again. Seriously though, I guess as you say we are putting things more into their proper perspective. Darling, I want you to understand one thing— inside I'm not measuring up to my problems and this awful separation as well as you might think. I resent it lots of times, hate everything and every-one, even the children . . . I can truthfully say I have not been really happy since you went away.

It was announced in yesterday's paper that all men up to thirty-five are to be conscripted—however it was not settled and Quebec may still balk.

Glad to hear you are on the wagon. If you fall off dear, don't worry about me not understanding. Fred dear, I'll understand anything you do and I won't blame you . . .

On the twelfth, last Friday, it was a year since I said good-bye to you in Hamilton. What a day and what a dreadful drive, back to London. But what a day when you return! . . . Darling, I appreciate your words of praise and declarations of love. Many a time when we lived in Toronto, I must confess I often wondered if you really loved me. You very seldom told me—but you were always very sweet to me and loved me as if you loved me, but never before have you told me quite how much I mean to you.

Darling, in these two letters you are very depressed and lonely, as I was in a couple that crossed yours. I may be mistaken, but I have a feeling you've done something that is worrying you and you want to get it off your chest, so to speak, to me but you don't know quite how to do it? Am I right? . . . I understand quite well when you said, "damned if I did not think I'd blow a fuse soon". I had the same feeling all winter. I'm just now beginning to be a bit normal . . .

Biologically a man is supposed to be different from a woman. Remember Napoleon and his femmes du guerre? Oh hell, what I'm trying to say is, if it would relieve the tension any, get yourself a girl for a night. I know one thing though, you won't feel much better because you are so constituted that you have to love the girl to whom you make love, and the girl you love happens to be me and I'm too far away.

Seriously dear, I really don't believe it is such a terrible sin. The tragedy would come if you had more than a physical experience—if your mind and heart and soul entered into it, like it did when you and I made love.

Fred dear, maybe I'm away off the track—please tell me if I am or not. And if you have anything to confess, please do so if it would make you feel better. I've felt better ever since I made my little confession, but maybe on the other hand it has worried you . . . Never hesitate to write me, no matter what kind of mood you're in—I certainly unburden my troubles to you, sweet . . .

Norah

Fred was wounded in action in Italy but returned safely to Canada in 1945.

165
1942: FRANCE
MAJOR GENERAL J.H. ROBERTS TO THE CANADIAN CORPS
HEADQUARTERS IN SUSSEX, ENGLAND

On August 19, 1942, the Western Allies launched Operation Jubilee, a reconnaissance mission on the French coast to test Hitler's defences. Nearly 5,000 Canadian troops took part in the ill-fated Dieppe offensive. The raiding party took carrier pigeons along as part of their communication equipment. A pigeon arrived back at HQ the same evening with this grim message.

Very heavy casualties in men and ships. Did everything possible to get men off but in order to get any home had to come to sad decision to abandon remainder. This was joint decision by [naval and military] Force Commanders. Obviously operation completely lacked surprise.

More than 900 Canadian soldiers were killed and 1,874 taken prisoner. There is no evidence that the Germans were expecting the attack: the failure was due to bad planning, inadequate training, and insufficient fire support.

166
1942: ENGLAND
ARTHUR WILKINSON TO HIS MOTHER,
ALTA WILKINSON, IN OTTAWA

Arthur Wilkinson was one of the 630,000 Canadians who donned the uniform of the Canadian Army. He was nineteen when he joined the Canadian Postal Corps and crossed the Atlantic in 1939. In regular letters to his mother in Ottawa, he described life in English barracks amid his high-spirited comrades and asked for cigarettes, gum, and sports news from home. His letters reflect both the gung-ho optimism of Canadian troops and his own private homesickness.

1st Canadian Corps Postal Unit,
Somewhere in England,
August 21, 1942

Dear Mother,

Was delighted with the news your letter contained, especially to hear that Richie [his brother] had been posted to a mine-sweeper. It would just be my luck to have him drop in at Edinburgh now that I am down here in southern England.

People are just getting over this Dieppe business and the Limey's attitude towards the Canucks seems to have changed considerably. They were tops in the raid and did their job well. There appears to have been quite a number of casualties on both sides, but you can be certain that before a Canadian went down he had a crack at Jerry which was really felt. The boys who came back were confident that the Canadians are good enough for any two square heads. The whole Canadian army will be in Jerry's occupied countries before this war ends, and they will be fighting for the lads who gave their all at Dieppe.

The air activities were colossal. Squadron after squadron passed over here on their way to and from the big show. It makes one feel secure to know that at last we have Spitfires, Hurricanes, etc., up there fitting in like linemen on a rugby team, making holes in the opposition's lines for the ground gaining backs. It won't be long now Mother, and we are going to score the touchdowns and convert them.

I received the parcel, for which thanks a million. In the field now again, that type of parcel is really welcome. I shall write Mrs. Muhlig and Aunt Doris immediately to thank them, too. I depend on you and Dad yet, Mom, and you have never let me down. I hope I shall never let you both down.

Cheerio for tonight.
Art

In 1944, Art transferred to the Black Watch, Royal Highland Regiment of Canada, and was sent to fight in France. In a last, nervous letter home, he wrote: "It is a gigantic business and we are fighting a tough enemy." Eight days later, Art was listed as missing in action, one of the 23,000 Canadian soldiers killed during the war.

167
1943: LONDON
KATHLEEN ROBSON ROE TO HER SISTER BESSIE IN CANADA

Military service included a few eye-opening experiences for some of the Canadians who worked in London, England, during the Blitz. In 1942, Kathleen Robson Roe, a member of the newly formed Canadian Women's Army Corps, started a desk job at the Canadian Military Headquarters in London, England. There she faced air raids, Spam sandwiches—and an anything-goes atmosphere unlike anything she had known back home.

London,
England
23 February 1943

Dear Bessie,

I don't know if you have read any of the letters I sent to Mother and Dad but I seldom mention one of the biggest things which struck me over here and that is the ubiquitous atmosphere of sex which seems to hang over this city like a pea soup fog and which pervades the atmosphere and the arts. They tell me it is always thus in times of war and great troop concentrations and I suppose that is so, what with the blackout etc.

A friend of mine, M., was coming home the other day and it was really black and foggy. She had her torch, as they call flashlights over here, with her and was flicking it on and off to get her bearings and find her way to South Street. Sometimes there is a chink of light showing when someone lifts a blackout curtain to go into a restaurant or pub and you get to know these various landmarks of light but in a pea-souper [thick London fog] it is so dark you literally can't see your hand in front of you. To get back to the point, M. shone her torch and it showed the figure of an American soldier busily making love to what we call "a Piccadilly Commando". She turned it off fast but as she did she noticed the girl's hand slowly withdrawing the soldier's wallet! These commandoes are really bold and sometimes they try to take our escorts away in broad daylight. Around Waterloo Station at night reminds me of Dante's Inferno. I forgot to mention the "commando" who seems to work the Shepherd's Market vicinity. She wears a tight black satin dress and we have nicknamed her "The General" and usually everyone returning to the barracks reports on her activities.

I must tell you about the squares. They are really what make the city so lovely. The planners of our cities should take note and instead of having big inaccessible parks they should have these little parks and should plan the streets so they run into squares. Anyway London is full of these most delightful squares and in these times I must say that sex literally "lies rampant" in these parks and if you don't keep to the paths you are liable to walk over what seems to be a fleshy carpet of bodies . . . *c'est la guerre.*

A great many soldiers who are married in Canada have a second family here. There are at least two cases in the office. I expect they will either stay here or calmly go home and leave the English girl literally "holding the baby(s)". Such behaviour really makes me ashamed. I must tell you that on the whole the Americans disgust me the most. The Canadians come a close second as all [that] most seem to think of is the usual drink-sex thing. I was talking to a soldier who had been here two years and had never seen anything of London except Grosvenor Square . . .

168
1944: ENGLAND
DONALD DUNCAN TO HIS FRIEND MAURINE STUART IN WINNIPEG

Even in rural England, there were surprises for Canadians accustomed to reliable plumbing and warm houses. Don Duncan was a radio announcer in Winnipeg who had been turned down three times by the navy when he was finally accepted into the Canadian Army. He crossed the Atlantic in 1944 and was billeted in a stately home which sounds uncomfortably like "Fawlty Towers."

21st May, 1944,
England

Dear Maurine,

Left my typewriter back at my unit, so please do your best to solve these hieroglyphics. Postal arrangements for we Canucks attached to the British Army have not been very satisfactory, so I am using my Uncle's address for the time being. If you answered my last note from Sussex, N. B., I am not likely to receive it for weeks, the way things are messed up.

I have been posted to a Welsh unit and am attending the Divisional Battle school at the moment. We are living on a former country estate in one of the loveliest parts of England, and whenever we find time, J. K.

[a fellow Winnipeg officer] and I take long walks through the countryside, refreshing ourselves with a glass of "bitters" at wayside inns.

The house is Victorian (very ugly therefore), spacious, and cold, I can visualize Lord and Lady Blatherstone retiring for the night in the Blue Room (where ten of us are billeted) with instructions for Jeeves to call them at eleven. I hope the Lord and Lady accepted the whimsical plumbing with more composure than I have. Water to wash and shave is served up by batmen in the morning in canvas buckets. The lavatories (if I may be so vulgar) are magnificent, colorful, and imposing; but when you pull the good old chain, anything is liable to happen and usually does . . .

London (one day there so far) is owned and occupied by the Americans. With their fists-full of money, and tendency to noisiness, many of them have gotten thoroughly into the hair of the English. All the same the English are very glad to have them here for the big job at hand. The Englishmen particularly resent the way the English girls go for the Americans' classy uniforms, and full pocket books. People don't know what to make of us Canadians wearing Welsh insignia, and talking with mid-west Canadian accents. If they look closer however, they'll still see the little "Canada" flashes of which, of course, we are very proud.

Hope to have a leave soon, when I plan on taking in a few plays and concerts in London. However time is short, and soon the grim business will be started on the other side of the channel. Keep your fingers crossed for me— for all of us—as there will be a lot of nasty stuff flying about. I'll write again if events allow but they may not. Please write if you are not rushed about too strenuously and give my morale a nice boost.

Cheers,
Don

"I am beginning to feel more and more like a character in a Gilbert and Sullivan opera," Don wrote to his parents as he awaited shipment to France, "although I don't expect the music to be exactly soothing." In July 1944, his parents received news that their twenty-eight-year-old son had been killed in Normandy, on the Caen front.

169

1944: BELGIUM
JACK GOUINLOCK TO HIS PARENTS IN ONTARIO

Imagine the reactions of Jack Gouinlock's parents when they received this letter! Four months earlier, they had opened a telegram from the Air Ministry telling them that his RCAF plane had not returned from a bombing mission over northern Europe. Now they were torn between relief that he had made a successful parachute landing in occupied Holland, and fear that he had not survived the Gestapo and this was the last communication they would ever have from him.

In a Farmhouse in NE Belgium
Sunday morning June 25, 1944

My Dearest Mom and Dad:

How strange it is to write those words again—yet never did they mean so much as now! It seems years since I wrote you, altho' actually my last letter was written just four weeks ago yesterday and I mailed it when Don and I went to mess for what was to be our last meal in England. You have been in my thoughts constantly and I could imagine the sadness with which you read that last letter, received, no doubt, several days after that fateful cable from Air Ministry. I have decided to write down a few thoughts and experiences since that night and will have these good people hide the letter and mail it to you when the war is over. Of course, I hope to be with you in person to tell you all these things but in case I'm not, I want you to know. I will not go to great length to give you all the details—I have done so in a narrative to Air Ministry and this will be more personal.

We had just dropped our bombs that night, May 27th, when the boys spotted a German night fighter. Before Howie [the rear gunner] even had time to start evasive action, the fighter opened fire and I think set the engines and gas tanks in the port wing on fire. Howie almost immediately gave the order to jump. I cannot say whether any of the crew had been hit as I was the first to jump—my seat is directly over the escape hatch—and I hope and pray I was quick enough to leave the other fellows time to jump. I never moved so quickly in all my life though, so I feel they must have had time. We were fairly low, only 8000', so the air was warm. My chute opened perfectly and I drifted gently to earth. Except for a slight nauseating feeling due to the swinging motion of the chute, I landed safely all alone in the middle of a field and had no idea where

Jack Gouinlock (second row, far left) spent months in hiding before the Allies liberated Belgium: he and other evaders are photographed here with their Belgian underground saviours.

I was. I knew I had to start walking because they would be out looking for us.

It turns out I had landed on the Holland border. I walked to Belgium and have spent the past few weeks hiding on a farm at Wychmaal. The people are extremely nice and very generous with the few things they have. But they have lots of food! There are sumptuous meals every day of the week, with wine and biscuits or a plate of milk pudding at the end. Oh, there is always a plate of soup too!

Friday and Saturday are spent in getting ready for Sunday. Six to ten pies and a batch of grand cookies, many "black head" loaves (big round ones) and a few of the forbidden light brown ones! Sunday is a day of rest if one could call having visitors all day a rest—what do you say, mother and Edie! Noon dinner there is always more elaborate chicken soup with noodles, roast chicken, potatoes, asparagus or beans etc, custard pudding with biscuits broken in it. I've already said what Sunday supper is usually. And so

you see, I am living in the land of plenty in a country where there is very little plenty in crowded areas—but on the farms it's different and this is one
of the best farms in the district. No person (even German soldiers) is sent
away empty handed—whether it's an egg or two or a piece of pie. Ah, these
are marvelous people! I hope to be able to express my appreciation in a
more concrete way after the war is over.

Well, my dearest ones (and all my relatives and friends) I hope this letter will never have to be read except to "check up" my own verbal account
of this incredible experience. My love to you all.

> Your loving son,
> Jack.

*This letter was received in Toronto on September 19, 1944. Jack arrived safely back in
Canada two weeks later, having been hidden by the Belgian underground until the end
of the war.*

170
1944: ITALY
**FARLEY MOWAT TO HIS PARENTS, ANGUS AND HELEN MOWAT,
IN ONTARIO**

*The writer Farley Mowat joined the Hastings and Prince Edward Regiment ("the Hasty
Pees") in 1940 and served with it in Europe for three years. Throughout the war, he and
his parents enjoyed a correspondence that sparkled with affection and cynical wit. After
the Allies' victory at Monte Cassino in Italy, Farley was a brigade intelligence officer
and an acting captain, writing the brigade's official war diary, questioning prisoners
and refugees, and greeting visiting journalists.*

> [near the Conca River, Italy]
> Sept 1, 1944

Dear Parents:
We are enjoying a couple of days in reserve although I am working twice as
hard as when the brigade is in the line. And I am not so fond of this HQ
any more. My principal grouse is that the new boss doesn't see eye to eye
with me on how battle histories and official war diaries should be written.
Somewhat to my surprise, I find that ill-informed (make that stupid) and

inept literary criticisms of even such run-of-the-mill stuff make me excessively annoyed. The temptation to tell him to write his own bumpf, if that's
what he wants, is almost irresistible. But then I'd be Lieut. Mowat again,
and poor old Doc [his father] would cry.

Also I find myself surrounded more and more by people with whom I can
get along only with great personal effort. Jobs at Div [Divisional
Headquarters] and even at Bde [First Brigade Headquarters] are being
increasingly filled from the rear rather than from the front. It seems there
is a fat surplus of non-combatant officers qualified for staff jobs. And a
shortage of same willing to serve in combat. And a lot of the newcomers
here are, you will have to excuse me, Maw, shit-headed. If I have to listen
to one more Grade 4 dirty joke I'll throw a slug into someone's smutty mug.
God knows I'm hardly a puritan, but slime is slime, and only to be excused
in adolescence. One serious drawback to army life is the inability to choose
your companions. This doesn't matter at the front, where circumstances
select the best, but to the rear it can become a real malaise.

Sept 5

I wait patiently for the appearance of *Carrying Place* [his father's novel]
which, despite Pop's pessimism about the reading public, is sure to have a
wide appeal. I am counting on this if only to free me from the drudgery of
slaving for a living when I get home.

Speaking of writers. One Mrs. Ernest Hemingway [Martha Gellhorn, a
war correspondent] arrived on my doorstep today in slacks, a bandanna, and
a U.S. combat jacket strung with cameras and notebooks. The Brig and the
BM were busy fighting a war so I got stuck with her and had to listen to and
try to answer a lot of asinine questions ("I hear your troops are mostly
Indians. What tribes do they represent?") and be properly impressed by The
Importance of Being Ernest's Wife. By good luck I had a bunch of
Turkoman POWs on hand (Mongols from beyond the Caucasus, impressed
into the German army) whom I introduced to her as some of our Native
Scouts just back from a sortie behind the Jerry lines. The silly bitch was
enthralled, but her "accompanying officer" from Army HQ smelled a rat.
Me. Hi ho, I did my best to give her what she wanted. God preserve me
from females in slacks who think war is a grand and glorious game.

The BBC news says that Jerry is fleeing from us in wild retreat. Like hell
he is! He is digging in his heels at every valley, every hill and casa, and staying put until we blast him out. Wish the silly bastards would listen to the

BBC. Would save us a lot of sweat and grief. We've had just two days out of range of hot stuff since this campaign started, and I am welching on my bet about [the war ending on] Nov. 15.

Have you heard from Susi yet? Maw, you had best start learning Austrian with a gypsy accent. And just wait until you meet Auntie. But before you have a fit, remember that monogamy is not going to be my style. I expect to have a house full of women which, I'm told, can be a paying proposition. I have decided to make my living *après la guerre* by writing for *Zippy Stories*, *Garter Tales* and *Forbidden Frolics*. I understand that the research required can be edifying. And I am growing a new moustache. I hope this one will be visible.

Sorry pals, it is getting too damn noisy up here . . . I think I'll make for a nearby cellar.

Farley Mowat returned to Canada in 1945. His accounts of his wartime experiences, The Regiment *(1961) and* And No Birds Sang *(1979), were both best-sellers.*

171

1945: GERMANY
BOB SANDERSON TO HIS PARENTS, NELLIE AND STANLEY
SANDERSON, IN ONTARIO

In early March 1945, Nellie and Stanley Sanderson of Chesley, Ontario, received a telegram informing them that their son Bob was missing in action in Germany. Bob, a popular local hockey hero and student at the University of Western Ontario, had enlisted in the Canadian Army in March 1943, and was assigned to the Essex Scottish Regiment in November 1944, just in time for the final Allied advance into Germany. Bob's family was desperately worried; although he had been captured and sent to a prisoner-of-war camp south of Hamburg in February, word that he was alive and safe did not arrive in Chesley until May 1945.

Kriegsgefangenenpost [prisoner of war mail]
Recovered in Germany 16.3.45–17
Stalag XI B
Vor- und Zuname [name and surname]: L/Cpl. Sanderson Robt.
Gefangenennummer [prisoner number]: 200978
Deutschland (Germany)

Dear Mother and Dad,

Just a note to let you know I'm well and a P. O. W. in Germany. Please don't worry about my condition or health—you know me, and I'm the same as ever. Your prayers have been with me, I know, and through my experiences I have been conscious of them and of you. I was captured late in the afternoon of Feb. 19. It was rather a rough time and I ended up on the wrong side of the line when the attack was over and things were more settled. I can receive all mail sent to me and the address is on the outside of this sheet. Hope war is over before I hear from you. Hope brothers and relatives are finding things o.k. Sorry if I caused you some extra worry with the "missing" report. It bothers me very much and I do hope you get this letter. I have sent a card previous to this by a few days. Wonder if you could let Marie know? Never once thought of this ever happening to me—but that's how I've ended up. Probably belated by the time this reaches you but congratulations on celebrating one more wedding anniversary. Often think of you all and am sending much love to you two particularly. All for now and will write again as soon as possible.

Your army son—Bob

Despite Bob's assurances, life in Stalag XI B was a nightmare: tuberculosis, bronchitis, and rheumatism were rampant, and food practically non-existent. On April 16, the camp was liberated by the British. Bob had lost 50 pounds from his 170-pound frame and contracted chronic dysentery. He returned to Canada a year later, married Marie, and trained as a dentist.

172

1945: MONTREAL
HUGH MACLENNAN TO WILLIAM DEACON IN TORONTO

At a time when Canadian literature was still struggling to establish itself, the Montreal writer Hugh MacLennan published a groundbreaking work of fiction, Two Solitudes. *Its significance lay in its focus on a national rather than international issue, and its treatment of English-French tensions in Quebec. It immediately caught the attention of Toronto critics and was reviewed by William Deacon in the* Globe and Mail *under the headline "French-Canadian Problem in Daring and Timely Novel."*

1178 Mountain Street
Montreal
April 8, 1945

My Dear Deacon:

Thanks for the grand review of *Two Solitudes* in yesterday's *Globe & Mail*. I know any writer is pleased by a good review, and delighted by the kind you gave me. But quite apart from my own personal pleasure, I think you deserve congratulations on your handling of a book which must have been nearly as difficult to review as it was to write. A sensational handling of it—as it got in many American reviews—would have been the last thing desirable, from many points of view, for, as you rightly said, it was not so much the Quebec problem, as a Canadian novel.

From my standpoint, I had to write that book to orientate myself toward any future work I might do. It is my complete conviction that no writer can function in a vacuum. As his point of view, his method of regarding phenomena, derives from his childhood environment, he can't help writing out of the society in which he was produced. It gradually dawned on me—very gradually, I'm afraid—that so far as I was concerned my own society was obscure, not clear-cut, a queer congeries of various subtle inner and outer relationships which in my own time were gradually coming into focus. Unless it were possible for me somehow to effect something of a fusion of this Canadian dichotomy, I felt myself stymied. *Two Solitudes* was the result of that, and now that it is finished, I feel greatly released. Whatever the book may have done for others, for me it has put something like solid ground under my feet.

You are certainly correct in assuming that the book will cause a lot of controversy. I knew it, I suppose, while I was writing it. But for me personally there was no sense of controversy at all; merely a prolonged and often mind-breaking effort to bring the various pieces into focus. So far among the French, and even among some of the clergy here, the reception has been much better than I had feared. There is no doubt that some aspects of French-Canadian life will loathe the book, for you know what a proud people they are. Yet if anyone is capable of understanding what he reads, he can hardly fail to detect a deep respect and affection for French-Canada within the book.

Undoubtedly, the treatment of English-Canada is less inclusive. It couldn't be [otherwise], for the artistic theme rendered it impossible. I was forced to deal with those English elements which, by working so much harm among the French, are in many cases cynically responsible for much of the trouble we have here. And while writing so largely of the situation which is at the core of Canada, I kept in mind that I was writing for English-Canadians, who so constantly make the error of regarding Quebec as a monolith, and not a society in rapid transition under the impact of modern industrialism.

This letter has run on far too long, and certainly has told you nothing you did not know anyway. I'm awfully sorry I missed seeing you when you were in Montreal, but Dorothy [Duncan, a writer to whom MacLennan was married] greatly enjoyed talking with you. Next time you come to town we may be able to have a drink together.

Sincerely,
Hugh MacLennan

Two Solitudes *won the Governor General's Award for Fiction. Hugh MacLennan received five Governor General's Awards and countless other honours before his death in 1990.*

173
1945: GERMANY
KING WHYTE TO DOROTHY ALT WHYTE IN BUFFALO, NEW YORK

King Whyte, born in Montreal, started his career in burlesque theatre in the United States. He was an established CBC Radio producer when he joined the Canadian Army as a war correspondent in 1943. Over the next three years he wrote more than 300 letters to his wife, Dorothy, a famous singer—letters filled with details about

London during the Blitz, the shortcomings of British toilet paper, and the state of Germany after its surrender.

April 22 [1945]
Somewhere In Germany

Things have been very hectic with me. Have been on the go night and day and I'm a bit weary. However, my lucky star is still shining even though it did rain to beat hell last night and it was very cold to be sleeping under canvas. Last night when I got into my camp bed that old song "Tenting Tonight" kept running through my head. Do you remember it? I kind of sighed and said to myself that I probably wasn't the only weary heart on the old camp ground.

Now that the war is in its final stages I can hardly wait to get home. Today I may be going up to that awful concentration camp you have been reading so much about—it is Belsen. I hate the thought of going to the scene of all that suffering. You have probably seen the pictures in the papers so you know what I am heading for. They are dying at the rate of four hundred a day there and nothing can be done about it. They are too far gone to even eat now that the food is available. God, what a war, and to think that so many of the folks back home have absolutely no idea of what it is all about. The things I have seen with these eyes of mine. No wonder I am getting a bit grey. I have one thing for which I am continually thankful and that is that you will never have to see them or go through the tortures of real war. At times there is only one thing that keeps me on an even keel and that is the fact that you are waiting for me.

I was only in Paris for two nights and a day. Paris was lovely. Everything they say about that place in the springtime is an understatement. The flowers were in bloom—the pretty girls were riding bicycles with abandon—the taxis and cars were hooting their horns like mad—spring was in the air and it was definitely very good to be alive. But, shortages are in vogue again. Believe it or not I tried to buy you some perfume and couldn't find anything worth buying.

My transport is here—must leave. Bye for now my sweet. I'll write again as soon as I can. I love you more than anything else in all the world.

April 24

Somewhere in Germany

Tonight I am a different man. I have spent the last two days in Belsen concentration camp, the most horrible festering scab there has ever been on the face of humanity. It was so horrible that I'm not going to tell you of it. I still cannot bring myself to write my reports to Radio Luxembourg. It makes me sick to my stomach even to imagine the smell, and I want to weep and go out in the streets and kill every Nazi I see when I think of what they have done to those countless thousands of people.

War correspondent King Whyte was so shocked and nauseated by his visit to Belsen concentration camp that he was unable to file his reports.

You have seen pictures in the paper but they cannot tell the story. You have to smell it and feel it and keep a stern look on your face while your heart tears itself into pieces and the tears of compassion drench your soul. My God, that there should be such suffering on the face of this earth. I have seen hundreds of people dying before my eyes. I have seen filthy green corpses used as pillows for the living. I have seen forty thousand people living and dying amongst their own fetid offal. They are dying faster than they can be buried. For most of them food is absolutely of no use. Their stomachs will not take it—they vomit or they have dysentery and it goes right through them. All over the camp, both men and women squat wherever they happen to be. There is no latrine and it is almost impossible to walk around without stepping in filth.

An American medical officer in charge of the Allied Typhus Commission told me that any one of the cases in the camp would put any hospital in the United States into a flap. I had to be sprayed with powder even in my hair and my beret before I could enter the place. It is a sinkhole of pestilence. The SS guards were left behind at the camp when the Germans retreated. They are burying the dead. I leave it to your imagination—the love the Tommies have for them. I could write you like this for hours my darling, but I said I wasn't going to tell you of the things I have seen. Only, in the years to come, if I am suddenly sick on the street it will be because some smell has wafted to my nostrils which my stomach remembers from Belsen.

I am with the same chaps I was with near Bremen and it is good to be back with them. I expect that I will only be here for another week and then it will be back to Luxembourg for reassignment. It will be good to go back to Luxembourg where I can get a good bath and put on a fresh uniform and get into my feather bed. I am lucky and I know it.

I do wish this letter wasn't like this darling, but you are the only one I can tell my thoughts to. I couldn't help thinking of your [German-Canadian] mother and father. If they were living in Europe they would have been in such a place. An English officer came up from Lux[embourg] with me. His grandmother and grandfather were German Jews and were expatriated from Germany to Holland. When the Germans took Holland they were put in concentration camps. The old man died two years ago at eighty-two, the old lady died in Belsen last August at seventy-three. The old man was gassed because he was too old to work. At Belsen there weren't many Jews, just plain ordinary people who didn't happen to be Nazis or in sympathy with the Germans. There were many Germans among them.

I don't know what I am going to do about an anniversary present for you honey. I just haven't been able to buy anything. I feel hellish about it, but that's the way it is. Please understand honey. *Verstehen du, bitte.* How I would love to be home tonight beside you. I know that you would soothe this head of mine and my heart, too. There is always the comfort for me knowing that you are waiting for me and that someday all will be well again.

Think of me often. I love you so.

174

1945: CALIFORNIA
ESCOTT REID TO HIS FATHER,
THE REVEREND ALFRED JOHN REID, IN ONTARIO

Canada's considerable contribution to the Allied war effort gave it a significant voice in post-war discussions about the future shape of the world. Escott Reid was one of several Canadian diplomats (Mike Pearson was another) who participated in debate in

San Francisco on a new league of nations that would make a third world war impossible. But he was beset with doubts as to whether the United Nations could repair historic splits and corrosive distrust.

[San Francisco]
24 May 1945. Thursday.

To father.

I think the final Charter is going to be better than the Dumbarton Oaks proposals [a design for the United Nations drawn up the previous year] but not as good as what was politically possible. The main obstacle is, of course, the suspicion between the western world and the Soviet Union. We have to tailor a charter not for Willkie's "One World" but for a globe which consists of two worlds. Our hope has to be that in the course of the next few decades the two worlds can learn to understand each other and to progress first to the point at which each does not believe the other is out to dominate it and then to the point at which a lack of mistrust becomes a positive trust.

There is nothing today to fear but fear. The Soviet Union is not, I am sure, planning how to secure world domination by force but they sometimes act in such a way as to frighten the western world. The western world is not planning to overthrow the Soviet Union by force but apparently we unknowingly do things which lead the Soviet Union to suspect that we do. Thus we both get frightened and fear is a bad counsellor. From false fears good Lord deliver us.

We all have a feeling here that what we are doing is merely writing marginal notes on the pages of history. The substance of history is being written not in San Francisco but in Poland, Germany, Czechoslovakia, Yugoslavia and so on. That is where the new world is taking shape and taking shape with terrifying speed . . .

Less than three months later, Escott Reid wrote to his wife, "I am in despair today about the kind of world our children are going to live in." The Americans had dropped an atomic bomb on Hiroshima, and Reid admitted, "I just haven't enough faith in man or god to believe that we have enough time or intelligence or goodwill to reach the goal of a world government before we obliterate civilization in another war." Nevertheless, he continued to work towards international harmony, and his ideas on a collective security alliance of Western democracies led to the establishment of NATO.

175
1949: QUEBEC
CÉLINE TO GERMAIN SICOTTE IN QUEBEC CITY

Life gradually reverted to normal after the war. Canadians returned to the serious business of complaining about the weather and enjoying winter sports.

Sherbrooke,
13 March 1949

Dear Germain,

Winter's come back to Sherbrooke. It hasn't stopped snowing since Friday night and it's still coming down, I think as much has fallen as we'd had all winter. I would have liked to have had this weather a week ago, when we could have skied as we pleased. I imagine that you must be getting ready to go skiing right now. Johanne asked me to go with her to Hillcrest but I was a bit tired and gave in to my laziness, besides I'll go to the lake and study a little.

Last night I went to the Ice Cycles show, which I found enchanting; I hadn't expected something so good, really, with magnificent costumes and very good skaters . . .

Yesterday afternoon while out in the car I went to the Beauclair farm with Johanne. There were several people skiing, including a nun from the congregation who was with some pensioners. It was a real comedy to see her descent, she shot down the hill at full speed and then once she got to the bottom she couldn't stop and fell flat on her face in the snow. Everyone made fun of how well she could do. When she was coming down, the wind filled out her cloak and she looked like the superman we saw the other day at the movies or something like the abominable snowman.

Looking forward to seeing you along with spring.

Céline

At Expo 67 in Montreal, Canadians lined up to travel on the sky train, admire Buckminster Fuller's geodesic dome, and embrace the future.

PART 4: HURTLING TOWARDS THE MILLENNIUM
1950-2000

WE'RE NOW INTO THE REALMS OF LIVING MEMORY. I FOUND THE concerns of letter writers from the second half of the twentieth century refreshingly familiar: I could imagine the excitement of Expo 67, and I recalled the grim television footage from Sarajevo in 1992 as I read a peace-keeper's description of children being shot there. At the same time, these modern voices echo the sentiments of so many earlier letter writers. Every generation exults over the difference a new invention can make, whether it is a Massey-Harris plow in the 1890s or a television in the 1960s. The home-sickness of the Canadian peacekeeper a few years ago mirrors the melan-choly of a soldier in the First World War trenches. A young woman's desire for a new coat in the 1950s reminded me of Sophia Ryerson Harris's craving for a diamond ring in 1865.

However, these very personal emotions now play out against the back-drop of a wealthier, more settled, and far more urban society than earlier generations could have imagined. In the 1950s, suburbs started to sprawl across farmland, cranes hovered over new steel-and-cement schools and hospitals, and yellow school buses trundled along country roads. Ordinary families found they could now afford cars, holidays, and an avalanche of labour-saving domestic appliances. The Depression did not return. A com-bination of public spending and private investment kept Canadians floating contentedly on a strong economy, although it took a while for Canadians to realize that the good times had arrived.

Not everybody shared the new-found affluence: native peoples, the eld-erly, and workers in moribund industries such as Nova Scotia's mines strug-gled at the margins of the post-war boom. But they were a minority. The majority luxuriated in unaccustomed affluence, for which they gave credit to the Liberal government of the Quebec lawyer Louis St. Laurent. "Uncle Louis," who had succeeded King in 1948, was elected with huge majorities in 1949 and 1953. There had been Liberal government for thirty-five of the first fifty years of the century; the party seemed set to beat its own record in the second half.

So much of what we take for granted in the arts today was a product of this period. Prosperity allowed the federal government to subsidize a young nation's budding cultural life. CBC Television and the Canada Council came into existence, making wages and grants available for the work of individual actors, dancers, artists, and writers. Orchestras, ballet companies, publishing houses, new arts organizations, and (in 1953) the Stratford Festival were founded. There was a robust belief that a wealthy, successful country like Canada deserved its own cultural institutions, not just British hand-me-downs or American soap operas. People like Glenn Gould and Marshall McLuhan became international stars (and reflected in their private correspondence, I noticed, the thin-skinned insecurity of many celebrities).

Prosperity also made the costs of defence and foreign aid more acceptable. Canadian diplomats had participated in the 1945 discussions on collective security and the emergence of the United Nations, and they had got the taste for an independent foreign policy. The phrase "quiet diplomacy" (usually accompanied by a little moue of pride) began to do the rounds. In the words of the historian Ramsay Cook, Canada was now regarded as "a 'middle power', with too little influence to claim a global voice but with too great a material strength to be ignored." A close relationship with the United States was inevitable, and in the face of the Cold War threat, Canadians quickly followed American soldiers into Korea in 1950. Canada and the United States jointly established the Distant Early Warning (DEW) radar line in the Far North in 1954. At the same time, Canada added important weight to organizations like NATO and the Commonwealth, to counterbalance the American pull.

Canada's "middle power" significance was confirmed in 1957, when Lester B. Pearson was awarded the Nobel Peace Prize. The Canadian secretary of state for external affairs had played a lead role within the United Nations, in developing the idea of a multinational peacekeeping force to bring the Suez Crisis under control. Pearson struck a chord with the voters back home when he remarked, in his Nobel acceptance speech: "The grim fact is that we prepare for war like precocious giants and for peace like retarded pigmies." The nation's old timorousness over national unity—a hangover from repeated conscription crises—was fading: we were confident at home and on the world stage. It was a great time to be a Canadian.

Despite these successes, the love affair with the Liberal Party began to wane. With affluence came self-reflection: the Grits in Ottawa seemed too laissez-faire to shape a distinctive national character. By 1957, the new Conservative leader, John Diefenbaker, had Louis St. Laurent on the run. In 1958, the small-town lawyer and brilliant orator from Saskatchewan won a decisive victory at the polls. Farmers, westerners, rural Quebeckers, and the owners of small businesses elected "the Chief." His government introduced a series of policies that would make them happy: agricultural subsidies, tax reform, pension increases. Most important, he captivated Canadians with a new national vision: Canada as a northern nation, with priceless natural resources in the frozen wilderness. For those who lived there, it was pretty bleak. "I have never seen a more desolate settlement," Jill Kidder, wife of a mining company's explosives expert, wrote to her mother from Labrador City, "flat and barren and bleak, a few straight rows of apartment buildings, hundreds of power poles, and a trailer village." But it was ours.

When I watch old footage of Diefenbaker's speeches, I am impressed with his rhetorical skills and appalled at his paranoid style. Flashing eyes, pointing finger, voice breaking with passion—in our television-savvy age, he is almost a caricature of a politician. His approach alienated many of his own contemporaries. Quebec chafed under his relentlessly unsympathetic, and unilingual, rule. His belief in "one Canada" grated on those who felt marginalized. Rising unemployment, a declining dollar, and Diefenbaker's embrace of U.S. military technology unnerved bankers and nationalists alike. When Diefenbaker killed the Avro Arrow, Canada's homegrown Cold War jet fighter, the "Northern Vision" congealed.

The Canadian political landscape of the 1960s rivals today's for instability. The New Democratic Party (NDP) was formed and, along with the Liberal Party (headed by Lester B. Pearson), pledged to make Canada non-nuclear. All this might have remained a passionate but essentially theoretical debate between peace groups and proponents of *realpolitik*, had it not been for John Kennedy and the 1962 Cuban Missile Crisis. The Diefenbaker government collapsed as the Chief wavered helplessly on both economic and defence issues. By 1963, the Liberals were back in power with Lester Pearson as prime minister.

The Pearson government started badly: the new prime minister stuttered in the House and his administration seemed to stumble on its two main initiatives, an improved pension plan and medicare. But the Liberals quietly

continued the social democratic reforms initiated by their Liberal predecessors, and also managed to secure parliamentary reform and the Auto
Pact, which allowed free trade with the United States in autos. In 1965,
after an agonized national debate, Pearson cemented the nation's post-war
sense of self with the introduction of a new Canadian flag, featuring a red
maple leaf. The committee responsible for coming up with a flag design had
been overwhelmed with drawings of beavers, moose, feathers, and
mountains. But, in the words of George Stanley, the man who first recom-
mended what became the final design: "The single leaf has the virtue of
simplicity; it emphasizes the distinctive Canadian symbol, and suggests the
idea of loyalty to a single country."

By the 1960s, Canadians were again taking post-war affluence for
granted, provoking them to ponder new and sometimes radical options
for the future. The most dramatic pressures came within Quebec. In 1960,
Liberal premier Jean Lesage announced, "Il faut que ça change!" (Things
must change!) The province transformed itself from a rural, church-
dominated culture into an urban, secular, and intensely nationalist society.
Events moved much faster than the elected officials could have imagined.
Soon young Quebeckers were embracing the idea of separation, and a
handful of extremists—the Front de Libération du Québec—were bombing
mailboxes and daubing "Québec Libre" on public buildings.

The year 1967 marked 100 years since Confederation, and the world's fair
which opened in Montreal that spring seemed at first to swamp Quebec's
anti-federalist anger. Expo 67 took the country by storm, and Canadians
were suffused with unfamiliar pride in their country and achievements. "It's
Gigantic, Splendid, Terrific, Marvellous, Unique," a young Montrealer
wrote to her sister. "All with Capital Letters." The planners anticipated
26 million visitors to the sixty national pavilions, including Buckminster
Fuller's geodesic dome; the final total was over 50 million. Letters about
Expo 67 have some of the same guileless confidence that I encountered in
the letters from western Canada before the First World War—a sense that
anything was possible, that Canada really was the promised land.

The euphoria didn't last long. One of the visitors was Charles de Gaulle,
president of France. He brought separatist frustrations back into clear focus
when he declared, in front of a vast rally at Montreal's City Hall, "Vive le
Québec libre!" By the end of the year, the former radio commentator and
provincial Liberal minister René Lévesque had set out to establish a separatist political party, the Parti Québécois. One of the most insistent themes

of the next three decades of Canadian politics—Quebec's struggle to become "maîtres chez nous"—had begun in earnest.

English Canada was also in transition during these years, although less dramatically than Quebec. From 1940 to 1980, the proportion of the population living in rural areas fell to 30 percent from 60 percent, and as urbanites multiplied, so did trends. Youth culture ruled: the music of the Guess Who, Neil Young, and Gordon Lightfoot blasted out (and still does—proving that it was not, as our parents insisted, "just noise"). Baby boomers demonstrated against American involvement in Vietnam, grew their hair, demanded less restrictive roles for women and votes for Indians—or at least, young people in cities like Toronto, Montreal, and Vancouver did, while their less affluent counterparts in small towns watched their antics on television. Church attendance fell, along with the birth rate (thanks in part to the contraceptive pill). And in 1968, Canadians elected a prime minister who seemed to symbolize a new kind of Canada: brash, bilingual, sophisticated, and sexy. Pierre Trudeau succeeded Lester Pearson, and promised to give the country a "just society" rooted in "participatory democracy." Great slogans, even if, today, they seem stripped of much meaning.

Throughout his years in power, Pierre Trudeau was preoccupied with the *indépendantiste* movement in Quebec. He made no secret of the fact that the workaday issues of businessmen, blue-collar workers, and farmers bored him. He inflamed public opinion with the insouciance of comments like "Just watch me" when asked how far he would go in dealing with Quebec separatists, and "Why should I sell your wheat?" to western farmers. The Trudeaumania of 1968 soon evaporated. Western Canada was going through a painful transformation: agricultural markets were wildly unstable. Resources were increasingly important to the Prairie provinces—oil in Alberta, potash in Saskatchewan—and provincial leaders did not trust a prime minister fixated on bilingualism to look after their interests. East-west bitterness intensified, the historic strains within Confederation multiplied, and once again regional disintegration threatened.

But the major threat to national unity continued to be Quebec. On November 15, 1976, René Lévesque led his Parti Québécois, a party committed to taking Quebec out of Confederation or at least renegotiating the terms of federalism, to victory at the polls. He promised to hold a referendum on independence. At first this seemed an idle boast. In 1979, Canadians went so far as to throw out the Trudeau government and elected a minority Progressive Conservative government, under the absurdly youthful leadership of Joe Clark. However, while Clark dithered, Lévesque struck, with the announcement of a referendum in 1980. In Ottawa, the Clark government was summarily defeated, and Pierre Trudeau returned, poised for battle. The Parti Québécois lost the 1980 referendum. Quebeckers, it seemed, saw the merit of challenging federal power, and they successfully wrested important powers from Ottawa. But they did not really want to walk away from Confederation.

Pierre Trudeau resigned from office in 1984. We are still arguing over his legacy. He championed individual rights over collective rights, gave his supporters a vision of a bilingual, multicultural country, and reminded us all that leadership is about more than balancing the books. At the same time, he revived the regional tensions that have always characterized Canada, and left us with a costly central government. The extraordinary impact he had on this country was vividly illustrated in 2000, when thousands of mourners lined the train tracks as his funeral cortège travelled from Ottawa to Montreal or watched his televised funeral service in tears. I think that the Trudeau funeral will remain lodged in the collective memory for years, as a moment when Canadians reflected on how far their nation had come in 200 years.

It is hard to get a perspective on the post-Trudeau years—a past too raw and recent to have settled in public memory. In national politics, the recurrent themes of Canadian history continued to reassert themselves. How could Canada preserve its independence in an interdependent world? How could regional tensions be absorbed? And as the millennium approached, new challenges emerged. Were "peace, order, and good government"—and the social programs on which citizens had come to rely— sustainable? Would the courts interpret the 1982 Charter of Rights and Freedoms in favour of groups such as gays and natives who have suffered years of discrimination?

During the Conservative government of Brian Mulroney (1984–1993), fears about Canada's economic dependence on the United States exploded in a corrosive debate in the late 1980s on the Canada-U.S. Free Trade Agreement. With the return of the Liberals to power in 1993, under Jean Chrétien, regional tensions escalated, with a new political party, the Reform Party, emerging in the west and a second referendum in Quebec. During the last two decades of the twentieth century, muscular provincial governments quietly whittled away the authority of the central government in Ottawa.

Political issues, however, rarely preoccupy letter writers. Now that so much information can be transmitted by phone or e-mail, letters have become largely the repositories of emotions—the hopes, fears, and passions that many people find it hard to talk about. The majority of letters I found for this period covered personal concerns: the joys of parenthood, the spread of HIV/AIDS, the changing nature of women's lives, the experience of being immigrants in a multicultural society or peacekeepers in distant parts of the world. In my introduction to the first fifty years of letters, I suggested that the creation myth for Canada was the struggle for survival on a raw and windswept landscape. Now, 217 letters later, I see that most Canadians take for granted the unity, prosperity, and security of the nation in which they live. However, as a compulsive letter reader, I am glad to report that they still feel the need to put pen to paper.

176
1951: ONTARIO
RUBY CRESS TO HER SISTER KAY IN LONDON, ONTARIO

As the nation settled into a peacetime rhythm, it was time to think about new clothes. Ruby Cress wrote to her sisters in London, Ontario, every week about anything that came into her head: housekeeping, schemes for making money (she and her husband, Fred, had very little), her two children, cherry pie, and her excitement that she could finally replace her old coon coat. I think most of us had a great-aunt like Ruby.

Barrie
Sept. 16/51

Dear Kay,

I'm so excited about the coat you ordered for me. My first new coat since I've been married—12 years. I've always wanted a Harris tweed and navy is just the color too cause most of my things are navy—least I've a navy hat and dress. And remember you're not paying for it. I am. I've exactly $74 in the bank so all I need extra is $1 and Fred can give me that.

Gee it's wonderful. I'm so thrilled cause I've kept thinking What will I wear this winter, I need a coat so badly. The grey one of yours you gave me is really too big, too long waisted and my coon that I've had since high school is as shabby as an old barn dog. But now, glory be, I'll be having a NEW one. When I get it and go to Western Alumnae dinner with Fred I won't feel ashamed. If only I had my B.A. too—how often I've wished I had that. I hope both my kids will one day get their's. I must tell them to concentrate hard and not let their minds run round in the cornfields like Mr. Muslin at London Collegiate said that mine did.

We've really been busy. I had the two school teachers in on Sunday for turkey and they gave us a pound of chocolates. Last nite Sally and I went to a mother and daughter banquet—she looked so cute in her middy. I washed this morning and baked 3 pies—wish you lived near us and I'd bring you one. This aft I made over slacks of mine for Sally and recovered her eiderdown, this morning I cleaned, washed up the bathroom and kitchen and waxed floors. Now I'm tired and fat. Wish I were slim and figurey for my new coat.

I only hope it fits. But with measurements taken all round surely the salesgirl can tell the size I need—waist 28, chest 34, hip 37 (isn't that horrible?) sleeves 27, skirt length 43. I know a 16 is too big, even at my fattest I've never been a 16. A 14 should be just right, shouldn't it? I should be a 12.

Oh—I nearly forgot—the most important thing. Fred gets the cast off his broken ankle today. Beans; darn it, I wanted to take a picture of it but there's no sun and I've no film for the camera.

Love, Ruby

Oh dear. The coat did not meet expectations: "My new coat is warm and a perfect fit except it's too long," Ruby wrote in her next letter. "I don't look dressed up pretty like I hoped I would."

177
1952: QUEBEC
MICHELINE TO HER SISTER RENÉE IN ARVIDA

Who can imagine life without television (except perhaps at summer cottages) today? Yet the square box arrived in the corner of most Canadian living rooms only in the early 1950s. It quickly revolutionized home life, as this Montreal woman, stricken with poverty and caring for a husband in ill health, explained.

Montréal,
18 April 1952

My dear Renée,

Unbelievable, you say? But it's true—it's me—ashamed [and] embarrassed not to have written sooner. However, even if it's not an excuse, I can assure you I've written you often, but I never finish the letter. Then, after a few days, I throw it out, saying I'll write her tomorrow. Oh! this tomorrow that I count on too often! However, haven't I had a terrible lesson. Don't count on tomorrow, don't put things off, because tomorrow doesn't belong to us.

Oh! Renée, you will never be able to understand what a trial Pierre and I are going through. Just when in our lives we were going to "turn the corner" and "breathe easy" . . . Wham! Pierre all of a sudden becomes totally helpless given his illness. He's suffered constantly for eight months. He never has less than 5 or 6 ulcers in his mouth, as big as a thumbnail, he has had some in his throat since the summer. He's a martyr every time he eats something, and the little food he does finally swallow gives him terrible stomach pains, brought on it seems by gas, making him feel nauseous. He then becomes so pale that I become all upset as you can imagine.

And the days carry on like this. There are special little meals for Pierre, several times a day, but very little at a time. And every night around midnight, he puts on his overcoat, scarf, hat, boots, to go along two doors to Dr. Rioux to get a shot of calves' liver, then again, day after day, without forgetting his medicines to which we often add pills for very bad pain or others against his frequent bouts of high fever.

Besides that, I have my three birds, which isn't nothing. They're noisy. At the least flare-up between them (which happens every day) I practically smother them in the back kitchen so as not to irritate Pierre because, being so weak, he really can't deal with anything requiring control. Besides I don't need to tell you that his suffering makes him very quiet, sad, smiling rarely, every worry being a drama, and God knows there is no shortage of worries!!! As you see, I've not got an easy job. I pray hard to God to give Pierre courage and me tact, patience, to keep my little ones serene, joyful, sensitive and kind and to find encouraging words for Pierre who still weighs 120 pounds. It's a very tough time, Renée, and I'm not looking any more to understand God's will because, there are times when I'm on the verge of rejecting everything. It's not pretty, is it? But Renée I get to that point . . . then all of a sudden I snap back with great strength, and I suppose a blessing from above, and I thank God!

Besides the misfortune that wears us down every day, we count on our pride. I wonder if I have any more . . . we're beaten down with humiliations from the fact that we live on the charity of our little sisters (I don't know if I will be able to go to the family reunion I'm so embarrassed about facing them all) and from those who hold out a hand to us, and we're stuck "receiving without giving." We've the sense of being in a vortex, will we get out? However, Pierre and I who have never thought of anything but giving to others, you can imagine . . . I'm overcome with despair. It's in the cellar, when I'm feeding the "damned furnace" that I cry my heart out. But what to do, we're powerless and can do nothing.

What permits us to forget all this Renée, it's this wonderful T.V. My God! how it passes the time for us who can't go out. I know you've been generous, even very generous, with this tremendous present Renée. Listen carefully. I'm on my knees before you with a big kiss, I thank you in the name of my family. It's with cries of joy [and] eyes full of tears that we received this beautiful object that matches our living room so well. Again, a thousand thanks to you and André, who I imagine had no idea how much a T.V. would overwhelm us. I can assure you it's a tonic every day for the low spirits in this house.

And this brings me to your superb Christmas gift. Oh! My God! I'll end my days with a weak heart, with so many pangs, fast palpitations, and missed beats! almost automatic! and there we are! I get back down on my knees Renée . . . and kiss you. By the way, during a chat today with Annie, I was saying that Dad called us "my two [little monkeys]", you and me, when we were teenagers . . . Annie asked, "Do you love Renée as much as in the past?" and I realized how much I still love you, but how much everything keeps us apart and that I would not even wish (supposing you lived in Montréal) that life would bring us back together, because of our lives being so opposite. I swear that I felt a great pity and I almost detested this wicked life. However, I've known some great times . . . will they come again?

I'm asked to say hello to you. Pierre especially says thank you, thank you again for all your kindness to us. He really hopes to get back to doing the trip that he'd planned last year to go see you in Arvida. His spirit isn't too bad tonight, what do you think?

> Once again, a big kiss,
> Micheline who loves you always and more and more.

178
1954: ONTARIO
EUGENE FORSEY TO THE EDITOR OF
THE *GLOBE AND MAIL* IN TORONTO

No collection of Canadian letters would be complete without a contribution from Eugene Forsey, whose witty and acerbic salvoes on letters-to-the-editor pages in the second half of the twentieth century were readers' favourites. Forsey, born in Newfoundland, was a Rhodes Scholar. He served as director of research at the Canadian Labour Congress from 1942 to 1966, and twice ran for Parliament for the CCF (Co-operative Commonwealth Federation, forerunner of the NDP). He combined economic radicalism with constitutional conservatism, so when he noticed that some of Canada's more idiosyncratically named institutions were being surreptitiously renamed by government officials, he protested loudly.

Ottawa
September 1954

Dear Sir,

The Department of External Affairs explains that its use of the term "Canada Day" for "Dominion Day" is for external consumption only, for "convenience," because the poor foreigners wouldn't know what "Dominion Day" meant: "it means very little abroad." I suppose the French, when they are talking to foreigners, call the 14th of July "France Day," and the Americans call the 4th of July "United States Day"? I hope the Department of External Affairs will be careful in future, if it has occasion to speak of June 24th, not to call it "St. Jean Baptiste Day" but "Quebec Day". "St. Jean Baptiste" might "mean very little abroad."

The principle seems to be that if foreigners don't understand any of our legal terms for our own institutions, we don't explain what they mean: we change the names. Perhaps this accounts for the Canada Year Book's funny work with "Ministry" and "House of Commons" and "Parliament." Henceforth, our "Parliament" can be "National Assembly" when we're talking to Frenchmen, and "Congress" when we're talking to Americans or Central or South Americans, and "Supreme Soviet" when we're talking to Russians.

And, of course, the foreigners would understand better if we called our "Secretary of State for External Affairs" "Foreign Minister," and our "provinces" "states." . . .

The Department of External Affairs explains also that "Dominion Day" could refer to any Commonwealth country. It certainly couldn't refer to India, which deliberately and by law struck out "Dominion" from its legal designation, and substituted "Republic." (That is the honest, manly, democratic way to make such changes; but some people prefer to sneak them into telephone books and Year Books and miscellaneous official documents when they think no one is looking.) So the poor foreigner, reading an official bulletin of the Canadian Department of External Affairs, and seeing the heading "Observance of Dominion Day Abroad," and finding the words "Canada" and "Canadian" twenty-five times in a page and a half, might have thought the Department was talking about Ceylon, or Pakistan, or the United Kingdom, or Australia, or South Africa or New Zealand? I hope the foreigners will be pleased by the Department's estimate of their intelligence . . .

If, as your editorial suggests, it is civil servants who are doing this sort of thing on their own, it is high time they were reminded that they are not entitled to repeal Acts of Parliament. It is not their business to impose on the public their own personal preferences for this, that or the other term, or their own opinion of foreigners' IQs. It is their business to obey the law. We need in Canada more of the spirit of the Englishman who, whenever he writes a letter to a civil servant, ends it with: "You have the honor to be, Sir, my obedient servant."

Eugene Forsey

Forsey lost some of these battles: Dominion Day became Canada Day, and the secretary of state for external affairs is now the foreign minister. But the Parliament and provinces of Canada have stuck to their names.

179

1959: ONTARIO

EUSTACE ROSS TO RALPH GUSTAFSON IN TORONTO

As Canadian literature matured, it left behind its roots in British romanticism. In fact, post-war poets had little but contempt for those old warhorses of Canadian literature: Confederation poets Charles G.D. Roberts, Bliss Carman, and Archibald Lampman. The poet and geophysicist W.W.E. Ross, often described as "the first

modern Canadian poet," was interested in imagism and surrealism. When his fel-
low poet the literary critic Ralph Gustafson included some of Ross's poetry in The
Penguin Book of Canadian Verse (1958), *Ross was less than enthusiastic about the*
company in which he found himself.

Lake Scugog,
August 19, 1959.

Dear Ralph,
I should have thanked you long ago for the cheque but for several months
I wrote, and read, practically nothing. Here, at the lake, I've been catching
up on both. We're here for three weeks and my address remains, of course,
62 Delaware.

Glad to learn a book of your poems will be coming out this fall. It wasn't
till after considerable delay that I got hold of a copy of the Penguin anthology. I haven't been going down town because of lack of time and the parking difficulties. Mary tried Eaton's unsuccessfully, finally secured a copy at
Simpson's. I've been going over it carefully, and find it somewhat more dif-
fuse than the first one [Gustafson had also edited an anthology in 1942],
more like [A.J.M.] Smith's—though the introduction is certainly breezier
than his. It's so much bigger, and with all that [Charles G.D.] Roberts,
[Bliss] Carman etc. it seems more literary-historical, less "modern". The
late nineteenth century English (and American) poetic annals (periodicals,
etc.) must have been filled with similar echoes of Keats, Shelley and others
and their recent anthologists have tended to drop most of it . . . Anyway, for
me, reading large gobs of Roberts and the others is like trying to swallow a
mass of feathers from slit pillow. I won't enlarge on this. Isn't [Archibald]
Lampman's "Life and Nature" (Oh, Life! Oh, Life!) simply one of the silli-
est pieces ever written, if you examine it closely—and all because he either
didn't like organ music or happened to run into some bad organists ("moan-
ing shrill")? And "The Piper of Arll" has always been one of my pet aver-
sions. (I could go on at great length but won't.) Anyway, I don't see how
those writers can have the faintest stimulating effect on young writers
nowadays, who very properly look elsewhere, and, if they want romanticism,
take it straight, from the best sources . . .

Of course I appreciate the difficulty a Canadian anthologist is up
against. The horrid fact is that Canada, differing from the U.S., England
and France, didn't have any first rate poets in the 19th century (and I'm
doubtful about the 20th century too, so far!). The situation must be the

same in Australia, New Zealand and South Africa. There must be "pet" earlier poets who are claimed to be essentially "Australian", etc., and are carefully preserved, rather to the bewilderment of the outside world. Here, since a country, to be a "nation" must have a great poet, or great poets, some of the most (apparently) modern minded have fallen back on Pratt [E. J. Pratt] . . . Similarly, in Germany, Goethe was hoisted into that position, since Germany had to have a great poet, but with considerable excuse . . . The thing to do, apparently, is to be really vociferous about one's talent—though there may be, finally, a big flop, as in the case of Amy Lowell . . .

I'll certainly be interested in learning how this collection sells, and in any critical comments, especially from the U.S. and England . . .

With best wishes for the success of your forthcoming book,

> Yours sincerely,
> Eustace Ross

180
1960: ONTARIO
GLENN GOULD TO HIS FRIEND
EDITH BOECKER IN HEIDELBERG, GERMANY

The Canadian pianist Glenn Gould (1932–1982) was one of the most brilliant pianists of his generation, best known for his championing of moderns such as Hindemith and Schoenberg and for his interpretations of Bach. His public persona was enigmatic and reclusive, but in private he was witty and warm. A letter to a German fellow musician reveals his delight in his own eccentricity.

> Toronto,
> January 27, 1960

Dear Edith:

Many thanks for your Christmas greetings. I did not send mine earlier because I had no way of knowing whether or not you still resided in Husumer Strasse.

. . . This past season has been one fraught by all kinds of curious adventures. Several months ago I began to develop a longing for grandeur which my establishment at Lake Simcoe was not fully able to satisfy. So, more or less on a whim, I became the tenant of an estate some fifteen miles above Toronto, known as "Donchery." It was love at first sight and it lasted until the day after the lease was signed! The estate, let me tell you, had 26 rooms, if one counts the 7 bathrooms, the breakfast room, the scullery, the dog kennel, and every other partition which could conceivably be construed as a room. It also had on the property, which by the way was beautifully wooded with a river running through it, a swimming pool and tennis court. The swimming pool was surrounded by a four-car garage and boys and girls dressing rooms (no bacchanalian revelries for us!). The house was situated some 60 steps above the river (known as the Don) and the view from down below looking up and especially at night with flood lights was like looking at Salzburg castle, from your own strawberry patch. Oh yes, there was one of those too on the other side of the Don.

Anyway, the lease was signed on December 13 and on December 19 I was suddenly struck with the realization of what I had done as well as with the intriguing puzzle of what I would ever do with 26 rooms in the first place. Of course everyone here put their own interpretation on it and the most fascinating stories were circulating about Toronto. Unfortunately someone let the news of this operation get to the newspapers and from that moment on the house began to be enlarged by one wing every day. The last time I was accosted on the street about it someone asked me whether it was really 40 rooms or just 38!! Mr. Homburger [Walter Homburger, his manager], I think, was terrified that I was giving up the piano to devote myself to the role of country squire and his secretary was convinced that I was having an affair with the upstairs maid (who hadn't yet been engaged—to do housework that is) and my mother, I'm sure, was convinced I was secretly married.

On the second day of the lease, I set out on a gigantic buying spree in a vain attempt to furnish 26 rooms in two days and, with all the ferocity of the plague at Oran, I descended with a group of advisors on one of the large department stores. It was my first exposure to household purchasing and I must say that I was rather intimidated by it. It was relatively easy in the kitchenwares where I was able, for the most part, to stand with my head inside an oven ostensibly examining the broiler and even in the towel and bathmat department, I managed to pick out some subdued specimens which I felt would go well in the master bedroom suite. (By the way, the master bedroom suite possessed a fully broadloomed bathroom!) But it was really in the bedroom furnishings that I began to show signs of weakness and, although mattress testing has always been among my favourite private pastimes, I began to feel rather conspicuous when a group of salesmen began to persuade me of the advantages of "Beautyrest" vs "Posturepedic." This little vignette was made the more dramatic because I was accompanied by a most elegant young lady, who was left over from the kitchenware blitz, and who tested the mattresses with such dignity that all of the salesmen were addressing her as "Madame."

The following day I was back at "Donchery" to welcome the movers as the various purchases began to arrive. I was alone at the time in the 26 rooms and at first, as the larger items such as the refrigerator and the stove arrived, I was grateful for the space which they filled and optimistic about the possibility of polishing off the other 25 rooms. But then suddenly it happened—the brooms and the pyrex dishes arrived and I was filled with all the horror of the domestic idyll I had been courting. Suddenly "Donchery" represented a snare, my lease commitment, the pyrex dishes—permanency—and my only escape seemed to flee with my trusty Buick, into which I sprang, and I streaked for Toronto.

Only last week, at considerable expense to the management, was I able to purchase my release and so now, when not occupying a newly acquired apartment in Toronto, I return with my tail between my legs to Lake Simcoe which somehow seems quite grand enough . . .

All the very best,

> Affectionately,
> Glenn

181

1960: LABRADOR
JILL KIDDER TO HER MOTHER, RUTH WILSON, IN VANCOUVER

Although Canada was by now primarily an urban society, adventurous spirits were still drawn to unexplored regions of this huge land mass. In 1958, the Iron Ore Company of Canada (IOC) began preparing to mine the massive iron ore deposits on the shores of Carol Lake in the bleak and rocky interior of Labrador. Two years later, the mining camp was a thriving little town which would eventually be named Labrador City, peopled by pioneer families such as the Kidders. Jill Kidder was used to the north: when she was eight months pregnant, she had lived in a tent 350 kilometres from Yellowknife,

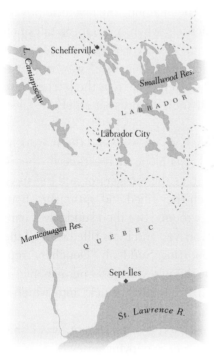

while her husband, Kendall, a mining prospector and explosives expert, prospected in the Northwest Territories. By 1960, the Kidders had five children (John, twelve, Margie, eleven, Ann, seven, Michael, six, and newborn Peter) and Jill decided she would like a break. It turned out to be a longer break than she expected.

Carol Project
Nov. 22, 1960

Dear Mum,

Well, for goodness sake, all sorts of things have happened . . .

Ten days ago I hoped I might get a week-end in Sept-Îles. Ken didn't get home on time that Friday night, but we decided it would be a good thing if I went out on the Saturday [scheduled flight] and came back on a special flight Monday morning. All very good. So I phoned the Booths to tell them I was coming, and off we went on Saturday afternoon to the airstrip. When we got there, the pilot had just had a radio message that he was to go to Knob Lake [later renamed Schefferville] and pick up a stretcher case to fly to Sept-Îles. I had to make up my mind immediately if I wanted to go—it meant about four hours of flying, instead of the hour and fifteen minutes it takes to get to Sept-Îles from here—so after debating with myself and Kendall for two minutes, I decided I might as well. I'd never seen Knob, and at least I'd be away from the little ones. So off we went into the wild blue yonder.

We got to Knob about five in the afternoon. I have never seen a more desolate settlement, flat and barren and bleak, a few straight rows of apartment buildings, hundreds of power poles, and a trailer village. We went into the hut at the airstrip and were standing around warming up at the Quebec heater, when the pilot announced that there'd been a change of plans, and we were flying the injured man right to Montreal! There were four men on the plane, and another woman who sat up at the front with the pilots, and was sick all the time. When we got back on, they had loaded the stretcher, and when I got on and looked at the injured man, I almost decided I'd rather stay at Knob. He had slipped while carrying a railroad tie and the tie had hit him on the head; they were flying him to the Neurological, and weren't sure he would make it. He made horrible gasping groans with every breath and kept coughing up blood. Fortunately he was unconscious. The trip was awful—I've never been so cold. The plane is an old DC-3, heated only in the pilot's compartment. I got my slacks and sweater out of my suitcase and put them on over my dress, and sat and shivered for five and a half hours. The aircraft had only bucket seats—benches, really—down the side, so we had to sit hunched over, because the side of the plane curves up from the seats. They put some sandwiches on for us at Knob, but we couldn't eat them because the man on the stretcher upset our stomachs. (There was a nurse with him, and she was wonderful—never took her eyes off him, and spent most of the trip mopping up blood.)

It was, of course, pitch dark, so we had nothing to look at, and I didn't even take a book. For three hours there was nothing at all, and when we saw the first lights of some mining camp we were all as excited as if we'd just made port after several months at sea. Before we got to Montreal the injured man regained consciousness, and the nurse said his pulse was strong, and that he would be alright. We sat and beamed at each other in a congratulatory way, as if we'd done it all ourselves. We made a dramatic entrance in front of the main terminal, greeted by ambulances and police cars—sirens and flashing red lights all over the place.

The pilot was taking the plane back that night to Mont Joli, on the south shore, but I didn't particularly want to spend a day or two in Mont Joli, and anyway, I couldn't have flown another inch.

So there I was in Montreal, with fifteen dollars and no-one expecting me. I phoned Ken, hoping to astound him with the news, but he already knew—so disappointing of him. He advised me to go to the Mount Royal Hotel, as that is where the IOC people always stay, and tell the assistant manager my story, and get him to cash me a cheque. So off I went—isn't it exciting?—and spent the night at the hotel, lying in my bed watching TV and eating chocolate bars, and having the time of my life.

On Sunday I went out to the Smiths and crashed a dinner party they were having. I spent all day Monday Christmas shopping at Simpson's, where I just happen to have a credit card. I was so delighted to be able to do this, as I had decided that Christmas shopping would just have to be passed up this year; and Christmas is no fun at all if you can't send off gifts in all directions . . . I got lots of vital winter clothes for my chicks, and some heavy boots for myself.

On Tuesday Rosemarie gave me a Toni, and that night I went to a session of our old bridge club, and won the prize—only time I ever won.

In the meantime, I kept phoning Timmins Aviation, who look after the IOC flights in Montreal, to find out when I could get home . . . I had been in touch with Ken, off and on, although he lost track of me several times, and he kept sending teletypes to the IOC office in Montreal, to see if they knew where I was. Margie was staying home from school to look after Peter, and they were all getting along beautifully. Fortunately, I had cleaned and baked and laundered before I left, and got in a big food order. I got to Sept-Îles Thursday evening, in time for choir practice and a party after at the Booths. There was nothing flying up here until the Saturday sched, so I stayed over at the Booths, and we had a bridge party Friday night.

Home at noon on Saturday, just a week after I had left to spend the weekend in Sept-Îles. Everything here was in excellent order, and all happy as could be. Marg ran the whole thing—washed and ironed, cleaned and cooked all the meals, and Ken has been boasting about her ever since. Her teacher didn't even bother sending her homework, since she is so far ahead of her class.

Now, isn't that a tale? All the women are full of envy and complaining that when they plan to spend a day in Sept-Îles, all they do is spend a day in Sept-Îles. I never had such a nice holiday . . .

Love,
Jill

Jill and Kendall's daughter Margie, who had run the household while Jill was stuck in Montreal, became the actress Margot Kidder, best known for her role as Lois Lane in the movie Superman.

182

1961: NEW BRUNSWICK
BEATRICE MAITLAND TO THE EDITOR OF
CHATELAINE IN TORONTO

I expect Doris Anderson, editor of Chatelaine, *roared with laughter when she received this letter. One of the most popular competitions of the 1960s was the "Mrs. Chatelaine" contest. More than 6,000 women, in English and French Canada, entered the competition, run by the country's largest-circulation magazine, for which they were graded on such traditional skills as baking, child-rearing, and community involvement. But even prizes such as ten days in Paris and a three-piece luggage set could not entice a reader such as Beatrice Maitland.*

Chatham, NB
1 November 1961

Dear Editor,

Yesterday was the closing date for your Mrs. Chatelaine contest, but I didn't enter.

I wish someone, sometime, would have a competition for "Mrs. Nothing"!! A person who isn't a perfect housekeeper, a faultless mother, a charming hostess, a loving wife, or a servant of the community. Besides being glamorous as a model, talented as a Broadway star and virtuous as a Saint.

I have studied your questionnaire carefully but my replies are hopelessly inadequate . . . To start with my appearance is absolutely fatal . . . I am overweight, pear-shaped and bow legged. Consequently, not having much to work on I don't bother and cover it up with comfortable, warm old slacks.

Now, housework. Failure there too as I am a lousy housekeeper. If I feel like sewing, or sleeping, or writing a letter, like this morning, the house has to wait.

Entertaining? Practically never. Hubby isn't particularly socially minded so anything is impromptu with close friends. A game of cards or just talk with a few beers. No fancy food, drinks or entertainment.

Meals? We prefer plain meat-potato-vegetable meals with no frills. For birthdays our children choose the dinner. What's the menu? Usually hamburgers and chips. You can't win. Make a fancy meal from a magazine and they look like they are being poisoned.

The decor is middle English European junk shop, especially v
children start doing their homework.

Community activities? I have always belonged to and worked with other organizations . . . but I have become so sick of and bored with meetings I quit. Home-and-School meetings where people sit like stuffed apes and look at anyone who gets up to make a suggestion as if he were a Martian . . .

My philosophy as a home-maker? I guess that is, be happy, don't worry. You do what you can with what you've got when you feel like it. Consequently I'm never sick and I've got no nerves or fears.

That is poor me. So if you want to run a contest for Mrs. Slob of 1961, I would be happy to apply and would probably win hands down. Thank you for your enjoyable magazine and my apologies for taking up your time.

Mrs. Beatrice Maitland

183
1963: ONTARIO
ARTHUR PATTILLO, QC, TO CHARLOTTE VANDINE,
NATIONAL CHAIRMAN OF THE CANADIAN FEDERATION OF
BUSINESS AND PROFESSIONAL WOMEN'S CLUBS, IN MONTREAL

Beatrice Maitland was not alone in her resentment of the 1950s "perfect housewife" image to which women were expected to conform. In 1930, the Canadian Federation of Business and Professional Women's Clubs was founded and immediately began to lobby for improvements in women's lives and rights. The "B.s and P.s" passed resolutions on abortion and divorce at their 1963 annual convention. But the response of the Canadian Bar Association to these resolutions reflects the prejudices yet to be overcome.

25 King Street West
Toronto 1, Ontario
November 1, 1963

Dear Miss VanDine:

I am sorry that I have been so long in acknowledging your letter of October 7th with enclosures. Unfortunately, when they arrived I was busily engaged in Court.

I really had a great deal of personal amusement in reading your resolutions and the submissions that you have made to the Hon. Lester B. Pearson. Perhaps the reason for this is that one of the two secretaries whom

I have had in my thirty years at the Bar was Mrs. Allie Ahern, a Past President of what I always knew as the B. and P.

Seriously speaking, do you think that Mr. Pearson or I or any of our sex are really interested in the question of abortion? I fully appreciate that "Canadian conditions of life and Canadian attitudes have changed greatly in the past thirty or forty years," but as far as my sex is concerned don't you really think that what you are talking about is inflation?

I was interested in your comment about the laws of divorce. With these I have a much more keen appreciation. The only thing that I regret is that your statement as to the present laws is not correct. It is true that in the provinces of Canada which did not have divorce laws prior to Confederation, adultery is the only grounds for divorce, but this is not so in the Province of Nova Scotia. When I practised law there I was engaged in several cases in which the ground for divorce was cruelty, and under the laws of the Province it was a valid ground.

Notwithstanding this, I do agree that the laws of divorce should be changed in this country, even though I do not personally agree with divorce but think rather that society would benefit more if we had judicial separation which did not permit remarriage. Again I may point out that in Nova Scotia under the laws of that Province you can obtain judicial separation.

My present secretary, who is a personal friend of Allie Ahern and came with me from Nova Scotia, thinks that I have been facetious in my reply. I hope you do not think that I have been because I am really pointing out, even though I perhaps have not been too serious in my manner, the difficulties that I see in both of your resolutions. However, the B. and P. is a worthwhile institution and has done a great deal and it may succeed where others have failed.

> Yours sincerely,
> Arthur S. Pattillo
> President, The Canadian Bar Association

184
1964: ONTARIO
GEORGE STANLEY TO JOHN MATHESON, MP, IN OTTAWA

As Canada approached the 100th anniversary of Confederation, Prime Minister Pearson pledged to replace the Red Ensign, a makeshift banner adapted from the Union Jack, with a new and distinctive national flag. Debate over national symbols erupted: the Royal Canadian Legion argued vehemently against such a break with British traditions, while Quebec nationalists campaigned noisily against symbols of English power. The federal Liberals were inundated with sketches of flags that could become rallying symbols. John Matheson, Liberal MP for Brockville, Ontario, and the prime minister's point man on the flag debate, received a particularly thoughtful letter from his old friend George Stanley, an eminent Canadian historian and dean of arts at the Royal Military College in Kingston.

Royal Military College of Canada
Kingston, Ontario
23 March, 1964

Confidential

John Matheson, Esq., M.P.,
Member of Parliament for Leeds,
House of Commons,
Ottawa, Ontario

Dear Mr. Matheson,
With reference to our conversation last week regarding flags and heraldry, I am sending you these few observations at your request.

1. Canadian Flag
   (a) There does not appear to have been any formal Canadian flag during the Ancien Régime. When required, the flag flown was the royal standard of France, three golden lilies on a white ground. During the British period the flag used was the union flag, known usually as the Union Jack.
   The Red Ensign, with the Canadian coat of arms on the fly was used for the merchant marine. It was authorized in 1924 by Parliament to be flown from Canadian buildings abroad in order to differentiate Canadian from British buildings . . . In 1945, the Red Ensign was

authorized to be flown in Canada from public buildings. This was done by Order-in-Council.

2. Canadian Emblems

(a) Two emblems are usually associated with Canada, the beaver and the maple leaf. The beaver goes back to the early days of the fur trade. A beaver was included in the coat of arms granted to Sir William Alexander by Charles I. Frontenac suggested the beaver as a Canadian emblem to Colbert in 1673. The beaver has been included in the coat of arms of the Hudson's Bay Company and the City of Montreal. However, after the middle of the nineteenth century the beaver was replaced by the maple leaf in common use and popularity.

(b) The maple leaf was first used by French Canadians as a French Canadian emblem. In 1806, the newspaper, Le Canadien, suggested that the maple leaf be adopted as an emblem for Canada. In 1834 it was adopted by the St. Jean Baptiste Society. However, we find the maple leaf being used in Upper Canada at the inauguration of the General Brock monument at Queenston Heights. In 1860 the maple leaf was widely worn as a Canadian symbol at the time of the visit of the Prince of Wales (later Edward II) to Canada. Many ladies wore silver maple leaf brooches similar to those used by the Queen mother (Elizabeth). It was subsequently embodied in the coat of arms of Quebec, Ontario and Canada . . .

5. Application of the above principles to a Canadian Flag.

(a) The Canadian flag should avoid the over-use of heraldic devices such as are to be found on coats of arms. A flag embodying the Canadian coat of arms might be properly devised for the use of the Governor-General as the head of the state in Canada. It seems to me that the Red Ensign is unsuitable because it lacks simplicity, and because it includes a complicated coat of arms on the fly.

(b) There should be no question of confusing the flag of one country with that of another. In selecting a Canadian flag, therefore, every effort should be made to avoid including on it symbols more properly associated with another country, i.e. stripes, stars. A Canadian flag must be sufficiently Canadian that it can be easily recognized at a distance as being Canadian. I believe that the Red Ensign, which is similar to the British merchant marine flag, the flags flown by several British colonies, is unsuitable for Canadian purposes, because it is not easily identifiable as Canadian at a distance.

(c) The colours now associated with Canada are Red and White. These are traditional colours in the sense that they are usually looked upon as representing Great Britain and France . . . Moreover, these colours were approved in 1921 as special Canadian colours and were included in the Canadian coat of arms approved at that time (Three red maple leaves on a white background).

(d) The traditional heraldic device or emblem of Canada is the maple leaf (See para. 2 (b)). This emblem has official sanction by its inclusion in two provincial coats of arms and in the official coat of arms of Canada. It has been used by Canadian troops in two world wars, and by Canadian Olympic teams (including the colours red and white). It appears to have universal acceptance both in and outside Canada as a distinctive Canadian emblem.

(e) If the flag is to be a unifying symbol it must avoid the use of national or racial symbols that are of a divisive nature. It in clearly inadvisable in a purely Canadian flag to include such obvious national symbols as the Union Jack or the Fleur de Lys. Racial feelings should be content with the use of the colours red and white, if it is essential to read these in such a light.

6. Suggestions

(a) The flag which would meet most of the requirements mentioned above would be a simple red and white flag bearing a stylized maple leaf on it. Such a flag might appear in this way:

(b) Of the two suggestions above, I would favour (A). This flag, admittedly, is very similar to that presently being flown at the Royal Military College. The basic difference being the inclusion of the RMC crest (armed fist) in the white third.

(c) The use of two thirds of red has no particular significance. What is in my mind is the availability of a white strip to carry the stylized maple leaf in red. If equal balance is given to red and white, then the symmetry and balance of the flag is destroyed once the maple leaf is inserted in the white portion.

(d) The use of the single stylized maple leaf is, in my view, preferable to the three maple leaves conjoined on a single stem. The single leaf has the virtue of simplicity; it emphasizes the distinctive Canadian symbol, and suggests the idea of loyalty to a single country. In this respect the leaf resembles the eagle, the star or the crescent used as national symbols in other countries . . .

I hope that these few observations will assist you in your labours. If there is anything else I can do to assist you, I shall be pleased to do it.

Yours sincerely,
G. F. G. Stanley
Dean of Arts

George Stanley's suggestion that the Canadian flag be a single maple leaf on a white stripe, bordered by two red stripes, was adopted by Parliament. The new Canadian flag was officially unfurled on February 15, 1965. George Stanley went on to become the lieutenant-governor of New Brunswick.

Exhausted Liberal MPs celebrate passage of the government's flag resolution after six months of bitter controversy. The maple leaf on the flag they hold has thirteen points, which would eventually be reduced to eleven.

185

1964: ONTARIO

**JOHN DIEFENBAKER TO HIS BROTHER, ELMER DIEFENBAKER,
IN SASKATCHEWAN**

*In 1964, former prime minister John Diefenbaker was an angry man. The previous
year, after only six years in office, his Progressive Conservative government had been
defeated by the Liberals, whom Dief abhorred, led by a former diplomat of whom Dief
had a low opinion. Day after day in the House of Commons, "the man from Prince
Albert" (so-called after his Saskatchewan riding) goaded Prime Minister Lester Pearson
about his proposal for a new Canadian flag, which Diefenbaker did not support.*

Office of the Leader of the Opposition
Ottawa
May 28, 1964

Dear Elmer,

I had just arrived in the office this morning when Olive phoned and advised
that her brother Don had passed away. He had been ill for some months but
nobody had expected his death. You remember him as a little boy in Saskatoon.

Olive as always is like a rock. This afternoon she and I were to go to
Toronto to a Variety Show in memory of the late Mayor Summerville. I do
not think she should go although she feels she should.

Last evening we went out to a Women's Conservative meeting in
Carleton and from all appearances there that is one of the constituencies
that will be won back.

It is impossible to follow the mental processes of Mr. Pearson. He was
going to have a distinctive flag. Now he is going to have two flags and two
anthems. Having already established the principle of two nations in his
speech at Murray Bay, Quebec, this latest step is a further divisive and dis-
ruptive force.

French Canada is not satisfied now because, while he is going to abolish
the Red Ensign, he is going to reinstate the Union Jack.

I hope I will be able to unite the Conservative Party in the House and
really put on a fight.

This man more and more is showing signs of egomania. After having seen
the film on me over [at] the CBC the Liberals decided they ought to have
one on him and they spent $35,000 of the Canadian people's money. While
the CBC wouldn't let me see or know of any part of the film they were going

to produce, they provided a preview for him, Paul Martin, [Mitchell] Sharp, [Maurice] Lamontagne and some of the Liberal organizers. Five runs were provided. I have often seen people who have enjoyed a picture stay for the second show, [but] the entertainment value of the Pearson picture must have been in a class by itself if after they had seen it and re-seen it four more times, the CBC decided not to produce it! According to the press it showed him to be too petulant and would leave a bad impression. What has happened reveals him in a truer light.

> With best wishes,
> Sincerely,
> John

In 1967, John Diefenbaker was forced to step down from the Progressive Conservative leadership. He was replaced by Robert Stanfield, whose willingness to go along with Liberal policies on bilingualism appalled his predecessor. But when the former prime minister died in 1979, thousands lined the railroad tracks in western Canada to say goodbye to "the Chief" as his cortège passed.

186
1964: ONTARIO
MARSHALL MCLUHAN TO ROBERT FULFORD IN TORONTO

One of the literary sensations of 1964 was the appearance of Understanding Media, *by the communications guru Marshall McLuhan, director of the University of Toronto Centre for Culture and Technology. Complex and paradoxical, it received mixed reviews. In* Maclean's *magazine, Robert Fulford suggested that the book was brilliant and provocative, but also "arrogant, sloppy [and] repetitious." McLuhan took offence . . .*

Toronto
June 1st, 1964

Dear Bob:

It's amazing that you got anything out of my writing at all, since you misconceive my entire procedure. I do not move along lines. I use points like the dots in a wire-photo. That is why I must repeat and repeat my points. Again, insights are not points of view. I do not have a point of view on anything. I am interested only in modalities and processes. You assume that I have a point of view. No wonder I sound "arrogant." My main theme is the extension of the nervous system in the electric age and thus the complete break with 5000 years of mechanical technology. This I state over and over again. I do not say whether it is a good or bad thing. To do so would be meaningless and arrogant.

I do value your friendly approach.

Cordially
Marshall McLuhan

187
1967: QUEBEC
NATHALIE TO HER SISTER FRANÇOISE

I am one of the rare Canadians of my generation who did not visit Expo 67, the international fair that marked the centenary of Confederation and won international acclaim. Quebeckers were among those who felt the most pride: Expo also celebrated for them the Quiet Revolution that had ended the province's long period of introversion. Relatives who were travelling abroad were urged to come home to enjoy the excitement.

Montréal,
30 April 1967

My dear Françoise,
Expo has started at last . . . If you saw how proud we are to be Montrealers. It's Gigantic, Splendid, Terrific, Marvellous, Unique. All with Capital Letters. There should be an even stronger word to really make the point. Dad and I spent the day on Sunday the 30th on the site—we knew there would be huge crowds but we were so keen we went anyway. There were around 400,000 people. Incredible! At about three o'clock they had to stop the Metro at the Berri-Demontigny station to . . . relieve the congestion and let out those who wanted to leave Expo. It's not only in the United States that it's the *biggest*—believe me it's here too. The weather was splendid, which put us in a terrific mood. So far we have visited the Russian pavilion, which will get a lot of visitors, the Thai and Burmese pavilions, both sculptured, you'd almost say in embroidery, really fascinating. As well, we went

to Africa Place, which includes several republics, namely the Ivory Coast, Cameroon, Uganda, and Togo; there'll also be the Congo, but it's not open yet. They're slow, they are. I recognize them even on the grounds of Expo. But of those we saw, the most beautiful, to my taste, is the Czechoslovakian pavilion. It's beautiful, but beautiful as in a dream. In any case, I can't wait until you come to see it all. I even suggest you come straight away, because your holidays won't be long enough for you to take it all in. You know we have a world tour right here on our doorstep.

> Affectionately,
> Nathalie

188

1968: ONTARIO

BLAIR FRASER TO HIS EDITOR DAVID MANUEL IN TORONTO

This letter contains the kind of "inside Ottawa" details that political junkies love. When Pierre Trudeau arrived in Ottawa, federal politics began to look a lot more interesting. And when the dashing Quebecker won an upset victory at the Liberal leadership convention in April 1968 and succeeded Lester Pearson as prime minister and leader of the Liberal Party, leading journalists realized he was an irresistible subject for a book. The distinguished Maclean's *political columnist Blair Fraser started laying out his book proposal to David Manuel, editor-in-chief of Doubleday Canada. Fraser began by tracking the new PM's leadership style and his decision to call an early election.*

> [Ottawa]
> April 28, 1968

Dear David,

I used to write long letters to Ralph Allen [editor of *Maclean's* magazine] that began "Don't read this if you're busy." This is one of that kind. It's an attempt to summarize a few recent conversations, in lieu of notes, and an aide-mémoire not only of what I have learned but also of important things I don't know, and must try to find out . . .

First, about the general state of play. I saw the PM briefly on Friday and he repeated what he had said before, that he had no objection to my writing the book nor to my talking to any of his people. However, he said some of them were reluctant to talk and he was equally reluctant to discourage their reticence, since he was urging it on all and sundry as a general rule . . .

Trudeau's technique of "keeping the options open" is no mere charade, it's real. All day Monday and up to noon on Tuesday April 23, his own staff continued to work as two separate task forces, one on the assumption that Parliament would sit, the other that it would be dissolved [and a June election called] . . . Allan MacEachen, House leader, apparently declined to tell the other party House leaders what the business would be, but this could only have been because he wasn't sure whether or not the House would sit . . . Anyway, [Trudeau] did arrange for the swearing-in on Saturday and did let it be known, on Friday, that an early election was at least being contemplated. The first Cabinet meeting, held on Saturday afternoon, was apparently devoted both to the putative legislative program and also to the election question. Several senior ministers are known to have opposed the early date, and this may have surprised Trudeau since up to then, I gather, the advice he had got was mostly hawkish.

. . . Trudeau may possibly have been influenced by the fact that some of his less admired colleagues and ex-colleagues were doves. Bob Winters, for one, told me he thought the new government should have proved itself in the House before going to the people; he also said, with an emphasis that Trudeau may have found rather unpleasantly challenging, that this time the Conservatives would be "much better financed" than the Liberals. Paul Martin, speaking to other people, gave as one of his reasons for wanting to leave the Commons his reluctance to take on the burdens of an election campaign at this time.

Both these men had attempted to bargain with Trudeau for their places and roles in the Cabinet. Martin said to a friend last weekend: "I've been fighting for the Liberal Party for 40 years, and the other day a man who only three years ago was fighting for the NDP against the Liberal Party, sat across the table from me and told me I couldn't handle Canada's external affairs." As for Winters, he was volubly upset by press reports that he had served an "ultimatum" on Trudeau as his price for entering the Cabinet, but it's now apparent that this was merely a blunt, impolite way of stating what actually happened. Martin wanted his choice of portfolios, Winters wanted what amounted to a veto power on policy. Trudeau paid no attention to either demand.

However, there were others opposed to an early election whom Trudeau had no reason at all to distrust. I'm told that one was Mitchell Sharp; I know at first hand that another was Bud Drury. John Nichol was a third. There was also a great flood of invited advice from across the country, by mail, telegram and telephone, much of it hostile to June election plans. The Cabinet broke up late Saturday afternoon with no decision.

. . . Next day, Sunday, was a day off and apparently second-thought day for many. Roméo LeBlanc told me that by Monday morning the tone of the mail and telegrams had changed abruptly, even in some cases from the same people. He got many messages that began, "Disregard earlier telegram stop Now feel . . ." Most of these second thinkers had swung around to a yes instead of a no on the early election. The same change took place, they both told me, in the minds of John Nichol and Bud Drury. I would guess, therefore, that the prevailing view in Cabinet on Monday must have been somewhat different from that of Saturday. However, there still was no decision pending the caucus on Tuesday morning at 11 . . .

I have no full story of what went on in caucus, but I know what was planned by a small group of hawks and I think it came off. The plan was to make sure that Russ Honey, the chairman, recognize about half a dozen reliable hawks before he recognized any doves. Thus the bewildered, the dubious and the wagon-climbers would already be at least half sold before the first dove had a chance to coo. The PM himself made no strong pitch either way, just set out the "options" with his usual clarity. (By this time, of course, the mere fact that an election had been talked about for four days had become a strong reason for having one.)

Caucus broke up about one o'clock. Still no decision, or anyway no announcement; Parliament to meet at 2:30. But Paul Martin must have had at least an inkling when the PM asked him to get his car and bring it round to the John A. Macdonald door on the west side of the West Block. Paul had to shake off Bobby Hull of the *Windsor Star*, which he did by asking Bobby if he hadn't better get back upstairs to be there when the PM came out of his office. Paul then got his car, met the PM by the "secret" exit, drove him to the rear of Government House so that he could enter through the garden and elude the press stake-out in front.

This game of hide-and-seek with the press was not entirely frivolous. He went to some trouble to make sure that the proper order of priority was observed in letting various people know of his decision. First of all, the Governor General; then Parliament; then the people, directly on live TV without the intermediary of the press. Newspapers were then free to write about it as much as they liked.

April 20

Yesterday I learned a bit more about the process of decision before the election was called . . .

Apparently three factors were important in converting doves to hawks:

1. A private poll conducted by Lou Harris . . . which showed almost incredibly favorable conditions. As my informant said: "We wouldn't have believed it except for one thing—he gave us zero in Nova Scotia [home province of the popular Conservative leader, Robert Stanfield] and this proved the poll was honest." But outside of the Atlantic Provinces (which would be substantially unchanged) it was Trudeau all the way—54% in Quebec, 51% in Ontario including 52% in Metro Toronto, over 50% in B.C., and even on the prairies a fair showing, over 50% in some places.

2. Realisation of how narrow the field of choice actually was. Trudeau's own original preference had been for a short continuation of the present session, with an agenda of items selected for urgency; then a summer recess, an autumn recall of Parliament with the Speech from the Throne serving as an election platform, and dissolution after the debate on the Address in Reply, or soon thereafter. He discovered that the "short" continuation would require a minimum of 56 sitting days, even without allowing for a Tory filibuster on the drug bill or an NDP one on the trade unions bill.

3. Rumors that Daniel Johnson [premier of Quebec] was about to call a snap election of his own. Whether these had any foundation in fact it's impossible to tell, but I understand some of the Quebec MPs believed them. In any event, the advantages of procuring a Quebec mandate for Trudeau, to use with both Johnson and De Gaulle, are too obvious to need bolstering . . .

I might as well bring this seemingly interminable document to an end. My original plan [for the book] is working out badly, but I have not abandoned it—i.e., to write the leadership campaign stuff before the election campaign begins. Trouble is, I keep getting new material about the leadership campaigns. Also, the organization problem is difficult when I don't know who is going to win the election. However, I think I shall start writing at the end of this week, at least a first draft which can be rewritten in July, and I shall organize on the assumption that Trudeau has won . . .

Your comment would be welcome.

Best,
Blair

Blair Fraser's instincts were right: the Liberals created the euphoric summer of "Trudeaumania" and Trudeau won the election. But an account of the election by Blair Fraser never appeared: on May 12, the fifty-nine-year-old journalist was drowned in a canoeing accident.

189

1968: ONTARIO

LEONARD GILBERT TO HIS FRIEND ANTHONY NETBOY
IN WASHINGTON STATE

Trudeaumania made Canada interesting to observers beyond our borders. Leonard Gilbert, a high school principal in Capreol, near Sudbury, Ontario, found himself explaining to an American friend the latest political developments in Canada, including the rising wave of aggressive Quebec nationalism. Demonstrations against the Vietnam War had convulsed the United States for some years; now the St. Jean Baptiste Day riot in Montreal suggested that Canada was not such a peaceable nation, either.

Sudbury,
29 June 1968

Dear Netboy:

I seem to be writing you too often, but I'll probably not write again for years . . . I thought you might be interested in a few comments on the recent election as seen from the centre of the country, one of the points where the two languages meet.

First, I would point out that the Sudbury area has six representatives in government at the federal and provincial levels, one senator, two M.P.'s, three M.L.A.'s. Two are Conservative, three are Liberal, one is NDP. All are French although the French are in a decided minority so this situation reflects both rising French nationalism and general good relations between the two groups. It is not to be found at all points of contact as in North-eastern Ontario or South-eastern N.B., and still less in the three western provinces—I omit Quebec itself. John and Angus [his sons] voted for the Conservatives, John helped Robert, my son-in-law, with a little Conservative electioneering in Brantford. God knows how David voted, I have not seen him since. We did not vote, but if we had we should have departed from the Tory faith and voted for Trudeau.

You may have seen some reports of the St. Jean Baptiste riot in Montreal. The Séparatistes began by declaring themselves entirely indifferent to the election, they ended by feeling increasingly desperate at the course of events, and this was their crowning act of folly. Ninety-six police hospitalized, more than two hundred rioters tossed into the cells in a rather battered condition . . . As soon as the action began the semi-traitorous Quebec premier [Daniel Johnson] left the reviewing stand and was seen no more, political tact or political cowardice depending on one's politics. American activities have a way of spilling over here in diminished intensity and Trudeau at whom the riot was aimed was being guarded as no Canadian political leader was ever guarded before, but he refused to leave the stand, watched with considerable interest and ducked the occasional missile. On election day he must have worried his protectors still more by insisting on rambling around from one voting booth to another, talking to whomever he met. The result? Out of the 25 ridings in Montreal, the dreadful metropolis, the Liberals won 24. Trudeau's personal result? A majority of rather more than 35,000 over his nearest opponent.

Apart from this self-destructive riot, and the suspicion is that the rioters received training from "outside", the election was as decorous as is usual, but with above average courtesy and good humour. Stanfield is a gentleman of the old school and one is sorry that circumstances threw him against the one Liberal leader whom he had no possibility of defeating. Both Liberals and Conservatives suppressed electioneering material which seemed in the slightest degree unchivalrous. But there was a minor underground smear campaign against Stanfield in Ontario and a much more ambitious country-wide one against Trudeau. There was apparently money behind it far beyond the hopes of Séparatistes. I would suspect that it was managed by the left-wing of the séparatistes and financed from France. And Lo! It backfired.

Trudeau is a gamble on the unknown, but perhaps the policy of drift has been carried far enough. This former student at the London School of Economics and Harvard was barred from lecturing at the Université de Montréal by the cardinal as suspect of dangerous thinking: was barred from the U.S. because he had been in Moscow at a "conference": has canoed from Hudson Bay to Montreal and down the MacKenzie to the Arctic: attempted to canoe from Florida to Cuba, etc., etc.,—this fashion-plate in his next mood brings scholarship and a breath of adventure, in short: panache, and the ability to capture the imagination.

The most serious problems he has to deal with are French-English relations and inflation. He has already indicated a firm line on the latter, something which has been sadly missing. I have always held that a French PM would be in a much stronger position than an English one in dealing with the former. So far events seem to be bearing me out. It is fiendishly difficult, especially at its core, Montreal, and cannot be solved or palliated as the Quebec premier wants, on any legal basis. What Trudeau seems to have accomplished in his election campaign is to win a great deal of support in English Canada, and, I think, in Quebec also, for an attitude of mutual good will without which legal formulae become mere grounds for strife. I think a great deal of his campaigning was a deliberate act and probably with that end in view. He has demonstrated plenty of courage and ability, he has not yet had opportunity to prove his judgement.

I have my own little bit of personal malice involved in all this. The Canadian school systems worship the subject of mathematics, which actually has no educational value at all, and have consistently belittled the importance of language study, especially the study of any second or third language. If the Séparatistes can get it through the thick heads of Anglo-Saxon Canadians that in this country a working knowledge of French is of vastly more importance even practically than perfection, even heavenly perfection, in the manipulation of cosines and tangents, then, I think, the whole country will owe them a great debt of gratitude. Is there any subject on the curriculum more calculated to shrivel a human soul than mathematics?

 . . . Enough of this. If I do not write again before your tour gets under way I hope that you find it successful and enjoyable. Your tour itinerary seems to take you through Waterford and Wexford. My grandfather as a boy set off from Kilkenny . . . My wife still toys with the hope that we shall get over some time, but health, health, neither of us can stand much knocking about.

Leonard

190

1969: ONTARIO
IRVING LAYTON TO DESMOND PACEY IN FREDERICTON

The poet Irving Layton, raised in Montreal and known for his volatile temper and provocative verse, won a Governor General's Award for A Red Carpet for the Sun *in 1959. Layton spent 1969 as writer-in-residence at the University of Guelph, while he hoped to get a teaching position at York University in Toronto. As Layton explained to his friend Desmond Pacey, head of the English department at the University of New Brunswick, he thoroughly enjoyed his period at Guelph.*

Russell Hall
University of Guelph
23 January 1969

Dear Desmond:

When I saw Eli Mandel in Toronto this Saturday, he was wearing a brilliantly white bandage on the right side of his face and he managed to look both sheepish and proud at the same time. John Saywell was present to look me over as a possible recruit to the English dept. at York University and so was his wife as an insurance against an over-hasty judgement. Women are much shrewder judges of character than men. Anyhow it seems I impressed them favourably . . . I've just been informed that I've been taken on either as Special Lecturer or professor, the title hasn't been settled yet . . .

If I told you about my schedule here you wouldn't believe it. The university and the students' council want to extract every ounce of good from their investment in this business of poet-in-residency. Also every bit of publicity. I don't blame them in the least. Luckily for them they lighted on someone who has immense reservoirs of energy, likes meeting people, above all students, and is still thrilled by the sound of his voice. There are many residences on the campus and the students in them take turns inviting me over for poetry readings. Last night I was over at Simcoe Hall where about 35 girls from South Ontario listened to me reading the erotic poems of Ovid, Cohen, Layton, Cummings. At first their royal and loyal posteriors stiffened them against the raw emotion and the raw words, they were embarrassed because they didn't know how they were expected to behave but after awhile they relaxed their guards and let their smiles and juices run naturally over their upper and lower parts. When at the end I said I'd better stop reading or they wouldn't be able to sleep at night, they all looked at one another with a knowing lasciviousness and broke into unrestrained laughter. In the meantime of course my hands had been stroking their hidden and delicious parts, squeezing them with an energy that only an imagination fired by erotic poetry and frustration can muster. If anyone spent a sleepless night I think it was I . . .

Write soon. Regards to Mary.

Irving Layton was professor of English at York from 1969 to 1978 and was nominated for a Nobel Prize in 1981.

191
1970: BRITISH COLUMBIA
GEORGE WOODCOCK TO JIM CHRISTY,
EDITOR OF *GUERRILLA* MAGAZINE, IN TORONTO

The flower power generation's motto was "Don't trust anyone over thirty." But for the author, poet, and essayist George Woodcock (1912–1995), the intellectual exuberance of student protesters was a refreshing reminder of the anarchism he had espoused in England in the 1930s. Woodcock was one of Canada's most influential and prolific writers; his intelligence and radicalism endeared him to several generations of readers. He published books on political movements (including a biography of the Russian anarchist Prince Peter Kropotkin), travel, history, and modern Canadian literature, and won a Governor General's Award for a book on George Orwell.

Vancouver
1st July 1970

Dear Jim Christy,
I know *Guerrilla* is run by a collective, but as your name is the first I came across, and as I enjoyed your articles, I am writing via you to thank the collective for sending me the first issue, and to congratulate you all on putting together the best underground paper I have yet seen in Canada. I send a cheque to cover a year's subscription and a few dollars extra for expenses. At the same time, perhaps I should be more explicit about the aspects of *Guerrilla* which I appreciate.

Fifteen years ago I made myself unpopular among the "orthodox" anarchists by telling them that in repeating Kropotkinist and Syndicalist arguments in the

1950s they were parading in a charade of dinosaurs. Last summer I raised a squall of abuse from the New Left by remarking that there was a great deal of fascist thinking among the elitists of the student "radicals".

Now I am delighted to realize that I am not so much isolated as I thought. In *Guerrilla* I find anarchists really keyed into the contemporary world, weaned of campus hangups, who recognize how far "revolution" has been taken over by the establishment, paid and neutralized by publishers, TV and the record companies, and how far leaders like [Jerry] Rubin and [Abbie] Hoffman . . . are diverting the young who think radically into the imitative conformity that delivers them ready bound. (Incidentally, you say nothing about how the coming legalization of soft drugs will be used to set up something very like the soma culture of *Brave New World*).

I like also in *Guerrilla* the abandonment of the kind of "head" jargon that makes a paper like *Georgia Straight* unreadable to anyone who knew about the *hashishim* [soft-drug users] thirty years ago, and of the constipated Marx-bound New Left manner that makes *Our Generation* so infinitely dull and complacent. In almost every article of *Guerrilla* I find independent thoughts clearly expressed. I am glad to get away from the mephitic atmosphere of drug obsession on the part of wouldbe Columbuses who do not realize there have been Leif Ericsons before them (though I believe in everybody's right to ingest what he likes, I in many cases resent the attempt to ram it into *my* nostrils), and perhaps most of all I like the atmosphere of mutual aid practicality that pervades the whole first issue. This is Kropotkin adapted to the modern world, Proudhon's ideal of dignified poverty brought up to date. I further appreciate the effort to get out of the generational pattern, which fundamentally is a pattern imposed by the divide and rule tactics of the establishment. (But—to sound the chord that links true anarchism to true aristocracy—good as the People's Revolutionary Concert Band may be, it's only a stage on the path everyone must take to understand what *Don Giovanni* really means).

I hope *Guerrilla* survives and succeeds.

> Yours for peace,
> George Woodcock

Guerrilla, *an anarchist underground newspaper published in Toronto by the poet Jim Christy and the designer Bob Macdonald, folded after a few years.*

192

1970: QUEBEC
PIERRE LAPORTE TO ROBERT BOURASSA,
PREMIER OF QUEBEC, IN QUEBEC CITY

This letter is central to the October Crisis, one of the most traumatic events in Canadian history. On Saturday, October 10, 1970, Pierre Laporte, Quebec minister of labour and immigration, walked across the street from his suburban Montreal home and was grabbed by hooded men who jumped out of a blue Chevrolet. He had been kidnapped by members of the Front de Libération du Québec (FLQ), the same separatist organization that five days earlier had kidnapped James Cross, the British trade commissioner. The kidnappings prompted the Quebec government to ask for the help of the Canadian Armed Forces, and the Trudeau government in Ottawa implemented the draconian War Measures Act. Meanwhile, held captive in a house near Saint-Hubert Airport, the minister scribbled an anguished note to Premier Bourassa.

Sunday, 3:00 p.m.

M. Robert Bourassa:

Dear Robert,

I believe I am writing the most significant letter of my life.

For the moment, I am in perfect health. I am treated well, even with courtesy.

I insist that the police stop all searches to find me. If it reaches that point, it would result in a shootout, which I would certainly not live through. This is absolutely urgent.

You have, in short, the power over my life. If there were nothing else to it but that, and my sacrifice might bring good results, one could accept it. But we are in the presence of a well-organized uprising, which will finish only with the release of the "political prisoners". After me, there would be a 3rd, then a 4th and a 20th. If all the politicians get protection, it will strike elsewhere, in other classes of society. Act immediately and thus avoid a quite useless bloodbath and panic.

You know my personal situation deserves some attention. I had two brothers; they are both dead. I remain the sole head of a large family which includes my mother, my sisters, my own wife and my children as well as Roland's children, for whom I am the guardian. My death would trigger irrevocable grief, as you know the ties which bind the members of my family. It is not I alone who is threatened, but a dozen people, all of them women and young children. I believe that you understand!

If the release of the "political prisoners" is organized and completed, I have a guarantee that my personal security will be assured. Mine . . . and that of the others who could follow.

This could be done quickly, as by taking more time I continue to die little by little in captivity.

Decide . . . on my life or my death . . . I depend on you and thank you.

Sincerely,
Pierre Laporte

P.S. I repeat, put an end to the search. And also ensure that the police are warned not to continue without your knowledge. The success of this search would be a death sentence for me.

On October 17, the body of Pierre Laporte was found in a car trunk on the outskirts of Montreal. Seven weeks later, police negotiated the release of James Cross in exchange for safe conduct to Cuba for his captors. Laporte's kidnappers were tried and convicted of kidnapping and murder.

193
1970: QUEBEC
NATHALIE TO A FRIEND

The murder of Pierre Laporte shocked Quebeckers. But many felt divided loyalties, as they heard first the polemics of the FLQ terrorists, then the platitudes of Premier Bourassa, and finally the tough-guy talk of Prime Minister Trudeau. In the opinion of this letter writer, only one voice captured the confused hopes of law-abiding Quebec nationalists.

19 October 1970

Hi,
I was surprised to get your letter. Your envelope and writing paper are really fun.

I'd love to be able to knit, but I've never been able to get it into my head. Every time I try, I can't remember it any more.

The FLQ has been pretty tough, eh? They shouldn't have killed Laporte, a Quebecker. But they see things differently. People are stunned, but I think everyone wants to at least half understand what's going on. Quite a few people have gone right round the bend, me for example. I'm not for PET [Pierre Elliot Trudeau], nor for little Bourassa, nor for the FLQ given what they've just done.

I think René Lévesque spoke best of all. His speech was masterful. It's really sad if all these events hurt the PQ because there are a lot of pig-headed types who still mix up the FLQ and the PQ or get confused over the aims of the two parties. Lévesque has every reason [to be upset]. The Quebec people are a really bizarre people anyway. The majority switches sides every week. What to make of it? It's hard.

To come back to knitting, I'd love it if you had the time to make me some wool socks. I like them and had some before and have always wanted another pair. Is there a size for these things? In any case, I take size 7 shoes and I think my ski boots are 9 ½ inches, but I think you'd better add ½ inch so that I could wiggle my [toes]. Is Lucien still wearing his sharp pajamas? I hope he's not shocked but I've never got over them.

Salut,
Nathalie

194
1970: ONTARIO
J. PIVIE TO THE EDITOR OF THE *OTTAWA CITIZEN*

The imposition of the War Measures Act on October 16, allowing the federal government to govern by decree in the face of an "apprehended insurrection," was approved almost unanimously in the House of Commons. According to opinion polls, the majority of voters, appalled by the FLQ's murder of Pierre Laporte, felt that the Trudeau government had made the right decision in implementing the War Measures Act.

Ottawa
21 October 1970

Dear Editor:
Our country is threatened by the violence of a handful of renegades. This is not a French versus English war, but an FLQ attempt to cause chaos for

all the people of Canada. I have lived in this wonderful country for 23 years among every nationality and found them to be proud Canadians.

If the police knock at my door, they are welcome to come in and search, I have nothing to hide. If they mistakenly arrest me I will gladly go to jail knowing they are doing their job and saving my country.

J. Pivie

195

1970: ONTARIO

GLENN CHERITON TO THE EDITOR OF THE *OTTAWA CITIZEN*

Not everybody agreed with Pivie. The sight of armed soldiers in Ottawa and Montreal and the suspension of civil liberties shook many people.

Ottawa
21 October, 1970

Dear Editor:

I am shocked at the tragic death of Pierre Laporte at the hands of his abductors. More than that, I am dismayed at the stupidity of the kidnapping tactics and grossly unreasonable demands.

There is another thing, however, which frightens me more than the above. That is the report that over 300 persons are being held in Quebec jails under provisions of the War Measures Act.

It is quite one thing to question people, to call out the army, to search for kidnappers and to guard the residences of our leaders, and to request the aid of the populace in finding the kidnappers, but it is another to imprison so many innocent people.

If my information is correct, which I believe it is, these people are held incommunicado, under no charge, certainly not that of kidnapping, with no bail and for an indefinite length of time. Surely they cannot all be kidnappers.

Their only "crime" appears to be affiliation with the FLQ or the Parti Quebecois at some time.

I still do not see the logic behind jailing known separatists as a response to what the prime minister calls a criminal act. No criminal act warrants such a far-reaching political response. At best it is a dangerous infringement on the basic rights of all Canadians. At worst it is legalized kidnapping of an opposition political group.

Glenn Cheriton

Over 450 Quebeckers were detained under the War Measures Act; most were released without the laying or hearing of charges. In subsequent years, many Canadians agreed that the federal government's firm response contributed to the end of terrorism in Quebec. But others suggest that its disappearance was due to public distaste for it and to the steady growth of the democratic separatist movement in the 1970s, which culminated in the election of a Parti Québécois government in 1976.

196
1971: ENGLAND
MARGARET LAURENCE TO MARGARET ATWOOD IN TORONTO

The women's movement was easy for 1960s student radicals to champion, but, as Margaret Laurence eloquently explains in this letter, harder for single mothers with small children to absorb. In 1971, the novelist was in the middle of writing a series of novels set in Manawaka, an imaginary town on the Canadian prairies. She herself had separated from her husband, had moved to England with their two children, and was struggling to make ends meet. She had met the novelist and poet Margaret Atwood, who was thirteen years younger than her, at a writers' conference.

Elm Cottage,
Bucks, England
10 Jan 71

Dear Peggy,
Very many thanks for sending me the Women's Lib. publication and the poems of bill bissett. Haven't read the poems yet, but read some of the Women's Lib this morning. I guess I really do not have an ambiguous attitude to Women's Lib this morning—basically, I am in great agreement. I can't go along with some of the attitudes, but probably quite a few women in the movement can't, either. I'm not a joiner in the sense that I shall never find a cause with which I agree over detailed beliefs 100%, but of course that isn't so important. I thought "The Politics of Housework" was great! I recognized all the arguments from way back, of course. Except that in my

case, I was too naive and uncertain (yeh, even at 34) to do much more than argue sporadically or resent silently. I suppose I do find it emotionally trying to read the Women's Lib stuff, not because I disagree with most of it, but because in many ways I wish so profoundly that such a general movement had existed let's say 15 years ago. I feel as tho' I have in fact fought every single one of these issues, but alone and therefore not effectually from the point of view of relationships. The only solution for me, therefore, was to take off and learn to accept the fact that at 44, now, and considering the men of my generation, and also considering that my own work is of enormous overwhelming importance to me, there's no way of having a partnership on the only terms I could now bear. Odd . . . I remember figuring it all out about 1962 when I was 36, and on my own for the first time in my life, but with 2 kids, whose presence saves me from despair, and when I got to England, thinking "the only relationship I could possibly now maintain would be a relationship of equals." It seems almost spooky to see the same things now being written about and yelled out loud . . . one really wants to say hurrah! Personally, from that point of view, I wish I were 15 yrs younger or else that there were a few more men of my own age or older who cottoned on to these views. They are, however, scarce as hen's teeth. Luckily, the acts of "managing" a household and its economy no longer scare me as I found I could really do all that without much trouble when I had to, and that I wasn't a financial nitwit after all, as I had always somehow believed.

You know, I think a lot of girls in Women's Lib nowadays tend to resent women like myself who have to some extent or other made their own professional lives, as this is like saying, "I'll make it for myself, never mind about the rest," but of course when I set about my own mini-revolution, I didn't know there were so many others who felt the same way. And that was less than ten years ago. Have noticed v[ery] sharply in those years, however, that after I'd had a couple of books published, my relationships with men always fell into 1 of 2 categories . . . those who saw me as a woman and would rather not know about my writing, and those who accepted me as a writer and equal (mostly writers these guys) but kind of a quasi-male figure or sort of neuter, and who would cringe slightly if I mentioned, e.g., my children.

The whole colonial situation, of course (i.e. the woman as black) I not unnaturally figured out years ago when living in Africa, helped somewhat by the French psychologist Mannoni, whose book *Prospero & Caliban: The Psychology of Colonization*, for a time was my bible.

Well. Didn't mean to go on like this, but all this is so damn relevant to what I'm praying for the grace to be able to write, but of course the character is not myself, altho' also is myself, and the dilemma is also slightly different. (Like Stacey in *The Fire-Dwellers* is both me and not me). But how to listen enough to be able to set people down and not theories? Real dilemmas (and god knows they are real) and not diatribes? That is one reason I probably won't read all the articles in the Women's Lib thing. I only want to rely on the sight of my own eyes. I remember refusing to read *The Feminine Mystique* by Betty Friedan, some years ago, because I thought the novel which was brewing might be kind of related, and I thought that reading a whole lot of stuff which might agree but was doing it from the journalistic angle, not fiction (which tries to approach by being, not talking) might screw me up. I feel kind of choked with this damn novel, but to do it only on one level—well, one might as well not bother . . .

Incidentally, one point with which I took issue, re: some of the Women's Lib articles [was] the feeling on the part of some women that it was kind of unnatural for women to want to have kids. I would say that if a woman doesn't want to have kids, that is her business and hers only. But if she deeply does, that does not mean she is not interested in anything else. I don't really feel I have to analyse my own motives in wanting children. . . . It's like (to me) asking why you want to write. Who cares? You have to, and that's that. But the kids, like the writing, belong ultimately to themselves, and not to you. In fact, they're very like the writing. A gift, given to you by life, undeserved like all grace is undeserved by its very nature, and not to be owned. . . .

Love to you and Jim [Polk], and please come out again soon.

197

1971: ONTARIO

CHIEF FREDERICK PLAIN TO THE EDITOR

OF THE *NATIVE PRESS* IN YELLOWKNIFE

Relations between non-natives and Canada's aboriginal peoples continued to deteriorate throughout the twentieth century, and in the 1960s, Indian political protests became better organized and more assertive. Careless and negative depictions of native history were particular targets of the new Indian leadership.

Sept 1971

Dear Sir,

The Union of Ontario Indians is calling a complete boycott of advertisers who sponsored the second television showing of the racist program, "The Taming of the Wild West."

The products you are asked not to buy are:
1. MAXWELL HOUSE COFFEE
2. YUBAN COFFEE
3. PROTEIN 21
4. DESITIN
5. SHELL GASOLINE
6. DU MAURIER CIGARETTES
7. ROLAIDS
8. JELLO

Native people who watched the program found it inaccurate, derogatory, discriminatory, and superficial in its treatment of our history and of our ancestors' relationship with the first white man who invaded our land.

The program, which used such derogatory terms as "savages", "redskins" and "scalpers" to refer to native people, was originally shown in March of 1970 and was rebroadcast July 18th this year by CTV despite widespread complaints from native people and attempts by the Union, working in conjunction with the National Indian Brotherhood, Indian-Eskimo Association and the Canadian Indian Centre of Toronto to have the Canadian Radio and Television Commission investigate the program. These attempts eventually led to court action which was still pending when the program was shown.

The Union also suggests that your Band or organization vigorously publicize this boycott and suggest to your members that they also boycott these products.

Native people across Canada spend a lot of money on these products; we will show the advertisers that there is no profit in sponsoring racist programs. I can think of no responsible reason for the CTV to show the program a second time. Their high handed, insulting attitude is inexcusable.

Yours for Indian Unity,
Frederick Plain
President—Union of Ontario Indians

198

1974: BRITISH COLUMBIA

JANE HENSON TO FRONTIER COLLEGE IN TORONTO

It was no easier being a pioneer in the twentieth century than it had been in the nine-teenth, as many barrier-breaking women discovered. Jane Henson went to work in Tasu, an isolated mining town in northern British Columbia, in late 1974, as a Frontier College volunteer. Frontier College (originally called the Canadian Reading Camp Association) was founded in 1899 to bring the benefits of literacy to men work-ing in the forests, mines, and railway gangs of the Canadian bush. Its volunteers worked alongside the labourers during the day, then taught them to read and argue in the bunkhouses at night. The first letter that Jane wrote back to Frontier College's Toronto headquarters was enthusiastic. "One of the bull-cooks told me this morning that he felt it was a good thing they had a woman in the bunkhouse—it seemed to increase morale among the men, spruce them up a bit, etc." Four months later, how-ever, she had a different story about being the only woman around.

Vancouver, B.C.
April 14, 1975

To all at Frontier—

This letter has been a long time in the writing and for its delay I must apologise. However, it has been thought about for a long time, and writ-ten over and over again in my head. After 4 months in Tasu, and now 2 weeks in Vancouver, I feel as if I can put down some measure of perspective . . .

Be that as it may, I feel extremely disillusioned because of the garbage, purely and simply, that I've had to cope with every single day of my exis-tence in Tasu. Coping emotionally with these problems seems to have taken up so much time and energy that I really feel that my effectiveness as a Frontier College teacher has been severely diminished. One has only so much emotional reserve, as every F. C. person knows, and drawing on it soon reveals one's limitations. I feel very saddened to think that I have not been able to take advantage of all these opportunities available to me as a result of the uniqueness of the situation—I can't really believe that just being here and coping is making an adequate contribution.

So far, I am still the only single female in the bunkhouse, though there are now 2 of us in the mine site workforce, the other being the wife of one of the engineers. Since the departure of my good friend, the nurse, this means that I am the only woman eating in the cookhouse as well. My greatest disappointment of all is to realize that after 4 months and all my efforts to blend in (ha!) I am still regarded as a conversation piece, to say nothing of a freak, and am still constantly watched. It is this watching, the constant unwanted and unavoidable attention that is the hardest of all to cope with. It has taken me this long to realize, much less accept the fact, that my private life can not be my own, that comings and goings at work are open to question by absolutely everyone, and that I am in a position of great emotional vulnerability. Perhaps the last needs a bit of explaining.

It seems to me that I am emotionally vulnerable because my personal relationship with the men is constantly changing, and it is I who has to make the adaptation. Come to think of it, it is this adaptation to constantly shifting ground that causes the greatest emotional drain. As an example, one hour, say Saturday night at a dinner, I can be buddy-buddy with the guys as we eat; two hours later at the singalong or in the bar, I have to relate to them in a totally different way; and Sunday morning I have to play the role of Mother Confessor and grant dispensations to the hung-overs and still-drunks who beg my forgiveness for stepping on my toes at the boogie last night. And so it goes . . .

How do you respond when you are humiliated beyond measure before a roomful of men by a mealy-mouthed, two-bit gangster of a union business representative? What do you say when, after 3 ½ months, you are insulted in the bar by a lonely old drunk lashing out at the world in bitterness and using you as his vehicle? How do you cope with the innuendo, the stares, the sexual come-on of lonely men who can't have you, know it, and retaliate the only way they know how? . . .

You become selfish and self-centred because you retreat into yourself as a result of being a mere player on a stage directed by someone else, in a world not of your own making. You put up barriers and tell yourself it's for your own protection. You lose a measure of sensitivity and sometimes your reactions reach a point of brittleness, without that oil of spontaneity that is the delight of human relationships. You are cut to the quick by a remark tossed off for the benefit of an audience you despise, and wonder why you die a little bit when the only course left is to cry, and you use it.

. . . I hope this letter has voiced adequately a number of the concerns that surround me in Tasu. More important, I hope that other people, and especially women, will gain something from my having expressed some of these things . . .

I will look forward to hearing from you upon my return April 30th to Tasu.

All the best,
Jane

Despite this outburst, Jane never questioned the benefits of Frontier College's work. After finishing her contract in Tasu, she became western regional coordinator for Frontier College.

199
1976: ONTARIO
ROBERTSON DAVIES TO HIS PUBLISHER
JACK MCCLELLAND IN TORONTO

The author Robertson Davies, who in 1963 became Master of Massey College, was frequently asked to provide endorsements for about-to-be-published books. He had no difficulty praising Marian Engel's novel Bear, *which describes an erotic relationship between a woman archivist staying in a backwoods cabin and a bear. However, he could not resist a few digs at the critics who had reviewed his own books.*

Massey College
University of Toronto
January 6, 1976

Dear Jack:
Thanks for your letter of December 24; it did not reach me until December 31, and I did not have time to read the ms. until last night. You ask for a comment you can use. Very well: here goes—

The theme of *Bear* is one of the most significant and pressing in Canada in our time—the necessity for us who are newcomers to the country, with hardly four hundred years of acquaintance with it, to ally ourselves with the spirit of one of the most ancient lands in the world. In our search for this spirit, we are indeed in search of ourselves.

There—that being done, let me say a few other things, not for quotation. I thought the book admirably written, spare and taut, with a good command of tone throughout; the changes from reality to fantasy are very well managed, and the pathos of the lonely woman is conveyed without too much agonizing and feminine self-pity. It reminded me of Margaret Atwood's *Surfacing* [published four years earlier], because it explores the same ground—the search for healing in the wilderness—but I thought it a much better book as a work of art. I am not surprised Margaret Laurence and Adele Wiseman urged you to publish it: it is, in the best sense, a woman's book, and they know what they are talking about. But—this must be put delicately—neither Margaret nor Adele, who are both dears, labour under the burden of a strong sense of humour, and when the book is published you had better prepare yourself for some explosions, not of outrage but of ribaldry.

Writing from my own recent experience [of reviews], I think you may run into a few things like this: [Roy] MacSkimming [of the *Toronto Star*] will like the book and understand it; [William] French [of the *Globe and Mail*] will not like the book and won't understand it, and will be vulgarly jocose about it; Brian Vintcent [of *Books in Canada*] will complain that it is elitist (not every woman has a bear, so why should any woman have one?) and will hint that bears are well-known to be homosexuals (like all sensitive people) and should not be bothered by importunate archivists. All critics, everywhere in Canada, will tell the whole plot in the course of what they think of as reviews, thereby spilling the beans. Gordon Sinclair [television commentator] will declare that he has never slept with a bear, but served under a sergeant who was a bear in World War One. Pierre Berton [moderator of Global TV debates] will have an evening of The Great Debate on the theme Why Not Bears? Peter Newman [editor of *Maclean's* magazine and author of *The Canadian Establishment*] will discover and publish the bear's Income Tax file. The Ontario Public Archives will be queried in the Legislature about what goes on there during lunchtime, anyway? The CBC will offer an hour-long (50 minutes, and 10 minutes of commercials) drama about Goldilocks, a social worker, who attempts to mend the marriage of Father Bear and Mother Bear, which has come to grief because Father Bear thinks Baby Bear looks altogether too much like Farley Mowat, and wants to know what has been going on in the den when he was out looking for acorns and honey. Peter Gzowski and 99 other TV and radio interviewers will lure Miss Engel to their studios and after a lot of humming and hawing, ask, "Now Marian, I hope you'll take this question as it's intended, but did you ever—

really—let me phrase this carefully—you know what I mean—with a bear?" Judy LaMarsh [politician and broadcaster] will ask a similar question, but not having read the book, will think it was a porcupine. The SPCA and the ecology people will protest against the sexual solicitation of bears, and the Gay Lib people will counter by asking what is wrong with a consenting bear, especially if it is a sailor-bear or a truck-driver-bear? . . .

All of this you and Miss Engel will have to endure philosophically. Where you will be driven to the uttermost pitch of endurance will be when the Society for the Advancement of Native Peoples—months after publication (slow readers because of the poor education imposed on them by unsympathetic governments) will demand that in the paperback the line "Shit with the bear" be changed to "Excrete with the bear, having first provided the bear with an ample supply of Face-Elle, preferably pink." You are all set for a lively Spring.

More seriously, I thought the book a fine treatment of a tricky theme— tricky because intercourse with a large animal is one of the commonest of feminine fantasies, and in a country like Canada one that is rarely given public voice. But it is recurrent in all mythologies, and its roots lie very deep. Men do not fantasize about large female animals, and books like *Wild Animals I Have Known* [by Ernest Thompson Seton] are quite free of such material—incidentally, Miss Engel must be prepared to meet ladies at cocktail parties whose names figure in Peter Newman's book who will think the popular work named above is the one she has written; rich women don't seem to read, and when they do, they don't read straight.

I wish you luck, and my congratulations to Miss Engel, whom I do not know, but whose work I have long admired.

> Yours sincerely,
> Rob.

PS: Of course this letter is for your eye alone.

Marian Engel's Bear *won the Governor General's Award for Fiction.*

200

1976: ONTARIO
JAMES HUTCHINSON TO THE
EDITOR OF THE *GLOBE AND MAIL* IN TORONTO

I hope James Hutchinson's tongue was firmly in his cheek when he wrote this. At the federal Progressive Conservatives' 1976 leadership convention, thirty-seven-year-old Joe Clark's victory was not the only surprise for long-time Tories. His wife's insistence that she be called Maureen McTeer, rather than Mrs. Joe Clark, was regarded as a definite drag on her husband's electoral hopes.

If Joe Clark seemed to some voters too young to be prime minister, Maureen McTeer seemed to others too feminist to play the role of leader's spouse.

Woodstock,
Ontario
February 27, 1976

Dear Sir,

We have more or less got used to Margaret Trudeau's idiosyncrasies and now we have Joe Clark's wife, whatever her name is. When we had W.L.M. King and R.B. Bennett things were so peaceful. I think now it was because they didn't have wives. At the risk of being called a male chauvinist might I suggest that if we ever succeed in repatriating the constitution, we amend it to require vows of celibacy from prospective Prime Ministers.

James F. Hutchinson

Despite Ms. McTeer's idiosyncrasy about her name, Joe Clark became prime minister of Canada in June 1979.

201

1977: ONTARIO
MARGARET LAURENCE TO GABRIELLE ROY IN QUEBEC CITY

I couldn't resist another letter by one of Canada's finest and most thoughtful writers,
Margaret Laurence (see Letter 196). The election of René Lévesque's Parti Québécois
government in 1976 shook many English Canadians, who had hoped that, in the wake
of the October Crisis, the independence movement would decline. However, there was
widespread sympathy within literary and left-wing circles for Quebeckers. Laurence
shared her own dismay with her friend Gabrielle Roy, a Franco-Manitoban then living
in Quebec who was one of the most important and most widely translated writers of
post-war Canada.

Lakefield,
17 Feb 77

Dear Gabrielle,

. . . When you last wrote, it was the eve of the Quebec elections. I don't
even presume to make any comments—I have not the right. I do feel, however, that Lévesque is a man of integrity. I wish with all my heart that in
Anglophone Canada (and yes, in the prairies which you and I both love so
much) that more people could have realized, really realized, long ago, the
way in which people in Quebec feel about their history, their language, their
heritage, their identity. I only pray (and I use that word advisedly) that it
may not be too late. I have never been in the slightest doubt about how
Francophone Canadians feel about their language. It is the same way I feel
about mine, even though for me, as for millions of Canadians not of English
background, it was not the language of my ancestors. But I never knew
Gaelic (or as the Scots say, "had the Gaelic"); English is my birth tongue,
and I love it. And yet I am always aware of the irony—here I am, writing to
you in my language, not in yours. I am as much to blame as any other
"Anglo". The ideal would be for me to write to you in English, and for you
to reply in French. And you could do it, that way, with full and complete
understanding, but I could not. And yet I feel it may be too late for me (and
for all those middle-aged civil servants taking crash courses in French), but
surely we could begin with the children? A family irony of mine—my
daughter, educated in England, is pretty fluent in French. But surely primary school is the place to begin, and not from duty, but from a desire to
know one another. Also, I believe that translations of books, from English

into French, and from French into English, is one area which can help. I know that some of the younger Quebec writers aren't anxious to have their books translated, but one can hope they may change their minds, ultimately. I believe that, national considerations not withstanding, writers should be as widely read as possible. When I think that without translations, to speak realistically, I would have been deprived of your work, and of the work of many others, it doesn't bear thinking about. And there are so many translations yet to be done, both ways . . .

There are times when I find I cannot think too long at once about all the problems which beset us. One turns, as you did in *Enchanted Summer*, to things which are simple (and enormously complex as well) and beautiful and perhaps joyful. Also, to the humorous stories—and my life seems to abound in these, thank God. It abounds in lots of other things as well, but I really do believe that laughter is a kind of gift of grace—I mean laughter that is warm, of course, not malicious (but that isn't true laughter, is it?) . . .

Love, and God bless . . .

202
1978: ONTARIO
S.H. GRANT TO THE EDITOR OF
THE *GLOBE AND MAIL* IN TORONTO

Plus ça change . . . Existential angst proved to be a continuing theme of post-war life, as Canada grew increasingly close to the United States in both its economy and culture. A "Buy Canadian" campaign by the federal government drew attention to the dependence of most consumers on imports.

London, Ontario
April 1, 1978

Dear Sir,
During my travels last summer, I saw a definition of a Canadian, applicable to the condition in which we find ourselves today. It went something like this:

"A Canadian is a man who leaves a French movie, climbs into his German car, drives to an Italian restaurant, orders Dutch beer and Danish cheese. Then, when he arrives home, doffs his Korean shirt, Romanian trousers, and

BROOKS'S
ST. JAMES'S STREET,
LONDON, SWIA ILN.

TEL. 01-499 0072

Friday, November 17, 1978

Dear Graham:

Let me, a few weeks late, welcome you to the Universe and to thank your Mother and Father for generously giving you the name I also share. It has been a good name to me and brought me a richly varied experience. I pray you will find it confers on you a still more full life. Of course it is not the name that does this, it is you yourself.

Graham Spry, one of the fathers of Canadian public broadcasting, was seventy-eight when he sent this note to his newborn godson, Graham Mann.

I wrote this in an old Club
in London during a holiday.
Many of the early makers of Canada
or its institutions have been members
and their portraits or biographies
adorn its walls. I hope some day
you will be as fortunate as I have
been in seeing other parts of the world,
and particularly Europe.

Please give my love to your
mother and Father and my gratitude
both for you and for your name.

Affectionately

Graham Spry

Graham Mann
Pakenham,
Ottawa Valley
Canada

Polish shoes, dons his Taiwanese dressing gown, turns on his Japanese stereo, picks up an American ballpoint pen and writes a letter to his Member of Parliament, complaining about the unemployment situation."

Not a particularly scholarly bit of prose, but the message comes through loud and clear.

S.H. Grant

203
1979: DOMINICAN REPUBLIC
CRAIG RUSSELL TO GINO EMPRY IN TORONTO

Craig Russell, from small-town Ontario, became the ambassador of Canada's gay culture when he starred as a drag queen in the 1977 independent movie Outrageous. *He had honed his transvestite skills while working as personal assistant to the aging Mae West But stardom had its costs: Russell was soon in a spiral of drugs and alcoholism. During a much-needed holiday in the Caribbean, he sent a* cri de coeur *to his publicist, personal manager, and good friend Gino Empry, the Toronto impresario.*

> Hotel Embajador Intercontinental,
> Dominican Republic.
> Nov. 14/79

Dearest Gino,
The weather is here and I wish you were too. Why don't you ever take two days off and GET REAL. Now that we're friends, you better take some of my messages—LIKE TAKE IT EASY, Honey, you last longer.

Love, Craig Russell

Russell himself never learned to take it easy. Aged forty-two, he died of AIDS-related complications in 1990.

204
1982: SOVIET UNION
LANDON PEARSON TO HER FAMILY IN CANADA

Don't you wonder about the surreptitious scrambles to prepare for the funerals of heads of state? Two years after Landon Pearson arrived in Moscow with her husband, Geoffrey, the newly appointed Canadian ambassador to the Soviet Union, President Leonid Brezhnev died. Heads of state and government from all over the world converged on the Russian capital, including Pierre Trudeau, who had been prime minister of Canada for thirteen years, and his ten-year-old son, Justin. The ambassador's wife managed to record a historic moment in Russian history, while coping with a large delegation of VIPs.

Canadian Embassy,
Moscow
November 23, 1982

Dear one and all,

After the aeroplane carrying Mr. Trudeau and his companions roared off last Tuesday into a whirl of snow, I thought I would be able to return to the Embassy and write to you immediately, for last week's bag, all about the momentous events that had just taken place. But I couldn't. As soon as I sat at my typewriter I realized that I would need some time to get a "fix" of my own on what had happened. After all, you will already have read almost all you ever wanted to know about Brezhnev's death and you will have been exposed to endless speculation about the changes at the top, to biographies of Andropov [the new Soviet president], to reflections about what's in store for the Soviet Union now, to queries about new directions in U.S. - U.S.S.R. relations. So I'll give you no more of that; just some very personal impressions of everything that I was able to witness.

For me, the sequence of events began on the 7th of November. The weather was cold and windy and I, at least, was quite happy to watch the parade yet again on television. However, by the time we arrived at the Kremlin Palace of Congresses for the official reception the clouds had cleared away and the golden domes were brilliant against the deep blue sky and the snow sparkled in a light layer on the grass. The old men looked ruddy from standing so long in the cold. Mr. Brezhnev read his brief speech firmly although I thought (I was standing with some of the other diplomatic wives directly facing the men) that Mr. Tikhonov was looking at him rather anxiously. Brezhnev and the other politburo members shook our hands with surprising vigour and attention, considering how many of us went through the line, and then they fell to the buffet with gusto. So I really was surprised on Wednesday night when the American Ambassador was called away twice to the phone in the middle of the delicious dinner we were eating at the Greek Embassy and came back with a worried look. And later, when we were dancing, we wondered whether we should. But there had been rumours before. It was only next morning when I drove back from gymnastics and a trip to the gastronome [the diplomats' grocery store] and saw that our flag was at half-mast that I realized it was true. So, being of a practical nature, I immediately rushed back to the gastronome to stock up. For the rest of that day life in the streets proceeded much as usual but on Friday the official mourning began; all the red flags sprouted black organdie ribbons, the centre of the city, within the garden boulevards, was sealed off, there were soldiers everywhere, and the weather turned grey and dreary and wet. We got the news that Mr. Trudeau would be coming on from Germany with quite a large group including a number of journalists.

The Embassy rallied in force during the next couple of days preparing both for the known and for the unpredictable. The Canadians were terrific, but so were the locals, particularly, from my point of view, Nikolai and Tamara and Zhenia. At 3 on Sunday we set off for Sheremetyevo [airport] where we shared the VIP waiting room with several other embassy groups each waiting for *their* delegation. Such a flurry of diplomatic activity, you can well imagine!

"Kanada", called out a plump, blue-uniformed Aeroflot lady, and she led us all on to a bus that drove us standing and swaying out onto the tarmac to the Canadian Armed Forces plane that had just taxied to a stop. The bright oblong of the door, the red-carpeted stairs, the official greeting by the Deputy Prime Minister, handshakes all around, photographs, and into the waiting Zil [limousine]. Then a rapid ride into the city along deserted streets, Mr. Trudeau leaning over occasionally to explain something to Justin in the jump seat, who was staring intently out of the window. After settling into the Rossiya Hotel and putting on suitable clothes (I reversed my padded coat from white to black) we went to the Dom Soyuzov, the House of Trade Unions, to pay our last respects to Mr. Brezhnev lying in state in the Hall of Columns, his body a little dwarfed by the banked wreaths and the display of his medals, each one on a separate piece of red satin 6-inches square. The Dom Soyuzov is a fine 18th-century building near the Bolshoi Theatre on Prospect Marxa. It used to serve the noble classes for social assemblies. With its handsome proportions and its great chandeliers swathed in black net it looked properly solemn and impressive for such an occasion. The orchestra was playing the sixth symphony of Tchaikowsky as we stood there silently and I was moved by the sight of the folded white hand that had shaken mine so briskly just seven days before. Justin was very quiet. I'm sure he was relieved to be able to run as we returned on foot to the hotel across the vast, unpeopled expanse of Red Square, so haunting and mysterious in the dim yellow light.

We had an excellent dinner on the 21st floor of the Rossiya . . . with its view down on St. Basil's and over the Kremlin walls . . . The conversation was about the major issues raised by Brezhnev's death and the change in leadership as well as about the gamut of bilateral concerns, but all the while Mr. Trudeau kept a weather eye out for Justin at a nearby table and occasionally got up to find out how he was getting along. When we had finished eating and talking he got up from the table and carried Justin piggyback out of the restaurant. The waiters were delighted! Pavel [the Embassy driver] still recalls with unfeigned admiration how Mr. Trudeau climbed onto one of the motorcycles belonging to his police escort when he was in Moscow ten years ago and roared off around Red Square!

Next morning Geoff went off to join Mr. Trudeau and the three or four others who were able to attend the funeral, and I settled myself in front of the television set along with Chris. Victoria and Elena joined us to translate the commentary and the speeches. Soon after it started George Hazen [the commercial counsellor in the Embassy] sent up Lorna (aged 11) to watch it with us and François [Mathys, the minister counsellor in the Embassy] brought Justin, who had decided that he would rather watch it in the Residence than at the hotel. They were both very patient. Justin buried himself in *Star Trek* during the funeral speeches and Lorna vanished into the bathroom as soon as the coffin was opened in front of Lenin's tomb and did not reappear until it had been closed after the final kisses of his family and safely lowered into the ground out of sight, and all the factory whistles had begun their three-minute salute. But otherwise they were quiet and attentive. There was very little commentary during the transmission so one's whole attention was focussed visually. One of the cameramen obviously had an eye for composition and I was much struck by the formal beauty of the aligned and balanced forms and colours; the red of the Kremlin wall, the red and black of the Lenin Mausoleum, the grey of pavement, of military squares marching in awesome synchrony, and the clear yellow of the 18th-century palaces beyond the Kremlin wall. But the most vivid image I retain of the funeral is the sight of the massed wreaths, two or three hundred of them, appearing up the slope alongside the blood-red brick wall of the towered and turreted historical museum, evoking, somehow, strange echoes of Burnham Wood . . .

After the funeral Geoff and the Prime Minister and the Senator went to St. George's Hall to meet Andropov, Tikhonov, Kuznetsov, and Gromyko and then back to the hotel for a late lunch. I joined them about 4 for a little sightseeing. We went up to the Lenin Hills in the rapidly fading daylight and the Soviet security officer assigned to Mr. Trudeau (a Lieut. Colonel at the very least) practically had a fit when Justin slipped over the red marble balustrade and somersaulted backwards down the slope! Then we went to Novodevichy and were able to make a quick visit to the rich golden interior of the Cathedral of the Virgin of Smolensk (1513), which was opened and illumined for us. Then we drove through the Kremlin gates to deposit Mr. Trudeau and Geoff at Mr. Tikhonov's office. Justin and I went back to the Embassy but at least he had had a chance to glimpse the churches of the Kremlin lit against the night sky. He disappeared immediately to the Domik [the minister counsellor's residence] where he joined Antoine (who is exactly his age) and Benoit at the Mathys' newly acquired pool table. I did not see him again for quite a long time!

At 6:30 the Embassy families began to drift upstairs with their children and the group arrived from the hotel, and Geoff arrived with Mr. Trudeau not long after. I think everyone managed to meet him, at least I did my best. He talked easily and pleasantly with everyone, particularly the older children, and had himself photographed with all kinds of combinations of young and old. He and his companions stayed on for dinner with the Embassy officers and their wives (except for the younger military, who were entertaining the plane crew down in the Club). This is when I was especially pleased with Nikolai and Tamara et al because a cocktail party for 100 plus kids followed by dinner for 40 is really quite an undertaking and they did it very well. If we had had more time to plan it might have been less spontaneous and therefore less successful. As soon as he had finished dessert, Mr. Trudeau slipped off to the Domik with Elaine [Mathys] and had a couple of games of pool with Justin and the other boys and then brought him back to say goodnight. Some of his group stayed on after he left so we were able to have a good talk about events in Canada as well as in the Soviet Union.

By next morning at 9 a real blizzard was blowing and the ride out to the airport was decidedly unnerving. Geoffrey and Mr. Trudeau were talking and didn't pay much attention but Justin was wide-eyed and I was hanging on tightly to the back of his seat! I'm sure I will never ride in a Zil again so the drive would have been memorable even if we hadn't driven so fast. However, it was rather a relief, after we heard the aeroplane take off (we couldn't see it through the snow), to ride back sedately to the city with Ilya. The snow stopped as we came down Gorky Street and by noon it had all melted. The weather has been unusually mild ever since but somehow all those extraordinary effects of light and weather that marked the days of the funeral and the hours of Mr. Trudeau's visit were totally appropriate. Events have taken place whose effect on both our public and our private lives will be profound even though it is still very difficult to guess what those effects will turn out to be . . .

> Love to everyone
> Landon

Within the next two years, there were state funerals for both President Yuri Andropov and his successor, President Konstantin Chernenko. With the arrival of President Mikhail Gorbachev in the Kremlin, the sclerotic Soviet empire began the process of collapse that led to the end of the Cold War. In 1983, the Pearsons left Moscow and Landon returned to her work in Canada on issues involving children. In 1994, she was appointed to the Canadian Senate.

205
1983: ONTARIO
LEONARD LEE TO HIS CUSTOMERS

History comes full circle, even in a land with as short a written history as ours. By the 1980s, sophisticated urbanites were on the lookout for the kind of antique doorknobs and window hinges with which, a century or more earlier, Canadian pioneers such as Catharine Parr Traill in Upper Canada (see Letter 25) and Willie Wallace in Manitoba (see Letter 80) had furnished log cabins and prairie homesteads. The Ottawa entrepreneur Leonard Lee, who had founded a mail-order business in 1977 selling well-made tools for home carpenters, was happy to feed the appetite. When he published the first edition of his antique hardware catalogue, he included this letter to his customers.

Lee Valley Tools Ltd.
2680 Queensview Drive
Ottawa
Ontario
March 1983

Dear Customers:

We have been in the process of collecting the hardware in this catalogue for more than two years. It has involved countless telephone calls and frequent trips to dusty warehouses in various parts of the continent. The results are shown in these pages.

In putting together what must be the largest collection of unused antique hardware in North America, there were many pitfalls. Buying old hardware is quite different from buying new hardware. There are no warm, well-lit showrooms in which to view the product. There are also no catalogues with photographs, list prices, and standard discounts. The business tends to be done in cold, dark warehouses in a hurry and with mutual suspicion. The seller is concerned that he may be quoting a price that is too low and the buyer is wondering if the unopened boxes contain products with the same finish as the sample he is looking at. The seller is trying to be enthusiastic about a product that has been a dog ever since his grandfather first bought it, and the buyer is trying to be diffident about something he knows is 100 years old and has been unavailable for decades. It is all high drama with bad acting.

In this process, there are certain truths about antique hardware to be kept in mind:

1. If you find a well designed item in several finishes, the largest number of them will be in the least desirable finish.

2. If items are "handed" (e.g. right or left) the majority will be in the least popular hand.

3. When you look for companion pieces (e.g. icebox latches and hinges) you will find both but always with incompatible finishes.

4. The most desirable pieces always occur in the smallest number.

5. Regardless of what you find, the customer wants it an inch longer in a different finish.

Within these limitations, there are few things that match the excitement of discovering a cache of old hardware (if you exclude finding a cache of old tools). To open a crumbling box and find ornate Victorian pieces in their original packing is a bit like an archaeological find. Even coming upon a simple item such as screen door springs can cause nostalgic reverie. The let-down comes when it is time to sell this hard-won item. It is not so much a question of price as whether or not the buyer will appreciate the item. So if you put our opalescent knobs on plastic drawer fronts or if you paint over one of our cast bronze pulls, please don't tell us. We'd rather think that they all went to good homes.

Yours sincerely,
Leonard G. Lee
President

206
1984: ONTARIO
PROFESSOR ELIZABETH ALLIN TO DR. ANN MCMILLAN,
CHAIR OF THE CANADIAN ASSOCIATION OF PHYSICISTS'
NEWLY FORMED COMMITTEE TO ENCOURAGE WOMEN
IN PHYSICS, IN TORONTO

Born in 1905, the daughter of a rural storekeeper, Elizabeth Allin attended a high school which boasted no electricity and less scientific equipment than any other secondary school in Ontario. When she was seventeen, she enrolled at the University of Toronto to study math and physics; by 1931 she had a doctorate and was teaching within the physics department. During these years the physics department required women to enter the labs by a separate door, and women were not admitted to Hart House, the student centre. During the 1930s, Allin's male classmates received rapid promotions. After the Second World War, she was finally promoted to the rank of professor, and she played a crucial role in the establishment of the Canadian Association of Physicists. In 1984, she reflected on the satisfactions of a career in physics—and the obstacles faced by anyone who wanted to study physics, especially women.

Department of Physics,
University of Toronto,
Toronto, Canada
January 26, 1984

Dear Madam:
I am replying to the letter I received recently from CAP over your signature and regret that circumstances have prevented me from replying sooner. I

agree that women should be encouraged to choose physics as a career. I have found it stimulating and satisfying and know other women who also have found it so . . .

In the period during which I was active, there was little opportunity for employment in physics for women graduates from the honours course in mathematics and physics. Most looked forward to teaching mathematics in High Schools or Collegiates in Ontario. Many were most successful and attained very well-paying positions. To teach physics in most Collegiates it was necessary to qualify as a science specialist and this involved further study in Chemistry. To become a research physicist required qualifying for the PhD and this meant four or five years of further work with very little pay. Only those really dedicated could be expected to make the sacrifice of time and money this demanded. Nevertheless, in Toronto of the 23 PhDs in physics awarded before Dr. McLennan's retirement, 4 [were] women. You mention that more women are entering engineering courses than courses in honours physics in the Faculties of Arts and Science. Physicists have always been at a disadvantage in industry, compared to graduates from Engineering Physics although their training in physics was at least as good. A graduate in Engineering Physics is automatically qualified as a "Professional Engineer" and the graduate in Honours Physics was not. This put the Engineering . . . graduate at a definite advantage over the Physicist, since Professional status plays an important role in industrial laboratories . . .

Over the years attempts . . . to win recognition for physicists based on their technical and scientific qualifications have continued and are still continuing. Since a woman has in addition to the above a further prejudice to overcome if she is to be accepted in industry, her preference for Engineering Physics as an under graduate training course is easily understood. Recognition of the Physicist as a Professional with privileges compatible with those of the [Professional Engineer] would, I believe, result in more women choosing physics as a career.

I have so far not mentioned the effect of social pressures in discouraging women from becoming physicists. For years, young girls were encouraged to say they couldn't do elementary and secondary school mathematics. Women were encouraged on entering University to enroll in language courses and household science. Pure science and medicine were barely permissible. To enter [math and physics] was to be regarded as scarcely human by many. I have yet to discover any evidence that women have less innate ability in mathematics and physics than men and I have seen a number of cases in which the women in the group have graduated in Honours Physics with higher standing than the men . . .

Admitting that I am not infallible I suggest that the two most important factors in limiting the number of women physicists are social pressures (probably less important now than earlier) and the difficulty of finding satisfactory employment as a physicist in a situation which promises opportunity for promotion.

Sincerely,
E.J. Allin
Emeritus Professor of Physics

207
1984: ONTARIO
AN ADOPTIVE MOTHER TO THE BIRTH MOTHER

After anxious years of waiting, a young couple in southern Ontario were handed a precious bundle: their adopted baby. Since the birth five months earlier, the birth mother had agonized over whether to relinquish the child. At the birth mother's request, the adoptive mother sent her a description of the home in which her daughter would be raised.

May 15, 1984

Dear Birth Mother,

I've been looking at this blank page for almost thirty minutes, wondering just how to express our joy and happiness. No words seem adequate to fully explain how my husband and I feel. How do you thank someone for giving you their baby?

We've been waiting for this little baby girl for a long, long time. Many years had gone by. We could hardly believe it when we got the telephone call to say our daughter (yours and ours) was born. It seemed surreal when she was put into my arms, for the first time, and we were allowed to bring her home.

We had a busy first few days. Everyone was eager to see her. She has two sets of grandparents, many aunts and uncles and cousins that will comprise her extended family. Everyone constantly kisses and cuddles her. Her new big brother is busy bringing his friends in to meet her and he and I took her into his Junior Kindergarten class, so he could present her during show and tell time.

When she is in her walker, she delights in being pushed by him around the kitchen. She giggles and coos and when he stops, she wriggles her legs and tries to jump to show she wants to be pushed more. She is being given such lovely gifts from all our friends and family: dresses with lace and frills and matching fancy pants, flowered tops and soft, pastel coloured rompers and many toys.

She is a good and happy wee soul. She is everything we prayed, hoped and wished for—and so much more! She is adjusting to her new routine and surroundings without any trouble. Her room is painted a soft mint green with white lace curtains on the window. It gets the morning sun. There are nursery rhyme posters on the wall. A musical mobile hangs above the crib and it plays "Around the World". There are stuffed toy animals and cloth dolls on a long shelf above the change table. Her room smells of baby powder, baby shampoo and lavender.

I can only imagine the strength and tremendous courage it took for you to relinquish her. I hope the pain of that isn't resurfacing as you read this letter and look at the enclosed picture. I promise you she will not want for anything. Please remember, always, that she is loved by us so very, very much. She always will be.

You have made our family complete and she will grow to know and understand what you've done for us and how very happy you've made us. Though it seems hardly enough, thank you. Thank you so much.

Sincerely,
Stan and Nancy

A series of learning and behavioural problems emerged in their adopted daughter, consistent with undiagnosed fetal alcohol spectrum disorder. Now nineteen, she has estranged herself from her parents and brother, but they hope she will find her way back to them.

208

1987: ONTARIO

EUGENE FORSEY TO THE EDITOR OF

THE *GLOBE AND MAIL* IN TORONTO

A milestone in Canada's legal history was the 1981 repatriation of the Canadian con-stitution. However, repatriation was not achieved painlessly: the province of Quebec refused to sign the newly Canadianized constitution. Three years later, Conservative leader Brian Mulroney became prime minister; one of his election promises was to ini-tiate a process of constitutional reform to satisfy some of Quebec's demands. Various provinces, particularly Alberta, promptly demanded that the reforms must include changes to the Canadian Senate that would make it a more representative institution. Eugene Forsey (see Letter 178), who served in the Senate from 1970 to 1979, was quick to reveal the impossibility of the proposed reform.

The Senate

Ottawa

April 1987

Dear Editor:

The proposal for a "triple-E" Senate (equal, elected, effective) includes pro-vision for six senators from every province. That alone is enough to prove that it is just flailing the air, whistling in the wind, blowing soap bubbles.

Nova Scotia and New Brunswick would drop from 10 seats to six. Quebec and Ontario would drop from 24 seats to six.

Anyone who believes that Nova Scotia and New Brunswick would con-sent to drop from 10 to six or Quebec and Ontario from 24 to six, is capable of believing that the moon is made of molasses.

But under the Constitution Act, 1982, any change in the number of sen-ators from any province must have the consent of the legislatures of at least seven provinces with at least half the population of the 10.

If four provinces balk, the proposal is dead.

Before 1982, it was possible to argue about how many provinces had to consent, or which ones. All? A majority? A "substantial number" or "sub-stantial majority"? Quebec? But now it is all set down in black and white in the supreme law of the land. For some amendments (for example, abolishing the Senate), you must have the consent of all 10 provinces; for most of the other amendments, the consent of seven representing half the total population of the 10. You don't even need a pocket calculator.

All you need is a copy of the latest census and the ability to count up to 10, or even to seven.

And if you can't get the consent of the 10, or the seven, within three years, your proposed amendment is dead. One province (for some amendments), four provinces (for most of the others) just dragging their feet, is enough to kill it.

It is astonishing how many people simply cannot get it into their heads that we now have a very rigid Constitution. It is going to be the devil of a job to get anything new of any importance into it, or anything old of any importance out of it.

Eugene Forsey

In April 1987, a marathon bargaining session with provincial premiers at the Meech Lake conference centre produced an accord that (among other provisions) would allow provinces to submit short lists of potential senators to Ottawa. But the Meech Lake Accord was never ratified, and the Senate (as Forsey predicted) never reformed. When Eugene Forsey died in 1991, the Globe and Mail *lost one of its most insistent correspondents.*

209
1987: ONTARIO
JEAN CAZABON TO HIS DAUGHTER, ANDRÉE CAZABON, IN MONTREAL

Sex, drugs, and rock 'n' roll, endlessly promoted in videos and movies, were parental nightmares by the 1980s. When Andrée Cazabon was thirteen, she ran away from home to live on the streets. Her parents, both teachers, were bewildered by their daughter's behaviour and horrified by her rapid slide into drug and alcohol use. Jean and Jo-Ann Cazabon made many attempts to bring Andrée home and re-establish the happy family atmosphere that they had previously known. But after six months of hell, they decided to hand over responsibility to the Children's Aid Society. The night before they signed the papers, Jean wrote to his daughter.

Ottawa

October 18, 1987

Andrée,

I am cleaning the kitchen, I'm thinking of you, of us, of the past, of the future, I sigh, I smile, I cry, I rage—so many ideas wise and crazy come to me; finally I tell myself it might be better to try to put it all on paper and try to make sense of it, if possible.

You know, when I was 19 or 20 years old and I was convinced that one day I would marry Jo Ann and together we would have a family I would catch myself at times dreaming a corny dream that I've had many times since and that I am sure that all fathers have. I would picture myself at church, on a beautiful spring or summer day. I would walk down the aisle, proud and as tall as I can stretch myself and accompanying me on my arm would be a beautiful young woman, radiating, beautiful, blossoming—my daughter. In the beginning, the first few times, I didn't know her name, her physique, her spirit, but always she was beautiful and I loved her and I was proud. And she loved me, and she loved her mother and her family—her grandfather, her grandmothers, her uncles, her aunts, her cousins and her best friends.

I know that it's a crazy dream—but what do you expect, it's an everyday dream. The expression that we used was "a father giving away his daughter" . . . and I would give you to a young man that you had chosen, that you loved and that we had learned to know and love also . . .

I have always accepted that I, as a father, would give you to another that you loved . . . But never in my worst dreams, have I ever imagined that my daughter could choose to live in another home, in another family. Never in my worst moments could I conceive that one day, I would give my daughter away to an institution, the Children's Aid Society.

Six months ago I knew nothing about the C.A.S., and yet, tomorrow, I find myself having to "give" my daughter to it. Like you, I'm learning that it may not be good to have dreams. Six months ago I didn't have a clue about punks, Billy Idol, The Sex Pistols, The Accused, Sid and Nancy. Six months ago I had no idea that you would choose to associate with Marc Caseault, Tyrant, Shomir, Ron Turner, James Dupont and Chris . . . and all the other girls and guys that you have chosen to be part of your life.

I think of the day when you were born and it will always be for me one of the three happiest days of my life. I remember how much I loved you when I gently held you in my arms that first time—you with your big ski feet, your little mouth in the shape of an "o", and your big owl eyes. I think about that sweet little girl, "chouette" like your grandma Fern baptised you. I think of our lovely Saturday mornings together, cuddling up and watching "Heidi" and "Candy", you and Julien [her younger brother] in pyjamas and me still in my robe at 11:00 or noon. I think of our summers at the cottage, at all the wonderful family trips we took—Oh, how much I would love one day to be as happy together as we were the four of us in that big restaurant in Acapulco . . . I have loved you and been so proud of you so many times: when you picked up your writing trophy in grade six, your dance perform-ances, your theatre play. What a tender and yet strong girl you have always been. And even with these past six months, I love you always and will always love you—in hell's darkness as well as in the sunlight—always you will be my daughter, our "chouette", our Andrée.

But Andrée, I know that the worst day of my life will come tomorrow. I would never have imagined that I would entrust my child to someone else because it would be preferable that way. Tomorrow I will be devastated, torn, humiliated but I choose, still, to take my child and "give her" to some-one else in the hope that she will be protected.

Tomorrow, Andrée, I am not abandoning you—I will *never* abandon you or Julien or Jo Ann. Tomorrow I will lend you to someone else, in the hope that I will see the day where you will choose to return completely to your family. I have chosen one day to have a child and it's God that has entrusted you to us. From tomorrow, I will live for the day where you will choose me as your father, and Jo Ann as your mother and Julien as your brother. I will live from now on, waiting for the day where we will be, once again, as a family.

> I love you and will love you always,
> Your father

Andrée finally told her parents that one of the precipitating events in her metamor-phosis from sunny youngster to street kid, living among heroin addicts and violent punks, was that she had been raped by an employer at their summer cottage. After sev-eral months at a Minnesota treatment centre, Andrée overcame her drug addiction and reconciled with her parents, with whom she remains in close touch. She went on to study film at Ryerson University in Toronto. Her NFB docudramas about street kids, No Quick Fix and Letters to a Street Child, have been widely shown at film festivals and in schools.

210

1990: ONTARIO
IRSHAD MANJI TO HER MOTHER,
IN RICHMOND, BRITISH COLUMBIA

Adolescence can be a tough time for anyone, but it is particularly challenging for an immigrant caught between two cultures. After changes to the Immigration Act in 1978, waves of immigrants from Asia, Africa, and the Caribbean transformed Canada (or at least its major cities) into a multiracial, multicultural country. Irshad Manji had arrived in Richmond from Uganda with her South Asian parents and two sisters in 1972, when she was four years old. Eighteen years later, after a move to Ottawa gave her distance from home, she published a letter to her now-divorced mother, explaining how her eagerness to "fit in" as a child complicated her feelings as a daughter.

Ottawa

1990

Dear Mum:

I am ashamed. I am an immigrant woman, like you. But because one of us is "more immigrant" than the other, one of us is more oppressed than the other. Thanks to me.

Since childhood, Mum, I have oppressed you. I have ridiculed your accent, told you not to cook curry, demanded that you speak English in public, called you "cute" when you made people chuckle, and thought you "stupid" when you made them uncomfortable.

Do you remember, Mum, the lunch my university [University of British Columbia] held to honor its scholarship winners? You sat next to the university president. We were discussing languages; after pointing out the smallest accents can cause the biggest misunderstandings, you explained how most people interpret your pronunciation of "beach" as "bitch". Do you remember that our entire table fell silent? The president cleared his throat and my shocked 80-year-old neighbor whispered, "Oh my!"

In retrospect, your story was funny. I should have laughed with you. Instead, I felt like crawling under the table and shouting, "Forgive her—she knows not what she does. She is an immigrant!"

Worse yet, Mum, one horribly racist and patronizing thought kept popping into my mind: "How many times have I warned my immigrant mother not to embarrass me like this?"

When Irshad Manji's mother fled Uganda in 1972, she brought beautiful saris and her own culture to Canada with her. Irshad (aged two in this photo) took time to come to terms with their immigrant status.

That, Mum, was one in a string of racist and patronizing thoughts about you. I can recall, as a 10-year-old at a sleepover with the Brownies, sharing Rice Krispie treats that you—"my Mum," I proudly said—had made for "the gang."

But when the all-white gang examined the treats with scrunched-up noses, then spat out what they had just bitten into, my heart sank. Rather than defending you, I ridiculed you. "My mum has got to be the yuckiest cook in the world," I giggled to break the tension.

"She probably put curry in these!" someone screamed above our laughter. That's right, our laughter. Mine included. I decided not to explain to them that the treats looked and tasted a bit different because you had made them with colored and not plain marshmallows. It was easier simply to laugh at your "dumb" and "gross" immigrant ways. It was easier to let my "friends" oppress me. It was easier to let them let me oppress you.

And, Mum, if this behavior is OK for a 10-year-old, it's not OK for a 22-year-old. So why, just last week, did I lecture you like an overworked immigration officer would? Why did I react this way to a Muslim woman whose guts and brains allowed her to divorce an abusive husband, stand up to manipulative lawyers, fill out her own tax forms and gather enough money to have a house built while dealing with contractors' delays?

I reacted this way because lurking within me is the memory of you as an Avon Lady: baby in one arm, make-up bag in the other, able to sputter only a few English words, and missing home profoundly. Mine is the memory of an immigrant image that my friends and their friends consider shameful.

Occasionally, at least, Mum, I have taken pride in watching you flaunt our immigrant past. When you appeared at parent-teacher nights in a sari, or brought samosas to my school parties, I didn't run for cover. How could

I run when I saw people gasp at your beauty in that sequined sari? How could I run when I heard them praising your samosas?

How could I oppress you when I sense approval, not oppression, from others?

Mum, please recognize—help all immigrant mothers to recognize that their raised-in-Canada kids can be just as oppressive as we can be oppressed. We will swallow the intimidation of others, then regurgitate it on those whom we believe, because others believe, least represent Canada, those who are most vulnerable yet most forgiving, our mothers.

That's why I wish I could stand atop a mountain and yell to every immigrant woman below about their children: "Learn to separate your children's constructive advice from your children's destructive criticism. Take their advice. Don't take their criticism!"

I opened this letter by confessing that I'm ashamed. Let me close, Mum, by saying I'm sorry.

> Irshad

Irshad Manji, now a successful author, broadcaster, and media entrepreneur in Toronto, says today, "I love Canada as much I love my mum. No matter what we immigrants go through, we know what the alternative is. I've had the freedom to outgrow the scars of racism, which is why I had to take the adult responsibility of apologizing to my mother."

211

1992: SARAJEVO
A SOLDIER TO JANE SNAILHAM, IN HALIFAX

Sometimes, when your life is filled with horrific experiences, it is easier to write to a stranger than to your own family. This was often true for peacekeepers, several of whom described in graphic detail the realities of their jobs to Jane Snailham, a Halifax wife and mother. Since 1992, Snailham has sent letters of comfort addressed to "A peacekeeper" to the various trouble spots in the world where Canadian troops in blue berets try to keep or make the peace. This is one of the replies she received.

Sarajevo,
Bosnia-Herzegovina
July 16, 1992

Hi Jane,

A note to acknowledge that I have been receiving your letters of support and [best] wishes. Thanks again for doing so. It sure is nice to receive mail. I get quite a bit from yourself and my family there. I'm sorry you haven't received any notes from myself in the past two to three weeks. I really couldn't come to write to anyone other than my wife.

Our trip to Sarajevo from Croatia was certainly a taste of things to come. We had so much trouble crossing [the border], our main problems came from the Serbs. In a small town called Novo Selo, we deployed to fight our way in or out, whichever came first, but it ended without a shot being fired. The convoy stretched five kilometres, and I was riding up front negotiating crossings [at the opposing checkpoints]. We got here a day late, but all arrived safe and sound.

There is really nothing good that I can say, other than the mail I get or a cold beer before I go to sleep. My job is to go out at 0600 and occupy an intersection and send reports higher [to headquarters]. This is to ensure that there is no fighting at that point, so the convoy of supplies can cross safely, to say the least. I have been shot at so many times that I'm wondering if I'm invisible to man, not only myself, but the rest of us that man the crossing points.

The sight of dead animals in Croatia has been changed only to the sight of dead humans [in Sarajevo] who litter the gutters and river which flows through the main city. I don't know if people just forget them or what. Normally, you would think there is no war here, if you were deaf, as people walk along the streets, only to break into a run between the buildings in fear of being shot. It's unbelievable to sit and watch people (regardless of their sex or age) be gunned down in the street. The sniper's favorite target is the buses, as they are full of people and you would have no trouble hitting someone. It is hard to look into the eyes of an old man, and try and tell him he's okay while you try and patch him up the best you can. We transport them to the UNPROFOR hospital for quicker response. This is only one situation of many that happen on the hour!

Two children were killed while talking to the soldiers in front of our head-quarters. Children [usually] gather [there] to receive candy and talk. Last night, the Serbs launched a mortar attack on the main street. The bombs land[ed] where the children were standing. Eight were injured and two dead.

At the airport, it is no better. The Serbs shoot at airplanes loading and taking off. We had no other choice but to deploy our own snipers to protect the relief flights from further attacks.

With all this happening, the relief supplies are still flowing. I often wonder if it is worth it. As of this date, no one was killed yet, but we have had some serious injuries and gunshot wounds. We all know someone is going to get it, it's just who and when, but it's going to happen. When I first got here and experienced the baptism by fire at myself and my friends, I was shocked, but now we no longer worry about getting hit. It's kind of like going to a circus when you were a child, and you were scared of a certain ride at the fair. Once you got on the ride, you lose the fear and end up expecting it . . .

The time is passing by very fast. We work 14 hour days, then head back to our sleeping quarters for [our] orders for the next day, then try to relax and go to sleep. Our camp is hit nightly with small arms fire and the odd artillery or mortar round. We have lost a lot of vehicles so far, but nothing serious.

I am really sorry as this is not a letter for anyone to read, but it helps to get it off my chest, as we don't talk about it among the soldiers. I wouldn't dare say this to my wife, so you are helping out a lot by reading this whether you realize it or not . . .

Well Jane, I must stop babbling and get ready for tomorrow. Sorry for a depressing letter, but if I didn't say what I said, I would only be lying and making up shit. Anyway, I'll sign off and I'll write again when I have time. Thanks so much for the support and prayers. May God bless you.

212

1995: ENGLAND
MORDECAI RICHLER TO HIS SON JACOB RICHLER IN TORONTO

For all his carefully cultivated image as a grump, Mordecai Richler was, I think, one of the funniest writers Canada has ever produced, as well as being one of our greatest authors. However, his family didn't always appreciate some of his better jokes. When his son Jacob became an editorial intern at Saturday Night *magazine, under editor Ken Whyte, Mordecai began to bombard him with faxes. The mischief-making messages, which arrived at a very public fax machine in the editorial offices, triggered some hilarity among Jake's colleagues.*

Feb 28, 1995

To: Jacob Richler, Esq.
   Private and Confidential
   Eyes Only

Dear Jacob

Thanks for all the stamps (half price is a good deal), but as they will only do for Canadian postage, in future please send them to my Montreal address, marked HOLD FOR ARRIVAL. Yes, I am interested in those office computers, but I find the price you suggest rather steep, seeing as they are second-hand and surely no longer state-of-the-art. Re Ken Whyte's desk: I can't make an offer until you advise me of dimensions, number of drawers etc. But I have no interest in the coffee-maker. Sorry about that.

   Your ever helpful

                  Dad

PS. I wouldn't worry about what could just be a harmless rash, but yes, I do think it would be considerate to wear gloves at the office, until you've checked it out.

PPS. I know you're strapped for money, but I don't think it's comme il faut for you to send on your editorial meeting notes to FRANK [a magazine of satire and gossip].

Mordecai Richler enjoyed practical jokes almost as much as he enjoyed fishing trips, such as the one he took with his youngest son Jacob in the early 1980s on the Restigouche, New Brunswick.

In 1996, Jacob was given a staff position on the magazine as assistant editor.

213

1995: BRITISH COLUMBIA
ANNE GIARDINI TO CAROL SHIELDS IN MINNEAPOLIS

By the 1990s, Canada's fiction writers were acknowledged as some of the finest in the world. Carol Shields is one of my favourite authors, and like all her readers, I was thrilled when she won the Pulitzer Prize for The Stone Diaries. *Carol was on a book tour when the announcement was heard; when her husband, Don, tried to phone her hotel to congratulate her, he was told he was "number 144 on hold." So her daughter Anne Giardini fired off a fax. Anne's message reflected both family pride and her father's dry sense of humour.*

By Fax

Vancouver
April 18, 1995

Dear Mum:

Congratulations and many, many hugs and kisses. We are all so proud of you we are bursting. I talked to Dad who is rueful he did not drive you to the airport. Also, he mentioned that you don't get prizes for setting alarms—just for setting the world on fire, which you have done. Words must be able to convey how happy I am; your work shows how powerful they can be in the right hands.

All the love in the world. We've made arrangements through Laura at The Hungry Mind [a St. Paul bookstore where Carol was scheduled to read] for champagne. Wish we were there to help celebrate. LOVE

Anne

214

1997: ONTARIO
STÉPHANE DION TO LUCIEN BOUCHARD,
PREMIER OF QUEBEC, QUEBEC CITY

The relentless Canadian obsession with the Constitution rumbled on through the 1990s. Lucien Bouchard, who had walked out of Brian Mulroney's cabinet over the constitutional proposals known as the Charlottetown Accord, emerged as the most powerful Quebec nationalist since René Lévesque. In 1995, he led the Yes forces in

Quebec's second referendum on sovereignty-association to within a percentage point of victory and then, on a wave of popularity, became leader of the Parti Québécois and premier in 1996. In Ottawa, Jean Chrétien named Stéphane Dion, a young Quebec academic, his minister of intergovernmental affairs. Dion's new strategy was to take on "separatist myths" by combating Premier Bouchard's statements and key premises with aggressive, sophisticated arguments.

Parliament Hill
Ottawa
August 11, 1997

Dear Premier:

The open letter you recently sent to the Premier of New Brunswick, Mr. Frank McKenna, was brought to my attention, and I read it with interest. I will consider it as a contribution to public debate about the procedure by which Quebec might eventually become an independent state, an issue of great importance to Quebecers and other Canadians.

Your argument is based on three rules that you claim are universally accepted: that a unilateral declaration of independence is supported by international law; that a majority of "50% plus one" is a sufficient threshold for secession; and that international law rejects any changes to the borders of the entity attempting to secede. We are convinced that such assertions are contradicted by international law and state practice.

Let me start with the question of a unilateral declaration of independence. The Government of Canada has always maintained that if Quebecers expressed very clearly a desire to secede from Canada, then their will would be respected. As you know, this position is highly unusual in the international community. Most countries do not allow constituent parts to secede under any circumstances. For example, the constitution of the French Fifth Republic, that of General de Gaulle, provides that "La France est une République indivisible," while the United States Supreme Court has found that our neighbour forms an "indestructible union."

The Government of Canada has never contested the right of the Government of Quebec to consult Quebecers on their future, but it has affirmed that the provincial government cannot have a monopoly on the establishment of a fair process that might lead to secession. There is no democratic country in the world where the government of a province or other constituent entity has been allowed to determine these procedures unilaterally.

The vast majority of international law experts, including the five experts consulted by the Bélanger-Campeau Commission, believe that the right to declare secession unilaterally does not belong to constituent entities of a democratic country such as Canada. If you believe otherwise, then I invite your government to ask the Supreme Court of Canada for the opportunity to submit your arguments on these questions as part of the present reference.

Quebecers and other Canadians should reflect on this fine statement by the Secretary-General of the United Nations, and I quote: "If every ethnic region or linguistic group claimed statehood there would be no limit to fragmentation, and peace, security and well-being for all would become even more difficult to achieve."

Canada is the last place in the world where identity-based fragmentation should be allowed to prevail. In the eyes of the world, this country symbolizes better than any other the ideal of how different people can live together in harmony in a single state. In this regard, let us listen to President Clinton, who said, and I quote: "In a world darkened by ethnic conflicts that literally tear nations apart, Canada has stood for all of us as a model of how people of different cultures can live and work together in peace, prosperity and understanding. Canada has shown the world how to balance freedom with compassion."

Many others have said the same thing about Canada. I will give just one other quotation: "Canada is a land of promise and Canadians are people of hope. It is a country celebrated for its generosity of spirit, where tolerance is ingrained in the national character. A society in which all citizens and all groups can assert and express themselves and realize their aspirations."

These words, which have the ring of truth and could have come from Sir Wilfrid Laurier or Pierre Trudeau, were pronounced on July 1, 1988, by the then Secretary of State, the Hon. Lucien Bouchard.

The Canadian government's priority is to help Quebecers and other Canadians achieve reconciliation. They must speak to one another, stay in closer contact, clear up misunderstandings, find ways to make their federation work better, and celebrate Quebec's distinctiveness within Canada. They must achieve reconciliation, not only as fellow citizens but also as inhabitants of this poor planet. Let us bet on democracy . . .

Turning to the "50% plus one" rule, it should be noted that it is customary in a democracy to require a consensus for serious, virtually irreversible changes that deeply affect not only our own lives but also those of future generations. Secession, the act of choosing between one's fellow citizens, is one of the most consequence-laden choices a society can ever make.

It is no accident that all instances of secession effected through referenda have been supported by a clear consensus. It would be too dangerous to attempt such an operation in an atmosphere of division, on the basis of a narrow, "soft" majority, as it is commonly called, which could evaporate in the face of difficulties.

If I had enough space, I would cite a series of examples from other countries in which a referendum verdict that was too uncertain was not acted on, for decisions much less important than the break-up of a country. But let us confine ourselves to your secession project.

In the white paper that led up to Quebec's Referendum Act, it is noted that, because of the consultative—and not decisive—nature of referenda, "it would be pointless to include in the law special provisions requiring a certain majority vote or rate of participation." When the bill was tabled on April 5, 1978, its sponsor, Mr. Robert Burns, spoke of the "moral weight" of a referendum won on the basis of "a clearly and broadly expressed popular will." You yourself acknowledged on June 15, 1994, that an attempt at sovereignty with a slim majority would adversely affect "the political cohesion of Quebec." And on September 12, 1992, in the case of a simple constitutional referendum (on the Charlottetown Accord), Mr. Bernard Landry linked the legitimacy of a "yes" vote to obtaining a substantial majority in Quebec.

As to the question of territorial integrity, there is neither a paragraph nor a line in international law that protects Quebec's territory but not Canada's. International experience demonstrates that the borders of the entity seeking independence can be called into question, sometimes for reasons based on democracy. For example, you are no doubt aware that France insisted on partitioning the island of Mayotte from the Comoros at the time the latter gained independence because the residents of Mayotte unequivocally expressed their desire to maintain their link with France.

Even the most prominent secessionists do not agree that Quebec's borders would be guaranteed if secession were being negotiated. When he was a professor of international law, Mr. Daniel Turp [Bloc Québécois MP] stated his belief that, in the event of Quebec separation, Quebec's Aboriginal peoples would have the right to remain in Canada if they so chose. During the recent federal election campaign, Mr. Gilles Duceppe [Bloc Québécois leader] also pointed to the special geographic position of Quebec territory occupied by Aboriginal peoples and suggested the issue might be referred to an international tribunal.

Neither you nor I nor anyone else can predict that the borders of an independent Quebec would be those now guaranteed by the Canadian Constitution.

These are crucial questions which, so that they can be better debated on their substance, require your government to choose between two contradictory positions. In effect, you are saying simultaneously: 1) that the procedure leading up to secession is a purely political matter, in which case the established law is not relevant; and 2) that the established law demonstrates you are right and those who contest the procedure you intend to follow are wrong.

If you hold the first assertion, you must alert our fellow citizens that you are prepared to plunge them into a situation of anarchy, outside the legal framework, which is not done in a democracy. If, on the contrary, you hold the second assertion, you must produce the rules of law that support your position and agree that our reference to the Supreme Court is a constructive and necessary exercise of clarification, whether or not its outcome is in your favour. One thing is certain: you cannot continue to deny the relevance of law while invoking it when it suits you.

The Government of Canada is convinced that Quebecers will never choose to renounce the deep-rooted solidarity that unites them with other Canadians within this great federation, which we must always strive to improve. Our being together gives us one of the best qualities of life in the world. We acknowledge, however, that the spirit and practice of democracy must be respected in all circumstances, even the very unlikely and sad prospect of Canada's partition.

Reconciling secession with democracy is such a difficult undertaking that no well-established democracy has yet attempted to do so. These grave questions cannot be avoided if you persist in your project of secession. Our fellow citizens expect their elected representatives to debate these issues in a calm and level-headed manner. This debate on the procedures that would apply concerns us as Quebecers first and foremost, because an attempt at secession in an atmosphere of confusion would profoundly divide our society; but it also concerns Canadians as a whole, all of whom would be affected by the break-up of their country.

Yours sincerely,
Stéphane Dion

In 2001, when Lucien Bouchard retired from politics, polls showed that support for independence was below 40 percent and that there was widespread reluctance to hold a third referendum.

215
1998: NOVA SCOTIA
JOHNNIE CLARK (CUSTOMER NUMBER 28544)
TO LEONARD LEE IN OTTAWA

Johnnie Clark savours the Lee Valley Tools catalogues of woodworking tools. His enthusiasm for the displays of lathes, hammers, and bits led him into a lengthy correspondence with the catalogue's founder, Leonard Lee (see Letter 205), in which the men share their pleasure in a well-balanced chainsaw or well-sharpened chisel. Johnnie always signs his letters with his customer number, and the two men have never met.

Dartmouth, N.S.
November 23, 1998

Dear Mr. Lee,

Just received my Christmas catalogue and was impressed with the coincidence of seeing another pocket wrench—your pocket wrench II, #25K1701.

For years I have had my own pocket wrench and I'd like to give it to you now to commemorate the coincidence of you selling one with such similarities to mine, (note the teeth in her gullet).

The hole was for a chain as the wrench was often worn on Saturday night in one's arse pocket to the Wellington dance. If one was suave enough to also have one of the big leather trucker's wallets on a chain, the wrench could be worn in the opposing arse pocket for symmetry of chains and overall balance to the arse.

I suppose I never explained the geography of my youth to you, but I grew up in Richmond [Prince Edward Island] with all the English crew while the French crew lived in Egmont Bay. Strategically located at the exact midpoint was the Wellington Immaculate Conception Church, horse shed, (later upgraded to hockey rink), and hall.

There's none of that uppity, "Never the twain shall meet" stuff in this story. Meet we did and ask me if we didn't do one fine job of it.

When one arrived at the dance hall parking lot, the first 6 vehicles were usually already there. One Ford van, owned by the DJ, and 5 late model full-sized Chevrolet cars especially decorated for the occasion with red and white lights, sirens, and the appropriate bilingual doorcrests—G.R.C.-R.C.M.P. The English boys hated the French boys and loved the French girls and the French boys loved to fight. Talk about your chemistry!

Believe me, the OK Corral had nothing on the Immaculate Conception parking lot. A lot of immaculate things happened on that parking lot, my survival being foremost among the miracles, but for sure, conception was not one of them. Any jeasles form of conception other than immaculate was what amused me. But I digress!

Big Barriault had a pocket wrench as did Bologna Hashie and, in the rough late night hours to the wails of Roy Orbison screaming out *Pretty Woman* between the needle jumping over the scratches in the record the pocket wrenches would flail. To suit this Neanderthal activity the record would usually skip just as Roy got to "pretty" and land back in the groove on the tail end of "woman" and all you got was "pre-man." To this day I wonder if the sacred heart of Jesus and the repose of the souls of the faithful departed in the mercy of God weren't teaming up to send us a message to get with the program. But I tell ya, those pocket wrenches were every bit as effective as a handful of HO-MI-DIGGERS in that application.

Last week I had dinner with one of the descendants of those beautiful French women and I was as thrilled to be in her presence as I was to chase those little French girls back when pocket wrenches were for real men and real men knew how to instinctively swagger in a manner befitting the arse pocket adornment.

If you do choose to wear it you can chain 'er to your belt or just run 'er naked in your rule pocket.

For me, I'm gonna get me one of your little darlins, chain her $1/4$" hex hole to me own belt and run 'er just like that from now on.

I'll let you know how I make out and let me know too how you like traveling with your new pocket wrench.

                    Yours sincerely,
                    Customer Number 28544

216

1999: BRITISH COLUMBIA
JIMMIE TO JANE FROST IN VANCOUVER

Of all the love letters I read during my research, this is the one that moved me most. This is in part because of the recipient's circumstances. Jane Frost was recovering from chemotherapy following a second episode of breast cancer, when she received a phone call out of the blue. It was a particularly low point in Jane's life. She was alone and frightened; all her hair had fallen out; she was grey with fatigue. A couple of days later, this letter from the caller arrived, explaining what had prompted the call.

The Coast Plaza Suite Hotel
1763 Comox Street
Vancouver B.C., Canada
June 5, 1999

Dear Jane,

There is a marvellous Canadian named Alice Munro who writes for the *New Yorker*. Her stories usually begin with something odd, like the phone call you received from me Thursday afternoon; a confusing chat with someone you never knew and only shared a few words with very long ago. Munro's stories usually get around to instinct, to things lost and things regained. It was in this spirit that I sat down in a sunny garden in San Francisco and finally made the call I wanted to make thirty years ago. I hope I can explain myself.

1965-66, the year I spent in Vancouver followed one where I had had my face disfigured after going through a windshield in a car wreck. I arrived at St. George's [School] determined not to be what I had been, an unread jock and make-out artist from a very small place. I threw myself, literally, into rugby and trying to memorize every word that had come out of Great Britain. At the same time I was bludgeoned with the narcissism of most 17 year-olds, compounded every time I looked in the mirror at my freshly plastic-surgeoned face.

That was the boy-man who, in late October, was finally invited to check out of the school on a Saturday night, to attend a real city party, with strong beer and wealthy, lovely girls . . . My new friends even supplied me with a date who did not find the tongue-tied sack of neuroses she had been paired with quite to her liking. Not long after entering the party, she fled into the dancing arms of a Leslie Howard look-alike.

It was about that time that you appeared, came over, and actually talked to me.

Given your current struggles you might find it hard to remember what a truly radiant young woman you were. The Jane I met had a classic New World beauty I'm sure people have remarked on all your life. That said, your real power came from your kindness. You spoke to me for a very long time. You told me about Vancouver, about ignoring the appearance of status in the room; you asked me about the beach where I grew up and—thankfully not avoiding it—where the scar that ran across my forehead had come from. When you finally rejoined whomever it is people rejoin in these situations, I felt about as good as it gets.

I left the party and the dancing couple and walked a very long way back to school where I spent the rest of a majestic, lonely year. I worked hard at a lot of things, including the courage to call you, to get on the bus and share some English tea in your English city. I believe it was towards the end of November that the boarders' grapevine informed me that you had become involved with the person you eventually married. It was my first lesson in lost chances, something I've learned to have no patience for.

. . . I [returned to the States and] was married myself at 36 and have two children who are the lights of my life. I live a fairly hectic life . . . trying to add to my assets and, at the same time, realize what true assets really are. I am here this weekend because I put some money [in a company here]. Truth told, I think the investment was based on other reasons. I still want to have tea with you.

I don't get nervous anymore, except in a situation calling a woman who has no reason to remember me. As I said, it wasn't ridiculous nostalgia, nor one of the misguided missiles of middle-aged men. It was a thank you, long overdue. As simple as your kindness was that night, it was something I lived on for a year.

I heard your spirit again Thursday when you said, *this phone call must be very hard for you.* You went on to say how you will beat your cancer. You will. But in days right now, in moments that must be so hard for you, I hope you remember the true beauty you really have. I was an incident in your life, but your heart must have been so extended for so many years that no loss of appearance will ever dim it for the people lucky enough to have known its glow.

Tonight, as you were this morning, you will be in my prayers.

Jimmie

Jane and Jimmie met a year later and picked up on the friendship that had started thirty years earlier. The letter, proving the enduring value of written rather than electronic messages, is one of Jane's greatest treasures, as her cancer remains in remission.

217

1999: ITALY

EDA BANNISTER TO HER SISTER MARIE BANNISTER IN SASKATOON

As the year 2000 approached, Canadians were increasingly mobile, increasingly caught up in world affairs, and more and more conscious of the fragility of international peace. When Eda Bannister, a thirty-eight-year-old master corporal in the Canadian Forces, volunteered to join the NATO peacekeeping mission in the former Yugoslavia, she was sent to the Aviano air base, in the Italian Alps. She worked with the Canadian pilots (nicknamed "jockeys") who were flying regular bombing missions over Kosovo. In regular e-mails to her sister Marie back home, she considered a hypothetical question that for many people, in the new century, would be all too real.

Aviano,
Italy
6/11/99
5:36 a.m.

Hi Yourself,

Well, you are right, there are lots of things happening over here, lots that I cannot talk about, but I am keeping a journal of events here. All the kinds of stuff that I cannot talk about over the phone, over e-mail, or any other method of mass communication. There are a lot of personal observations too about my life here, and general Dear Diary kinds of things. If I sometimes seem evasive on my e-mails, it is because we are channelled through the American system, and have to be careful about what we say. Big brother is watching me.

Yes, I try to stay upbeat over here. We have enough people bitching about every little thing, and it just lends to a general feeling of bummer. So I try to be cheerful. But it is wearing. The days are long, the work never ends, and the other things are stressful. It is unsettling for me to be involved in this event. It seems so often like I am detached from it all and that I am not really involved, but yes, sometimes when I see the jockeys go, I wonder if they will all come back. It is difficult. This is another reason why I am keeping a journal . . .

I do not know what is going to happen with the peace initiative. There is a long history of strife in this area of the world, and Milosovic [the Serbian leader] is a very sly man . . . The ethnic hatred over there is so strong that a friend commented he had seen it well-developed in three and four year olds. It would probably take three generations of non-events for them to be able to forget their anger, and it would only really take after all the elders were gone and there was no one left to tell the tales of long unavenged wrongdoings.

Yes, it would be interesting to see what one would pack as a refugee. I think that I have a different perspective than you do. I have lived a much more mobile life, and I have been on exercises and courses with the military when all the personal items you brought with you had to fit in a barrack box. I was even on a course where the only personal items you could have other than military kit and toiletries, had to be able to fit in a shoe box. You become very clear on what it is you need that is a necessity, a luxury, and just a want. My camping experience really helps too. I would probably grab a pot, knife, can opener, ranger blanket (a lightweight army blanket, very warm and packs down to nothing). Wear all your clothes in layers. Bring a mug or bowl, both are multi purpose. A large tin basin, good for cooking, washing, bathing, and carrying food and water. A strong pack, a camp tarp, a large spoon. All the food I could carry, that was easy to cook and light for its nutritional value, (couscous, dried fruit).

For personal items: I would bring, my sewing kit, for both practicality, and so I could pass time embroidering my clothes if I wished. Jewellery, some for sentimental value, the rest for trade. And the baby sock of [her daughter] Adelle's that got mixed into my clothes when I went away to basic training ten years ago, and I have carried with me always, anywhere I travel, ever since then.

That is about it. Everything else would just be stuff, and extra weight to carry.

Anyways, I will write, a real letter, soon.

Yours,
Eda.

SOURCES OF LETTERS

The following abbreviations are used in the sources.

AM   Archives of Manitoba
AO   Archives of Ontario
NAC   National Archives of Canada
NLC   National Library of Canada
NSARM   Nova Scotia Archives and Records Management
PAA   Provincial Archives of Alberta
SAB   Saskatchewan Archives Board

1   1800: PETER RUSSELL TO SERJEANT SHEPHERD
The Town of York, 1793–1815: A Collection of Documents of Early Toronto. Edited by Edith G. Firth. Toronto: Champlain Society, 1962. Pages 231–32. Reprinted by permission of the Champlain Society, Toronto, Canada.

2   1800: DR. JOHN CALEFF TO MAJOR HAILES
Winslow Papers, A.D. 1776–1826. Edited by W.O. Raymond. Printed under the Auspices of the New Brunswick Historical Society. Saint John, N.B.: Sun Printing, 1901. Pages 449–50.

3   1800: JOSEPH WILLCOCKS TO RICHARD WILLCOCKS
Ottawa, NAC, Joseph Willcocks Memorandum and Letter Book, MG24 C1.

4   1801: COLONEL THOMAS TALBOT TO THE DUKE OF CUMBERLAND
The Talbot Papers. Edited by James H. Coyne. Ottawa: Royal Society of Canada, 1907. Pages 75–77.

5   1802: EDWARD WINSLOW TO THE *ROYAL GAZETTE AND NEW BRUNSWICK ADVERTISER*
Winslow Papers, A.D. 1776–1826. Edited by W.O. Raymond. Printed under the Auspices of the New Brunswick Historical Society. Saint John, N.B.: Sun Printing, 1901. Pages 468–72.

6   1807: THOMAS RIDOUT TO THOMAS AND MARY RIDOUT
Ten Years of Upper Canada in Peace and War, 1805–1815: Being the Ridout Letters. Edited by Matilda [Ridout] Edgar. Toronto: William Briggs, 1890. Pages 21–22.

7   1807: JOHN BLAND TO GOVERNOR JOHN HOLLOWAY
Howley, James P. *The Beothuks, or Red Indians: The Aboriginal Inhabitants of Newfoundland.* Cambridge: Cambridge University Press, 1915. Reprint, Toronto: Prospero Books, 2000. Pages 65–66.

8   1808: TIMOTHY NIGHTINGALE TO QUETTON DE ST. GEORGE
Toronto, AO, Baldwin Papers, MS88 (1).

9   1811: THOMAS RIDOUT TO GEORGE RIDOUT
Ten Years of Upper Canada in Peace and War, 1805–1815: Being the Ridout Letters. Edited by Matilda [Ridout] Edgar. Toronto: William Briggs, 1890. Pages 38–39.

10   1811: SHERIFF JOHN BEIKIE TO THE CHAIRMAN OF THE QUARTER SESSIONS
The Town of York 1793–1815: A Collection of Documents of Early Toronto. Edited by Edith G. Firth. Toronto: Champlain Society, 1962. Page 107. Reprinted by permission of the Champlain Society, Toronto, Canada.

11   1813: PENELOPE BEIKIE TO JOHN MACDONELL
The Town of York 1793–1815: A Collection of Documents of Early Toronto. Edited by Edith G. Firth. Toronto: Champlain Society, 1962. Pages 299–300. Reprinted by permission of the Champlain Society, Toronto, Canada.

12   1815: JOHN BALDWIN TO QUETTON DE ST. GEORGE
Toronto, AO, Baldwin Papers, MS88 (1).

13   1818: A LANCASHIRE FARMER TO HIS MINISTER
The Emigrant's Guide to the British Settlements in Upper Canada and the United States of America. London, 1820. Pages 163–65.

14   1819: COLIN ROBERTSON TO GEORGE MOFFATT
Colin Robertson's Correspondence Book, September 1817 to September 1822. Edited by E.E. Rich and R. Harvey Fleming. Toronto: Champlain Society, for The Hudson's Bay Record Society, 1939. Pages 100–01. Reprinted by permission of the Champlain Society, Toronto, Canada.

15   1821: A. BOAG TO HIS SISTER
Lamond, Robert. *A Narrative of the Rise and Progress of Emigration from the Counties of Lanark & Renfrew to the New Settlements in Upper Canada, on Government Grant.* Glasgow, 1821. Pages 103–04.

16   1821: ANNIE POWELL TO GEORGE W. MURRAY
Letters of Mrs. Wm. Dummer Powell, 1807–1821. Niagara Historical Society, no. 14. [1905]. Page 39. Reprinted by permission of the Niagara Historical Society and Museum.

17   1822: JOHN FRANKLIN TO ADMIRAL JOHN BARROW
Sir John Franklin's Journals and Correspondence: The First Arctic Land Expedition, 1819–1822. Edited by Richard C. Davis. Toronto: Champlain Society, 1995. Pages 420–23. Reprinted by permission of the Champlain Society, Toronto, Canada.

18   1822: EDWARD BLEWETT TO THE REVEREND JOHN STRACHAN
The Town of York, 1815–1834: A Further Collection of Documents of Early Toronto. Edited by Edith G. Firth. Toronto: Champlain Society, 1966. Page 268. Reprinted by permission of the Champlain Society, Toronto, Canada.

19   1829: MISSISSAUGA INDIANS OF RICE LAKE TO SIR JOHN COLBORNE
Muskoka and Haliburton, 1615–1875: A Collection of Documents. Edited by Florence B. Murray. Toronto: Champlain Society, 1963. Pages 104–05. Reprinted by permission of the Champlain Society, Toronto, Canada.

20   1831: FRANCES STEWART TO LOUISA BEAUFORT
Our Forest Home: Being Extracts from the Correspondence of the Late Frances Stewart. Edited by E.S. Dunlop. Montreal: Gazette Printing, 1902. Pages 122–23.

21   1832: MARY RYERSON TO JAMES LEWIS
Sissons, C.B. *Egerton Ryerson: His Life and Letters.* Toronto: Clarke, Irwin, 1937. Pages 159–60.

22   1832: JOHN CAPLING TO HIS BROTHER
English Immigrant Voices: Labourers' Letters from Upper Canada in the 1830s. Edited by Wendy Cameron, Sheila Haines, and Mary McDougall Maude. Montreal: McGill-Queen's University Press, 2000. Pages 43–44. Reprinted by permission of the publisher.

23 1832: THOMAS SIMPSON TO JAMES HARGRAVE
The Hargrave Correspondence, 1821–1843. Edited by G.P. de T. Glazebrook. Toronto: Champlain Society, 1938. Pages 95–97. Reprinted by permission of the Champlain Society, Toronto, Canada.

24 1833: JOSEPH HOWE TO SUSAN HOWE
My Dear Susan Ann: Letters of Joseph Howe to His Wife, 1829–1836. Edited by M.G. Parks. St. John's: Jesperson Press, 1985. Pages 130–33.

25 1834: CATHARINE PARR TRAILL TO JAMES AND EMMA BIRD
I Bless You in My Heart: Selected Correspondence of Catharine Parr Traill. Edited by Carl Ballstadt, Elizabeth Hopkins, and Michael A. Peterman. Toronto: University of Toronto Press, 1996. Pages 39–42. Reprinted with permission of the publisher.

26 1836: WILLIAM ROBINSON TO THE REVEREND T. SOCKETT
English Immigrant Voices: Labourers' Letters from Upper Canada in the 1830s. Edited by Wendy Cameron, Sheila Haines, and Mary McDougall Maude. Montreal: McGill-Queen's University Press, 2000. Pages 230–33. Reprinted by permission of the publisher.

27 1837: FANNY BRIDGMAN TO FANNY WEST
Toronto, AO, Miscellaneous, 1837, no. 10, MU2107.

28 1837: CHIEFS JOSHUA WAWANOSH, EDWARD OGEEBEGUN, AND GORDON MEGEZEEZ TO CHIEFS KANOODUNG, MAUSHKENOOZHA, WANNEDEGOOSH, AND JOHN KIYA RYLEY
The Rebellion of 1837 in Upper Canada. Edited by Colin Read and Ronald J. Stagg. Toronto: Champlain Society, 1985. Pages 326–27. Reprinted by permission of the Champlain Society, Toronto, Canada.

29 1838: LADY DURHAM TO LADY MARY GREY
The excerpt from *Letters & Diaries of Lady Durham,* edited by Patricia Godsell, is reprinted by permission of Oberon Press.

30 1838: THE REVEREND JAMES EVANS TO MRS. EVANS
Letter from Reverend James Evans to Mrs. Evans (Oct–Nov 1839), first published in *Papers and Records of the Ontario Historical Society,* Vol. 27 (1932). Pages 60–63. Reprinted with permission of the Ontario Historical Society.

31 1838: EUGENIE SAINT-GERMAIN TO LADY COLBORNE
Pioneer and Gentlewomen of British North America, 1713–1867. Edited by Beth Light and Alison Prentice. Toronto: New Hogtown Press, 1980. Pages 165–66.

32 1839: JAMES ROBB TO JANE ROBB
The Letters of James and Ellen Robb: Portrait of a Fredericton Family in Early Victorian Times. Edited by Alfred Goldsworthy Bailey. Fredericton: Acadiensis Press, 1983. Pages 24–28.

33 1839: SUSANNA MOODIE TO JOHN DUNBAR MOODIE
Letters of Love and Duty: The Correspondence of Susanna and John Moodie. Edited by Carl Ballstadt, Elizabeth Hopkins, and Michael A. Peterman. Toronto: University of Toronto Press, 1993. Pages 136–39. Reprinted with permission of the publisher.

34 1840: JOSEPH HOWE TO JOHN MORRIS
Pre-Confederation. Edited by Peter B. Waite. Scarborough, Ont.: Prentice-Hall, [1965]. Page 183. Vol. 2 in Canadian Historical Documents Series.

35 1840: LETITIA HARGRAVE TO FLORENCE MACTAVISH
The Letters of Letitia Hargrave. Edited by Margaret Arnett Macleod. Toronto: Champlain Society, 1947. Pages 64–68. Reprinted by permission of the Champlain Society, Toronto, Canada.

36 1840: JAMES GUNN TO GEORGE GUNN
Winnipeg, AM, Hudson's Bay Company Archives, E.31/2/4, folios 9–9d.

37   1840: ROBERT BALDWIN TO LOUIS-HIPPOLYTE LAFONTAINE
My Dear Friend: Letters of Louis Hippolyte LaFontaine & Robert Baldwin. Edited by Yolande Stewart. Whitby, Ont.: Plum Hollow Books, 1978. Pages 5–7.

38   1842: GEORGE CHILD TO LYDIA CHILD
The Child Letters: Public and Private Life in a Canadian Merchant-Politician's Family, 1841–1845. Edited by J.I. Little. Montreal: McGill-Queen's University Press, 1995. Pages 48–49. Reprinted by permission of the publisher.

39   1843: MARCUS CHILD TO LYDIA CHILD
The Child Letters: Public and Private Life in a Canadian Merchant-Politician's Family, 1841–1845. Edited by J.I. Little. Montreal: McGill-Queen's University Press, 1995. Pages 84–85. Reprinted by permission of the publisher.

40   1843: SOPHIA EASTWOOD TO THE STANDENS
A New Life in Canada: The Letters of Sophia Eastwood, 1843–1870. Edited by Susan Beattie. Toronto: Canadian Scholars' Press, 1989. Pages 20–22.

41   1846: WILLIAM HUTTON TO HIS MOTHER
Boyce, Gerald E. *Hutton of Hastings: The Life and Letters of William Hutton, 1801–1861.* Belleville, Ont.: Hastings County Council, 1972. Pages 44–48. Reprinted by permission.

42   1846: HENRY CHANTLER TO JOSEPH CHANTLER
English Immigrant Voices: Labourers' Letters from Upper Canada in the 1830s. Edited by Wendy Cameron, Sheila Haines, and Mary McDougall Maude. Montreal: McGill-Queen's University Press, 2000. Pages 368–70. Reprinted by permission of the publisher.

43   1847: ELIZA STACEY TO EDWARD STACEY
Lifelines: The Stacey Letters, 1836–1858. Edited by Jane Vansittart. London: P. Davies, 1976. Pages 67–69.

44   1847: JAMES THOMSON TO ALEXANDER THOMSON
For Friends at Home: A Scottish Emigrant's Letters from Canada, California and the Cariboo, 1844–1864. Edited by Richard Arthur Preston. Montreal: McGill-Queen's University Press, 1974. Pages 105–07.

45   1848: LORD ELGIN TO EARL GREY
The Elgin-Grey Papers, 1846–1852. Edited by Sir Arthur G. Doughty. Ottawa: J.O. Patenaude, 1937. Pages 45–47.

46   1849: THE REVEREND WILLIAM RUFUS SEAVER TO MEHITABLE HOMER SEAVER
Foster, Josephine, ed., "The Montreal Riot of 1849." *Canadian Historical Review.* Vol. 32, no. 1 (March 1951), pages 62–63.

47   1851: THOMAS H. JONES TO DANIEL FOSTER
The Black Abolitionist Papers. Vol. 2, *Canada, 1830–1865.* Edited by C. Peter Ripley. Chapel Hill, N.C.: University of North Carolina Press, 1986. Pages 133–34.

48   1852: TUNIS SNOOK TO HIS FATHER
Thanks to Christopher Moore, Toronto.

49   1853: MARY BIBB TO HORACE MANN
Quoted in Afua B. Cooper, "Black Women and Work in Nineteenth-Century Canada West: Black Woman Teacher Mary Bibb." In *"We're Rooted Here and They Can't Pull Us Up": Essays in African Canadian Women's History.* Edited by Peggy Bristow et al. Toronto: University of Toronto Press, 1994. Pages 151–52. Reprinted with permission of the publisher.

50   1853: HENRY TUZO TO ANNA MARIA TUZO
Thanks to Susan Loetitia Wilson, Toronto.

51   1855: WILLIAM DAVIES TO JAMES DAVIES
Letters of William Davies, Toronto, 1854–1861. Edited by William Sherwood Fox. Toronto: University of Toronto Press, 1945. Pages 37–39. Reprinted with permission of the publisher.

52   1855: FREDERICK ROBB TO ELIZABETH ROBB
The Letters of James and Ellen Robb: Portrait of a Fredericton Family in Early Victorian Times. Edited by Alfred Goldsworthy Bailey. Fredericton: Acadiensis Press, 1983. Page 119.

53   1856: ROBERT JONES TO WILLIAM STILL
Still, William. *The Underground Railroad.* New York: Arno Press, 1968. Page 272.

54   1856: JAMES ROSS TO HIS SISTERS
Winnipeg, AM, MG2 C14, Alexander Ross Family Papers, item 200.

55   1857: GEORGE CANN TO ANN CANN
Thanks to Lois Daly, Calgary.

56   1858: LOUISA STACEY TO EDWARD STACEY
Lifelines: The Stacey Letters, 1836–1858. Edited by Jane Vansittart. London: P. Davies, 1976. Pages 164–65.

57   1858: CRITCHLOW HARRIS TO MARTHA CRITCHLOW HARRIS
The Island Family Harris: Letters of an Immigrant Family in British North America, 1856–1866. Edited by Robert Critchlow Tuck. Charlottetown: Ragweed Press, 1983. Pages 74–75.

58   1859: SIR JAMES DOUGLAS TO SISTER SUPERIOR
Pioneer and Gentlewomen of British North America, 1713–1867. Edited by Beth Light and Alison Prentice. Toronto: New Hogtown Press, 1980. Pages 34–35.

59   1859: FIELDING SMITHEA TO THE BRITISH COLONIST
The Black Abolitionist Papers. Vol. 2, *Canada, 1830–1865.* Edited by C. Peter Ripley. Chapel Hill, N.C.: University of North Carolina Press, 1986. Pages 412–14.

60   1860: W.R. BARTLETT TO JAMES BEGAHMIGABOW
Muskoka and Haliburton, 1615–1875: A Collection of Documents. Edited by Florence B. Murray. Toronto: Champlain Society, 1963. Page 124. Reprinted by permission of the Champlain Society, Toronto, Canada.

61   1863: LIEUTENANT EDMUND VERNEY TO SIR HARRY VERNEY
Vancouver Island Letters of Edmund Hope Verney, 1862–1865. Edited by Allan Pritchard. Vancouver: University of British Columbia Press, 1996. Pages 169–73. Reprinted with permission of the publisher. © University of British Columbia Press, 1996. All rights reserved by the publisher.

62   1864: ARTHUR BIRCH TO JOHN BIRCH
The Beaver. Autumn 1976, pages 43–44.

63   1864: GEORGE BROWN TO ANNE BROWN
The Atlantic Advocate. May 1962, pages 74–79.

64   1865: ANN SLATTERY TO HER SISTER
Pioneer and Gentlewomen of British North America, 1713–1867. Edited by Beth Light and Alison Prentice. Toronto: New Hogtown Press, 1980. Pages 46–47.

65   1865: EGERTON RYERSON TO SOPHIA HARRIS
My Dearest Sophie: Letters from Egerton Ryerson to His Daughter. Edited by C.B. Sissons. Toronto: Ryerson Press, 1955. Pages 76–77.

66   1866: NATHANIEL CARROTHERS TO WILLIAM CARROTHERS
Houston, Cecil J. *Irish Emigration and Canadian Settlement: Patterns, Links, and Letters.* Toronto: University of Toronto Press; Belfast: Ulster Historical Foundation, 1990. Pages 262–64. Reprinted with permission of the publisher.

67 1868: CHARLES MAIR TO HOLMES MAIR
Alexander Begg's Red River Journal and Other Papers Relative to the Red River Resistance of 1869–70. Edited by W.L. Morton. Toronto: Champlain Society, 1956. Pages 395–99. Reprinted by permission of the Champlain Society, Toronto, Canada.

68 1869: LOUIS RIEL TO *LE NOUVEAU MONDE*
Alexander Begg's Red River Journal and Other Papers Relative to the Red River Resistance of 1869–70. Edited by W.L. Morton. Toronto: Champlain Society, 1956. Pages 399–402. Reprinted by permission of the Champlain Society, Toronto, Canada.

69 1869: SIR JOHN A. MACDONALD TO JAMES O'REILLY
Correspondence of Sir John Macdonald: Selections from . . . Edited by Sir Joseph Pope. Garden City, N.Y.: Doubleday, 1921. Pages 101–02.

70 1869: WILLIAM MCDOUGALL TO SIR JOHN A. MACDONALD
Correspondence of Sir John Macdonald: Selections from . . . Edited by Sir Joseph Pope. Garden City, N.Y.: Doubleday, 1921. Pages 101–02.

71 1871: SARA RIEL TO LOUIS RIEL
To Louis from Your Sister Who Loves You, Sara Riel. Edited by Mary V. Jordan. Toronto: Griffin House, 1974. Pages 31–33.

72 1871: ALEXANDER ROBB TO SUSANNA ROBB
Houston, Cecil J. *Irish Emigration and Canadian Settlement: Patterns, Links, and Letters.* Toronto: University of Toronto Press; Belfast: Ulster Historical Foundation, 1990. Pages 326–28. Reprinted with permission of the publisher.

73 1872: THE MARQUESS OF DUFFERIN TO SIR JOHN A. MACDONALD
Correspondence of Sir John Macdonald: Selections from . . . Edited by Sir Joseph Pope. Garden City, N.Y.: Doubleday, 1921. Pages 189–92.

74 1874: SAMUEL ANDERSON TO JANET ANDERSON
Letters from the 49th Parallel, 1857–1873: Selected Correspondence of Joseph Harris and Samuel Anderson. Edited by C. Ian Jackson. Toronto: Champlain Society, 2000. Pages 418–21. Reprinted by permission of the Champlain Society, Toronto, Canada.

75 1875: ANNIE DAVEY TO ADAMS DAVEY
Thanks to Elaine Deschenes, Greely, Ontario.

76 1871: LOUIS-A. DESSAULES TO A FRIEND OF LOUIS-JOSEPH PAPINEAU
Chers nous autres : un siècle de correspondance québécoise. Vol. 2. Edited by Robert Blondin and Gilles Lamontagne. Montreal: VLB éditeur, 1978. Pages 67–68. Translated from the French.

77 1879: LOVISA MCDOUGALL TO HER MOTHER
Letters of Lovisa McDougall, 1878–1887. Edited by Elizabeth M. McCrum. [Edmonton]: Alberta Culture, Historical Resources Division, 1978. Occasional Paper (PAA), no. 1. Pages 25–27.

78 1879: ELLIOT GALT TO ALEXANDER GALT
Den Otter, A.A. "Letters from Elliott Galt: Travelling the Prairies 1879–1880." *Alberta History.* Vol. 26, no. 23 (Summer 1978), pages 24–27.

79 1880: TED FFOLKES TO MRS. HENRY FFOLKES
Reprinted by permission from *Letters from a Young Emigrant in Manitoba.* Edited by Ronald A. Wells. Published by the University of Manitoba Press, 1981. Pages 58–60.

80 1881: WILLIE WALLACE TO MAGGIE WALLACE
Wallace, William. *"My Dear Maggie . . .": Letters from a Western Manitoba Pioneer.* Edited by Kenneth S. Coates and William R. Morrison. [Regina]: University of Regina, 1991. Pages 39–42. Reproduced with permission of the Canadian Plains Research Center, University of Regina.

81   1882: ANNIE AFFLECK THOMPSON TO JOHN THOMPSON

Ottawa, NAC, Sir John S.D. Thompson Papers, MG26 D, vol. 277, microfilm C-10706.

82   1884: JESSIE MCLEAN TO LILIAN SHARPE

Buck, Ruth M. "In the Midst of Life." *The Beaver*. December 1991/January 1992, pages 42–44.

83   1885: LOTTIE DALKIN AND LEILA GEGGIE TO ADOLPHE CARON

Telegrams of the North-West Campaign 1885. Edited by Desmond Morton and Reginald H. Roy. Toronto: Champlain Society, 1972. Page 171. Reproduced by permission of the Champlain Society, Toronto, Canada.

84   1885: JOHN MCDOUGALL TO CHARLES AMEY

Letters of Lovisa McDougall, 1878–1887. Edited by Elizabeth M. McCrum. [Edmonton]: Alberta Culture, Historical Resources Division, 1978. Occasional Paper (PAA), no. 1. Pages 73–76.

85   1885: CAPTAIN J. DROLET TO HIS FATHER

Drolet, J. "A Rebellion Letter." *Alberta History*. Vol. 30, no. 3 (Summer 1982), pages 27–28.

86   1885: LOUIS RIEL TO JAMES WICKES TAYLOR

The Collected Writings of Louis Riel. Vol. 3. Edited by Thomas Flanagan. Edmonton: University of Alberta Press, 1985. Pages 134–35. Reproduced with permission.

87   1888: ANNIE LEAKE TO SARAH GIBBS GOODERHAM AND ELIZABETH SUTHERLAND STRACHAN

The Life and Letters of Annie Leake Tuttle: Working for the Best. Edited by Marilyn Fardig Whiteley. Waterloo, Ont.: Wilfrid Laurier University Press, 1999. Pages 77–80. Reprinted with permission of Wilfrid Laurier University Press.

88   1888: I.A. YEREX TO HIS PARENTS

"On Board the Steamer 'Northwest', Saskatchewan River." *Manitoba History*. No. 17 (Spring 1989), pages 17–18.

89   1889: PAULINE JOHNSON TO ARCHIBALD KAINS

Ottawa, NAC, Archibald Kains Papers. 2000–01315-5.

90   1890: HENRY SWIFT TO R. COWANS

Halifax, NSARM, RG 21, A, vols. 32 and 35 (Henry Swift letter books). Thanks to Professor Ian McKay.

91   1890: ALEXANDER LYLE TO LEVI THOMAS

Letters to Levi: A Young Fisherman's Mail. Edited by Joan Stephenson. Lockeport, N.S.: Roseway Publishing Co., 1991. Page 27.

92   1891: DAISY MACDONALD TO SIR JOHN A. MACDONALD

Affectionately Yours: The Letters of Sir John A. Macdonald and His Family. Edited by J.K. Johnson. Toronto: Macmillan, 1969. Pages 190–91.

93   1892: WILFRID LAURIER TO ÉMILIE LAVERGNE

Dearest Émilie: The Love-Letters of Sir Wilfrid Laurier to Madame Émilie Lavergne. Edited by Charles Fisher. Toronto: NC Press, 1989. Pages 111–12.

94   1895: CLAUDE GARDINER TO MRS. EDWARD JAMES GARDINER

Letters from an English Rancher. Edited by Hugh A. Dempsey. Calgary: Glenbow-Alberta Institute, 1988. Pages 40–41. Reprinted by permission of the Glenbow Museum.

95   1898: ISABEL MACKENZIE KING TO WILLIAM LYON MACKENZIE KING

Ottawa, NAC, King Papers, J7 H2245.

96   1899: ALMON JAMES COTTON TO W.F. MCCREARY

The Wheat King: The Selected Letters and Papers of A. J. Cotton, 1888–1913. Edited by Wendy Owen. Winnipeg: Manitoba Record Society, 1985. Pages 11–13.

97   1899: D.C. BLACK TO THE *GLOBE*

Shocked and Appalled: A Century of Letters to "The Globe and Mail." Edited by Jack Kapica. Toronto: Lester & Orpen Dennys, 1985. Page 14.

98   1900: MALI TO *ALL HALLOWS IN THE WEST*

All Hallows in the West. Vol. 2, no. 3 (Christmas 1900).

99   1900: WILLIAM OGILVIE TO CLIFFORD SIFTON

Whitehorse, Yukon Archives, Gov. 1619, file 1443, pt. 3.

100   1901: WINSTON CHURCHILL TO LADY RANDOLPH CHURCHILL

Churchill, Randolph S. *Winston S. Churchill.* Companion Volume 1, Part 2 (1896–1900). London: Heinemann, 1967. Pages 1231–32. Reproduced with permission of Curtis Brown Ltd., London on behalf of the Estate of Sir Winston Churchill. © Winston S. Churchill.

101   1902: BERTIE LECKIE TO ALICE LECKIE

Thanks to Rosemary Partridge, Toronto.

102   1904: ANNIE BURBIDGE TO ELLA LATHROP

Canadian Women on the Move, 1867–1920. Edited by Beth Light and Joy Parr. Toronto: New Hogtown Press and OISE, 1983. Pages 121–24.

103   1906: "BIG MIKE" TO *WESTERN HOME MONTHLY*

Dear Editor and Friends: Letters from Rural Women of the North-West, 1900–1920. Edited by Norah L. Lewis. Waterloo, Ont.: Wilfrid Laurier University Press, 1998. Page 50. Reprinted with permission of Wilfrid Laurier University Press.

104   1907: JACOB PENNER TO HIS FAMILY

Doerksen, Victor G., trans. "A Letter from Winnipeg in 1907." *Journal of Mennonite Studies.* Vol. 15 (1997), pages 192–96.

105   1907: LUCY MAUD MONTGOMERY TO EPHRAIM WEBER

The Green Gables Letters: From L.M. Montgomery to Ephraim Weber, 1905–1909. Edited by Wilfrid Eggleston. Ottawa: Borealis Press, 1981. Pages 51–54. Reprinted with permission of Ruth Macdonald. *L.M. Montgomery* is a trademark of the Heirs of L.M. Montgomery Inc.

106   1907: JOHN DAVIS TO MAGGIE NICKLE DAVIS

Thanks to Frances Daunt, Peterborough, Ontario, granddaughter of John Davis.

107   1908: WANDA WYATT TO JAMES (NED) WYATT

Kessler, Deidre. *A Century on Spring Street: Wanda Lefurgey Wyatt of Summerside, Prince Edward Island, 1895–1998.* Charlottetown: Indigo Press, 1999. Pages 73–74.

108   1909: LOIS SYBIL HARRINGTON TO EDWARD WINSLOW-SPRAGGE

Life and Letters of Lois Sybil Harrington & Edward Winslow-Spragge: Love, Family and Travel in Canada, 1908–1950. Edited by Anne V. Byers. Ottawa: Euros Publications, 2000. Page 14.

109   1910: WILLEM DE GELDER TO HIS FAMILY

A Dutch Homesteader on the Prairies. Edited and translated by Herman Ganzevoort. Toronto: University of Toronto Press, 1973. Pages 9–11. Reprinted with permission of the publisher.

110   1910: MONICA HOPKINS TO HER FRIEND GILL

Hopkins, Monica. *Letters from a Lady Rancher.* [Calgary]: Glenbow Museum, 1981. Pages 84–94. Reprinted by permission of the Glenbow Museum.

111 1910: "IN-THE-DEPTHS" TO THE FARMER'S ADVOCATE

Dear Editor and Friends: Letters from Rural Women of the North-West, 1900–1920. Edited by Norah L. Lewis. Waterloo, Ont.: Wilfrid Laurier University Press, 1998. Pages 92–93. Reprinted with permission of Wilfrid Laurier University Press.

112 1910: THE REVEREND MARTIN WEBBER HOLDOM TO GRACE HOLDOM

A Preacher's Frontier: The Castor, Alberta Letters of Rev. Martin W. Holdom, 1909–1912. Edited by Paul Voisey. Calgary: Historical Society of Alberta, 1996. Page 78.

113 1914: CLARE LOUISE CAMPBELL TO DINAH MEREDITH

Thanks to James O'Reilly, Toronto, son of Dinah Meredith.

114 1915: LEA PANQUIN TO THE FAMILY HERALD AND WEEKLY STAR

"I Want to Join Your Club": Letters from Rural Children, 1900–1920. Edited by Norah L. Lewis. Waterloo, Ont.: Wilfrid Laurier University Press, 1996. Page 28. Reprinted with permission of Wilfrid Laurier University Press.

115 1915: PERCY WINTHROP MCCLARE TO GERTRUDE WINTHROP

The Letters of a Young Canadian Soldier During World War I: P. Winthrop McClare, of Mount Uniacke, N.S. Edited by Dale McClare. Kentville, N.S.: Brook House Press, 2000. Page 1. Reprinted by permission.

116 1915: ALWYN BRAMLEY-MOORE TO DOROTHY BRAMLEY-MOORE

The Path of Duty: The Wartime Letters of Alwyn Bramley-Moore, 1914–1916. Edited by Ken Tingley. Calgary: Historical Society of Alberta, 1998. Page 44.

117 1916: SIR ROBERT BORDEN TO SIR GEORGE PERLEY

Robert Laird Borden: His Memoirs. Edited by Henry Borden. Toronto: Macmillan, 1938. Pages 622–23.

118 1916: STUART TOMPKINS TO EDNA CHRISTIE TOMPKINS

A Canadian's Road to Russia: Letters from the Great War Decade by Stuart Ramsay Tompkins. Edited by Doris H. Pieroth. Edmonton: University of Alberta Press, 1989. Pages 92–93. Reproduced with permission.

119 1916: GEORGE HADDOW TO THE REVEREND ROBERT HADDOW

Thanks to Douglas Haddow, Cobourg, Ontario, son of George Haddow.

120 1916: MAYO LIND TO THE DAILY NEWS

Lind, Francis T. *The Letters of Mayo Lind: Newfoundland's Unofficial War Correspondent, 1914–1916.* 1919. Reprint, with a foreword by Peter Neary. St. John's: Creative Publishers, 2001. Pages 138–44. Reprinted by permission of the publisher. All rights reserved.

121 1916: FRANÇOIS-XAVIER MAHEUX TO ANGÉLIQUE MAHEUX

Ottawa, NAC, MG30, E297, file 7. Thanks to Professor Desmond Morton.

122 1917: PRIVATE DONALD ROSS TO MABLE ROSS

Thanks to Stephen Workman, Halifax, great-nephew of Donald Ross.

123 1917: AGAR ADAMSON TO MABEL ADAMSON

Letters of Agar Adamson, 1914–1919. Edited by N.M. Christie. Nepean, Ont.: CEF Books, 1997. Page 274.

124 1917: TOM THOMSON TO JOHN THOMSON

Murray, Joan. *Tom Thomson: The Last Spring.* Toronto: Dundurn Press, 1994. Page 90.

125 1917: EVELYN KELLY ALBRIGHT TO FRED ALBRIGHT

Brooke, Lorna. *An Echo in My Heart: The Letters of Elnora Evelyn (Kelly) Albright and Frederick Stanley Albright.* London, University of Western Ontario, D.B. Weldon Library, J.J. Talman Regional Collection. Also available at http://members.rogers.com/echoinmyheart.

126   1917: MARY DOHERTY TO MRS. H.A. DOHERTY
Thanks to Rob McCleave, Kingston, great-nephew of Mary Doherty.

127   1917: BERTHA BOND TO SANDY WOURNELL
Kitz, Janet F. *Shattered City: The Halifax Explosion and the Road to Recovery*. Halifax: Nimbus Publishing, 1989. Pages 39–40.

128   1917: JANIE SMYTHE TO FLORA DENISON
Canadian Women on the Move, 1867–1920. Edited by Beth Light and Joy Parr. Toronto: New Hogtown Press and OISE, 1983. Pages 226–27.

129   1918: "DISCOURAGED WOMAN" TO THE *FREE PRESS PRAIRIE FARMER*
Dear Editor and Friends: Letters from Rural Women of the North-West, 1900–1920. Edited by Norah L. Lewis. Waterloo, Ont.: Wilfrid Laurier University Press, 1998. Page 139. Reprinted with permission of Wilfrid Laurier University Press.

130   ALEXANDER GORDON TYRRELL TO JESSIE ROBERTSON TYRRELL
Thanks to Cavell Tyrrell, Toronto, daughter-in-law of Alexander Tyrrell.

131   1919: KENNETH LYON TO THE *FREE PRESS PRAIRIE FARMER*
"I Want to Join Your Club": Letters from Rural Children, 1900–1920. Edited by Norah L. Lewis. Waterloo, Ont.: Wilfrid Laurier University Press, 1996. Page 76. Reprinted with permission of Wilfrid Laurier University Press.

132   1919: GEORGES VANIER TO PHILIAS VANIER
Georges Vanier, Soldier: The Wartime Letters and Diaries, 1915–1919. Edited by Deborah Cowley. Toronto: Dundurn Press, 2000. Pages 290–91.

133   1919: SARAH RAMSLAND TO HER PARENTS
Regina, SAB, Sarah Ramsland Papers, S-A191. Thanks to Professor Bill Waiser.

134   1920: KOST KLYM TO HIS UNCLE
Reflections and Reminiscences: Ukrainians in Canada, 1892–1992. Edited by Michael Ewanchuk. Winnipeg, 1994. Pages 61–62.

135   1922: DR. J.B. COLLIP TO DR. H.M. TORY
University of Alberta, H.M. Tory Papers. Thanks to Professor Michael Bliss and Alison Li.

136   1922: GERTRUDE CHASE TO HER MOTHER
No Easy Road: Women in Canada, 1920s to 1960s. Edited by Beth Light and Ruth Roach Pierson. Toronto: New Hogtown Press, 1990. Pages 222–23.

137   1923: A YOUNG MOTHER TO MARGARET SANGER
No Easy Road: Women in Canada, 1920s to 1960s. Edited by Beth Light and Ruth Roach Pierson. Toronto: New Hogtown Press, 1990. Page 122.

138   1924: NORMAN ROBERTSON TO FLORA ROBERTSON
Thanks to Judith Robertson, Toronto, daughter of Norman Robertson.

139   1924: EMILY MURPHY TO WILLIAM DEACON
Dear Bill: The Correspondence of William Arthur Deacon. Edited by John Lennox and Michèle Lacombe. Toronto: University of Toronto Press, 1988. Pages 45–48. Reprinted with permission of the publisher.

140   1925: WILLIAM LYON MACKENZIE KING TO ELIZABETH CLOUGH
Neatby, H. Blair, *William Lyon Mackenzie King, 1924–32: The Lonely Heights*. Toronto: University of Toronto Press, 1963. Pages 54–55. Reprinted with permission of the publisher.

141   1925: DUTCH IMMIGRANTS TO *DE NIEUWE TILBURGSCHE COURANT*
The Last Illusion: Letters from Dutch Immigrants in the "Land of Opportunity," 1924–1930. Edited by Herman Ganzevoort. Calgary: University of Calgary Press, 1999. Pages 43–45.

142 1927: AMELIA CARVER TO SCHOOL DAYS

No Easy Road: Women in Canada, 1920s to 1960s. Edited by Beth Light and Ruth Roach Pierson. Toronto: New Hogtown Press, 1990. Pages 36–37.

143 1927: EDGAR CHRISTIAN TO HIS PARENTS

The except from *Death in the Barren Ground* by Edgar Christian, edited by William James, is reprinted by permission of Oberon Press.

144 1927: WILLIAM DEACON TO B.K. SANDWELL

Dear Bill: The Correspondence of William Arthur Deacon. Edited by John Lennox and Michèle Lacombe. Toronto: University of Toronto Press, 1988. Pages 91–92. Reprinted with permission of the publisher.

145 1929: DR. MARY PERCY TO HER PARENTS

Suitable for the Wilds: Letters from Northern Alberta, 1929–1931. Edited by Janice Dickin McGinnis. Toronto: University of Toronto, 1925. Pages 122–28. Reprinted with permission of the publisher.

146 1930: EMILY CARR TO NAN CHENEY

Dear Nan: Letters of Emily Carr, Nan Cheney and Humphrey Toms. Edited by Doreen Walker. Vancouver: University of British Columbia Press, 1990. Pages 3–4. Reprinted with permission of the publisher. © University of British Columbia Press, 1990. All rights reserved by the publisher.

147 1931: "A DISHEARTENED MAN" TO R.B. BENNETT

The Wretched of Canada. Edited by L.M. Grayson and Michael Bliss. Toronto: University of Toronto Press, 1971. Page 5. Reprinted with permission of the publisher.

148 1931: VERA ERNST TO HER PARENTS

McNichol, Vera Ernst. *Smiling Through Tears.* Vol. 2. Bloomingdale, Ont., 1971. Pages 32–36.

149 1933: BERTRAM BROOKER TO LEMOINE FITZGERALD

University of Manitoba Archives, Brooker Papers. Thanks to Doreen Millin.

150 1933: MRS. THOMAS PERKINS TO R.B. BENNETT

The Wretched of Canada. Edited by L.M. Grayson and Michael Bliss. Toronto: University of Toronto Press, 1971. Pages 53–54. Reprinted with permission of the publisher.

151 1934: LADY HOPE SIMPSON TO HER DAUGHTER BETTY

White Tie and Decorations: Sir John and Lady Hope Simpson in Newfoundland, 1934–1936. Edited by Peter Neary. Toronto: University of Toronto Press, 1996. Pages 49–51. Reprinted with permission of the publisher.

152 1934: WILLIAM KINGSMAN TO MITCHELL HEPBURN

Toronto, AO, RG3 series 9, Hepburn Papers, box 180, file 105: Unemployment (Relief Requests for Aid), no. 1. Thanks to Lara Campbell.

153 1935: GREY OWL TO WILLIAM DEACON

Dear Bill: The Correspondence of William Arthur Deacon. Edited by John Lennox and Michèle Lacombe. Toronto: University of Toronto Press, 1988. Pages 162–66. Reprinted with permission of the publisher.

154 1936: JEWISH IMMIGRANT AID SOCIETY OF CANADA TO THOMAS A. CRERAR

Belkin, Simon. *Through Narrow Gates: A Review of Jewish Immigration . . .* [Montreal: Canadian Jewish Congress & the Jewish Colonization Association, 1966]. Pages 218–19.

155 1936: C. GARDINER TO MARY SUTHERLAND

No Easy Road: Women in Canada, 1920s to 1960s. Edited by Beth Light and Ruth Roach Pierson. Toronto: New Hogtown Press, 1990. Pages 280–81.

156   1938: FRANK PICKERSGILL TO HELEN MAGILL
The Pickersgill Letters. Edited by George H. Ford. Toronto: Ryerson Press, 1948. Pages 76–80.

157   1939: FRANK PICKERSGILL TO SARA PICKERSGILL
The Pickersgill Letters. Edited by George H. Ford. Ryerson Press, 1948. Pages 127–29.

158   1939: DR. NORMAN BETHUNE TO JOHN BARNWELL
Stewart, Roderick. *The Mind of Norman Bethune*. Toronto: Fitzhenry & Whiteside, 1977. Pages 133–35. © 1977. Reprinted by permission of Fitzhenry & Whiteside, Ltd.

159   1939: DOROTHY MACKENZIE TO HER SISTER RUTH
Thanks to Heather Elliot, Toronto, niece of Dorothy Mackenzie.

160   1940: MARIE WILLIAMSON TO MARGARET TOUT SHARP
Thanks to Mary Williamson, daughter of Marie Williamson, Toronto, and Tom Sharp, son of Margaret Sharp, in England.

161   1940: LESTER PEARSON TO MARYON PEARSON
Thanks to Patricia Hannah, Toronto, and Geoffrey Pearson, Ottawa.

162   1941: MINNIE PAYZANT WARD TO MRS. STAN GILBERT
Thanks to Margaret Gilbert, Newmarket, Ontario.

163   1942: MURIEL KITAGAWA TO WES FUJIWARA
Reprinted from *This Is My Own: Letters to Wes and Other Writings on Japanese Canadians, 1941–1948*, Muriel Kitigawa edited by Roy Miki. © 1985, Talon Books Ltd., Vancouver B. C.

164   1942: NORAH EGENER TO FRED EGENER
Permission to republish this letter is granted by Norah Egener, author of *A Time Apart: Letters of Love and War 1941–1945*, edited by Joan Barfoot and published by The Ginger Press, Owen Sound.

165   1942: MAJOR GENERAL J.H. ROBERTS TO CANADIAN CORPS HEADQUARTERS
Historical Documents of Canada. Vol. 5, *The Arts of War and Peace, 1914–1945*. Edited by C.P. Stacey. Toronto: Macmillan, 1972. Page 620.

166   1942: ARTHUR WILKINSON TO ALTA WILKINSON
Ottawa to Caen: Letters from Arthur Campbell Wilkinson. Edited by Alta R. Wilkinson. [Ottawa]: Tower Books, 1947. Pages 71–72.

167   1943: KATHLEEN ROBSON ROE TO HER SISTER BESSIE
Roe, Kathleen Robson. *War Letters from the C.W.A.C. (Canadian Women's Army Corps)*. Toronto: Kakabeca Publishing, 1975. Pages 42–43.

168   1944: DONALD DUNCAN TO MAURINE STUART
Some Letters and Other Writings of Donald Albert Duncan. Halifax: [Halifax Imperial Publishing, 1945]. Pages 155–56.

169   1944: JACK GOUINLOCK TO HIS PARENTS
Thanks to Blake Heathcote, Toronto.

170   1944: FARLEY MOWAT TO ANGUS AND HELEN MOWAT
Mowat, Farley. *My Father's Son: Memories of War and Peace*. New York: Houghton Mifflin, 1992. Pages 136–38. Reprinted with permission from the author.

171   1945: BOB SANDERSON TO NELLIE AND STANLEY SANDERSON
Sanderson, Robert Miles, and Marie Sanderson. *Letters from a Soldier: The Wartime Experiences of a Canadian Infantryman, 1943–1945*. Waterloo, Ont.: Escart Press, 1993. Pages 1-4, 101-24, 166-92. Translations from the German by Dr. Marie Sanderson.

172   1945: HUGH MACLENNAN TO WILLIAM DEACON

Dear Bill: The Correspondence of William Arthur Deacon. Edited by John Lennox and Michèle Lacombe. Toronto: University of Toronto Press, 1988. Pages 200–01. Reprinted by permission of the publisher.

173   1945: KING WHYTE TO DOROTHY ALT WHYTE

Letters Home 1944–1946. Edited by Tanya Nanavati and Maureen Whyte. Toronto: Seraphim Editions, 1966. Pages 55–56.

174   1945: ESCOTT REID TO THE REVEREND ALFRED JOHN REID

Reid, Escott. *On Duty: A Canadian at the Making of the United Nations.* Kent, Ohio: Kent State University Press, 1983. Pages 49–50.

175   1949: CÉLINE TO GERMAIN SICOTTE

Chers nous autres : un siècle de correspondance québécoise. Vol. 1. Edited by Robert Blondin and Gilles Lamontagne. Montreal: VLB éditeur, 1978. Pages 32–33. Translated from the French.

176   1951: RUBY CRESS TO HER SISTER KAY

Haven't Any News: Ruby's Letters from the Fifties. Edited by Edna Staebler. Waterloo, Ont.: Wilfrid Laurier University Press, 1995.

177   1952: MICHELINE TO HER SISTER RENÉE

Chers nous autres : un siècle de correspondance québécoise. Vol. 1. Edited by Robert Blondin and Gilles Lamontagne. Montreal: VLB éditeur, 1978. Pages 157–58. Translated from the French.

178   1954: EUGENE FORSEY TO THE *GLOBE AND MAIL*

Globe and Mail. September 7, 1954, page 6.

179   1959: EUSTACE ROSS TO RALPH GUSTAFSON

A Literary Friendship: The Correspondence of Ralph Gustafson and W.W.E. Ross. Edited by Bruce Whiteman. Toronto: ECW Press, 1984. No. 51. Reprinted by permission of ECW Press and Bruce Whiteman.

180   1960: GLENN GOULD TO EDITH BOECKER

Glenn Gould: Selected Letters. Edited by John P. Roberts and Ghyslaine Guertin. Toronto: Oxford University Press, 1992. Pages 26–28.

181   1960: JILL KIDDER TO RUTH WILSON

Thanks to Jill Kidder, Vancouver.

182   1961: BEATRICE MAITLAND TO *CHATELAINE*

Toronto, AO, Maclean Hunter Collection, MHRS F-4-3-a, box 434.

183   1963: ARTHUR PATTILLO TO CHARLOTTE VANDINE

No Easy Road: Women in Canada, 1920s to 1960s. Edited by Beth Light and Ruth Roach Pierson. Toronto: New Hogtown Press, 1990. Pages 390–91.

184   1964: GEORGE STANLEY TO JOHN MATHESON

Ottawa, NAC, Beddoe Papers, MG30 D252, vol. 9.

185   1964: JOHN DIEFENBAKER TO ELMER DIEFENBAKER

Personal Letters of a Public Man: The Family Letters of John G. Diefenbaker. Edited by Thad McIlroy. Toronto: Doubleday, 1985. Page 152.

186   1964: MARSHALL MCLUHAN TO ROBERT FULFORD

Letters of Marshall McLuhan. Edited by Matie Molinaro, Corinne McLuhan, and William Toye. Toronto: Oxford University Press, 1987. Page 300.

187   1967: NATHALIE TO HER SISTER FRANÇOISE

Chers nous autres : un siècle de correspondance québécoise. Vol. 2. Edited by Robert Blondin and Gilles Lamontagne. Montreal: VLB éditeur, 1978. Pages 83–84. Translated from the French.

188   1968: BLAIR FRASER TO DAVID MANUEL

Thanks to John Fraser and Graham Fraser, Ottawa, Blair Fraser's sons.

189   1968: LEONARD GILBERT TO ANTHONY NETBOY
Thanks to John Gilbert, Toronto, Leonard Gilbert's son.

190   1969: IRVING LAYTON TO DESMOND PACEY
Wild Gooseberries: The Selected Letters of Irving Layton. Edited by Francis Mansbridge. Toronto: Macmillan, 1989. Pages 241–42.

191   1970: GEORGE WOODCOCK TO JIM CHRISTY
Woodcock, George. *Taking It to the Letter*. Dunvegan, Ont.: Quadrant Editions, 1981. Pages 22–24.

192   1970: PIERRE LAPORTE TO ROBERT BOURASSA
Available at www.cbc.ca/news/indepth/october/timeline.html.

193   1970: NATHALIE TO A FRIEND
Chers nous autres : un siècle de correspondance québécoise. Vol. 2. Edited by Robert Blondin and Gilles Lamontagne. Montreal: VLB éditeur, 1978. Pages 89–90. Translated from the French.

194   1970: J. PIVIE TO THE OTTAWA CITIZEN
Ottawa Citizen. October 22, 1970.

195   1970: GLENN CHERITON TO THE OTTAWA CITIZEN
Ottawa Citizen. October 22, 1970.

196   1971: MARGARET LAURENCE TO MARGARET ATWOOD
© Margaret Laurence, from *A Very Large Soul: Selected Letters from Margaret Laurence to Canadian Writers*. Toronto: Cormorant Books, 1995. Pages 1–4. Used by permission. All rights reserved.

197   1971: CHIEF FREDERICK PLAIN TO THE NATIVE PRESS
Native Press. September 17, 1971.

198   1974: JANE HENSON TO FRONTIER COLLEGE
Ottawa, NAC, Frontier College Collection, MG28 I 124, vol. 456. Thanks to Frontier College.

199   1976: ROBERTSON DAVIES TO JACK MCCLELLAND
From *Robertson Davies, For Your Eyes Alone: Letters 1976–1995*, ed. Judith Skelton Grant. Used by permission, McClelland & Stewart Ltd. *The Canadian Publishers*.

200   1976: JAMES HUTCHINSON TO THE GLOBE AND MAIL
Shocked and Appalled: A Century of Letters to "The Globe and Mail." Edited by Jack Kapica. Toronto: Lester & Orpen Dennys, 1985. Page 242.

201   1977: MARGARET LAURENCE TO GABRIELLE ROY
© Margaret Laurence, from *A Very Large Soul: Selected Letters from Margaret Laurence to Canadian Writers*, edited by J.A. Wainwright. Toronto: Cormorant Books Inc., 1995. Pages 178–79. Used by permission. All rights reserved.

202   1978: S.H. GRANT TO THE GLOBE AND MAIL
Shocked and Appalled: A Century of Letters to "The Globe and Mail." Edited by Jack Kapica. Toronto: Lester & Orpen Dennys, 1985. Page 74.

203   1979: CRAIG RUSSELL TO GINO EMPRY
Ottawa, NLC, Gino Empry Papers, MG31–D47, vol. 45, file 8.

204   1982: LANDON PEARSON TO HER FAMILY
Thanks to Senator Landon Pearson, Ottawa.

205   1983: LEONARD LEE TO HIS CUSTOMERS
Thanks to Leonard Lee, Ottawa.

206   1984: PROFESSOR ELIZABETH ALLIN TO DR. ANN MCMILLAN
University of Toronto Archives, Elizabeth Josephine Allin Papers, B93–0035 (001–004).

207   1984: AN ADOPTIVE MOTHER TO THE BIRTH MOTHER

Thanks to the writer.

208   1987: EUGENE FORSEY TO THE *GLOBE AND MAIL*

Globe and Mail. April 25, 1987, page 7.

209   1987: JEAN CAZABON TO ANDRÉE CAZABON

Thanks to Andrée Cazabon, Ottawa. Translated from the French.

210   1990: IRSHAD MANJI TO MUMTAZ MANJI

Thanks to Irshad Manji, Toronto.

211   1992: A SOLDIER TO JANE SNAILHAM

This letter is taken from the book *Eyewitness to Peace: Letters from Canadian Peacekeepers* by Jane Snailham. It is published by the Canadian Peacekeeping Press, Pearson Peacekeeping Centre, P.O. Box 100, Clementsport NS, Canada, B0S 1E0.

212   1995: MORDECAI RICHLER TO JACOB RICHLER

Thanks to Jacob Richler, Toronto.

213   1995: ANNE GIARDINI TO CAROL SHIELDS

Thanks to Carol Shields, Victoria, and Anne Giardini, Vancouver.

214   1997: STÉPHANE DION TO LUCIEN BOUCHARD

From *Straight Talk: On Canadian Unity* by Stéphane Dion. Montreal: McGill-Queen's University Press, 1999. Pages 189–93. Published in French under the title *Le pari de la franchise*. Reprinted by permission of the author.

215   1998: JOHNNIE CLARK TO LEONARD LEE

Thanks to Johnnie Clark, Lower Sackville, New Brunswick, and Leonard Lee, Ottawa.

216   1999: JIMMIE TO JANE FROST

Thanks to Jane Frost, Vancouver.

217   1999: EDA BANNISTER TO MARIE BANNISTER

Thanks to Eda Bannister, in the Armed Forces, and Marie Bannister, Saskatoon.

ILLUSTRATION CREDITS

BHS: Brant Historical Society, The Brant Museum Archives
CMC: Canadian Museum of Civilization
NAC: National Archives of Canada
NL: National Library of Canada
PAA: Provincial Archives of Alberta
THA: Testaments of Honour Archives

p. viii: NL 15559
p.5: NAC C150505
p.6: Copyright (c) Canada Post Corporation. 1851, reproduced with permission.
p.9: CMC 82000–5668
pp.10 and 11: Courtesy of Edith Cody-Rice, Ottawa
p.14: NAC C41067
p.46: NAC C3257
p.51: *Muskoka and Haliburton, 1615–1875: A Collection of Documents*. Edited by Florence B. Murray. Toronto: Champlain Society, 1963. p. 105. Reprinted by permission of the Champlain Society, Toronto, Canada.
p.52 NAC PA201405
p.53: NAC C1993
p.57: NAC 16826
p.63: NAC C67346
p.66: NAC C11811
p.86: NAC C67337
p.88: NAC C7158
p.91: NAC C150740
p.95: NAC C31493
p.101: NAC C150716
p.120: NAC C606
p.135: Courtesy of Susan Wilson, Toronto
p.163: NAC C26415
p.166: NAC NMC10330
p.188: NAC C3884
p.197: NAC C21005
p.199: PAA A3495
p.200: PAA 71.365/3
p.203: NAC PA48475
p.227: NAC C16307

p.231: BHS 634; Photographer, J. Fraser Bryce
p.240: NAC C7353
p.244: NAC C30620
p.255: NAC PA63175
p.257: NAC PA13284
p.260: NAC PA16431
p.292: Private collection
p.303: NAC PA120121
p.307: NAC PA1020
p.335: NAC PA195653
p.343: Private collection
p.358: Private collection
p.361: NAC C29397
p.364: NAC PA122483
p.377: NAC PA157630
p.382: Courtesy of Margaret Sharp
p.388: NAC C46355
p.398: THA GNL-05
p.406: THA
p.410: NAC PA169833
p.438: NAC PA142624
p.465: NAC PA142624
p.468: Private collection
p.486: Courtesy of Irshad Manji
p.490: Courtesy of the Richler family

Acknowledgments

MY FIRST DEBT OF GRATITUDE GOES TO DEBORAH VAN SETERS, WHO trolled through libraries and archives for the raw material from which this portrait of Canada was assembled. Without Deborah's extensive knowledge of both Canadian history and the Dewey system, I could not have produced this book. Her research skills, hard work, and good judgment were invaluable. I would also like to thank Adam Crerar for his support to us both, and his good ideas.

I am immensely grateful to those who made suggestions or sent material for inclusion. Triage was painful: as you can see, I didn't meet my goal of 200 letters covering 200 years. Instead, I ended up with 217 letters to include and a huge pile of other letters that deserved inclusion too. I would like to extend my thanks, and my apologies if your suggestions and submissions were not included, to Tannis Baker, Marie Bannister, Margaret Blank, Professor Michael Bliss, Jim Bowman at the Glenbow Museum Archives, Lorna Brooke, Lara Campbell, Andrée Cazabon, Johnnie Clark, Ron Cohen, June Copeland, Lois Daly, Frances Daunt, Elaine Deschenes, Heather Elliot, Graham Fraser, John Fraser, Jane Frost, John Gilbert, Margaret Gilbert, Nan Gray, Douglas Haddow, Patricia Hannah, Blake Heathcote, Kathy Hooke, Heather Jones at the Yukon Archives, John Kidder, Arthur Kroeger, Bill Lankin, Leonard Lee, Dr. Ian Mackay, Irshad Manji, Graham Mann, Erica Martin of Frontier College, Sandra Martin, Rob McCleave, Sally McLean, Professor J.S. Miller, Doreen Millin, Christopher Moore, Professor Desmond Morton, Mary Mundle, Penelope Noble, John Daniel O'Leary of Frontier College, James O'Reilly, Dr. Bryan Palmer, Rosemary Partridge, Geoffrey Pearson, Senator Landon Pearson, Alison Prentice, Chris Raible, Jennifer Raiche, Jim Rainer, Alan Rayburn, Judith Robertson, Susan Evans Shaw, Carol and Don Shields, David Silcox, Dorothy Davies Snyder, Kevin Tompkins, Cavell Tyrrell, Judy van Raalte,

Professor Bill Waiser, Professor Peter Waite, Mary Williamson, Susan Loetitia Wilson, Tony Wilson, Stephen Workman, and Ian Young.

I am particularly grateful to four friends for scholarly advice: Professors Duncan McDowell, Sandy Campbell, and Norman Hillmer of Carleton University, and Professor Roger Hall of the University of Western Ontario. As usual, I relied heavily on the resources and staff at three of Canada's great institutions: the National Archives of Canada, the National Library of Canada, and the Library of Parliament. In addition, I drew extensively on several invaluable reference books: *The Illustrated History of Canada*, edited by Craig Brown (3rd ed., Key Porter, 1997); *The Canadian Encyclopedia* (Hurtig, 2nd ed., 1988); *Dictionary of Canadian Biography* (University of Toronto Press, 1966–); *Historical Atlas of Canada* (University of Toronto Press, 1987–1993).

The idea for an anthology of Canadian letters came originally from John Pearce and Pamela Murray of Random House, who gave me free rein to shape it as I wished. My editors Meg Masters and Martha Kanya-Forstner, together with the creative director, Scott Richardson, were supportive and helpful. The copy editor, Barbara Czarnecki, did a superb job in ensuring accuracy and consistency. Professor J. Barnard Gilmore prepared a useful index. I would like to thank my former agent, Jan Whitford, my current agent, Jackie Kaiser, and my friend Ernest Hillen for their good advice.

Wayne McAlear, Monic Charlebois, and Violeta Hollmann-Bonales provided invaluable help while I was writing this book. My sons, Alexander, Nicholas, and Oliver, reminded me that there is more to life than a keyboard. My husband, George Anderson, provided not only the love and encouragement he has consistently given me but also English translations of letters originally written in French.

Thank you, all.

Index

Page citations in *italic* refer to *illustrations* in this book
Page citations in **boldface** refer to **editorial passages** and **commentary** in this book